GREAT TALES
FROM
ENGLISH
HISTORY

"Lacey has taken up the call for a modern, accessible, narrative history of Britain and has come up trumps."   —*BBC History*

"Eminently readable, highly enjoyable. . . . *Great Tales from English History* should appeal to the reader who appreciates individuals and their personalities more than mere mass movements."
                                    —*St. Louis Post-Dispatch*

"A delight to dip into, with plenty to rescue a last-minute assembly or a Friday afternoon lesson."   —*Times Educational Supplement*

"Superb. . . . Lacey helps to bring our national story to life."
                                    —*Daily Express*

GREAT TALES
FROM
ENGLISH
HISTORY

*A Treasury of True Stories
about the Extraordinary People—
Knights and Knaves, Rebels and
Heroes, Queens and Commoners—
Who Made Britain Great*

ROBERT LACEY

BACK BAY BOOKS
Little, Brown and Company
New York   Boston   London

Great Tales from English History was first published in the United States by Little, Brown and Company in three volumes: *The Truth about King Arthur, Lady Godiva, Richard the Lionheart, and More* in 2004; *Joan of Arc, The Princes in the Tower, Bloody Mary, Oliver Cromwell, Sir Isaac Newton, and More* in 2005; *Captain Cook, Samuel Johnson, Queen Victoria, Charles Darwin, Edward the Abdicator, and More* in 2006. This omnibus edition contains the complete text of the three books.

Back Bay Books / Little, Brown and Company
Hachette Book Group
237 Park Avenue, New York, NY 10017
Visit our Web site at www.HachetteBookGroupUSA.com

First Published in Great Britain by Abacus, 2007
First North American Edition, November 2007

Back Bay Books is an imprint of Little, Brown and Company. The Back Bay Books name and logo are trademarks of Hachette Book Group, Inc.

Illustrations and family trees © 2006 by Fred van Deelen 2003, 2004, 2006
The author gratefully acknowledges permission to quote from: *Bede: Ecclesiastical History of the English People* (Penguin Classics, 1995; revised edition, 1968): translation copyright © Leo Sherley-Price, 1955, 1968; *The Ecclesiastical History of Orderic Vitalis* (Oxford, Clarendon Press, 1978), translator Marjorie Chibnall, © Oxford University Press, 1978; *The Anglo-Saxon Chronicle* (J. M. Dent, 1966), translator M. J. Swanton, © J. M. Dent, 1966; *Piers the Ploughman* by William Langland (Penguin Books, 1996), translation © J. F. Goodridge, 1959, 1966; Souvenir Press for 'The Life That I Have' from the poetry collection of the same name. Methuen Publishing Ltd. for the use of a facsimile of the illustration by John Reynolds from the cover of *1066 and All That* by W. C. Sellar and R. J. Yeatman.

ISBN 978-0-316-06757-7
LCCN 2007936758

10 9 8 7 6 5 4 3

RRD-C

Printed in the United States of America

FOR SASHA, SCARLETT AND BRUNO

CONTENTS

England's Norman and Angevin, or Plantagenet, Kings		xv
Wars of the Roses: The Houses of York, Lancaster and Tudor		xvi
England's Tudor and Stuart Monarchs		xvii
The Stuart and Hanoverian Monarchs		xviii
Victoria, Edward VII and the House of Windsor		xix
Storytelling		1
c.7150 BC	Cheddar Man	3
c.325 BC	Pytheas and the Painted People	4
55 BC	The Standard-bearer of the 10th	7
AD 1–33	And Did Those Feet? Jesus Christ and the Legends of Glastonbury	10
AD 43	The Emperor Claudius Triumphant	13
AD 61	Boadicea, Warrior Queen	14
AD 122	Hadrian's Wall	17
AD 410–*c*.600	Arthur, Once and Future King	20
c.AD 575	Pope Gregory's Angels	23
AD 597	St Augustine's Magic	25
AD 664	King Oswy and the Crown of Thorns	27
c.AD 680	Caedmon, the First English Poet	30
AD 672/3–735	The Venerable Bede	32
AD 878	Alfred and the Cakes	35
AD 911–18	The Lady of the Mercians	40
AD 978–1016	Ethelred the Unready	43
c.AD 1010	Elmer the Flying Monk	46

CONTENTS

AD 1016–35	King Canute and the Waves	48
AD 1042–66	Edward the Confessor	51
c.AD 1043	The Legend of Lady Godiva	55
1066	The Year of Three Kings	58
1066	The Death of Brave King Harold	62
1070	Hereward the Wake and the Norman Yoke	66
1086	The Domesday Book	69
1100	The Mysterious Death of William Rufus	72
1120	Henry I and the *White Ship*	76
1135–54	Stephen and Matilda	80
1170	Murder in the Cathedral	83
1174	A King Repents	89
1172	The River-bank Take-away	91
1189–99	Richard the Lionheart	93
1215	John Lackland and Magna Carta	98
1225	Hobbehod, Prince of Thieves	104
1265	Simon de Montfort and his Talking-place	106
1284	A Prince Who Speaks No Word of English	112
1308	Piers Gaveston and Edward II	115
1346	A Prince Wins His Spurs	121
1347	The Burghers of Calais	125
1347–9	The Fair Maid of Kent and the Order of the Garter	128
1348–9	The Great Mortality	131
1376	The Bedside Manner of a Plague Doctor	134
1377	The Dream of Piers the Ploughman	136
1381	The 'Mad Multitude'	139
1387	Geoffrey Chaucer and the Mother Tongue	146
1399	The Deposing of King Richard II	149
1399	'Turn Again, Dick Whittington!'	153

CONTENTS

1399	Henry IV and His Extra-virgin Oil	156
1415	We Happy Few – the Battle of Azincourt	158
1429	Joan of Arc, the Maid of Orleans	161
1440	A 'Prompter for Little Ones'	165
1422–61, 1470–1	House of Lancaster: the Two Reigns of Henry VI	166
1432–85	The House of Theodore	169
1461–70, 1471–83	House of York: Edward IV, Merchant King	172
1474	William Caxton	174
1483	Whodunnit? The Princes in the Tower	177
1484	The Cat and the Rat	181
1485	The Battle of Bosworth Field	182
1486–99	Double Trouble	186
1497	Fish 'n' Ships	188
1500	Fork In, Fork Out	191
1509–33	King Henry VIII's 'Great Matter'	193
1525	'Let There Be Light' – William Tyndale and the English Bible	198
1535	Thomas More and His Wonderful 'No-Place'	201
1533–7	Divorced, Beheaded, Died . . .	204
1536	The Pilgrimage of Grace	206
1539–47	. . . Divorced, Beheaded, Survived	210
1547–53	Boy King – Edward VI, 'The Godly Imp'	214
1553	Lady Jane Grey – the Nine-day Queen	217
1553–8	Bloody Mary and the Fires of Smithfield	220
1557	Robert Recorde and His Intelligence Sharpener	224
1559	Elizabeth – Queen of Hearts	225
1571	That's Entertainment	228
1585	Sir Walter Ralegh and the Lost Colony	231

CONTENTS

1560–87	Mary Queen of Scots	234
1588	Sir Francis Drake and the Spanish Armada	238
1592	Sir John's Jakes	241
1603	By Time Surprised	242
1605	5/11: England's First Terrorist	244
1611	King James's 'Authentical' Bible	248
1616	'Spoilt Child' and the Pilgrim Fathers	249
1622	The Ark of the John Tradescants	252
1629	God's Lieutenant in Earth	254
1642	'All My Birds Have Flown'	257
1642–8	Roundheads v. Cavaliers	261
1649	Behold the Head of a Traitor!	264
1653	'Take Away This Bauble!'	267
1655	Rabbi Manasseh and the Return of the Jews	270
1660	Charles II and the Royal Oak	273
1665	The Village That Chose to Die	276
1666	London Burning	278
1678/9	Titus Oates and the Popish Plot	280
1685	Monmouth's Rebellion and the Bloody Assizes	284
1688–9	The Glorious Invasion	286
1687	Isaac Newton and the Principles of the Universe	289
1690	John Locke and Toleration	293
1690	'Remember the Boyne!' – the Birth of the Orangemen	296
1693	Britannia Rules the Waves – the Triangular Trade	298
1701	Jethro Tull's 'Drill' and the Miner's Friend	301
1704	Marlborough Catches the French Sleeping at the Village of the Blind	303

CONTENTS

1707	Union Jack	306
1714	Made in Germany	308
1720	South Sea Bubble	309
1721–42	Britain's First Prime Minister	311
1738	Born Again	314
1739	Dick Turpin – 'Stand and Deliver!'	316
1745	God Save the King!	318
1755	Dr Johnson's Dictionary	321
1759	General Wolfe and the Capture of Quebec	324
1766	James Hargreaves and the Spinning Jenny	327
1770	Captain Cook – Master of the Pilotage	329
1773	The Boston Tea Party	332
1785	Thomas Clarkson – the Giant with One Idea	334
1788	The Madness of King George III	337
1789	'Breadfruit Bligh' and the Mutiny on the *Bounty*	340
1791	Thomas Paine and the Rights of Man	343
1792	Mary Wollstonecraft and the Rights of Woman	347
1805	England Expects . . .	350
1811	Fanny Burney's Breast	353
1812	Who Was Ned Ludd?	355
1815	Wellington and Waterloo	358
1823	Stone Treasures – Mary Anning and the Terror Lizards	361
1830	Blood on the Tracks	363
1819–32	The Lung Power of Orator Hunt	366
1834	The Tolpuddle Martyrs	369
1837	'I Will Be Good' – Victoria Becomes Queen	371

1843	'God's Wonderful Railway' – Isambard Kingdom Brunel	373
1843	*Rain, Steam & Speed* – the Shimmering Vision of J. M. W. Turner	376
1851	Prince Albert's Crystal Palace	378
1852	'Women and Children First!' – the *Birkenhead* Drill	380
1854	Into the Valley of Death	382
1854–5	The Lady of the Lamp and the Lady with the Teacup (plus the Odd Sip of Brandy)	386
1858	Charles Darwin and the Survival of the Fittest	391
1878	The Great Stink – and the Tragedy of the *Princess Alice*	394
1887	Lord Rosebery's Historical Howler	397
1888	Annie Besant and 'Phossy Jaw' – the Strike of the Match Girls	398
1897	Diamond Jubilee – the Empire Marches By	400
1900	Slaughter on Spion Kop	403
1903	Edward VII and the Entente Cordiale	406
1910	Cellar Murderer Caught by Wireless – Dr Crippen	409
1912	'I May Be Some Time . . .' – the Sacrifice of Captain Oates	411
1913	The King's Horse and Emily Davison	414
1914	When Christmas Stopped a War	418
1915	Patriotism Is Not Enough – Edith Cavell	421
1916	Your Country Needs You! – the Sheffield Pals	423
1926	A Country Fit for Heroes?	426
1930	The Greatest History Book Ever	429
1933	Not Cricket – 'Bodyline' Bowling Wins the Ashes	431

CONTENTS

1936   Edward the Abdicator   434

1938   Peace for Our Time! – Mr Chamberlain
Takes a Plane   437

1940   Dunkirk – Britain's Army Saved by the
Little Boats   440

1940   Battle of Britain – the Few and the Many   443

1943   Code-making, Code-breaking –
'The Life That I Have'   446

1945   Voice of the People   448

1953   Decoding the Secret of Life   450

Exploring the Orginal Sources   455

Acknowledgements   501

Index   505

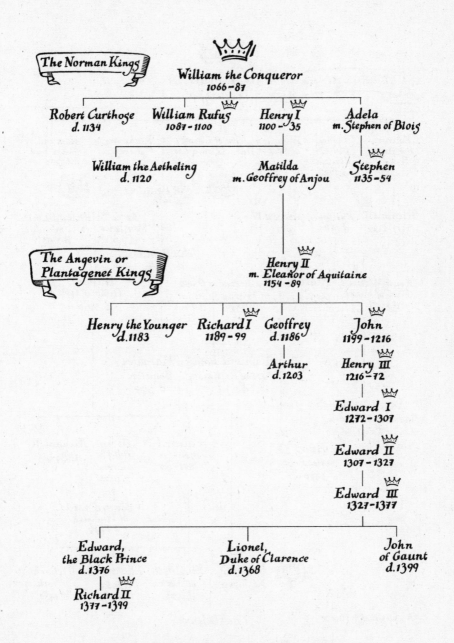

The Norman Kings

William the Conqueror
1066–87

Robert Curthose
d. 1134

William Rufus
1087–1100

Henry I
1100–35

Adela
m. Stephen of Blois

William the Aetheling
d. 1120

Matilda
m. Geoffrey of Anjou

Stephen
1135–54

The Angevin or
Plantagenet Kings

Henry II
m. Eleanor of Aquitaine
1154–89

Henry the Younger
d. 1183

Richard I
1189–99

Geoffrey
d. 1186

John
1199–1216

Arthur
d. 1203

Henry III
1216–72

Edward I
1272–1307

Edward II
1307–1327

Edward III
1327–1377

Edward,
the Black Prince
d. 1376

Lionel,
Duke of Clarence
d. 1368

John
of Gaunt
d. 1399

Richard II
1377–1399

England's Norman and Angevin,
or Plantagenet, Kings

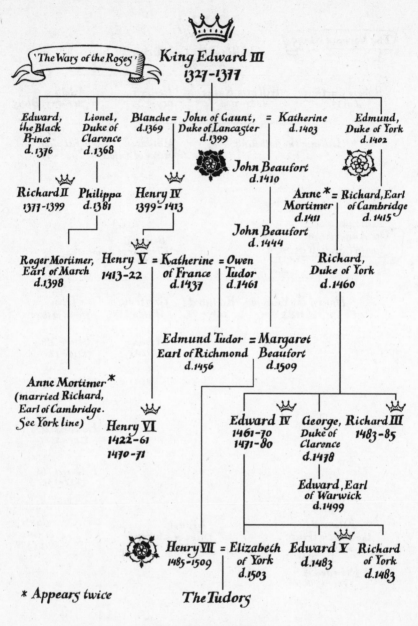

Wars of the Roses:
The Houses of York, Lancaster and Tudor

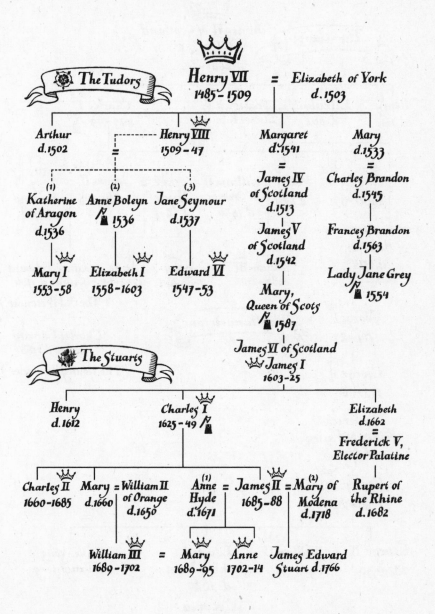

The Tudors

Henry VII
1485 - 1509
= Elizabeth of York
d. 1503

Arthur
d. 1502

Henry VIII
1509 - 47

Margaret
d. 1541
=
James IV
of Scotland
d. 1513

Mary
d. 1533
=
Charles Brandon
d. 1545

(1)
Katherine
of Aragon
d. 1536

(2)
Anne Boleyn
⚔ 1536

(3)
Jane Seymour
d. 1537

James V
of Scotland
d. 1542

Frances Brandon
d. 1563

Mary I
1553 - 58

Elizabeth I
1558 - 1603

Edward VI
1547 - 53

Mary,
Queen of Scots
⚔ 1587

Lady Jane Grey
⚔ 1554

The Stuarts

James VI of Scotland
James I
1603 - 25

Henry
d. 1612

Charles I
1625 - 49 ⚔

Elizabeth
d. 1662
=
Frederick V,
Elector Palatine

Charles II
1660 - 1685

Mary =
d. 1660

William II
of Orange
d. 1650

Anne (1)
Hyde = James II = Mary (2)
d. 1671   1685 - 88   of
Modena
d. 1718

Rupert of
the Rhine
d. 1682

William III
1689 - 1702
= Mary
1689 - 95

Anne
1702 - 14

James Edward
Stuart d. 1766

England's Tudor and Stuart Monarchs

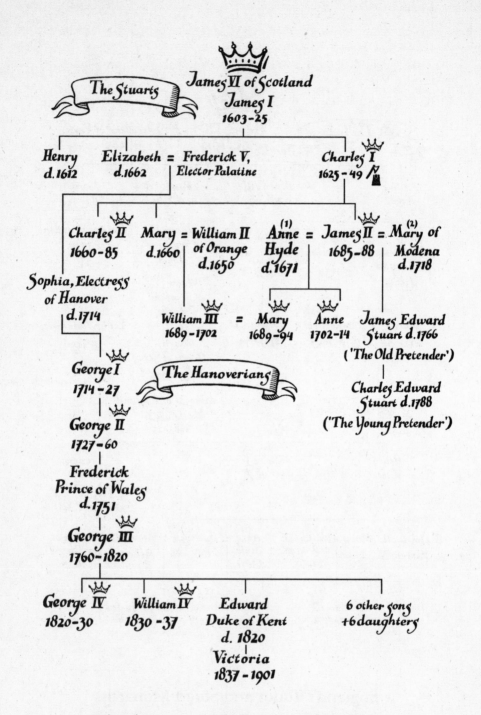

The Stuarts

James VI of Scotland
James I
1603-25

Henry
d.1612

Elizabeth = Frederick V,
d.1662   Elector Palatine

Charles I
1625-49

Charles II
1660-85

Mary = William II
d.1660   of Orange
         d.1650

Anne (1) = James II = Mary of (2)
Hyde   1685-88   Modena
d.1671   d.1718

Sophia, Electress
of Hanover
d.1714

William III = Mary
1689-1702   1689-94

Anne
1702-14

James Edward
Stuart d.1766

('The Old Pretender')

George I
1714-27

The Hanoverians

Charles Edward
Stuart d.1788

('The Young Pretender')

George II
1727-60

Frederick
Prince of Wales
d.1751

George III
1760-1820

George IV
1820-30

William IV
1830-37

Edward
Duke of Kent
d. 1820

6 other sons
+6 daughters

Victoria
1837-1901

The Stuart and Hanoverian Monarchs

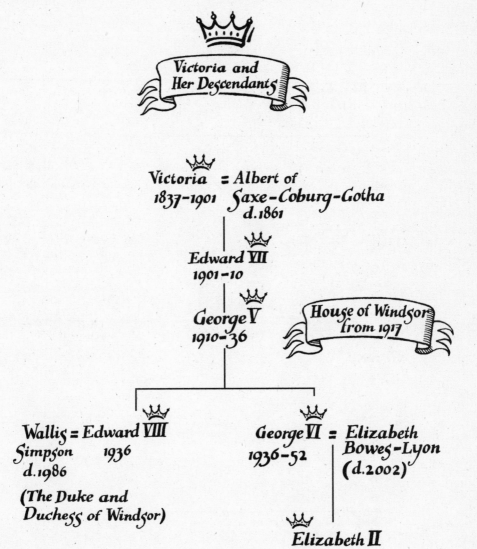

Victoria, Edward VII and the House of Windsor

STORYTELLING

The first history book that I remember reading with pleasure was a stout, blue, exuberantly triumphalist volume, *Our Island Story – A History of England for Boys and Girls* by H. E. Marshall. It had a red and gold crested shield embossed on the cover, and it told tales of men, women and often children whom it dared to describe as 'heroes' and 'heroines'. It was accompanied by a companion volume, *Our Empire Story*, which was even more politically incorrect, relating the sagas of the heroes and heroines who adventured 'across the seas' to paint much of the globe pink. I must confess that I loved it still more – even though I discovered, at the beginning of the second chapter, that the author had a vivid imagination.

John Cabot's ship the *Matthew* was described by Marshall as sailing out from Bristol harbour one bright May morning, 'followed by the wishes and prayers of many an anxious heart . . . until it was but a speck in the distance'. Old H. E. – who, I later learned, was an Edwardian lady, Henrietta Elizabeth, living in Australia – was clearly not aware that the port of Bristol is several muddy miles inland from the Bristol Channel. As a pupil at Clifton National Infants School, a few hundred yards from the Bristol docks, I could have told her that if there had been a crowd waving goodbye to Cabot, they would have lost sight of the doughty mariner as he tacked round the first corner of the Avon Gorge.

It was my first lesson in the imperfections of history. There may be such a thing as pure, true history – what actually, really, *definitely* happened in the past – but it is unknowable. We can only hope to get somewhere close. The history that we have to make do with is the story that historians choose to tell us, pieced together and filtered through every handler's value system.

Making due allowance for the Avon Gorge factor, all the tales you are about to hear are *true*. I have consulted the best available contemporary sources and eyewitness accounts. But telling stories that are 'true' does not exclude England's legends – the romances of King Arthur or Hereward the Wake. You will find them examined here as myths that illustrate a truth about the age from which they spring – while also revealing how we today like our Englishness to be.

The lessons we derive from history inevitably resonate with our own code of values. When we go back to the past in search of heroes and heroines, we are looking for personalities to inspire and comfort us, to confirm our view of how things should be. That is why every generation needs to rewrite its history, and if you are a cynic you may conclude that a nation's history is simply its own deluded and self-serving view of its past.

Great Tales from English History is not cynical: it is written, and recounted for you now, by an eternal optimist – albeit one who views the evidence with a sceptical eye. Sir Walter Ralegh, one of the heroes of these tales – and one of mine – is said to have given up writing his *History of the World* when he looked out of his cell in the Tower of London one day and saw two men arguing in the courtyard. Try as he might, he could not work out what they were quarrelling about: he could not hear them; could only see their angry gestures. So there and then, we are told, he abandoned his ambitious historical enterprise, concluding that you can never establish the full truth about anything.

In this sobering realisation, Sir Walter was displaying unusual humility – both in himself and as a member of the historical fraternity: the things we do not know about history far outnumber those that we do. But the fragments that survive are precious and bright. They offer us glimpses of drama, humour, incompetence, bravery, apathy, sorrow and lust – the stuff of life. There are still a few good tales to tell . . .

CHEDDAR MAN

C.7150 BC

T HERE WAS A TIME, AS RECENTLY AS NINE THOUSAND YEARS
ago, when the British Isles were not islands at all. After the bleak-
ness of the successive ice ages, the south-eastern corner of modern
England was still linked to Europe by a wide swathe of low-lying
marshes. People crossed to and fro, and so did animals – including
antelopes and brown bears. We know this because the remains of these
creatures were discovered by modern archaeologists in a cave in the
Cheddar Gorge near Bristol. Scattered among numerous wild horse
bones, the scraps of bear and antelope had made up the larder of
'Cheddar Man', England's oldest complete skeleton, found lying nearby
in the cave with his legs curled up under him.

According to the radiocarbon dating of his bones, Cheddar Man
lived and died around 7150 BC. He was a member of one of the small
bands of hunter-gatherers who were then padding their way over the
soft forest floors of north-western Europe. The dry cave was his home
base, where mothers and grandmothers reared children, kindling fires
for warmth and lighting and for cooking the family dinner. We don't
know what language Cheddar Man spoke. But we can deduce that
wild horsemeat was his staple food and that he hunted his prey across
the grey-green Mendip Hills with traps, clubs and spears tipped with
delicately sharpened leaf-shaped flints.

Did Cheddar Man have a name of his own? A wife or children? Did
he have a god to whom he prayed? The answers to all these basic questions remain mysteries. Bone experts tell us that he was twenty-three or
so when he died – almost certainly from a violent blow to his head. So
our earliest semi-identifiable ancestor could have been a battle casualty,

or even a murder victim. And since the pattern of cuts on his bones is the same as the butcher's cuts made on the animal bones around him, we are confronted with another, still more gruesome possibility – that our early ancestors were cannibals. According to some archaeologists, the reason why so few human skeletons survive from these post-ice-age years is because relatives must have eaten the dead, cracking up the bones to suck out the nourishing marrow inside.

Nowadays, the grief of losing Grandma is softened by inheriting her house in the suburbs – a legacy, at modern property values, worth several years of going to the office. Nine thousand years ago, a death in the family would let you off one day's horse chasing at least.

PYTHEAS AND THE PAINTED PEOPLE
c.325 BC

CHEDDAR MAN HAD LIVED IN AN ERA OF GLOBAL WARMING. As the glaciers of the last ice age melted, sea levels were rising sharply, and this turned high ground like the Isle of Wight, the Isle of Man, and modern Ireland into separate islands. The waters flooded over the land bridge, severing the physical link with Europe.

Thus was created the great moat that we now call the English Channel. As you approached England by boat across the narrowest point where marshes had once been, you were confronted by the striking prospect of long, tall cliffs of bright chalk – the inspiration, according to one theory, for the country's earliest recorded name, Albion, from the Celtic word for 'white'. Europe's great white-capped mountain chain, the Alps, are thought to have derived their name from the same linguistic root.

It was Pytheas, a brave and enquiring Greek navigator, who probably wrote down the name around 325 BC. Nearly seven thousand years after the death of Cheddar Man, Pytheas travelled north from the Mediterranean to investigate the islands that were by now supplying the tin which, when smelted and alloyed with copper, produced the bronze for the tools and weapons of southern Europe. These offshore 'tin islands' were so remote that they were said to be occupied by one-eyed men and griffins. But unafraid, Pytheas followed the customary trade routes to Cornwall, and set about composing the earliest written description of this land that lay on the edge of the known world.

The Greek explorer seems to have covered large areas of the country on foot. Placing his gnomon, or surveying-stick, into the ground at noon each day, he was able to measure the changing length of its shadow and hence calculate latitude and the distance north he had travelled. He almost certainly sailed around the islands, and was the first to describe the shape of Britain as a wonky triangle. Rival geographers scorned Pytheas. But his findings, which survive today only in fragments through the writings of others, have been confirmed by time – and by modern archaeologists, whose excavations tell us of a population that had advanced spectacularly since the days of Cheddar Man.

The inhabitants of Albion by now spoke Celtic, a lilting, flexible language distantly related to Latin. They shared it with the Gauls across the water in the Low Countries and France. They still hunted, as Cheddar Man had done. But now their spears and arrows were tipped with bronze or iron, not sharpened flint, and they no longer depended on hunting for survival. They hunted for pleasure and to supplement a diet that was derived from their farms, since they had learned how to tame both plants and animals. By 300 BC surprisingly large areas of the landscape were a patchwork of open fields – the classic English countryside that we recognise today. Iron axes had cut down the forests. Iron hoes and ploughs had scratched and cross-hatched fields whose boundaries were marked, on the uplands, by firm white furrows that, in some cases, still serve as boundaries for farmers in the twenty-first century.

Compared with Cheddar Man the Celts were quite affluent folk, with jewellery, polished metal mirrors and artfully incised pots decorating their homes. Some lived in towns. The remains of their bulky earth-walled settlements can still be seen in southern England, along with the monuments of their mysterious religion – the sinuous, heart-lifting white horses whose prancings they carved into the soft chalk of the Downs.

They were a people who enjoyed their pleasures, to judge from the large quantities of wine jars that have been dug from their household debris. They brewed their own ale and mead, a high-alcohol fermentation of water and honey which they ceremoniously passed from one to another in loving-cups. And while their sips might be small, it was happily noted in the Mediterranean, where the wine jars came from, that this sipping took place 'rather frequently' – as one ancient historian put it.

But there was a darker side. The religious rituals of these Celts were in the hands of the Druids – high priests or witch doctors, according to your point of view. Travellers told tales of human sacrifice in their sacred groves of oak and mistletoe, and modern excavations have confirmed their altars must have reeked of carrion. One recent dig revealed a body that had been partially drowned and had its blood drained from the jugular vein. Death, it seems, was finally administered by the ritual of garrotting – a technique of crushing the windpipe by twisting a knotted rope around the neck.

The Celts were fearsome in battle, stripping down to their coarse woven undershorts and painting themselves with the greeny-blue dye that they extracted from the arrow-shaped leaves of the woad plant. Woad was the war paint of Albion's inhabitants, and it is thought to have inspired a name that has lasted to this day. *Pretani* is the Celtic for painted, or tattooed folk, and Pytheas seems to have transcribed this into Greek as *pretanniké*, meaning 'the land of the painted people'. When later translated into Latin, *pretanniké* yielded first *Pretannia*, then *Britannia*.

Diodorus Siculus, a historian working in Rome in the first century BC, described a less ferocious aspect of these blue-painted warriors. They were, he said, 'especially friendly to strangers' – always happy to do business with the many foreign merchants who now travelled to Pretannia to purchase Cornish tin, wolfhounds and the odd slave. Hide-covered boats carried the tin across to France, where pack-horses and river barges transported it along the trade routes that led southwards through Italy to Rome. By the first century BC Rome had supplanted Greece as the Western centre of learning and military might. The Roman Empire circled the Mediterranean and had reached north into France and Germany. The wealth of the distant tin islands sounded tempting. As the Roman historian Tacitus later put it, the land of these painted people could be *'pretium victoriae'* – 'well worth the conquering'.

THE STANDARD-BEARER OF THE 10TH
55 BC

S O FAR IN OUR STORY ALL THE DATES HAVE BEEN estimates – much better than guesses, but not really precise. Radiocarbon dating, for example, measures the rate of decay of the radioactive isotope carbon 14, which is found in all living things but which starts to decay at the moment of death at a precisely predictable rate. Using this method, scientists have been able to calculate the age of Cheddar Man to an accuracy of one hundred and fifty years.

But now, in 55 BC, we can for the first time set a British date precisely in months and days. Two centuries after the travel jottings of Pytheas, our history finally collides full tilt with the culture of writing – and what a writer to start with! Gaius Julius Caesar not only shaped history – he also wrote about it. Reading his vivid account of his invasion of Britain, we can feel ourselves there with him in the early hours of 26 August 55 BC, rocking in the swell in his creaking wooden vessel off the white cliffs of Albion – and contemplating the unwelcome sight at the top of them.

'Armed men,' he wrote, 'could be seen stationed on all the heights, and the nature of the place was such, with the shore edged by sheer cliffs, that javelins and spears could be hurled onto the beach.'

The Roman force had sailed from France the previous night, cruising through the darkness with a fleet of eighty ships bearing two battle-hardened legions – about ten thousand men. Trying to control the western corner of Europe for Rome, Caesar had found his authority challenged by the Celtic peoples of Gaul, and he had a strong suspicion they had been receiving help from their cousins in Britain. He had tried to get to the bottom of it, calling together the merchants who traded with the Britons across the channel, but he had received no straight answers. His solution had been to spend the summer assembling his invasion fleet, and now, here at the top of the cliffs, was the reception committee.

Caesar ordered his ships to sail along the coast for a few miles to where the cliffs gave way to a sloping beach, somewhere near the modern port of Deal. But the Britons kept pace with him along the cliff top on horseback and in chariots, then coming down to mass together menacingly on the beach. The Roman legionaries faced the unappealing prospect of leaping into chest-high water in their heavy armour and battling their way ashore.

'Our troops,' admitted Caesar, 'were shaken, and they failed to show the same dash and enthusiasm as they did in land battles.'

But then the standard-bearer of the 10th legion leapt down into the waves, brandishing high the silver eagle that was the symbol of the favour in which the gods held the regiment. Dressed in a wild-animal pelt, with the snarling head of a lion, bear or wolf fixed to the top of his helmet, the standard-bearer was guardian of the legion's morale. While the eagle remained upright, the legion's honour lived.

'Jump down, men!' cried the standard-bearer. 'Unless you want the enemy to get your standard! You will not find me failing in my duty to my country or my leader!'

According to Caesar, the Roman footsoldiers were transformed by the gallantry of the standard-bearer. Crashing down into the water after him, they fought their way up the shingle to regroup and form the disciplined lines of shields, spears and swords that made up the basic Roman battle formation. The Britons withdrew, and Caesar sent home news of a mighty victory. When his report reached Rome, the Senate voted an unprecedented twenty-day holiday of celebration.

But the Roman conqueror then spent less than twenty days in

Britain. A storm wrecked many of his ships, so Caesar headed smartly back to France before the weather got any worse. Next summer, in July 54 BC, he tried again, with redesigned landing craft whose shallow keels could be driven through the waves and up on to the beach. With more cavalry than at their first attempt, the Romans were able to secure their beachhead, march inland and cross the River Thames, fighting off hit-and-run attacks. The Celtic chiefs that Caesar managed to corner offered the conqueror their allegiance. But once again the winter storms threatened, and the Romans had to hurry back to France. This time the Senate did not call a holiday.

Julius Caesar was one of the towering figures of Western history. Tall and sharp-featured, with the thinning brushed-forward hairstyle immortalised in countless marble statues, he was a man of extraordinary charisma. A brilliant general, he fought off his rivals to gain control of the entire Roman Empire before being murdered by opponents of his absolute power. Later Roman emperors tried to borrow his glory by calling themselves Caesar, and his memory has been perpetuated into recent times by the German and Russian titles of Kaiser and Czar.

In 45 BC he reformed the Western calendar. Known henceforward as the Julian calendar, this used the device of the leap year to keep the earthly year in pace with the sun. The month of July is named after him, as is the Caesarean method of delivering babies, deriving from the story that his mother died while giving birth to him and that he had to be cut out of her womb.

Ever the self-publicist, he is famous for his declaration '*Veni, vidi, vici*' – 'I came, I saw, I conquered' – after his victory at Zela in central Turkey in 47 BC, and he conveyed a similar message of triumphant conquest when writing the history of his two brief, and only moderately successful, trips to Britain. Describing events in words had made the historical record more vivid and accurate in many ways – but words clearly provided no guarantee that history would now become more truthful.

AND DID THOSE FEET?
JESUS CHRIST AND THE
LEGENDS OF GLASTONBURY

AD 1–33

And did those feet in ancient time
Walk upon England's mountains green?
And was the Holy Lamb of God
On England's pleasant pastures seen?

SUNG AT RUGBY MATCHES AND PATRIOTIC OCCASIONS LIKE the Last Night of the Proms, the hymn 'Jerusalem' has become England's unofficial national anthem. Its uplifting lines conjure up the wild idea that Jesus Christ himself, 'the Holy Lamb of God', set foot in England at some moment during his thirty-three years on earth. If Pytheas the Greek and Julius Caesar could make it from the Mediterranean, why not the Saviour?

It could not possibly be. If Christ had had the time and means to travel the five thousand miles all the way from Palestine across Europe to England and back again in the course of his brief life, it would certainly have been recorded in the Gospels. And would not Christ himself have referred to the great adventure somewhere in his teaching?

The myth has entered the folk memory sideways, through the fables inspired by Joseph of Arimathea, the rich disciple who provided the tomb for Christ's body after the crucifixion. The Gospels tell us quite a lot about Joseph (not to be confused with Christ's father, Joseph the carpenter). A well respected member of the Sanhedrin, or Supreme Council of the Jews, Joseph had kept secret his dangerous conversion to the message of Jesus. It was only a man of such standing who could have gone to Pontius Pilate, the Roman governor of Judaea, and asked for Christ's dead body.

But over the centuries – and we are talking of more than a dozen centuries – extra exploits were attributed to this substantial and intriguing character. Joseph is said to have been one of the disciples who travelled to northern Europe preaching the gospel. He was credited with founding the first monastery in Britain. Other tales supposed that he had made his wealth in the metals trade, and had been in the habit of visiting the south-west in search of Cornwall's tin and Somerset's high-quality lead. It was even imagined that Joseph was the uncle of the Virgin Mary, and therefore the great-uncle of Christ, and so might have brought the boy along on one of his business trips to the region.

In 1502 came the first mention of a living relic that might lend some substance to these extraordinary tales – a hawthorn bush growing at Glastonbury Abbey in Somerset. Blossoming unusually around Christmastime, in the depths of winter and on Christ's birthday, it was known as the Holy Thorn and was said to have been planted by Joseph of Arimathea himself when he stuck his staff into the ground and it took root. It was further said that Joseph had cut his staff from the same bush as Christ's crown of thorns – and modern botanists have established that the Glastonbury thorn, a pinkish-flowered hawthorn known as *Crataegus monogyna praecox*, is indeed a plant that originated in the Middle East. It blooms in Glastonbury to this day and the first sprig of blossom is ceremonially cut every year and presented to the Queen, who keeps it on her desk over Christmas.

In 1808, at the height of Britain's bitter wars against Napoleon, the artist and poet William Blake pulled together the elements of the various Jesus and Glastonbury legends to create the poem that we now know as 'Jerusalem'. Blake was a mystic and a radical, then making his living in a grimy engraving workshop in the sooty slums of London, where he dreamed of angels. He abhorred what he memorably described as the 'dark satanic mills' of industrial Britain, and he nursed the vision that a shining new society might be built. Jerusalem in our own day may be a sadly afflicted and tragically unholy place, but to Blake it was something glorious:

Bring me my bow of burning gold!
Bring me my arrows of desire!
Bring me my spear! O clouds, unfold!
Bring me my chariot of fire!
I will not cease from mental fight,
Nor shall my sword sleep in my hand,
Till we have built Jerusalem,
In England's green and pleasant land.

Two centuries later during the horrors of World War I, when the flower of Europe's youth was being slaughtered in the trenches of northern France, the composer Hubert Parry set the visionary words to music. The first time the stirring strains of 'Jerusalem' were heard in public was at a 'Votes for Women' concert in 1916, setting the note of reform and regeneration that the anthem retains to this day.

Let us say it one more time – we can be as sure as the sun rises that Jesus Christ did not set foot in Glastonbury, or anywhere else in England. The legend of Joseph of Arimathea is not history. But over the centuries the story would play its part in inspiring history. In words and music, 'Jerusalem' gives wing to the sense of hope and shared endeavour that a community needs if it is to believe in itself – the vision of a national spirit as clean and pure as England's beautiful green countryside. Things may be good, but let us not get complacent – 'better must come'.

THE EMPEROR CLAUDIUS
TRIUMPHANT
AD 43

AFTER CAESAR'S HASTY DEPARTURE IN 54 BC, IT WAS MORE than ninety years before the Romans tried to conquer Britain again – and when they eventually landed, they made the most of their triumph. In AD 43 the forty-thousand-strong army pushed resistance aside as it rolled up through Kent to the Thames, where the men were ordered to halt. The emperor Claudius wanted to catch up with them, and he duly arrived in splendour for the advance into modern Colchester, the principal British settlement of the south-east. The Roman victory parade featured a squadron of elephants, whose exotic appearance must have been greeted with amazement as they plodded through the Kent countryside.

Swaying a dozen feet above the ground, the club-footed but canny Claudius proudly claimed Colchester as the capital of Rome's latest province. Straight streets were laid down, with a forum and amphi-theatre, and the showpiece was a high, rectangular, white-pillared temple. Roman veterans were given land around the town, in the centre of which rose a statue of the emperor. With firm chin, large nose and slicked-down hair, the statue made Claudius look remarkably like Julius Caesar.

Claudius was considered a rather comical character by his con-temporaries, who secretly mocked his physical handicaps. His dragging right foot was probably the result of brain damage at birth – his head and hands shook slightly – and he had a cracked, throaty and scarcely intelligible voice which, according to one of his enemies, belonged 'to no land animal'. But as someone who had often found himself in the hands of doctors, he had a high regard for healing. He managed a soothing tone when dealing with the local chieftains of Britain, acknowledging that they had rights. He honoured them as 'kings' – which, in turn, boosted his own status as their emperor. Then in AD 54 Claudius died, to be succeeded by his stepson Nero, whose name would become proverbial for wilfulness and cruelty.

BOADICEA, WARRIOR QUEEN
AD 61

ANY BRITISH 'KING' WHO LIVED UNDER THE ROMANS HAD to pay a price for his protection. So when Prasutagus, the leader of the Iceni people, died in AD 60 he prudently left half his wealth and territories to the emperor Nero as a form of 'death duty'. The Iceni occupied the flat fenlands that stretched down from the Wash across modern Norfolk and Suffolk and, like other Celtic peoples, they accepted the authority of female leaders. Dying without a son, Prasutagus had left his people in the care of his widow, Boadicea (or Boudicca), until their two daughters came of age.

But women had few rights under Roman law, and Nero's local officials treated Boadicea's succession with contempt.

'Kingdom and household alike,' wrote the Roman historian Tacitus, author of the first history of Britain, 'were plundered like prizes of war.'

The lands of the Iceni nobles were confiscated and Boadicea was publicly beaten. Worst of all, her two daughters were raped. Outraged, in AD 61 the Iceni rose in rebellion, and it was Boadicea who led them into battle.

'In stature she was very tall, in appearance most terrifying,' wrote a later Roman historian, Dio Cassius. 'Her glance was fierce, her voice harsh, a great mass of the most tawny hair cascaded to her hips.'

Joined by other Britons, Boadicea with her rebel Iceni fell on

Colchester in fury, slaughtering the inhabitants and smashing the white-pillared temple and other symbols of Roman oppression. Over eighteen hundred years later, in 1907, a boy swimming in the River Alde in Suffolk, deep in what had been Iceni territory, was astonished to discover the submerged bronze head of the emperor Claudius. Looking at the jagged edges of the severed neck today, one can almost hear the shouts of anger that have attended the satisfying ritual of statue-toppling over the centuries.

The rebels now turned towards Londinium, the trading settlement that was just growing up around the recently built bridge over the Thames. The vengeance they wreaked here was equally bitter. Today, four metres below the busy streets of the modern capital, near the Bank of England, lies a thick red band of fired clay and debris which archaeologists know as 'Boadicea's Layer'. The city to which the Iceni set the torch burned as intensely as it would in World War II during the firebomb raids of the Germans. Temperatures rose as high as 1000 degrees Celsius – and, not far away, in the Walbrook Stream that runs down to the Thames, has been found a grisly collection of skulls, violently hacked from their bodies.

Boadicea's forces had wiped out part of a Roman legion that had marched to the rescue of Colchester. But the bulk of the Roman troops had been on a mission in the north-west to hunt down the Druids and destroy their groves on the island of Anglesey, and it was a measure of Boadicea's self-assurance that she now headed her army in that north-westerly direction. Her spectacular victories had swollen her ranks, not only with warriors but with their families too, in a vast wagon train of women and children. She laid waste to the Roman settlement of Verulamium, modern St Albans, then moved confidently onwards.

Meanwhile the Romans had been gathering reinforcements and the two forces are thought to have met somewhere in the Midlands, probably near the village of Mancetter, just north of Coventry.

'I am fighting for my lost freedom, my bruised body and my outraged daughters!' cried Boadicea, as she rode in her chariot in front of her troops. 'Consider how many of you are fighting and why – then you will win this battle, or perish! That is what I, a woman, plan to do! Let the men live in slavery if they want to.'

These fighting words come from the pen of Tacitus, who describes the fierce showdown in which the much smaller, but impeccably armed and drilled, Roman army wore down the hordes of Boadicea. At the crux of the battle, it was the wagon train of British women and children that proved their menfolk's undoing. The camp followers had fanned out in a semicircle to watch the battle, fully expecting another victory. But as the Britons were driven back, they found themselves hemmed in by their own wagons, and the slaughter was terrible – eighty thousand Britons killed, according to one report, and just four hundred Romans. Boadicea took poison rather than fall into the hands of her enemies, and, legend has it, gave poison to her daughters for the same reason.

It was only when some of Tacitus' writings, lost for many centuries, were rediscovered five hundred and fifty years ago that Britain found out that its history had featured this inspiring and epic warrior queen. Plays and poems were written to celebrate Boadicea's battle for her people's rights and liberties, and in 1902 a stirring statue in her honour was raised in the shadow of the Houses of Parliament. There on the banks of the Thames you can see Boadicea thrusting her spear defiantly into the air, while her daughters shelter in the chariot beside her.

But the menacing curved blades on Boadicea's chariot wheels are, sadly, the invention of a later time. Remains of the Britons' light bentwood chariots show no scythes on the wheels. Nor is there evidence of another great myth, that Boadicea fought her last battle near London and that her body lies where she fell – in the ground on which King's Cross Station was built many years later. Her supposed grave beneath platform ten at King's Cross is the reason why Harry Potter's Hogwarts Express leaves, magically, from Platform Nine and Three-Quarters.

In fact, the bones of the great queen probably do lie near a railway line – albeit more than a hundred miles north of King's Cross, near Mancetter in modern Warwickshire. The trains on the Euston line between London and the north-west rumble through the battlefield where, historians calculate, Boadicea fought her last battle.

HADRIAN'S WALL
AD 122

THE ROMANS EXACTED FIERCE REVENGE FOR BOADICEA'S revolt. Reinforcements were sent over from Germany and, as Tacitus put it, 'hostile or wavering peoples were ravaged with fire and sword'.

But tempers cooled, and in AD 77 a new governor arrived in Britain, Gnaeus Julius Agricola. His daughter was married to the historian Tacitus and it seems likely that Tacitus himself came with his father-in-law and served on his staff. In which case, it was from first-hand observation that he described how Agricola, to promote peace, 'encouraged individuals and helped communities to build temples, market-places and houses. Further, he trained the sons of the chiefs in the liberal arts and expressed a preference for British natural ability.'

The result, wrote the reporter-historian, was that 'the people, who used to reject the Latin language, began to aspire to being eloquent in it. Even the wearing of our Roman robes and togas came to be esteemed. And so, little by little, the Britons were seduced into alluring vices – colonnades, baths and elegant banquets.'

Then, as now, the well-to-do locals showed themselves suckers for Italian trendiness. Beautiful mosaics, underfloor heating, villas, law courts, council chambers, sports stadiums, bath-houses, amphitheatres, roads – handsome stone structures of all kinds sprang up in the main Roman settlements, especially in the south of the island. But the most massive construction project of all was the Empire's huge northern frontier wall, started in AD 122 and some six years in the building.

The great wall was the work of the emperor Hadrian, a patient and thorough man who spent half of his twenty-one-year reign systematically travelling the boundaries of his vast Empire, sorting out problems. In Britain, Rome's problem was the warlike peoples in the north of the island – the Picts and the Caledonians – whom the legions had found it impossible to subdue.

Running seventy-three miles from the River Tyne on the east coast to the Solway Firth on the west, Hadrian's Wall was 3 metres thick and 5 metres high, a huge stone-faced rampart with a succession of full-scale frontier forts along its length. In 143, Hadrian's successor Antoninus built another row of ditches and turf defences a hundred miles further north, and for as long as this, the Antonine Wall, held, it created a broad northern band of Roman-dominated territory.

Excavations show that Hadrian's Wall was a centre of bustling colonial life where soldiers and their families lived, traded and, to judge from the scraps of letters that survive, invited each other to dinner parties. To the rolling windswept hills of northern Britain the Romans brought *garum*, the dark, salty fish sauce that was the ketchup of the Roman legionary, poured over everything. For the sweet tooth there was *defrutum* – concentrated grape syrup that tasted like fruit squash. Another scrap of letter refers to the thermal socks and underwear that a Roman soldier needed to keep himself warm on the northern border.

It is not likely that many of Britain's border farmers wore togas or conversed in Latin. But they must have learned a few words as they haggled over the price of grain with the Roman quartermaster or bit on the coins that bore the current emperor's head. It was during Britain's Roman centuries that cabbages, peas, parsnips and turnips came to be cultivated in the British Isles. The Romans brought north bulkier, more meat-bearing strains of cattle, as well as apples, cherries, plums and walnuts for British orchards – plus lilies, roses, pansies and poppies to provide scent and colour for the island's early gardens. The British were famous for their trained hunting dogs, which they bred, trained and sold to Europe. But it was probably thanks to the Romans that now appeared, curled up by the second-century fireside, the domestic cat.

The Romans were proud of what they called *Pax Romana*, 'the Roman peace'. They cultivated the life of the city – *civitas* in Latin – the root of our word civilisation, connecting city to city with their superb, straight, stone and gravel roads. Some Britons joined the Roman army and were sent off to live in other parts of the Empire. Soldiers from the Balkans and southern Europe came to Britain, married local girls and helped create a mingled, cosmopolitan way of life. In AD 212 the emperor Caracalla granted full citizenship to all free men in the Empire, wherever they might live.

But the comforts of Roman civilisation depended on the protection of the tough, battle-ready legions that had built the Empire and now guarded its frontiers. Organised in units of a hundred (hence the title of their commanding officer, the centurion), Roman legionaries drilled every day – 'cutting down trees, carrying burdens, jumping over ditches, swimming in sea or river water, going on route marches at full pace, or even running fully armed and with packs,' as one fourth-century reporter described them. Could a modern SAS man emulate the crack Roman cavalrymen who had mastered the art of vaulting on to their horses' backs in full armour?

Those who remained outside the Empire were warriors too – and of them there were many more. The Romans called them *barbari*, from a Greek word that originally meant 'outsiders' but which came to be tinged with notions of savagery and fear. In AD 197, less than seventy years after its massive fortifications were completed, Hadrian's Wall was overrun by the Picts, the warlike barbarians of the north. Many of its forts had to be reconstructed.

A hundred years later southern Britain faced another threat. Sailing across from the low coastal islands of northern Germany came the Angles and Saxons – pirates who preyed on the prosperous farms and villas of the south-east in lightning hit-and-run-and-row raids. In 285 the Romans started fortifying a line of defences and watchtowers to keep them at bay. Eventually the fortifications stretched all the way from Norfolk down to the mouth of the Thames and round the south coast to the Isle of Wight. The Romans called it the Saxon Shore.

But there was only so much that forts and soldiers could achieve. The pressures of peoples are hard to resist. The Angles, Saxons and other raiders from across the sea were part of the great swirlings of populations that were bringing change to every part of Europe. These barbarians – most of them Germanic peoples – penetrated the Empire willy-nilly, and by the early years of the fifth century they were sweeping southwards, threatening the survival of Rome itself. The legions were called home. In AD 410 the British asked the emperor Honorius for help against the continuing inroads of the seaborne raiders. But the bleak answer came back that from now on the inhabitants of Britannia must fend for themselves.

ARTHUR, ONCE AND FUTURE KING
AD 410–c.600

'THE DARK AGES' IS THE LABEL HISTORIANS USED TO APPLY to the centuries after the legions left Britain. With the departure of the Romans, civilisation literally departed as well. If any written records of this time were made, virtually none has survived, and to this day we can only guess at exactly who did what to whom from 410 until nearly 600. Unlike Julius Caesar, the Anglo-Saxons did not keep invasion diaries.

What we do know for sure is that the Angles, Saxons and other peoples of northern Germany kept on rowing across the water to the white cliffs and sheltered harbours of Albion. Their poems tell of their brave exploits cresting the waves in their oar-powered, plank-built boats. Within a century and a half of the Romans' departure, the south-east corner of the island had indeed become the Saxon Shore. The newcomers had moved in and were busy creating their new kingdoms of Essex, Sussex and Wessex – the lands of the East, the South and West Saxons. They came, they saw, they settled.

The settlement extended widely. The Angles gave their name to East Anglia, and they founded more kingdoms up the coast – Lindsey (now Lincolnshire) and Northumbria, literally the land of the people north of the Humber, the wide estuary that separates modern Hull and Grimsby. In the Midlands lay the kingdom of Mercia, the people of the borders or boundaries. By the time this mosaic of little sovereignties was complete, the newcomers held most of the land.

But modern excavation has uncovered little evidence that this was a violent ethnic takeover. Hundreds of Roman villas and settlements have been dug up, with no severed skulls or suggestions of blood spilt on the tiles. No equivalent of Boadicea's fire-scorched layer has yet been found in what was becoming Anglo-Saxon England.

It would seem that most of the people who were left behind by the legions – the Romano-Britons – made some sort of peace, more or less grudging, with their new masters. Settlements along one river in Sussex show the Romano-Britons on one side and the Saxons on the other. The earliest law code of the West Saxons, drawn up by King Ine in the late seventh century, allowed the British who held land in his domain to keep some of their own customs.

It was further west and to the north that the violence occurred, in Cornwall, Wales and Scotland – the great crescent of sea, moors and mountains later called the Celtic fringe. Roman influence had been relatively slight here and the Celts had preserved their traditional identity. There is evidence of fortification and battles in these border areas, drawing a bitter boundary of blood and language between Celt and Anglo-Saxon. *Wælisc*, from which we get the word 'Welsh', was an Anglo-Saxon term applied to foreigners and also to slaves. And when the Welsh talk of England today they use a word that means 'the lost lands'.

It is from the so-called Dark Ages that some of Britain's most potent legends have sprung. As later chroniclers looked back, they pieced together scraps of memory and folklore – like the tales of the Saxon warriors Hengist ('the stallion') and Horsa ('the horse'), who were invited to Britain to help the locals and who then turned on their hosts. Did Hengist and Horsa really exist? The great modern expert on the subject was J. R. R. Tolkien, Professor of Anglo-Saxon at Oxford University from 1925 to 1945, who, having soaked up the atmosphere of these mysterious years, made up some legends of his own: Tolkien's tales of *The Hobbit* and *The Lord of the Rings* resound with the clash of swords in dark forests, where fantastical characters flit half-seen through a vanished landscape.

It took Tolkien twenty years to create his epic saga – 'saga' is the Norse word for 'tale' – but England's greatest Dark Age legend was generations in the making. In 1113 some French priests visiting Devon and Cornwall were astonished to be told of a great king – Arthur – who had once ruled over those parts and who would one day return from the grave to rule again. When the educated visitors laughed at the story, they found themselves pelted with vegetables by the irate locals.

The stirring legend of Arthur stems from fleeting references in a chronicle of around 829 – three or four centuries after he was supposed to have existed – attributed to a Welsh scholar called Nennius. There we read of a brave warrior who is said to have fought and won no less than twelve battles against the Saxons, and of that historical Arthur we know little more. But over the years, poets, painters, storytellers – and, in our own day, composers and filmmakers – have striven to embellish the Arthur of legend. Merlin, Guinevere, Sir Galahad, the Round Table, the Holy Grail, the Sword in the Stone and the Mists of Avalon were all later additions to the story. Tourist sites like Glastonbury, Tintagel, Winchester and the ancient hill fort of South Cadbury in Somerset have added their own local details as they have each staked their claim to having been Camelot, the mythical seat of Arthur's court.

The legend of Arthur has struck a chord with every age, but his tale is strongly tinged with melancholy. Though chivalrous and brave, the King Arthur of poem and fable is defeated in his final battle, surrendering his sword, as he dies, to the Lady of the Lake. His knightly Round Table was overthrown, just as Romano-British culture was swamped by the new realities of the fifth and sixth centuries. So both in history and legend Arthur embodies a theme that has proved dear to patriotic hearts over the centuries – the heroic failure.

POPE GREGORY'S ANGELS

c. AD 575

I T IS EASY TO FORGET HOW MANY HAZARDS LIFE HELD IN previous centuries. Nowadays, if you get blood-poisoning from a bad tooth or an infected cut, you take antibiotics. In those days you died. For that reason, outright death in battle was almost preferable to the slow, agonising end that came with a gangrenous wound. And there was another battle hazard – if you were captured, you could well end up a slave.

Imagine yourself living in a village in the fifth or sixth century and seeing a strange boat coming up the river filled with armed men. You would run for the woods at once, for fear that you might be taken captive, never to see your family again. That's what happened to the young St Patrick, the son of a town councillor living on the west coast of Britain in the early fifth century. Kidnapped by raiders when he was sixteen, Patrick suffered six years of slavery in Ireland before he finally escaped.

Along the trade routes of Europe travelled merchants carrying with them the hot items for which the rich would pay good money – gold, jewels, wine, spices and slaves, a number of them captured in the battles between the Slavic peoples of the Balkans. The medieval Latin word *sclavus* ('captive') is the root of the modern words 'Slav' and 'slave'. In the principal European markets there was a corner where you could buy yourself a maidservant, a labourer, or even a scribe to take care of your writing and accounting chores. Teeth were inspected and limbs prodded by would-be purchasers, just as buyers today kick the tyres of cars.

It was in such a slave market in Rome that Abbot Gregory, a priest well known for his piety, was strolling one day around 575. Though Gregory had been born into a wealthy Roman family that owned slaves, he had sold off his estates to found monasteries and had become popular for his good deeds and his sense of humour – he had something

23

of a weakness for wordplay and puns. Struck by the unusual appearance of a group of young captives with fair complexions and golden hair, he asked where they came from.

'From the island of Britain,' he was told, and specifically from the kingdom of Deira in Northumbria, the moorland area around the town of York, roughly equivalent to modern Yorkshire. At the mention of Deira, Gregory was tempted to one of his puns. In Latin, *de ira* means 'from wrath'.

'Then let us hope they will be rescued from wrath,' he said, 'and that they will be called to the mercy of Christ.'

But it was the news that these captives were Angles that inspired the pun that has been polished and repolished over the centuries. '*Non Angli sed angeli*,' Gregory is supposed to have said – 'They are not Angles, but angels.'

In fact, Gregory did not say that. His wordplay was more complicated. 'They have angelic faces,' he said in the most widely circulated version of this story, recorded about a hundred and fifty years later, 'and it is right that they should become joint heirs with the angels in heaven.' They might look like angels, in other words, but they were not angels yet. Christian conversion of these Anglish was called for.

Abbot Gregory, who became Pope Gregory I in 590, was a major figure in the growth of the Catholic Church. He is revered in Catholic and Greek Orthodox history as Gregory the Great – and, indeed, as a saint. His keen political sense and the popularity that he cultivated with the people of Rome contributed greatly to making the popes more than religious leaders. In due course the papacy would take over the city of Rome and would rule all of central Italy. Gregory also reformed the Church's services and rituals, giving his name to the solemn chanting inherited from Hebrew music, the 'Gregorian' chant or plainsong, whose haunting cadences could spread the faith across language barriers, making music possible without the need for musical instruments.

But it is for his wordplay in the slave market that he is remembered in English history. The sight of the fair Anglish captives in Rome inspired Pope Gregory to send missionaries northwards. He made history's pun come true – by giving the Angles (as well as the Saxons and the Britons) a chance to join the angels.

ST AUGUSTINE'S MAGIC
AD 597

IN THE HIGH SUMMER OF 597 POPE GREGORY'S MISSIONARIES
landed on the Isle of Thanet in Kent bearing painted banners, silver
crosses and holy relics. The man that Gregory had picked to lead the
mission to the Angles was a trusted old colleague, Augustine – and his
first target was cleverly chosen. King Ethelbert of Kent was a pagan,
but his wife Bertha was a Christian, a Frankish princess who had
brought her own chaplain from Paris. If Kent's king was allowing his
wife to practise her Christian faith in Kent's capital (Kent-erbury or
Canterbury), he must be a promising prospect for conversion.

Ethelbert greeted the missionaries with caution, insisting that their
first meeting should be out of doors – he did not want to be trapped
by their alien magic.

'I cannot abandon the age-old beliefs that I have held,' he declared
in his speech of welcome. 'But since you have travelled far, and I can
see that you are sincere in your desire to share with us what you believe
to be true and excellent, we will not harm you.'

In fact, the King let Augustine and his forty followers base themselves in Canterbury at an old church where Bertha worshipped – clear
evidence that Christianity was by no means new to a country which had
previously been a Roman province. Some time in the third century St
Alban had become Britain's earliest saint and martyr when he suffered
execution for protecting a Christian priest – and after the emperor
Constantine was converted in 312, Christianity had been tolerated
across the empire. But then the Anglo-Saxons had imported their pan-
theon of Germanic gods, a collection of very human deities inspired
by storms, victory in battle and the forces of nature. The word 'pagan'
comes from *pagus*, Latin for a country district and its inhabitants.
When the Anglo-Saxon ploughman went out to cut his first furrow of

25

the year, he would kneel and say a prayer as he buried a fertility cake baked from the last harvest's grain, asking the gods to allow the seed to germinate again.

Back in Rome, Pope Gregory had told Augustine to treat such pagan customs with respect. 'For in these days,' he explained, 'the Church corrects some things strictly and allows others out of leniency . . . By doing so she often succeeds in checking an evil of which she disapproves.'

The Pope wisely suggested that churches should be built where the old pagan temples had been – 'in order that the people may the more familiarly resort to the places with which they have been accustomed'.

Rather than sacrifice to Mother Earth, the pagans were encouraged to pray to the mother of Jesus, the Virgin Mary. And our modern calendar shows the live-and-let-live interaction between old and new: Sun-day and Moon-day were followed by Tiw's-day, Woden's-day, Thor's-day and Freya's-day, named after the Germanic gods of war, wisdom, thunder and love respectively. Saturn's-day was another pagan hangover – from the Romans in pre-Christian times. The feast of Easter gets its name from Eastre, the Anglo-Saxon goddess of dawn and fertility.

As Ethelbert cannily studied Augustine and his companions, he came to the conclusion that the Christians posed no threat to him. On the contrary, he liked what they had to offer – learning, piety, discipline, and a ready-made band of activists who were keen to go out and spread these solid virtues among his people. Augustine helped the king draw up the first Anglo-Saxon law code. The Christian magic was a potent and modern magic, and he had a special reason for urgency – Augustine and his missionaries warned all they met that the end of the world was nigh and that God's terrible judgement was at hand. Fourteen hundred years later we speak of the *early* Church, but Gregory, Augustine and their fellow-believers did not know they were only at the beginning of a very long story. They believed that time was short. Jesus could be coming back to earth at any moment – maybe that very night, 'like a thief', as he promised in the Bible – and King Ethelbert decided not to take the chance that these learned newcomers with their documents and paintings might be wrong.

Ethelbert was baptised, and he invited Augustine to make

Canterbury the headquarters of his missionary efforts, giving him the land and money to build the first Canterbury Cathedral. To this day, Canterbury remains the headquarters of the Church of England, and Archbishops of Canterbury sit on the throne of St Augustine.

KING OSWY AND THE CROWN OF THORNS
AD 664

AUGUSTINE AND HIS FOLLOWERS WERE NOT THE ONLY missionaries at work converting the pagans of Anglo-Saxon England in the years around AD 600. For nearly half a century, Celtic monks from the island of Iona off the shore of western Scotland had been travelling around, preaching Christianity to the inhabitants of northern England. Their teachings were inspired by the kidnapped St Patrick (see p. 23), who, after escaping from slavery in Ireland, could not rid himself of the 'cry of unbaptised children'. He had returned to convert his Irish captors – and, according to legend, had also rid Ireland of snakes in the process.

The graphic emblem of the Irish missionaries was the Celtic cross, the symbol of Christianity surrounded by a sunburst. Irish monks happily sought inspiration in Celtic culture, incorporating the sinuous geometric patterns of its imagery into their Christian manuscripts. They shaved the front of their heads in the tradition of the Druids and had their own date for Easter. So in the early seventh century England's patchwork of Anglo-Saxon kingdoms was being converted from two directions, with north and south practising Christianity in different ways.

The problem came to a head when King Oswy of Northumbria

married Eanfled, a princess from Kent, who came north with her own chaplain and other followers. They practised their religion in the manner that Augustine had established – including the latest Roman way of calculating when Easter should fall. Christ had been crucified in Jerusalem as the Jews were gathering for the feast of Passover, so Easter's timing had to relate to the Jewish lunar calendar which ran from new moon to new moon in a cycle of $29\frac{1}{2}$ days. But the Christian church used Rome's Julian calendar, which was based on the annual $365\frac{1}{4}$-day cycle of the sun – and whichever way you try, $29\frac{1}{2}$ into $365\frac{1}{4}$ does not go.

'Such was the confusion in those days', related the historian Bede, 'that Easter was sometimes kept twice in one year, so that when the king [Oswy] had ended Lent and was keeping Easter, the queen [Eanfled] and her attendants were still fasting and keeping Palm Sunday.'

Oswy decided to call a conference to sort out this clash of timing and to resolve the whole range of differences between the rival bands of priests – among them the vexed question of the correct religious hairstyle, or tonsure. Down in the south clergy shaved a bald patch on the top of their heads, leaving a thin circle of hair all round the head just above the temples, in memory of Christ's crown of thorns. This was the Roman tonsure that contrasted with the Druid-like hairstyle of the Celtic monks, who shaved the front of their heads along a line going over the top of the scalp from ear to ear, with the hair behind their ears tumbling down in long, flowing and sometimes greasy locks. Not for the last time in English history, hairstyles were vivid and visible symbols of divided loyalties.

The two sets of holy men squared off at a synod, or church council, held in 664 at the Abbey of Whitby, high on a hill overlooking the rugged Yorkshire coast.

'Easter is observed by men of different nations and languages at one and the same time in Africa, Asia, Egypt, Greece, and throughout the world,' argued the Roman, southern English side. 'The only people who stupidly contend against the whole world are those Irishmen . . .'

'It is strange that you call us stupid,' retorted the Irish spokesman, citing the support of the gospel writer St John, and, more pertinently, St Columba, who had founded the great monastery of Iona from which so many of the Irish monks had come.

In the end it was the King who resolved the arguments. The Canterbury side had based their case on the authority of St Peter, who was believed to have brought Christianity to the city of Rome and to whom Jesus Christ had said, 'I will give unto thee the keys of the kingdom of heaven.' These words from the Bible impressed King Oswy mightily.

'I tell you,' said the King, 'if Peter is guardian of the gates of heaven, I shall not contradict him. Otherwise when I come to the gates of heaven, there may be no one to open them.'

Heaven and earth seemed very close in a world where life was so fragile. King Oswy plumped for the Roman Easter, the Roman tonsure and the overall authority of the Pope in Rome, tying England more firmly to the church's 'world headquarters', with Canterbury confirmed as the local 'head office'. The first reaction of the long-haired monks who had argued the Celtic case was to leave Northumbria disgruntled, returning to Iona and eventually to Ireland. There they discovered, however, that some Irish churches were already calculating Easter according to the latest Roman system – and the Roman tonsure eventually followed. In due course razors would shave the necks and scalps of all Irish monks in the Roman crown-of-thorns style.

Six years later, in 670, King Oswy, whose voice had been so decisive in Rome's victory, died as he was setting out on a pilgrimage to the Holy See of St Peter in Rome. His body was brought back to Whitby to be buried at the site of the historic synod by the sea, and if his spirit did manage to find its way to the gates of heaven, we must presume that St Peter was waiting there for him with the keys.

CAEDMON, THE FIRST ENGLISH POET

c.AD 680

CAEDMON WAS A HERDSMAN WHO LOOKED AFTER THE FARM animals at the monastery of Whitby. His Celtic name tells us he was of native British descent, like so many others, as a labourer for the new Anglo-Saxon masters of the land.

Caedmon was something of a dreamer – and very shy. When guests gathered for the firelit evenings of song and recitation with which the people of the time entertained themselves he would shrink away when he saw the harp heading in his direction. He would slip quietly back to his home in the stables – and it was on one such evening, lying down in the straw to sleep among the animals, that he had a dream. The cowherd saw a man beside him.

'Caedmon,' said the stranger, 'sing me a song.'

'I don't know how to sing,' he replied. 'I left the feast because I cannot sing – that's why I'm here.'

'But you shall sing to me,' insisted the man.

'What shall I sing?' asked Caedmon.

'Sing the song of creation,' came the answer.

At once, in his dream, Caedmon found himself singing to God in a rush of poetry that he was astonished to hear coming from his own mouth – 'Nu scylun hergan, haefaenricaes uard' – 'Now shall we praise the keeper of the kingdom of heaven.'

When he awoke next morning, Caedmon found that he could remember the whole verse from his dream, and that he could compose more. There and then he created an entire song, the 'Hymn of Creation'. He recited it that same morning to his boss the reeve – the manager of the abbey farm – who was so impressed that he took the cowherd along for a meeting with the head of the monastery, the abbess Hilda.

Hilda was a lively and welcoming woman. As Abbess of Whitby she had been hostess of the great synod that had argued over Easter and hairstyles some twenty years earlier, and now she gathered together a group of clerics to audition this cowherd who could sing. When they heard Caedmon's 'Hymn of Creation', the learned panel agreed that his gift of composing could only have come from God, and that the stranger in his dream must have been an angel. To test him, they picked out another theme, a story from the Bible, and next day he brought them more visionary verses that had come to him in the stable during the night.

Hilda was delighted. Caedmon should give up tending the cattle, she suggested. He must become a monk – and as the cowherd came to know the great stories of the Bible, so the inspiration flowed. He sang of the creation of the world, of how the human race had started and how the children of Israel had found themselves entering the Promised Land. He sang of Christ coming down to earth, of how God's son was crucified and then rose miraculously from the dead. And he also sang darker songs – warnings against the flames of hell and the terrors of the Last Judgement. Caedmon was like one of the cows that he used to tend, wrote a fellow-monk. He transformed everyday words into poetry, just as a cow, by chewing and ruminating, turns humble grass into green, fresh-smelling cud.

The cowherd stunned his listeners because his sacred verses were in the earthy language of ordinary people. By tradition, holy things had to be said in Latin, the language of the Church. In those days church services were all in Latin – as was the Bible. Speaking Latin was the sign of being educated and therefore superior. But now Caedmon was daring to sing hymns in Anglish, or *englisc*, the racy and rhythmic language of the Angles that was spreading across the island. *Englisc* was the language of the Anglo-Saxons' pagan sagas. In making poetry from the language of the less privileged, Caedmon, who died in the year 680, could be compared to a folksinger or even a modern rapper – and in Anglo-Saxon terms his 'Hymn of Creation' was certainly a popular hit. It survives as part of his story in no fewer than twenty-one hand-copied versions.

Every modern pop song bears a credit line – 'Copyright: Lennon–McCartney', or whatever. Below the earliest surviving poem in English, composed one night in a stable on the edge of the Yorkshire moors, are written the words: 'Caedmon first sang this song.'

31

THE VENERABLE BEDE
AD 672/3–735

WE KNOW ABOUT CAEDMON THE COWHERD, HILDA THE abbess, the Angles and the angels, and the insults that the Irish and English monks hurled at each other as they argued about hairstyles and the timing of Easter, thanks to the writings of the very first English historian, the Venerable Bede. To modern ears, it is a weird and even pompous-sounding name – 'venerable' meaning ancient and worthy, 'Bede' being an old word for prayer. But Bede the man was anything but pompous. He was a down-to-earth and rather humorous character – as you might expect of a Geordie lad, born in Northumbria near Monkwearmouth, now part of modern Sunderland. Bede spent most of his life in Jarrow on the banks of the River Tyne, where the modern Geordie accent, according to linguists, can be traced back to the Old English dialect spoken by Bede and his fellow-Northumbrians in Anglo-Saxon times.

The boy was just seven, and quite possibly an orphan, when he was handed into the care of the local monastery. In Anglo-Saxon England monks operated the only schools, and they trained their pupils in harsh conditions. In winter it was so cold in the Jarrow cloisters that pens slipped from the fingers of the priestly hands – while summer brought flies and infection. When plague struck the monastery in 685, the only survivors who could scratch up a choir were the twelve-year-old Bede and the old abbot, who managed to keep the services going between them, chanting and responding to each other across the chapel.

Today there is a Bede Station on the Newcastle to South Shields line of the Tyne and Wear Metro. If you get off the train and walk past the oil tanks and electricity power lines of modern Jarrow you soon come to the very chapel where Bede and the abbot kept the singing alive thirteen hundred years ago. Sometimes there is only a thin curtain between the past and ourselves. In those days the Jarrow monastery was surrounded by green fields, and from its ruins you can get an idea of how Bede lived his life, studying and writing by candlelight for more than fifty years in his small stone cell.

He wrote with a sharpened goose quill that he dipped in acid. 'Encaustum' was the monks' word for ink, from the same Latin word that gives us 'caustic', meaning 'biting' or 'burning'. Darkened with iron salts, Bede's ink literally bit into his writing surface, which was not paper but parchment – scraped animal skin. The parchment would have been stretched out initially on a wooden frame that prevented the skin from shrinking back into the shape of the lamb, calf or kid from which it came. It could take as many as five hundred calfskins to make one Bible.

On this primitive but very effective and durable surface, Bede worked magic. He wrote no less than sixty-eight books – commentaries on the Bible, a guide to spelling, works on science, the art of poetry, mathematics, astronomy, philosophy, grammar, the lives of Christian martyrs and a book of hymns. From his bright and simple Latin prose we get to know a man who was also interested in carpentry, music and the movement of the tides, which he studied and measured on long walks along the sands and rockpools of the blowy Northumbrian coast. Bede took a particular interest in cooking. He kept his own store of peppercorns, precious spices transported by traders from the other side of the world, to pound and sprinkle on the bland monastery food. He could be frank about the drawbacks of the monkish life. Writing of King Saul's two wives, he ruefully admitted: 'How can I comment on this who have not even been married to one?'

It is largely thanks to Bede that today we date our history from the birth of Christ – the AD method of dating that gets its name from the Latin *anno domini* ('in the year of our Lord'). The Romans had based their dating system on the accession dates of their emperors, but in his work *On the Reckoning of Time*, written in 725 AD, Bede took up the idea that the Church should not rely on this pagan system, particularly since it was the Romans who persecuted Christ. How much better to date the Christian era from the birth of Our Saviour himself! Six years later Bede put the system into practice when he wrote the book for which he is principally remembered – *The Ecclesiastical History of the English People*.

To this day, Bede's vivid narrative brings alive the texture of a turbulent time. He was a storytelling monk with a human touch, describing the terrible effects of famine in the land of the South Saxons where whole families, starving, would hold hands and jump off the white Sussex cliffs in tragic suicide pacts. In a credulous age he had a sceptical wit, poking fun, for example, at the legend that St Patrick had rid Ireland of snakes. This must mean, he wrote, that if any snakes happened to come over in a boat from Britain, they only had to inhale the scented Irish air to breathe their last.

This gentle dig at the Irish Christians reflected Bede's prejudices. He was English and proud of it. For him, the Angles and Saxons were God's chosen people, and his history tells us little about the Scots, and still less about the Welsh, of whom he disapproved heartily as troublesome heretics. He believed that life had a purpose, that men and women can shape their own destiny through hard work and faith – and for him that destiny was Christian and English.

But Bede's proudly local story contains scenes and ideas with which anyone could identify today. Imagine yourself among a group of Anglo-Saxon nobles discussing the pros and cons of the new Christian faith, when one of them comes up with this interpretation of life:

It seems to me that the life of man on earth is like the swift flight of a single sparrow through the banqueting hall where you are sitting at dinner on a winter's day with your captains and counsellors. In the midst there is a comforting fire to warm the hall. Outside, the storms of winter rain and snow are raging. This sparrow flies swiftly in through one window of the hall and out through another. While he is inside, the bird is safe from the winter storms, but after a few moments of comfort, he vanishes from sight into the wintry world from which he came. So, man appears on earth for a little while – but of what went before this life, or of what follows, we know nothing.

Bede's own sparrow flight across the hall of life was lengthy by Anglo-Saxon standards. He died when he was sixty-two, surrounded by his pupils, who were helping him finish his last work, a translation of the Gospel of St John into 'our language', that is, from Latin into *englisc*.

'Learn quickly now,' he told them, 'for I do not know how much longer I will live.'

He dictated the final chapter, then turned to one of his pupils. 'I have a few treasures in my little box,' he said. 'Run quickly and fetch the priests of our monastery, so I can distribute to them these little gifts which God has given me.'

And so, before he died, the Venerable Bede handed out to the monks his store of worldly treasures – some handkerchiefs, some incense and the remains of his beloved peppercorns.

ALFRED AND THE CAKES
AD 878

ANGLO-SAXON ENGLAND SOUNDS QUITE A CHEERY place, as described by the gentle and generous Bede from the security of his monastic cell. But we read of quite another country in the blood-drenched pagan sagas of the age. Winter howls. Ravens wheel over trees that are bent and blasted by the sea winds. Storms crash against rocky slopes. Darkness draws on. It was a perilous and threatening world that lay outside the torchlit circles of Anglo-Saxon settlements. No wonder their inhabitants declaimed courage-stirring poems of defiance of which the epic tale of Beowulf is an early example. Shepherds guarded their flocks against the wolf – 'grey ganger of the heath' – and long-tusked boar ran wild in the forests. Vast areas of the country were trackless watery wastelands.

These inaccessible brackish expanses were the main difference between the English countryside then and now. In East Anglia the Wash flowed into Middle England, a fenland of more than a thousand square miles where cattle had to be rounded up by boat. Half of Staffordshire consisted of peat and moss swamps, and much of the Thames Valley was a marsh. To the west lay the Somerset Levels, acre after misty acre of bullrush and sedge extending from Glastonbury to Bridgwater Bay. Pelicans, herons and the huge European crane took refuge in its wastes, along with fugitives and runaways – and, on one famous occasion, a king.

He was Alfred, King of the West Saxons, driven into the Somerset no man's land by the Vikings, the seaborne raiders who had started their attacks on England at the end of the previous century. They came from Denmark, Norway and the Baltic in their sleek and deadly longboats, crossing the North Sea as the Angles and Saxons had crossed it before them, pushed by the same pressures of population and attracted by easy pickings. One day around the year 800, the royal tax collector at Dorchester rode down to Portland to meet a fleet of Norse trading ships that had landed. But when he explained to the visitors how to pay their customs duties, they split his head open with a battle-axe. In the north the invaders captured and burgled the defenceless Abbey of Lindisfarne, drowning the old monks and taking away the young ones to sell as slaves.

The raids continued, decade after decade – and not just in England. In the course of the ninth century, Viking armies sacked Paris, Hamburg, Antwerp, Bordeaux and Seville. Moving fast in packs of five hundred or more, sometimes shouldering their lean-planked ships overland from river to river, the raiders even reached Russia – whose name comes from the Rus, the community of Vikings who set up their own kingdom in Novgorod, just south of the Gulf of Finland, in 852.

It was around this time that the Vikings in England adopted a worrying change of tactic: instead of returning home in the autumn, their armies started to settle. They took over the north of England, making York their own Danish-speaking, Danish-run capital, then extended their 'Danelaw', as the land they occupied came to be known, south into East Anglia, where in 870 they defeated Edmund, King of the East Angles. Refusing to renounce his Christian faith, King Edmund was tied to a tree and shot to death with arrows, according to one tradition. According to another, he was subjected to the inhuman Norse rite of 'carving the blood eagle', whereby the victim's ribs were cut away from his spine while alive. His lungs were then pulled out, to be spread like wings across his back. In the following century the martyred king's remains were moved to the Suffolk town of

Bedricsworth, which in due course became a centre of worship and pilgrimage under the name of Bury St Edmunds.

Down in the south-west in Wessex, the last remaining centre of Anglo-Saxon resistance, King Alfred could certainly have expected a grisly end to match Edmund's. He was a devout Christian – he had travelled to Rome as a boy. When he succeeded his brother in 871, at the age of twenty-three, Alfred was more noted for his learning and piety than for warfare. His name meant 'elf wisdom', and while he did enjoy some success in battle his most successful tactic was to buy off the enemy. In return for payments later known as 'Danegeld', the Vikings would agree to go home for the winter.

But the next year they would reappear, and early in 878 an army led by the Danish king Guthrum drove Alfred westwards into the marshes of Somerset. It was Easter time and the King retreated with a small band of followers, dodging from islet to islet through the splashy bogs. They had nothing to live on except what they could forage from the local population – and from Alfred's desperate plight came one of the most famous tales of English history.

Taking shelter in the poor home of a swineherd whose wife was baking some bread, went the story, the refugee king was sitting by the fire, so preoccupied by his problems that he did not notice that the loaves were burning.

'Look here, man,' exclaimed the woman, who did not know that her bedraggled guest was the king, 'you hesitate to turn the loaves which you see to be burning, yet you're quite happy to eat them when they come warm from the oven!'

The endearing story ends with the apologetic king meekly submitting to the woman's scolding and setting to work to turn the bread; but the account does not, unfortunately, come down to us from Alfred's lifetime. The earliest manuscript that recounts the burning of the loaves (which turned into 'cakes' in the course of many subsequent retellings) was written about a hundred years after his death.

It is most likely a folk tale, handed on by word of mouth. Much was written about the heroic Alfred in the course of his life, and it seems surprising that such a very good story did not find its way on to parchment at the time. By the strictest laws of historical evidence, the story of Alfred and the cakes must be rated a myth.

But while myths may be factually untrue, they can help convey a deeper truth – in this case the humbling of the great king hiding in the marshes. So down-and-out that he had to suffer the scolding of a peasant woman, Alfred showed grace under pressure. He resisted the temptation to pull rank and lash out when rebuked – and he also made good use of his weeks in the wilderness. In May 878 Alfred rode out of his fortified camp in the marshes at Athelney, met up with his people and, just two days later, led them to a famous victory at Edington in Wiltshire. Guthrum was compelled to renounce his bloodthirsty Norse gods and to accept Christianity. He withdrew to the Danelaw with his forces, and for a dozen years the Vikings left Wessex largely in peace.

Alfred made good use of the respite. He built a defensive network of forts and fortified towns known as *burhs*, from which comes the modern word 'boroughs'. No one in Wessex was more than twenty miles from a *burh* where they could take refuge, and many of these military settlements later grew into towns. Taking on the Vikings at their own game, he designed and built a fleet of longships – in later centuries Alfred came to be described as the 'Father of the Royal Navy' – and he also reorganised his army. As the *Anglo-Saxon Chronicle* reported in 893, 'the king had divided his army in two, so that always half his men were at home and half out on service, except for those men who were to garrison the burhs'.

The *Anglo-Saxon Chronicle* was one of Alfred's great creations, a history of England up to his own reign, which then turned into a sort of yearly newspaper, regularly updated, recording that year's events in a forthright and sometimes quite critical fashion. The first updating was in the early 890s, and from then on monasteries around the country added their own instalments to a project that was one of the most remarkable of its kind in Europe. The *Chronicle* reported battles, famines, floods, political back-stabbing, triumphs and disasters in lively prose – not in Latin but in English, the language, as Alfred put it, 'that we can all understand'.

Alfred felt passionately that his kingdom must be educated. 'The saddest thing about any man,' he once wrote, 'is that he be ignorant, and the most exciting thing is that he knows.'

He put together a panel of scholars and started to learn Latin himself so that he could translate some of the great Latin texts into

English. In a world without clocks, the King was anxious to work out the exact time of day, inventing a graduated candle on which the hours were marked off. Then he came up with the idea of a ventilated cow's-horn lantern to stop the candle blowing out.

When Alfred died in 899, Wessex was a thriving and dynamic kingdom, and it is not surprising that he should have become the only king in English history to be known in later centuries as 'the Great'. But he himself was modest about his achievements. He suffered as an adult from the agonies of swollen veins in and around the anus, the embarrassing complaint we call piles, along with other pains that baffled his doctors. These infirmities seem to have contributed to a strong sense of his own imperfections, and his account of his life ended on a tired and rueful note. Comparing his life to a house built out of whatever timber he could forage from the forests of experience, he described how 'in each tree I saw something that I required'. He advised others 'to go to the same woods where I have cut these timbers' so that they could construct their own house of life, 'with a fair enclosure and may dwell therein pleasantly and at their ease, winter and summer, as I have not yet done'.

Reading these words, it does seem reasonable to assume that such a spiritual and modest man would have accepted the reproof of a peasant woman when he let her loaves burn in the wilderness. But Alfred himself would surely expect us to be rigorous about the truth.

THE LADY OF THE MERCIANS
AD 911–18

THERE IS A BATTERED SILVER PENNY FROM KING ALFRED'S reign on which is inscribed the grand Latin title rex anglo[rum] – 'King of the English'. But the claim was only half true. Alfred had been King of those Angel-cynn, the kin or family of the English, who lived in Wessex, and his resourcefulness had kept Englishness alive in the dark days when the Viking forces drove him and his people into the Somerset marshes. The work of extending Anglo-Saxon authority across the whole of Engla-lond, as it would come to be known, was done by Alfred's children and grandchildren – and of these the most remarkable was his firstborn, his daughter Aethelflaed, whose exploits as a warrior and town-builder won her fame as the 'Lady of the Mercians'.

'In this year English and Danes fought at Tettenhall [near Wolverhampton], and the English took the victory,' reported the *Anglo-Saxon Chronicle* for 910. 'And the same year Aethelflaed built the stronghold at Bremsbyrig [Bromsberrow, near Hereford].'

Women exercised more power than we might imagine in the macho society of Anglo-Saxon England. The Old English word *hlaford*, 'lord', could apply equally to a man or a woman. The abbess Hilda of Whitby (Caedmon's mentor, p. 31), who was related to the royal families of both Northumbria and East Anglia, had been in charge of a so-called 'double house', where monks and nuns lived and worshipped side by side and where the men answered to the abbess, not the abbot.

The assets and chattels of any marriage were legally considered the property of both husband and wife, and wills of the time routinely describe landed estates owned by wealthy women who had supervised the management of many acres, giving orders to men working under them. King Alfred's will distinguished rather gracefully between the 'spear' and 'spindle' sides of his family. It was women's work to spin wool or flax with a carved wooden spindle and distaff, and the old king bequeathed more to his sons on the spear side than to his wife and daughters with their spindles. But he still presented Aethelflaed with one hundred pounds, a small fortune in tenth-century terms, along with a substantial royal estate.

Aethelflaed turned out to be an Anglo-Saxon Boadicea, for like Boadicea she was a warrior widow. Her husband Ethelred had ruled over Mercia, the Anglo-Saxon kingdom that had spread over most of the Midlands under the great King Offa in the late 700s. Extending from London and Gloucester up to Chester and Lincoln, Mercia formed a sort of buffer state between Wessex in the south and the Danelaw to the north and east, and the couple had made a good partnership, working hard to push back Danish power northwards. But Ethelred was sickly, and after his death in 911 Aethelflaed continued the work.

'In this year, by the Grace of God,' records the *Anglo-Saxon Chronicle* for 913, 'Aethelflaed Lady of the Mercians went with all the Mercians to Tamworth, and built the fortress there in early summer, and before the beginning of August, the one in Stafford.'

It does not seem likely that Aethelflaed fought in hand-to-hand combat. But we can imagine her standing behind the formidable shield wall of Saxon warriors, inspiring the loyalty of her men and winning the awed respect of her enemies. She campaigned in alliance with her brother Edward, their father's successor as King of Wessex, and together the brother and sister repulsed the Danes northwards to the River Humber, thereby regaining control of East Anglia and central England. To secure the territory they captured, they followed their father's policy of building fortified *burhs*.

Aethelflaed built ten of these walled communities at the rate of about two a year, and their sites can be traced today along the rolling green hills of the Welsh borderland and across into the Peak District. They show a shrewd eye for the lie of the land, both as defensive sites and as population centres. Chester, Stafford, Warwick and Runcorn all developed into successful towns – and as Aethelflaed built, she kept her armies advancing northwards. In the summer of 917 she captured the Viking stronghold of Derby, and the following year she took

Leicester 'and the most part of the raiding-armies that belonged to it', according to the *Chronicle*. This was the prelude to a still more remarkable triumph: 'The York-folk had promised that they would be hers, with some of them granting by pledge or confirming with oaths.'

The Lady of the Mercians was on the point of receiving the homage of the great Viking capital of the north when she died, just twelve days before midsummer 918, a folk hero like her father Alfred. She had played out both of the roles that the Anglo-Saxons accorded to high-born women, those of 'peace-weaver' and 'shield-maiden', and her influence lived on after her death. Edward had had such respect for his tough and purposeful big sister that he had sent his eldest son Athelstan to be brought up by her – a fruitful apprenticeship in fortress-building, war and busy statecraft that also helped to get the young Wessex prince accepted as a prince of Mercia. After his father's death in 924, Athelstan was able to take control of both kingdoms.

Athelstan proved a powerful and assertive king, extending his rule to the north, west and south-west and becoming the first monarch who could truly claim to be King of all England. In his canny nation-building could be seen the skills of his grandfather Alfred and his father Edward, along with the fortitude of his remarkable aunt, tutor and foster-mother, the Lady of the Mercians.

ETHELRED THE UNREADY
AD 978–1016

ETHELRED THE UNREADY IS A FIGURE OF FUN IN ENGLISH history. It is now considered old-fashioned to classify monarchs as good kings or bad kings, but by almost any measure Ethelred was a bad one. In 978 he inherited the rich and respected kingdom of Engla-lond that had been pulled together by Aethelflaed, Edward, Athelstan and the other descendants of his great-great-grandfather Alfred. By 1016 Ethelred had lost it all, from Northumbria down to Cornwall, in the course of a reign that made him a byword for folly, low cunning and incompetence.

Perhaps the one sphere in which he deserves some sympathy is his unfortunate nickname, a mistranslation of the gibe made after his death by chroniclers who dubbed him Ethelred 'Unred'. In fact, *unred* was an Old English word that meant 'ill-advised', and it made a rather clever pun on the meaning of Ethelred's name, 'of noble counsel', rendering Ethelred Unred 'the well-advised, ill-advised'.

In Anglo-Saxon 'ethel' (also spelt 'aethel') denoted someone well born or royal – hence the vast number of Ethel-related names, from Ethelbert to Aethelflaed. All the offspring of a king, down to his great grandchildren, were known as *aethelings* – 'throne-worthies' – and it was from this gene pool that the *aetheling* who seemed most qualified for the job was selected. It would be many years before the rule of primogeniture, whereby the king would be automatically succeeded by his eldest son, came to prevail. If the Anglo-Saxon *aetheling* system still operated today, it might be decided that Prince William was more qualified than Prince Charles to succeed the Queen.

Ethelred, however, did not become king through discussion or consensus. He owed his throne to murder. One day when he was only ten, his older half-brother Edward – his father's son by a previous wife – rode through the gates of Corfe Castle in Dorset to quench his thirst

43

after an afternoon's hunting. The young Ethelred was staying in the castle with his mother, and out in the courtyard a quarrel developed between her followers and Edward. They handed him a drink, then stabbed him to death before he could dismount.

Did Ethelred, inside the castle, hear his half-brother hit the ground in the courtyard? His mother was suspected of inspiring the stabbing, but Ethelred never investigated the murder that handed the crown to him as a ten-year-old, and it cast a shadow of suspicion over his entire reign.

The great challenge facing England during Ethelred's years was a new round of Danish invasions. Having left the island in peace for decades, the Vikings now returned with more rapacious raiding parties than ever. In fact, the raids were so ferocious that the Anglo-Saxons inserted a prayer in their church services every Sunday imploring God to spare them from the terror of the invaders. Ethelred resorted to Alfred's time-honoured tactic of paying them off, but he failed to take advantage of the time the Danegeld payments gave him to strengthen and reorganise his defences. The King seemed devoid of leadership qualities.

'When the invaders were in the East,' recorded one of the scribes of the *Anglo-Saxon Chronicle* with ill-concealed disgust, 'the English army was kept in the West, and when they were in the South, our army was in the North . . . If anything was then decided, it did not last even a month. Finally there was no leader who would collect an army, but each fled as best he could, and in the end no shire would even help the next.'

For many of their raids, the Danes got help from their kinsmen in northern France. In 912 the French Channel coast had fallen to the Norsemen – *Normanni* in medieval Latin – and the sheltered harbours of Normandy provided ideal staging-posts for the Danes as they raided the south coast of England. Ethelred complained to the Pope, who got Duke Richard of Normandy to promise to stop helping the Danish raiders. To strengthen his links with the Normans, Ethelred later got married to Duke Richard's sister Emma.

But the invaders kept coming, and in 1002 Ethelred took a desperate step: he ordered the massacre of all Danes living in England. It was a foolhardy and wretched measure that gave the excuse for some Anglo-Saxons to settle local scores – the community of Danes living in Oxford were burned to death in the church where they had taken shelter. But even Ethelred's massacre was incompetent. There is little evidence that this dreadful ethnic cleansing was widely carried out – with one exception. Among the Danes who were killed was Gunnhilda, the sister of Sweyn Forkbeard, the King of Denmark.

It was a fatal mistake. The following year Sweyn led a huge Danish army up the River Humber, to receive a warm welcome from the inhabitants of the Danelaw. He returned in 1006 and again in 1013, fighting a campaign that eventually gave him control of all of England. England became a Danish possession, and Ethelred fled into exile in Normandy.

History books usually conclude Ethelred's story with the confused fighting that consumed the years 1013-16, ending with the deaths of both Ethelred and his son Edmund Ironside. But one episode tends to be overlooked. Sweyn died in 1014, and in a desperate attempt to regain his throne Ethelred offered to turn over a new leaf. Harking back to the conditions that Danish communities demanded when giving their allegiance to English rulers, Ethelred negotiated a sort of contract with the leading Anglo-Saxon nobles and clerics.

It was the first recorded pact between an English ruler and his subjects. Ethelred promised that 'he would govern them more justly than he did before', reported the *Anglo-Saxon Chronicle*. The king parleyed a comeback deal whereby 'he would be a gracious lord to them, and would improve each of the things which they all hated'. In return the nobles and clergy agreed to obey him, 'and full friendship was secured with word and pledge on either side'.

This contract, which appears to have been sealed in writing, was one of several last-ditch measures to which Ethelred had been driven in his weakness. As his authority eroded he had turned for help to the council of great lords and bishops who traditionally gave advice to Anglo-Saxon kings, the *witan* (plural of the Old English *wita*, meaning 'wise man'). Ethelred had used the prestige of the *witan* to bolster his appeals for taxes, for a national day of prayer against the heathen Danes and even for a nationwide fast during which just water and herbs would be consumed.

None of these frantic steps saved him. Though Ethelred was allowed back to England, he died in April 1016, and following the death of his son Edmund later that year the throne of England passed to the Danes in the shape of Sweyn's warrior son, Canute (Cnut). But some good came of the disaster. The incompetence that had compelled Ethelred to enlist the *witan* and that had inspired his last-gasp promise of good behaviour helped sow the seeds of a notion that would be crucial for the future – that English kings must rule with the consent of their people.

ELMER THE FLYING MONK
C.AD 1010

E LMER WAS AN ENQUIRING YOUNG MONK WHO LIVED AT Malmesbury Abbey, and who loved to gaze up at the stars. During the troubled early decades of the eleventh century, he would look to the heavens for signs and portents of things to come. But while many of his contemporaries were content to draw simple lessons of doom and disaster, Elmer gazed with a scientific eye. He noted that, if you were fortunate to live long enough, you could see a comet come round again in the sky.

Elmer applied his experimental mind to classical history, making a particular study of Daedalus, the mythical Athenian architect and engineer who was hired by King Minos to build his sinister labyrinth in Crete. To preserve the secret of his maze, Minos then imprisoned Daedalus and his son Icarus, who only escaped by building themselves wings of feathers and wax. Their escape plan was working beautifully until Icarus, intoxicated by the joy of flying, flew too close to the sun, which melted the wax in his wings. The boy fell into the Aegean Sea below, where the island of Ikaria perpetuates his legend to this day.

Elmer decided to test the story of Daedalus by making wings for himself, then trying to fly from the tower of the abbey. In an age when Britain was still suffering Viking raids, many Saxon churches had high bell-towers, both to serve as a lookout and to sound the alarm. Whenever the Vikings captured a church, the bell was always the first thing they tore down. Its valuable metal could be beaten into high-quality swords and helmets – and anyway, to capture the Christians' unique sound was a triumph in its own right.

Modern aeronautic experts have recreated Elmer's flight, and they calculate that his launch platform must have been at least 18 metres high, which corresponds to the height of surviving Saxon church towers. They also presume that he built his paragliding equipment from willow or ash, the most lightweight and flexible of the woods available in the copses of the nearby Cotswolds. To complete his bird-man outfit, the monk must have stretched parchment or thin cloth over the frame, which, we are told, he attached to both his arms and his feet. Today the ravens and jackdaws that live around Malmesbury Abbey can be seen soaring on the updraughts that blow up the hill between the church and the valley of the River Avon, and Elmer may have tried to copy them as he leapt off the tower and glided down towards the river.

According to William of Malmesbury, the historian who recorded Elmer's feat in the following century, the monk managed a downward glide of some 200 metres before he landed – or, rather, crash-landed. He did catch a breeze from the top of the tower, but was surprised by the atmospheric turbulence and seems to have lost his nerve.

'What with the violence of the wind and the eddies and at the same time his consciousness of the temerity of the attempt,' related William, 'he faltered and fell, breaking and crippling both his legs.'

William of Malmesbury probably got his story from fellow-monks who had known Elmer in old age. The eleventh-century stargazer was the sort of character dismissed as mad in his lifetime, but later seen as a visionary. In his final years Elmer's limping figure was a familiar sight around the abbey – and the would-be birdman would explain the failure of his great enterprise with wry humour. It was his own fault, he would say. As William told it, 'He forgot to fit a tail on his hinder parts.'

KING CANUTE AND THE WAVES
AD 1016–35

KING CANUTE (CNUT) WHO RULED THE ENGLISH FROM 1016 until 1035 and who tried to turn back the waves, has gone down in folklore as the very model of arrogance, stupidity and wishful thinking.

One day the King invited his nobles down to the beach as the tide was coming in, ordering his throne to be placed where the waves were advancing across the sands. 'You are subject to me,' he shouted out to the water, 'as the land on which I am sitting is mine . . . I command you, therefore, not to rise on to my land, nor to presume to wet the clothing or limbs of your master.'

Not surprisingly, the sea paid no attention. According to the earliest surviving written version of the story, the tide kept on coming. The waves 'disrespectfully drenched the king's feet and shins', so he had to jump back to avoid getting wetter.

King Canute's soaked feet are a historical image to rival King Alfred's smoking cakes, and, as with the story of the cakes, we get our evidence not from an eyewitness but from a manuscript that was not written until about a hundred years later. In the case of Canute we can identify the storyteller precisely as Henry of Huntingdon, a country clergyman who lived on the edge of the Fens around 1130 and who wrote a *History of the English* in praise of 'this, the most celebrated of islands, formerly called Albion, later Britain, and now England'. An enthusiast for his local wetlands – 'beautiful to behold . . . green, with many woods and islands' – Henry compiled his history from other manuscript histories, most notably Bede and the *Anglo-Saxon Chronicle*, and from the personal memories of people who had lived through the great events.

Henry was a conscientious reporter. His account of his own times has a careful ring, and if I were putting money on it I would feel safer

KING CANUTE AND THE WAVES

betting that Canute got his feet wet than that Alfred burned the cakes. History's mistake has been the belief that Canute really did think he could stop the waves – according to Henry, the King thought quite the opposite.

'Let all the world know,' cried Canute as he retreated from his throne and contemplated his wet feet, 'that the power of kings is empty and worthless!' He shouted at the waves, in other words, to convey the message that he was *not* as all-powerful as he might seem, and he embellished his point with an additional, religious, lesson. 'There is no king worthy of the name,' he proclaimed, 'save God by whose will heaven, earth and sea obey eternal laws.'

The King of Heaven was the king who mattered, was his second message; and after this episode on the beach, according to Henry of Huntingdon, Canute never wore his golden crown again, placing it instead atop a figure of Jesus Christ. This tallies exactly with what we know of Canute's entire reign. As the son of the Viking Sweyn Forkbeard who had ousted Ethelred the Unready, he was anxious to emphasise that his family had converted from paganism and was now Christian. He gave generous gifts to embellish the cathedrals at Winchester and Canterbury, and also donated royal estates to support the abbey at Bury where pilgrims were starting to pray to Edmund, the saintly king who had been so cruelly murdered by a previous generation of Danish invaders (see p. 36). It was a matter of reconciliation.

Canute was a battle-hardened Viking who had slaughtered mercilessly to secure his power. In later years he liked to take the helm of the royal ship, Viking-style, so he could steer himself when he was travelling along the Thames, and if you attended his court you were likely to be jostled by Icelandic bards ready to declaim the latest epic poem. In the course of his reign he took control of both Denmark and Norway, to create a huge North Sea empire that stretched from Greenland to the Baltic and from the White Sea off north-western Russia to the Isle of Wight. But Canute had a touching wish to be considered English. He always saw England as his power base, and he understood that the key to success there was reconciliation between Anglo-Saxon and Dane.

He achieved it. Realising he could not hope to control the whole of Engla-lond, Canute delegated his powers to trusted local governors, *jarls* in Danish, the origin of our word 'earl'. His reign saw the consolidation of England's counties and shires, with their own courts and adminis- trators – the shire-reeves, or sheriffs. He produced a law code embodying the idea behind the contract to which Ethelred had agreed in the last moments of his reign: that a sort of bargain should exist between the King and his subjects. He wrote newsletters to the people of his adopted country, describing his personal impressions and feelings, for example, after a long trip when he had met the Pope in Rome.

'I have never spared,' he wrote, 'nor will I in the future spare, to devote myself to the well-being of my people.'

Canute was especially keen to discourage superstition, and anxious to educate those of his people who had not seen the light. For the sake of their souls he urged them to forsake their surviving pagan habits – the worship of trees, wizards and weather prophets, together with the magic charms that people offered up when they were trying to track down stolen cattle. Some of his laws sound barbaric today: 'If a woman during her husband's life commits adultery with another man,' read law 53, 'her legal husband is to have all her property, and she is to lose her nose and her ears.' But one hundred years later the comprehensive law code of Canute, with its respect for both Anglo-Saxon and Dane, was still regarded as an authority.

After the chaos of Ethelred's reign, this rough, tough Dane proved to be England's best king since Alfred – both wise and realistic. Realism was one of the lessons he was aiming to teach when he had tried to turn back the waves, and it is one of history's injustices that the monarch who took his throne down to the beach in order to spread wisdom has ended up looking an idiot.

EDWARD THE CONFESSOR
AD 1042-66

Edward the confessor is the only english king to have been declared a saint by the Pope. When people 'confess' anything nowadays, it is to actions they are ashamed of – their mistakes, their sins and, perhaps even, their crimes. If you hear someone say, 'I must confess', you know there is some sort of an apology coming up. But in Old English the word had an altogether more positive meaning. Confessors were a particular category of saint who had not been martyred but who had demonstrated their saintliness by testifying actively to their faith – in the case of King Edward, to the spiritual happiness that Christianity had brought to his not-always happy life. He was Edward the Testifier.

King Edward's testifying took the form of the immense abbey that he constructed in the fields a mile or so to the west of the walled city of London – the west minster (or monastery church), as opposed to the east minster of St Paul's that was London's cathedral. The soaring grandeur of the Westminster Abbey that we know today reflects the reshaping of the building in later centuries. But Edward's original abbey was grand enough. Built of stone, nearly 100 metres long and towering above the banks of the Thames, it was the largest church – in fact, the largest building of any sort – in Anglo-Saxon England. Edward modelled his great minster on the impressive new Romanesque architecture of Normandy where he had spent most of his youth.

He had had a lonely childhood. He saw little of his parents, Ethelred the Unready and Emma, the Norman noblewoman whom Ethelred married in 1002 (see p. 44). Through most of his boyhood Edward's distracted father was busy with the losing battle that he was fighting against the Danes, and after Ethelred's death in 1016 and

Canute's Danish conquest of England, the boy took refuge with his mother's relatives in Normandy.

Emma, however, did not join her eleven-year-old son in exile. Following the custom of conquerors, Canute secured his hold on his new kingdom by marrying the widow of his defeated enemy, and Emma seemed to enjoy the experience. In the eighteen years that she was married to Canute, she became so Danish it was as if she had never been married to Ethelred. When Canute died and Edward finally returned to England, his mother scarcely welcomed her son. She had had another son by Canute, Hartha Canute, whom she preferred. So after Hartha Canute died in 1042, clearing Edward's path to the throne, it was hardly surprising that once he had established his power the new king rounded up his earls, rode to Winchester where his mother was living, and confiscated all her treasure.

By now Edward was thirty-seven. He was a tall, skinny man with blond or prematurely white hair. Some later accounts suggest that he may have been lacking in normal pigmentation in skin, hair and eyes – an albino. One description hints at a pale, almost translucent complexion, so that the blood vessels in his cheeks would show bright pink beneath his skin. Looking otherworldly, speaking Norman French and spending much of his time at prayer, the Confessor was something of an outsider among the hard men of Anglo-Saxon England – a choirboy in a den of gangsters.

Edward owed his throne to the consent of the three great earls who controlled the country – Siward of Northumbria, Leofric of Mercia and Godwin of Wessex. Their landholdings were such that they could dictate terms to someone like Edward who was, in many ways, a foreigner. Of the three powerbrokers Godwin was the wealthiest and most powerful. In gangster terms, he was the boss of bosses, and in 1045 he received the pay-off for his role as kingmaker: Edward married Godwin's daughter Edith, and gave her brother Harold the earldom of East Anglia.

Six years later, Edward rebelled against his minders. He ordered old Godwin, Harold and the rest of the Godwins into exile, and packed Edith off to a nunnery. But his independence was short-lived. While Earls Siward and Leofric had been happy to see the back of the scheming Godwins, they were rapidly antagonised by the pro-Norman policies that the King now adopted. Edward had spent most of his life among Normans. They were the people he really understood and trusted. So to his Norman nephew Ralf the Timid he gave large estates in Herefordshire, where Ralf started building a mini-Normandy, complete with castles.

Edward also worried the English with the favour he showed to his forceful and ambitious relative, William the Bastard. William was the son of Emma's nephew, Duke Robert of Normandy, and was known as 'the Bastard' because his father never married his mother Herlève, a tanner's daughter, whose beauty, according to later legend, was said to have caught Robert's eye while she was washing clothes, bare legged, in a stream. After his father's death, William built Normandy into a dynamic military power, displaying ambitions that many English found disturbing. It was rumoured that, out of gratitude for Norman hospitality during his days of exile, Edward had even promised this distant kinsman that he could inherit the English throne after his death.

When old Godwin and his son Harold sailed defiantly up the Thames the following summer, the fleet that Edward raised against them refused to fight. The confessor king was humiliated. He had no choice but to accept the restoration of Godwin power, which Harold wielded after his father's death in 1053. Harold now took his father's title as Earl of Wessex. Edward was also compelled to bring his wife Edith back to court from the nunnery, though it was rumoured that he refused to have sexual relations with her. The loveless marriage certainly proved to be childless, and Edith's family was denied the satisfaction of welcoming into the world an heir who was both royal *and* half Godwin.

With the return of the Godwins, Edward scaled down his bid to be an effective king. Delegating his military power to Harold, he took consolation in his beloved minster, to which he devoted a tenth of his royal income.

On the riverbank nearby he built himself a home, the Palace of Westminster – the site of today's Houses of Parliament; and he spent his days there, praying with his monks and reading the Bible.

Edward's saintliness was confirmed when he started laying his hands on sufferers from scrofula, a form of tuberculosis that causes swellings in the lymph glands of the neck. Victims testified that their swellings decreased after the king had touched them, and it became a tradition for English monarchs to lay their hands on sufferers from this disease, later known as the 'King's Evil'. The ceremony of kings and queens 'touching for the King's Evil' continued into the eighteenth century and the reign of Queen Anne, who touched the infant Dr Johnson in 1712, without effecting a cure.

Edward's great Abbey of Westminster became the spot where the English monarchy did its business with God, the place where every monarch would be crowned except the twentieth-century king, Edward VIII – Edward the Abdicator, as he would have been called in the Middle Ages. Many kings and queens were also buried there, to be joined over the centuries by the nation's non-royal headline-makers. In Poets' Corner lie the writers, beside a historic cavalcade of statesmen, soldiers, scientists and other heroes – with just a few heroines – in a marble forest of statues and tombs. The Confessor's abbey has become England's hall of fame.

Edward himself was too ill to attend the dedication of his minster when it was finally completed in December 1065, and a week later he was dead, leaving England up for grabs. Since the saintly Confessor had failed to produce any children, the succession came down to a contest between Godwin's son Harold and the Duke of Normandy, William the Bastard. Harold had no blood connection at all, and William had only a distant claim. But both men knew how to fight a good battle.

THE LEGEND OF LADY GODIVA
C.AD 1043

THE IDEA OF A BEAUTIFUL NAKED LADY RIDING HER HORSE through the streets in broad daylight has an appeal that extends far beyond history. Today the name 'Godiva' is used as a trademark all over the world for striptease clubs and skimpy underwear, advertised by smiling young women with long, rippling hair. Yet these modern Godivas do not deploy their long hair to conceal their nakedness. On the contrary, they seem rather keen to reveal it – and they would certainly shock the pious Anglo-Saxon lady to whom they offer their naughty tribute.

The original Godiva was generous, kind-hearted and, by all accounts, highly respectable. In Anglo-Saxon her name was Godgifu, or 'God's gift'. She was a prominent figure in Edward the Confessor's England, owning large estates in her own right in the Midlands and East Anglia, and she was married to Leofric of Mercia, one of the three powerful earls who had placed Edward on the throne in 1042. Leofric effectively controlled most of central England, and he was selected by Edward to join the posse that raided the property of the King's mother Emma (see p. 52).

Godgifu and Leofric followed Edward's example of giving generously to the Church. Nowadays ambitious bigwigs buy the local football team and spend their money trying to help it to success. In the Middle Ages they showered their riches on the local church – or churches, in the case of Godgifu. In Coventry she devoted a great deal of her wealth to making its humble abbey the pride of the county of Warwickshire and beyond. 'There was not found in all England a monastery with such an abundance of gold and silver, gems, and costly garments,' wrote the chronicler Roger of Wendover in the early thirteenth century. And it was Roger who first wrote down the tale:

Longing to free the town of Coventry from the oppression of a heavy tax, Lady Godiva begged her husband with urgent prayers, for the sake of Jesus and his mother Mary, that he would free the town from the toll, and from all other heavy burdens. The earl rebuked her sharply. She was asking for something that would cost him much money, and he forbade her to raise the subject with him again. But, with a woman's persistence, she would not stop pestering her husband, until he finally gave her this reply. 'Mount your horse, and ride naked before all the people, through the market of the town, from one end to the other, and on your return you shall have your request.' To which Godiva replied, 'But will you give me permission if I am ready to do it?' 'I will,' her husband replied. Whereupon the countess, beloved of God, loosed her hair and let down her tresses, which covered the whole of her body like a veil. And then, mounting her horse, and attended by two knights, she rode through the market place, without being seen, except her fair legs. And having completed the journey, she returned with gladness to her astonished husband, and obtained of him what she had asked. Earl Leofric freed the town of Coventry and its inhabitants from the taxes.

So there you have the story, translated from the Latin that Roger scratched into his parchment around the year 1220 – and you will notice that, like Alfred's 'cakes' and Canute's waves, this colourful episode was not recorded until many years after it was supposed to have happened. Roger of Wendover's description of Lady Godgifu is rather like Trevor McDonald reporting on the Battle of Trafalgar. Long before Roger was born a number of historians had mentioned Godgifu in their chronicles, and not one of them had anything to say about naked horseback riding.

But there are several reasons for believing that Roger did not make the whole thing up. He was a monk at the Benedictine Abbey of St Albans, which had close links with the abbey founded in Coventry by Leofric and Godgifu. The monks went for prayer and study sessions at each other's abbeys, and their libraries exchanged manuscripts. So it is quite possible that the St Albans chronicler might have come across some since-vanished Coventry document that recounted Godgifu's stratagem for relieving the community's over-taxed poor.

Taxation was certainly a bitter and controversial local issue in 1043 when Leofric and Godgifu built their abbey at Coventry (a small part of which is now the site of the modern Coventry Cathedral). Just two years earlier feelings had been running so high in nearby Worcester that a couple of royal tax collectors had been set upon and murdered by the irate townsfolk. Leofric had been a commander of the army sent to discipline the community, and the brutal punishment he exacted involved ravaging the town for five days, before setting it alight and, according to the chronicler, John of Worcester, retiring 'with great booty'.

What did Godgifu think of her husband's role in slaughtering Worcester's tax protesters? It is tempting to wonder whether the 'gold and silver, gems, and costly garments' that she presented to her abbey two years later might, perhaps, have come from the booty of Worcester – Godgifu's own quiet way of making amends. But did her protest go as far as we have been led to believe?

In recent times, respectable members of the Women's Institute have stripped off so as to raise money for good causes, strategically placing apple pies and cookery books to substitute for Godiva's legendary long hair. But one cannot, sadly, imagine a grand and pious medieval lady doing any such thing. Godiva was one of the last great Anglo-Saxon women landowners. She inherited Leofric's vast estates after his death in 1057, and her possessions were listed in the Domesday Book. This God-fearing founder of monasteries and nunneries would hardly have ridden naked through rows of gawping peasants, however complete the camouflage of her luxuriant hair.

What does seem possible, however, is that Godiva may have ridden out *symbolically* naked – that is, stripped of the fine jewellery and sumptuous costume that denoted her status as one of the great of the land. Roger's source for the story may have used the Latin word *denudata*, which means 'stripped' – not necessarily total nudity. Maybe the jewels and fine outer clothes that Godiva took off for her ride were the very treasures that she was presenting to the abbey – and without fancy hairpins, of course, her hair would have come tumbling down voluptuously.

Symbolism was a powerful force in the Middle Ages. Riding penitentially through Coventry, an unadorned Lady Godiva would have made a forceful and startling statement by the standards of 1043. Her performance would have been well understood as a gesture of the sympathy she felt with the people of the community – which we should not, by the way, think of as much of a town. According to the Domesday Book, eleventh-century Coventry was scarcely a village: just sixty-nine families are listed as living there.

But real nudity is much more fun, and that is how the story has not just endured, but developed. As Coventry grew into a bustling centre of trade, the citizens became so proud of their naked lady that they started their own annual Godiva pageant, a saucy cut above the attractions of any other Midlands market town. An account of 1678 describes a Godiva procession that attracted tens of thousands of visitors, and it was around this time that another detail was added to the legend. According to the seventeenth-century version, the medieval villagers had shown their solidarity with Godiva's protest by staying indoors on the day of her ride, with their shutters decently closed so that she could pass by unobserved. No one, it seems, was so cheeky as to look out at her, with the single exception of a tailor called Thomas, who was promptly punished for his curiosity by being struck blind (or even struck dead, depending on the storyteller). And this is the origin of another English folk character – Peeping Tom.

THE YEAR OF THREE KINGS
1066

A S EDWARD THE CONFESSOR LAY ON HIS DEATHBED, TOO ill to attend the dedication of his beloved west minster, he summoned Earl Harold of Wessex to his side. Harold had no blood claim to the throne, but he was Edward's brother-in-law. He had helped run England for a dozen years and he was the candidate preferred by the other Anglo-Saxon earls, so now the dying king named him as his successor. That, at any rate, was the story according to Harold, and on 6

January 1066, the day that Edward was buried, he had himself crowned King of England.

The story was rather different according to William the Bastard, Duke of Normandy, who thought the succession was rightfully his through his French connections with the dead king. Out hunting in Normandy when the news of Harold's enthronement reached him, he was so angry that he could not speak. His followers kept their distance while the imperious Duke, in his wordless fury, kept tying and untying the fastenings on his cloak. (It is just a detail, but buttons and buttonholes had not been invented in 1066.)

William's view of events and of why he should succeed to the English throne was to be set out in a stupendous piece of graphic evidence and propaganda, the Bayeux Tapestry – a unique work of art and one of history's most remarkable documents. Stitched to the orders of William's half-brother, Bishop Odo, to decorate his new cathedral at Bayeux near the Normandy coast, the tapestry is a vast panorama, 50 centimetres high and some 70 metres long – the width of a football field. It features 37 buildings, 41 ships, 202 horses and no less than 626 characters, including lifelike images of Edward, William and Harold, who act out the drama in a wide-screen production of seventy-three picture sequences.

The tapestry tells us the Norman story, starting in England where Edward is still on the throne, and shows Earl Harold sitting proudly in his stirrups, a hunting hawk on his wrist, as he rides to set sail for France. Here the tapestry gives a comic-strip version of a journey that Harold probably made to Normandy in 1064, when he is thought to have sworn some sort of oath to William. Harold's supporters maintained that it was a simple pledge of friendship between the two strong men who controlled the different sides of the Channel.

The story according to William, however, was that Harold's pledge involved much more than mere friendship. The tapestry shows Harold making a deeply serious oath of allegiance – we see his hands outstretched, and he is swearing on not just one, but two large boxes of holy relics. Later Norman chroniclers had no doubt that Harold had promised to support William's claim to the English throne once the Confessor was dead.

For nine centuries people have argued fiercely about what Harold did or did not promise. It hardly seems likely that the ambitious and dynamic earl would have sworn away a kingdom voluntarily, and if the oath had been forced out of him, then he clearly did not feel bound by it when he took over England on Edward's death. But we know from the tapestry what happened next: a flaming ball of fire, described by the *Anglo-Saxon Chronicle* as a 'hairy star', appeared in the heavens.

Modern astronomers have identified this hairy star as Halley's Comet, named after the seventeenth-century astronomer Sir Edmund Halley, who identified it when it passed over England in 1682. Elmer the flying monk saw the comet pass over England in both 989 and 1066, and realised that it was the same 'star' returning (see p. 46). Halley was able to work out the other dates when the comet's seventy-six-and-a-half-year-long circlings of the solar system would have brought it close to the earth – and April 1066 was one of those moments. But William of Normandy was certain that the hairy star was a sign of God's anger at Harold for breaking his oath, and it served as God's authorisation for the busy picture that soon follows on the tapestry – a tableau of Norman axemen chopping down trees and building an invasion fleet.

In England, meanwhile, Harold was trying to strengthen his position. His lover for many years had been the beautiful Edith Swan-Neck – they had had five sons and two daughters together. But to cement his power within the English aristocracy, Harold now arranged a marriage of convenience with Ealdgyth, the sister of two of the country's most powerful earls. Ealdgyth and her brothers were grandchildren of Leofric and Godgifu of Mercia. In other words, brave King Harold's legal wife, the last queen of Anglo-Saxon England, was the granddaughter of Lady Godiva.

Harold might have done better to foster his relationships within his own family. The previous autumn, with ghastly timing, he had fallen out with his fiery brother Tostig who had stalked off indignantly into exile. And in the summer of 1066 Harold learned that his brother had teamed up with Harald Hardraada, the King of Norway. Hardraada believed he had a claim on England through a treaty concluded by his father with Hartha Canute, and in September 1066 Harold heard that Tostig and Hardraada had landed their forces in Northumbria and had taken control of York.

Harold knew that William's fleet was poised on the other side of the Channel ready to sail at any moment, but he had no choice. He marched his army north, covering no less than 180 miles in four days and making such good time that he took the invaders by surprise. On 25 September, outside York, he won a fierce and brilliant battle at Stamford Bridge in which both Tostig and the King of Norway were killed. The remains of their army were driven back to their ships.

Harold's lightning triumph at Stamford Bridge was one of the great victories of early English history. His Saxon army could claim to be the nimblest and most lethal fighting force in Europe. But just three days later, on 28 September 1066, William of Normandy landed with his troops in Sussex, and when Harold received the news he knew he had to march south at once. He reached London, again in record time, picked up reinforcements and proceeded towards Hastings, where William had established his headquarters. Harold and the English army took up their position on the ridge above the valley of Sandlake, or Senlac, just north of Hastings, at the spot now known as Battle.

The Bayeux Tapestry shows the Norman knights riding their horses into battle on the morning of Saturday, 14 October. In modern movies Norman soldiers, who are usually depicted as 'baddies', are identified by the sinister long, flat nose-guards that project downwards from their pointed, dome-shaped helmets. In fact, both sides at Hastings wore these helmets, along with chainmail armour, and they are both shown carrying the same long, kite-shaped shields.

One thing that does distinguish Saxon from Norman is their hair-cuts: the Anglo-Saxons are shown with long hair and with even longer droopy moustaches, while the Normans are moustacheless and are coiffed in 'short back and sides' mode, the backs of their necks shaved bare to the crown of the heads. This gave them an advantage in hand-to-hand fighting – they could not be grabbed by their hair or moustaches.

The more significant difference is that the Normans are shown fighting from horseback, while the Anglo-Saxons are fighting on foot. Harold's army did have horses – they rode them to the battle. But then they tethered them and found they were facing the formidable cavalry that William had shipped over the Channel. The Normans had bred themselves a compact and powerful warhorse, the destrier, whose arched neck and small head indicate that it may have had Arab blood, and this battle-bred charger would play a crucial role at Hastings.

The Norman cavalry rode powerfully out of Senlac valley, casting their javelins into the Anglo-Saxon shield wall, then retreating. The battle wavered both ways, and there were moments when it seemed that victory could be Harold's. But the English had not regained their strength after their extraordinary forced marches to Stamford Bridge and back, and now they were worn down by the charges of the Norman horsemen. Armchair generals have criticised Harold for the speed with which he rushed south to confront the Normans, staking all on his stand north of Hastings. He could have held back closer to London, it has been argued, thereby regaining energy and forcing William to come to him.

But dash and courage were always Harold's way, and as the sun went down the Norman army found itself master of the field. Lasting more than six hours, the Battle of Hastings was one of the longest-recorded military encounters of the Middle Ages, and its outcome changed the course of English history. England became Norman. Duke William of Normandy became England's third king in the tumultuous year 1066. And his defeated enemy, Harold, lay dead on the battlefield, slain by an arrow to the eye. Or so we have always thought . . .

THE DEATH OF BRAVE KING HAROLD
1066

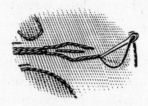

THE IMAGE OF THE LAST ANGLO-SAXON KING ON THE HILL ABOVE Senlac, staggering back tragically with a Norman arrow through his eye, has come to epitomise the drama of the Battle of Hastings. It is graphically depicted on the Bayeux Tapestry – but in this instance Bishop Odo's epic is not quite the reliable witness that it seems. Over its long nine centuries of existence, the tapestry has been hidden, stolen, damaged, restored, and finally displayed as a money-spinning tourist attraction. The stitching we see today is not always the original – and, indeed, some of it might be described as a stitch-up.

In 1729, when the tapestry was already over six centuries old, a French artist, Antoine Benoît, carried out a full-scale tracing to serve as the basis for a set of engravings to be sold in France. Nearly a hundred years later, the Society of Antiquaries sent over an English artist, Charles Stothard, to prepare another series of facsimile prints. Then came the age of the camera, and the newly founded Victoria and Albert Museum in London despatched a photographer to make a photographic record of the tapestry. So we have three sets of images, dating from 1729, 1819 and 1872 showing how it looked in the past at three different points – and there are some dramatic variations.

Two British historians, David Hill and John McSween, have recently compared the three versions and have discovered no less than 379 differences. Swords and stirrups appear and disappear. A griffin becomes an angel. A horse that was a mare in 1729 has by 1819 become a stallion. Freckles – or maybe acne – appear on a Norman shipbuilder's face as a result of some creative darning. Three shields become two, and fish turn into seals. Continuity seems to have gone by the board.

The most significant differences are in the successive depictions of Harold's slaying. In 1729 the King is grasping at the shaft of a spear that he could be trying to throw – or might, alternatively, be pulling out of his forehead. In 1819 the shaft has sprouted feathers, to become an arrow pointing towards his forehead. But fifty-three years later, in the photograph of 1872, the angle of the arrow has shifted downwards: now it is pointing directly into the King's right eye, which is hidden from us by the nose-piece of his helmet. This is what you see if you visit Bayeux today.

The reason for this literal re-embroidering of history lies with the industrious ladies of Bayeux. It is thought that the original embroiderers of the tapestry were English, working at Canterbury in the early 1070s to the orders of Bishop Odo of Bayeux. But once the tapestry crossed the Channel to France it was cared for by local seamstresses – among them, from the nineteenth century onwards, the chambermaids of the town's principal hotel. This was appropriate since the tapestry had become Bayeux's main tourist attraction, and the chambermaids seem to have made sure that it showed visitors the romantic picture they expected.

The earliest version of the arrow-in-the-eye story has been found in an Italian chronicle written by 1080, but the more likely account of Harold's death, written only the year after Hastings, is less romantic. According to the 'Song of the Battle of Hastings' by Guy, bishop of the French town of Amiens, the crucial moment came when the Normans finally broke through the Saxon shield wall that fateful Saturday afternoon. With Harold and a few of his retainers still holding out, William handpicked a hit squad to go off and kill the King.

The Duke had once boasted that he would meet Harold in single combat. But now he was taking no chances. Four Norman knights tracked Harold down and overpowered him, the first striking him in the breast, the second cutting off his head, and the third running a lance through his belly to disembowel him. According to Guy of Amiens, the fourth knight then performed the difficult operation of hacking off one of the dead king's legs.

Now the story gets even more gruesome. A poignant tradition originating at Waltham Abbey in Essex, where Harold's tomb lies, describes the lovely Edith Swan-Neck picking her way through the heaps of corpses and eventually discovering the dead king's remains. They were so horribly mutilated that Edith alone could identify them as Harold's, 'by certain marks on the body, known only to her'. The standard battlefield mutilation that accompanied beheading and disembowelling was full castration – chopping off the penis as well as the testicles – so Bishop Guy was almost certainly being polite when he wrote of a severed 'leg'.

That ugly interpretation seems borne out by the reported reaction of Duke William when he found out what had happened. According to William of Malmesbury, he was both furious and horrified at the final shaming detail of the assault on Harold, demanding to know who had carried it out. When he discovered the culprit, he promptly stripped him of his knighthood and sent him home in disgrace. Ruthless warrior though he was, William evidently felt that this atrocity had dishonoured his victory.

Posterity has agreed with him. In the last analysis, we cannot be sure whether Harold was shot through the eye with an arrow or dismembered by a hit squad of Norman thugs. It is, of course, possible that both calamities befell him, one after the other. But over the centuries people have tended to nurture the less horrendous version of events. The Norman Conquest was a disaster for Anglo-Saxon society, a bitter defeat that involved subjugation, famine, ethnic atrocities and humiliation – it was one of the most brutal times in English history, in fact. After such a trauma it is natural for a community to look for some sort of healing, and re-embroidering history can go some way towards achieving it.

The Bayeux Tapestry gives us 70 metres of proof that history can be just about anything you care to make it – or 64.45 metres, according to the Nazi historians who examined its slightly shrunken form after it had been taken down for safety during the Second World War. In 1940 German forces had occupied Normandy along with the rest of northern France, and as Hitler prepared to invade England a team of scholars were dispatched to Bayeux. After all, the famous tapestry depicted the last successful cross-Channel invasion, and the academics were commissioned to investigate what lessons might be learned.

They sent back an encouraging report to Hitler's henchman Heinrich Himmler, head of the German secret police, the Gestapo, and founder of the SS. The decorative animals woven into the tapestry's borders derived from German mythology, they stated. Better still, the whole message of the saga symbolised three 'characteristic German traits . . . the joy of fighting, the love of war, and the chivalric respect of the enemy'. So this Norman tapestry that had been woven in England, they concluded, was actually 'a sort of German royal saga'. Heil Hitler!

HEREWARD THE WAKE AND THE NORMAN YOKE

1070

WITH HIS VICTORY AT HASTINGS, WILLIAM THE BASTARD became William the Conqueror, and he staged his crowning as King William I of England in the Confessor's great abbey on Christmas Day 1066. In terms of the law and of blood descent the Duke of Normandy knew that his claim to the throne was slight, so he introduced a new element into the Anglo-Saxon coronation ceremony – a call for the people's consent to his rule. Questioned in both English and French as to whether they freely accepted William as their lord, the assembled congregation obediently burst into shouts of '*Vivat Rex!*' – 'Long live the King!' But outside the abbey, William's guard of Norman knights misinterpreted the pandemonium. Maybe they panicked, or maybe they wanted an excuse to panic. The mounted warriors went on a rampage, setting fire to the surrounding buildings and slaughtering any Saxon not quick enough to get out of their way.

England's first Norman king might have asked for popular consent inside Westminster Abbey, but the burned houses nearby made it clear that the Conqueror was well named – his power rested on force of arms. William's first project in the New Year was to throw up a wooden fortress on the banks of the Thames, the original Tower of London. The new arrival wished to make clear who England's new boss was, and castles became the trademark of his reign. The weathered stone towers and battlements of Norman England remain romantic landmarks to this day. But they were anything but romantic to the Anglo-Saxons who were conscripted to dig the ditches for the moats, raise and ram solid the great mound of earth on which the central fort would stand, then live the rest of their lives with the fortifications towering above them.

In the twenty-one years of his reign, William and his followers built hundreds of castles. Wherever there was trouble or discontent, the Normans rode in on their destriers, taught the agitators a lesson, then raised a castle to make sure it did not happen again. They built in wood to start with, throwing up palisades of sharpened stakes that were replaced with stone in later years. And if a community had been particularly irksome, the castle would be built on the site of Saxon homes that had been trashed.

There is some evidence that William's original intent was to be conciliatory. He tried to learn some English, and for several years he kept most of the local English sheriffs in place. The new king's early official documents bear the names of senior Anglo-Saxon office-holders, still in positions of high trust at court. But when William went home to Normandy in 1067 to check on the affairs of his duchy, a series of uprisings broke out. Three of Harold's sons by Edith Swan-Neck tried to raise Devon and Cornwall in revolt. Danish raiding parties sailing up the east coast found themselves being welcomed by the anti-Norman locals. The north rose, and Mercians on the Welsh border joined forces with the ever-defiant Welsh.

It was time to take off the kid gloves. Back in England, criss-crossing the Midlands and the north with his armies, William mercilessly punished neighbourhoods that had risen against him. Villages were destroyed and the countryside burned so that it remained derelict and uninhabited for years. Scorched earth, ethnic cleansing – all the horror words apply. It was a time of famine and tears that seared itself on the folk memory as the tyranny of the 'Norman Yoke'.

Just one centre of resistance held out. In the tradition of King Alfred, it was only in the Fens, in England's watery wastelands of treacherous swamp and brackish lagoons, that some local defiance survived. Hereward of Peterborough, a Saxon gentleman who had been deprived of his lands by the Normans, retreated into the East Anglian marshes around Ely with a band of fellow freedom fighters.

For a time Hereward received help from the Danish raiders in the area – and in 1070 he joined forces with them to plunder the Abbey of Peterborough. But when William bought the Danes off, the English kept on fighting. Hereward's guerrilla warfare became the symbol of native resistance. As the Saxon squire used the mists and marshes of the Fens to outwit his lumbering enemy, folk tales multiplied of his bravery and cunning, and of his legendary sword, which he nicknamed 'Brainbiter'. The folk hero gained a nickname of his own, Hereward the Wake – ever alert, luminous, elusive, the enduring Saxon embodiment of the fight for justice.

Not every Anglo-Saxon was impressed with Hereward. The monk who compiled the Peterborough version of the *Anglo-Saxon Chronicle* was scathing that an Englishman should help the Danes plunder the treasures of his local abbey with the excuse of denying it to the Normans – 'they said they did it,' he wrote sarcastically, 'out of loyalty to this minster'. The sacrilege prompted William to take action. Refusing to be defeated in the Fens by mere pools of water, the Normans built siege causeways – bridges of wood and earth embankments whose traces can still be found today in villages around Ely – and they flushed out the resistance. 'The outlaws all came to hand,' reported the *Chronicle* – with the exception of Hereward who, spry and nippy as ever, masterminded an escape.

What happened next is a mystery. According to one tradition, King William forgave the outlaw on account of his gallantry. That does not sound like the Conqueror, particularly after resistance that had cost him such expense and difficulty. The alternative story has Hereward betrayed into the hands of cowardly Norman assassins who stabbed him in the back with their lances. Either way, the Wake passed rapidly from history into legend. We do not know how long he lived or how he died, but within a generation or so the tales about him had been gathered into a Latin story book entitled *Gesta Herwardi Incliti Exulis et Militis* – 'The Exploits of Hereward the Celebrated Outlaw and Soldier'.

Starting from a grain of truth, the *Gesta Herwardi* expanded into yarns of wild fantasy that seem to have found a wide audience among both Normans and Saxons, many of whom would have listened to the tales as they were read aloud in Latin, or retold in instant translation. The plot lines followed some eternal stereotypes. In one exciting episode, Hereward returns to his family home to discover it full of Normans, with the head of his younger brother stuck on a pole beside the gate. In the style of Ulysses – or indeed of Ratty, Mole and Badger when they recapture Toad Hall from the wicked weasels and stoats –

Hereward sneaks back into the house that night while the Normans are celebrating, and takes them by surprise. With the aid of just one follower, he kills the new lord and fifteen of his companions, cuts off *their* heads, and sticks them all up on poles where he found his brother's.

This was adventure fiction at its best – sheer wish fulfilment. But it was nonetheless popular for that, one imagines, when recounted around the firesides of the Anglo-Saxons.

THE DOMESDAY BOOK
1086

B Y 1085 WILLIAM THE CONQUEROR WAS NEARLY SIXTY, AND he had long since settled into an annual routine. When he was in England he usually spent Easter at Winchester, the old capital of Wessex, which remained his working headquarters. For the Whitsun holiday he went to London, already the hub of English trade and on its way to becoming the country's capital; and he liked to celebrate Christmas in Gloucester, the old Mercian settlement on the border of Wales. William had ruled England for the best part of twenty years, and now, around New Year's Day 1086, it was time to take stock. Let the *Anglo-Saxon Chronicle* take up the story:

> *The king had much thought and very deep discussion with his council about this country – how it was settled, and with what kind of people. Then he sent his men all over England, into every shire, and had them find out how many hides [units of land] there were in the shire, or what land and cattle the king himself had in the country, or what dues [tax] he ought to have each year.*

The Norman Conquest has been described in today's terms as a 'corporate takeover'. Twenty to thirty thousand Normans, a comparatively small number, became the new managers and controllers of the two million or so Anglo-Saxons and Danes who inhabited England. Modern managers take over a company's accounting system. The Normans took over the land – and now William wanted to know 'what or how much everyone who was in England had'.

The result of this countrywide investigation was the Domesday Book, so nicknamed by the native English as a sort of put-down, a resentful joke. William's great survey invaded everyone's lives, winkling out their secrets, they complained. Like God's Day of Judgement, it left people helpless in the face of such total knowledge – there was no way they could avoid paying the tax.

The book contained nine hundred pages of hand-written Latin – some two million words – describing more than thirteen thousand places in England and some parts of Wales, all examined in the most extraordinary detail. 'So very strictly did [William] have it investigated,' wrote the *Anglo-Saxon Chronicle*, 'that not a yard of land, nor indeed one ox nor one cow nor one pig was left out.' Leaving us in no doubt about their Anglo-Saxon origins, the monks added a sarcastic footnote: 'Shame it is to relate, but it seemed no shame to him to do.'

These critical monks understood the bottom line. Domesday was all about control and money. William had taken possession of all England, every square inch of it. As far back as anyone could remember, the Anglo-Saxons had held and farmed their land in a variety of ways. But now nobody owned land without obligations to the King: they held it as William's tenant, and had to pay for the privilege with 'service', which could take the form of a basket of eggs, some chickens, bacon, honey, a barrel of herrings, money, or supplying armed soldiers when the King called for war.

Many centuries later this system became known as 'feudalism', from the medieval Latin *feudum*, meaning 'fee' or 'payment'. The economist Adam Smith first coined the phrase the 'feudal system' in 1776 – long after feudalism itself was dead – and it has been talked about in highflown, almost philosophical terms. In practice, it was the crude means whereby William and the Normans shared out England among themselves. It was a land-grab. Domesday makes clear that by 1087 all the major landholders were Normans or French – the original group of investors. The Anglo-Saxons had been cut out of the picture. If they held land at all it was as tenants to the invaders.

It is now more than nine hundred years since the English experienced subjugation: taking orders from people who don't speak your language, being forced to pay for land you thought you owned, and probably having some of your relatives killed into the bargain. There was one law for the Normans and another for the natives. William's laws gave special protection to 'all the men I have brought with me, or who have come after me'.

This legal discrimination is reflected in the language that we speak today, a mixture of Anglo-Saxon or *englisc*, and Norman French. Our modern English words of control and authority – 'order', 'police', 'court', 'judge', 'trial', 'sentence', 'prison', 'punishment', 'execution' – all come from Norman French. And there is a similar linguistic apartheid in the way we describe food. When it came to the hard work of rearing and tending the animals, the words used were English – cow (*cū*), pig (*pigge*), sheep (*scēap*). When it came to eating them, they were French – beef (*bœuf*), pork (*porc*), mutton (*mouton*). It is not hard to see who produced the fruits of the earth, and who enjoyed them.

You can see the Domesday Book today in the airy glass and concrete National Archives building in Kew in south-west London. It is England's oldest public record, and anyone can go and look at it. The first known legal dispute that used the great document as evidence occurred in the 1090s, almost as soon as it was completed, and Domesday still has legal authority when it comes to the ownership of English land. For centuries it was kept in a rat-proof iron chest. Now it is carefully preserved, in four volumes, in an air-conditioned, shatterproof glass case.

The parchment looks soft, almost pinkish, the ink faded to brown with people's names picked out in rusty red. Here is Leofgyth, a Saxon woman of Knook in Wiltshire, 'who made and still makes gold embroideries for the king and queen'. We can trace the size of the estates that Godgifu, Lady Godiva, owned in Worcestershire at the beginning of January 1066, 'the day King Edward lived and died'. And here are the details of the land held by the troublesome Hereward before he fled in 1071.

The Domesday Book is living history. To start with, the massive survey was known as 'The King's Roll' or 'The Winchester Book', reflecting where it was made and stored. But within less than a century it had come to be known officially by its rude English nickname, and has remained so ever since. The Anglo-Saxons might have lost the land for the time being, but they had the last word on it.

THE MYSTERIOUS DEATH OF WILLIAM RUFUS

1100

King WILLIAM I DIED AS HE HAD LIVED – a-conquering. In the high summer of 1087 he led his troops to punish the town of Mantes on the River Seine, which had dared to send a raiding party into Norman territory. As the Normans torched Mantes, some burning object caused William's horse to rear up in fright. Now sixty years old, the Conqueror was grossly overweight, and as his horse lurched backwards the high pommel at the front of his battle-saddle was driven into his soft belly, puncturing his intestines. Bleeding internally, the King was carried away to die, and as the priests gathered round him he set about disposing of his empire.

William had three sons, and he didn't think much of any of them. Ridiculing the short stature of his eldest, Robert, he had nicknamed him 'Curthose' (Short-stockings) or 'Jamberons' (Stubby-legs), and he had not been on speaking terms with him for years. William saw no way of preventing Robert becoming Duke of Normandy, because of the Norman rule of primogeniture. But for England he picked his second son, William Rufus, and from his deathbed the old man sent Rufus riding hard towards the Channel. To his third son Henry he presented a huge sum of money, five thousand pounds of silver, which Henry set about counting there and then so as to make sure he had not been short-changed.

Before he breathed his last, William ordered his prisoners-of-war to be freed and gifts of money to be made to selected churches – his admission fee to heaven. But as his followers rode off to secure their property ahead of the conflict that they could sense coming between the two elder sons, his servants plundered his personal possessions. The final indignity came when the gases that had accumulated in the Conqueror's rotting, corpulent body exploded – it had been forced into a coffin that was too small for it.

Usually respected, often feared, William the Conqueror had never been loved, and William Rufus was to rule in his father's tradition. He got his name, William the Red, from his florid complexion, which the superstitious saw as symbolising blood and fire. Historians disagree as to whether his hair was ginger or flaxen yellow, but there is no doubt about his complexion – red, the witches' colour – and William played up to this by sneering openly at religion. Why should he pray to God, he once asked after suffering a severe illness, since God had caused him such pain and trouble? When senior churchmen – abbots and bishops – died, Rufus blocked the appointment of a successor, so he could take over their lands and keep the income for himself. It was scarcely surprising that the churchmen who wrote the history of the times should have given him a bad press. On the basis of their criticisms, William the Red has gone down in history as one of England's 'bad' kings.

In fact, he ruled England quite effectively, if harshly, in the Norman style. He defeated the attempts of his elder brother Robert Curthose to claim England, taking the battle to Robert in Normandy. In London William built ambitiously, constructing the first stone bridge over the River Thames, and a huge banqueting hall down the river in Edward the Confessor's Palace of Westminster.

Westminster Hall stands to this day, and is the most ancient section of the Houses of Parliament. The tall and echoing hall was the home of the law courts for centuries and, since 1910, the place where dead kings and queens lie in state. In April 2002 some two hundred thousand mourners queued for hours to file silently through William

Rufus's nine-hundred-year-old banqueting hall to pay their last respects at the coffin of Queen Elizabeth the Queen Mother.

The Red King loved hunting. It was a passion with all the Norman monarchs, and a deep source of grievance to their English subjects. More than seventy forests around England were eventually to be designated royal hunting preserves where special forest laws were fiercely enforced by the King's foresters and 'wood-wards'. Anyone caught hunting deer, boar or other game there was punished with blinding or mutilation. You could be punished just for carrying a bow and arrow. People inside the royal forest areas, which included open fields and whole villages, were not allowed to keep dogs, unless the animal had been disabled from hunting by having three digits cut from one of its front paws. These are the years when rabbits and pheasants first appeared in England, introduced by the Normans to add to their hunting pleasures. But for Saxon farmers these new arrivals, like the royal deer, were simply crop-consuming pests.

The New Forest, south of Winchester, was the subject of a particular grievance. It was quite literally new, recently created by expelling people from their farms and villages, and William Rufus was hunting there on 2 August 1100 when a curious accident occurred. It was late in the afternoon, the sun was setting, and the King had to shade his eyes against the light. The royal hunting party was strung out at different stands in the forest, waiting for the rangers to chase up and drive the deer through the undergrowth across their line of fire. The King was with one of his favourite hunting companions, Walter Tyrel, a Norman nobleman who was an excellent shot. But somehow the usually accurate Tyrel missed his deer and fired directly into William's chest. Reaching to tear out the arrow, William succeeded only in breaking off the shaft, and as he fell to the ground the arrowhead was driven deeper into his chest.

It was what happened next that suggests that this shooting was no accident, for Tyrel rode straight out of the forest and headed for the coast, where he took a boat to France. He had left the King's body lying on the forest floor, where it was retrieved by local farm labourers and thrown on to a cart, to be trundled over the rutted lanes to Winchester. 'Blood dripped freely the whole way', according to William of Malmesbury, writing a few years later.

Tyrel's strange behaviour could be explained in terms of sheer panic. But panic was anything but the reaction of William's younger brother Henry, who was one of the royal hunting party that day. Henry had been at another stand in the forest with Tyrel's brothers-in-law, Gilbert and Roger of Clare. We do not know who brought Henry the news of his brother's death, but his reaction was as instant as Tyrel's. He rode straight to Winchester to secure the royal treasury, and was proclaimed king next day. He then rode on to London, where he was solemnly crowned in Westminster Abbey on 5 August – just three days after the death of his brother, who was buried with scant ceremony at Winchester.

The chroniclers had no doubt that the death of William Rufus was inspired by God himself, to punish a monarch who had derided and exploited the Church. At the time, Rufus was enjoying the income of no less than twelve abbeys that he had deliberately kept abbotless – 'without shepherds', as William of Malmesbury put it. No wonder God should strike down 'a soul who could not be saved'.

Today we might scan the evidence for a more earthly plotter. William's brother, Henry, now sat securely on the throne of England. Walter Tyrel was never investigated or punished for the slaying of William the Red; and it was curious that among those to whom the new king showed special favour were Walter Tyrel's brothers-in-law, Gilbert and Robert of Clare.

HENRY I AND
THE WHITE SHIP
1120

TEN YEARS BEFORE HE BECAME KING, WILLIAM THE Conqueror's youngest son Henry was helping to put down an uprising in the Norman city of Rouen. It was the late autumn of 1090, and after the fighting had ended he invited the leader of the rebellion to a high tower where he could look out over the walled city and admire the beautiful river and surrounding green fields and woods that he had been trying to conquer. Then he personally threw the man out of the window.

Henry I was thirty-two when he became King of England, and had shown himself to be both decisive and single-minded after the mysterious shooting of his brother Rufus. Now he set about capturing Normandy from his other brother, Robert Curthose. In 1106 he defeated Robert at the Battle of Tinchebrai, south of Bayeux – fought, by coincidence, on 28 September, the date on which William the Conqueror had landed his troops in Sussex in 1066. So forty years later to the day, William's youngest son had reunited his father's cross-Channel empire. Henry consigned his brother Robert to successive prisons at Wareham, Devizes, Bristol and finally Cardiff, where the unhappy Short-stockings would spend the last months of his twenty-eight-year imprisonment learning Welsh.

'Woe to him that is not old enough to die,' declared Robert Curthose, who finally expired in 1134 at the age of eighty, and whose tomb can be seen today in Gloucester Cathedral.

'Exchequer' is a modern word that comes to us from the reign of Henry I – a king with a sharp eye for a penny. We have seen him counting the silver his father gave him on his deathbed for his inheritance, then galloping straight to the treasury when his brother died;

he was the last king for four hundred years shrewd enough to die with-out any debts. Now, sometime after 1106, he introduced the exchequer as a revolutionary new method of government accounting and of cen-tralising royal power. Based on the Middle Eastern abacus or counting-frame, the exchequer was a chequered cloth like a chessboard. Counters were piled on the different squares, rather as croupiers handle chips on a gaming table. Twice a year, at Easter and Michaelmas (the feast of St Michael on 29 September), the sheriffs and royal officials from the shires had to bring their money to be checked and counted. To this day, the cabinet minister in charge of the nation's finances is known as the Chancellor of the Exchequer, and we all write and, if we are lucky, also sometimes cash 'cheques'.

By 1120 Henry I controlled a well-financed empire on the two sides of the English Channel. He travelled quite frequently from England to Normandy in his own longboat or *snecca*, a Norse word literally meaning 'snake' or 'serpent'. Merchants and nobles criss-crossed the channel on these medieval equivalents of the cross-Channel ferry, which, according to records from the next century, charged two pence for an ordinary passenger and twelve for a knight with his horse. In tapestries and paintings of the time the boats are depicted with striped sails, complete with masts, rigging, tillers and anchors. Often their prows were decorated with figureheads of dragons and other beasts.

As Henry was preparing to set sail from the Norman port of Barfleur at the end of November 1120, he was approached by a young seafarer, Thomas FitzStephen. Thomas's father, Stephen, had been William the Conqueror's personal sea captain, taking him on the his-toric voyage of 1066 to fight against Harold, and he had ferried him back and forth across the Channel to the end of his life. Now his son Thomas had a newly fitted-out snakeship of which he was particularly proud, the *White Ship*, and he offered it to the King for his voyage.

Henry had already made his travelling arrangements, but he suggested it would be a treat for his son and heir, William, to sail on this state-of-the-art vessel. William was just seventeen and a young man on whom many hopes rode. He was popularly nicknamed 'the Aetheling', the old Anglo-Saxon title meaning 'throne-worthy' (see p. 43), because his mother Edith-Matilda was descended from King Alfred's royal house of Wessex. Here was a part-Saxon heir – some much-cherished English blood – who would one day inherit the Normans' empire.

Henry set sail for England, leaving William the Aetheling to follow in the *White Ship*, with many of the court's most lively young blades, among them William's half-brother Richard and his half-sister Matilda du Perche, two of the numerous illegitimate children that Henry had fathered outside his marriage to Edith-Matilda. Spirits were high as the *White Ship* loosed its moorings. Wine flowed freely among passengers and crew, and as darkness fell, the princely party issued a dare to the captain – that he should overtake the King's ship, which was already out at sea.

The *White Ship*'s fifty oarsmen heaved with all their might to pull clear of the harbour, but as the vessel made its way through the night its port side struck violently against a rock that lay hidden just below the surface of the water. This rock was a well-known hazard of the area, uncovered each day as the tide ebbed, then submerged at high tide. It can be seen to this day from the cliffs of Barfleur, a dark shadow lurking beneath the water. But Captain Thomas FitzStephen, like his passengers, had been drinking, and the ship's wooden hull shattered on the rock, the vessel capsizing almost immediately. It was still close enough to the shore for the cries and screams of its three hundred passengers and crew to be mistaken for drunken revelry. According to one account the passengers on the royal snakeship heard the cries behind them, but sailed on, unheeding, towards England, through the night.

The *White Ship* was the *Titanic* of the Middle Ages, a much-vaunted high-tech vessel on its maiden voyage, wrecked against a foreseeable natural obstacle in the reckless pursuit of speed. The passenger list constituted the cream of high society, cast into the chilly waters. Orderic Vitalis, an Anglo-Norman chronicler of the time, described the scene:

> *The rays of the moon lit up the world for about nine hours, showing up every-thing in the sea to the mariners. Thomas, the skipper, gathered his strength after sinking for the first time and, remembering his duty, lifted his head as he came to the surface. Seeing the heads of the men who were clinging some-how to the spar, he asked, 'The king's son, what has become of him?' When the shipwrecked men replied that he had perished with all his companions, he*

said, 'It is vain for me to go on living.' With these words, in utter despair, he
chose rather to sink on the spot than to die beneath the wrath of a king
enraged by the loss of his son, or suffer long years of punishment in fetters.

Orderic was wrong about the full moon. Sky tables show that on 25
November 1120 the moon was new, so the night must have been dark.
But the chronicler does seem to have gathered his information, directly
or indirectly, from the wreck's only survivor, a butcher from Rouen who
had jumped on to the *White Ship* to collect some debts that were due
to him from members of the court. The butcher was saved from the
exposure that killed the others on that still, frosty night by the thick, air-
retaining ram-skins he was wearing. Three fishermen plucked him out
of the water next morning and took him back to dry land.

Over in England next day, King Henry became puzzled when the
White Ship did not dock or even appear on the horizon. But the news
of the catastrophe reached the nobles at his court soon enough, and
everyone discovered they had lost family and friends. Stewards, cham-
berlains and cupbearers had all died – wives and husbands, sons and
daughters. As the court mourned, no one dared break the dreadful
news to the King, and a whole day and night went by before a young
boy was finally pushed into the royal presence, weeping, to throw himself at the King's feet. When Henry realised what had happened, he
fell to the ground himself, grief-stricken at the news. He had to be
shepherded away to a room where he could mourn privately – this
stern Norman king did not care to display weakness in public.

In the years following the death of his cherished son, King Henry I
governed his realm as busily as ever, and also found time for his pleasures. He founded England's first zoo, where he kept lions and leopards,
and a porcupine of which he was particularly fond. But he did confess
to nightmares that terrified him so much that he would leap out of his
bed and reach for his sword. He dreamed that his people – those who
worked, those who fought, and those who prayed – were attacking him.
The Conqueror's shrewd, harsh, penny-pinching youngest son had provided England and Normandy with firm government, but the wreck of
the *White Ship* meant that Henry left no legitimate male heir to succeed
him. The drowning of William the Aetheling was not just a personal
tragedy – it would lead to England's first real and prolonged civil war.

STEPHEN AND MATILDA
1135–54

KING HENRY I HAD A GREAT WEAKNESS FOR LAMPREYS, small, eel-like creatures that sucked the blood of other fishes and were considered a delicacy in the Middle Ages. Worried at the havoc this oily parasite could wreak on the digestive system, Henry's doctor had banned the fish from the royal diet. But the King could not resist the temptation when his chefs served him up a plate of lampreys one late November evening in 1135 at the end of a day's hunting in the forest near Rouen in Normandy. The sixty-seven-year-old king was stricken with chills and convulsions on the Monday night, and by Sunday 1 December he was dead.

It was fifteen years since the tragic wreck of the *White Ship*, and Henry had not managed to solve the succession problem caused by the death of William the Aetheling, his only legitimate son. In 1127 he had got his barons to swear allegiance to his only other legitimate child, his daughter Matilda, then aged twenty-five, and, hoping to make doubly sure of their pledge, the old king had them repeat the exercise four years later. The unlikely prospect of a woman controlling the male-chauvinist barons of the Anglo-Norman realm might just have been feasible if Matilda had not been married to Geoffrey of Anjou, an ambitious young nobleman whom many Normans distrusted, and if Matilda herself had not been so heavy-handed. At the moment of Henry's death she had been quarrelling – not for the first time – with her father, and her absence from the deathbed cost her dear. The moment was seized by her nimble cousin Stephen of Blois, the son of Henry's sister Adela.

Controlling territory to the south of Normandy, the counts of Blois were powerful magnates with whom the Normans tried to stay on good terms. Stephen was an affable and well-liked character, popular with many of the Anglo-Norman barons. He was fortunate to have had a narrow escape in 1120 when he turned down an invitation to join the young hell-raisers on William the Aetheling's booze cruise. Stephen was then in his early twenties, and the chroniclers give two reasons why he decided not to board the *White Ship*: he disapproved of so much drinking, and he was suffering at the time from diarrhoea.

Maybe the diarrhoea had been an excuse, since it had not stopped him boarding the King's ship that night. Stephen was a quick-thinking man. The moment he realised in December 1135 that there was a crown for the taking, he followed the example of his uncles William Rufus and Henry himself and headed hell-for-leather for the royal treasury in Winchester. Three weeks later, England's first and last King Stephen was crowned in Westminster Abbey, just in time for Christmas.

But Matilda had her father's ferocious bloody-mindedness, and she was not willing to let her cousin steal her inheritance without a fight. The next twenty years would see Stephen and Matilda battling for control of England and Normandy, raising armies and bribing towns, bishops and barons to consolidate their cause. Matilda captured and imprisoned Stephen, then Stephen besieged her. In the winter of 1141, Matilda and her followers made a dramatic escape from Oxford Castle, dressed in white so they could not be seen against the snow. When Matilda held power, she alienated people with her overbearing ways. When Stephen had the whip hand he proved too soft and good-natured.

To start with, the barons saw themselves as the beneficiaries of this family rivalry, and they used the widespread unrest to settle old scores, often switching sides without a qualm. Loyalty hardly seemed to come into it. The *Anglo-Saxon Chronicle* described the situation in a famous passage on the woes of a land torn apart by civil war:

> *Every powerful man built himself castles and held them against the king . . .*
> *They sorely burdened the unhappy people of the country with forced labour,*
> *and when the castles were built, they filled them with devils and wicked men.*
> *By night and by day they seized those whom they believed had any wealth,*
> *ordinary men and women, and put them in prison to get their gold and silver*
> *and tortured them . . . They hung them up by their feet and smoked them with*

foul smoke. They hung them by the thumbs or by the head, then hung coats of mail [weighing about 25 kg] on their feet. They put knotted strings round their heads and twisted till it went to the brains. They put them in dungeons where there were adders and snakes and toads . . . Then when the wretched people had no more to give, they plundered and burned all the villages, so that you could easily go a day's journey without ever finding a village inhabited or field cultivated . . . Wherever the ground was tilled, the earth bore no corn, for the land was ruined by such doings. And men said openly that Christ and his saints slept.

Written by 1154, these vivid words come to us from Peterborough on the edge of the Fens, from the last monastery that was still producing editions of the *Anglo-Saxon Chronicle* – and which would itself stop the updatings at the end of Stephen's reign. The description quoted here was clearly based on the cruelty and destruction that the monks witnessed in their own neighbourhood; other parts of England may not have been so badly affected by what came to be known as the 'great anarchy'. But by the early 1150s, exhaustion had set in. The nobles were refusing to fight for either side, and there was a clear need for a settlement.

By then Matilda's cause was being fought by her forceful son, the red-headed Henry Plantagenet, so named after the bright-yellow broom flower known as the *planta genesta* that was the emblem of the counts of Anjou, his father's home territory to the south-west of Normandy. These Angevin rulers had a history of rivalry with the Normans, and Matilda's marriage to Geoffrey of Anjou had always hampered her cause. But Geoffrey died in 1151, and, having succeeded to the title, his son Henry married Eleanor of Aquitaine, whose vast territories to the south of Anjou included Gascony and the rich wine district of Bordeaux.

Henry Plantagenet was only twenty when he arrived in England in 1153, but through inheritance and marriage he controlled almost half of France, a wide swathe down the western, Atlantic coast, and he had the soldiers to match. That winter he struck a deal for the succession, allowing the old and weary Stephen to remain on the throne for the rest of his lifetime, which lasted, in the event, barely a year. In December 1154 Matilda's son became King Henry II, the first ruler of England's new Angevin and Plantagenet dynasty.

Matilda had never been able to enjoy her inheritance. The closest she had come to being queen was to be styled the 'Lady of the English' during one of her brief periods of power. But she was to outlive her rival Stephen by a dozen years, and she had the pleasure of seeing her son, the new king, reign over a vast empire that stretched from Hadrian's Wall to the Pyrenees.

MURDER IN THE CATHEDRAL
1170

KING HENRY II AND HIS CHANCELLOR THOMAS BECKET were the closest of friends. People declared the two men 'had but one heart and one mind'. The new Plantagenet king was twenty-one when he came to the throne in 1154. Thomas Becket, a London merchant's son, was in his mid-thirties, but the difference in their ages and status did not seem to matter. They hunted and played chess together – and both were furious workers. Henry was consumed by the challenge of holding together his diverse and disorderly collection of territories in England and France. Thomas, appointed his chancellor at the start of the reign, was in charge of the royal writing office, drawing up official documents and firing off letters. One clerk later recalled that before taking dictation from Becket he would have to get at least sixty, and sometimes as many as a hundred, quill pens cut and sharpened in advance – he knew there would be no time for sharpening during the session.

Business from all over Henry's Angevin empire passed through Thomas's hands, and he revelled in the glory of his position. Imitating his master's grandfather, Henry I, Thomas kept exotic animals – monkeys, and a couple of wolves that he had trained for hunting their own kind, which still lurked in the royal forests. When he went to France in 1158 to negotiate a marriage treaty for one of Henry's daughters, he travelled in fabulous luxury.

'If this be only the Chancellor,' marvelled onlookers, 'what must be the glory of the King himself?'

Henry would tease Thomas wryly about his grandeur. As the two men rode together through London one winter's day, the King saw a poor man shivering in the cold and suggested that he needed a coat. Thomas agreed – whereupon Henry grabbed at his chancellor's magnificent fur-lined scarlet cloak, and the two friends wrestled together until Thomas gave way.

Henry II was proud of the law and order that he had brought to his so recently chaotic realm. He would refer contemptuously to the reign of his predecessor as the years of 'disorder', as if King Stephen had never been. It was in Henry's reign that the legal status of the jury, first introduced by the Danes, took firm root, and from this time comes the word 'assizes', from the Norman French for 'sitting'. The King's judges would travel from county to county, sitting in justice over the people to administer the common law – the law that applied to all free men.

The exception was the Church, which had its own courts and a law of its own. If a priest murdered or raped or stole, he could avoid the common-law penalties of hanging or mutilation by claiming 'benefit of clergy', the right to be tried in the bishop's court, which could do no worse than defrock him – expel him from the priesthood – and impose a penance. Common law stopped at the church door, and some clerics were major powers in the land. Rich bishops and abbots enjoyed the revenues of large estates, with their own retinues and sometimes mini-armies. Although they swore loyalty to the King, they insisted that their earthly oaths must rank below their loyalty to God and to his supreme earthly representative, the Pope in Rome.

When the Archbishop of Canterbury died in 1161, Henry saw the chance to tackle the problem. He would give the job to his best friend, who would use his energy and loyalty to put the Church in its place while at the same time remaining his chancellor. But Henry – along with almost everyone who had ever seen the two men together – was astonished when the new archbishop insisted on resigning his position as chancellor and almost immediately started to champion the rights of the Church. Becket publicly opposed Henry's attempts to levy a tax that applied to bishops as well as to barons, and when it came to the vexed question of Church versus common law, he took the position that priests should never be subject to the death penalty. With the donning of his archbishop's robes, the King's worldly comrade had become his pious and prickly opponent, dedicated to frustrating the very changes he had been put in place to implement.

What made Becket change? The elegant chancellor's startling transformation has been debated ever since, not least by playwrights and poets from Alfred Lord Tennyson to T. S. Eliot, who have created stirring dramas from the change in character that turned dear friends into mortal enemies. Thomas had been 'born again', it seemed. From being the King's man, he became God's man – as he saw his God, at least. But there were those in the Church who suggested that the change had not been as total as it seemed. There had always been something artificial about the glittering Thomas, something of the actor. Becket could never resist catching the public eye: he loved being a celebrity. Gilded companion of the King or sackcloth servant of the Church, he never failed to act his part – or to overact it – superbly.

'An ass he always was,' remarked Gilbert Foliot, the Bishop of London, 'and an ass he'll always be.'

Foliot was a broad-minded churchman in the tolerant tradition of Bede. He understood the need for compromise between Church and state, and, like other senior clerics, he openly opposed the obstinacy of the new archbishop.

But compromise had never been a word in Thomas's vocabulary, and he now pursued God's cause in a succession of confrontations that came to a head in October 1164. Becket arrived at Northampton Castle to answer Henry's complaints, with a large retinue of clerks and monks and an armoured bodyguard. He insisted on carrying the massive silver cross of Canterbury in his own hands to signify that he was claiming God's protection against the King.

'Perjurer!' shouted the barons who supported Henry and felt that Thomas had broken his oath of loyalty to him. 'Traitor!'

Born-again Becket gave as good as he got, temporarily forsaking his saintly demeanour to retort 'Whoremonger!' at the baron who organised the King's mistresses, and 'Bastard!' at Henry's illegitimate brother.

Anticipating arrest and captivity, Thomas then slipped out of the castle before dawn by an unguarded gate, and made his way in disguise to the south coast where he took a small boat to Flanders, and then on to France.

In the six years of exile that followed, Henry and Thomas met three times in France to try to patch up their differences – encounters that were fraught with emotion. In July 1170 in a field near the banks of the River Loire, Thomas was so overcome that he jumped off his horse and threw himself to the ground in front of Henry. The King responded by himself dismounting. Then he took hold of his old friend and forced him back into the saddle, holding his stirrup so as to help him up.

On this occasion the two men had been arguing over a crowning ceremony that Henry had arranged for his eldest son earlier that summer in an attempt to solidify the royal succession. In Thomas's absence, Henry had called in the Archbishop of York and Gilbert Foliot of London, with other bishops, to consecrate the ceremony. The crowning hijacked a job that archbishops of Canterbury had always jealously preserved as their own, but Becket agreed to return to England, all the same.

Back in Canterbury, however, and preaching from the cathedral pulpit on Christmas Day, the restored archbishop denounced the bishops who had taken part in the illegal crowning.

'May they all be damned by Jesus Christ!' he cried, hurling flaming candles to the floor.

Over in Normandy, Henry flew into a tantrum of his own. 'Will no man rid me of this turbulent priest?' is the cry that legend has attributed to the furious king.

In fact, these words come from many centuries later, and there is much better evidence from closer to the time. Within two years of the episode Edward Grim, a priest on Becket's staff who was personally involved in the drama, reported Henry railing even more bitterly. 'What miserable drones and traitors have I nourished and promoted in my household, who let their lord be treated with such shameful contempt by a lowborn cleric?'

Four of his knights took this cry as a summons to action. They crossed the Channel to Kent, stopping at Saltwood Castle to mobilise an arrest party, then rode on to Canterbury. When they arrived at the cathedral on 29 December 1170, the archbishop had just finished his lunch. It was around three in the afternoon when the visitors were ushered into his bedroom, and though they had taken off their sword-belts as a gesture of courtesy, Thomas studiously ignored them at first. He certainly knew at least three of the knights personally, but he chose to treat them with disdain, angrily rejecting their request that he should accompany them to Winchester.

A shouting match ensued. As tempers rose, the knights waved their arms about and twisted their heavy gloves into knots, according to one eyewitness. Their leader Reginald FitzUrse – literally Reginald 'Bearson' – ordered the archbishop's followers to leave, and when they refused, led his own men out of the room to get their weapons. Thomas seemed almost disappointed that they were retreating.

'Do you think I'm going to sneak off?' he cried. 'I haven't returned to Canterbury in order to run away. You'll find me here. And in the Lord's battle, I'll fight hand to hand, toe to toe.'

'Why should you annoy them further,' remonstrated one of his followers, 'by getting up and following them to the door?'

'My mind is made up,' replied Thomas. 'I know exactly what I have to do.'

'Please God,' came the reply, 'that you have chosen well.'

By four o'clock Thomas was in the cathedral. It was getting dark. In the candlelit church, the monks were just finishing their devotions and townsfolk were arriving for public evensong. Meanwhile, the knights were out in the cloisters, pulling on their armour and strapping on their sword-belts.

'Where is the traitor?' they shouted as they broke into the cathedral. 'Where is the archbishop?'

'Here I am,' replied Becket. 'No traitor to the king, but a priest of God!'

We know these words and all the dramatic details of what happened next in the cathedral that fading December evening, because no less than four of Becket's followers recorded their own accounts of the tragedy – with first-hand vividness, and considerable honesty as well. One admitted that he ran off and hid behind the altar as soon as the fighting started. But Edward Grim was made of sterner stuff, and he stayed beside Becket as the knights moved in to lay hands on the arch-bishop. Becket, a strong man, robustly wrestled them off, and as Grim put up a hand to shield his master, a sword struck through his arm to the bone, then rebounded, flying onwards to slice into the top of Becket's head.

'He received a second blow on the head,' wrote Grim, 'but still stood firm. At the third blow he fell on his knees and elbows, offering him-self a living victim and saying in a low voice, "For the name of Jesus and the protection of the church, I am ready to embrace death."'

Grim described the grisly details as a further blow cut Becket's skull right open, spilling 'blood white with the brain, and the brain red with the blood' on to the cathedral floor.

'Let's be off, knights!' cried one of the assassins. 'This fellow won't be up again!'

The eyewitness accounts make clear that in the initial terrible shock of such violence, few people saw the slaying as a martyrdom. It was Becket's own confrontational style that had turned the arrest party into murderers – and some even suggested that Becket had provoked the disaster through his own arrogance.

'He wanted to be a king – he wanted to be more than a king,' was one angry reaction. 'Let him be a king now!'

But then the monks started readying Thomas's body for burial, and as they cut away his bloodstained outer vestments, the surprising gar-ment they discovered underneath changed their attitude entirely.

'Look,' cried one, 'he's a true monk!'

A KING REPENTS
1174

I F THOMAS BECKET HAD BEEN WEARING SILK UNDERPANTS
when he died, he might never have become a martyr. Luxurious
clothing would have confirmed all the worst suspicions about his vain-
glorious pride. But as Thomas's confused followers stripped off his
bloodied vestments on the evening of 29 December 1170 to prepare his
body for burial, they discovered the very opposite of luxury. Next to
the skin of the murdered archbishop was a shirt of the roughest goat's
hair, extending from his neck to his knees. It was the ultimate monkish symbol of humility, the painfully itchy garment that the pious wore
when they wished to punish themselves – and Thomas had taken self-
punishment to extremes. His hair shirt was crawling with maggots and
lice.

This was the moment when the process of sainthood began. The
discovery of the hair shirt, we are told, astonished everyone except
Thomas's private chaplain Robert of Merton, the archbishop's spiritual
confidant, who had been in charge of his private devotions. These
included, it now turned out, the trussing-up of the heavy hair shirt as
many as three times a day, so the chaplain could whip the archbishop's
back until the blood flowed – and if the man tired, Thomas would tear
at his flesh with his own fingernails.

We might well say today that such appalling masochism was reason
in itself for Thomas's incurably prickly attitude towards the world. But
in Canterbury Cathedral that evening in 1170 the monks knew they
had been confronted with proof of the dead archbishop's saintliness.
Thomas had mortified his body in order to master his carnal desires.
Otherworldly in this last stage of his life, Becket had moved to the ultimate dimension in the manner and place of his dying, and the monks
promptly set about collecting his blood in a basin. The martyr was

decked out for burial in the cathedral crypt, wearing his hair shirt below his glorious robes, and carrying his ceremonial shepherd's staff of office.

All Europe was shocked by the murder in the cathedral. The tale reached as far as Iceland, where it became the 'Thómas Saga', and in the scandalised retellings the complexity of Becket's love–hate relationship with his former friend became simplified. Henry Plantagenet was cast as the villain. The Pope declared Thomas a saint, and ordered the King to do penance.

In the summer of 1174, dressed for the occasion in a hair shirt of his own, Henry went humbly to Canterbury, where he spent a day and a night fasting on the bare ground beside Thomas's tomb. Around him lay ordinary pilgrims, so the news of the royal humiliation would be publicly known and spread. The King offered himself for five strokes of the rod from every bishop present, and three from each of Canterbury's eighty monks. Then, wearing around his neck a phial of water that had been tinctured with drops of Becket's blood, Henry dragged himself on to his horse and rode back to London, where he took to his bed.

'Canterbury Water' became a must-buy for the countless pilgrims who flocked to Becket's tomb in the centuries that followed. The precious pink liquid was said to heal the blind and raise the crippled, and the streets around the cathedral became crammed with souvenir stalls selling badges and highly coloured images of the martyr. The tomb itself was a stupendous sight, sparkling with jewels and hung about with the sticks and crutches of those whom the visit had revivified – a gaudy spectacle of salvation. From relative obscurity, Canterbury became one of Europe's premier religious destinations, ranking with Rome, Jerusalem, Santiago de Compostela and the continent's other great centres of pilgrimage.

England took pride in its home-grown hero who so enhanced the country's spiritual status in Christendom, and no one embraced the devotion of Thomas more enthusiastically than the royal family. Henry II's three daughters, married to the rulers of Sicily, Saxony and the Spanish kingdom of Castile, spread the cult of the English saint with chapels, lavish wallpaintings and mosaics. The obstinate individual who had dared to defy their father was no longer a villain – he was an icon of English identity – and in later centuries even the name of this London merchant's son became fancified. He came to be known as Thomas 'à' Becket.

The prestigious new cult and enhanced tourist business were some consolation for the fact that Henry had lost his great battle with the Church. It had been a major defeat. In addition to his public penance, the King had to agree that England's church courts should remain independent of the common law. Priests continued to enjoy the 'benefit of clergy' for centuries, and from a modern perspective clerical privilege might not seem a worthy cause for which to die. But the archbishop had spoken his mind. He had stood up to authority he considered unjust and he had been prepared to lay down his life for his beliefs. Goat-hair shirt or silk underpants – either way, Thomas Becket had walked the path of the hero.

THE RIVER-BANK TAKE-AWAY

1172

IN 1172 WILLIAM FITZSTEPHEN, ONE OF THE EYEWITNESSES AT the death of Thomas Becket, described what you would see if you visited the bustling city of London in the reign of England's first Plantagenet king:

> On the east stands the Tower, exceeding great and strong, whose walls and bailey rise from very deep foundations, their mortar being mixed with the blood of beasts. On the west are two strongly fortified castles, while from them there runs a great continuous wall, very high, with seven double gates, and towers at intervals along its north side. On the south, London once had similar

walls and towers. But the Thames, that mighty river teeming with fish, which runs on that side and ebbs and flows with the sea, has in the passage of time washed those bulwarks away, undermining them and bringing them down . . . On all sides, beyond the houses, lie the gardens of the citizens that live in the suburbs, planted with trees, spacious and fair, laid out beside each other. To the north are pasturelands and pleasant open spaces of level meadow, inter- sected by running waters, which turn millwheels with a cheerful sound.

FitzStephen wrote this description as a prologue to his life of Becket. He wanted to explain the background from which his hero had sprung and, as a fellow Londoner, he was clearly proud of England's largest city, which he praised for its Christian faith, for the whole- someness of its air – and for its ability to enjoy itself.

At Easter, they make sport with tournaments on the river. A shield is firmly tied to a stout pole in midstream and a small boat, rowed with the current by many oarsmen, carries a young man standing in the bows, who has to strike the shield with his lance. His object is to break the lance by striking the shield and keeping his footing. But if he strikes it and does not splinter the lance, he falls into the river, and the boat goes on without him.

When the great marsh along the northern walls of the city is frozen, crowds of young men go out to amuse themselves on the ice. Some run to gather speed, and slide along the ice with feet apart covering great distances. Others make seats of ice shaped like millstones, and get a group of others who run in front of them, holding hands to drag them along. Sometimes they go too fast, and all fall flat on their faces. Others more skilled in ice sports fit the shin-bones of beasts to their feet, lashing them to their ankles, and use an iron- shod pole to propel themselves, pushing against the ice. They are borne along as swiftly as a bird in flight.

If England had had a tourist board in the twelfth century William FitzStephen would surely have been employed to write its brochures. A man of strong opinions, he contended that the men of London were famous for their honour and the women for their chastity. He produced no evidence to back up these claims, but he did describe a city with at least one facility that sounds both modern and convenient:

Moreover there is in London on the river-bank, amid the wine sold from ships and wine cellars, a public cook-shop. There daily you can find the seasonal foods, dishes roast, fried and boiled, fish of every size, coarse meat for the poor and delicate for the rich, such as venison and various kinds of birds. If travel-weary friends should suddenly call on any of the citizens, and do not wish to wait until fresh food is bought and cooked and 'till servants bring water for hands and bread', they hasten to the river-bank, where everything that they could want is ready and waiting . . . Those who desire to fare delicately need not search to find sturgeon or guinea-fowl . . . since every sort of delicacy is set out for them here.

RICHARD THE LIONHEART
1189–99

JUST ONE ENGLISH KING HAS BEEN ACCORDED THE honour of a statue outside the Houses of Parliament – Richard Coeur de Lion, the Lionheart, who sits magnificently on horseback, larger than life, wearing chain mail and brandishing his great sword over the car park between the Commons and the Lords. Richard is England's muscular hero king – our only ruler to have been captured and flung into a foreign dungeon – and it is not surprising that he has generated some fairytales. While in jail, according to one medieval legend, he had a love affair with the daughter of the German king who had captured him – to the fury of her father, who decided to stage an 'accident'. He gave orders for a lion in his private zoo to be starved for a few days, then to be allowed to 'escape' into Richard's cell. Hearing of the plan, the distraught princess begged her lover to flee, but Richard asked her instead for forty silk handkerchiefs. These he bound around his right forearm, and thus protected, when the beast broke into his

93

cell, he thrust his arm down the lion's throat. Reaching inside its chest to tear out the heart, Richard strode to the Great Hall and flung it, still beating, on to the table in front of the astonished king. He then proceeded to sprinkle salt over the pulsating flesh and ate it with great relish – the Lionheart in deed and name.

Two years before he succeeded his father Henry II in 1189, Richard had sworn to 'take the Cross' – that is, to go on crusade – and his crusading oath defined almost everything about him. For a hundred years, Christian Europe had been consumed by the compulsion to clear Palestine of the Muslims, who controlled access to Jerusalem, Bethlehem and the other sites sacred to Christians in the Holy Land. The crusaders believed they possessed the one and only true faith, and that they were fighting in a just cause when they destroyed non-Christians. If they risked their lives in battle they increased their chances of going to heaven – a crusade was a pilgrimage with bloodshed added. Throw in a dash of vengeance and a call to liberation involving a simply identified but distant place: here were the eternal constituents for self-righteous homicide.

At the moment when Christianity was securing its greatest ever hold over the hearts and minds of Europe – its mastery carved into the stone of the continent's great cathedrals – non-believers were being seen by ordinary Christians as deeply threatening. Richard's accession was marked by England's first violent persecution of a minority group in the name of religion, when the Jews living in London and a number of other towns were attacked. The Jews had come to England with the Normans. They were a means by which the Normans financed their warfare, and they provided banking services to the rest of the community. They lent money on which they charged interest to merchants, landowners and also to the Church – many of England's great cathedrals and monasteries were built with money lent by the Jews.

But dependency provoked resentment among those who had borrowed, and they seized on the foreigners' unfamiliar costume, diet and other non-Christian practices as an alibi for taking revenge. Killing the lender was also a simple way of removing the debt. At Lynn in Norfolk and Stamford in Lincolnshire it was members of the local establishment – gentry and knights – who led the plundering of Jewish property. In York many of the several-hundred-strong Jewish community barricaded themselves inside the castle tower, whereupon they were besieged not only by rioters but by the sheriff's men who were supposed to protect them. Fearing their wives and children would be raped and mutilated, they killed them, then set fire to the tower and killed themselves.

To his credit, Richard tried personally to stop the anti-Semitic atrocities and made sure that the perpetrators of the York attack were punished. But when he arrived in Palestine on his crusade the following year, he showed no mercy to the Muslim infidels that he encountered.

In June 1191 he landed with his army at the port of Acre, which crusaders from several European countries had been besieging to no avail. Immediately, his powerful personality and his well organised forces gave him effective command of the attack. The city surrendered within five weeks. It was one of the great and rare triumphs in the two-hundred-year history of European crusading, establishing Richard as a solid-gold hero throughout Christendom. But when he felt that the Arabs were being slow in implementing the surrender agreement, he had no hesitation in parading 2700 hostages in front of the city and then having them slaughtered.

It is the folk-memory of such killings that has led Osama bin Laden and Arab leaders such as Saddam Hussein and Muammar Gaddafi to describe modern Western invaders of the Middle East, particularly Britain and America, as 'crusaders'. They see a direct connection, and they view the modern state of Israel, sponsored and so heavily supported by America, as the West's revenge for the failure of its crusades. In the Middle Ages the Arab inhabitants of Palestine generally extended more tolerance to Christians – and to the small number of Jews then living there – than the Christians were prepared to show to them. Saladin, the Kurdish leader of the Muslim forces, was conspicuous for his gallantry, entertaining enemy leaders with courtesy and generosity – though his soldiers, like the crusader armies, were ultimately held together by religious fanaticism. Muslims who died in this jihad, or holy war, were promised instant entry to heaven.

In his sixteen months of campaigning, Richard failed to capture his main goal, Jerusalem. But he did secure Acre and a strip of territory that provided a toehold for Christian influence. And when it came to hand-to-hand combat, he proved himself a royal Rambo: 'With no armour on his legs, he threw himself into the sea first . . . and forced his way powerfully on to dry land', according to one account of how the Lionheart relieved the town of Jaffa in August 1192, showing no mercy to his opponents. 'The outstanding king shot them down indiscriminately with a crossbow he was carrying in his hand, and his elite companions pursued [them] as they fled across the beach, cutting them down.'

Richard's fame as a warrior owed as much to his organisational skills as to his bravery. Thanks to the care he took with the logistics, the English were the best-supplied, fed and watered of all the crusader armies. Before he left London, the King had arranged the manufacture and delivery of sixty thousand horseshoes – most from the iron forges of the Forest of Dean – along with fourteen thousand cured pig carcasses from Lincolnshire, Essex and Hampshire. He seldom let sentiment obstruct practicality. In England he had been presented with an ancient and mighty sword found in Glastonbury and said to be King Arthur's Excalibur. But when he reached Sicily Richard exchanged the mythical weapon for four supply ships. The Lionheart was so busy creating his own legend he had no need of anyone else's.

It was on his way back from the Holy Land that he inspired the most memorable legends of all. Hugging the shore in an attempt to avoid the winter storms of the open Mediterranean, he was shipwrecked in December 1192 on the northern Adriatic coast (now Slovenia), and travelling north towards home he entered the territory of the Austrian duke Leopold with whom he had quarrelled during the siege of Acre. The English king and his companions tried to disguise themselves in hoods and cloaks as returning pilgrims, but they were captured and flung into the dungeons of Castle Durnstein, high on a crag above the River Danube.

Richard did not spend long behind bars. As Christendom's most famous warrior, he was a high-profile bargaining chip to be paraded by Leopold and the German emperor – the king in the fairytale of the forty handkerchiefs. But it was over a year before England came up with the 100,000 silver crowns – the equivalent of three years' taxation – required to ransom its walkabout king, and from this captivity came both the legend of the hungry lion and the story of Blondel the royal minstrel.

Richard was music-mad. He loved to conduct the choir in his

chapel, and he composed ballads in the style of the courtly troubadours of Aquitaine, where he grew up and which he always considered his home. According to the legend, he had composed a ballad to a lady of the court with the help of Blondel, a ministrel who was devoted to him. The moment Blondel heard of his master's captivity, he set off for Germany, singing the first line of the ballad outside every castle he passed, until finally he reached Castle Durnstein. There he heard, wafting through the bars of the dungeon, the melodious voice that told him that Richard was alive and well.

Like the tale of the silk handkerchiefs and the lion's heart, this story sprang up within a few decades of Richard's death. When people later recalled the imprisonment of their crusader king they opted for fantasy, forgetting the unprecedented expense that his ransom had imposed on England. The ransom tax swelled the considerable sums already shelled out by those back home to finance his crusade, and it was followed by even heavier taxes to sustain the battles that Richard started fighting in France as soon as he got back to Europe. But as we smile, perhaps patronisingly, at the thought of these poor put-upon medievals, let us reflect on the disposal of our taxes today. In the spring of 2003 Tony Blair promised he would spend 'whatever it takes' to support the British troops fighting in Iraq, and, despite people's doubts about the war, the opinion polls showed broad agreement with that particular use of taxpayers' money. Who would dare to put a price on patriotism?

The abandonment of reason that national feeling can provoke seems the likeliest explanation of England's fondness down the years for the warlike Lionheart – a character venerated enough to be played on the screen by Sir Sean Connery. In reality, England's hero king did not speak English. His native language was French, and he saw himself as an Angevin, building up the French empire of his father Henry and his mother, Eleanor of Aquitaine. As he lay dying in 1199, aged only forty-one, following a crossbow wound he had received during the siege of the French castle of Chalus, Richard arranged that his body, disembowelled and salted, should be sent for burial beside his parents at the abbey of Fontevrault in Anjou. As a final touch, he instructed that his famous Coeur de Lion – which turned out to be 'of great size' – be cut out and sent, not to England, but to Normandy.

Yet Richard did bequeath to England an enduring emblem of the martial qualities he embodied. As the English crusaders fought in the Holy Land they often heard the French soldiers cry out to their patron saint, St Denys, and they decided they would like a patron of their own. There was a whole gallery of English martyrs they could have invoked, from St Alban to the recently canonised St Thomas of Canterbury. But none of these was warlike enough, and so they lighted on a local campaigner. St George was a Christian martyr, thought to be of Turkish or Arab descent, who had died at Lydda in Palestine around AD 303. Many centuries later, the legend that he slew a dragon to save a damsel in distress was attached to his name, together with the symbol of a striking red cross on a plain white field – and the tale evidently caught Richard's fancy. The King placed himself and his army in the Holy Land under George's protection.

It was several hundred years before St George became fully established as England's patron saint, and he has never been exclusively ours. Portugal regards him as its patron, as do the great Italian seaport cities of Venice and Genoa. But Richard spread himself pretty thin as well. In the course of his ten-year reign he spent just six months in England. So a king who was not English helped supply us with the saint who was not English – hybrid symbols for a mongrel race.

JOHN LACKLAND AND MAGNA CARTA

1215

BEFORE HE DIED, HENRY II, THE FATHER OF RICHARD THE Lionheart, commissioned a painting that showed an eagle being pecked to death by its young.

'Those are my sons,' Henry would say.

The painting hung in his palace at Winchester, and showed one of the eaglets poised on its father's neck, waiting for the moment to peck out its eyes. That particularly vicious nestling was John, explained the old king – 'the youngest of them, whom I now embrace with so much affection' – and he predicted that his favourite son would one day betray him.

So it proved. Henry had four adult sons (two of whom, Henry the Younger and Geoffrey, would predecease their father), and he worried that the youngest had no inheritance. He nicknamed the boy 'Jean sans Terre' – John Lackland – and the fond father provoked a series of bitter family battles by trying to pare off bits of the other brothers' inheritances to give to John. In the Middle Ages a royal family battle could be just that. In 1189 the furious Richard led an army against his ailing father so as to compel him to hand over his birthright. As he marched across France his forces were swelled by many who calculated that the old man had become a lost cause and that they had nothing to lose by rallying to the Lionheart.

'Woe, woe,' Henry muttered, 'on a vanquished king!'

Just a few days from death, Henry II was compelled to surrender, asking only that he be told the names of those who had switched sides to support Richard. The old man was shown the list – and John's name was at the head of it.

Having betrayed one member of the family, John then set about betraying another. If Richard is the Prince Charming of English history, John is the pantomime villain. No sooner had Richard left on crusade for the Holy Land in 1189, than John started plotting to steal England from him. When the news came through of Richard's capture and imprisonment in Germany, he conspired with King Philip II of France to keep Richard in jail.

'Look to yourself,' Philip warned John when he discovered their plot had failed, 'the devil is loosed!'

It was a measure of the Lionheart's chivalry that he forgave his younger brother when he arrived back in England and John pleaded for mercy.

'Think no more of it, John,' he said. 'You are only a child' – and the King took the twenty-seven-year-old child off for a feast of freshly caught salmon.

John succeeded Richard in 1199 when the Lionheart died without legitimate offspring, and for most people their experience of the new reign was no different from the old. Nobles, townspeople, farmers – all were taxed and taxed again as John went about campaigning in an effort to hold together the extensive family lands in France. But while Richard's military adventures had yielded romantic glory, John had little to show but defeat. *Mollegladium* (Softsword) became his Latin nickname according to the monkish chroniclers, who paint a disapproving picture of an idle and luxury-loving king, gloating over his jewels and spending long hours in bed.

As churchmen they were biased witnesses, since much of John's reign was dominated by long-running conflict with the Church. In 1205 a dispute arose over the election of a new Archbishop of Canterbury, and John refused to accept the Pope's candidate. His Holiness responded with an interdiction on the whole of England – a general 'lock-out' by the clergy. Churches were closed, the bells tied up and silenced. For six years the clergy held no services in church, refusing to perform baptisms, weddings or funerals. You might get the priest to come to your home privately to bless your baby or your son's marriage, and masses with sermons were still held once a week. But these had to take place outside the shuttered churches, in the often damp and chilly churchyard. The priest might also attend deathbeds to administer the last sacraments, but after that the people had to bury their loved ones in ditches or woodlands, making do with their own improvised prayers.

If religion is the opium of the people, Britain went without its fix for six years. People were in fear for their immortal souls. Without being fully welcomed into the Church, they believed, their children could be possessed by devils; without proper burial they might not get to heaven. For a faith-based society, the years of the interdiction were a grievous and demoralising time. In the Holy Land the English had recently been numbered among God's heroes. Now they were cast out among the goats.

In 1209 John was singled out personally by the Pope for excommunication – a total rejection by the Church, even worse than interdiction, and a badge of shame that condemned him to hellfire and damnation. Every bishop but one left the country, and in the end John caved in. He accepted the Pope's candidate as Archbishop of Canterbury and the interdiction was lifted in mid-1214. But when

England suffered military disaster that summer, the humiliation could not help seeming like the judgement of God. John had already lost control of Normandy to the King of France, and the French victory at Bouvines on 27 July 1214 made the loss final.

Softsword had something of the snake about him. It was not unusual for a medieval king simply to eliminate rivals, as John had done early in his reign when he imprisoned the son of his late brother Geoffrey – Arthur, who was never to be seen again. But when John later heard that a noblewoman had been gossiping about Arthur's disappearance, he had the culprit jailed with one of her sons and left them both to starve to death. The King gave the impression that he did not know how to play fair, that he would not hesitate to ride roughshod over anyone who crossed him. This, combined with his military failure, the church interdiction and his unrelenting tax demands, set the stage for the momentous and historic events of 1215.

In January of that year, a group of disgruntled barons who had gathered for the Christmas court called for the restoration of their 'ancient and accustomed liberties'. They seem to have been thinking of the sort of contract promising better behaviour on the part of the monarch that Ethelred the Unready had struck with his nobles and bishops in 1014. These ideas had been repeated by William the Conqueror's two sons, William Rufus and Henry I, when, in 1087 and 1100 respectively, they were canvassing for support after their throne-grabbing gallops to Winchester. It was Henry's coronation charter that now provided John's critics with a model.

In the spring of 1215 the barons decided to act. Assembling at Stamford in Lincolnshire, they started marching south, gathering support along the way. On 17 May sympathisers welcomed them to London, and their occupation of the city seems to have persuaded John to come to terms. After some preliminary discussions, the two sides met in the middle of June to negotiate on the banks of the Thames near Windsor in a meadow named Runnymede – literally, the 'soggy meadow' – and the result of several days' hard bargaining was the famous Magna Carta and a rather optimistic declaration of peace.

History has romanticised the Great Charter as the far-reaching document that established the people's liberties, when in many respects its purpose was scarcely grander than to protect the rights of the rich warrior landowners who were fed up with being so heavily taxed. The barons were certainly not fighting for the rights of the often down-trodden labourers, the serfs and villeins who worked on their estates ('serf' from the Latin word *servus* – 'slave' or 'servant'; 'villein' from *villa* – the country house that owned them). But, willy-nilly, the rights for which the barons fought had a universal application.

'No free man shall be seized, imprisoned, dispossessed, outlawed, exiled or ruined in any way . . .' read clause 39, 'except by the lawful judgement of his peers and the law of the land.' Here was a call for fair play and justice that would resonate in later years – and the following clause backed it up: 'To no one will we sell, to no one will we deny or delay right or justice.'

Other clauses regulated feudal landholding and inheritance, guaranteed towns their freedoms, and gave merchants the right of free travel. A start was made on reforming the hated laws that protected the royal hunting forests (see p. 74), and a serious attempt was made to check abuses of power by local officials. Clause 35 set up the first countrywide system of standardised weights and measures – a bonus to trade and to all consumers.

All through the last days of June 1215, the clerks at Runnymede scribbled away furiously, making copies of the charter to be taken and read out in every shire of the land. Magna Carta was the first written document limiting the powers of the king to be backed up by practical enforcement. A watchdog council of twenty-five barons was set up to make sure the king obeyed the charter, and a commission of twelve knights in each county was charged to look into local abuses of the law.

It was the watchdog council that proved the snag. John refused to accept that a non-royal body should infringe his sacred power, while several of the twenty-five barons started to throw their new-found weight around. By the autumn, England was engulfed in civil war. The following spring Philip II of France sent an army under his son Louis to help the barons – if the English could invade France, why not vice versa? – and John spent the last months of his reign tramping the country in a vain attempt to quell the rebellion.

The final scene was staged that October in the misty wetlands of East Anglia, where the royal baggage train struggled to cross the four-and-a-half-mile estuary of the Nene River (then known as the

Wellstream) near Wisbech on the Wash. Misjudging the tide, the King's horses, wagons and riders were caught by the incoming waters. Jewels, gold and silver goblets, flagons, candelabra – even John's crown and coronation regalia – all were swallowed up by the sucking eddies of the Wash. The lost jewels of King John remain undiscovered treasure trove to this day.

The King himself was already sick with dysentery. After weeks of camp-fire food, he had overeaten when entertained by the townsfolk of Lynn and, according to one chronicler, his idea of a cure was to consume quantities of peaches and fresh-brewed cider. It was one delicacy too many. Borne to the nearby town of Newark on a stretcher of branches cut from Fen willows, John Lackland breathed his last on 18 October 1216.

Furious over the indignities of the interdiction, caused by John's refusal to do his Christian duty as they saw it, the monkish chroniclers of the time had no doubt which way his soul was headed. Hell was a foul place, wrote one, but it would now be rendered still more foul by the presence of King John. Disapproving of such moralistic judgements, 'value-free' modern historians have pointed to the growth of royal record-keeping during John's reign as evidence of how efficient his government administration was – as if bureaucratic efficiency was not one of our own modern gods.

But John's painstaking record-keeping has certainly provided us with some interesting insights into his life. The detailed inventory of what he lost in the watery East Anglian wastes included pieces of glass, which seem to have been portable windowpanes ready to be cut and fitted into the castles he visited. John was clearly a man who loved his comforts. We read in his accounts of William his bathman, paid a halfpenny a day for his services, with a few extra pence as a tip when he actually prepared a bath. The record shows us that John was unusually clean for his time – he took a bath every three weeks – while an entry describing 'an over-tunic for when his Lordship the King gets up in the night' reveals a further claim to distinction. John was England's first king to be recorded as owning a dressing-gown.

HOBBEHOD, PRINCE OF THIEVES
1225

WHEN THE ROYAL JUDGES ARRIVED IN YORK IN THE summer of 1225, they found that one of the cases before them involved a certain Robert Hod (or Hood), an outlaw. Hod had failed to appear in court, so the judges duly confiscated his worldly goods, valued at the sum of thirty-two shillings and sixpence, which was about what it cost in the thirteenth century to live modestly for a year. Hod, or Hood, continued to steer clear of the justice system, for his penalty remained unpaid, and it was carried forward to the ledger for the following year under the name of 'Hobbehod' – which could mean 'that devil Hood', or might have been a spelling mistake for 'RobbeHod'.

That is the extent of the historical evidence we have for the possible existence of Robin Hood, the dashing outlaw of Sherwood Forest. But court records from Berkshire in 1261 tell us of another outlaw, this one described as 'William Robehod', and in the years that follow the Robehods or Robynhods proliferate in the records. Whether or not this particular bandit actually existed, his exploits were so famous that 'Robin Hood' became the medieval nickname for a fugitive from justice. Some outlaws chose notoriety; others had it thrust upon them. By around 1400 a priest was complaining that people would rather hear 'a tale or a song of Robyn Hood' than listen to a sermon.

Robin and his Merrie Men have proved to have a timeless appeal, but in their own day they had a specific significance. You were proclaimed an outlaw if you repeatedly failed to show up at court to answer a charge. As with Hobbehod, a fugitive from the judges in 1225, your goods and chattels and any land you held were confiscated, and you would then have to take your chances outside the law. If you were captured, your death by hanging would be ordered without further trial, and if you resisted arrest anyone was entitled to kill you. To be a

legally proclaimed fugitive was a perilous state of affairs, so no wonder
that people's imaginations were captured by the dream of life under the
greenwood tree, where you could live according to your own laws. It
was a particularly satisfying option if the forest was one of those preserved for the king's hunting.

There had been legends about heroic brigands, bandits, and resistance fighters before Robin Hood, notably the stories surrounding
Hereward, the Saxon nobleman deprived of his lands by the Normans.
But Robin came a step or two down the social ladder from Hereward.
The tales of the time described Hood as a 'yeoman', from the Danish
word *yongerman*, a free peasant of the artisan class. He was a 'yeoman
of the forest', spending his days in harmony with nature. And if the
primitive philosophy of this 'good life' did not quite make Hobbehod
a working-class hero, it could fairly be claimed that he was the original 'green' warrior.

Today you can visit the huge hollow oak tree in Sherwood Forest
where Robin Hood and his band are supposed to have hidden from
the wicked Sheriff of Nottingham. Sadly, the tree was not even an
acorn at the end of the twelfth century, when legend claims the outlaw
roamed the forest. King Richard was certainly in Nottingham in
March 1194. He made a beeline for the town when he returned from
imprisonment after the Crusades, for Nottingham had supported
Prince John's attempts to supplant him, and its castle was the last to
hold out for John's cause.

Richard instantly set up gallows in front of the castle walls, and proceeded to hang several soldiers, whose resistance may be attributed to their
not knowing, or their refusal to believe, that the King was finally back.

'Well, what can you see?' asked Richard when at last the defenders
sent envoys to negotiate. 'Am I here?'

The garrison promptly surrendered, and the King went off to celebrate with a day's hunting in Sherwood Forest. But there is no record
of him ever meeting Robin Hood – and he cannot possibly have met
Little John, Friar Tuck, Will Scarlet, Much the Miller's son, or any
other of the subsequently named Merrie Men. Maid Marion would
not appear in the proliferating network of Robyn Hood ballads,
masques, and morris dances until the beginning of the sixteenth century, when she was often played for laughs by a male impersonator –

an early example of the pantomime dame. It was around this period, three hundred years after Hobbehod's first non-appearance in court, that the national anti-hero's penchant for relieving passers-by of their spare cash was finally given a serious social purpose. In all his early portrayals Robin was a sturdy rascal – jovial, maybe, but basically a robber. Not until 1589 do we first read the claim that his followers 'tooke from rich to give the poore'.

So that devil Hood finally became England's symbol of resistance to tyranny, the archer of the green wood, daredevil justice maker, with his own programme of wealth redistribution in the days before the welfare state. Those are the noble and romantic aspects of the legend. But it is surely ironic that the national heart has been so stirred down the centuries by a man who started out a thief.

SIMON DE MONTFORT AND HIS TALKING-PLACE

1265

MAGNA CARTA DID NOT VANISH INTO THE WASH WITH THE rest of King John's baggage in October 1216. On the contrary, his death revived the Great Charter – along with the fortunes of the monarchy. John's heir was his nine-year-old son Henry, and the prospect of this child being in charge of England somehow purged the bitterness between Crown and barons. The country's quarrel had been with John, and few people had welcomed the French army that had come to the aid of the rebels. It is often said that no foreign army has set foot on English soil since 1066, but from May 1216 French troops were tramping over much of south-east England, and during John's last desperate months Louis, the son of the French king, was holding court in London.

To win over domestic opinion and help get rid of the French, who finally departed in September 1217, the young Henry III's guardians rapidly reissued the Great Charter – in modified form. They reworded or deleted a number of clauses, removing the controversial watchdog council of twenty-five barons that had sparked the civil war, but promised that the new king would rule according to the remaining provisions. When the boy king presided over a council meeting at Westminster the following year the charter was issued again, then affirmed for a third time in 1225 when Henry, by then seventeen, had been declared old enough to play a formal role in government. So, triply restated and confirmed, the idea of a contract between king and subjects became once more the basis of rule and law. When lawyers started collating English law in later centuries they listed the 1225 version of Magna Carta as the first in the Statute Book.

The trouble was that the new king himself had not the slightest intention of being accountable. A regulation-bound monarchy was not for Henry III. Humiliated by what he knew of his father's unhappy end, a fugitive in his own country skulking around the Fens, the latest Plantagenet was dedicated to the vision of glorious and absolute kingship. As he saw it, he was a ruler consecrated by God, with enough divinity in his fingertips to cure the sick with his touch.

The keynote project of Henry's reign was the rebuilding of Edward the Confessor's Westminster Abbey, which he demolished and had redesigned in the new, soaring gothic style – a temple to the historic past and, he hoped, to the magnificent future of England's kings. Henry installed the Confessor as the patron saint of this triumphal cult of royalty, reburying his remains in a shrine behind the high altar, the centrepiece of the new abbey. Henry even had a mural of Edward painted in his bedroom, so his saintly hero was the last thing he saw before he went to bed and the face that he woke up to in the morning.

Gazing up at the vaulted arches of Westminster Abbey, one can see that Henry III had a fine taste in architecture. But his judgement was poor when it came to just about everything else. A court jester is said to have remarked that, like Jesus Christ himself, Henry was as wise on the day of his birth as he would ever be. The contemporary chronicler Matthew Paris described him as 'of medium stature and compact in body. One of his eyelids drooped, hiding some of the dark part of the eyeball. He had robust strength, but was careless in his acts.'

In the eyes of England's barons, Henry was particularly careless in the choice of advisers and favourites, who, like his wife Eleanor of Provence, were almost all from southern France. In previous reigns, French dominance at court had reflected the powerbase of William the Conqueror. But King John had lost Normandy, Anjou and all of Aquitaine except for Gascony, the wine region around Bordeaux, and in trying to regain the lost territories Henry proved as much a 'Softsword' as his father. His wars, coupled with his ambitious building and the grandiose style of his court, got him hopelessly into debt. His predictable solution – taxation – provoked the predictable response.

While Henry was formulating his lofty view of royal power, reform was in the air. The notion of a 'community of the realm' was taking shape among the thinking classes who were getting more numerous. Educated at the growing number of cathedral schools and in the colleges that were just starting up in the market towns of Oxford and Cambridge, the increasing ranks of graduates went into the Church for the most part. But some found work in the Exchequer and in the other developing offices of government, where the leading lights among the 'king's clerks' took pride in their work. They saw good and efficient government as an aim in itself, and they were starting to ask how this could be maintained when the King himself did not practise it.

The daring idea of controlling an unreliable monarch had been inherent in the thinking behind Magna Carta's twenty-five-strong watchdog committee, and as discontent mounted during Henry's long reign, calls grew to bring back this crucial feature of the Great Charter. By 1258 the fifty-one-year-old king was virtually bankrupt following an expensive foreign-policy adventure in which he had tried to make one of his sons king of Sicily. Now, under pressure from his barons, he finally gave way. Twelve of his nominees met at Oxford with twelve of the discontents to hammer out, Runnymede-style, how 'our kingdom shall be ordered, rectified, and reformed in keeping with what they think best to enact'.

The twenty-four-man think tank convened on 11 June 1258 at a moment of great national distress. The previous year's harvest had been catastrophic, and as the 'hungry month' of July approached, famine was becoming widespread. 'Owing to the shortage of food,' wrote Matthew Paris, 'an innumerable multitude of poor people died and dead bodies were found everywhere, swollen through famine and livid, lying by fives and sixes in pigsties and dunghills in the muddy streets.'

Extreme times produce extreme measures – in the summer of 1258, a 'New Deal' for England. The Provisions of Oxford which the twenty-four wise men produced that summer effectively transferred England's government from Henry to a 'Council of Fifteen'. These men would appoint the great officers of state, control the Exchequer, super-vise the sheriffs and local officials, and have the power of 'advising the King in good faith regarding the government of the Kingdom'. The Provisions, which count alongside Magna Carta as milestones in England's constitutional history, were drawn up loyally in the name of the King. But they made a crucial distinction between the human fal-libility of any particular king and the superior institution of the Crown, whose job it was to guarantee the well-being of *all* the people, the 'community of the realm'.

One of the twenty-four wise men who had gathered at Oxford and subsequently a member of the Council of Fifteen was the Earl of Leicester, Simon de Montfort – a prickly and imperious Thomas Becket-like character, who, like Becket, began as his king's close friend but would end up as his nemesis. Years earlier, de Montfort had secretly wooed and won Henry III's sister, another Eleanor, and he was never afraid to take on his royal brother-in-law. The two men had savage stand-up rows in public, which de Montfort, with his overbearing manner, tended to win. Henry was rather in awe of him. Being rowed along the Thames one day, the King was over-taken by a thunderstorm and, terrified, ordered his watermen to make for the nearest landing-steps, which happened to belong to a house where de Montfort was staying. 'I fear the thunder and light-ning beyond measure, I know,' the King candidly confessed as de Montfort came out to greet him. 'But by God's head, Sir Earl, I dread you even more.'

De Montfort came from northern France and had grown up in the same martial atmosphere as Richard the Lionheart. Like Richard, he went on crusade to the Holy Land, and distinguished himself there in battle. He was an inspiring general – and a pious one. He would frequently rise at midnight to spend the hours until dawn in silent vigil and prayer. His best friend was Robert Grosseteste, the Bishop of Lincoln, who wrote a treatise setting out the difference between good rule and tyranny. De Montfort, who had sipped self-righteousness, it sometimes seemed, with his mother's milk, came to believe over the years that his royal brother-in-law was little more than a coward and a tyrant. Furthermore, he had no doubt that he alone knew the way to achieve just rule.

In the aftermath of the Provisions of Oxford this unbending sense of morality got de Montfort in trouble with his fellow-barons. Why should the King alone be subject to outside controls? he asked. What about those barons and lords who abused their authority at the expense of the ordinary people? Needless to say, this was not at all what the barons wanted to hear. When the King, with their backing, enlisted the Pope to absolve him from his oath to the Provisions of Oxford, de Montfort's coalition fell apart. His critics had complained, with some justification, that he was not above exploiting his eminence for the benefit of his own family, and in October 1261 the earl stalked off to France in disgust, swearing never to return.

Less than two years later he was back. Henry had reverted to his bad old ways, and now his popularity was lower than ever. On one occasion when his wife tried to sail down the Thames in the royal barge, Londoners went to scoop up the manure that filled the streets in the days before sanitation and expressed their feelings by pelting the Queen with pungent missiles from London Bridge.

When de Montfort called for a restoration of the Provisions of Oxford, many rallied to his cause. Between 1263 and 1265 England was convulsed by civil war, with de Montfort championing the cause of reform. In May 1264, facing the royal army at Lewes on the Sussex Downs, he ordered his men to prostrate themselves, arms spread out in prayer, before donning armour that bore the holy crosses of the crusaders. The general himself, having injured his leg in a riding accident, had been transported to the battlefield in a cart. His forces were heavily outnumbered. But the rebels' fervour carried the day. De Montfort took the King's eldest son Edward (named after the Confessor) as a hostage, and set about putting the Provisions of Oxford into practice.

The Provisions had called for the regular summoning of 'parliament' – literally a 'talking-place' (from the French word *parler*, to speak) – and it was Simon de Montfort's Parliament of January 1265 that secured his place in history. This was by no means the first English parliament to be summoned. The term had been used in 1236 to describe the convention of barons, bishops and other worthies whom the King summoned to advise him – it was not unlike the old Anglo-Saxon *witan*, the council of wise men. But we should not think of this extended royal council as anything like our modern Parliament, with its own identity and its own permanent buildings. In the thirteenth century parliament was called at the king's pleasure, wherever he happened to be in the country – it was an event rather than an institution.

But in January 1265, for the first time, came two knights from every shire, along with two burgesses (town representatives) from York, Lincoln and other selected boroughs to parley in London with the barons, bishops and clergy. Here was the seed of the modern body that now holds the ultimate political authority over our lives, and the gathering was invited to discuss a major question – what to do with Prince Edward, the King's son, whom Simon had taken hostage after the Battle of Lewes.

For townsfolk and country landowners to be conferring on the fate of a future king was heady stuff. In the climate of the times it could not last – and Simon's own followers took fright at the thought of meddling in such mighty matters. In the event, the twenty-five-year-old Edward escaped from captivity and took command of the royal forces, to confront the earl's depleted troops at Evesham that August. The outcome was a foregone conclusion.

'God have mercy on our souls,' cried the old general as the immensely larger royal army approached, 'for our bodies are theirs.'

Simon de Montfort was killed in the brief and bloody slaughter that followed. His testicles were cut off, to be hung around his nose, and his body was then dismembered, with his feet, head and hands being sent around the country as an object lesson to other rebels. But his dream did not die. What was left of him was buried at Evesham and became a place of pilgrimage. Miracles were reported, and songs were sung about this fearless, awkward, self-righteous French-born grandee, who had undoubtedly enriched himself in his campaigning, but who did at least have a vision of a fairer, more representative land.

'Simon, Simon, you are but sleeping,' sang the faithful. One day Simon would wake, went the dream, and with him the cause of liberty in England.

A PRINCE WHO SPEAKS NO WORD OF ENGLISH
1284

IN MAY 1265 THE FUTURE KING EDWARD I WAS BEING HELD hostage in Hereford Castle. Since the Battle of Lewes the previous May his uncle Simon de Montfort had been detaining him under house arrest. It was a courteous kind of detention – the twenty-five-year-old prince was not actually a prisoner – so when a dealer brought some horses to the castle, his guards saw no harm in letting the young man try them out. The men walked him down to an open space, where he gave them a superb display of horsemanship. The athletic young man, over six feet tall, put each of the animals vigorously through its paces, wheeling, galloping, spurring them on and yanking them into sudden stops and turns, until all but one were exhausted. Then he sprang on to the last remaining fresh horse and rode off to freedom.

Shrewd calculation and physical prowess were the hallmarks of Edward I, who came to the throne in 1272. His father Henry III had managed the longest reign of any English sovereign yet, but had run the Crown's authority and its finances into the ground. So when Edward finally succeeded his father, he cannily presented himself as a reformer, ready to implement at least some of the parliamentary principles championed by de Montfort. Edward also looked beyond

England, to the island's furthest shores, ambitious to win control of all Britain. It was this lofty aim that inspired one of the enduring stories of his reign.

The Normans had always laid theoretical claim to Wales, but the middle years of the thirteenth century had seen a series of native freedom fighters robustly dispute this. In Welsh they called themselves *tywysogion*, which in the official documents was translated into Latin as *principes*. So the English – their traditional enemies – described them as 'princes' of Wales. In a series of brilliant and brutal campaigns, Edward I defeated the last two Welsh 'princes' and ringed north-west Wales with a chain of massive stone castles which stand to this day. They represent the pinnacle of the castle-builder's art, and it was to the building-site that would be Caernarfon Castle, looking across at the island of Anglesey, that the King brought his pregnant wife Eleanor in the spring of 1284.

According to the story, Edward had promised the conquered Welsh that he would give them 'a prince born in Wales who speaks no word of English', and that April Eleanor duly produced a son, another Edward. From the battlements of Caernarfon Castle, the proud father presented the Welsh with their newborn prince – who spoke not a word of anything. Tradition has it that, far from being insulted, the Welsh were thoroughly delighted by King Edward's little joke, and that from that day to this all heirs to the English throne have been called Princes of Wales.

That was the legend, first recorded some two hundred years later, and it is true that the baby prince was born in Wales. But there were no battlements at Caernarfon at that date, only some muddy excavations. More important, the new-born Edward of Caernarfon was not his father's heir – that distinction belonged to his eleven-year-old brother, Alfonso. It was not until 1301, after Alfonso's death, that, shortly before his seventeenth birthday, the future Edward II was declared Prince of Wales, and that was in Lincoln, just about as far from Caernarfon as you could get. When Edward became king, he did not name his own son, the future Edward III, Prince of Wales, and in the centuries that followed a number of heirs to the English throne were not given the title.

It was not until the twentieth century, in fact, that an heir to the

English throne was invested as Prince of Wales *in Wales*. In 1911 the demagogic Welsh politician David Lloyd George invented a fake medieval ceremony especially for the purpose, complete with a striped 'crusader tent' and a princely costume that the seventeen-year-old future king, Edward VIII, described as a 'preposterous rig'. In 1969 Prince Charles wore a more conventional, military uniform, and the crusader tent was replaced by a transparent Perspex awning, the better to televise the pageant, which, commentators told millions of viewers around the world, had been inspired by King Edward I in 1284.

Edward Longshanks, as he was nicknamed, was a man of impressive capacity, a tall, lean warrior, every inch a king. Like his great-uncle the Lionheart, he went to Palestine as a crusader and displayed both bravery and an ability to organise. With him to the Holy Land he took his wife Eleanor, to whom he was deeply attached. When she died in Northamptonshire in 1290, the King mounted a procession to carry her back to London, marking the occasion by having a series of tall, highly decorated stone crosses built at every spot where the cortège stopped along the way. The last stopping-point before Westminster was in the neighbourhood of Charing, and a replica of the cross stands in front of Charing Cross Station in London today.

Edward was a man of ferocious temper, notorious for boxing the ears of his children when they displeased him. The royal account book lists repairs to his daughter Elizabeth's coronet in 1297, after he had hurled it into the fire. His tomb in Westminster Abbey bears the inscription *Malleus Scottorum*, the 'Hammer of the Scots'. But his attempts to conquer Scotland did not yield the success that he had enjoyed in Wales, and in a series of bloody campaigns he was held off by the Scottish heroes William 'Braveheart' Wallace and Robert the Bruce.

These setbacks did not deter his people from rating Edward I an English hero, and they even applauded the act of bigotry that is the enduring blot on his reputation to this day. In the course of his unsuccessful Scottish campaigns and his Welsh castle-building programmes, the King found himself in dire financial difficulties and he resorted to desperate measures. Monarchs such as Richard I had traditionally tried to protect England's Jewish communities of merchants and moneylenders against popular prejudice, but in 1290, in return for a large subsidy from Parliament, Edward I agreed to expel England's Jews. There were some three thousand, it has been estimated, living in about fifteen communities. Some were killed, many were robbed, and Edward himself took about £2000 in proceeds from the houses they were compelled to abandon.

It was the ugly face of the faith that had inspired Longshanks to go crusading. When a Jew, before the expulsion, went to Parliament to complain about the case of a Jewish boy who had been forcibly baptised a Christian, Edward did not see the problem. 'The king does not want to revoke the baptism,' reads the ledger. 'No enquiries are to be made of anyone, and nothing is to be done.'

It is a comment to ponder as you look at the beautiful Charing Cross.

PIERS GAVESTON AND EDWARD II

1308

FAIR OF BODY AND GREAT OF STRENGTH, EDWARD OF CAERNARFON, England's first Prince of Wales, was widely welcomed when he came into his inheritance as King Edward II at the age of twenty-three. But as he made his way down the aisle of Westminster Abbey at the end of February 1308 with his young queen Isabella, daughter of the French king Philip IV, all eyes turned to the individual behind him – Piers Gaveston, a young knight from Gascony. The new king had awarded Gaveston pride of place in his coronation procession, bestowing on him the honour of carrying the crown and sword of Edward the Confessor, and Gaveston, in royal purple splashed with pearls, was certainly dressed for the occasion. His finery was such, wrote one chronicler, that 'he more resembled the god Mars, than an ordinary mortal'. According to the gossips, King Edward was so fond of Gaveston that he had given him the pick of the presents that he had received at his recent wedding to Isabella. The Queen's relatives went back to France complaining that Edward loved Gaveston more than he loved his wife.

Edward's father, Edward I, the pugnacious 'Hammer of the Scots', had been infuriated by his son's closeness to the flamboyant young Gascon. The old king had made Gaveston, the son of a trusted knight, a ward in the prince's household, but there were complaints that the two men got up to mischief together, frequenting taverns and running up debts. On Edward I's last unsuccessful campaign against the Scots in Carlisle in the winter of 1306–7, the prince had suggested giving Gaveston some of the royal estates in France. His father exploded, seizing Edward by the hair and tearing it out in tufts. He ordered Gaveston into exile.

On coming to the throne, Edward II's first concern had been to expedite the return of his friend Piers. When he went off to France to marry Isabella in January 1308, a few weeks before the coronation, he placed Gaveston in charge of England, and, to the fury of just about every baron in the land, he also bestowed on him the rich earldom of Cornwall.

The reckless passion of Edward II for Piers Gaveston ranks as the first of the momentous love affairs that have shaken England's monarchy over the centuries. Homosexuality was deeply disapproved of in medieval England. It was considered a form of heresy – a ticket to hell – though there is enough evidence to suggest that many a monk and priest qualified to pass through the ticket barrier. 'The sin against nature' was usually referred to indirectly, with comparisons to the Old Testament love of King David for Jonathan – 'a love beyond the love of women'. When writing specifically of Edward's love for Gaveston, the chroniclers of the time would call it 'excessive', 'immoderate', 'beyond measure and reason'. But one source referred directly to a rumour going around England that 'the King loved an evil male sorcerer more than he did his wife, a most handsome lady and a very beautiful woman'.

It should be stressed that the details of Edward's physical relationship with Gaveston are as unknowable as those of any other royal bedchamber, and we should not forget that the King had four children by Isabella. It has even been argued that the two men were totally chaste, cultivating their relationship as devoted 'brothers'. Certainly, none of this would have been an issue if Edward had not allowed his private affections to intrude so fiercely into his public role. Other kings had no problems with same-sex relationships. It is generally assumed that William Rufus (who ruled from 1087 to 1100) was gay – he produced no children and kept no mistresses – and the same has been said of Richard Coeur de Lion, though this is hotly denied by recent biographers. Whatever their predilections, these monarchs did not allow their private passions to impinge on their royal style or, more important, to influence their decisions when it came to handing out land and other largesse.

Edward II, however, displayed an assortment of characteristics that were viewed as unkingly. For a start, he dressed like his friend Piers, a little too extravagantly. He enjoyed the unusual sport of swimming and also rowing, which was considered demeaning – kings traditionally showed their power by getting others to row *them*. He kept a camel in his stables. He pursued a whole range of 'common' pursuits such as digging, thatching, building walls and hedges, and he enjoyed hammering away at the anvil like a blacksmith. Nowadays England might welcome a DIY king, but in the fourteenth century such activities, not to mention the pleasure Edward took in hobnobbing with grooms and ploughmen, were considered abnormal.

The major grievance, however, was the disproportionate favour that Edward showed Piers Gaveston. When the barons in Parliament called for the exile of the favourite, Edward's response was to endow him with still more castles and manors. He did agree, reluctantly, that Gaveston should go over to Ireland for a while as his representative, but he was clearly unhinged by his departure. The King took his entire household to Bristol to wave Gaveston off and pined for him in his absence, getting personally involved in such petty problems as the punishment of trespassers on Gaveston's property on the Isle of Wight.

When, in an attempt to curb the King's aberrations, Parliament presented him with a set of 'Ordinances' in 1311, along the lines of Simon de Montfort's Provisions of Oxford, Edward took the extraordinary step of offering to agree to any restriction on his own powers provided that his favourite was in no way affected.

The muscular Gaveston did not make things any easier. He took delight in defeating the barons in jousts and tournaments, and then rubbed salt in their wounds by mimicking his critics and giving them derisive nicknames. The Earl of Gloucester was 'whoreson', Leicester was 'the fiddler', and Warwick the 'black hound of Arden'.

'Let him call me"hound",' the earl exclaimed. 'One day the hound will bite him.'

As approved by Parliament and reluctantly agreed by the King, the Ordinances of 1311 imposed stringent controls on royal power. Building on Magna Carta and the Provisions of Oxford, championed by Simon de Montfort, it was now laid down that the King could not leave the kingdom without the consent of the barons, and that parliaments must be held at least once or twice a year and in a convenient place. Clearly, the immediate purpose of the Ordinances was to deal with Gaveston, who was promptly sent out of the country for a second time. But he sneaked quietly back, and by the end of November there were reports of the favourite 'hiding and wandering from place to place in the counties of Cornwall, Devon, Somerset and Dorset'. That Christmas he appeared openly at Edward's side at Windsor.

For the indignant barons, this act of defiance was the last straw. Using the authority of the Ordinances, they summoned troops, while Edward and Gaveston headed north to rally forces of their own. Cornered at Newcastle, they managed to escape, Edward to York and Gaveston to Scarborough, where the barons besieged him. Lacking supplies, Gaveston surrendered, and under promise of safe conduct he was escorted south. But just beyond Banbury the party was ambushed by the Earl of Warwick, who whisked the favourite back to his castle and delivered the promised 'bite'. On 19 June 1312, Piers Gaveston was beheaded at Blacklow Hill on the road between Warwick and Kenilworth.

The killing of Edward II's beloved 'brother' devastated the King and prompted a backlash of sympathy in his favour. But two years later, finally doing what a king was supposed to do and leading his army north against Scotland, Edward was heavily defeated between Edinburgh and Stirling in June 1314. Robert the Bruce's brave and cunning victory at Bannockburn is one of the great tales of Scottish history, but in England its consequence was a further blow to Edward's authority. Early in 1316 at the Parliament of Lincoln, the King humbly agreed to hand over the running of the country to the barons.

The trouble was that Edward had found himself another Gaveston. Hugh Despenser was an ambitious young courtier whose father, also named Hugh, had been an adviser and official to Edward I and still wielded considerable power. The Despensers came from the Welsh borders or Marches, and they used their influence shamelessly to extend their lands. Once again the barons found themselves rallying together to restrict the power of a royal *familiaris* – a favourite – and this time a new element came into play. In 1325 Edward's long-suffering wife Isabella seized the chance of a journey to France to take a stand against the husband who had humiliated her, first with Gaveston and now with the younger Despenser. She took a lover, Roger Mortimer, another powerful Welsh Marcher lord, who had taken up arms against the King and the Despensers in 1322, and who, after being imprisoned in the Tower of London, had been lucky to escape to France with his life.

When Mortimer and Isabella landed in England in 1326, they had only a few hundred men, but they held a trump card – Isabella's elder son by Edward, the thirteen-year-old Prince Edward. As heir to the throne, the boy represented some sort of hope for the future, and London welcomed the Queen, whose cause, according to one chronicler, was supported by 'the whole community of the realm'. In a widespread uprising, the hated Despensers were tracked down and executed – in the case of Edward's favourite, at the top of a ladder in Hereford, where his genitals were hacked off and burned in front of his eyes.

England now set about doing something it had never attempted before – the deposition of a king by legal process. Prelates prepared the way. Early in January, the Bishop of Hereford preached to a clamorous London congregation on the text 'A foolish king shall ruin his people', and a parliament of bishops, barons, judges, knights and burgesses was convened in Westminster. Preaching to them on 15 January 1327, the Archbishop of Canterbury took as his text '*Vox populi, Vox dei*' – 'The voice of the people is the voice of God.' By the unanimous consent of all the lords, clergy and people, he announced, King Edward II was deposed from his royal dignity, 'never more to govern the people of England', and he would be succeeded by his first-born son, the Lord

Edward. So Edward III would be the first English monarch appointed by a popular decision in Parliament.

It remained to break the news to the King himself, then imprisoned at Kenilworth Castle, and a deputation of lords, churchmen, knights and townsfolk set off forthwith for the Midlands. Dramatically clad in black, Edward half fainted as he heard William Trussell, a Lancastrian knight, read out the verdict of the whole Parliament. It grieved him, he said in response, that his people should be so exasperated with him as to wish to reject his rule, but he would bow to their will, since his son was being accepted in his place. Next day Trussell, on behalf of the whole kingdom, renounced all homage and allegiance to Edward of Caernarfon, and the steward of the royal household broke his staff of office, as if the King had died. The deputation returned to Parliament and the new reign was declared on 25 January 1327.

Now formally a non-king, Edward was imprisoned in the forlorn and ponderous Berkeley Castle overlooking the River Severn just north of Bristol. It is possible that, with time, his imprisonment might have been eased so as to allow him to potter around the grounds, digging his beloved ditches and hammering out a horseshoe or two. But in the space of just a few months there were two attempts to rescue him, and the Queen's lover, Mortimer, decided that he was too dangerous to be left alive. In September 1327 a messenger took instructions down to Berkeley, and two weeks later it was announced that Edward of Caernarfon, only forty-three and of previously robust health, was dead. Abbots, knights and burgesses were brought from Bristol and Gloucester to view the body, and they reported seeing no visible marks of violence. Edward had had 'internal trouble' during the night, they were informed.

But in the village of Berkeley, tales were told of hideous screams ringing out from the castle on the night of 21 September, and some years later one John Trevisa, who had been a boy at the time, revealed what had actually happened. Trevisa had grown up to take holy orders and become chaplain and confessor to the King's jailer, Thomas, Lord Berkeley, so he was well placed to solve the mystery. There were no marks of illness or violence to the King's body, he wrote, because Edward was killed 'with a hoote brooche [meat-roasting spit] putte thro the secret place posterialle'.

A PRINCE WINS HIS SPURS
1346

IN THE AUTUMN OF 1330 THE BARONS WERE SUMMONED TO A Parliament in Nottingham. The writs went out in the name of the king, but everyone knew that the eighteen-year-old Edward III was not really running the country. Control over the young monarch was lodged firmly in the hands of his mother's lover, Roger Mortimer, who had awarded himself an earldom in his three years of power since the deposition of Edward II – along with land and money that he flaunted extravagantly.

Mortimer's ruthless elimination of his enemies had made him widely feared, and when the barons rode into Nottingham they found themselves under the forbidding eye of the earl's Welsh archers, stationed in the battlements of the castle up on the rocks above the River Trent. Inside the castle were Mortimer, Queen Isabella and the young king, on whom Mortimer kept a close eye.

Unknown to the earl, however, the rocks on which the castle stood were warrened with caves and crevices, and Edward had a plan that would cut short his tutelage. On the night of Friday 19 October 1330 a group of lords crept into the fortress via a secret passage. Waiting there for them was the young King who led them to Mortimer's chamber where, according to one source, he himself struck down the door with a battle-axe. As they finished off the two knights who were guarding the earl, the Queen rushed into the room.

'Bel fitz! Bel fitz!' she cried. 'Ayez pitié du gentil Mortimer!' – 'Fair son, fair son, have pity on sweet Mortimer!'

Her cries went unheeded, and the raiding party hustled the 'sweet' earl back down through the secret passage below the rocks, leaving his archers none the wiser up on the battlements. Next day Edward III proclaimed himself fully king and started off back to London, where

Mortimer was found guilty on a string of charges that included the murder of Edward II. On 29 November the earl was hanged as a common criminal beneath the elms at Tyburn, having been spared the more hideous penalties of 'drawing' (disembowelling) and quartering that were prescribed by law for treason. Edward also showed restraint towards his mother Isabella, despatching her to comfortable retirement at Castle Rising in Norfolk and sending her, the royal accounts reveal, a steady flow of treats – a wild boar for roasting, a pair of lovebirds which she fed on hemp seeds, and generous quantities of wine from Gascony.

Decisiveness and generosity, delivered in style, were the hallmarks of the reign of Edward III. He was one of England's most dynamic monarchs, and much of his energy was devoted to war – specifically the conflict which history textbooks would later call the 'Hundred Years War'. In reality, this was a series of wars that lasted more than a hundred years, growing out of England's claims to lands in France – and at this moment in the 1330s, from a dispute over the rich territory of Gascony which Henry II had acquired nearly two centuries earlier through his marriage to Eleanor of Aquitaine.

Nestling in the south-west of France, just above the Pyrenees, Gascony was a prosperous region that produced revenue for the English king, largely on the strength of its subtle and cheering red *vin claret* ('clear wine'). In the fourteenth century the English drank more claret from the Gascon vineyards of Bordeaux than we do today, per head of the population, and the Gascons, who spoke their own language, liked their profitable relationship with England. Its distant kings threatened less interference than did the French kings in Paris, who had pushed the English out of Normandy and Anjou and were now nibbling away at the English holdings in south-west France. There had been a series of skirmishes involving the *bastides*, the walled towns along Gascony's borders, and in May 1337 King Philip VI went the whole hog. He announced that he was confiscating all Gascon territories – to which Edward III responded by restating his claim to the French throne itself through his mother Isabella.

Edward had enjoyed remarkable military success since seizing power in 1330. He was a charismatic leader, strikingly handsome with a pointed yellow beard – he had 'the face of a God', according to one contemporary. A fan of jousting, he was constantly honing his own warlike skills in tournaments, along with those of the men around him, who came to form the tough core of his military campaigns. Starting in Scotland, he had reversed the inept record of his father with a spectacular victory at Halidon Hill, near Berwick on the banks of the Tweed, where the firestorm of arrows from the English and Welsh longbowmen shattered the Scots.

The two-metre longbow, both longer and heavier than the bows that had been used at Hastings, was to revolutionise military tactics in the fourteenth century. The English encountered it when fighting the Welsh, whose capacity to pierce chain mail and even a thick oak door with their iron-tipped arrows had been mightily impressive. In his enthusiasm, Edward I had called for villagers to practise archery every Sunday and holy day, and Parliament passed laws forbidding tennis, dice and cock-fighting as well as various forms of cricket and hockey (described as 'club-ball') because they diverted men from their target practice. Football was particularly disapproved of, as leading to hooliganism and riots.

In contrast, French laws prohibited peasants from possessing any arms at all. French military tactics still centred on the mounted knight, and the difference showed when the French and English armies met on the battlefield of Crécy near the French Channel coast in 1346. The French far outnumbered the English, by nearly thirty thousand to ten or fifteen thousand according to one estimate, with the French forces including some six thousand Genoese mercenaries wielding crossbows. A formidable weapon made of wood banded with iron – almost a machine – the crossbow fired a lethal bolt with great velocity and had a greater range than the longbow. But while a crossbow archer could load and trigger off only four bolts in a minute, the much more flexible longbowman could fire eight or even ten arrows in the same time. The French knights, furthermore, despised the foreign mercenaries that their King had engaged, and even rode down their own crossbowmen at one stage in the battle.

The entire outcome of Crécy seems to have been determined by the arrogance of the French horsemen. The 'flower of France', as the knights liked to call themselves, arrived in front of the English position on the hill of Crécy on the evening of 26 August 1346. Raring for battle, they ignored their king's orders to halt and make camp for the night. The sun was setting as they charged up the hill, and under their onslaught the English archers wasted not a single arrow. If they did not strike riders, they struck horses, wreaking havoc. According to Jean le Bel, one of the chroniclers of the battle, the dead and wounded horses piled on top of one another 'like a litter of piglets'.

As the French recoiled in confusion, they were struck by another of Edward III's secret weapons – Welsh and Cornish knifemen, armed only with daggers. Their speciality was to creep under the enemy's horses and cut open their bellies, and they took advantage of the dusk to slink up and 'murder many [men] as they lay on the ground, both earls, barons, knights and squires'.

It was not till the sun rose the next morning that the English realised what a massive victory they had achieved. Edward III sent out his heralds – the clerks who were experts in coats of arms – and, picking their way through the corpses on the battlefield, they identified more than fifteen hundred slain lords and knights, in addition, perhaps, to some ten thousand enemy footsoldiers and crossbowmen, who, unlike the knights, were not counted. Among the dead lay John, the blind King of Bohemia, who had brought his troops to support the French and had ordered his knights to lead him forward, 'so that I may strike one stroke with my sword'. The discovery of his corpse, still tied to the bodies of his knights by their reins, became one of the legends of the victory.

The other concerned Edward's son, the sixteen-year-old Edward Prince of Wales, said to have worn black armour. Thrown to the ground by the French charge, the 'Black Prince' was rescued by his standard-bearer, who covered his body with the banner of Wales. Messengers asking for help were sent post-haste to Edward, who had set up his headquarters in a windmill overlooking the field, but the King refused. 'Let the boy win his spurs,' he said, 'for I want him, please God, to have all the glory.'

When help did reach the prince, they found him with his standard-bearer and companions 'leaning on lances and swords, taking breath and resting quietly on long mounds of corpses, waiting for the enemy who had withdrawn'. Someone had brought from the battlefield the crest of the King of Bohemia, three tall white ostrich plumes, and the prince took them as his badge there and then. He also adopted the blind hero's motto, which Princes of Wales bear to this day – *Ich Dien*, 'I serve.'

THE BURGHERS OF CALAIS
1347

THE ENGLISH VICTORY AT CRÉCY ASTONISHED EUROPE. 'Nobody thought much of the English, nobody spoke of their prowess or courage,' wrote the chronicler Jean le Bel. 'Now, in the time of the noble Edward, who has often put them to the test, they are the finest and most daring warriors known to man.'

It was less, in truth, a matter of personalities than of military technology. The light, mobile bowmen of England and Wales, trained on their village greens and selected at archery contests, had challenged the superiority of the mounted knight – and, fortunately for England, it took the French a remarkably long time to work it out. Edward III, by contrast, was a canny leader, and he proved it after Crécy when he decided to head north towards Calais.

The English king understood that, if he was to maintain his position in France, he needed a secure deep-water port on the French side of the Channel. Visible from Dover on a clear day, Calais would give him a stranglehold on the sea-lanes, with a chance of controlling both trade and the growing problem of freelance piracy. Edward knew marching from Crécy to Paris to besiege the French capital would have been a step too far, whereas making Calais an English port would yield a solid dividend from his victory.

Calais, however, was not going to give in without a struggle. The port had strong natural defences of sand dunes and marshes, and as a walled town it was not just a centre of trade but had a semi-military status. It was customary for medieval rulers to provide incentives for communities to live in strategic fortresses on the understanding that they would make it their job to defend the fortress when it was attacked. This meant, in turn, that the men, women and children of a fortress town like Calais were treated as combatants if an enemy besieged them. They could expect no mercy if their resistance was breached.

Edward settled down for a long siege. Gunpowder was just making its appearance in European warfare, but the primitive cannon of the time had neither the range nor the power to demolish town walls. Out of range of the defenders' crossbow fire, Edward now built his own settlement of wooden huts, and to brighten up the winter he brought over his wife and the ladies of the court. The English king enjoyed female company, and he had encouraged his men to bring their wives, too. In addition, merchants came twice a week from Flanders to hold markets in the English camp.

Inside Calais itself, however, life was not so comfortable. In the early months of the siege, the inhabitants succeeded in smuggling in supplies by sea. But Edward was able to blockade the harbour mouth, and in late June 1347, nearly a year after the siege had begun, the English defeated a French convoy that had tried to break through with supplies. In the wreckage was found an axe head that had been thrown overboard to avoid capture. Attached to it was a desperate message that the town's governor, Sir John de Vienne, had intended for the King of France:

> *Know, dread Sir, that your people in Calais have eaten their horses, dogs, and rats, and nothing remains for them to live upon unless they eat one another. Wherefore, most honourable Sir if we have not speedy succour, the town is lost!*

Edward III read the document, sealed it with his own seal and sent it on to its destination.

When, four weeks later, King Philip of France finally appeared with his army on the sand dunes within sight of Calais, cheers and sounding trumpets were heard from inside the town. The King's banner with the fleur-de-lis was run up on the castle tower, and the famished inhabitants lit a great fire. But on the second night the fire was somewhat less, and on the third night, after no rescue, it was just a flicker. Wails and groans were heard from inside the walls.

The French king had camped at Sangatte – notorious at the beginning of the twenty-first century as the site from which thousands of foreign immigrants smuggled themselves illegally into Britain – but Philip did not have their appetite for penetrating the English defences. After taking a good look at Edward's impressive encampment and the rested, well supplied English troops, he decided to retreat.

The following day Sir John de Vienne appeared on the battlements offering to negotiate, and shortly afterwards, barely able to hold himself erect, he rode out of the gates on a starving, wasted horse, to surrender his sword and the keys of the city. Round his neck the governor wore a rope, offering himself up to be hanged; and behind, roped to him, straggled a bizarre procession – the leading knights and burghers of the town, emaciated and in tatters, offering their own lives so that those of their fellow-citizens might be saved.

Edward acted mercifully – up to a point. One chronicler says that it was his wife, Philippa of Hainault, who persuaded him to spare the burghers of Calais. But on 4 August 1347 the English king entered the town with his soldiers and ordered the evacuation of virtually all the inhabitants, whose property he confiscated. To replace them, he shipped a colony of settlers over from England and built a ring of forts around the town. Calais would remain English for more than two hundred years.

THE FAIR MAID OF KENT AND THE ORDER OF THE GARTER
1347-9

SEEKING DIVERSION DURING THE ELEVEN LONG MONTHS that he was camped outside Calais, King Edward III held a grand ball to celebrate the victory at Crécy. The ladies of the court were decked out in all their finery, but as they danced, one of them lost her garter, the elegant circlet of blue silk that was holding up one of her stockings. It fell to the floor, and the King, in expansive mood, picked it up and tied it round his own well shaped leg.

Edward III's flamboyant gesture has gone down in history, though it was only recorded a century later. If the lady in question had been his wife, there would have been no special reason for comment. But Queen Philippa was pregnant at the time. She may not have been at the ball or she may have been sitting out the dancing. What is certain is that the soldier king had an eye for the ladies, and in 1347, according to some historians, his fancy had alighted on the great beauty of the day, Joan of Kent, wife of the Earl of Salisbury.

Although she was only nineteen, this remarkable young woman had already managed to acquire two husbands at once. This same year the 'Fair Maid of Kent' was embroiled in a bigamy case, and was faced with having to explain to the Pope how and why she had married an earl when she was already married to a knight. The Pope's judgement was that she should return to her first husband, Sir Thomas Holland, and Joan seems to have made the best of it. She had five children with Holland before he died in 1360. The next year, she and the Black Prince, then thirty-one, fell in love and married (and had two children of their own, one of them the future King Richard II). The 'Fair Maid of Kent' would be the first beautiful and controversial Princess of Wales.

In 1347 much of this lay in the future, but the lady whose blue silk garter the king had snaffled was clearly a figure of such interest that eyebrows were raised – and Edward must have felt that some comment was required. '*Honi soit qui mal y pense*,' he declared in his medieval French, which is usually translated as 'Shame on him who thinks shameful thoughts.' But the message could be simply interpreted – 'No sniggering, please.'

Back at Windsor the following year, Edward III made the blue silk garter the focus of an extraordinary ceremony, when he founded an order of chivalry – the Order of the Garter – a brotherhood of just twenty-four knights who would serve the King as a veritable Round Table. Four years earlier Edward had staged a Round Table dinner at Windsor, and now he formalised the idea of himself as a latter-day King Arthur, who was firmly established by this date as an English folk hero.

The myth of Arthur had been extensively popularised over the previous two hundred years by the writings of Geoffrey of Monmouth, a Welsh priest living in Oxford whose *Historia Regum Britanniae*, 'History of the Kings of Britain', became the bestselling English history book of the Middle Ages. No less than 220 handwritten copies survive to this day. Geoffrey incorporated the Welsh traditions of Merlin the Magician into the Arthur legend, setting it within the mainstream of Britain's story and going back to the days of Albion when the island, he claimed, was inhabited by giants.

Geoffrey's fanciful stories were denounced in his lifetime by more orthodox chroniclers as 'shameless and impudent lies', and there were a good number of those, starting with the giants. His history was rather like a modern television docudrama, weaving facts with fantasy. His fables of the legendary British kings Lear (probably derived from a folk tale) and Cymbeline (based on a pre-Roman British chieftain Cunobelinus) were to inspire William Shakespeare. Geoffrey's entire saga caught the imagination of a community growing conscious of itself and searching for a sense of national purpose and identity.

This was exactly what Edward III wished to harness with his Order of the Garter. In the months after his return from Crécy, he took his Round Table show on the road in a series of tournaments held at Windsor, Reading, Eltham, Canterbury, Bury and Lichfield. Here was all the fun of the fair, with tents and flags and trampled grass, stalls laden with food and drink, lords and ladies showing off and the populace watching and cheering. The tournaments were a travelling victory celebration for the stunning conquests in France – national morale-boosters to get people smiling for when the tax collectors next came knocking.

The King added one extra touch: in 1349 he held the first formal meeting of his new order on 23 April, St George's Day, adopting the dragon-slaying saint brought back by the crusaders. The pious and anaemic St Edward the Confessor, a reasonably genuine Englishman, continued to preside at Westminster Abbey, but out at Windsor the chapel of the Garter brotherhood was dedicated to George, the warrior Turk. Edward called his knights 'The Fraternity of St George', and it is from this date that people started thinking of St George as the patron saint of England.

Edward's knightly fraternity, England's first gentlemen's club, was copied across Europe. France tried the short-lived Order of the Star, the Dukes of Burgundy the more durable Order of the Golden Fleece, and today there is not a country in the world, whether republic or monarchy, without its medal-and-ribbon-bedecked honours system. The Order of Lenin, the Order of the Chrysanthemum, the Order of the Elephant – all are solemn and thoroughly self-important institutions. How very English of Edward III to apply a name that injected humour, with a touch of scandal, into the country's ultimate social distinction. You might even imagine, as the King's eyes twinkled across the dance floor at the Fair Maid of Kent, that he was making fun of the whole ridiculous business.

THE GREAT MORTALITY
1348-9

AS ENGLAND CELEBRATED ALL THROUGH THE HEADY victory summer of 1348, a merchant ship from Gascony was docking in the port of Melcombe in Weymouth Bay. It was 23 June, the eve of St John, celebrated across the country as a fertility festival, when the village maidens dressed in their finery and bonfires were lit. But, disembarking from the vessel with the crew, to be borne along the drovers' paths and through the marketplaces of the ripening Dorset countryside, were the germs of an island-wide disaster.

In later centuries it was called the Black Death. At the time people talked of 'the Pestilence' or 'the Great Mortality'. Either way, the imagery was dark enough. 'We see death coming into our midst like black smoke,' wrote the Welsh poet Euan Gethin, 'a plague which cuts off the young, a rootless phenomenon which has no mercy for fair countenance.'

Gethin himself was laid low by the infection, like one third of the five million or so other inhabitants of England and Wales, and he described the ghastly symptoms:

> Woe is me of the shilling in the armpit. It is seething, terrible, wherever it may come, a head that gives pain and causes a loud cry, a burden carried under the arms, a painful angry knob, a white lump. It is of the form of an apple, like the head of an onion, a small boil that spares no one. Great is its seething, like a burning cinder, a grievous thing of an ashy colour.

It would be more than five centuries before the plague bacillus was isolated and identified by the French bacteriologist Alexandre Yersin in 1894 – hence its name, *Yersinia pestis*. But its contagious nature was recognised from the start. In 1346 Mongol forces besieging the Black Sea port of Caffa lobbed the bodies of their plague victims over the walls into the city – an early example of biological warfare. It was trade that had brought the infection from the East, and in at least two varieties. Pneumonic plague was spread on the breath from contaminated lungs, and resulted in a ghastly choking death, with bloody froth bubbling at the mouth. Bubonic plague was spread by fleas and by the black rat, *Rattus rattus*, an agile creature that could run up and down the mooring ropes of ships. One symptom of the disease was ravening hunger in both flea and rat, which made them the more likely to bite. As the rats scurried along the rafters and through the thatched roofs of fourteenth-century England, the infected fleas would drop down off their backs on to the humans below.

The symptoms of plague were swollen lymph nodes in the armpits and groin known as buboes – Euan Gethin's apples and onions – and death followed within hours, or a few days at most. Victims suffered from bad breath – 'a loathsome, cadaverous stink from within', according to one contemporary, and other symptoms included high fever, acute stomach pains and bluish-black spots on the body.

'The sick are served by their kinsfolk as dogs would be,' wrote one chronicler. 'Food is put near the bed for the sick to eat or drink, after which all fly.' Another related how 'fathers and mothers refused to see and tend their children, as if they had not been theirs'.

It was not surprising that such a trauma induced agonised soul-searching across the whole of Europe. When King Philip VI of France demanded an official explanation from the medical faculty of the University of Paris, he was told that God, in his anger, had ordained a fatal conjunction of the planets. This had sucked up the waters of the sea, creating an invisible but lethal 'miasma' (from the Greek word for 'pollution' or 'defilement'), a poisonous cloud that infected all who inhaled it.

Divine retribution also figured heavily in England's diagnosis, with the monkish chroniclers pointing a finger at the debauchery that went on at the royal tournaments. Between jousts the crowds would be entertained by female cheerleaders, some of them dressed like men in tight-fitting costumes that showed off their figures.

'We are not constant in faith,' complained Thomas Brinton, the great preacher who thundered his denunciations from the pulpit of

Rochester Cathedral in Kent in the 1370s and '80s. 'We are not honourable in the eyes of the world.'

Not even the King himself was spared. Edward III's second daughter Joan, barely thirteen years old, was struck down in Bordeaux that September. She was on her way to Spain to marry Pedro, the heir to the kingdom of Castile, and had been travelling with her dowry, which included her own huge red silk marriage bed.

'No fellow human being could be surprised,' wrote Edward to King Alfonso, as one father to another, 'if we were inwardly desolated by the sting of this bitter grief, for we are human too.'

After the initial attack of 1348 and 1349, the plague returned to England five more times before the century was out – in 1361, 1368, 1374, 1379 and 1390. The fall-out was catastrophic, seeping into every aspect of life, from the way the land was farmed, after a third – or even a half – of the workforce had been smitten, to the relaxation of regulations governing feudal service and marriage: fewer tenants, fewer spouses, fewer rules. Grasping at the notion that the plague was an airborne 'miasma', more houses were now fitted with closed windows, shutters and heavy tapestries, while frequent bathing went out of fashion: the hot water was thought to open the pores to airborne infection.

Recent medical research shows that some effects of the Black Death have lasted into present times. Doctors researching the AIDS epidemic have discovered that there are certain, relatively rare, people who will never come down with AIDS, however much they are exposed to it. What these people have in common has been identified as a gene mutation known as CCR5-delta 32, found mostly in white Europeans and especially in Swedes. Doctors suspect that the ancestors of these people were precisely those who were infected and managed to survive the plagues of the fourteenth century. The mutation does not appear to exist in African and East Asian populations that did not suffer the Black Death.

Bubonic plague – identified by its underarm swellings – still exists today. It can be treated with antibiotics if diagnosed early enough, but two thousand deaths are reported worldwide each year, and a recent case in Madagascar showed a worrying resistance to antibiotics. AIDS, SARS, deadly influenza epidemics – the plagues are still with us.

THE BEDSIDE MANNER OF
A PLAGUE DOCTOR
1376

JOHN ARDERNE MADE HIS REPUTATION BY DEVISING A treatment for an embarrassing ailment that was suffered by many in the age of chivalry. Knights spent hours, days, even months in the saddle – the mounted heroes of Crécy bumped their bottoms all the way to France and back. *Fistula in ano*, an unpleasant abscess between the base of the spine and the anus, was an occupational hazard of their apparently glamorous profession, and Arderne developed a surgical technique for treating it. He cut out the abscess, using opiates to deaden the pain, and wrote up his method in a precisely illustrated treatise of 1376 that ranks as one of the earliest professional medical articles. The basic principles of his treatment are followed by surgeons to this day.

Arderne learned his craft as a doctor by tending to the wounds of English soldiers in the French wars, and he favoured experimentation. He prided himself on knowing better than the old medical dogmas dating back to Greek times, though he did acknowledge that he had made some mistakes early on. On one occasion he tried sprinkling leg wounds with powdered arsenic that ate away at the bone. Fortunately for Arderne, suing for compensation was not yet a national pastime. People were well aware they could die in almost any medical situation, and were grateful for whatever help the doctor could give them.

After the failure of his arsenic powder, Arderne concocted gentler dressings using mutton fat, which he christened *salus populi*, the 'balm of the people', and he came to specialise in herbal remedies. His remedy for gout was a poultice of green laurel and honey mixed with the lard of a male pig – he claimed to have cured a gouty abbot overnight with a single application – and his remedy for kidney stones was a plaster of pigeon's dung and honey applied hot to the body. These cures might sound outlandish to modern ears, but his patients came back for more, and the astrological spells that he used while dispensing his treatments seem to have had a calming effect. One of his most popular was a charm he originally came up with to tackle the hangovers suffered by the guests who caroused too freely at the wedding of Lionel, the Black Prince's younger brother. The hangover cure worked so well he tried it for epilepsy, and reported success.

The good doctor should not boast, advised Arderne, nor should he pass comment on his colleagues. It was better to err on the safe side when discussing prospects of recovery, and he should always be modest and discreet. Also, he should always keep his nails clean. When it came to fees, the rich should be charged as much as possible – high fees inspired their confidence – and while the poor should be treated free as a matter of professional prestige, there was no harm done if they provided the odd chicken or duck.

When attending the bedside, there was nothing wrong in deploying a little flattery, and better still if the doctor could tell a few good stories that would make the patient laugh. It induced anxiety in a patient if the physician took his relatives aside to whisper in a corner, nor should he be too familiar with 'fair women in great men's houses'. He should certainly avoid greeting them in public by thrusting his hands about their bosoms – which would seem, on the face of it, to raise the question of what form a private greeting from the jolly Dr Arderne might take.

When it came to the plague, Arderne did not pretend to have a solution. He offered patients who suffered from heart attacks an expensive cure that involved gold dust and a powder made from pearls. But he advised his colleagues to try to avoid hopeless cases as a matter of principle. An honest doctor risked losing his fee *and* his reputation – and, worse, could find himself accused of poisoning.

John Arderne was proudest of the remedies he devised for the battlefield, and particularly a salve for arrow wounds that he called '*sangue d'amour*' – the blood of love. This ideally required the blood of a maiden aged twenty, drawn at the full moon in Virgo (mid-August to mid-September).

It would then be mixed with myrrh, aloes and other ingredients before being boiled up with olive oil. But the doctor had confected a red powder to take the place of the maiden's blood – 'for now,' he explained, 'in this time, virgins come full seldom to twenty years'.

THE DREAM OF PIERS THE PLOUGHMAN
· 1377 ·

One summer season when the sun was warm, I rigged myself out in shaggy woollen clothes as if I were a shepherd; and in the garb of an easy-living hermit I set out to roam far and wide through the world, hoping to hear of marvels. But on a morning in May, among the Malvern Hills, a strange thing happened to me, as though by magic. For I was tired out by my wanderings, and as I lay down to rest under a broad bank by the side of the stream, and leaned over gazing into the water, it sounded so pleasant that I fell asleep. And I dreamt a marvellous dream . . .

S O BEGINS PIERS THE PLOUGHMAN, A RAMBLING EPIC POEM that takes a stroll through plague-stricken England in the declining years of Edward III. We read of monks and friars, proud barons and burgesses in fur-trimmed coats, poor parish priests who can no longer scrape a living from their death-diminished parishes, and, of course, a ploughman. Piers is a brave, plain-spoken innocent, a good-hearted man of the people, who seeks to make sense of the world.

Piers the Ploughman was the life's work of William Langland, a quirky and impoverished churchman who spent many years working and reworking his saga, his one and only known creation, in colloquial verse. Langland grew up in the Malvern Hills in Worcestershire where his first 'vision' is set, but then moved to London to scratch a living by singing masses for the souls of the rich and transcribing legal documents. He must have had some difficulty in supporting his wife Kit and their daughter Collette in their cottage in Cornhill, between London Bridge and the modern Bank of England. He himself features prominently in the poem – he is the dreamer – and the poem is the source for just about all that we know about him. 'Long Will' describes himself as tall, lean and disrespectful. He sometimes dressed in rags like a beggar so that he could experience the life of the poor, and when he encountered pompous or self-important people he would take pride in being almost insolent.

In his very first vision, Langland dreams of a gathering of rats and mice that are terrified of an overbearing cat who is playfully batting them about – 'scratching and clawing us and trapping us between his paws until our lives are not worth living'. At the suggestion of one elderly rat they solemnly debate the old folk-fable idea of securing a bell to the monster's collar in order to protect themselves against it, but end up with the famous dilemma – 'Who will bell the cat?'

'Now what this dream means,' says Langland, 'you folk must guess for yourselves, for I haven't the courage to tell you.'

The guess was an easy one for Langland's fourteenth-century readers. The poet was referring to the parliaments of his time. The cat was the King – the ageing and ailing Edward III, on the throne for more than half a century. The rats and mice were the knights and burgesses who made up Parliament.

After Crécy, the war with France had gone well for a while. In 1356 the Black Prince, who had taken over England's armies on behalf of his father, won a brilliant victory at Poitiers against all the odds. The French King John II was actually captured and held to ransom. But since 1369 it had been all downhill, with retreats and loss of territories. The Black Prince fell ill, and the senile Edward III had fallen under the influence, since the death of his wife Philippa, of his mistress Alice Perrers. The royal demands for taxes kept on coming, and all this amid the strain and turmoil of the Black Death.

In 1376 the 'Good Parliament', as they boldly called themselves, had tried to stop the rot. They elected themselves a Speaker – Parliament's first – who presided over business that included scathing attacks on royal ministers and favourites, Alice Perrers among them. The Commons expected the King to 'live off his own', they declared, and not to assume he could just go on squeezing his people – hence the wise old rat's idea of a 'bell'. But no sooner had Parliament broken up than the 'cat', in the form of Edward's younger son John of Gaunt, had had the Speaker arrested and the Acts of the Good Parliament annulled.

'Even if we kill the cat,' remarks one of Langland's mice cynically, 'another like him would come to scratch us, and it would be no use our creeping under the benches. I advise all commoners to leave him alone and let's not be so rash as even to show him the bell.'

Piers the Ploughman was less a political tract than a spiritual adventure. Langland's vision was that life's purpose is the seeking of truth, and that truth when explored turns out, rather beautifully, to be the same as love, dwelling in the human heart. This unconventional man who dressed as a beggar to sample the life of the disadvantaged had a keen eye for injustice, and there are angry passages in his poem that give us a unique view of how some people lived in late fourteenth-century England:

> *The poorest folk are our neighbours if we look about us – the prisoners in dungeons and the poor in their hovels, overburdened with children, and rack-rented by landlords. For whatever they save by spinning they spend on rent, or on milk and oatmeal to make gruel and fill the bellies of their children who clamour for food. And they themselves are often famished with hunger, and wretched with the miseries of winter – cold sleepless nights, when they get up to rock the cradle cramped in a corner and rise before dawn to card and comb the wool, to wash and scrub and mend . . .*
>
> *There are many more who suffer like them – men who go hungry and thirsty all day long, and strive their utmost to hide it – ashamed to beg, or tell their neighbours of their need. I've seen enough of the world to know how they suffer, these men who have many children and no means but their trade to clothe and feed them. For many hands are waiting to grasp the few pence they earn, and while the friars feast on roast venison, they have bread and thin ale, with perhaps a scrap of cold meat or stale fish.*

In the story of *Piers the Ploughman*, as in the brief poem of Caedmon the cowherd, we get a rare chance to hear the early voice of an ordinary

Englishman – transfused in Langland's case with a burning anger. It would not be long before this voice of the people – and their anger – would be more loudly heard.

THE 'MAD MULTITUDE'
1381

When Adam delved and Eve span
Who was then a gentleman?

JOHN BALL'S QUESTIONING AND PROVOCATIVE COUPLET excited the crowds gathered on the green heights of Blackheath overlooking London in the early summer of 1381. As the fiery preacher conjured up the image of Adam, the original man, painfully delving— or digging – in the fields, while his wife laboured with her spindle in their mud-and-wattle hovel, twisting piles of sheep's wool into yarn, his audience knew exactly what he was getting at.

'In the beginning,' cried Ball, 'all men were equal. Servitude of man to man was introduced by the unjust dealings of the wicked. For if God had intended some to be servants and others lords, He would have made a distinction between them at the beginning.'

John Ball's sermon was inspired by a plague-stricken land. His restive audience had dutifully obeyed both the lord of the manor and their Lord in heaven, and they had been punished with death – in 1348, 1361, 1368, 1374 and again five years later. But they also had a self-confidence and assertiveness they had not known before, since, by the brutal laws of economics, the survivors of the plague years were actually better off than they had ever been. A drastically reduced labour force meant higher wages – and if you could scrape together some savings, you could also pick up land cheaply. Modern archaeologists have noticed how smart metal utensils began to replace earthenware pots in quite ordinary homes during these years. Higher living standards, lower rents, a more diversified economy – all this from a flea on a rat's back. And with these changes came a resonating cry for social justice.

'What can they show,' asked Ball, 'or what reasons give why they should be more the masters than ourselves? Except, perhaps, in making us labour and work, for them to spend.'

The Great Rising of 1381 sought to break the cycle of feudal bondage, the system whereby men gave their labour and their loyalty – and, in many ways, their very being – to the local lord of the manor in return for land and protection. For this reason later generations called the uprising the Peasants' Revolt.

But to judge from the records, it might better have been called the Ratepayers' Revolt, since the ledgers of the time show that the leaders and mouthpieces of the rebellion like John Ball, Wat Tyler and Jack Straw were substantial, tax-paying folk. Anything but peasants, they came from the upwardly mobile yeoman classes. They were village leaders who sat on juries – and their rebellion first exploded not in the poor and downtrodden areas of England but in the very richest counties, the fruitful orchards of Kent and Essex, close to London with its alluring wealth and progressive ideas.

Discontent had been stirred by a general conviction that things were awry at the top. Edward III had died in 1377, after the debacle of the 'Good Parliament', leaving the throne to his ten-year-old grandson Richard II. 'I heard my father say,' remarked one of William Langland's dream mice, 'that when the cat is a kitten the court is a sorry place.'

While Richard was a child, the court was in the hands of his uncle John of Gaunt, so named because he was born during a royal visit to Ghent in the Low Countries. Gaunt lacked the charisma of his elder brother, Richard's father, the Black Prince, whose premature death was the more mourned because he was widely thought to be a reformer. Gaunt, by contrast, positively prided himself on his lack of the common touch. 'Do they think that they are kings and princes in this land?' he had asked as he annulled the reforms of the Good Parliament. 'Have they forgotten how powerful I am?'

Gaunt had maintained the dreary pursuit of war with France and Scotland, and the huge expenditure that this necessitated had kept the tax demands coming. The final provocation was the poll tax of 1380 – the third in four years. 'Poll' meant 'head' (thus counting per head, the same word we use for elections), and it was a new way of raising money. Previously, taxes had been levelled per household. They were known as 'tenths', 'thirteenths' or 'fifteenths', reflecting the fraction of your household wealth you were expected to pay. Now people were supposed to pay according to the number of heads polled in their homes – which automatically doubled your tax burden if you were married, and increased it still more if you had parents living with you, or children over the age of fourteen.

Not surprisingly, many people conveniently 'lost' members of their family when the tax collectors came to call. Between 1377 and 1381, the Exchequer was faced with a mysterious fall of 33 per cent in the adult population, and correctly suspecting tax evasion, the government sent out fresh teams of examiners, with powers of arrest and escorts of armed guards, to root out the hidden evaders.

It was the arrival of one such commission in the Essex town of Brentwood at the end of May 1381 that provided the spark for rebellion. Led by John Bampton, the local Member of Parliament, the commissioners started summoning representatives from the area to account for the deficits in their payments. But those from the villages of Fobbing, Corringham and Stanford-le-Hope felt they were being threatened. They refused to cooperate, and when Bampton's armed escort attempted to arrest the villagers there was uproar. The tax commissioners were expelled from Brentwood, and Bampton fled to London in fear for his life.

Within days, much of Essex had risen in rebellion. Several thousand protesters headed for London, while down in Kent the standard of revolt was flown by Wat Tyler, who then lived in Maidstone but had earlier lived in Essex. Tyler may have been a link between the surprisingly well coordinated uprisings now occurring in these counties to the north-east and south-east of the capital.

On Monday 10 June, Tyler led some four thousand rebels to Canterbury, where they broke into the cathedral during the celebration of high mass, demanding that the monks depose the archbishop,

Simon Sudbury. Sudbury was a leading member of the government, and Tyler's followers denounced him as 'a traitor who will be beheaded for his iniquity'. During these years, radical religious thinking was marching in step with social revolution. The Oxford philosopher John Wycliffe was teaching that men could find their own path to God without the help of priests, whose riches, power and worldliness he denounced. His followers, most of them from poor backgrounds, were called Lollards – literally, in Middle English, 'mumblers', a reference to their constant mouthing of their own private prayers to God.

When the rebels got to London they soon tracked down Archbishop Sudbury, who was hiding in the Tower along with Sir Robert Hales, the King's treasurer. Both men were dragged out, to be beheaded by the crowds, who paraded their severed heads on poles in a triumphant procession to Westminster Abbey. In the bloody mayhem that followed, the protesters looked for more scapegoats – and found them in the immigrant merchant communities from Flanders and Lombardy, who had taken over royal money-raising from the Jews. It was lucky for John of Gaunt that he was away from London on yet another military campaign. But the mass looted his sumptuous palace by the Thames anyway, and even cornered the King's mother, Joan, and asked her to kiss them. Now an elderly lady, the Fair Maid of Kent, whose beauty was said to have inspired the Order of the Garter all those years before, fainted clean away from the shock.

The one member of the court to rise bravely to the occasion turned out to be the 'kitten' – the fourteen-year-old King Richard II. On Saturday 15 June 1381, the boy rode out to the north-west of the city to the meadows of Smithfield, London's meat market then as now. A small but self-assured figure, he was accompanied by about two hundred courtiers and men-at-arms, facing a much larger party of rebels on the other side of the field.

Wat Tyler came riding proudly out from the rebel ranks on a little horse, a lone figure, with just a dagger in his hand for protection. As he dismounted, he half bent his knee and took the boy king's hand in a rough and jocular fashion. 'Brother,' he said, 'be of good comfort and joyful!'

The rallying cry of the masses as they marched towards London had been 'For King Richard and the true commons!', for they nursed the fantasy attending the monarchy to this day that, personally, the monarch is somehow without fault. Royal mistakes are the fault of royal advisers and, at heart, the monarch is the people's friend – 'We shall be good companions,' Tyler promised the king.

Richard evidently bridled at this familiarity. 'Why will you not go back to your own country?' he asked – by 'country' he meant Tyler's own place or neighbourhood – and at this rejection, the rebel leader flared up angrily. Neither he nor his companions would leave, he swore vehemently, until they had got agreement to their demands. He then launched into his manifesto:

'There should be equality among all people,' he proclaimed, 'save only the king . . . There should be no more "villeins" in England, and no serfdom or villeinage.' All men should be 'free and of one condi-tion' – and when it came to the Church, all its worldly goods should be confiscated. A reasonable amount should be set aside to provide the clergy with 'sufficient sustenance', but the remaining church property should be divided among the people of the parish.

It was a wish list of breathtaking idealism and impossibility, bolder than any Englishman has ever demanded face to face with his king. If Tyler really did deliver the people's demands with the fluency and power with which the chronicler wrote it down, he was a man of remarkable eloquence and courage. He seems to have been the key to the revolt – and what happened next has been fiercely debated by his-torians. Was there a prearranged plan to set Wat Tyler up, or was it his own arrogance that provoked the denouement?

According to one chronicler, he concluded his great speech by calling for a flagon of water, then 'rinsed his mouth in a very rude and disgust-ing fashion' in Richard's face. According to another, he was tossing his dagger from hand to hand 'as a child might play with it, and looked as though he might suddenly seize the opportunity to stab the king'.

Tyler was 'the greatest thief and robber in all Kent,' called out one of the royal retainers, thereby provoking the rebel leader – as was per-haps the intention – to lunge at his accuser with his dagger. When the Mayor of London intervened, Tyler started to stab him, and would have injured him severely if the mayor had not been wearing armour beneath his costume – another clue that the royal party had come to Smithfield ready for trouble.

It was all the royal bodyguard needed. One promptly fell on Tyler, running him through with his sword. Mortally wounded, Tyler pulled himself up on to his horse and headed back towards his comrades. Then, crying out for help, he fell to the ground in the no man's land separating the two sides. Angry archers in the watching rebel ranks began to flex their bows, and were only prevented from loosing their arrows by the sight of the boy King himself, spurring his horse forward and calling out to them with a personal appeal – they should come with him to the nearby fields of Clerkenwell, he cried, for further discussion.

Even allowing for the exaggeration of loyal chroniclers, Richard's bravery and presence of mind were remarkable. He defused a moment that could have led to wholesale bloodshed, and his composure turned the tide which, until then, had been flowing in the rebels' favour.

Wat Tyler's followers took their grievously wounded leader to the nearby St Bartholomew's Hospital, but the mayor had him dragged out and beheaded. No one stepped forward to take Tyler's place, and the men of Kent – 'enveloped', as one observer put it, 'like sheep within a pen' – allowed themselves to be ushered homewards over London Bridge.

The great revolt continued to rage in other parts of the country. In St Albans, Cambridge and Bury St Edmunds, merchants and craftsmen rose to free their towns from the control of local abbeys, fighting for the right to function as independent communities. In Norfolk men rose up in town and countryside alike. But at the end of June royal troops advanced on Essex and mercilessly crushed all resistance they encountered. According to one chronicle, five hundred men perished. More reliable figures indicate that some thirty-one ringleaders were identified, tried and hanged on the gallows.

'Rustics you were and rustics you are still,' declared the young Richard later, on his tour of Essex. 'You will remain in bondage, not as before, but incomparably harsher.'

The juvenile hero of Smithfield rescinded every concession he had granted under the pressure of rebellion – in his value system, promises made under duress did not count. The blithe courage that he had shown at Smithfield sprang from the mantle of divine appointment in which he would wrap himself for the rest of his reign. John Ball and Jack Straw were tracked down, tried and hanged, and in a Parliament that was summoned at the end of the year the knights, gentlemen and burgesses wasted no time in reaffirming the social restrictions that had provoked the uprising in the first place. Now that it was safe again to sneer, the rebels with their high-flown ideas of freedom and equality were dismissed as 'the mad multitude'.

But Parliament never again tried a poll tax – well, at least not for another six hundred and nine years, when Margaret Thatcher's Conservative government imposed a 'per head' community charge on a reluctant country. Once again the electoral rolls displayed mysterious 'disappearances' – 130,000 names went missing in London alone – and once again the protesters came to the capital to fight pitched battles in the streets. In 1990, however, the rebels got their way. Mrs Thatcher was jettisoned by her colleagues – for their own survival. Her successor John Major wasted no time in dropping the poll tax, and was returned to power in the next general election.

The processes of democracy and consultation that we enjoy today saw their origins in these years. From the wise men who advised the Anglo-Saxon kings, via the first 'social contract' reluctantly agreed by the hapless Ethelred the Unready, the green shoots of freedom had started to flourish. The Norman Conquest seemed a setback, but that too enriched England's cross-bred culture, not least her potent, subtle language: some of the most English things about England, we discover, have come from abroad.

In the Peasants' Revolt we have heard cries for liberty and equality that resound to this day, and we have seen those demands brutally suppressed. Two steps forward, one step back. Adam would be delving and Eve would be twirling her spindle for many a year before Englishmen and women became close to being 'free and of one condition', as Wat Tyles had demanded of King Richard II. But the economic power that the Black Death had paradoxically spread in the direction of able-bodied working people would, with time, generate new ways of living – and new ways of thinking as well.

GEOFFREY CHAUCER AND
THE MOTHER TONGUE
1387

Whan that Aprill with his shoures soote
The droghte of March hath perced to the roote . . .

GEOFFREY CHAUCER'S *CANTERBURY TALES* OPENS ON A green spring morning beside the River Thames, towards the end of the fourteenth century. Birds are singing, the sap is rising, and a group of travellers gathers in the Tabard Inn – one of the rambling wooden hostelries with stables and dormitory-like bedrooms round a courtyard, that clustered around the southern end of London Bridge. At first hearing, Chaucer's 'English' sounds foreign, but in its phrasing we can detect the rhythms and wording of our own speech, especially if we read it aloud, as people usually did six hundred years ago: 'Thanne longen folk to goon on pilgrimages . . .'

The pilgrimage was the package holiday of the Middle Ages, and Chaucer imagines a group of holidaymakers in search of country air, leisurely exercise and spiritual refreshment at England's premier tourist attraction, the tomb of St Thomas Becket at Canterbury: a brawny miller tootling on his bagpipes; a grey-eyed prioress daintily feeding tit-bits to her lapdogs; a poor knight whose chain mail has left smudgings of rust on his tunic. To read Geoffrey Chaucer is to be transported back in time, to feel the skin and clothes – and sometimes, even, to smell the leek- or onion-laden breath – of people as they went about their daily business in what we call the Middle Ages. For them, of course, it was 'now'.

The host of the Tabard, the innkeeper Harry Bailey, suggests a story-telling competition to enliven the journey – free supper to the winner – and so we meet the poor knight, the dainty prioress and the miller, along with a merchant, a sea captain, a cook, and twenty other deeply believable characters plucked from the three or four million or so inhabitants of King Richard II's England. Chaucer includes himself as one of the pilgrims, offering to entertain the company with a rhyming tale of his own. But scarcely has he started when he is cut short by Harry the host:

> 'By God,' quod he, 'for pleynly, at a word,
> Thy drasty ryming is nat worth a toord!'

It is lines like these that have won Chaucer his fondly rude niche in the English folk memory. People's eyes light up at the mention of *The Canterbury Tales*, as they recall embarrassed schoolteachers struggling to explain words like 'turd' and to bypass tales of backsides being stuck out of windows. 'Please, sir, what is this "something" that is "rough and hairy"?'

In one passage Chaucer describes a friar (or religious brother, from the French word *frère*) who, while visiting hell in the course of a dream, is pleased to detect no trace of other friars, and complacently concludes that all friars must go to heaven.

'Oh *no*, we've got millions of them here!' an angel corrects him, pointing to the Devil's massively broad tail:

> 'Hold up thy tayl, thou Satanas!' quod he,
> 'Shewe forth thyn ers, and lat the frere se . . .'

Whereupon twenty thousand friars swarm out of the Devil's *ers* and fly around hell like angry bees, before creeping back inside their warm and cosy home for eternity.

In gathering for a pilgrimage, Chaucer's travellers were taking part in a Church-inspired ritual. But the poet's message was that the Church – the massive nationalised industry that ran the schools and hospitals of medieval England as well as its worship – was in serious trouble. While his imaginary company of pilgrims included a pious Oxford cleric and a parish priest who was a genuinely good shepherd to his flock, it also included men who were only too happy to make a

GREAT TALES FROM ENGLISH HISTORY

corrupt living out of God's service on earth: a worldly monk who liked to feast on roast swan; a pimpled 'Summoner' who took bribes from sinners *not* to summon them to the church courts; and a 'Pardoner' who sold bogus relics like the veil of the Virgin Mary (actually an old pillowcase) and a rubble of pig's bones that he labelled as belonging to various saints. Buy one of these, was the message of this medieval insurance salesman, and you would go straight to heaven.

Chaucer humorously but unsparingly describes a country where almost everything is for sale. Four decades earlier England's population had been halved by the onslaught of the 'Black Death' – the bubonic plague that would return several more times before the end of the century – and the consequence of this appalling tragedy had been a sharp-elbowed economic scramble among the survivors. Wages had risen, plague-cleared land was going cheap. For a dozen years before he wrote *The Canterbury Tales* Chaucer had lived over the Aldgate, or 'Old Gate', the most easterly of the six gates in London's fortified wall, and from his windows in the arch he had been able to look down on the changing scene. In 1381 the angry men of Essex had come and gone through the Aldgate, waving their billhooks – the 'mad multitude' known to history as the ill-fated Peasants' Revolt. During the plague years the city's iron-wheeled refuse carts had rumbled beneath the poet's floorboards with their bouncing heaps of corpses, heading for the limepits.

Chaucer paints the keen detail of this reviving community in a newly revived language – the spoken English that the Norman Conquest had threatened to suppress. Written between 1387 and 1400, the year of Chaucer's death, *The Canterbury Tales* is one of the earliest pieces of English that is intelligible to a modern ear. For three hundred years English had endured among the ordinary people, and particularly among the gentry. Even in French-speaking noble households Anglo-Saxon wives and local nursemaids had chattered to children in the native language. English had survived because it was literally the mother tongue, and it was in these post-plague years that it reasserted itself. In 1356 the Mayor of London decreed that English should be the language of council meetings, and in 1363 the Lord Chancellor made a point of opening Parliament in English – not, as had previously been the case, in the language of the enemy across the Channel.

148

Geoffrey Chaucer's cheery and companionable writing foreshadows the modern world. In the pages that follow we shall trace the unstoppable spread of the English language – carried from England to the far side of the world. We shall see men and women reject the commerce of the old religion, while making fortunes from the new. And as they change their views about God, they will also change their views profoundly about the authority of kings and earthly power. They will sharpen their words and start freeing their minds – and in embarking upon that, they will also begin the uncertain process of freeing themselves.

THE DEPOSING OF
KING RICHARD II
1399

T HE LAST TIME WE MET RICHARD II HE WAS A BOY OF fourteen, facing down Wat Tyler and his rebels at the climax of the Peasants' Revolt. 'Sirs, will you shoot your king? I will be your captain!' the young man had cried in June 1381 as the 'mad multitude' massed angrily on the grass at Smithfield outside the city walls. His domineering uncle John of Gaunt was away from London, negotiating a truce in Scotland, and Richard's advisers had shown themselves wavering. But the boy king had said his prayers and ridden out to face the brandished billhooks.

An uncomplicated faith brought Richard II a brave and famous triumph, and it was small wonder that he should grow up with an exalted idea of himself and his powers. While waiting for vespers, the evening prayer, the young man who had been treated as a king from the age of ten liked to sit enthroned for hours, doing nothing much more than wearing his crown and 'speaking to no man'. People who entered his presence were expected to bow the knee and lower the eyes. While previous English kings had been content to be addressed as 'My Lord', now the titles of 'Highness' and 'Majesty' were demanded.

Richard came to believe that he was ordained of God. He had himself painted like Christ in Majesty, a golden icon glowing on his throne – the earliest surviving portrait that we have of any English king. When the King of Armenia came to the capital, Richard ordered that Westminster Abbey be opened in the middle of the night and proudly showed his visitor his crown, his sceptre and the other symbols of regality by the flicker of candlelight.

But Richard's public grandeur was a mask for insecurity. The King suffered from a stammer, and by the time he was fully grown, at nearly six feet tall, his fits of anger could be terrifying. Cheeks flushed, and shaking his yellow Plantagenet hair, on one occasion Richard drew his sword on a noble who dared to cross him, and struck another across the cheek. When Parliament was critical of his advisers, he declared that he 'would not even dismiss a scullion' from his kitchens at their request. When Parliament was compliant, he proclaimed proudly that he had no need of Lords or Commons, since the laws of England were 'in his mouth or his breast'.

Richard's dream was to rule without having to answer to anyone, and to that end he made peace with France, calling a truce in the series of draining conflicts that we know as the Hundred Years War. No fighting meant no extra taxes, calculated Richard – and that meant he might never have to call Parliament again.

Some modern historians have frowned on Richard II's ambition to rule without Parliament. They condemn his attempts to interrupt the traditional story of England's march towards democracy – only six Parliaments met during his reign of twenty-two years. But it is by no means certain that Richard's subjects saw this as regrettable. On the contrary. The summoning of Parliament was invariably followed by the appearance of tax assessors in the towns and villages. So there was much to be said for a king who left his people in peace and who managed to 'live of his own' – without levying taxes.

Richard's gilded, image-dazzled style, however, won him few friends. He made no pretence to love the common man, and it was his attempt to 'live of his own' that brought about his downfall. When John of Gaunt died in 1399, aged fifty-eight, Richard could not resist the temptation to seize his uncle's lands. Gaunt's Duchy of Lancaster estates were the largest single landholding in England, and his son Henry Bolingbroke had recently been sent into exile, banished for ten years following a dispute with another nobleman.

Bolingbroke, named after the Lincolnshire castle where he was born in 1366, was the same age as Richard. The two cousins had grown up at court together, sharing the frightening experience of being inside the Tower of London at one stage of the Peasants' Revolt as the angry rebels had flocked outside the walls, yelling and hurling abuse. Some rioters who broke through managed to capture Henry, and he had been lucky to escape the fate of the Archbishop of Canterbury, who was dragged outside to be beaten, then beheaded.

Henry was not one jot less pious than his royal cousin. In 1390, aged twenty-four, he had been on crusade to fight alongside Germany's Teutonic Knights as they took Christianity to Lithuania, and in 1392 he travelled on a pilgrimage to Jerusalem. A tough character, the leading jouster of his generation, he was not the sort to surrender his family inheritance without a fight. Land was sacred to a medieval baron, and many magnates supported Bolingbroke's quarrel with the King. No one's estates were safe if the great Duchy of Lancaster could be seized at the royal whim.

When Richard decided to go campaigning against Irish rebels in the summer of 1399, his cousin grabbed his chance. Bolingbroke had spent his nine-month exile in France. Now he landed in Yorkshire, to be welcomed by the Earl of Northumberland and his son Henry 'Hotspur', the great warriors of the north. Henry had won control of most of central and eastern England, and was in a position to claim much more than his family's estate. Richard returned from Ireland to find himself facing a coup.

'Now I can see the end of my days coming,' the King mournfully declared as he stood on the ramparts of Flint Castle in north Wales early in August 1399, watching the advance of his cousin's army along the coast.

Captured, escorted to London and imprisoned in the Tower, Richard resisted three attempts to make him renounce in Henry's favour, until he was finally worn down – though he refused to hand the crown directly to his supplanter. Instead, he defiantly placed the gold circlet on God's earth, symbolically resigning his sovereignty to his Maker.

Sent north to the gloomy fortress of Pontefract in Yorkshire, Richard survived only a few months. A Christmas rising by his supporters made him too dangerous to keep alive. According to Shakespeare's play *Richard II*, the deposed monarch met his end heroically in a scuffle in which he killed two of his would-be assassins before being himself struck down. But the truth was less theatrical. The official story was that Richard went on hunger strike, so that the opening that led to his stomach gradually contracted. His supporters maintained that the gaolers deliberately deprived him of food. Either way, the thirty-three-year-old ex-monarch starved to death. According to one account, in his hunger he gnawed desperately at his own arm.

> *Of comfort no man speak . . .*
> *Let us sit upon the ground*
> *And tell sad stories of the death of kings!*

Writing two hundred years later, Shakespeare drew a simple moral from the tale of Richard II. Richard may have been a flawed character, but the deposition of an anointed monarch upset the ordained order of things. The playwright knew what would happen next – the generations of conflict between the families of Richard and Henry that have come to be known as the 'Wars of the Roses'.

'TURN AGAIN, DICK WHITTINGTON!'
1399

A S HENRY IV TOOK CONTROL OF HIS NEW KINGDOM AT THE end of 1399, he pointedly promised that, unlike his wilful predecessor, he would rule with the guidance of 'wise and discreet' persons. Richard II had been criticised for shunning the advice of his counsellors. He was nicknamed 'Richard the Redeless' – the 'uncounselled'. So Henry made sure that the advisers he summoned to his early council were a sober mixture of bishops and barons.

Then on 8 December that year the new King sent for a different sort of expert – a merchant and businessman, the first ever to sit on the Royal Council. Sir Richard Whittington was a cloth trader and moneylender from the City of London, who had served as Mayor of the City and who would, in fact, be elected Mayor no less than three times.

'Oh yes he did! Oh no he didn't!' Every Christmas the adventures of Dick Whittington still inspire pantomime audiences in theatres and church halls around the country. We see Whittington, usually played by a pretty girl in tights, striding off from Gloucestershire to seek his fortune in London, only to leave soon afterwards, dispirited to discover that the streets are not paved with gold. But sitting down to rest with his cat, the only friend he has managed to make on his travels, Dick hears the bells of London pealing out behind him.

'Turn again, Dick Whittington,' they seem to be calling, 'thrice Lord Mayor of London!'

Reinvigorated, Dick returns to the city, where he gets a job in the house of Alderman Fitzwarren and falls in love with Fitzwarren's beautiful daughter, Alice. Disaster strikes when Dick is falsely accused of stealing a valuable necklace. So, deciding he had better make himself scarce, he and his cat stow away on one of the alderman's ships trading silks and satins with the Barbary Coast. There Puss wins favour with the local sultan by ridding his palace of rats, and Dick is rewarded with sackfuls of gold and jewels, which he bears home in triumph – more than enough to replace the necklace, which, it turns out, had been stolen by Puss's mortal enemy, King Rat. Alice and Dick are married, and Dick goes on to fulfil the bells' prophecy, becoming thrice Lord Mayor of London.

Much of this is true. Young Richard Whittington, a third son with no chance of an inheritance, did leave the village of Pauntley in Gloucestershire sometime in the 1360s to seek his fortune in London. And there he was indeed apprenticed to one Sir Hugh Fitzwarren, a mercer who dealt in precious cloth, some of it imported from the land of the Berbers, the Barbary Coast of North Africa. Dick became a mercer himself (the word derives from the Latin *merx*, or wares, the same root that gives us 'merchant'). He supplied sumptuous cloth to both Richard II and Henry IV, providing two of Henry's daughters with cloth of gold for their wedding trousseaus. He also became a friendly bank manager to the royal family, extending generous over-drafts whenever they were strapped for cash. In the decades around 1400 Dick Whittington made no less than fifty-three loans to Richard and Henry, and also to Henry's son Henry V. He routinely took royal jewels as security, and on one occasion lost a necklace, whose value he had to repay.

Dick was elected mayor of London in 1397, 1406 and 1419. With the populist flair that a mayor needs to go down in history, he campaigned against watered beer, greedy brewers who overcharged, and the destruction of old walls and monuments. There was a 'green' touch to his removal from the Thames of illegal 'fish weirs', the standing traps of basketwork or netting that threatened fish stocks when their aper-tures were too small and trapped even the tiniest tiddlers.

Less kind to the river, perhaps, was the money that he left in his will for the building of 'Whittington's Longhouse'. This monster public lavatory contained 128 seats, half for men and half for women, in two very long rows with no partitions and no privacy. It overhung a gully near modern Cannon Street that was flushed by the tide. Dying child-less in 1423, Dick spread his vast fortune across a generous range of London almshouses, hospitals and charities.

The trouble is the cat. There is not the slightest evidence that Dick Whittington ever owned any pets, let alone a skilled ratter who might have won the favour of the Sultan of Barbary. Puss does not enter the story for another two hundred years, and was probably introduced into the plot by mummers in early pantomimes.

'To Southwark Fair,' wrote Samuel Pepys in his diary for 21 September 1668. 'Very dirty, and there saw the puppet show of Whittington which was pretty to see.'

Stories of clever cats are found in the earliest Egyptian and Hindu myths; Portuguese, Spanish and Italian fables tell of men whose fortunes are made by their cats. *Puss in Boots*, a rival pantomime, also celebrates the exploits of a trickster cat that magically enriches his impoverished master.

Experts call this a 'migratory myth'. Blending the cosy notion of a furry, four-legged partner with the story of the advancement of hard-nosed Richard Whittington, England's biggest moneylender, took the edge off people's envy at the rise of the merchant class in the years after the Black Death – these new magnates who mattered in the reign of King Money. And when it comes to our own day, Dick's tale of luck and ambition provides a timeless stereotype for the pop stars and celebrities who play him in panto: the classless, self-made wannabes who leave their life in the sticks and reinvent themselves in the big city.

HENRY IV AND HIS
EXTRA-VIRGIN OIL
1399

WHEN PARLIAMENT FIRST WELCOMED HENRY IV AS KING in September 1399 with cries of 'Yes, Yes, Yes', he told them to shout it again. The first round of yeses had not been loud enough for him. At that moment the deposed Richard II, just a mile or so down-river in the Tower of London, was still alive. The new King quite understood, he told the company who assembled that day in Westminster, that some of them might have reservations.

This may have been a joke on Henry IV's part – he had a self-deprecating sense of humour. But the fact that he had usurped the throne was to be the theme of his reign. For his coronation in October, he introduced a new 'imperial' style of crown consisting of a circlet sur-mounted by arches that English kings and queens have worn ever since. He commissioned a book to emphasise the significance of England's coronation regalia – and he had himself anointed with an especially potent and prestigious oil that Richard II had located in his increasing obsession with majesty. The Virgin Mary herself, it was said, had given it to St Thomas Becket.

The fancy oil delivered its own verdict on the usurper – an infes-tation of headlice that afflicted Henry for months. He spent the first half of his reign fighting off challenges, particularly from the fractious Percy family of Northumberland who plotted against him in the north and were behind no less than three dangerous rebellions. In Wales the English King had to contend with the defiance of the charismatic Owain Glyndwr, who kept the red dragon fluttering from castles and misty Celtic mountain-tops.

Henry defeated his enemies in a run of brisk campaigns that con-firmed his prowess as a military leader. But he was not able to enjoy his triumphs. In 1406, at the age of forty, the stocky and heavy-jowled monarch was struck down by a mystery illness that made it difficult for him to travel or to communicate verbally.

Modern doctors think that Henry must have suffered a series of strokes. For the rest of his reign he was disabled in both mind and body, though he went to great lengths to conceal his infirmity. Letters went out to the local sheriffs ordering the arrest of those who spread rumours of his sickness, while his bishops received letters requesting prayers to be said for his physical recovery. Depressed and speaking of himself as 'a sinful wretch', Henry came to believe that his salvation rested in a repeat of his youthful pilgrimage to Jerusalem.

One cause of his melancholy was the conflicts that arose with his eldest son, Henry of Monmouth. A brave and forceful warrior who fought alongside his father against the Percys and took charge of the campaign against Owain Glyndwr, 'Prince Hal' was not the dissolute hell-raiser portrayed by Shakespeare. But he was an impatient critic of the ailing King. In 1410 he elbowed aside Henry's advisers to take control of the Royal Council for a spell – it seems possible he was even pushing his father to abdicate.

In 1413 the old King collapsed while at prayer in Westminster Abbey. Carried to the abbot's quarters and placed on a straw mattress beside the fire, he fell into a deep sleep, with his crown placed, as was the medieval custom, on the pillow beside him. Thinking he had breathed his last, his attendants covered his face with a linen cloth, while the Prince of Wales picked up the crown and left the room.

Suddenly the King woke. As he sat up, the cloth fell from his face, and he demanded to know what had happened to the crown. Summoned to his father's bedside, the prince did not beat about the bush.

'Sir,' he said, 'to mine and all men's judgement, you seemed dead in this world. So I, as your next heir apparent, took that as mine own.'

'What right could you have to the crown,' retorted Henry wryly, 'when I have none?'

Richard's usurper never lost his sense of guilt – nor his sense of humour. Looking round the room, the King asked where he was, and was told that he had been brought to the Jerusalem Chamber.

'Praise be to God,' he said, 'for it was foretold me long ago that I would die in Jerusalem.'

WE HAPPY FEW – THE BATTLE OF AZINCOURT

1415

THE NEW KING HENRY V WAS A TWENTY-FIVE-YEAR-OLD IN a hurry. He had been impatient with his disabled father, and he was impatient with just about everyone else. Watching a Lollard blacksmith suffering the recently introduced penalty of being burned at the stake, he had the man dragged out of the flames, then invited him to recant. When the blacksmith refused, the prince thrust him back on to the pyre.

Henry saw himself as God's soldier, and he had a soldier's haircut to match: shaved back and sides with a dark-brown pudding-basin of hair perched on top. This pallid young warrior, with his large, fiercely bright, almond-shaped eyes, brought intense religious conviction to England's long-running quarrel with France.

'My hope is in God,' he declared as he stood with his troops in the pouring rain on the night of Thursday 24 October, 1415. 'If my cause is just I shall prevail, whatever the size of my following.'

He was addressing his small, damp and beleaguered army outside the village of Agincourt in northern France. Here the English had been disconcerted to find their route back to Calais blocked by an immensely larger French army. Modern estimates put the English at 6000, facing as many as 20,000 or even 25,000. Henry's cause looked hopeless. A large number of his men were suffering from dysentery, the bloody diarrhoea that was a major hazard of pre-penicillin warfare. The French were so confident that night that they threw dice, wagering on the rich ransoms they would be extorting for the English nobility they would capture next day.

In contrast to the rowdy chatter and singing around the French campfires, there was silence in the English ranks, where Henry walked among his intimidated little army, doing his best to raise their morale.

'He made fine speeches everywhere,' wrote Jehan de Wavrin, a French knight who fought in the battle and collected eyewitness accounts of how Henry set about encouraging his men:

> They should remember [the King said] that they were born of the realm of England where they had been brought up, and where their fathers, mothers, wives, and children were living; wherefore it became them to exert themselves that they might return thither with great joy and approval . . . And further he told them and explained how the French were boasting that they would cut off three fingers of the right hand of all the archers that should be taken prisoners, to the end that neither man nor horse should ever again be killed with their arrows.

Archers made up nearly four thousand of the English force – double the number of men-at-arms – and the English archers were crucial to what happened next day.

The French had chosen the ground on which they wished to fight – an open field, bordered by thick woods. But as their knights advanced in their heavy armour, the effect of the woods was to funnel them into the English bowmen's line of fire. The torrential rain the night before had turned the ground into mud, so the French slithered and stumbled, falling in their dozens beneath the fusillades of arrows. The white-feathered quills littered the battlefield, protruding from the bodies of both horses and men. It looked as if snow had fallen, according to one observer.

At the end of the encounter the English casualties were minimal, no more than two hundred. By contrast, more than seven thousand French lay dead, though many of their nobility died in circumstances their descendants would not forget. Under the pressure of a surprise counterattack, Henry ordered the summary execution of several hundred French noblemen who had surrendered but had not been disarmed. He considered them a threat. But in France to this day, the Battle of Azincourt – as the French call it – is remembered for this shaming betrayal of the traditional rules of chivalry. Modern visitors to the area are told that the battle saw the death not just of thousands of men, but of 'un certain idéal de combat' – a foretaste of modern mass warfare.

For England, Agincourt has inspired quite a different national myth. London welcomed Henry home with drums, trumpets and tambourines and choirs of children dressed as angels. Flocks of birds were released into the air and gigantic carved effigies spelled out the meaning of the victory – a David defeating Goliath.

'We few, we happy few, we band of brothers', were the words with which Shakespeare would later enshrine Agincourt's model of bravery against the odds – the notion that the English actually do best when they are outnumbered. This phenomenon came to full flower in 1940 during the Battle of Britain, when Britain faced the might of Germany alone and Churchill spoke so movingly of the 'few'. To further fortify the bulldog spirit, the Ministry of Information financed the actor Laurence Olivier to film a Technicolor version of Agincourt as depicted in Shakespeare's Henry V. 'Dedicated to the Airborne Regiments', read a screen title in medieval script as the opening credits began to roll.

Henry V's own patriotism was deeply infused with religion. Dreaming of England and France unified beneath God, he had crusader ambitions similar to those of Richard the Lionheart, the warrior king he so resembled in charisma and ferocity. Like the Lionheart, Henry could not keep away from battle and, like him, he was struck down, young and unnecessarily, by a hazard of the battlefield when besieging a minor castle in France. Gangrene claimed Richard. Henry was felled by dysentery, contracted at the siege of Meaux. His boiled and flesh-free bones were borne back to England in a coffin topped with his effigy – a death mask of his head, face and upper body that had been moulded in steamed leather.

Just before he died Henry had called for charts of the harbours of

Syria and Egypt, and was reading a history of the first Crusade. He was getting ready for his great expedition to Palestine. His wish to link England and France in this pious joint venture went beyond the simple jingoism of a modern soccer or rugby crowd. But one thing that modern fans might share with holy Henry is the two-fingered, 'Up yours' V-sign, directed derisively at the enemy. It has been suggested, though without any evidence, that this gesture originated with fifteenth-century archers who wished to demonstate that their bow-string fingers had not been cut off – hence its modern nickname, 'the Agincourt salute'.

JOAN OF ARC, THE MAID OF ORLEANS
1429

J OAN OF ARC WAS THREE YEARS OLD WHEN HENRY V WON his famous victory in the mud of Azincourt. She was the daughter of a prosperous farmer whose solid stone-built house can still be seen in the village of Domrémy, near the River Meuse in Lorraine, France's eastern border country.

Today the border is with Germany. In 1415, it was with the independent and ambitious Duchy of Burgundy, whose territory stretched down from the prosperous Low Countries towards Switzerland. Joan's village was right in the path of the Burgundians when they came raiding, often in alliance with the English, as the two countries carved out conquests from the incompetently governed territories of France.

Henry V's famous victories, which continued after Agincourt, owed much to the weakness of France's rulers. The French king Charles VI suffered from long periods of madness, when he would run howling like a wolf down the corridors of his palaces. One of his fantasies was to believe himself made of glass and to suspect anyone who came too near of trying to push him over and shatter him. His son Charles, who bore the title of Dauphin, had a phobia about entering houses, believing they would fall down on him (as one once did in the town of La Rochelle).

The title of Dauphin, meaning literally 'dolphin', is the French equivalent of Prince of Wales, a title relating to the heir to the throne. England's heir had three feathers on his crest – the banner of France's sported a playful dolphin. But in the early 1400s the shifty and hesitant Dauphin of France did no credit to the bright and intuitive animal whose name he bore. The Dauphin's court was notorious throughout Europe for harbouring such undesirables as the paedophile Gilles de Rais – the model for the legendary Bluebeard – in whose castle were found the remains of more than fifty children.

France degenerated into civil war. King and Dauphin were at loggerheads, and England reaped the benefit in 1420 when the unstable Charles VI disinherited his equally unbalanced son. On 20 May, in the Treaty of Troyes, the French king took the humiliating step of appointing England's Henry V as 'regent and heir' to his kingdom, marrying his daughter Catherine to the English warrior monarch. So five years after Agincourt, Henry V had within his grasp the glorious prospect of becoming the first ever King of both France and England – only to die just six weeks before his father-in-law, in August 1422, leaving his title to the long-dreamed-of double monarchy to his nine-month-old son.

It was three years later that the thirteen-year-old Joan first heard God talking to her in her home village of Domrémy.

'And came this voice,' she later remembered, 'about the hour of noon, in the summertime, in my father's garden . . . I heard the voice on the right-hand side, towards the church, and rarely do I hear it without a brightness. This brightness comes from the same side as the voice is heard. It is usually a great light.'

Anyone today who reported hearing voices would probably be sent to a psychiatrist and might well be diagnosed as schizophrenic. But Joan had no doubt who was talking to her. 'After I had thrice heard this voice, I knew that it was the voice of an angel. This voice has always guided me well and I have always understood it clearly.'

The fascination of Joan's story is that a teenage girl should have per-suaded ever-widening circles of people to agree with her. 'You are she,' said her angel, 'whom the King of Heaven has chosen to bring repa-ration to the kingdom.'

It was just what a divided and demoralised France needed to hear. After months of badgering, Joan finally won an audience with the Dauphin, and she galvanised the normally melancholic prince, who was now technically Charles VII but had so far lacked the push to get him-self crowned. Dressed in men's clothes, Joan had been led into court as a freak show. But the Dauphin was inspired. After hearing her, recalled one eyewitness, the would-be king 'appeared radiant'. He sent the girl to be cross-examined by a commission of learned clerics, and she con-fronted them with the same self-confidence.

'Do you believe in God?' asked one theologian.

'Yes,' she retorted, 'better than you.'

The practical proof of Joan's divine mandate came in the spring of 1429 when, aged seventeen, she joined the French army at the town of Orleans, which the English had been besieging for six months. Her timing was perfect – the English, weakened by illness, had been deserted by their Burgundian allies. Within ten days of Joan's arrival they had retreated.

What the English saw as a strategic withdrawal on their part, their opponents interpreted as a glorious victory inspired by 'La Pucelle' – 'the Maid', as the French now called her. Joan symbolised the purity that France had lost and was longing to regain. Her virginity was a curious source of pride to her fellow-soldiers, among whom she dressed and undressed with a remarkable lack of inhibition. Several later testified that they had seen her breasts 'which were beautiful', but found, to their surprise, that their 'carnal desires' were not aroused by the prospect.

Joan's voices had told her to dress as a soldier of God, and her appearance in a specially made suit of armour created a stirring image around which her legend could flourish. As her authority grew, she demanded that France's soldiers should give up swearing, go to church and refrain from looting or harassing the civilians through whose towns and villages they passed.

Volunteers stepped forward in their hundreds, inspired by the idea of joining an army with a saint at its head, while the demoralised

English, once so confident that God was on their side, also began to believe the legend. When Joan was captured by Burgundian forces in May 1430, both the Burgundians and the English 'were much more excited than if they had captured five hundred fighting men', wrote the French chronicler de Monstrelet. 'They had never been so afraid of any captain or commander in war.'

The English promptly set up a church tribunal where Joan was condemned as a witch – her habit of wearing men's clothes was taken as particular proof of her damnation. If the Dauphin had exerted himself he might have negotiated her ransom, as was normal with high-profile prisoners-of-war. But he did nothing to help save the girl who had saved *him*. On 30 May 1431 Joan of Arc was led out into the marketplace in Rouen by English soldiers, tied to a stake and burned to death. She was nineteen years old.

'We are all ruined,' said one English witness, 'for a good and holy person was burned.'

Over the centuries England has chosen to remember the Hundred Years War for its great victories like Crécy and Agincourt: but, thanks to Joan of Arc, the bloody 116-year enterprise actually ended, for the English, in miserable defeat. According to one account, a white dove was seen in the sky at the moment of the Maid's death, and the French took this to symbolise God's blessing. They felt inspired to campaign with even more righteous certainty, and by 1453 all that survived of England's once great French empire was the walled port of Calais.

Joan of Arc's scarcely credible adventure remains eternally compelling. The simplicity and purity of her faith have inspired writers and dramatists over the centuries – particularly in times when it has become fashionable not to believe in God.

A 'PROMPTER FOR LITTLE ONES'
1440

THE LONG LISTS OF LATIN WORDS IN GEOFFREY OF LYNN'S *Promptorium Parvulorum* would offer tedious reading for modern fans of Harry Potter, but his 'Prompter for Little Ones' has a good claim to being England's first child-friendly book.

Geoffrey was a friar from the Norfolk town known today as King's Lynn, and his 'Prompter' reads like the work of a kindly schoolmaster. It was a dictionary which set out the words that a good medieval pupil might be expected to know – many of them to do with religion. But defying the solemn tone, Geoffrey also listed the names of toys, games and children's playground pastimes. We read of rag dolls, four different types of spinning top, a child's bell; of games of shuttlecock, tennis and leapfrog, three running and chasing games, and games to be played on a swing or seesaw (which Geoffrey calls a 'totter', or 'merry totter').

All this gives us a rare glimpse into childhood in the Middle Ages. Medieval books were for grown-ups – most chronicles tell us of war and arguments over religion. But Geoffrey of Lynn takes us into the world of children, and shows us something of their preoccupations and imaginings.

In recent times this picture has been made real for us thanks to the chirps and bleepings of the modern metal detector. The Thames Mud Larks, named after the Victorian children who used to scavenge flotsam from the banks of the river, are a group of enthusiasts who scour the mudflats of the Thames at low tide. During London's construction boom of the 1980s they were also to be seen raking over the city's building sites, and what they came up with was an extraordinary treasure trove – large numbers of ancient toys.

One Mud Lark, Tony Pilson, retrieved hundreds of tiny pewter playthings dating back as early as AD 1250 – miniature jugs, pans, other kitchen and cooking utensils and even bird-cages. He and his fellow-searchers turned up just about everything you would need to equip a doll's house – along with small metal soldiers that included a knight in armour. Mounted on horseback, the little figure had been cast from a mould, so he must originally have been produced in bulk.

When we look at portraits of children in the Middle Ages, they usually stare out at us with formal and stern expressions. But in the pages of Geoffrey's 'Prompter for Little Ones' and in the modern discoveries of the Mud Larks, we find evidence of so much infant fun and laughter. And since all these toys were made by adults, and must, for the most part, have been purchased and given as presents by parents and other fond relations, we can presume that medieval grown-ups recognised and cherished the magic world of childhood.

HOUSE OF LANCASTER: THE TWO REIGNS OF HENRY VI
1422–61, 1470–1

HENRY VI WAS THE YOUNGEST EVER KING OF ENGLAND, succeeding his warrior father Henry V at the age of just nine months. When the little boy attended his first opening of Parliament, aged only three, it was hardly surprising that he 'shrieked and cried and sprang', as one report described.

The problem was that in the course of his fifty troubled years, this king never really grew up. Henry VI went from first to second childhood, according to one modern historian, 'without the usual interval'.

This is unfair. Henry was a kindly and pious man who financed the building of two gems of English architecture – the soaring Perpendicular chapel of Eton College across the Thames from

Windsor, and the chapel of King's College, Cambridge. He also ran a court of some magnificence, to which his naïvety brought a charming touch. The 'Royal Book' of court etiquette describes Henry and his French wife Margaret of Anjou waking up early one New Year's morning to receive their presents – then staying in bed to enjoy them.

But Henry showed a disastrous lack of interest in the kingly pursuits of chivalry and war. Faced with the need to command the English army in Normandy at the age of eighteen, three years after he had taken over personal control of government from his father's old councillors, his response was to send a cousin in his place. Henry felt he had quite enough to do supervising the foundation of Eton College. It was not surprising he developed a reputation for namby-pambiness. Riding one day through the Cripplegate in London's city walls, he was shocked to see a decaying section of a human body impaled on a stake above the archway – and was horrified when informed it was the severed quarter of a man who had been 'false to the King's majesty'. 'Take it away!' he cried. 'I will not have any Christian man so cruelly handled for my sake!'

Unfortunately for Henry, respect for human rights simply did not feature in the job description of a medieval king. Toughness was required. In the absence of a police force or army, a ruler depended on his network of nobles to ensure law and order, and if people lost confidence in the power of the Crown, it was to their local lord that they looked. They wore their lord's livery and badge – and it was these rival badges that would later give the conflicts of this period its famous name.

A memorable scene in Shakespeare's play *Henry VI, Part 1* depicts the nobility of England in a garden selecting roses, red or white, to signify their loyalty to the House of York or the House of Lancaster. It did not happen – Shakespeare invented the episode. 'The Wars of the Roses', the romantic title we use today for the succession of battles and dynastic changes that took place in England between 1453 and 1487, was also a later invention, coined by the nineteenth-century romantic novelist Sir Walter Scott. The Yorkists may have sported a rose on occasion, but there is no evidence that the Lancastrians ever did – at the Battle of Barnet in 1471, they started fighting each other because they did not recognise their own liveries. To judge from the profusion of badges and banners that were actually borne into battle during these years, men were fighting the wars of the swans, dogs, boars, bears, lions, stars, suns and daisies.

The struggle for power, money and land, however, certainly revolved around York and Lancaster, the two rival houses that developed from the numerous descendants of King Edward III (you can see the complications in the family tree on p. xvi). The Lancastrians traced their loyalties back to John of Gaunt, Duke of Lancaster, while the Yorkists rallied round the descendants of Gaunt's younger brother Edmund, Duke of York. Shakespeare dated the trouble from the moment that Gaunt's son Henry Bolingbroke deposed his cousin Richard II. But York and Lancaster would have stuck together under a firm and decisive king – and if Henry V had lived longer he would certainly have passed on a stronger throne. Even the bumbling Henry VI might have avoided trouble if, after years of diminishing mental competence, he had not finally gone mad.

According to one account, in August 1453 the King had 'a sudden fright' that sent him into a sort of coma, a sad echo of his grandfather, Charles VI – the French king who had howled like a wolf and imagined he was made of glass. After sixteen months Henry staged a recovery, but his breakdown had been the trigger for civil disorder, and in the confused sequence of intrigue and conflict that followed he was a helpless cipher. In February 1461 he was reported to have spent the second Battle of St Albans laughing and singing manically to himself, with no apparent awareness of the mayhem in full swing around him. It was hardly a surprise when, later that year, he was deposed, to be replaced by the handsome, strapping young Yorkist candidate, Edward IV (see p. 172).

In this change of regime the key figure was the mightiest of England's over-mighty subjects – Richard Neville, Earl of Warwick, who fought under the badge of the Bear and Ragged Staff. With no claim to the throne, but controlling vast estates with the ability to raise armies, the earl has gone down in history as 'Warwick the Kingmaker'. 'They have two rulers,' remarked a French observer of the English in these years, 'Warwick, and another whose name I have forgotten.'

When Warwick and Edward IV fell out in the late 1460s, the Kingmaker turned against his protégé, chasing him from the country.

To replace him, Warwick brought back the deposed Henry VI who had spent the last six years in the Tower: the restored monarch was paraded around London in the spring of 1471. But the confused and shambling king had to be shepherded down Cheapside, his feet tied on to his horse. Never much of a parade-ground figure, he now made a sorry sight, dressed in a decidedly old and drab blue velvet gown that could not fail to prompt scorn – 'as though he had no more to change with'. This moth-eaten display, reported the chronicler John Warkworth, was 'more like a play than a showing of a prince to win men's hearts'.

It was the Kingmaker's last throw – and a losing one. Warwick was unable to beat off the challenge of Edward IV, now returned, who soon defeated and killed the earl in battle, regaining the crown for himself.

As for poor Henry, his fate was sealed. Two weeks later he was found dead in the Tower, and history has pointed the finger at his second-time supplanter, Edward. Henry probably *was* murdered – but there is a sad plausibility to the official explanation that the twice-reigning King, who inherited two kingdoms and lost them both, passed away out of 'pure displeasure and melancholy'.

THE HOUSE OF THEODORE
1432–85

IF THE WARS OF THE ROSES WERE FOUGHT BY THE MEN, IT was the women who eventually sorted out the mess. By the late 1400s the royal family tree had become a crazy spider's web of possible claimants to the throne, and it took female instinct to tease out the relevant strands from the tangle. The emotions of mothers and wives were to weave new patterns – and eventually they produced a most unlikely solution.

Owain ap Maredudd ap Tydwr was a silver-tongued Welsh gentleman who caught the eye of Henry V's widow, Catherine of France. He was a servant in her household in the 1420s – probably Clerk of her Wardrobe – and being Welsh, he had no surname. The 'ap' in his name meant 'son of', so he was Owen, son of Meredith, son of Theodore.

But once he had captured the heart of the widowed Queen, Owen had needed a surname. According to later gossip, Catherine would spy on her energetic Welsh wardrobe clerk as he bathed naked in the Thames, and she decided she liked what she saw.

The court was outraged. An official inquiry was held. But Catherine stuck by her Owen and in 1432 their marriage was officially recognised. 'Theodore' became 'Tudor', and Owen went through life defiantly proud of the leap in fortune that he owed to love. Thirty years later, in 1461, cornered by his enemies after the Battle of Mortimer's Cross, he would go to the block with insouciance. 'That head shall lie on the stock,' he said jauntily, 'that was wont to lie on Queen Catherine's lap.'

From the outset, the Tudors confronted the world with attitude. Catherine and Owen had two sons, Edmund and Jasper, who were widely viewed as cuckoos in the royal nest. But the dowager Queen resolutely brought up her Welsh boys with her first-born royal son Henry VI, nine or ten years their senior, and the young King became fond of his boisterous half-brothers. In 1452 he raised them both to the peerage, giving Edmund the earldom of Richmond and making Jasper Earl of Pembroke. The two young Tudors were given precedence over all the earls in England, and Henry, who had produced no children, was rumoured to be considering making Edmund his heir. The new Earl of Richmond was granted a version of the royal arms to wear on his shield.

The Tudors rose still higher in the world a few years later, when Edmund married the twelve-year-old Lady Margaret Beaufort, who had her own claim to the throne. The great-granddaughter of John of Gaunt, she proved to be one of the most remarkable women of her time. Bright-eyed and birdlike, to judge from the portraits still to be seen in the several educational establishments she endowed, she was a woman of learning. She translated into English part of *The Imitation of Christ*, the early-fifteenth-century manual of contemplations in which the German monk Thomas of Kempen (Thomas à Kempis) taught how serenity comes through the judicious acceptance of life's problems. 'Trouble often compels a man to search his own heart: it reminds him he is an exile here, and he can put his trust in nothing in this world.'

Diminutive in stature, Lady Margaret was nonetheless strong in both mind and body. She was married, pregnant and widowed before the age of thirteen, when Edmund died of plague. In the care of his brother Jasper, Margaret gave birth to Edmund's son, Henry, in Jasper's castle at Pembroke in the bleak and windswept south-west corner of Wales. But some complication of the birth, probably to do with her youth or small frame, meant that she had no more children. For the rest of her life she devoted her energies to her son – 'my only worldly joy', as she lovingly described him – although circumstances kept them apart.

The young man's links to the succession through his mother – and less directly through his grandmother, the French queen Catherine – made England a dangerous place for Henry Tudor. He spent most of his upbringing in exile, much of it in the company of his uncle Jasper. At the age of four he was separated from his mother, and he scarcely saw her for twenty years.

But Lady Margaret never abandoned the cause. She would later plot a marriage for her son that would make his claim to the throne unassailable, and she had already arranged a marriage for herself that would turn out to be the Tudor trump card. In 1472 she married Thomas, Lord Stanley, a landowner with large estates in Cheshire, Lancashire and other parts of the north-west. The Stanleys were a wily family whose local empire-building typified the rivalries that made up the disorderly jostlings of these years. Allied to Lady Margaret, the Stanleys would prove crucial partners as her son Henry Tudor jostled for the largest prize of all.

HOUSE OF YORK: EDWARD IV,
MERCHANT KING
1461–70, 1471–83

THE FLAMBOYANT EDWARD IV SHARES WITH HIS LUCKLESS
rival Henry VI the dubious distinction of being the only king of
England to reign twice. In 1461 and 1471, thanks to Warwick the
Kingmaker, the two men played box and cox in what turned out to be
a humiliating royal timeshare. But after Edward had defeated Warwick
and disposed of Henry, he ruled for a dozen prosperous and largely
undisturbed years, during which he achieved another distinction. He
was the first king for more than a century and a half who did not die
in debt – in fact, he actually left his successor a little money in the kitty.

Edward was England's first and last businessman monarch. Clapping
folk around the shoulders and cracking dirty jokes, he was also an
unashamed wheeler-dealer. He set up his own trading business, making
handsome profits on exporting wool and tin to Italy, while importing
Mediterranean cargoes like wine, paper, sugar and oranges. He ran the
Crown lands with the keen eye of a bailiff, and when it came to PR with
the merchant community he was a master of corporate hospitality.

One day in 1482 Edward invited the Lord Mayor of London, the
aldermen and 'a certain number of such head commoners as the mayor
would assign' to join him in the royal forest at Waltham in Essex.
There, in today's golf-course country, they were treated to a morning
of sport, then conveyed 'to a strong and pleasant lodge made of green
boughs and other pleasant things. Within which lodge were laid certain tables, whereat at once the said mayor and his company were set
and served right plenteously with all manner of dainties . . . and especially of venison, both of red deer and of fallow.' After lunch the King
took his guests hunting again, and a few days later sent their wives 'two
harts and six bucks with a tun of Gascon Wine'.

It could be said that Edward IV invented the seductive flummery of the modern honours list when he made six London aldermen Knights of the Bath. Like the Order of the Garter, the Order of the Bath, which referred to the ritual cleansing that a squire underwent when he became a knight, was primarily a military honour. Now the King extended the bait to rich civilians that he wanted to keep on side: a moneylender would kneel down as Bill Bloggs, the sword would touch his shoulder, and he arose Sir William.

Edward understood that everyone had his price – himself included. In 1475 he had taken an army across the Channel where he met up with the French King at Picquigny near Amiens – and promptly did a deal to take his army home again. For a down payment of 75,000 crowns and a pension of 50,000 a year, he cheerfully sold off his birthright – England's claim to the French territories for which so many of his ancestors had fought so bloodily over the years.

The Treaty of Picquigny brought peace and prosperity to England, but not much honour. Edward's reign was too undramatic for Shakespeare to write a play about – one reason, perhaps, why Edward is sometimes called England's 'forgotten king'. But the beautiful St George's Chapel at Windsor, designed to outshine the chapel that his rival Henry VI had built at Eton College in the valley below, remains his memorial. And the Royal Book reveals a sumptuous court – along with a diverting little insight into how comfortably this fleshly monarch lived. After he had risen every morning, a yeoman was deputed to leap on to his bed and roll up and down so as to level out the lumps in the litter of bracken and straw that made up the royal mattress.

In 1483, Edward IV retired to his mattress unexpectedly, having caught a chill while fishing. He died some days later, aged only forty. Had this cynical yet able man lived just a few years longer, his elder son Edward, only twelve at the time of his death, might have been able to build on his legacy. As it was, young Edward and his younger brother soon found themselves inside the Tower of London, courtesy of their considerate uncle Richard.

WILLIAM CAXTON
1474

WARS AND ROSES ... WE HAVE SEEN THAT ROSES WERE rare on the battle banners of fifteenth-century England. Let's now take a closer look at the 'wars' themselves. In the thirty-two years that history textbooks conventionally allot to the 'Wars of the Roses', there were long periods of peace. In fact, there were only thirteen weeks of actual fighting – and though the battles themselves were bitter and sometimes very bloody, mayhem and ravaging seldom ensued.

'It is a custom in England,' reported Philippe de Commynes, a shrewd French visitor to England in the 1470s, 'that the victors in battle kill nobody, especially none of the ordinary soldiers.' In this curiously warless warfare, defeated noblemen could expect prompt and ruthless execution, but 'neither the country nor the people, nor the houses were wasted, destroyed or demolished'. The rank and file returned home as soon as they could, to continue farming their land.

In towns and cities people also got on with their lives. Trade and business positively flourished, generating contracts, ledgers and letters that called for a literate workforce – and it was the 'grammar' schools that taught this emerging class of office workers the practical mechanics of English and Latin. The grammar schools multiplied in the fifteenth century, and the demand for accessible low-price books that they helped generate was met by an invention that was to prove infinitely more important than considerations of who was nudging whom off the throne.

In 1469 William Caxton, an English merchant living in the prosperous Flemish trading town of Bruges, was finishing a book that he had researched. Caxton was a trader in rich cloths – a mercer like Richard Whittington – and books were his passion. He collected rare books, and he wrote for his own pleasure, scratching out the text laboriously with a quill on to parchment. The book he was currently completing was a history of the ancient Greek city of Troy, and the mercer, who was approaching his fiftieth birthday, was feeling weary. 'My pen is worn, mine hand heavy, my eye even dimmed,' he wrote. The prospect of copying out more versions of the manuscript for the friends who had expressed an interest was too much to contemplate. So Caxton decided to see what he could discover about the craft of printing, which had been pioneered by Johann Gutenberg in the 1440s in the Rhine Valley.

Travelling south-east from Bruges, he arrived on the Rhine nearly thirty years after Gutenberg had started work there. And having 'practised and learned' the technique for himself, the mercer turned printer went back to Bruges to set up his own press. In 1474 his *History of Troy* became the first book to be printed in English, and two years later he brought his press to England, setting up shop near the Chapter House, in the precinct of Westminster Abbey, where Parliament met.

Caxton had an eye for a good location. Along the route between the Palace of Westminster and the Chapter House shuttled lawyers, churchmen, courtiers, MPs – the book-buying elite of England. The former cloth trader also had an eye for a bestseller. The second book he printed was about chess, *The Game and Play of the Chesse*. Then came in fairly quick succession a French–English dictionary, a translation of Aesop's fables, several popular romances, Malory's tale of Camelot in the *Morte D'Arthur*, some school textbooks, a history of England, an encyclopaedia entitled *The Myrrour of the Worlde*, and Chaucer's bawdy evergreen, *The Canterbury Tales*.

More than five hundred years later a copy of Caxton's first edition of Chaucer became the most expensive book ever sold – knocked down at auction for £4.6 million. But in the fifteenth century the obvious appeal of the newly printed books lay in their value for money. Books became so commonplace that snobs sometimes employed scribes to copy Caxton's printed editions back into manuscript – while both Church and government became alarmed at the access to new ideas that the printing press offered to a widening public.

Over the centuries Caxton's innovation would marvellously stimulate diversity in thinking, but in one important respect its impact was to standardise. Caxton loved to write personal prefaces to his publications, explaining the background of the new book he was shar-ing with his readers, and in one of these he describes the difficulties of being England's first mass publisher. He was in his study, he relates, feeling rather bereft, looking for a new project to get his teeth into, and happened to pick up the recently published French version of Virgil's *Aeneid*. The editor in him couldn't resist trying to translate the great epic poem into English. Taking a pen, he wrote out a page or two. But when he came to read through what he had written, he had to wonder whether his customers in different corners of England would be able to understand it, since 'common English that is spoken in one shire varies from another'.

To make the point he recounted the tale of a group of English mer-chants who, when their ship was becalmed at the mouth of the Thames, decided to go ashore in search of a good breakfast. One of them asked for some '*eggys*', to be told by the Kentish wife that she did not understand French. Since the merchant himself only spoke and understood English, he started to get angry, until one of his compan-ions said he would like some '*eyren*' – and the woman promptly reached for the egg basket.

'Loo,' exclaimed Caxton, 'what sholde a man in thyse dayes now wryte – egges or eyren?'

Even in this account you may notice that Caxton himself first spelled the word '*eggys*', then '*egges*' a few lines later. As the printer-publisher produced more and more books – and when he died in 1491 he was on the point of printing his hundredth – he made his own decisions about how words should be spelled. His choices tended to reflect the language of the south-east of England, with which he was familiar – he was proud to come from Kent, 'where I doubt not is spoken as broad and rude English as is in any place of England'.

Many of Caxton's spelling decisions and those of the printers who came after him were quite arbitrary. As they matched letters to sounds they followed no particular rules, and we live with the con-sequences to this day. So if you have ever wondered why a bandage is 'wound' around a 'wound', why 'cough' rhymes with 'off' while 'bough' rhymes with 'cow', and why you might shed a 'tear' after seeing a 'tear' in your best dress or trousers, you have William Caxton to thank for the confusion.

WHODUNNIT? THE PRINCES IN THE TOWER
1483

WHEN EDWARD IV DIED EARLY IN APRIL 1483, HIS ELDER son Edward was in Ludlow on the Welsh border, carrying out his duties as Prince of Wales. The twelve-year-old was duly proclaimed King Edward V, and leisurely arrangements were made for him to travel to London for his coronation. But on the 30th of that month, with little more than a day's riding to go, the royal party was intercepted by the King's uncle, Richard, Duke of Gloucester, at Stony Stratford on the outskirts of modern-day Milton Keynes.

The thirty-year-old Richard was the energetic and ambitious younger brother of Edward IV. He had been ruling the north of England with firm efficiency, and he claimed to have uncovered a conspiracy to seize control of the new King. He took charge of his nephew and escorted him back to London where, after a spell in the bishop's palace, the young Edward V was dispatched for safekeeping into the royal apartments in the Tower. There the boy was joined on 16 June by his nine-year-old brother, Prince Richard of York.

But only ten days later, claiming that the two boys were illegitimate, Uncle Richard proclaimed himself King. It was an outlandish charge, but he was formally crowned King Richard III on 6 July 1483, and the children were never seen at liberty again. With a poignant report in the Great Chronicle of London that they were glimpsed that summer 'shooting and playing in the garden of the Tower', the young Edward V and his brother vanished from history.

Few people at the time doubted that the King had disposed of them. But there was no solid evidence of foul play until, nearly two centuries later, workmen digging at the bottom of a staircase in the Tower of London discovered a wooden chest containing the skeletons of two children. The taller child was lying on his back, with the smaller one face down on top of him. 'They were small bones of lads . . .' wrote one eyewitness, 'and there were pieces of rag and velvet about them.'

The reigning monarch of the time, Charles II, ordered an inquiry. All agreed that the skeletons must be those of the boy king Edward V and his younger brother, murdered in 1483 by their wicked uncle. In 1678 the remains were ceremonially reburied in Westminster Abbey, with full dignity, in an urn beneath a black-and-white marble altar.

But over the years historians and physicians queried the authenticity of the bones. Did they really belong to the so-called 'Princes in the Tower'? And even if they did, what proof was there that they were murdered by anybody, let alone by their uncle? By 1933 the controversy was such that King George V, grandfather of the present Queen, authorised the opening of the tomb.

The two medical experts who examined the contents came to the conclusion that the remains of the young skeletons were almost certainly those of Richard III's nephews. Both indicated a slender build, with very small finger bones. Dental evidence set the age of one at eleven to thirteen years old, the smaller at between nine and eleven. Professor W. Wright, a dental surgeon who was president of the Anatomical Society of Great Britain, declared that the structure of the jaws and other bones in both skeletons established a family link, and he further suggested that a red mark on the facial bones of the elder child was a bloodstain caused by suffocation.

The notion of the victims having been suffocated made a neat connection with the first detailed account of the boys' deaths by Sir Thomas More back in 1514. Writing thirty years after the event, More pieced his story together through first-hand research – plus a certain amount of what he honestly described as 'divining upon conjectures'. Acting on Richard's orders, he alleged, two men had crept into the princes' bedchamber about midnight, 'and suddenly lapped them up among the clothes, so bewrapped them and entangled them, keeping down by force the feather bed and pillows hard into their mouths, that within a while, smothered and stifled, their breath failing, they gave up to God their innocent souls'. More went on to describe how the murderers then buried the bodies 'at the stair foot, meetly deep under the ground, under a great heap of stones'.

We shall meet Thomas More again in a later chapter. His name has become a byword for both learning and courage in standing up for principle, and his unpublished account was written at the behest of no particular patron. While clearly disapproving of Richard III, he nonetheless made several attempts in his story to separate fact from rumour. But his research was seized on by others for commercial and political reasons – most notably by William Shakespeare, whose *Tragedy of King Richard III*, first performed in 1597, gave birth to one of the most exquisitely chilling villains of English drama: 'Conscience is but a word that cowards use . . .'

In Shakespeare's play we see the King ruthlessly order the murder of his two nephews, along with the deaths of a whole catalogue of other rivals and opponents – actually uttering at one point the immortal words 'Off with his head!' The evil that festers in the usurper's mind is graphically symbolised by his twisted and deformed body, reflecting sixteenth-century superstitions that Richard spent a full two years in his mother's womb, before emerging with teeth fully developed, a mane of black hair and a hideously hunched back.

In reality, King Richard III was lean and athletic. His portraits show quite a handsome-looking man, who may possibly have carried one shoulder a little higher than the other but who was certainly not the crookback of legend. Modern X-rays show that the higher shoulder in one portrait was painted in afterwards. He was a devout Christian – something of a Puritan. He was an efficient administrator. And while he was certainly ruthless in sweeping aside those who stood in his path to the throne – including his helpless nephews – he was not the hissing psychopath of Shakespeare's depiction. The popular image of 'Crookback Dick' is quite certainly a defamation – one of history's most successful hatchet jobs – and it is not surprising that over the centuries people have come to Richard's defence. Founded in 1924, the Fellowship of the White Boar, now known as the Richard III Society, has become the most thriving historical club in the entire English-speaking world, with branches in Britain and North America.

In a testament to the English sense of fair play, the Ricardians, as they call themselves, campaign tirelessly to rescue their hero's reputation, and central to their argument is the absence of solid evidence linking Richard III directly to the disappearance of his nephews. More himself wrote, for example, that, having initially been buried beneath the staircase in the Tower, the princes' bodies were later dug up and reburied some distance away. So, argue the Ricardians, the skeletons discovered in the 1670s could not possibly have been the princes – who might even have escaped from the Tower.

As for the 'experts' of 1933, their techniques do not stand modern forensic scrutiny. To take one instance, there is no possibility that a single stain on an ancient bone could be plausibly linked to suffocation. In 1984 no less than four hours of television were devoted to a court-room inquest and trial in which this evidence and much more was minutely dissected and argued over by prominent lawyers and histo-rians. Did Richard III murder the Princes in the Tower? The jury reached a verdict of 'not guilty'.

The debate will doubtless go on for ever – or, at least, until some conclusive new evidence is discovered. Modern DNA analysis could determine, for example, whether or not the bones that have lain in Westminster Abbey since 1678 are genetically linked to those of the boys' father, Edward IV, lying for over five centuries in his tomb at Windsor – though that would not tell us who disposed of the children.

Richard III's contemporaries had little doubt: 'There was much whispering among the people,' recorded the Great Chronicle, 'that the king had put the children of King Edward to death.'

'I saw men burst into tears when mention was made of [the boy king] after his removal from men's sight,' wrote the Italian traveller, Dominic Mancini, 'and already there was suspicion that he had been done away with.'

Medieval folk were not surprised by skulduggery and death at the top. In the previous two centuries England had seen three kings deposed (Edward II, Richard II, Henry VI), and all were subsequently disposed of in sinister circumstances. But to eliminate children – and your own brother's children – went one big step beyond that. Even if the physical evidence to convict Richard III of murder was missing, he was guilty of appalling neglect, for he had had a duty of care to his nephews. When it came to explaining what had happened to them, he never even tried to offer a cover story.

In any case, history's debate over the 'Princes in the Tower' lets Richard off too lightly. The younger boy was indeed a prince, but the elder one, Edward V, was a properly proclaimed and fully acknowl-edged king, until his uncle went riding out to meet him at Stony Stratford on that late spring day in 1483. Richard might wriggle off the hook of modern TV justice. But he was found guilty in the court of his own times, and he was soon made to pay the full penalty.

THE CAT AND THE RAT
1484

EUROPE WAS SCANDALISED BY RICHARD III'S SEIZURE OF power. 'See what has happened in England since the death of King Edward,' declared Guillaume de Rochefort, the Chancellor of France, to the Estates-General, France's Parliament, in a speech that positively oozed gloating disapproval. 'His children, already big and courageous, have been slaughtered with impunity, and their murderer, with the sup-port of the people, has received the crown.'

In fact, the support of England's people for their self-appointed monarch was anything but whole-hearted. The opening months of Richard's reign, as he disposed of his critics and enemies, saw five exe-cutions, and this made London an uneasy place to be. 'There is much trouble,' reported one newsletter to the provinces, 'and every man doubts the other.'

The new king's favourites ruled the roost, and Richard's roster of unpopular sidekicks prompted a famous piece of doggerel:

> *The Cat, the Rat, and Lovell our Dog*
> *Rule all England under the Hog.*

The Cat was Sir William Catesby, a sharp-witted lawyer who was

Speaker of the House of Commons – his job it was to make sure that MPs toed the line with the new regime. The Rat was Sir Richard Ratcliffe, one of Richard's oldest cronies; Francis, Lord Lovell, who had a silver dog on his crest, had grown up with Richard in the household of Warwick the Kingmaker; and the Hog was Richard himself – a derisive reference to the white boar of his crest.

Today it is our sacred right to make fun of our rulers. Satirists and cheeky impersonators make up a major branch of the entertainment business, sometimes becoming so famous in their own right that they outshine the national leaders they deride. But things were very different in 1484, when the authorities tracked down Sir William Collingbourne, the Wiltshire gentleman who had dared pen the scornful verse that had ended up pinned to the door of St Paul's Cathedral. Collingbourne was one of several West-Countrymen accused of plotting rebellion, and while the others were spared, the lampooner received special treatment for his 'rhyme [in] derision of the king and his council'. He was strung up on the gallows, then cut down while still breathing, to be castrated and disembowelled.

To his credit, Collingbourne seems to have retained his sense of humour to the end. 'Oh Lord Jesus, yet more trouble,' he sighed, as the executioner reached inside his body to yank out his intestines.

THE BATTLE OF BOSWORTH FIELD
1485

ONE DAY IN THE SUMMER OF 1485, THE FRENCH chronicler Philippe de Commynes encountered Henry Tudor at the court of the King of France. It was the young Welshman's latest port of call in more than twenty years of exile. Moving from castle to castle across Brittany and France, he knew what it was to live from hand to mouth. From the time he was five years old, Henry told the Frenchman, he 'had always been a fugitive or a prisoner'.

Now all this was about to change. With his faithful uncle Jasper Tudor beside him, Henry was preparing his bid for the English throne. Since Richard III had seized power two years earlier, an increasing trickle of Englishmen had been making their way across the Channel to throw in their lot with the young man whose descent through his mother Lady Margaret Beaufort – and, to a lesser extent, through his grandfather Owen's romantic marriage to Queen Catherine of France – made Henry the best alternative to Richard.

On 1 August Henry set sail with a force of a thousand or so soldiers, including a group of French pikemen he was paying with borrowed funds. They were heading for the south-west tip of Wales, Jasper's home territory, where Henry himself had been born, and they dropped anchor in Milford Haven on Sunday the 7th. Their plan was to head north in a loop across Wales, gathering support as they marched. Local poets, we are told, had been primed to proclaim the coming of *y mab darogan*, 'the man of destiny'.

In the event, the response was far from overwhelming. Few Welshmen were willing to risk their lives on Henry's threadbare enterprise, and when he reached Shrewsbury and the English Midlands there was further disappointment. Henry had been counting on the support of his stepfather, his mother's third husband Thomas, Lord Stanley. But anticipating such a move, Richard III had seized Stanley's eldest son and was holding him hostage.

The Stanley family certainly had the power to determine the course of the forthcoming conflict – they were the major magnates in the area. But they had not achieved their standing by taking chances. In battle, they had a history of holding back their troops till the very last possible moment – and in the high summer of 1485 this was as far as they were prepared to go for young Henry. When the armies of Henry Tudor and Richard III finally confronted each other on Monday 22 August, Henry's forces were considerably outnumbered by those of the King – though Richard's army also lacked the reinforcements he had been promised, with the Stanleys keeping their troops on the side.

Tradition has set the momentous Battle of Bosworth Field not far from Leicester. But modern research suggests that the armies may have clashed several miles further west near the modern A5 and the village of Mancetter, just north of Coventry, where Boadicea made her last stand fourteen hundred years earlier. The A5 follows the great curve of Watling Street, the Roman road connecting London with north Wales. So as Henry's pikemen made their uncertain way towards Richard's army, they were tracing the route of the Roman legions.

By one account, Richard was plagued by bad dreams and premonitions on the night before the battle. But he put on a brave face. He clad himself ostentatiously in glorious kingly armour, setting the gold circlet of the crown over his helmet. Then, when he caught sight of his rival's standard at the back of the Tudor army, he launched a cavalry charge directly at it.

'This day I will die as a king,' he cried, 'or win.'

There is some speculation as to why Henry was stationed to the rear of his men. The cautious claimant seems to have had an eye to cutting his losses if the battle went against him – he had left his uncle, Jasper, even further to the rear to cover his getaway. But Henry was saved by his French pikemen, who presented Richard's charging horsemen with a tactic never before seen in England. Swiftly, they formed their five-metre-plus steel-headed staves into a bristling defensive wall around their leader, and as Richard's cavalry hit the pike wall, the King was unhorsed. An eyewitness account by one of the mercenaries, written the day after the battle and recently rediscovered in a nineteenth-century transcription, describes Richard crying out in rage and frustration: 'These French traitors are today the cause of our realm's ruin!'

This seems to have been the moment that prompted the Stanleys, at last, to intervene. Cagey as ever, Lord Stanley himself continued to hold back, but his brother Sir William deftly moved his troops across the battlefield, overpowering Richard's soldiers and cornering the King. Richard fought on, bravely refusing his friends' offer of a horse on which to flee.

'A horse! A horse! My kingdom for a horse!' Shakespeare's *Tragedy of King Richard III* dramatically portrays the hunchback monarch screaming for a fresh mount to carry him to the personal showdown he craved with Henry Tudor. And in this depiction of defiant courage, the playwright finally does right by the King. By most eyewitness and contemporary accounts, Richard fought to the very last, until he was finally overpowered and cut down, his crown rolling off his helmet as he fell. Sir William Stanley picked up the gold circlet and placed it on Henry Tudor's head. 'Sir, here I make you King of England.'

As always after a battle, the victors turned to plunder. Stanley was allowed to take whatever he wished from the dead king's tent – he picked out a set of royal tapestries for the Stanley residence, enduring evidence of the family's decisive, if less than heroic, doings on Bosworth Field. Richard's miniature Book of Hours, his beautifully illustrated personal prayer book, went to Henry's mother Lady Margaret – while Henry himself chose to keep the delicate gold crown.

Richard's corpse, meanwhile, was stripped of all clothing – 'naught being left about him so much as would cover his privy member'. The body was then slung over a horse, with arms and legs hanging down on both sides, 'trussed . . . as a hog or other vile beast and so all bespattered with mire and filth'. He was taken to the Greyfriars Church at Leicester, and there he was buried 'without any pomp or solemn funeral'.

Five decades later the tomb was broken open when the friary was destroyed during the Dissolution of the Monasteries. To this day, the bones that are said to have belonged to the little Princes in the Tower rest in honour in Westminster Abbey. But sometime in the 1530s the bones of Richard III were thrown into a river in Leicestershire.

DOUBLE TROUBLE
1486-99

ON 18 JANUARY 1486 THE NEW KING HENRY VII, THE twenty-eight-year-old victor of Bosworth, married nineteen-year-old Princess Elizabeth of York, the elder sister of the tragic Princes in the Tower. Plotted by Henry's mother, Margaret Beaufort, the marriage was a step towards mending the bitter and bloodstained rift between the House of Lancaster and the House of York.

But the mysterious disappearance of the little princes had left a curious legacy. No one could be quite sure what had happened to them – and, if they *had* been murdered, who was to blame. Despite the suspicion attaching to Richard III, there were no bodies and no closure: the poison had not been drawn. For a dozen years England was haunted by conspiracy theories made flesh. It was the age of the pretenders.

The first was Lambert Simnel, an Oxford tradesman's son who became the tool of Richard Symonds, an ambitious local priest. Symonds took his twelve-year-old protégé to Ireland, claiming that Simnel was Edward, Earl of Warwick, the young nephew of Richard III (see Wars of the Roses family tree, p. xvi). On Whit Sunday 1487 'King Edward VI' was crowned by dissident Irish noblemen in Dublin.

The real Edward was in the Tower of London. Henry had made it a priority to put Warwick away when he came to the throne, and now he lost no time in bringing him out to be paraded through the streets of London. When Simnel and his Irish followers landed at Furness in Lancashire later that June, Henry marched north to defeat them in a rerun of the previous years of disorder.

But the Tudor response in victory was a new departure. Instead of executing 'Edward VI', Henry gave Simnel a job in the royal kitchens, turning the spit that roasted the royal ox. The boy made such a good job of his duties as a scullion that he rapidly earned promotion, rising to take care of Henry's beloved hunting hawks and finishing up as royal falconer.

In his humane, rather humorous treatment of Lambert Simnel, Henry was making a point – this new king did not kill children. He even spared the boy's Svengali, Symonds, who had planned to have himself made Archbishop of Canterbury. But Henry might have done better to be more severe, for within a few years he was confronted with another pretender. This one declared himself to be Richard, Duke of York, the younger of the Princes in the Tower. Apparently, he had made a miraculous escape following his elder brother's murder and had now returned to claim the throne.

'King Richard IV' – by this account, Henry's brother-in-law – would later confess that he was, in fact, one Pierquin Wesbecque (Perkin Warbeck) from Tournai in the Netherlands, the son of a boat-man. But it suited all manner of people to believe he was indeed the nephew of Richard III, and he did the rounds of Henry's enemies and neighbours, being treated to banquets and hunting excursions and given money to buy troops. King James IV of Scotland even found him an attractive wife, his own cousin Lady Katherine Gordon.

This pretender's six-year odyssey came to grief in the autumn of 1497, after a failed attempt to raise the West Country against Henry. Captured at Beaulieu in Hampshire, he finally admitted his humble origins. But having heard his confession, Henry again took a concil-iatory line, inviting Warbeck and his charming Scottish wife to join his court. It was as if the King was enjoying the fairytale himself. Even when Warbeck tried to escape the following summer, Henry was con-tent merely to put him in the stocks and have him repeat his confession. It was not until Warbeck tried to escape yet again that the King lost patience. On 23 November 1499 the false claimant was hanged, and a few days later the true claimant, the hapless Earl of Warwick, was beheaded on Tower Hill.

Henry gave Warbeck's noble widow a pension and made her lady-in-waiting to the Queen. Lady Katherine Gordon became quite a figure at the Tudor court, marrying no fewer than three more husbands and surviving until 1537. But the King's sharp dose of reality in 1499 had the desired effect – no more pretenders.

FISH 'N' SHIPS
1497

In fourteen hundred ninety-two, Columbus sailed the ocean blue
And found this land, land of the Free, beloved by you, beloved by me.

FOURTEEN NINETY-TWO IS THE FAMOUS DATE WHEN Christopher Columbus is credited by history with the 'discovery' of America. But modern archaeologists have shown that the Vikings must have crossed the Atlantic long before him. The remains of Viking homes, cooking pits and metal ornaments on the island of Newfoundland have been dated to around the year 1000. And there is every reason to believe that Columbus was also preceded to the Americas by several shiploads of weather-beaten Englishmen.

The men had set sail from Bristol, heading out from the prosperous port on the River Avon in the west of England, first towards Ireland, then further westwards into the Atlantic. They were fishermen, searching for cod that they could salt and trade for wine, and they brought back tales of remote islands that they called 'The Isle of the Seven Cities' and 'The Isle of Brasil'. Late in the 1490s an English merchant called John Day reported their discoveries to the 'Grand Admiral' of Spain – the *Almirante Major* – who may have been Columbus himself. In a letter that was misfiled for centuries in the National Archives at Simancas, Day pointed out that the New World across the Atlantic had, in fact, already been 'found and discovered in other times by the men of Bristol . . . as your Lordship knows'.

The problem with this English claim to transatlantic discovery is that these West Country fishermen had kept their find to themselves, as cagey fishermen tend to do. Harbour records make clear that in the 1480s, if not earlier, ships from Bristol had located the fabulously fecund Grand Banks fishing grounds that lie off New England and Newfoundland. But they did not wish to attract competitors or poachers. Their only interest in terra firma of any sort was as a landmark to guide them to the fishing waters. So Christopher Columbus has retained the glory for 1492 – and in any case, 'discovery' now seems the wrong word for landing on a continent that was already occupied by hundreds of thousands, if not millions, of indigenous American Indians.

When a contingent of Bristolians did finally set foot in America in a properly documented fashion, they did so under royal patronage. Around 1494 an Italian navigator, Zuan Caboto, arrived at the court of King Henry VII. Like Columbus, Caboto came from Genoa and he was a skilled propagandist for the exploding world of discovery. Brandishing charts and an impressive globe, he persuaded Henry to grant him a charter to 'seeke out, discover and finde whatsoever isles, countries, regions or provinces of heathens and infidels . . . which before this time have been unknown to all Christians'.

The prudent king was not about to invest any of his own money in the project. On the contrary, royal approval carried a price tag – 20 per cent of the profits. But Zuan, now 'John Cabot', was granted permanent tax exemption on whatever he might bring back from the New World for himself. So he went down to Bristol in search of investors. There he was able to fit out a small wooden sailing ship, the *Matthew*, with a crew of eighteen, most of them 'hearty Bristol sailors'.

It might seem surprising that the clannish West-Countrymen should team up with an Italian, an outsider, but there was a fraternity among those who risked their lives on the mysterious western ocean. Cabot was skilled in the latest navigational techniques using the stars, and he needed a crew who would not lose their nerve when out of sight of land for four weeks or more.

In the event, the journey took five. On 24 June 1497, thirty-five days after leaving England, the *Matthew* sighted land and dropped anchor somewhere off the coast of modern Newfoundland, Labrador or Nova Scotia. Cautiously, Cabot and his landing party rowed ashore, where they found the remains of a fire, some snares set for game, a needle for making nets and a trail that headed inland. Obviously, there were humans around; but Cabot was not keen to meet them. 'Since he was with just a few people,' John Day later explained in his letter to the Spanish Grand Admiral, 'he did not dare advance inland beyond the shooting distance of a crossbow.'

The landing party planted four banners: the arms of St George, on behalf of King Henry VII; a papal banner on behalf of the Pope; the flag of Venice, since Cabot had taken Venetian citizenship; and a cross intended for the local 'heathens and infidels'. Then the English mariners set off down the coast in pursuit of their great passion: the waters were 'swarming with fish', Cabot later boasted to the Milanese Ambassador, and there was no need of a net to catch them; they could just lean over the ship's rail and 'let down baskets with a stone'.

Heading for home around the middle of July, captain and crew used the same method that had got them there – the so-called 'dead reckoning'. This involved fixing on one particular angle to the stars and preserving that angle as they sailed, effectively staying on one line of latitude as they moved around the curve of the globe. Contrary to received wisdom, fifteenth-century sailors did not believe the world was flat. Indeed, its roundness was the basis of their adventurous navigation techniques.

By 23 August, Cabot was back in London, reporting on his finds to the King who, never careless with his money, doled out an immediate ten pounds – about four times the average annual wage at the time. Henry also granted the mariner an annual pension of twenty pounds for life, to be paid by the port of Bristol out of its customs receipts. But John Cabot did not live to claim it. The next year he set out on another expedition westwards where, as the Tudor historian Polydore Vergil heartlessly put it, the 'newe founde lande' he discovered was 'nowhere but on the very bottom of the ocean'. Cabot and his ship vanished without trace.

But his death did not discourage other adventurers. In 1501 Henry VII commissioned six more Bristolians to head westwards, and they returned with Arctic hunting falcons – perhaps the King gave them to Lambert Simnel to train – along with a few of the native inhabitants that Cabot had been careful to avoid encountering four years earlier: 'They were clothed in beasts' skins and ate raw flesh,' recorded one awestruck chronicler, 'and spake such speech that no man could understand them . . . In their demeanour [they were] like . . . brute beasts.'

Falcons, fish and Eskimos – as the Inuit people came to be called at the end of the sixteenth century – were interesting enough, but they bore no comparison to the gold, jewels and, above all, silver that Spain would soon be carrying home in heaving galleon-loads from the southerly lands discovered by Columbus. It would be more than seventy years before England made a determined effort to settle the northern parts of the continent that, after 1507, would be described on the maps as 'America'.

But the Eskimos settled in nicely, thank you. They evidently found themselves a tailor, for just two years after they had first appeared at Henry's court in their animal skins, England's first New World immigrants were spotted by a chronicler strolling around the Palace of Westminster, 'apparelled after the manner of Englishmen'. They were no longer 'brute beasts', he admitted – 'I could not discern [them] from Englishmen.'

FORK IN, FORK OUT
1500

FOR MORE THAN HALF HIS REIGN, HENRY VII'S CHIEF minister was Cardinal John Morton, Archbishop of Canterbury and one of the great church statesmen who shaped England's story during the Middle Ages. Often of lowly birth, these clever individuals rose through the meritocratic system of ecclesiastical education to make their names – in Morton's case, via the challenging task of national fund-raising.

When collecting money for the King, Morton's commissioners are said to have confronted their targets with a truly undodgeable means test. If a likely customer appeared prosperous, he obviously had surplus funds to contribute to the King's coffers. If, on the other hand, he lived modestly, he must have been stashing his wealth away. Either way the victim was compelled to pay – impaled, as it were, upon one or other of the twin prongs of a pitchfork.

Like many of history's chestnuts, the facts behind what came to be known as 'Morton's Fork' are not quite as neat as the story. It was more than 130 years later that the statesman-philosopher Francis Bacon coined the phrase, and the documents of the time make clear that Morton did not wield the pitchfork personally. But the cardinal certainly did work hard to satisfy the appetite of a money-hungry monarch. As well as helping Henry to tighten up parliamentary taxation, he presided over the collection of 'benevolences' – 'voluntary' wealth taxes that invited subjects to show their goodwill towards the King. Not surprisingly, these forced loans soon became known as 'malevolences', and Henry himself developed a reputation as a miser. 'In his later days,' wrote the normally loyal Polydore Vergil, 'all [his] virtues were obscured by avarice.'

Henry VII's account ledgers would seem to bear this out. At the foot of page after page are the royal initials, scratched by the careful bookkeeper monarch as he ran his finger down the columns. But Henry could spend lavishly when he wanted to, particularly when it came to making his kingship visibly magnificent. In November 1501 he spent £14,000 (over £8 million today) on jewels alone for the wedding in St Paul's Cathedral of his eldest son Arthur to Katherine of Aragon, daughter of Ferdinand and Isabella of Spain. Ten days of tournaments were staged at Westminster and the feasting went on night after night beneath the hammer-beam roof of the Great Hall, the walls hung with the costliest cloth of Arras.

Two years later Henry splashed out again when he sent his daughter Margaret north to marry King James IV of Scotland, with an escort of two thousand horsemen, a train of magnificently clad noblemen and £16,000 (another £9 million or so) in jewels. Henry VII's marriage-broking proved portentous. It was Margaret's marriage that would one day bring the Stuart dynasty to England, while Katherine of Aragon, following the death of Arthur in 1502, would be passed on as wife to his younger brother Henry, with equally historic consequences.

Henry VII had done well by England when he died, aged fifty-two, in April 1509. You can see his death mask in Westminster Abbey, his face lean and intelligent, his eyes sharp and his mouth shut, concealing the teeth which, according to contemporary description, were 'few, poor and black-stained'. He lies in splendour in the magnificent chapel that he built at the south end of the abbey – another notable item of dynastic extravagance. Beside him lies his wife Elizabeth of York, and not far away, his mother Lady Margaret Beaufort, who had schemed so hard and faithfully to bring her Tudor son to power.

The soaring stone pillars of the chapel are decorated with the Beaufort portcullis and with the double rose that would become the symbol of the Tudors, giving graphic shape to the healing, but over-simplified, myth that the warring flowers, red and white, had been melded into a flourishing new hybrid. One of the chapel's stained-glass windows shows a crown wreathed in a thorn bush, and later legend relates how Henry actually plucked his crown from such a bush at Bosworth. In fact, contemporary accounts of the battle made no mention of bushes – they describe the crown as simply being picked up off the ground. But it is fair enough to think of Henry as the King who redeemed England from a thorny situation.

KING HENRY VIII'S 'GREAT MATTER'

1509–33

AFTER THE PENNY-PINCHING WAYS OF HENRY VII, THE profligate glamour of his red-blooded, redheaded son, the new King Henry VIII, exploded over England like a sunburst. Just seventeen years old, the shapely and athletic young monarch was the nation's sporting hero.

'It is the prettiest thing in the world to see him play,' purred an admirer of Henry's exertions at tennis, 'his fair skin glowing through a shirt of the finest texture.' When the young King, tall and energetic, joined the royal bowmen for target practice, his arrow 'cleft the mark in the middle and surpassed them all'. He was a superlative horseman, a champion in the jousts, an all-round wrestler – and when the music started, he could pluck a mean string on the lute. Recent research has revealed that Henry may even have played football, a game usually considered too rough and common for the well born. In February 2004 a fresh look at the inventory of his Great Wardrobe discovered that alongside forty-five pairs of velvet shoes the King kept a pair of purpose-made football boots.

The other side of bluff King Hal was evident within three days of his accession. With the vicious eye for a scapegoat that was to characterise his ruling style, the King authorised the show trials of Richard Empson and Edmund Dudley, two of his father's most effective and unpopular money-raisers. The pair had done nothing worse than carry out royal orders and line their own pockets. But Henry had both men executed – then promptly embarked on a spending spree with his father's carefully hoarded treasure. He had an insatiable capacity for enjoying himself. Masques, mummeries, jousts, pageants – the festivities went on for days when Henry was crowned in June 1509 alongside his fetching and prestigious new Spanish wife Katherine of Aragon.

Four years older than Henry, Katherine was embarking on her second marriage. Having married Henry's brother Arthur in November 1501, she had found herself widowed before that winter was out. Young Henry had stepped forward to take Arthur's place both as Prince of Wales and as Katherine's betrothed, and when he came to the throne he made their marriage his first order of personal business. The couple exchanged vows and rings in a private ceremony at Greenwich on 11 June 1509, and set about the happy process of procreation. When, after one miscarriage, a son was born on New Year's Day 1511, Henry's joy knew no bounds. As bonfires were lit and salutes cannonaded from the Tower, the proud father staged a vast tournament, mingling with the crowds and delightedly allowing them to tear off as souvenirs the splendid gold letters 'H' and 'K' that adorned his clothes.

But the baby boy, who had been christened Henry, died within two months, and disappointment would prove the pattern of Katherine's childbearing. One daughter, Mary, born in 1516, was the only healthy survivor of a succession of ill-fated pregnancies, births and stillbirths, and after ten years of marriage without a male heir, Henry came to ponder on the reasons for God's displeasure.

He thought he found his answer in the Bible. 'Thou shalt not uncover the nakedness of thy brother's wife,' read chapter 18 of the Old Testament Book of Leviticus – and two chapters later, the consequences were set out clearly: 'If a man shall take his brother's wife, it is an unclean thing . . . they shall be childless.' This apparently firm prohibition had been overruled at the time of Henry and Katherine's betrothal in 1504 by special licence from the Pope, who based his action on the contradictory instruction in the Book of Deuteronomy that it was a man's duty to take his brother's widow 'and raise up seed for his brother'. Katherine, for her part, firmly maintained that she was free to marry Henry because her five-month marriage to the fifteen-year-old Arthur had never been consummated.

But as Katherine remained childless through the 1520s, her discontented husband started to lend a ready ear to those who suggested that his wife could easily have been lying. 'Bring me a cup of ale,' brother Arthur was said to have cried out contentedly on the first morning of his married life, 'I have been this night in the midst of Spain!'

To Henry the solution seemed simple. Since a pope had fixed his improper, heirless marriage to Katherine, a pope should now unfix it, freeing the English King to take the fertile young wife his dynastic duty required – and by the spring of 1527 the thirty-six-year-old Henry knew exactly who that wife should be. He had fallen in love with Anne Boleyn, a self-assured beauty ten years or so his junior, notable for a pair of mesmeric dark eyes and a steely sense of purpose.

But as Henry set his mind to making a new marriage, events in Italy made it highly unlikely that the Pope would give him any help. In May that year Rome was captured and sacked by the troops of Charles V, the powerful Habsburg ruler who was also Katherine's nephew. Charles controlled Spain, the Netherlands, much of Germany and Italy – and now the Pope. There was no way he would allow his aunt to be humiliatingly cast aside by the King of England.

Until now Henry had been content to leave the handling of his divorce to Cardinal Thomas Wolsey, the talented church statesman who ran the country for him, as Cardinal Morton had taken care of business for his father. But the normally competent cardinal was left helpless after the shift of power in Rome – and he had made the mistake of offending the now powerful Anne Boleyn. He called her, among other things, the 'night crow'. After fourteen years of effectively running England, Wolsey was disgraced. Charged with treason, he died from the shock. Henry took over Hampton Court, the magnificent palace the portly cardinal had built for himself down the Thames from Richmond – and started lending an ear to advisers who were considerably more Popo-sceptic.

Chief among these was Anne herself, who had a radical taste in reading. Sometime in 1530 she placed in Henry's hands a copy of the recently published *Obedience of a Christian Man* by the reformer William Tyndale, a controversial little volume that had been denounced as 'a holy boke of disobedyence' by Thomas More, Wolsey's successor as Lord Chancellor. *How Christian Rulers Ought to Govern* was Tyndale's subtitle, and he argued that, since the Bible made no mention of the Pope (nor of bishops, abbots, church courts or of the whole earthly edifice of church power and glory), the Church should be governed like the state, by a 'true Christian prince' – without interference from the so-called 'Bishop of Rome'.

'This book is for me and for all Kings to read,' mused Henry – here was the solution to his troublesome 'Great Matter'. Why should the King not effectively award himself his own divorce, as governor of the English Church, in order to secure the heir that his country needed?

'England cares nothing for popes,' Anne's brother George Boleyn would declare to a papal official visiting England in the summer of 1530. 'The king is absolute emperor and pope in his own kingdom.'

The Boleyns were thrusting members of the rising Tudor gentry – landowners and former merchants whose personal beliefs were traditional but who had no special fondness for the Pope, and still less for the power and privileges of the clergy with their unearned wealth and their special exemptions from the law. Scrounging was the Church's speciality, according to a scurrilous tract of the time, *A Supplication for the Beggars*, which pretended to be a petition from the 'Beggars of England' to the King, complaining that crafty churchmen were putting them out of business by begging so much better than they could. Stealing land, money and even, on occasion, the virtue of good men's wives and daughters, the clerics had filched 'the whole realm', complained the *Supplication*.

This jeering anticlerical sentiment was mobilised in the autumn of 1529, when Parliament gathered for what was to prove an historic series of sessions. Discontented laymen were invited to draw up lists of their grievances against the clergy, and the result, finally codified in May 1532, was a formidable roundup of just about everything that people found irritating about the often complacent and greedy ways of the all-too-earthly Church.

It was exactly what the King wanted to hear. 'We thought that the clergy of our realm had been our subjects wholly,' declared Henry menacingly as he studied the list of complaints. 'But now we have well perceived that they be but half our subjects.'

Here was an area where the King and a fair number of the merchants, lawyers, country gentlemen and landed magnates who dominated Parliament clearly felt as one. England, they argued, should have control over its own Church – and between 1529 and 1536 Parliament passed a series of laws to accomplish that, transferring the many aspects of church life and business to the Crown.

The immediate consequence was that Henry was able to marry Anne and cast off Katherine. But the long-term consequence of these new laws went far beyond Henry and his need for a son. 'This realm of England is an empire . . .' declared the Act in Restraint of Appeals of 1533, 'governed by one supreme head and king . . . furnished with plenary, whole and entire power . . . without restraint or provocation to any foreign princes or potentates of the world'.

Henry's 'Great Matter' turned out to be greater than anyone, including himself, had guessed. English kings now acknowledged no superior under God on earth.

'LET THERE BE LIGHT' –
WILLIAM TYNDALE AND
THE ENGLISH BIBLE
1525

Henry VIII's historic break with Rome was fundamentally about earthly power, not spiritual belief. Even while Henry was demolishing the Pope's authority over the English Church in the early 1530s, a Sunday service in the average English parish was still shaped by the comforting chants and Catholic rituals hallowed by the centuries.

But in Europe, belief was changing more radically. In October 1517 the rebellious German monk Martin Luther, a miner's son turned theologian and philosophy professor, had nailed his famous ninety-five theses – or 'propositions' – to the church door in Wittenberg in Saxony. Luther was appalled by the materialism of the Roman Church, and his ninety-five propositions were a particular attack on the sale of 'indulgences', Church-approved coupons that people purchased in the belief that they were being let off their sins – printed tickets to heaven. The Pope had no authority to forgive people's sins, argued Luther, let alone offer forgiveness for sale, like bread or beer. It was faith alone that would bring salvation, and men had no need of priests to mediate with God. Believers could commune directly with their Maker through prayer, and by reading God's word in the Bible. Within a few years several dozen of Germany's duchies and principalities had thrown off papal authority and signed up to Luther's protests and to his call for reform – generating the movement that historians would later call the Protestant Reformation.

Henry VIII was outraged. He thought that Luther's views undermined civil obedience, and left people with no reason to be good. When Luther's message reached England, the King was still on warm terms with the Pope, and with the help of Thomas More he fired off an indignant diatribe against the heretical German, earning himself the title *Fidei Defensor*, 'Defender of the Faith'. To this day the abbreviations *Fid. Def.*, or *F.D.*, appear on the face of every English coin, commemorating the title by which in 1521, only a decade before the break with Rome, the grateful Pope declared Henry his favourite and most faithful prince in Europe. On Henry's orders, Cardinal Wolsey organised public burnings of Luther's books, and even hunted down the reformer's translation of the New Testament into German.

The Roman Church's own version of the Bible was in Latin – the fourth-century Latin of St Jerome, whose precise meaning might be accessible to learned priests and scholars but which floated sonorously over the heads of most churchgoers, rather like a magical incantation, heavy on comfort and light on explanation. The Roman priesthood's control over faith relied heavily on its virtual monopoly of Latin, and most churchmen felt deeply threatened by the idea of people reading the Bible in their own language and interpreting it for themselves.

But this was precisely the ambition of the young priest, William Tyndale, who was working in Gloucestershire in the early 1520s. This area, on the border with Wales, had long been a stronghold of the Lollards, the prayer-mumbling disciples of John Wycliffe who, back in the 1380s, had argued that the Bible should be made accessible to ordinary people in their own tongue. 'If God spare my life,' declared Tyndale in a heated argument with an establishment cleric who had railed against the translating of the Bible, ''ere many years, I wyl cause a boye that dryveth the plough, shall know more the Scripture than thou dost.'

The talented and scholarly Tyndale had command of eight languages, notably Greek and Hebrew, which were virtually unknown in England at this time. He was also blessed with an extraordinary ability to create poetic phrases in his native tongue, and his memorable translations live on to this day – 'the salt of the earth', 'signs of the times', 'the powers that be' and even 'bald as a coot' we owe to William Tyndale. All these vibrant expressions flowed from his pen as, through the 1520s, he laboured to render the word of God into ploughboy language. When he could not find the right word, he invented it –

'scapegoat' and 'broken-hearted' are two of his coinages. As he translated, he was helping to shape the very rhythm and thought patterns of English: 'eat drink and be merry' – 'am I my brother's keeper?' – 'fight the good fight' – 'blessed are the meek for they shall inherit the earth' . . .

To avoid the wrath of Wolsey, who was having heretics whipped and imprisoned, Tyndale had to compose his fine phrases abroad. In 1524 he travelled to Europe, where he dodged from printing press to printing press in cities like Hamburg and Brussels – shadowed by the cardinal's agents, who had identified this prolific wordsmith as a home-grown heretic quite as dangerous as Luther. In 1526, Tyndale managed to get three thousand copies of his New Testament printed in the German city of Worms, and within months the books were circulating among freethinkers in England, smuggled in by Hull sailors in casks of wax and grain. It was four years later that a copy of Tyndale's *Obedience of a Christian Man* reached Anne Boleyn, providing encouragement for Henry's break from the Pope.

But then in 1530, Tyndale dared to address the great question of the King's marriage from a biblical point of view, and with the perversity of the dyed-in-the-wool nonconformist he concluded in his book *The Practice of Prelates* that the Bible did *not* authorise Henry to jettison his wife.

It was his death sentence. The growing number of reformers among the English clergy were advocating the use of the Bible in English, and Tyndale's accurate and powerful translation was the obvious version to use. But the King was infuriated by Tyndale's criticism of his divorce and of his proposed marriage to Anne. The English agents kept up their pursuit of the fugitive, and in May 1535 they got their man. Now aged about forty, he was captured in Antwerp, to be condemned as a heretic and sentenced to be burned to death.

On 6 October 1536, William Tyndale was led out to his execution. As a small token of mercy he was granted the kindness of being strangled in the moments before the fire was lit. But the executioner bungled the tightening of the rope, painfully crushing Tyndale's throat while leaving him still alive as the flames licked around him.

'Lord, open the King of England's eyes!' cried the reformer as he died.

The executioner piled on more fuel until the body was totally consumed, since the purpose of burning heretics was to reduce them to ashes that could be thrown to the winds – no trace of their presence should be left on earth. But William Tyndale left more than ashes: 'In the begynnynge was the worde and the worde was with God and the worde was God . . . In it was lyfe and the lyfe was the light of men. And the light shyneth in the darknes, but the darknes comprehended it not.'

THOMAS MORE AND HIS WONDERFUL 'NO-PLACE'

1535

YOUNG HENRY VIII LOVED THE COMPANY OF THE LEARNED and witty Thomas More. The King would take him up on to the roof of his palace to gaze skywards and 'consider with him the diversities, courses, motions and operations of the stars'. Travelling in his barge down the Thames one day, he decided to drop in unexpectedly on the Mores' sprawling riverside home in Chelsea. He invited himself for dinner, then walked in the garden with his host 'by the space of an hour, holding his arm about his neck'.

More's son-in-law William Roper was much impressed by this intimacy with the King, but More himself had no illusions. 'Son Roper, I may tell thee . . .' he confided, 'if my head could win His Majesty a castle in France it should not fail to go.'

Thomas More was literally a Renaissance man, playing his own part in the great 're-birthing' of the fifteenth and sixteenth centuries. South of the Alps, the Renaissance was famously embodied by such artists as Michelangelo and Leonardo. In the north, it was the so-called 'Christian humanists' like More and his Dutch friend Erasmus who struck sparks off each other – to memorable effect. In 1509, Erasmus dedicated his great work *In Praise of Folly* to Thomas (its Latin name, *Encomium Moriae*, was a pun on More's name). More responded with his own flight of intellect, *Utopia* – his inspired combination of the Greek words for 'no' and 'place'.

Utopia is the tale More claimed to have heard when, coming out of church one day, he bumped into an old seaman: 'his face was tanned, he had a long beard, and his cloak was hanging carelessly about him'. This philosopher-sailor had been travelling with the Italian explorer Amerigo Vespucci, after whom the Americas would shortly be named. Having chatted with More for a while about all that was presently wrong with the kingdoms of Europe, he started describing his experiences on the island of 'Utopia' where, he said, there was no shortage of life's essentials. When people went to the market, everything was free, and because of that 'there is no danger of a man's asking for more than he needs . . . since they are sure that they shall always be supplied. It is the fear of want that makes any of the whole race of animals either greedy or ravenous.'

Like space travel in our own day, the sixteenth century's voyages of discovery were stirring people's imaginations, and More's *Utopia* was a sort of science fiction, a fantasy about a super-perfect society where thoughtful people had worked out a life of benevolent equality. In this ideal 'No-Place', couples who were 'more fruitful' shared their children with those who were not so blessed, while lawyers were totally banned – they were a profession who disguised the truth, explained More, whose own wealth came from his prosperous legal practice. Living according to nature, striving for health and dying cheerfully, the Utopians offered a satirical commentary on the 'moth-eaten' laws and the hypocrisy of European society – and More himself tried to put some of Utopia's ideas into practice, encouraging his daughters to debate philosophy in front of him. 'Erudition in women is a new thing,' he wrote, 'and a reproach to the idleness of men.'

But More's visionary thinking was tethered to a deep religious conservatism – he was steadfastly loyal to the Pope and to the old ways of the Church. In the style of Thomas Becket, he wore a hair shirt beneath the glorious liveries of the public offices that he occupied – though unlike Becket, he kept his prickly garment maggot-free: it was regularly laundered by his daughter Margaret Roper. Thomas shared his royal master Henry VIII's indignation at Martin Luther and his reforming ideas, outdoing the King in his furious invective. In one diatribe, More described Luther as *merda, stercus, lutum, coenum* – shit, dung, filth, excrement. And for good measure, he then denounced the German as a drunkard, a liar, an ape and an arsehole who had been vomited on to this earth by the Antichrist.

More joined Henry's Council in 1517, the same year that Luther nailed his theses to the church door in Wittenberg, and set about waging a personal war on the new ideas for reform. He had a little jail and a set of stocks built in his garden so he could cross-question heretics personally, and he nursed a particular hatred for the translations of William Tyndale, whom he described as 'a hell-hound in the kennel of the devil'. When More got back to Chelsea after his work on the King's Council he would spend his evenings penning harangues denouncing Tyndale, while defending the traditional practices of the Church.

But while More and Tyndale might differ over popes and sacraments, they were agreed on the subject of kings' wives. More actually shared Tyndale's opinion that the Bible did not authorise Henry VIII's annulment of his marriage with Katherine – and their highly inconvenient conviction set both men on a tragic collision course with the King. When, after the disgrace of Wolsey, Henry invited Thomas to become his new Lord Chancellor, More at first refused. He could see the danger ahead. He only accepted after Henry promised not to embroil him in the divorce, leaving the 'Great Matter' to those 'whose consciences could well enough agree therein'.

But detachment became impossible as Henry's quarrel with the Pope grew more bitter. By the early 1530s royal policy was being guided by the gimlet-eyed Thomas Cromwell, a former agent of Wolsey's who, in the spring of 1534, pushed a new statute through Parliament, the Act of Succession. This required men to swear their agreement to the settlement, rejecting the rights of Katherine and her daughter Mary. When More refused to swear, he was promptly escorted to the Tower.

'By the mass, Master More,' warned the Duke of Norfolk, an old friend and one of several visitors who tried to persuade him to change his mind, 'it is perilous striving with princes . . . I would wish you somewhat to incline to the king's pleasure for, by God's body, *indignatio principis mors est* – the wrath of the king is death.'

'Is that all, my lord?' responded Thomas. 'Then in good faith is there no more difference between your Grace and me, but that I shall die today and you tomorrow.'

More was led out to the scaffold early on the morning of 6 July 1535, and he kept up his graceful, ironic humour to the end. 'I pray you, Master Lieutenant, see me safe up,' he said as he mounted the ladder, 'and [for] my coming down, let me shift for myself.'

Worn and thin from his months in prison, loose in his clothes, with a skullcap on his head and a long straggling beard, the former chancellor looked not unlike the old sailor-philosopher he had once imagined telling stories of 'No-Place' – and that name he invented for his imaginary island remains to this day the word people use when they want to describe a wonderful but impossible dream.

DIVORCED, BEHEADED, DIED ...
1533-7

ANNE BOLEYN SAILED DOWN THE THAMES TO HER coronation at the end of May 1533 in a Cleopatra's fleet of vessels. Anne herself rode in Katherine of Aragon's former barge – from which the discarded Queen's coat of arms had been hacked away – and her costume made clear the reason for her triumph. The new Queen had added 'a panel to her skirts' because she was visibly pregnant. In just four months she would be delivered of the heir for which her husband had schemed so hard.

But the child born on 7 September that year turned out to be a girl. She was christened Elizabeth, and the pre-written letters announcing

the birth made embarrassingly clear that this had not been the plan –
a last-minute stroke of the pen had made the word 'Prince' into
'Princes[s]'. The jousting that had been organised to celebrate the new
arrival was cancelled, and it was noted ominously that Henry did not
attend the christening. Anne Boleyn might 'spurn our heads off like
footballs', prophesied Thomas More, 'but it will not be long ere her
head will dance the like dance'.

When Anne's second pregnancy ended in a miscarriage in January
1536 her fate was sealed, since Tudor medical science – or the lack of
it – meant that one miscarriage might well be the first of an unbreak-
able series. This had been the case with Katherine, and once again
Henry had not been slow in lining up a possible replacement for his
non-productive Queen. He had set his cap at Jane Seymour, a soft-
spoken young woman who was as meek and submissive as Anne had
proved complicated and assertive.

Having made the Boleyn marriage possible, Thomas Cromwell was
now given the job of destroying it. Anne had always been flirtatious, and
this proved the route to her undoing. Playful glances and gestures were
interpreted as evidence of actual infidelity. Men were tortured and 'confessions' produced. A court musician pleaded guilty to adultery. Her own
brother was charged with incest. The facts were outlandish, but the servants of a Tudor government knew that 'proof' had to be found so that
the defective Queen could be condemned. As Anne Boleyn prepared to
step out on to Tower Green on 19 May 1536, the first Queen of England
ever to be executed, she seemed to have reached her own peace. 'I hear
the executioner is very good,' she said, 'and I have a little neck.' Then she
put her hands around her throat and burst out laughing.

Henry wasted no time. No sooner had he received the news of
Anne's beheading than he set off upriver on his barge to see Jane
Seymour. Engaged the next day, the couple were married ten days later,
and Jane was formally enthroned on Whit Sunday 4 June 1536 – in the
very chair where Anne had sat only five weeks earlier.

From Henry's point of view, it was third time lucky. A kindly and
level-headed woman in her late twenties, Jane worked hard to reconcile Henry with his elder daughter Mary, whose place in the succession
he had given to Anne's daughter Elizabeth, and the lottery of fertility
finally yielded the King the male heir that he wanted. At Hampton

Court on 12 October 1537, Queen Jane was delivered of a healthy baby boy, whom Henry christened Edward, after the Confessor, the patron saint of English royalty. Henry at last had the token of divine blessing he had sought.

But his wife had suffered a disastrous delivery. According to one account, she had undergone the then primitive and almost invariably fatal surgery of a Caesarean section. Other evidence suggests blood poisoning of the placenta – puerperal fever. Either way, Prince Edward's mother died after twelve days of blood loss and infection that the royal doctors were helpless to reverse.

Henry was prostrated with unaccustomed sorrow. Jane Seymour lay in state for three weeks, and then, alone of Henry's wives, she was buried in pomp and glory in St George's Chapel at Windsor. It was later said that her name was on Henry's lips when he died, and certainly his will was to direct that he should be buried beside her. When the King of France sent his congratulations on the birth of a healthy heir, Henry's reply was uncharacteristically subdued. 'Divine Providence,' he wrote, 'hath mingled my joy with the bitterness of the death of her who brought me this happiness.'

Diplomatic dispatches are seldom to be taken at their face value, still less when worded by Henry VIII. But in this case we might, perhaps, give Henry the benefit of the doubt.

THE PILGRIMAGE OF GRACE
1536

EARLY-SIXTEENTH-CENTURY LIFE WAS INTERWOVEN WITH the joy of religious rite and spectacle – effigies of saints, stained-glass windows; the washing of feet on Maundy Thursday, the 'creeping to the cross' on Good Friday. In London every Whit Sunday, doves were released from the tower of St Paul's Cathedral to symbolise the Holy Spirit winging its way to heaven. This age-old texture of symbol and ritual provided a satisfying structure to most people's lives. The English were devout folk, reported one European traveller: 'they all attend mass every day'.

The miracle of the mass – the Holy Communion service when bread and wine were offered up at the altar – was graphically described in Thomas Malory's *Morte D'Arthur*, the bestselling epic first printed and published by Caxton in 1485. As the bishop held up a wafer of bread, 'there came a figure in likeness of a child, and the visage was as red and as bright as any fire, and smote himself into the bread, that all they saw it that the bread was formed of a fleshly man'.

This was the moment of 'transubstantiation' when, according to Catholic belief, the bread and wine on the altar were literally transformed into the body and blood of Christ. It provided the awe-inspiring climax of every mass. Bells rang, incense wafted, and heads were bowed as Jesus himself, both child and 'fleshly man', descended from heaven to join that particular human congregation – to be devoured as the people ate his flesh and the priest alone drank his blood (the liquid that had once been wine was too precious to risk being passed around and spilled).

By the 1520s and 30s, the evangelical followers of Luther and Tyndale were openly scoffing at this potent but, to their mind, primitive and sacrilegious Catholic theatre. How could the Lord's sacred body be conjured up on earth by imperfect men in gaudy vestments? The exhilarating idea at the heart of the Reformation, that every man could have his own direct relationship with God, challenged the central role of the priest in religious ceremonies – and from this spiritual doubt followed material consequences. By what right did the clerics control their vast infrastructure of earthly power and possessions, notably the vast landed estates of the monasteries? The Church was by far the largest landowner in England.

In 1535 Henry VIII's chief minister, Thomas Cromwell, seized on this appetising question: if the Church was corrupted by its involvement with worldly goods, why should he not relieve it of the problem? So he sent out his 'visitors', crews of inspectors who descended on the eight hundred or so monasteries and nunneries in England and duly discovered what they were sent to find. Laziness, greed and sexual peccadilloes: it was not difficult to unearth – or indeed, invent – evidence that some of the country's seven thousand monks, nuns and friars had been failing to live up to the high ideals they set themselves. Cromwell's inquisitors gleefully presented to their master plenty of examples of misconduct, along with some improbable relics – the clippings of St Edmund's toenails, St Thomas Becket's penknife. Their hastily gathered dossiers provided the excuse for the biggest land grab in English history, starting in 1536 with the dissolution of the smaller monasteries.

But the destruction of the country's age-old education, employment and social welfare network was not accomplished without protest. The monasteries represented everything that, for centuries, people had been taught to respect, and in October 1536 the north of England rose in revolt. Rallying behind dramatic banners depicting the five wounds of Christ, some forty thousand marchers came to the aid of Mother Church in a rebellion they proudly called the Pilgrimage of Grace.

The 'pilgrims' set about reinstating the monks and nuns in sixteen of the fifty-five houses that had already been suppressed. They demanded the legitimisation of Queen Katherine's daughter, Mary. They also called for the destruction of the disruptive books of Luther and Tyndale, and for the removal of Thomas Cromwell along with his ally Thomas Cranmer, the reforming Archbishop of Canterbury. The rebels had a fundamental faith in the orthodoxy of their monarch – if only King Henry's wicked advisers were removed, they believed, he would return to the good old ways.

This loyalty proved their undoing when Henry, unable to raise sufficient troops against them, bought time by agreeing to concede to the 'pilgrims' some of their demands; he invited their leader, Robert Aske, to come down to London and present his grievances in person, under safe conduct. But once the rebels were safely dispersed back home in their villages, Henry seized on the excuse of new risings in the early months of 1537 to exact revenge. 'Our pleasure,' he instructed his army commander, the Duke of Norfolk, '[is] that you shall cause such dreadful execution to be done upon a good number of every town village and hamlet that have offended as they may be a fearful spectacle to all others hereafter that would practise any like matter.'

Norfolk carried out his orders ruthlessly. Some seventy Cumberland villagers were hanged on trees in their gardens in full sight of their wives and children; the monks of Sawley, one of the monasteries reopened by the pilgrims, were hanged on long timber staves projecting from their steeple. Aske was executed in front of the people who had so enthusiastically cheered him a few months earlier.

The rebels had not been wrong in their hunch that Henry was at heart a traditional Catholic – the King believed in the miracle of transubstantiation to the day he died. Even as the Reformation progressed, he burned the reformers who dared to suggest that the bread and wine of the communion were mere symbols of Christ's body and blood. But he needed to fill his coffers. By 1540 England's last religious house, the rich Augustinian abbey of Waltham, had been closed and the royal treasury was richer by £132,000 (more than £50 million today) from the sale of the monastery lands.

Even richer in the long term were the squires, merchants and magnates who had been conscripted into the new order of things, picking up prime monastic acres all over the country. The Dissolution of the Monasteries was Henry's payoff to the landed classes, and it helped make the Reformation permanent.

But to this day we find corners of the English countryside curiously sanctified by the remains of high gothic arches, haunted towers and long-deserted cloisters. Rievaulx in north Yorkshire, Tintern in the Wye Valley, and Whitby on the windswept North Sea coast where St Hilda preached and the cowherd Caedmon sang: all these ghostly ruins are visible reminders of what was once the heart of English learning, education and history-making – a civilisation that consoled and inspired rich and poor alike for centuries.

... DIVORCED, BEHEADED, SURVIVED
1539-47

IN THE SUMMER OF 1539 HENRY VIII STAGED A PAGEANT ON the River Thames. Two barges put out on to the water, one manned by a crew representing the King and his Council, the other by sailors in the scarlet costumes of the Pope and his cardinals. As Henry and crowds of Londoners looked on, the two boats met and engaged in mock battle, with much capering and horseplay until the inevitable happened – the scarlet-clad Pope and his cardinals were pitched into the river.

Real life was not so simple. In 1538 the Pope had issued a call to the Catholic powers of Europe to rally against England's 'most cruel and abominable tyrant' and England now found herself dangerously isolated. Thomas Cromwell's solution was to look for support among the Protestant princes of Germany. He could see how his royal master had been moping since the death of Jane Seymour a year or so earlier: perhaps business and pleasure could be combined by marriage to a comely German princess.

Inquiries established that there were two promising candidates in Cleves, the powerful north German duchy with its capital at Düsseldorf. The duke had a pair of marriageable sisters, Anne and Amelia, and early in 1539 Cromwell asked the English ambassador Christopher Mont to investigate their beauty. Mont reported back positively, and two locally produced portraits were sent off for the King's inspection. But were the likenesses trustworthy?

The answer was to dispatch the King's own painter, Hans Holbein, the talented German artist whose precise and luminous portraits embody for us the personalities and textures of Henry's court. Working quickly as usual, Holbein produced portraits of both sisters in little more than a week. That of Anne showed a serene and pleasant-looking woman, and legend has it that Henry fell in love with the portrait. In fact, the King had already decided that now, at forty-eight, he should go for the elder of the two sisters – the twenty-four-year-old Anne. The gentle, modest face that he saw in Holbein's canvas simply confirmed all the written reports he had received.

When Henry met his bride-to-be, however, he found her downright plain. 'I see nothing in this woman as men report of her,' he said, speaking 'very sadly and pensively' soon after he had greeted Anne on New Year's Day 1540. 'I marvel that wise men would make such report as they have done.'

Four days later Henry VIII went to his fourth marriage ceremony with a heavy heart. 'If it were not to satisfy the world and my realm,' he told Cromwell reproachfully on their way to the service, 'I would not do that I must do this day for none earthly thing.'

Next morning, Henry was in a thoroughly bad mood: there were still more grounds for reproach.

'Surely, as ye know,' he said to Cromwell, 'I liked her before not well, but now I like her much worse, for I have felt her belly and her breasts, and thereby, as I can judge, she should be no maid.' He added the indelicate detail that Anne suffered from bad body odour, and went on to describe the deflating effect this had on his ardour. 'I had neither will nor courage to proceed any further in other matters . . .' he confessed. 'I have left her as good a maid as I found her.'

The royal doctors were called in. It was a serious matter when a king could not consummate his marriage, but all they could offer was the age-old advice in such circumstances – not to worry too much. They advised Henry to take a night off.

But when the King returned to the fray, he found that nothing had changed – as Anne confirmed with charming innocence. 'When he comes to bed,' she told one of her ladies-in-waiting, 'he kisses me and taketh me by the hand and biddeth me "Goodnight, sweetheart". And in the morning [he] kisses me and biddeth me "Farewell, darling". Is this not enough?'

We know these extraordinary details because, not for the first time, Thomas Cromwell was allotted the task of undoing what he had done. A widely unpopular figure, he had pushed the reforming agenda too far for the tastes of many, and landing his master with a wife that Henry disparagingly called 'the Flanders Mare' proved the last straw.

In June 1540 Cromwell became the latest of Henry's scapegoats, condemned for treason by act of Parliament and facing the dreadful penalties of hanging, drawing and quartering. If he wished to avoid this particular fate, the minister's final duty was to set down on paper the circumstantial evidence that would make possible the annulment of Henry's non-marriage to Anne.

Thomas Cromwell was executed – with an axe – on 28 July 1540; the paperwork he produced at the eleventh hour helped Henry secure annulment of the Cleves marriage. Just ten days later the King was married again, to Katherine Howard, the twenty-year-old niece of his fierce general in the north, the Duke of Norfolk. For nearly a year the traditionalist duke, a Catholic and a bitter enemy of Cromwell's, had been pushing the enticing Katherine into Henry's path while plotting his rival's downfall.

Unfortunately, the new Queen's lively allure was accompanied by a lively sexual appetite, and little more than a year after her marriage, rumours circulated about Katherine's promiscuity. As an unmarried girl in the unsupervised surroundings of the Norfolk household, she was said to have romped with Henry Manox her music teacher and also with her cousin Thomas Dereham – whom she then had the nerve to employ as her private secretary when she became Queen. In the autumn of 1541, during a royal progress to the north, inquiries revealed that she had waited till Henry was asleep before cavorting with another young lover, Thomas Culpeper.

Henry wept openly before his Council when finally confronted with proof of his wife's betrayal. Katherine was beheaded in February the next year, along with Culpeper, Manox the music teacher, her cousin Dereham and Lady Rochford, the lady-in-waiting who had facilitated the backstairs liaisons after the King had gone to sleep.

Henry was by now a gross and lumbering man-mountain, 'moved by engines and art rather than by nature', as the Duke of Norfolk put it. Arthritic and ulcerous, the ageing King had to be manhandled up staircases – a little cart was built to transport him around Hampton Court. His apothecary's accounts list dam-busting quantities of liquorice, rhubarb and other laxatives, along with grease for the royal haemorrhoids.

What Henry needed was a reliable and experienced wife, and he finally found one in Catherine Parr, thirty-one years old and twice wid-owed – which gave her the distinction of being England's most married Queen. In July 1543 she embarked sagely on the awesome challenge of life with England's most married king, bringing together his children Mary, Elizabeth and Edward to create, for the first time, something like a functional royal family household. Catherine was sympathetic to the new faith, and her most significant achievement, apart from surviving, was probably to ensure that the two younger children, Edward and Elizabeth, were educated by tutors who favoured reform.

When Henry died on 28 January 1547, the news was kept secret for three days. It was difficult to imagine England without the lustful, self-indulgent tyrant who had once been the beautiful young sportsman-king. In moral terms the tale of his reign was one of remorseless decline, of power corrupting absolutely. By no measure of virtue could Henry VIII be called a good man.

But he was a great one – and arguably England's greatest ever king. Take virtue out of the equation, and his accomplishments were for-midable. He destroyed the centuries-old medieval Church. He revolutionised the ownership of English land. He increased the power of central government to unprecedented heights, and though he ruled England as a despot, he did so without the support of an army. The new Church of England was Henry VIII's most obvious legacy. And in the turbulent years that followed his death the country's destiny would also be decisively shaped by the institution that he had enlisted – and thus, in the process, strengthened – to help him break from Rome: the Houses of Parliament and, in particular, the House of Commons.

BOY KING – EDWARD VI,
'THE GODLY IMP'
1547–53

AFTER ALL THE TROUBLE THAT HENRY VIII AND ENGLAND had gone through to get a male heir, Henry made sure that his son Edward received the best education that could be devised for a future king. The boy's tutors, Richard Cox and John Cheke, were the leading humanist scholars of the day, and they redoubled their efforts with the nine-year-old when he succeeded his father in January 1547. In his geography lessons Edward learned by heart the names of all the ports in England, Scotland and France, together with the prevailing winds and tides; in history he studied the long and disastrous reign of Henry VI, an object lesson in how *not* to rule. By the age of twelve, the 'godly imp' was reading twelve chapters of the Bible every day and taking notes as he listened to the Sunday sermon. In a display of cunning reminiscent of his grandfather Henry VII, the boy king devised his own secret code of Greek letters so no one could read his personal jottings.

Except for rejecting the authority of the Pope, Henry VIII had gone to his grave a pretty traditional Catholic. But he seems to have accepted that change must come: the two tutors he engaged for his son were prominent evangelicals, and he was well aware of the radical sympathies of his Archbishop of Canterbury Thomas Cranmer, who had been secretly preparing a programme of Protestant reform. For nearly twenty years Cranmer had hidden from his master the fact that he was married – Henry did not approve of married priests – but with Henry's death the archbishop's wife became public, and so did his programme of reform.

Out went the candles, the stained-glass windows, the statues of the Virgin and the colourful tableaux that had embellished the walls of the churches, which were now slapped over with a virtuous coat of white-wash. No more ashes on Ash Wednesday, no palms on Palm Sunday, and no creeping to the cross on Good Friday. Bells were pulled down from belfries, altar hangings and vestments were cut up to be used as saddle-cloths – and doves no longer flew from the tower of St Paul's on Whit Sunday. In just six years the changes were remarkable.

Today we delight in the beautiful and sonorous phrases of the Book of Common Prayer, first framed by Thomas Cranmer in 1548–9, then revised in 1552. But this was a strange, discordant new language to the people of the time. While reformers obviously welcomed the change, they were in the minority. Most people felt themselves deprived of something they had known and loved all their lives.

Times were already unsettling enough. Inflation was rampant. By 1550, a silver penny contained a fifth of the silver content of 1500, having been so debased by the addition of red copper that, as Bishop Latimer put it, the coin literally 'blushed in shame'. Farming, the main-stay of the economy, was being transformed by rich landowners fencing in the common land. Large flocks of sheep, tended by a single shepherd boy, now grazed on pasture that had once supported half a dozen families ploughing their own strips.

These new fields, or 'enclosures', were helping enrich the Tudor squirearchy, but less affluent country-dwellers – the vast majority of the population – felt dispossessed. In the summer of 1549, villagers in East Anglia started uprooting hedges and seizing sheep by the thousand. They gathered on Mousehold Heath, outside Norwich, around a massive oak tree they called the Reformation Oak. Since Christ had died to make men free, they reasoned, they were demanding an end to bondage. In the West Country, the Cornish-speaking men of Cornwall had already risen in revolt, calling for the restoration of the mass in Latin, since they spoke little English. They had marched eastwards, besieging Exeter for thirty-five days.

Edward's tough councillors dealt with these and other risings in the traditional way – promising to listen to grievances, then meting out mortal punishment as soon as they had mustered their military strength. But inside his own family, Edward found a nut that could not be cracked. His elder sister Mary, thirty-two years old in January 1549, was an unashamed champion of the old faith, and she refused to prohibit the reading of the mass in her household as her brother requested. 'Death shall be more welcome to me,' she declared, 'than life with a troubled conscience.'

Edward's councillors tried for a compromise, but the boy king refused to give in on the matter. 'He would spend his life,' he said, 'and all he had, rather than agree and grant to what he knew certainly to be against the truth.'

His sister tried a mixture of flattery and condescension. 'Although your Majesty hath far more knowledge and greater gifts than others of your years, yet it is not possible that your Highness can at these years be a judge in matters of religion.'

Edward confirmed what a child he still was by breaking down in a fit of sobbing, 'his tender heart bursting out'. All the same, he refused to budge, as did Mary, who responded to his tears by repeating her willingness to be a martyr. 'Take away my life,' she said, 'rather than the old religion.'

This bitter clash between brother and sister showed that the obstinacy of Henry VIII lived on in both of them – as it did, for that matter, in their strong-willed half-sister Elizabeth, in 1553 approaching her twentieth birthday. It also suggested that the religious differences in their respective parentings might, in the future, cause turbulence and division. When Edward came down with a feverish cold in the spring of that year and could not shake it off, the whole programme of evangelical reform was suddenly in jeopardy. Edward's Protestant advisers had no doubt that if the boy were to die and Mary succeed him, she would immediately set about dismantling all the changes they had put in place. England would once again be subject to the Bishop of Rome. So what was to be done?

LADY JANE GREY –
THE NINE-DAY QUEEN
1553

AS THE FIFTEEN-YEAR-OLD EDWARD VI LAY SICK AT Greenwich in April and May 1553, his doctors were baffled by his 'weakness and faintness of spirit'. They noted a 'tough, strong, straining cough' – a possible sign of tuberculosis. Edward was coughing up blood; his body was covered with ulcers. In addition, there had been rumours that he was a victim of poison, so to protect themselves the doctors formally notified the Council that they feared the King had less than nine months to live.

On the death of Henry VIII, Edward's uncle Edward Seymour, Duke of Somerset, had taken charge of the boy king as 'Protector of the Realm'. Seymour was the elder brother of Henry's beloved third wife Jane, and it was under his auspices that the new Prayer Book of 1549 was introduced. But the risings of that year had marked the end of the Protector's power and provided an opening for John Dudley, son of Edmund Dudley, the overzealous fund-raiser that Henry VIII had executed at the beginning of his reign.

His father's fate had not deterred John Dudley from the perilous path of Tudor royal service. In the autumn of 1549 his contribution to the crushing defeat of the Norfolk rebels at the Battle of Dussindale opened the way to him becoming Lord President of Edward's Council, and two years later he awarded himself the dukedom of Northumberland. With a boy king on the throne, the new duke was the effective ruler of England.

Yet Northumberland's power rested entirely on the fragile health of the real King, and as Edward sickened, the duke resorted to desperate measures. He persuaded the fevered young monarch to keep the throne from his Catholic sister by altering the succession in favour of Lady Jane Grey, Edward's cousin and great-granddaughter of Henry VII (see

Tudor family tree, p. xvii). Jane was intelligent and well educated, versed in Greek, Latin and Hebrew – and reliably Protestant. Born in October 1537, the same month as Edward, she had been brought up with him in the reform-minded household of Henry VIII's last Queen, Catherine Parr – Jane and Edward often attended the same lessons.

But the young woman's greatest attraction, from the Lord President's point of view, was that she offered a way of entrenching the Northumberlands in the royal succession. On 26 May 1553 the sixteen-year-old Lady Jane was married, against her will, to Northumberland's fourth son Guildford Dudley – her protests overruled by her father Henry Grey, Duke of Suffolk, who owed his elevated title to his old crony Northumberland.

Most of Northumberland's fellow-councillors were aghast at his naked grab for power. Archbishop Cranmer said he could not agree to the change until he had spoken personally with the King – but Edward, though drifting in and out of consciousness, was still set on denying England to Rome. He ordered Cranmer to endorse his Protestant cousin, and the archbishop reluctantly obeyed. The rest of the Council went along with him.

As letters patent were hastily drawn up declaring that Edward's two elder sisters Mary and Elizabeth were illegitimate, writs went out to summon a Parliament that would confirm the new succession. But the royal health was fast failing. By now Edward's digestion had ceased to function, and his hair and nails were dropping out. When he coughed he brought up foul-smelling black sputum. Death came, on 6 July, as a merciful release.

Two days earlier, Northumberland had summoned Princesses Mary and Elizabeth to their brother's deathbed. But Elizabeth declined the trap and Mary would move only cautiously. The moment the news of Edward's death reached her, she retired to Framlingham Castle in East Anglia and defiantly proclaimed her right to the throne. Down in London, meanwhile, Northumberland was proclaiming the new Queen Jane. But as two heralds and a trumpeter made their way through the city, they met with a cold and indifferent response.

'No one present showed any sign of rejoicing,' reported one diplomat. When one herald cried, 'Long live the Queen', the only response came from the few archers who joined the sad trio.

In East Anglia it was equally clear where people's sympathies lay. Local gentlemen flocked to Framlingham with horsemen and retainers to pledge their loyalty to Mary. People who were unable to fight sent money or carts full of beer, bread and freshly slaughtered meat for the volunteer army, which by 19 July numbered nearly twenty thousand. When Mary rode out to thank them, she was greeted with 'shouts and acclamations' as men threw their helmets in the air. The noise frightened her horse so much she had to dismount and continue on foot through the mile-long encampment, greeting the soldiers personally and thanking them for their goodwill. Across the country there were enthusiastic demonstrations of support for Henry VIII's firstborn child, and local forces were quickly mustered.

It did not take long for the Council in London to get the message. Northumberland had headed north to arrest Mary, but his venture was clearly doomed. To save their own skins the colleagues he left in London, in a deft about-turn, offered a reward for his capture and proclaimed Mary's accession. In an explosion of popular joy people ran wild, crying out the news and dancing in the streets. As darkness fell, bonfires were lit. 'I am unable to describe to you,' wrote one visiting Italian, 'nor would you believe the exultation of all men. From a distance the earth must have looked like Mount Etna.'

When Mary entered London on 3 August 1553, the celebrations knew no bounds. By then Northumberland had surrendered and had been sent to the Tower, where he was executed before the month was out. Lady Jane Grey was also imprisoned, but spared by Mary – she had clearly been only a pawn in the game.

Unfortunately for Jane, however, one of Mary's first decisions as Queen was to arrange a marriage for herself to the Catholic Philip of Spain. Early in 1554 the unpopularity of this 'Spanish match' prompted an uprising by Kentish rebels who reached the walls of London, and it became clear that the nine-day Queen, who embodied the hope for a Protestant succession, was too dangerous to be kept alive.

On 12 February 1554, Lady Jane Grey was led out to the block. It was some sort of poetic justice that along with her went Guildford Dudley, the husband she had not wished to marry, and Henry Grey, the father who had forced her into it.

BLOODY MARY AND THE
FIRES OF SMITHFIELD
1553-8

THE SPONTANEOUS REVOLT THAT PUT MARY TUDOR ON THE throne of England was the only popular uprising to succeed in the 118 years of her dynasty's rule. 'Vox Populi, Vox Dei', read the banners that welcomed the daughter of Henry VIII and Katherine of Aragon to London in the summer of 1553 – 'The voice of the people is the voice of God.'

England had always felt sympathy, and perhaps a little guilt, over the way that both Mary and her mother had been treated during the break from Rome. Both women had stayed true to their faith, and now the old religion was back. The altars and vestments came out of hiding, and once again on feast days people could process and chant in church.

Mary believed in putting her intense personal piety into practice. She took the ceremonies of Maundy Thursday especially seriously, covering her finery with a long linen apron to kneel in front of poor women, humbly washing, drying and kissing their feet. She would turn up at the door of needy households and of poor widows, in particular, dressed not as a queen but as a gentlewoman with offers of help. She liked to mingle with ordinary villagers, asking if they had enough to live on and, if they lived on royal estates, whether they were being fairly treated by the officers of the Crown. To judge by the folk tales told of Mary Tudor's charitable exploits, the Catholic Queen was a sixteenth-century combination of Mother Teresa and Diana, Princess of Wales.

But that is not, of course, how 'Bloody Mary' has been remembered by history, for there was a fanatical and unforgiving core to her faith. On 30 November 1554, the long and complicated legal process of reuniting the English Church with Rome was finally completed, with

Parliament reinstating the medieval heresy statutes. If condemned by the church courts, heretics would now be handed over to the civil authorities to endure the grim penalty of burning to death at the stake. Less than three months later, the executions began.

Before the Reformation the public burning of heretics, which horrifies us today, was generally accepted – even popular. Since 1401, when the activities of the Lollards put burning on the Statute Book, the orthodox Catholic majority had felt strengthened in their own prospects for salvation by the sight of dissidents being reduced to ashes. Even as Henry VIII was breaking with Rome in the 1530s, his burning of especially vocal Protestants could be taken as demonstrating a sensible middle way. But by the 1550s the Protestants were no longer a crazy fringe. They made up a solid and respected minority of believers, and it was on them that Mary's zeal now focused.

From an early date, Mary's fervour worried those around her. In July 1554 she had provoked Protestant sensibilities by her marriage to the Catholic Philip of Spain – the Kent uprising that cost Lady Jane Grey her life only made Mary more determined – and even Philip's Spanish advisers counselled her against inflaming feelings further. But Mary felt she had compromised enough. Under pressure from her English councillors, many of them inherited from her brother Edward, she had reluctantly agreed to leave the monastery lands with those who had purchased them. But when it came to dogma, she had God's work to do. The burnings started in February 1555 with a selection of heretics both humble and mighty, among them the puritanical former Bishop of Gloucester, John Hooper.

Hooper was a victim of the local authorities' inexperience at the practicalities of this rare and specialised form of execution. They had supplied only two saddle-loads of reeds and faggots – and because the wood was green it burned slowly. Hooper desperately clasped bundles of reeds to his chest in a vain attempt to hasten the process, but only the bottom half of his body was burning. 'For God's love, good people,' he cried out, 'let me have more fire!'

In these early days the burnings were well attended. For the citizens of Gloucester there was a novelty value, and perhaps even a ghoulish attraction, in watching their once high-and-mighty bishop agonise in front of their eyes. But the very suffering began to alter opinion – the smell of burning human flesh turns even the strongest stomach – and the executions of Bishops Hugh Latimer and Nicholas Ridley at Oxford on 16 October that same year came to symbolise the tragedy of good men being tortured for their sincere beliefs.

Ridley had been Bishop of London and had played a major role in drafting the Book of Common Prayer of 1549. Latimer was a populist preacher well known for his sympathy for the poor. Famous for blending theology with everyday social concerns in open-air sermons that he delivered to large crowds, he had proudly refused the escape route that many radicals took to the German states and Swiss cities where Protestants were safe. As he and Ridley were being trussed to the same stake, he uttered the words that would forever evoke Mary's martyrs: 'Be of good comfort, Master Ridley, and play the man; we shall this day, by God's grace, light such a candle in England as I trust shall never be put out.'

Though Latimer died quite quickly, suffocated by the smoke and losing consciousness, the fire burned more slowly on Ridley's side. As was becoming the custom, his family had bribed the executioner to tie a bag of gunpowder around his neck, but the flames were not reaching high enough to trigger this ghastly if merciful release. 'I cannot burn,' Ridley cried, screaming in pain until a guard pulled away some of the damp faggots. Immediately the flames leapt upwards, and as Ridley swung his head down towards them the gunpowder exploded.

Watching this excruciating agony was the former Archbishop of Canterbury, Thomas Cranmer. The Catholic authorities were trying to terrify him into recanting his faith – and they succeeded. Under the pressures of prison life, constant hectoring and sheer fear, Cranmer signed no less than six recantations, each more abject than the one before. The great architect of England's Protestant Reformation was even driven to accept the Catholic doctrine of transubstantiation and the authority of the Pope.

But Cranmer still was not spared. Mary's determination to punish the archbishop who had annulled her mother's marriage and proclaimed her a bastard was unassailable. His burning was set for 21 March 1556, on the same spot in Oxford where Ridley and Latimer had died, and he was led into the university church to pronounce his final, public recantation.

But having embarked on the preamble that the authorities were expecting, Cranmer suddenly changed course. He wished to address, he said, 'the great thing which so much troubleth my conscience', and he began to explain that the recantations he had signed were 'contrary to the truth which I thought in my heart'. As uproar broke out in the church, he raised his voice to a shout: 'As for the Pope, I refuse him, as Christ's enemy and Antichrist!'

The white-bearded ex-archbishop was dragged out and hurried to the stake, where fire was put to the wood without delay. As the flames licked around him, he extended towards them the 'unworthy right hand' with which he had signed his recantations.

Cranmer's death was a propaganda disaster for Mary's government. Even loyal Catholics could see the unfairness in someone who had repeatedly recanted being punished just the same. In the forty-five killing months between 4 February 1555 and 10 November 1558, 283 martyrs – 227 men and 56 women – were burned alive for their faith. By June of that final year Londoners were reacting with anger and distaste: the burnings, hitherto held in front of St Bartholomew's Hospital in Smithfield, had to be shifted to secret places of execution. And elsewhere, things were looking no better for Henry VIII's eldest child. Earlier in 1558 her armies had been driven out of the fortified port of Calais, the last vestige of England's empire across the Channel; and she herself was mortally ill, dying of a stomach tumour that she had imagined to be a baby that would keep the Catholic cause alive.

The very opposite proved the case – for the reign which began with such popular promise ended by inspiring a hostility to 'popery' in England that is embedded to this day. It is still impossible for a British king or queen to be Roman Catholic or to marry a Roman Catholic, and the roots of the bitter hatreds that have divided Northern Ireland can be similarly traced back to the fires of Smithfield. Stubborn, pious, Catholic Mary had helped make England a Protestant nation.

ROBERT RECORDE AND HIS
INTELLIGENCE SHARPENER
1557

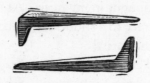

R OBERT RECORDE WAS A WELSHMAN WHO STUDIED AT BOTH Oxford and Cambridge in the reign of Henry VIII, before moving down to London to work as a doctor – he was consulted, on occasion, by both Edward VI and Mary. But it is for his maths that he is remembered. In 1543 he published *The Ground of Arts*, the first ever maths book in English, which ran through over fifty editions and introduced English schoolchildren to the tortured delights of such problems as: 'If a horse has four shoes, each with six nails, and you pay half a penny for the first nail, one penny for the second, two for the third, four for the fourth, and so on, doubling every time, how much will the shoeing of the horse cost?'

The modern historian Adam Hart-Davis has pointed out that there are, in fact, two answers to this problem: 126 pence, if the shoes are counted separately – that is, 4 lots of 6 nails – or 8,388,607.5 pence (£34,952) if you continue the doubling process as you move through all the shoes and nails.

In 1556, in *The Castle of Knowledge*, Recorde set out some of the revolutionary ideas of the Polish astronomer Nicolaus Copernicus who had died in 1543. After a lifetime of studying the stars, Copernicus had come to the conclusion that the earth is *not* the centre of the universe, but moves around the sun, while also spinning on its own axis. Copernicus had been careful to keep his heretical observations to himself in his lifetime – it was an article of Catholic faith that the heavens moved around God's earth – and Recorde, writing in the reign of Bloody Mary, exercised similar prudence: 'I will let it pass till some other time,' he wrote.

But the innovation for which the Welshman is remembered today appeared the following year in his algebra book, *The Whetstone of Wit* ('The Intelligence Sharpener'). Until 1557, mathematicians had finished off a calculation by laboriously writing out the words '. . . is equal to . . .', which was sometimes abbreviated to *ae* (or *oe*), from the Latin word for equal – *aequalis*. But Recorde had a better idea: why not use a symbol? 'To avoide the tedious repetition of these woords', he proposed the use of a pair of parallel lines: =.

Using the simple device that we now call 'the equals sign' released an enormous log jam in the efficient handling of numbers, and the implications extended far beyond pure maths. It immensely speeded up the calculations of astronomers and navigators – even shopkeepers – and what could be more satisfying for everyone than to round off a calculation with two elegant little parallel lines? As Recorde himself put it – 'noe two things can be moare equalle'.

ELIZABETH – QUEEN OF HEARTS
1559

ELIZABETH I WAS CROWNED IN WESTMINSTER ABBEY ON 15 January 1559 – a date selected by her astrologer, Dr John Dee. Cheering crowds had lined the route as she set off from the City of London the previous day, and the red-haired Queen had time for everyone, holding hands, cracking jokes and watching with rapt attention the loyal pageants staged in her honour. When the figure of Truth approached her, carrying a Bible, the twenty-five-year-old monarch kissed the holy book fervently and clasped it to her breast.

Flamboyant and theatrical, Elizabeth was very much her father's daughter – with the dash and temper (as well as the piercing dark eyes) of her mother Anne Boleyn. Tudor to the core, she was spiky, vain and bloody-minded, with the distrustfulness of her grandfather Henry VII whose penny-pinching she also matched. At the receiving end of arbitrary power during her youth, she had lived with rejection and danger and survived to boast about it. 'I thank God,' she told her Members of Parliament a few years after she came to power, 'that I am endued with such qualities that if I were turned out of the Realm in my petticoat, I were able to live in any place in Christendom.'

On the first day of her reign, the new Queen selected as her principal adviser William Cecil, her efficient estate manager whom she liked to call her 'spirit'. In fact, this hardworking servant of the Crown was anything but airy-fairy – Cecil provided ballast to the royal flightiness. At nine o'clock on the dot, three mornings a week, the dry little secretary summoned the Council to plough through the detail of administration. One early reform was to call in the much-debased 'pink' silver pennies for re-minting: within two years the coinage was so well re-established that the government actually made a profit. Her reign also saw the creation of England's first stock exchange. And to build up the nation's shipping capacity – as well as its seafarers – it became compulsory in Elizabeth's England to eat fish on Wednesdays and Saturdays.

But it was religion that was the priority after the trauma of Mary's excesses. Traditionally minded, like her father, Elizabeth favoured beautiful vestments, crucifixes and candlesticks, insisting there should be ceremony at the heart of Sunday worship. Also like her father, she disliked the new-fangled Protestant notion of allowing the clergy to marry, and made clear her disapproval of their wives. England's Catholics were also reassured when she declined to reclaim her father's title as Supreme Head of the Church. It was a subtle distinction, but she settled for Supreme Governor.

For their part, Protestants were pleased to see the powerful rhythms of Cranmer's Book of Common Prayer restored, and hear again William Tyndale's robust English ringing out when the gospel was read. Elizabeth offered both sides a compromise, and she promised no trouble to those who would live and let live – she did not wish to make, in Francis Bacon's words, 'windows into men's souls'. Elizabeth's attempt at a tolerant middle way came to define a certain strand of Englishness.

One subject on which she disagreed, however, with virtually every man in England – including William Cecil – was on her need to take a husband. It was inconceivable in the sixteenth century that a woman could lead a proper life, let alone run a country, without a better half: in 1566, in a telling display of insubordination, Parliament threatened to refuse to levy taxes unless the Queen took a husband. But Elizabeth was only too aware that if she married a foreign prince England would get embroiled in European wars, while an English husband could not help but provoke domestic jealousies. 'I am already bound to a husband,' she liked to say, 'which is the kingdom of England.'

Thus came into being the powerful myth of Gloriana the Virgin Queen – bedecked in jewels and an endless succession of spectacular dresses that took on the status of semi-sacred vestments. Homage to this stylised, white-faced icon became compulsory – a draft proclamation of 1563 sought to insist that all portraits of Elizabeth had to be copied from one approved template. When John Stubbs, an evangelical pamphleteer, dared to criticise the Queen's marriage policy in 1579, he was sentenced to have his writing hand chopped off with a cleaver. 'God save the Queen!' he cried out after his right hand was severed, raising his hat with his left.

This tyrannical, capricious monarch was the inspiration for the most glittering and creative court England has ever seen. Every year Elizabeth would embark on her 'progresses' – glorified summer holidays – in which the Queen, accompanied by her court and by a veritable army of horses and carts, set off to cadge free hospitality from the great of the land in their magnificent new windowed country houses.

Well before the end of the century, Elizabeth's accession day, 17 November, had come to be celebrated as a national holiday. Bells would be rung, toasts drunk, and poems composed in praise of the Faerie Queene who had made herself the embodiment of a dynamic and thrusting nation. And if by the end of the century the physical reality of Elizabeth in her sixties, lined and black-toothed, scarcely matched the idealised prints and portraits of the young monarch she once had been, people willingly suspended disbelief.

In 1601 she received a deputation from the House of Commons, furious at the many abuses and shortcomings of her government in these her declining years. But when, bewigged, bejewelled and beruffed, she responded to them directly yet again, they fell willingly under her spell. 'Though God has raised me high,' she declaimed, in what became known as her 'Golden Speech', 'yet this I count the glory of my crown, that I have reigned with your loves . . . Though you have had and may have many mightier and wiser princes sitting on this seat, yet you never had nor shall have any that will love you better.' The frail and fractious old lady was sixty-seven years old. But to her listeners she remained Gloriana, and one by one they shuffled forward to kiss her hand.

THAT'S ENTERTAINMENT

1571

A S YOU APPROACHED QUEEN ELIZABETH'S LONDON FROM the south you were confronted by a ghastly sight. Down from the stone gateway above London Bridge grimaced a row of rotting and weathered skulls – the severed heads of traitors, some of them generations old. Every sixteenth-century town had its hanging place, a purpose-built gallows or a tree where malefactors were executed and left to putrefy, dangling there as a warning to others. There were several gallows in London. Twenty to thirty offenders were hanged every day the law courts sat, reported one Swiss-German traveller in 1599, who was clearly rather impressed.

In a field to the west of London stood Tyburn Tree, the capital's busiest hanging place – and hence a major venue for popular entertainment, where rowdy crowds gathered and children, straining to get a glimpse, would be hoisted on to their parents' shoulders to cheer and jeer. Food and drink stalls did a brisk trade in pies, fruit and sweetmeats at the spot that is marked today by an iron plaque in the middle of the traffic island, near Speakers' Corner, just across from the fast food and takeaway shops of Marble Arch.

By 1571 the gallows traffic was such that a large wooden contraption had to be built on which as many as twenty-four bodies could be strung at once. The executioner was a local butcher who would tie a rope round the criminal's neck while he sat in a cart. When the cart moved on, the victim was left dangling, and his friends ran forward to hang on his legs and try to hasten his painful strangulation. In 1577 the topographer-chronologist William Harrison's *Description of England* listed the hanging crimes as buggery, murder, manslaughter, treason, rape, felony, hawk-stealing, witchcraft, desertion in the field of battle, highway robbery and the malicious letting-out of ponds.

Many Elizabethan amusements were brutal by our tastes. In 1562 an Italian visitor, Alessandro Magno, described a Sunday-afternoon session at one of London's animal-baiting pits, where admission cost the modern equivalent of £2 for standing room and £4 for a seat:

> *First they take into the ring a cheap horse . . . and a monkey in the saddle. Then they attack the horse with 5 or 6 of the youngest dogs. Then they change the dogs for more experienced ones . . . It is wonderful to see the horse galloping along . . . with the monkey holding on tightly to the saddle and crying out frequently when he is bitten by the dogs. After they have entertained the audience for a while with this sport, which often results in the death of the horse, they lead him out and bring in bears – sometimes one at a time, sometimes all together. But this sport is not very pleasant to watch. At the end, they bring on a fierce bull and tie it with a rope about two paces long to a stake fixed in the middle of the ring. This sport is the best one to see, and more dangerous for the dogs than the others: many of them are wounded and die. This goes on until evening.*

It is a relief to turn to descriptions of the innovative wooden structures that were being built among the bear-pits of Southwark – the playhouses. In the early Tudor decades, pageants and rudimentary plays had been performed in tavern courtyards and in noble households by touring companies of players. But 1587 saw the construction of England's first modern theatre, the Rose, an open-air stage and arena surrounded by wooden galleries – an enlarged and exalted version, in effect, of the tavern courtyard. 'They play on a raised platform,' wrote the Swiss traveller Thomas Platter, 'so that everyone has a good view. There are different galleries and places, however, where the seating is better and more comfortable and therefore more expensive . . . During the performance food and drink are carried round the audience . . . The actors are most expensively and elaborately costumed.'

Today one can get a taste of Elizabethan theatregoing by visiting the Globe, a modern reconstruction of the original theatre that opened in Southwark in January 1599. By that date there was a little clutch of playhouses on the south bank of the Thames, safely outside the jurisdiction of London's City Fathers, who disapproved of the low and licentious shows that tempted people away from work in the afternoons. The best-designed playhouses faced south-west so they could catch the afternoon sun as it set; the outstanding productions were honoured by an invitation to go and perform at court in the presence of Elizabeth.

William Shakespeare is the most famous of an entire school of English playwrights who were the equivalent of the TV programme makers of today, churning out soap operas, thrillers, comedies and even multi-part series: we watch docudramas on the world wars and on twentieth-century history – the Elizabethans sat through *Henry VI Parts 1, 2* and *3*. To appeal to the groundlings in the pit, the playwrights wrote slapstick comedies at which the Queen herself was known to slap a thigh – Shakespeare's most farcical play, *The Merry Wives of Windsor*, was written at her request. But they also invented a new dramatic form – the introspective soliloquy that showed how a harsh age was also becoming reflective and questioning: 'To be, or not to be – that is the question . . .'

SIR WALTER RALEGH AND
THE LOST COLONY
1585

WALTER RALEGH WAS A SWAGGERING WEST COUNTRY lad who started his career as a soldier of fortune. He was only sixteen when he crossed the Channel to fight on the side of the Huguenots, the French Protestants, in the religious wars that divided France for much of the sixteenth century. Later he fought against the Catholics in Ireland.

Ralegh was six feet tall by the time he came to court in the late 1570s, handsome and well built, with a jutting chin and dark curling hair shown off to perfection with a double pearl drop-earring. He has gone down in history for his rich and flashy clothes, and for many twentieth-century British schoolchildren the name Ralegh (or Raleigh – the 'i' was added in later years) stood for sturdy bicycles and for cloaks in the mud:

> *This Captain Ralegh, [runs the earliest version of the famous story] coming out of Ireland to the English court in good habit – his clothes being then a considerable part of his estate – found the Queen walking, till, meeting with a plashy place, she seemed to scruple going thereon. Presently Ralegh cast and spread his new plush cloak on the ground; whereon the Queen trod gently over, rewarding him afterwards with many suits for his so free and seasonable tender of so fair a foot cloth.*

This gallant tale was not recorded for another eighty years, but something like it almost certainly happened: one version of Ralegh's coat of arms featured a visual pun on the story – a plush and swirling cloak. Sir Walter epitomised the peacockery that danced attendance on the Virgin Queen, and Elizabeth was entranced by the style with which he played her game. She made him her Captain of the Guard. She liked 'proper men' and Ralegh was certainly one of those – though, not quite properly, 'he spake broad Devonshire till his dying day'.

As a West Countryman, Ralegh made himself the champion at court for the growing number of Elizabethans who were drawn towards the New World. Among these were relatives like his half-brother Humphrey Gilbert, who vanished in 1583 while searching for a route that would lead him to the riches of China through the ice floes and mist-laden inlets that lay beyond Newfoundland – the 'North West Passage'. Adventurers such as Francis Drake and Richard Grenville saw good Protestant duty, as well as piracy and plunder, in capturing Spanish galleons and challenging the Catholic King of Spain (who after 1581 also took over Portugal and its colonies). The guru of the New World enthusiasts was Dr John Dee, the Merlin-like figure who had cast the Queen's coronation horoscope. Dee put forward the ambitious idea of a 'British Impire' across the Atlantic – a land first dis-covered, he said, not by John Cabot in 1497 but by Madoc, a Welsh prince in the King Arthur mould, who was said to have crossed the Atlantic centuries previously.

In the early 1580s Dee provided Ralegh with a map of the American coastline north of Florida. Ralegh dispatched scouts to search for a suitable settlement, and in 1585 he presented the results of their prospecting to Elizabeth – two native Indians, some potatoes, and the curious leaf smoked by the natives: tobacco.

The Elizabethans considered the potato an exotic and aphrodisiac vegetable. When Sir John Falstaff was attempting to have his wicked way with the merry wives of Windsor, he called on the sky to 'rain potatoes'. As for tobacco, the 'herb' was considered a health-giving medicine, which 'purgeth superfluous phlegm and other gross humours and openeth all the pores and passages of the body'.

Sir John Hawkins had introduced tobacco to England twenty years earlier, but it was typical of Ralegh to hijack the brand identity with a stunt to match the cloak and puddle. Talking to the Queen one day he boasted he could weigh tobacco smoke. Not surprisingly, Elizabeth challenged him, and he called for scales. Having weighed some tobacco, he smoked it in his long-stemmed pipe, then weighed the ashes and calculated the difference. As a final flourish, he proposed that the land

where this remarkable plant grew should be named in her honour –
Virginia.

Ralegh's prospective colonists set sail for the New World in May
1587 – ninety men, seventeen women and nine children – with all the
supplies they needed to establish a self-sustaining and civilised community, including books, maps, pictures and a ceremonial suit of
armour for John White, who was to be the governor. They landed on
the island of Roanoke off modern North Carolina, and established
what seemed to be relatively friendly relations with the local Croatoan
Indians. But only a month after landing it became clear that more supplies would be needed, so Governor White set sail to organise a relief
expedition for the following spring.

White arrived home to find England transfixed by the threat of
Spanish invasion. Though chief promoter of the Virginia colony,
Ralegh had not sailed himself with his adventurers, and now he was
tied up organising ships to combat the threat of King Philip's Armada.
There was not a vessel to be spared, so it was August 1590 before
Governor White could finally drop anchor off Roanoke again – nearly
three years after he had departed. To his delight he saw smoke rising
from the island, but when he landed he discovered it was only a forest
fire. There was no trace of the colonists.

'We let fall our grapnel near the shore,' White related poignantly,
'and sounded with a trumpet and call, and afterwards many familiar
English tunes of songs, and called to them friendly. But we had no
answer.'

Locating the ruins of the palisade and cabins that he had helped to
build, White discovered only grass, weeds and pumpkin creepers. But
there were fresh native footprints in the sand – and one sign of
Western habitation: a post on which were carved the letters, 'CROA-
TOAN'. White had agreed with the colonists that if they moved to a
new settlement, they would leave its name carved somewhere on
Roanoke. But when he investigated the nearby Croatoan Island, he
found no sign of human habitation.

In later years archaeologists and historians would search for evidence of what might have happened to Walter Ralegh's 'lost colony'.
Recent diggings have uncovered the English fort and what appears
from the assembled samples of flora and fauna to be a primitive science

and research centre, North America's first. But the only clue to what happened to the colonists – and that is tenuous – has been found in modern Robertson County in North Carolina. Survivors of an Indian tribe there, called the Croatoans, speak a dialect containing words that sound a little like Elizabethan English – and some of these modern Croatoans have fair skin and blue eyes.

MARY QUEEN OF SCOTS
1560–87

WHEN IT CAME TO DEALING WITH THE OTHER KINGDOM that occupied their island, English monarchs sometimes sent armies north of the border, and sometimes brides. Henry VII's daughter Margaret Tudor had been the last bridal export – she had married James Stuart, King of the Scots, in 1503 (see p. 192), and her glamorous but troubled granddaughter Mary was to provide Elizabeth I with the longest-running drama of her reign.

Mary's life was dramatic from the start. Her father James V of Scotland died when she was only six days old – and for the rest of her life she bore her famous title Queen of Scots. She was Queen of France too for a time, thanks to her brief first marriage to the French King François II. But François died in 1560, and his eighteen-year-old widow returned to the turmoil of the Scottish Reformation.

The young Queen was not well received by John Knox, the fiery leader of Scotland's evangelicals, who had just published his virulent denunciation of female rulers, *The First Blast of the Trumpet against the Monstrous Regiment of Women*. Mary's Catholicism was another black mark against her in Knox's eyes, and as Protestantism became the official religion of Scotland in the early 1560s she had to pick her way carefully, prudently confining her beliefs to her own household.

But after several years of delicate and quite skilful balancing, Mary succumbed to the first of the headstrong impulses that would turn her promising young life to tragedy. In July 1565, she plunged into a passionate marriage with her cousin Henry Stuart, Lord Darnley, whose good looks masked a vain, drunken, jealous and violent nature – as he proved within months, when he arranged for a gang of cronies to set upon Mary's Italian private secretary, David Rizzio. Darnley's possessiveness could not tolerate the trust that his wife placed in her chief of staff, and as the hapless Italian clung screaming to the Queen's skirts – she was now six months pregnant – he was murdered in front of her eyes.

Compared to the canniness with which her English cousin Elizabeth steered clear of marital entanglement, Mary was worse than impulsive: she was self-destructive. Within a year of Rizzio's murder she was romantically involved with another homicidal aristocrat, James, Earl of Bothwell, who devised nothing less than the blowing-up of the bedridden Darnley who, after a youth of debauchery, had been laid low by the ravages of syphilis. Mary herself may even have been complicit in the murder. She had spent the evening of 10 February 1567 visiting her ailing husband in his house at Kirk o' Field, Edinburgh, before leaving for Holyrood Palace between ten and eleven o'clock. Two hours after midnight all Edinburgh was rocked as the house exploded. Darnley's lifeless body was found in the garden.

Mary's marriage to Bothwell only three months later confirmed Scottish suspicions of her involvement, and ended her last chance of being a credible ruler. In July that year she was compelled to abdicate in favour of her thirteen-month-old son James (Darnley's child), and in May 1568 at the age of twenty-five she fled from Scotland in disgrace to throw herself on the mercy of her cousin Elizabeth.

Elizabeth had been viewing Mary's melodramatic adventures across the border with fascination – and not a little rivalry. Nine years younger than Elizabeth, Mary was generally reckoned a beauty, and this piqued the jealousy of the English Queen. In 1564 she had cornered the Scottish ambassador Sir James Melville, putting his diplomacy to the test as she cross-questioned him on the looks of his

Scottish mistress. Elizabeth got crosser and crosser as Melville dodged her traps – until he let slip that Mary was taller. 'Then she is too high,' exclaimed Gloriana in triumph. 'I myself am neither too high, nor too low!'

Mary's arrival as an uninvited asylum seeker placed Elizabeth in a dilemma. England could hardly provide money, still less an army, to restore the deposed Queen – this would impose an unpopular Catholic monarch on Scotland's staunch Protestants. But since blood made Mary next in line to Elizabeth's own throne, she could not, either, be allowed to leave England lest she fall into the clutches of France or Spain. The Queen of Scots would have to be kept in some kind of limbo.

To start with, the fiction was maintained that Mary, as a cousin and anointed monarch, was being received in England as Elizabeth's honoured guest. Yet Elizabeth did not visit Mary – the two women never met – and as the Queen of Scots was shifted across the north of England from one residence to another, it became clear that she was under house arrest. With a bodyguard that was curiously large for a cousin who was supposed to be trusty and beloved, Mary was shuttled from Carlisle to Bolton, then on to Tutbury in Staffordshire.

The transfer that made her captivity plain occurred late in 1569, when the Catholics of the north rose in revolt. As the rebels burned the English prayer books and Bibles, restoring church altars so as to celebrate the Roman mass in all its splendour, the earls who headed the rising dispatched a kidnap squad to Tutbury. Only in the nick of time did William Cecil have Mary whisked southwards to the fortified walls of the city of Coventry. Though the revolt collapsed, the Queen of Scots was now clearly identified as the focus of Catholic hopes. In February 1570, Pope Pius V formally excommunicated Elizabeth and called on all Catholics to rise up, depose and, if necessary, murder the 'heretic Queen'.

The papal decree was to become Mary's death sentence, but Elizabeth could not bring herself to go along with the simple but ruthless solution proposed by her anxious councillors, and particularly by her spymaster Sir Francis Walsingham – England would not be safe, in their opinion, until the Queen of Scots was dead. In the meantime, the bodyguards kept moving Mary onwards – from Coventry to

Chatsworth, then on to Sheffield, Buxton, Chartley, and finally to Fotheringhay Castle in Rutland, now Northamptonshire. As she travelled, Walsingham's network of secret agents kept working to entrap her and, after a decade and a half, in October 1586 they had finally secured the evidence they required.

Imprudently, Mary had been plotting with fellow-Catholics through coded letters smuggled in waterproof pouches hidden in beer casks. But the whole scheme was of Walsingham's invention – a sting devised to incriminate Mary – and when she was put on trial at Fotheringhay it was revealed that his cipher clerks had been decoding her messages within hours of her sending them off.

Mary Queen of Scots was found guilty of treason and sentenced to death on 4 December that year. But again Elizabeth hesitated, and for weeks she could not bring herself to sign the death warrant – and then only in a contradictory fashion, first ordering her secretary William Davison to seal it, then instructing that it should not be sealed until further ordered. It was her councillors who took matters into their own hands by sealing the warrant and sending it north without informing the Queen.

On 8 February 1587, in the great hall at Fotheringhay, Mary went to the block with dignity, dressed dramatically in a blood-red shift, her eyes blindfolded with a white silk cloth. She was praying as the axe descended, and as the second blow severed her head, some witnesses maintained they could see her lips still moving in silent prayer.

'God save the Queen!' cried the executioner – but as he reached down to grasp Mary's head, her auburn hair came off in his hands: her wigless, grey-stubbled head fell to the ground and rolled unceremoniously across it.

Down in London, Elizabeth threw a fit of sorrow, surprise and anger at the death of her royal cousin. She raged at the councillors who had sent off the warrant without her final authority. She dispatched Secretary Davison to the Tower for eighteen months, and he was never restored to royal favour. When it came to the necessary brutalities, Gloriana was as skilled at finding scapegoats as her father Henry VIII.

SIR FRANCIS DRAKE AND
THE SPANISH ARMADA
1588

IN ENGLAND HIS NAME DESCRIBED A MALE WATERFOWL THAT might be seen bobbing placidly on the village pond – but in Spanish the drake became a dragon. El Draque was a name with which to frighten naughty children, a fire-breathing monster whose steely, glittering scales 'remained impregnable', wrote the sixteenth-century dramatist Lope de Vega, 'to all the spears and all the darts of Spain'.

By the 1580s, Francis Drake's reputation provoked panic in the seaports of Spain and in its New World colonies. In a series of daring raids, the rotund Devon-born pirate had pillaged Spanish harbours, looted Catholic churches and hijacked King Philip's silver bullion as it travelled from the mines of the Andes to the Spanish treasury in Seville. In his most famous exploit, during 1577–80, Drake had sailed round the world claiming California for Queen Elizabeth and arriving home laden with treasure. No wonder she knighted him – and that his ship the *Golden Hind*, moored at Deptford near London, became the tourist attraction of the day.

Now, on 20 July 1588, Sir Francis was taking his ease at Plymouth with the other commanders of the English navy, preparing to confront the great war fleet – *armada* in Spanish – that Philip II had marshalled to punish the English for their piracy and Protestantism. According to the chronicler John Stow, writing a dozen years after the event, the English officers were dancing and revelling on the shore as the Spanish Armada hove into sight.

It was not until 1736, 148 years later, that the famous tale was published of how Drake insisted on finishing his game of bowls before he went to join his ship. But the story could well be true. The tide conditions were such on that day in 1588 that it was not possible to sail out

238

of Plymouth Sound until the evening, and the Spanish ships were scarcely moving fast. Indeed, their speed has been calculated at a stately walking pace – just two miles an hour – as they moved eastwards in a vast crescent, heading for the Straits of Dover, then for the Low Countries, where they were planning to link up with the Duke of Parma and his army of invasion.

According to folklore, the Spanish galleons were massive and lumbering castles of the sea that towered over the vessels of the English fleet. In fact, the records show the chief fighting ships on both sides to have been of roughly similar size – about a thousand tons. The difference lay in the ships' designs, for while the English galleons were sleek and nippy, custom-made for piracy and for manoeuvring in coastal waters, the Spanish ships were full-bellied, built for steadiness as they transported their cargo on the long transatlantic run.

More significantly, the English ships carried twice the cannon power of their enemies', thanks, in no small part, to the zeal of Henry VIII. Elizabeth's polymath father had taken an interest in artillery, encouraging a new gun-building technology developed from bell-founding techniques: in 1588 some of the older English cannon that blasted out at the Spanish galleons had been recast from the copper and tin alloy melted down from the bells of the dissolved monasteries.

Popular history has assigned Francis Drake the credit for defeating the Spanish Armada. In fact, Drake almost scuppered the enterprise on the very first night: he broke formation to go off and seize a disabled Spanish vessel for himself. The overall commander of the fleet was Lord Howard of Effingham, and it was his steady strategy to keep pushing the Spanish up the Channel, harrying them as they went. 'Their force is wonderful great and strong,' wrote Howard to Elizabeth on the evening of 29 July, 'and yet we pluck their feathers by little and little.'

Ashore in England, meanwhile, the beacons had been lit. A chain of hilltop bonfires had spread the news of the Armada's sighting, and the militia rallied for the defence of the shires. Lit today to celebrate coronations and royal jubilees, this network of 'fires over England' dated back to medieval times. Seventeen thousand men rapidly mustered in the south-east, and early in August Queen Elizabeth travelled to inspect them at Tilbury as they drilled in preparation for confronting Parma's invasion force. According to one account, the fifty-four-year-old Queen strapped on a breastplate herself to deliver the most famous of the well-worded speeches that have gilded her reputation:

> *I am come amongst you, as you see . . . in the midst and heat of the battle, to live and die amongst you all . . . I know I have the body of a weak and feeble woman, but I have the heart and the stomach of a king, and a king of England too, and think it foul scorn that Parma, or Spain, or any prince of Europe should dare to invade the borders of my realm . . . We shall shortly have a famous victory over those enemies of my God, my kingdom and my people.*

By the time Elizabeth delivered this speech, on 9 August 1588, the famous victory had already been won. Several nights previously, Howard had dispatched fire ships into the Spanish fleet as it lay at anchor off the Flanders coast, and in the resulting confusion the Spanish had headed north, abandoning their rendezvous with Parma. Fleeing in front of their English pursuers, they took the long way home, heading round the top of Scotland and Ireland. Almost half the Armada, including many of the best warships, managed to make it back to Spain. But over eleven thousand Spaniards perished, and the great crusade to which the Pope and several Catholic nations had contributed ended in humiliation.

Drake himself died eight years later on a raiding expedition in the Caribbean that went disastrously wrong. He was buried at sea, and great was the celebration when the news of his death reached Spain. In England, however, he became an instant hero, inspiring implausible tales of wizardry. According to one, he increased the size of his fleet by cutting a piece of wood into chips, each of which became – hey-presto! – a man-o'-war.

His legend has been revived particularly at times of national danger. In the early 1800s, when Napoleon's troops were poised to cross the Channel, an ancient drum was discovered which was said to have travelled everywhere with Drake, and the Victorian poet Sir Henry Newbolt imagined the old sea dog dying in the tropics on his final voyage, promising to heed the summons whenever England had need of him:

Take my drum to England, hang et by the shore,
Strike et when your powder's runnin' low;
If the Dons sight Devon, I'll quit the port o' Heaven,
An' drum them up the Channel as we drummed them long ago.

SIR JOHN'S JAKES
1592

Today we associate sewage disposal with water – the push of a button, the pull of a chain and whoosh . . . But conveniences were rarely so convenient in Tudor times. A few castles had 'houses of easement' situated over the waters of the moat, and Dick Whittington's famous 'Longhouse' (see p.154) had been built over the River Thames. One of the advantages of occupying the hundred or so homes built on the sixteenth-century London Bridge was the straight drop from privy to river – though this was also a hazard for passing boatmen.

For most people, a hole in the earth did the job – inside a fenced enclosure or little hut at the back of the house. Moss or leaves served for toilet paper and a shovelful of earth for a flush. When the hole was full, you simply upped sticks and found, or made, a new hole.

At the other end of the social scale, Henry VIII had a private throne to suit his style and status. Decorated with ribbons, fringes and two thousand gold nails, his 'close stool' was a black velvet box concealing a pewter chamber pot whose regular clearing and cleaning was the job of the 'groom of the stool'.

His daughter Queen Elizabeth probably had a similar device, but in 1592 she was offered a novel alternative. While staying with her godson Sir John Harington at Kelston near Bath, she was invited to test his invention – the first modern water closet, complete with a seat and a lever by means of which you could flush water down from a cistern above. The Queen liked it so much she had one installed in her palace at Richmond.

Harington publicised his invention in a joke-filled book, *The Metamorphosis of Ajax*. The title itself was a pun – 'jakes' was the Elizabethan slang for lavatory – and the author supplied a helpful diagram for do-it-yourselfers showing how, for 30s 8d (around £250 today), you could build your own WC. It would make 'your worst privy as sweet as your best chamber', he promised – and his drawing showed that you could even keep your pet goldfish in the cistern.

Harington's WC was not the first. The Romans had flushing cisterns. But his design does seem to have been the original product of a lively mind. Elizabeth's multi-gifted godson amused her court with his translations of risqué foreign verses and, not surprisingly, bold wit that he was, he was never afraid to mention the unmentionable:

> *If leeks you leake, but do their smell disleeke, eat onions and*
> *   you shall not smell the leek.*
> *If you of onions would the scent expel,*
> *Eat garlic – that shall drown the onion smell.*
> *But against garlic's savour, if you smart,*
> *I know but one receipt. What's that? A fart.*

BY TIME SURPRISED
1603

BY MARCH 1603 IT WAS CLEAR THAT ELIZABETH WAS DYING. The faithful Doctor Dee had looked at the stars and advised her to move from Whitehall to her palace at airy Richmond. There she sat on the floor for days, propped up with embroidered cushions. With her finger in her mouth and her features, as ever, plastered with white, lead-based make-up, the sixty-nine-year-old monarch refused to eat, sleep or change her clothes.

'Madam, you must to bed,' urged Robert Cecil, who had become her chief minister following the death of his father William, Lord Burghley, in 1598.

'Little man! Little man!' retorted the Queen. 'Your father would have known that "must" is not a word we use to princes.'

The closing years of her reign had not been happy ones. The great triumph of the Armada had been followed by still more warfare – with Spain, in Ireland, in France and in the Netherlands. War cost money, and three times more taxes had been levied in the fifteen years since 1588 than in the first thirty years of her reign. Harvests had been poor, prices high, trade depressed. Parliament complained bitterly at the growth of 'monopolies', the exclusive trading licences the Queen granted to favourites like Ralegh, who controlled the sales of tin and playing cards, and also the licensing of taverns. Steel, starch, salt, imported drinking glasses . . . the list of these privately controlled and taxed commodities was read out one day in Parliament. 'Is not bread there?' called out a sarcastic voice.

In 1601 discontented citizens had marched through the streets of London in support of the Earl of Essex, the arrogant young aristocrat who had dared to criticise and defy Elizabeth. She sent him to the block – a last flourish of the standard Tudor remedy for trouble-makers – but that did not stop people laughing at her behind her back. Even her godson John Harington, the Jakes inventor, sniggered unchar-itably at the out-of-touch monarch 'shut up in a chamber from her subjects and most of her servants . . . seldom seen but on holy days'. Sir Walter Ralegh put it more gallantly. The Queen, he said, was 'a lady whom time had surprised'.

Elizabeth had always refused to nominate an heir. She had no wish, she said, to contemplate her 'own winding sheet'. But by 1603 it was clear there could be only one successor – King James VI of Scotland, the son of Mary Queen of Scots. Now thirty-six, James had proved himself a canny ruler north of the border, and his bloodline was impec-cable. He was the great-great-grandson of the first Tudor, Henry VII.

Robert Cecil had been corresponding secretly with James for months, and all through February and March the horses stood ready, staged at ten-mile intervals so that news of the Queen's death would reach Scotland without delay. On the evening of 23 March she fell unconscious and, waking only briefly, she died in the small hours of the 24th. As the messenger headed north, trumpeters, heralds, judges and barons were already processing through the streets of London to proclaim the new King James I.

Elizabeth I, Queen of Shakespeare, Ralegh, Drake and the Armada, had presided over one of the most glorious flowerings of English history and culture, and her success owed not a little to the adroitness with which she had avoided marriage. But this also meant that she was the last of her line. Her successor James Stuart and every subsequent English and British monarch has taken their descent not from Gloriana, but from Elizabeth's hated rival, Mary Queen of Scots.

5/11: ENGLAND'S FIRST TERRORIST

1605

WITH HIS FLOWING MOUSTACHE AND LUXURIANT BEARD, Guy Fawkes cut an elegant figure – he looked like anything but a household servant as he lurked in one of the cellars-to-rent below the Houses of Parliament on the afternoon of 4 November 1605. He was wearing a dark hat and cloak, and had strapped his spurs on to his riding boots, ready for a quick escape. But when the Lord Chamberlain's guards came upon Guy in the candlelit cellar, they believed his story. He was a domestic servant, he told them – 'John Johnson' was the cover name he had prepared – and he had been checking on the piles of firewood stacked against the wall. The search party went on their way, not thinking to rummage behind the dry kindling, where, if they had looked, they would have discovered thirty-six large barrels of gunpowder . . .

The notorious Gunpowder Plot was born of the injustice and disappointment that many English Catholics came to feel at the beginning of the reign of King James I. Their hopes had been high that the son of Mary Queen of Scots, their Catholic champion and martyr, would ease the legal persecution from which they suffered – and James duly had his mother's body dug up and reburied in Westminster Abbey. Mary lies there to this day, in a splendid tomb alongside Elizabeth – the two cousins, Catholic and Protestant, honoured equally in death.

But James knew he must live with the reality of a nation that defined itself as Protestant, and soon after his arrival in England he summoned a conference at Hampton Court to submit the Church of England to review by the growing number of evangelicals who wanted to weed out the 'impure' practices left over from Catholicism. As far as doctrine was concerned, the new King gave these 'Puritans' less than they wanted, but he did bow to their demands to enforce the anti-Catholic laws that Elizabeth had applied with a relatively light touch.

These laws were fierce. Anyone caught hearing the mass could be fined and sent to jail. Priests – many of whom survived in 'priest holes' hidden behind the panelling in the homes of rich Catholics – were liable to be punished by imprisonment or even death. Catholic children could not be baptised. The dying were denied the ceremony of extreme unction, their crucial step to heaven. Catholics could not study at university. If they failed to attend their local Anglican church they were classed as 'recusants' (we might say 'refuseniks'), and became liable to fines of £20 a month. The enforcement of recusancy fines was patchy, but £20 was a quite impossible penalty at a time when a yeoman, or 'middling', farmer was legally defined as someone whose land brought him forty shillings, or £2, per year.

'Catholics now saw their own country,' wrote Father William Weston, 'the country of their birth, turned into a ruthless and unloving land.'

State-sponsored oppression, frustration, hopelessness – from these bitter ingredients stemmed the extravagant scheme of Guy Fawkes and a dozen aggrieved young Catholics to blow up the King, his family, the Royal Council and all the members of the Protestant-dominated Houses of Parliament in one spectacular blast. Modern explosives experts have calculated that Guy's thirty-six barrels (5,500 pounds) of gunpowder would have caused 'severe structural damage' to an area within a radius of five hundred metres. Not only the Houses of Parliament, but Westminster Abbey and much of Whitehall would have been demolished in a terrorist gesture whose imaginative and destructive power stands comparison, for its time, with the planes that al-Qaeda's pilots crashed into New York's World Trade Center on 11 September 2001.

But as the Gunpowder Plotters' plan for scarcely imaginable slaughter became known in Catholic circles, someone felt they had to blow the whistle:

> My Lord, out of the love I bear to some of your friends, I have a care of your
> preservation ... [read an anonymous letter sent to a Catholic peer, Lord
> Monteagle, on 26 October 1605] I would advise you, as you tender your life,
> to devise some excuse to shift of your attendance at this Parliament ... [and]
> retire yourself into your country where you may expect the event in safety.

Delivered at dusk by a tall stranger to a servant of Monteagle's outside his house in Hoxton on the north-east outskirts of London, this 'dark and doubtful letter' can be seen today in the National Archives, and has inspired fevered debate among scholars: who betrayed the plot? The letter's authorship has been attributed to almost every one of Guy Fawkes's confederates – and even to Robert Cecil, Lord Salisbury, James's chief minister, who organised the investigation after Monteagle handed over the letter.

'John Johnson' fooled the first search party on the afternoon of 4 November, but not the second, who, lanterns in hand, prodded their way through the cellars in the early hours of the 5th, the very day Parliament was due to assemble. Once arrested, he made no secret of his intention to blow up King and lords. His only regret, he said, was that his plan had not succeeded. It was 'the devil and not God' who had betrayed the plot.

Torture soon extracted from Guy Fawkes that he was a thirty-four-year-old Catholic from York who had fought in the Netherlands on the Spanish side against the Dutch Protestants. Like the letter that betrayed him, his successive confessions can be read today: his signature starts off firm and black, then degenerates to a tremulous and scarcely legible scratching as the rack does its dreadful work. Once Parliament had been destroyed, it turned out, the conspirators were planning to seize the King's nine-year-old daughter Princess Elizabeth, and install her as their puppet ruler.

Guy and his fellow-plotters suffered the ghastly penalties prescribed for traitors: they were hung, drawn and quartered. When Parliament reassembled, the first order of business was to institute 'a public thanksgiving to Almighty God every year on the fifth day of November' – the origin of our modern 'Bonfire Night'.

But furious Protestants were not content with executions and prayers. 'This bloody stain and mark will never be washed out of Popish religion,' declared Sir Thomas Smith, one of the many who called for vengeance. Half a century after the fires of Smithfield, the Gunpowder Plot marked a further stage in the demonising of English Catholics, who, in the years that followed, were banned from practising law, serving in the army or navy as officers, or voting in elections. In 1614 one MP suggested Catholics be compelled to wear a yellow hat and shoes so they could be easily identified and 'hooted at' by true Englishmen.

This last proposal was, happily, judged to be unEnglish and went no further. But the Gunpowder Plot raises important moral issues to this day. Is violence permissible to a persecuted minority? And if you do strike back against a government that subjects you to state-sponsored terror – why are you the one who is called a terrorist?

KING JAMES'S
'AUTHENTICAL' BIBLE
1611

'NO MOR ENGLAND BOT GRATE BRITAINE,' NOTED A patriotic Scot in his diary, as James VI of Scotland and I of England rode out from Edinburgh to claim his southern kingdom in the spring of 1603. When the new King opened his first Parliament in London, he urged his English subjects to join more closely with Scotland – he called for a 'Union of Love' – and on 16 November he signed a decree creating a new Anglo-Scottish currency featuring a twenty-shilling piece called 'the Unite'. Sadly for James, his McPound proved impractical, but in 1604 he did initiate a project that would, over the years, make for unity in another sense, and in a context far wider than England and Scotland.

As the clerics debated at the Hampton Court conference in 1604 one of them suggested that there should be 'one only translation of the Bible to be authentical', and the King seized on the idea. 'One uniform translation' should be produced, he agreed, 'by the learned of both universities', to be reviewed by the 'chief learned of the church', then ratified by himself. 'Were I not a King,' he informed his bishops proudly, 'I would be a University man.'

Seven years, fifty-four translators and six committees later, the result of the King's initiative was the 'Authorised Version' that bears his name – the so-called King James Bible, 'Newly Translated out of the Originall tongues & with the former Translations diligently compared and revised by his Maiesties Speciall Comandement – Appointed to be read in Churches'.

For two hundred and fifty years the King James Bible would set the standard for phraseology, rhythm and syntax wherever in the world English speakers gathered – an English grammar and literature lesson in its own right. Sunday after Sunday its sonorous cadences filtered into the English consciousness, shaping thought patterns as well as language – and this was just as King James's scholarly committees intended: the surviving records of their deliberations make clear that they searched constantly for the words that would not only read better but *sound* better, for this was a lectern Bible, designed above all to be read out and listened to.

The dream of William Tyndale – and before that of John Wycliffe – had finally come true. Here was a Bible that could be understood by every ploughboy, built on a spare and simple vocabulary of only eight thousand different words – and time after time the reviewing committees decided that William Tyndale's translations were the best. They made only small changes to his original phrases, so that, in the end, eighty per cent of this royally 'authorised' version came from the man who had been tracked down by Henry VIII's agents seventy-five years earlier and had been burned at the stake.

'Our Father, which art in heaven, hallowed be thy name . . .' Even today, in our relatively non-religious age, these memorable Tyndale-King James lines may well be the most frequently repeated set of sentences in the English language.

'SPOILT CHILD' AND THE PILGRIM FATHERS
1616

IN THE SPRING OF 1616 THE TOAST OF LONDON WAS AN exotic young arrival from the New World – 'Pocahontas', the beautiful twenty-one-year-old daughter of Powhatan, chief of the Algonquins of coastal Virginia. Her tribal name had been Matoaka,

but her family had nicknamed her the 'naughty one', or 'spoilt child' –
and it was under her nickname that she had been brought to London
to celebrate the nine-year survival of Jamestown, Virginia. This was
England's first permanent colony in North America, established in
Chesapeake Bay, a hundred miles or so north of Ralegh's 'lost colony'
of Roanoke.

Wined and dined and taken to London's flourishing theatres,
Pocahontas was presented to King James I, after whom the new settlement had been named. Her visit spearheaded a publicity drive by
the investors of the Virginia Company who were looking for new
colonists and partners. Much was made of the young woman's conversion to Christianity and her marriage to a wealthy tobacco planter,
John Rolfe, by whom she had a son. Even before Pocahontas died of
pneumonia (or possibly tuberculosis) in March 1617, to be buried at
Gravesend in Kent, the Indian 'princess' had come to symbolise the
prospect of good relations between the new colonists and the native
population.

That hope, we now know, was a cruel illusion. The modern United
States of America has been built upon the systematic destruction and
dispossession of its native population – and the few reliable facts we
possess about the life of Pocahontas place a question mark over her
myth. In 1612 she had been captured and held to ransom in the course
of a savage series of attacks and reprisals between colonists and locals,
and according to the Powhatan nation of American Indians who
champion her cause today, the marriage of Pocahontas to the older,
wealthy widower John Rolfe was anything but a love match: it was the
price of her release.

The Never-Never Land aspects of transatlantic exploration were
made clear the following year when Sir Walter Ralegh, now sixty-seven
and a creaking relic of the glory days of Elizabeth, sailed into Plymouth
after a failed attempt to locate El Dorado, the fabled city of gold that
was said to lie in the rainforests of South America. Having flirted with
ill-judged notions of conspiracy in the early months of James's reign,
Ralegh had spent a dozen years imprisoned in the Tower before winning temporary release on his far-fetched promise to bring back the
treasures of El Dorado. But he failed to locate the city. Furthermore,
his frustrated followers attacked a Spanish settlement, and it suited

James to sacrifice the old Elizabethan to the Spanish protests that followed. ''Tis a sharp remedy,' Ralegh remarked as he felt the edge of the axe in New Palace Yard on 29 October 1618, 'but a sure one for all ills.'

The flamboyant champion of England's empire overseas went to his death not long before his dream took another step towards reality. In September 1620 the Pilgrim Fathers set sail from Plymouth in their merchant ship, the *Mayflower*. They came mainly from the village of Scrooby in Nottinghamshire, where they had pursued a category of Puritanism known as 'Separatism'. Abandoning the hope that they could 'purify' the Church of England of its papist taints, the Scrooby Separatists looked abroad, and in 1608 had exiled themselves to Protestant Holland. Among their leaders were the local postmaster William Brewster, and a fervent Yorkshireman, William Bradford, who would later write the story of their great adventure.

But Bradford, Brewster and their companions did not find the welcome they expected in Holland. While they were allowed to practise their religion, Dutch guild regulations prevented them from practising their trades. So they were after economic as much as religious freedom when they boarded the *Mayflower* in the summer of 1620, landing on Cape Cod, in modern Massachusetts, on 9 November. To govern themselves they drew up the 'Mayflower Compact', the first written constitution in the Americas – indeed, the first written constitution in the English language, in which the authority of government was explicitly based on the consent of the governed. And having sailed from Plymouth, they named their colony Plymouth.

In the next two decades Plymouth Colony inspired more than twenty thousand settlers to create new lives for themselves in the stockaded villages of 'New England' – and it also inspired the great American festival of Thanksgiving. Tradition dates this back to November 1621 when, after half Plymouth's pilgrims had died of disease and famine, the local Indians came to their rescue with a feast of turkey, corn on the cob, sweet potatoes and cranberries.

The rescue of 1621 is well documented, but more than two centuries were to elapse before we find Thanksgiving being celebrated routinely on an annual basis. Not until 1863 was Abraham Lincoln encouraged by the rediscovery of William Bradford's history *Of Plymouth Plantation* to reinvent the tradition and declare Thanksgiving a national holiday.

We should also, perhaps, revise our image of the Pilgrim Fathers all wearing sober black costumes with white collars and big buckles on their shoes. Shoe buckles did not come into fashion until the late 1660s, and, as for the colonists' costumes, as inventoried on their deaths by the Plymouth plantation court, they sound more like those of pixies than pilgrims: *Mayflower* passenger John Howland died with two red waistcoats in his travelling chest; William Bradford also owned a red waistcoat, along with a green gown and a suit with silver buttons, while the wardrobe of William Brewster, the former postmaster of Scrooby, featured green breeches, a red cap and a fine 'violet' coat.

THE ARK OF THE
JOHN TRADESCANTS
1622

Ananas comosus

THE JOHN TRADESCANTS, FATHER AND SON, WERE England's first master gardeners. John Sr made his name in the final years of Elizabeth's reign, and was then hired in 1609 by Robert Cecil, 1st Lord Salisbury, to beautify the gardens of his grand new home, Hatfield House in Hertfordshire. John travelled to Holland to purchase the newly fashionable flower, the tulip, and spent no less than eighty shillings of Cecil's money (the equivalent of £440 today) on sacks of bulbs. In search of more exotic plants, he joined a trading expedition to Russia in 1618, and two years later accompanied a squadron of English warships sent to North Africa to quell the Barbary pirates. Among the specimens he brought home was the hardy perennial beloved of modern gardeners, tradescantia.

But John was interested in more than plants. He started collecting local artefacts and curiosities on his travels, and this passion of his received a powerful boost in 1622 when he became gardener to George Villiers, Duke of Buckingham, the controversial favourite of King James I. Buckingham was Lord Admiral, and it was not long before the navy was instructing all English merchants engaged in trade with the New World to be on the lookout for a lengthy list of rarities – in fact 'any thing that is strange' – drawn up by John Tradescant.

By the 1630s, the Tradescant collection filled several rooms of the family house at Lambeth, just across the Thames from Westminster, and John decided to open his 'rarities' to the public. Taking biblical inspiration, he called England's first ever museum 'The Ark'. The public flocked to gaze at such novelties as the hat and lantern taken from Guy Fawkes when he was arrested under the Houses of Parliament, alongside over a thousand named varieties of plants, flowers and trees – an apparently odd but enduring combination of English enthusiasms that lives on in the popularity of such TV programmes as *Gardeners' World* and *Antiques Roadshow*.

After John's death in 1638, his son took over the collection, proving an even more adventurous traveller than his father. He crossed the Atlantic three times to bring back the pineapple, the yucca and the scarlet runner bean, along with the Virginia creeper whose green leaves go flame-red in autumn. In his later years John Jr joined forces with Elias Ashmole, an ambitious lawyer who had helped catalogue the collection, but after John's death Ashmole became embroiled in a series of disputes with Tradescant's widow Hester.

One morning, in April 1678, Hester Tradescant was found dead, apparently drowned in the garden pool at her Lambeth home. Foul play was ruled out, but Ashmole took control of Tradescant's Ark. The collection came to form the nucleus of the Ashmolean Museum at Oxford– where you can still see Guy Fawkes's hat and lantern.

GOD'S LIEUTENANT IN EARTH
1629

WHEN JAMES I'S SECOND-BORN SON PRINCE CHARLES arrived in London at the beginning of his father's reign, courtiers hesitated to join his retinue. The child was sickly and backward – he could easily die and his household vanish, leaving them high and dry. By his fourth birthday in November 1604 the young prince was still not walking properly, and his father was so worried by his slow speech and stutter that he 'was desirous that the string under his tongue should be cut'.

But Charles was not a quitter. The plodding prince worked hard at overcoming his disabilities, particularly after 1612 when his more obviously gifted elder brother Henry died of typhoid. By the time Charles I succeeded his father in March 1625, he was a young man of some grit, principle and piety, already displaying the taste that would make him, arguably, England's greatest royal patron of the arts. But the admirable determination he had shown in his childhood now verged on obstinacy, which was fed by the big idea that would eventually bring disaster on his family – the Divine Right of Kings.

The notion had been planted by his writerly father, James, who quoted lengthy passages from the Bible in his pamphlet *The Trew Law of Free Monarchies* in support of his argument that an anointed monarch was 'God's Lieutenant in earth'. This view was taken for granted by the absolute monarchs of early modern Europe, but the self-righteous James had turned it into a lecture directed at his 'honest and obedient subjects'. A people could no more depose their King, he told them, than sons could replace their father. 'I have at length prooved,' he concluded, 'that the King is above the law.'

When it came to practical politics, James himself had never pushed his ideas to the limit, particularly when, south of the border, he found himself dealing with the touchy squires and merchants who dominated England's House of Commons. But Charles lacked his father's subtlety. He felt personally affronted when on his accession Parliament declined to vote him the usual supply of customs revenues for life, granting the money for one year only. Puritan MPs were suspicious of Charles's French Catholic wife and of his personal preference for church cere-monial – and no one liked his reliance on the Duke of Buckingham, the unpopular favourite he had taken over from his father. 'In the gov-ernment,' complained one member, 'there wanteth good advice.'

But rather than negotiate in the style of his father – or cajole, as the imperious Queen Elizabeth would have done – Charles lost his temper. He dissolved Parliament in August 1625 and the following year started raising funds with 'forced loans', the ancient, discredited tactic of Empson and Dudley (see p. 194) which Charles now extended from a handful of rich targets to most of the tax-paying community. When his Chief Justice, Sir Randolph Crew, questioned the legality of this non-parliamentary levy, Charles dismissed him; more than seventy non-payers were sent to prison.

These were serious issues to the MPs whose predecessors had made the laws that had helped Henry VIII break with Rome. James had written about kings being above the law – Charles was trying to put theory into practice. When a shortage of funds compelled him to summon Parliament again in 1628, an angry House of Commons wasted no time in preparing a statement of fundamental principles, the Petition of Right, which prohibited non-parliamentary taxation and arbitrary imprisonment. After some prevarication, Charles signed the petition, but he did so with ill grace – and then, that August, his friend and confidant Buckingham was assassinated in Portsmouth.

The murder was the work of a deranged Puritan, John Felton, who had been incited by parliamentary denunciations of Buckingham as 'the grievance of all grievances', and Charles blamed his critics in Parliament for the killing. He felt bitterly wounded by the explosion of popular joy that greeted the news of Buckingham's death, and it turned his deepening dislike of Parliament into a grudge match that came to a head in the spring of 1629.

The issue was religion. Sir John Eliot, the eloquent Puritan MP who had led the assaults on both Buckingham and forced loans, had produced a resolution against what were known as 'Arminian' church practices, so-called after the Dutch theologian Jacob Arminius whose English admirers had called for a return to church ceremonial. This cause was championed by Charles's recently appointed Bishop of London, William Laud, who was busy restoring neglected rituals to the Church of England. In what we would describe as a battle between High and Low Church, Charles sided enthusiastically with ritual, and rightly interpreted the Puritan attack on Arminianism as a snub to his royal authority. He sent orders to Westminster to halt all discussion immediately.

The Commons responded with a defiance that would become historic. Heedless of the King's words, the debate continued. One MP, Sir Miles Hobart, locked the door against the indignant hammerings of the King's messenger, while the burly MP for Dorchester, Denzil Holles, forcibly held down the Speaker, Sir John Finch, in his chair. The Speaker was the Commons' servant, not the King's, Finch was told, and Sir John Eliot took the floor to denounce 'innovations in religion' and royal interference with Parliament's right to speak. 'None had gone about to break parliaments,' he declared, 'but in the end parliaments had broken them.'

Cries of 'Aye, Aye, Aye' rang out around the chamber, and Eliot's resolution against 'Popery or Arminianism' was duly acclaimed, along with a further condemnation of taxation without parliamentary assent. Anyone who disagreed or disobeyed – and this presumably included the King – 'shall be reputed a capital enemy to this kingdom and commonwealth . . . He shall likewise be reputed a betrayer of the liberties of England.'

But two days later, Hobart, Holles, Eliot and six other leaders of the protest were on their way to the Tower. Charles had the dissidents arrested, then dissolved Parliament on 10 March. God's Lieutenant had decided he could rule England more smoothly without it.

CHARLES I ATTEMPTED TO RULE ENGLAND WITHOUT Parliament for eleven years, from 1629 to 1640, and he started off well enough. He made peace with Spain and France and, alongside his French wife Henrietta Maria, presided over a well-ordered court where art, music and drama flourished. Under his auspices, the Church of England was stringently administered by William Laud who, as Archbishop of Canterbury after 1633, organised diocesan inspections that tested the conformity of every priest and parish. Laud's efficient policy style came to be known as 'Thorough', and it was matched by Sir Thomas Wentworth, a former Member of Parliament who administered first the north and then Ireland for Charles, before rising to become his principal minister, ennobled as the Earl of Strafford.

Back in 1628, as MP for Yorkshire, Wentworth had spoken out in favour of the Petition of Right, yet he came to feel that many of his fellow-parliamentarians went too far in their attacks on King and Crown – a view that was shared by many. The austere and driven Puritans whose voices rang out loudest in the Commons were even calling for the removal of bishops from the Church of England. Such extremism fortified moderate support for the King, and it was Charles's tragedy that he would waste England's deep-rooted conservatism and loyalty to the Crown. As his own man Laud later put it, Charles I was 'a gracious prince who neither knew how to be, nor to be made, great'.

One of the virtues of raising money through Parliament was that it minimised direct conflict between taxpayer and King. But as Charles exploited ancient and obscure sources of revenue like the duty of seaport towns to supply the King with ships, solid citizens came into head-to-head conflict with the Crown. To widespread support, the opposition to 'ship money' was led by a prosperous Buckinghamshire landowner, John Hampden, who fought the tax in court, effectively contending that it was the King who was the law-breaker here.

As so often, religion provoked even deeper issues of due process and fair play. When in 1634 the Puritan lawyer William Prynne denounced as immoral the court masques in which the King and his wife liked to dance, Charles's arbitrary Court of Star Chamber (evolved from the Royal Council of earlier times) ordered that his ears be cut off. Three years later the incorrigible Prynne turned his holy criticism on the bishops – only to have what survived of his ears sliced away.

Hampden and Prynne became national heroes thanks to the printed newsletters – early versions of newspapers – that were beginning to circulate between London and the provinces. These publicised the political and religious issues at stake, usually favouring the underdog, while primitive woodcuts provided dramatic images that got the message to the two-thirds of the population who could not read. One cartoon showed a smiling Archbishop Laud dining off a dish of Prynne's severed ears.

Feelings were running high in 1640 when Charles reluctantly resumed dealing with Parliament. His attempt to take 'Thorough' to Scotland and to impose the English Prayer Book (against Laud's better judgement) on Scotland's Presbyterians had led to the so-called Bishops' Wars that drained the royal treasury dry. The early months of 1640 had seen an army of rebellious Scots occupying the north of England, and the King was urgently in need of money. But his parliamentary critics were bitterly determined that he should pay a price for it.

Strafford and Laud were their first targets, both indicted for treason as Charles's accomplices in what would later be known as the 'Eleven Years Tyranny'. Strafford was sent to trial in March 1641, charged with being the 'principal author and promoter of all those counsels which had exposed the kingdom to so much ruin'. When he defended himself so ably in court that an acquittal seemed possible, the Commons contrived another way to get him. They quickly passed a bill of attainder, a blunt instrument that baldly declared Strafford's guilt without need of legal process, and as Charles hesitated to sign the attainder, mobs of shaven-headed apprentices roamed the London streets baying for the blood of 'Black Tom the Tyrant'.

The campaign against Thomas Strafford was directed by John Pym, the veteran MP for Calne in Wiltshire who, a dozen years earlier, had been Sir John Eliot's principal lieutenant in the battle for the Petition of Right. Now Pym masterminded the entire parliamentary assault on royal powers, plotting with the Scottish rebels to maintain pressure on the King while also stirring up the London mobs. On 10 May 1641, fearing for the safety of his wife and children, Charles signed Strafford's attainder, and two days later his faithful servant went to the block in front of a jubilant crowd over one hundred thousand strong.

Having secured one victim, Parliament's radicals turned to the practical business of ensuring that personal rule could never be revived. In February that year the Triennial Act had held that Parliament, if not summoned by the King, must automatically reassemble after three years. Now followed an act against dissolving Parliament without its consent, another to abolish ship money, and acts to shut down the Court of Star Chamber, which had sliced off Prynne's ears, along with the Court of High Commission through which Laud had exercised his control over the Church.

On 1 December came the climax – a 'Grand Remonstrance on the State of the Kingdom', which set out no less than 204 complaints against Charles and his eleven years of personal rule. As the Commons went through their list of grievances, the debates escalated into a raucous public event to match the dragging-down of Strafford, with delegations riding in from Essex, Kent and Sussex to shout their protests outside Parliament. Many moderates became alarmed. They rallied to the royal cause. Pym's Remonstrance only just scraped through the Commons, by 159 votes to 148.

One hundred and forty-eight worried MPs was a workable base on which Charles I might have moved towards compromise – and there was every possibility that the Lords would reject the Remonstrance. But God's Lieutenant did not do compromise, and his hurt pride would not let him delay. Bitterly remorseful and blaming himself for Strafford's fate, on Monday 3 January 1642 Charles instructed his Attorney General to commence treason proceedings against his five bitterest critics in the Commons: John Pym, John Hampden, Denzil Holles, Arthur Hazelrig and William Strode, along with Viscount Mandeville, a leading reformer in the House of Lords.

Next day Charles marched to the Parliament House in Westminster with a party of guards, intending to lay hands on the culprits himself – an extraordinarily risky and melodramatic gesture into which he was tempted by Pym and his four companions, who had set themselves up as bait. Having advertised their presence in the Commons that morning, the five Members then monitored the King's progress down Whitehall.

When Charles entered the Commons chamber, he requested the Speaker, William Lenthall, to yield him his seat and to point out Pym and the others. Falling to his knees, Lenthall replied that it was not for him to either see or speak but as the House desired. There was no precedent for this situation. No King of England had ever interrupted a session of the House of Commons. ''Tis no matter,' declared Charles, 'I think my eyes are as good as another's', and he cast his eyes along the benches as the MPs stood bareheaded and in silence. Through the open door they could see the royal guards, some of whom were cocking their pistols, playfully pretending to mark down their men – until melodrama turned to anticlimax.

'All my birds have flown,' admitted Charles, disconsolately conceding defeat. Having set their trap, the five had made good their escape, slipping down to the river, where a boat took them into hiding in the City. As the crestfallen King turned on his heel to leave the chamber, the suddenly emboldened Members reminded him of their rights and let out catcalls of 'Privilege! Privilege!' at his retreating and humiliated back.

The debacle marked a breaking point. Compromise was no longer possible between an obstinate monarch and a defiant Parliament, and six days later, on 10 January 1642, Charles slipped out of Whitehall with his family. He stopped briefly at Hampton Court. Then Henrietta Maria headed for Holland with the crown jewels, hoping to raise money, while Charles rode towards York, intent on raising the army he would need to fight the Civil War.

ROUNDHEADS V. CAVALIERS
1642–8

LADY MARY BANKES WAS A FORMIDABLE WOMAN, THE mother of fourteen children. When the Civil War broke out in August 1642 it fell to her to defend the family home at Corfe Castle in Dorset. Her husband was a senior judge and a privy councillor, so when the King had gone north to raise his standard that summer Sir John Bankes followed. He soon found himself, like all the King's councillors, denounced by Parliament as a traitor.

Down in Dorset, the local parliamentary commander anticipated little trouble when he arrived at Corfe to take the surrender of the Bankes's home. But he had not reckoned on the valiant Lady Mary, who shut the gates against him. When his men attempted to scale the walls they found themselves showered with rocks and burning embers thrown by the family's loyal retainers – cooks and chambermaids included. Even a prize of £20 (£2,240 today) offered to the first man to reach the battlements attracted no takers. Hearing of royalist troops in the nearby town of Dorchester, the parliamentarians slunk away.

It took an act of treachery to capture Corfe three years later. One February night in 1646, an accomplice in the garrison opened the gates to fifty parliamentary troops disguised as royalists, and Lady Bankes, a widow since her husband's death at Oxford two years previously, was arrested. Parliament confiscated their lands and decided to 'slight' Corfe Castle: they stacked the main towers with gunpowder barrels, then exploded them.

The bravery of Lady Mary and the spectacular ruins of her castle that loom over Corfe to this day illustrate the drama of England's Civil War and the damage it wreaked. Modern estimates suggest that one in every four or five adult males was caught up in the fighting: 150 towns suffered serious destruction; 11,000 houses were burned or demolished and 55,000 people made homeless – these were the years when the German word *plündern*, to plunder, came into the language, brought over by Charles's loot-happy cavalry commander, his nephew Prince Rupert of the Rhine. Nearly 4 per cent of England's population died in the fighting or from war-related disease – a higher proportion, even, than died in World War I. 'Whose blood stains the walls of our towns and defiles our land?' lamented Bulstrode Whitelock to the House of Commons in 1643. 'Is it not all English?'

The Civil War was not like the Wars of the Roses, when everyday life had largely carried on as normal. The clash between King and Parliament involved the most fundamental question – how should the country be ruled? And to this was added the profound differences in religion that bitterly divided families and split friend from friend. Sir William Waller and Sir Ralph Hopton had been comrades-in-arms in the early 1620s, fighting Catholics on the continent. But now they found themselves on opposing sides, Sir William supporting Parliament because of his Puritan beliefs, Sir Ralph feeling that he must stay loyal to his monarch. 'That great God which is the searcher of my heart knows with what a sad sense I go upon this service,' wrote Waller in distress to his old friend in 1643, 'and with what a perfect hatred I detest this war without an enemy . . . [But] we are both upon the stage and must act those parts that are assigned us in this tragedy.'

Both 'Roundhead' and 'Cavalier' were originally terms of abuse. Before the war began, royalists derided the 'round heads' of the crop-haired London apprentices who had rioted outside Parliament in late December 1641 calling for the exclusion of bishops and Catholic peers from the House of Lords. In retaliation the parliamentarians dubbed their opponents *caballeros*, after the Spanish troopers notorious for their brutality against the Dutch Protestants. When Charles I heard this rendered into English as 'cavalier' he decided that he liked the associations of nobility and horsemanship, and encouraged his followers to adopt the word.

In October 1642 came the first great battle of the Civil War, at Edgehill, north of the royal headquarters at Oxford. Outcome: indecisive. In the year that followed, the balance swung the King's way. But in July 1644 the two sides met en masse at Marston Moor, outside York, and Parliament was triumphant.

'God made them as stubble to our swords,' boasted the plain-spoken commander of the parliamentary cavalry, Oliver Cromwell. In a famous letter to his fellow-officers from East Anglia, this stocky gentleman farmer who was fast becoming the inspiration of the parliamentary cause described what he looked for in his soldiers: 'I had rather have a plain russet-coated captain what knows what he fights for, and loves what he knows,' he wrote, 'than that which you call a gentleman and is nothing else.' When it came to recruiting, explained the Puritan preacher Richard Baxter, 'none would be such engaged fighting men as the religious'.

Religion was the inspiration of the New Model Army, the 22,000-strong professional fighting force that Cromwell and the parliamentary commander Sir Thomas Fairfax were now organising to replace the system of regional militias. Its regiments sang hymns, refrained from drinking, and made a point of listening to sermons. Royalists nicknamed this new army the 'Noddle' in mockery of its constant godly head-bobbing in prayer, but sober discipline and holy certainty brought results. On 14 June 1645 at Naseby, just south of Leicester, the red-tunicked Noddle won the decisive victory of the Civil War, taking some five thousand prisoners, securing £100,000 in jewels and booty, and – worst of all from Charles's point of view – capturing the King's private correspondence. Soon published in pamphlet form, The King's Cabinet Opened revealed that Charles had been plotting to hire foreign mercenaries and to repeal the laws against Roman Catholics.

For Oliver Cromwell and the Puritan members of the New Model Army, this was the ultimate betrayal. It was proof that the King could never be trusted. Righteous voices were raised demanding the ultimate accounting with 'Charles Stuart, that man of blood'.

The Battle of Naseby left Charles I at the mercy of an army as convinced of their divine right as he was.

BEHOLD THE HEAD
OF A TRAITOR!
1649

EARLY IN JUNE 1647 CORNET GEORGE JOYCE LED FIVE hundred horsemen of the New Model Army to Holmby House in Northamptonshire. In civilian life, Joyce was a tailor. Now he was a cornet of horse, an officer who carried the flag – and his orders were to capture the King.

The Battle of Naseby had finished the Cavaliers as a fighting force, and having vainly tried to play off his English and Scottish enemies against each other, Charles had ended up in parliamentary custody at Holmby. But Parliament and the army had fallen out over what should be done with their tricky royal prisoner, and now the army took the initiative. They would seize Charles for themselves. At dawn on 3 June, the King walked through the gates of Holmby to find Cornet Joyce waiting for him, with his fully armed fighting men lined up at attention.

'I pray you, Mr Joyce . . .' asked the King, 'tell me what commission you have?'

'Here is my commission,' replied the cornet of horse.

'Where?' asked the King.

'Behind,' replied Joyce, pointing to his ranks of red-coated troopers.

The dramatic break between army and Parliament had occurred four months earlier, in February 1647, when MPs had voted to disband the New Model Army and to send its members home. England was exhausted by war, and reflecting the national mood, Parliament's leaders set about negotiating a settlement with the King.

But the men who had risked their lives and seen their companions fall in battle were incensed. Parliament was not only dismissing them with pay owing, it was negotiating with the Antichrist, planning to restore Charles – along with his popish wife and advisers – to the throne. 'We were not a mere mercenary army,' complained 'The Declaration of the Army' of June that year, 'hired to serve any arbitrary power of the state, but [were] called forth . . . to the defence of the people's just right and liberties.'

Radical ideas had flourished in the war years. Once the army had taken custody of the King it had the power to shape the way England would be governed, and in October 1647 the Council of the Army met at St Mary's Church in the village of Putney, south-west of London, to discuss future action. The agenda was set by the utopian ideas of the 'Levellers', who were demanding that Parliament be elected by all men, not just on the existing franchise of property-holders and tradesmen. The Levellers wanted no less than to get rid of the lords and the monarchy. 'The poorest he that is in England has a life to live as the greatest he,' declared Colonel Thomas Rainsborough, as he kicked off discussion in what became known as 'the Putney Debates'.

The case for the 'grandees' – the established property-holders and others who held a 'fixed interest in the kingdom' – was put by Cromwell's son-in-law Henry Ireton. But the army's groundbreaking discussions were cut short. Ensconced upriver at Hampton Court, Charles took fright at the reports reaching him from Putney, and on 11 November he escaped under cover of darkness, riding south towards the Channel.

There is no telling what might have happened if, having reached the coast, Charles had then taken ship for France. But, not for the first time, the King turned in the wrong direction, heading for the Isle of Wight, where he had been informed – incorrectly – that the governor had royalist sympathies. In no time Charles found himself behind bars, in Carisbrooke Castle, his abortive escape bid the prelude to what became known as the Second Civil War. Royalists now rose in revolt in Kent, Essex, Yorkshire and Wales, to be followed by an invasion by a Scottish army, lured south on a secret promise from Charles that he would introduce Presbyterianism to England and suppress the wilder Puritan sects.

It was the last straw. Parliament and the New Model Army were reunited in their fury at Charles's enduring intransigence, and these risings of the Second Civil War were put down with unforgiving savagery. When the King's chaplain, Michael Hudson, was cornered on the roof at Woodcroft Hall in Lincolnshire, parliamentary troopers refused his appeal for mercy, flinging him and his companions into the moat below. As Hudson clung on to a drainage spout, his fingers were slashed off, and he was retrieved from the moat only to have his tongue cut out before being executed.

The King was treated no less ruthlessly. Cromwell and the generals were now resolved to bring him to trial, and realising that a majority of MPs still favoured some sort of compromise, they organised a *coup d'état*. Early on the morning of 6 December 1648, a detachment of horsemen and foot-soldiers under Colonel Thomas Pride surrounded both Houses of Parliament and arrested or turned away all suspected compromisers and royalist sympathisers – more than 140 members.

'Pride's purge' made possible the final act of the drama. On New Year's Day 1649, the hard core of MPs remaining voted 'to erect a high Court of Justice to try King Charles for treason', and on 20 January the trial began. The only judge who would risk the terrible responsibility of presiding over the court was an obscure provincial justice, John Bradshaw. But even he, despite being a committed republican, was so fearful that he wore armour beneath his robes and had had his beaver hat lined with steel. The King, for his part, contemptuously declined to remove his own hat as he took his seat beneath the hammer-beam roof of Westminster Hall. This contrived court, he maintained doggedly during one hearing after another, had no right to try him: he, more than his judges, stood for the liberties of the people. 'If power without law may make laws . . .' he declared, 'I do not know what subject he is in England that can be sure of his life.'

It was to no avail. Witnesses were summoned to testify they had seen the King rallying his troops at Edgehill, Naseby and on other battlefields, thus proving him guilty of waging war on Parliament and people. He was thus found guilty as a 'Tyrant, Traitor, Murderer, and Public Enemy to the good people of this Nation'. Death 'by severing the head from his body' was to be his fate.

Ten days later, on 30 January, Charles walked out on to the raised scaffold outside his splendid Banqueting House that stands to this day, just across Whitehall from Downing Street. It was a piercingly cold afternoon. The Thames had frozen, and the King had put on an extra shirt so he should not be seen to shiver.

'A subject and a sovereign are clean different things,' he declared defiantly in a long oration in which he denounced the arbitrary power of the sword that had made him 'the Martyr of the People'. Then, more prosaically, he asked the executioner, 'Does my hair trouble you?' – tucking his straggling grey locks into a nightcap to leave his neck bare.

The axe fell, severing the King's head with a single blow, and the executioner leaned down to pick it up with the standard cry – 'Behold the head of a traitor!' But the crowd, estimated at several thousand, scarcely cheered. Instead, recalled one seventeen-year-old boy later, the cry was greeted with 'such a groan as I have never heard before and desire I may never hear again'.

'TAKE AWAY THIS BAUBLE!'
1653

T HE EXECUTION OF CHARLES I WAS THE SINGLE MOST remarkable event in the course of English history – and the person who brought it to pass has a claim to being England's most remarkable man. Until almost the last moment, Oliver Cromwell had shared the fears many felt at the enormity of cutting off the King's head. But when the death warrant was finally presented for signature to the apprehensive judges, it was Cromwell who bullied the requisite number into signing. He shouted down the waverers, flicked ink at them, and, in one case, actually held down a doubter's hand to the page until he signed.

In a portrait by the painter Samuel Cooper we can study the features of the fifty-year-old Cromwell at the moment he became the most powerful living Englishman. His nose is bulbous, his eyes large and strikingly blue; a dusting of salt-and-pepper whiskers conceals a mole beneath his lower lip and there is another, the size of a pea, dark and shiny, above his right brow. 'The mirror does not flatter me,' he told the painter. 'Nor should you, Mr Cooper. I'll have it warts and all.'

Cromwell was a curious mixture of arrogance and humility, ruthlessly sweeping aside obstacles, while also prey to depression in the opinion of some modern historians – he was once treated for 'melancholy' by the exiled Huguenot physician Turquet de Mayerne. In addition, he suffered from bronchitis, though his wheeziness didn't inhibit the 'eloquence full of fervour' with which he came to the attention of the House of Commons; the MP for Huntingdon was sometimes seen with a piece of red flannel wrapped comfortingly around his throat.

His certainty of the rightness of his cause came from a deep and austere Puritan faith that set him on an inescapable collision course with the High Church policies of Charles I. At one stage Cromwell contemplated joining the thousands of Separatists who were seeking their religious freedom in the Americas. Instead he stayed, rising meteorically through the ranks of the parliamentary armies to find himself charged with the task of creating a New World at home.

Following Charles I's execution, a series of votes in the purged House of Commons abolished the House of Lords and the monarchy, and on 16 May 1649 England was declared a 'Commonwealth', ruled through Parliament by a Council of State of which Cromwell was a member. He was appointed Lieutenant General of the Commonwealth's armies, and in 1649–50 commanded ruthless campaigns against revolts in Ireland – where he massacred Catholics with a brutality that stirs resentful memories to this day – and also in Scotland, which had briefly dared to crown Charles's twenty-year-old son as Charles II. These successes capped a military career that gave Cromwell a victory tally of won 30, lost 0. As he returned triumphantly from each campaign, he was fêted like Caesar.

Like Caesar, too, he was drawn irresistibly towards political power. 'Take away this bauble!' he angrily declared in April 1653, as he strode into the House of Commons with a company of musketeers and pointed at the symbol of parliamentary authority, the ceremonial golden staff, or mace, which was set on the table in front of the Speaker.

Since 1648, when Colonel Thomas Pride had excluded those MPs likely to oppose putting Charles I on trial, the House of Commons had been a wildly unrepresentative body. Derided as the 'Rump', or remnant, its little clique of surviving members – just 140 or so – had only paid lip service to the problem, solemnly debating the surrender of their power for more than four years, while greedily hanging on to its perks and profits. 'You are no parliament, I say you are no parliament,' declaimed the exasperated Cromwell. 'I will put an end to your sitting.'

His alternative fared no better. The Nominated, or 'Barebones', Parliament (so nicknamed after the MP for London, the leather-seller turned preacher, Praise-God Barbon) was an assembly of Puritan worthies selected by local churches on such criteria as how many times the candidates prayed each day. First meeting in July 1653, this 'Parliament of Saints' dissolved itself after only five months, pushing Cromwell ever closer towards the option by which he had been tempted, but had been resisting, for so long.

King Oliver I? Cromwell's critics had long accused him of desiring nothing less; and his supporters urged him to take the crown. A royal House of Cromwell was not an impossible concept in a society that found it difficult to imagine life without a king. But Cromwell's conscience would not let him. It would have betrayed everything he stood for – and the idea was, in any case, totally unacceptable to the army. In December 1653 he was proclaimed Lord Protector of England, and when he accepted this new dignity he was careful to dress in a plain black outfit with grey worsted stockings to emphasise that this was not a coronation.

The new Lord Protector believed that government should be 'for the people's good, not what pleases them', and for nearly five years he force-fed England a diet of godliness. Since the start of the Civil War, Parliament's Puritans had been legislating for virtue, and now Cromwell put this into practice – particularly after July 1655 when he set up a network of military governors, the 'major generals'. Sunday sports were quite literally spoiled: horseracing, cockfighting, bearbaiting, bowling, shooting, dancing, wrestling – all were banned on the Sabbath. It was an offence on any day to dance around a maypole or to be caught swearing: children under twelve who uttered profanities could be whipped. Fornicators were sent to prison, and for the only time in English history (apart from the reign of King Canute), adultery was punishable by death.

Human nature won through, of course. In many localities these Puritan regulations were scarcely enforced. But they have rather unfairly defined Cromwell's place in history. He never became King Oliver, but he *was* crowned King Kill-Joy – and when he died of malaria in September 1658 there was dancing in the streets. It was 'the joyfullest funeral that ever I saw', wrote John Evelyn, 'for there was none that cried but dogs'.

Today the statue of Cromwell – sword in one hand, Bible in the other – rightly enjoys pride of place outside the Houses of Parliament. But the father of the great English Revolution actually proved how little revolution England could take, inoculating us permanently against deposing monarchs, rule by armies or morality by decree. It is the measure of his achievement that there are more roads and streets in England named after Oliver Cromwell than anyone except Queen Victoria – and none in Ireland.

RABBI MANASSEH AND THE RETURN OF THE JEWS
1655

MANASSEH BEN ISRAEL MADE IT HIS MISSION TO SECURE freedom of worship for his fellow Jews. He was a rabbi living in Amsterdam during the years of the English Commonwealth, and, like many in Europe, he was fascinated by England's great experiment in the aftermath of killing its king. He particularly pondered the burgeoning of cults and religions that followed the Civil War, for

Parliament's victorious Puritans had wasted no time in abolishing the Church of England and its monopoly over worship. Bishops, prayer books and compulsory churchgoing – all the mechanisms of an established state religion – were swept away: people were free to work out their own route to salvation.

'After the Bible was translated into English,' wrote the political theorist Thomas Hobbes, 'Everyman, nay, every boy and wench that could read English, thought they spoke with God Almighty and understood what he said.' An outspoken royalist, Hobbes had spent the Civil War in exile in Paris. There he gave maths lessons to Charles, the teenage Prince of Wales, while writing his great work of philosophy, *Leviathan*. Human life, said Hobbes, was 'solitary, poor, nasty, brutish and short'. In his opinion, humans needed a strong ruler – a Leviathan or giant – to impose order upon their unruly natures. A king was the obvious candidate, but England's King had been destroyed, and two years after Charles's execution the inquiring philosopher went bravely back to England to investigate life in the absence of the royal Leviathan.

Hobbes found the Commonwealth teeming with the new faiths, many with names that reflected their aims. The Levellers (see p. 265) were fighting for social equality; the Diggers prayed and campaigned for land reform; the Baptists favoured adult baptism; the Quakers trembled at the name of the Lord; the Ranters, for their part, believed that nothing human was wrong, permitting them to 'rant' – meaning to swear blasphemously – while also smoking and drinking and practising free love. The Muggletonians took their name from their spokesman Ludovicke Muggleton, who claimed to be one of the godly witnesses mentioned in the Book of Revelation; while the Fifth Monarchists derived their theories from Daniel's Old Testament dream: they interpreted the four beasts he saw as the four great empires of the ancient world, which were now being succeeded by a fifth, the reign of Christ – whose saints they were.

Hobbes threw up his hands at this bewildering array of creeds. These manifestly contradictory views of God confirmed his amoral and very post-modern view of life's essential chaos. But the Commonwealth's closest thing to Leviathan, Oliver Cromwell, rather welcomed the diversity. 'I had rather that Mahometanism were permitted amongst us,' he said, 'than that one of God's children should be persecuted.'

When the Diggers and Levellers had threatened property and public order immediately after the death of the King and again during the Protectorate, Cromwell had gone along with the army's suppression of their disorder. He expected his major generals to be stern in their enforcement of the new regime. But when it came to the faith inside a man's heart and head, he held firmly that freedom of worship was the right of 'the most mistaken Christian [who] should desire to live peaceably and quietly under you, [and] soberly and humbly desire to live a life of godliness and honesty'. Liberty of conscience was 'a natural right, and he that would have it ought to give it'.

This was the cue for Rabbi Manasseh Ben Israel. In 1654 he sent his son to see the Lord Protector, and the following year he left Amsterdam for London and was granted a personal audience. The Jews had been expelled from England three hundred and fifty years earlier by Edward I (see p. 115), and prejudice still lingered. Indeed, rumours of the letters the rabbi had been sending to Cromwell had prompted speculation that the Lord Protector might be planning to sell St Paul's to the Jews, to be turned into a synagogue: Christian merchants, it was feared, would be elbowed aside by ringleted Shylocks.

Cromwell was too clever to exacerbate such feeling with a formal decree or invitation of readmission to Jews. But he used his personal authority to make sure that they could now benefit from the toleration being enjoyed by other religious groups. In 1656 Jews started worshipping openly in their own synagogue in Creechurch Lane, near London's Aldgate, and within a few years there were thirty to forty Jewish families, mostly of Portuguese origin, operating in the capital as bankers and as dealers in gold and gemstones. The centuries of exclusion were over.

CHARLES II AND THE ROYAL OAK
1660

IN SEPTEMBER 1651, KING CHARLES II CLIMBED UP A makeshift wooden ladder to hide in the branches of a leafy oak tree near Boscobel House in Shropshire. His face was blackened with soot scraped from inside a chimney and his hair had been hastily cropped. Wearing the rough breeches and shirt of a simple woodman, he carried enough bread, cheese and beer to sustain him till nightfall. The twenty-one-year-old, who had been claiming the English throne since the execution of his father eighteen months earlier, was on the run. The royalist army he had led down from Scotland had been routed at Worcester two days earlier, and now the Roundhead search parties were scouring the countryside. 'While we were in this tree,' he later recalled, 'we see soldiers going up and down in the thicket of the wood, searching for persons escaped, we seeing them, now and then, peeping out of the wood.'

In later life, Charles loved telling the story of his refuge in the Royal Oak – how sore his feet had felt in his badly fitting shoes and how he had actually spent most of his time in the tree asleep. Thirty years later he related the full story: on one occasion he had hidden in a barn behind mounds of corn and hay, on another the sound of galloping hooves had made him dive behind a hedge for cover.

Charles was a fugitive for no less than six weeks, first heading north from Worcester, then doubling back south, finally making his escape to France from the little port of Shoreham in Sussex. Along the way he was sheltered by dozens of ordinary folk – millers, shepherds, farmers – as well as by prosperous landowners, many of them Catholics, who would hide him behind the panelling in their priest holes. There was a price of £1,000 on Charles's head, and the death penalty for anyone who helped him. But the King, as this young man already was in the eyes of most, would not be betrayed.

The Crown exercised an enduring hold on England's affections. The many faults of Charles I were forgotten in the shock of what came to be seen as his martyrdom, and the succession of republican experiments from Commonwealth to Protectorate made a restoration of the monarchy seem the best guarantee of stability. But the death of Cromwell in September 1658 did not immediately lead to the return of Charles II. Power rested with the thirty thousand officers and men of the Puritan army who were, for the most part, fiercely opposed to the return of the monarch, not to mention the 'popish' Church of England. The title of Protector had been taken over by Oliver's son Richard, and so long as the victors of the Civil War hung together it seemed likely that Charles would remain in exile. As his shrewd adviser Edward Hyde put it, for the monarchy to be restored, its enemies – Puritans, parliamentarians and soldiers – would have to become 'each other's executioners'.

It happened more quickly than anyone had imagined. Richard Cromwell was no leader – he lacked his father's sense of purpose and the very particular prestige that old 'Ironsides' had always enjoyed with his fellow-generals and other ranks too. After only seven months the army removed Richard, and May 1659 saw the return of the forty or so remaining members of the 'Rump' Parliament. This little band of veterans who had survived Pride's purge and dismissal by Oliver Cromwell could claim a distant, if slightly tortuous, legitimacy that went back, through all the travails of the Commonwealth and Civil Wars, to England's last full-scale elections in 1640. But they handled their comeback no more competently than their previous spell in power. By the end of 1659 they were again presiding over chaos, with taxes unpaid and rioters calling for proper elections.

Watching this slide into disorder was George Monck, commander of the English army occupying Scotland. Of solid Devon stock, the fifty-one-year-old Monck was a tough professional soldier, but he hated what he called the 'slavery of sword government' as fiercely as any civilian. In the closing days of the year he mobilised his forces at Coldstream, where they were stationed on the Scottish border, and started the march south. When he reached London in February 1660, he insisted that Parliament's deliberations could not continue without the participation of the MPs who had been excluded by Pride's purge and he finally put an end to the infamous Rump. London celebrated with revelling and barbecues. That night, 11 February, the streets smelt of roasting meat as rumps were turned on open-air spits in every corner of the city – thirty-one bonfires were counted on London Bridge alone.

Monck was now England's undisputed ruler, but he refused to make himself Lord Protector. Instead he opened negotiations with Charles II, whose little government-in-exile was gathered at Breda in Holland, and on 4 April 1660, Charles issued the Declaration of Breda, effectively his contract for restoration. Shrewdly heeding the advice of Edward Hyde, he kept his promises vague, placing his destiny in the hands of 'a free parliament'. Charles undertook to grant liberty to 'tender consciences' and a free pardon to all who had fought for Parliament – with the exception of the 'regicides' who had signed his father's death warrant. The army was promised settlement of all pay arrears in full.

The following month, the diarist and naval administrator Samuel Pepys joined Charles and his brother James, at Scheveningen near The Hague, on the ship that would bring them back to a triumphant reception in London. It was the Commonwealth's flagship the *Naseby*, named after the parliamentary victory in the Civil War, and after dinner its name was repainted – as the *Royal Charles*. England was royal again.

As sailors shinned up the rigging, setting the sails for England, Pepys fell into conversation with the tall, dark thirty-year-old who would shortly be crowned Charles II. Walking up and down the quarterdeck with him, the diarist was impressed. He found Charles 'very active and stirring . . . quite contrary to what I thought him to have been' – and scarcely able to believe quite how dramatically his fortunes had been transformed in a mere nine years. 'He fell into discourse of his escape from Worcester . . . where it made me ready to weep to hear the stories that he told of his difficulties that he had passed through.'

THE VILLAGE THAT CHOSE TO DIE
1665

Xenopsylla Cheopis

PLAGUE CAME TO ENGLAND WITH THE BLACK DEATH IN 1348, and it stayed. According to London's 'bills of mortality', people died quite regularly from the infection, which had ballooned to epidemic proportions in 1563, 1593, 1603, 1625 and 1636. The rich studied the bills of mortality as a guide to their holiday plans. When the weekly plague rate started rising, it was time for a trip to the country.

The Latin *plaga* means a blow or knock, and in those days people often interpreted the erratic pattern of plague infections as punishing blows from an angry God. A more earthly explanation was that poisonous vapours lurked beneath the earth's crust, symptom of a cosmic constipation that could only be cured 'by expiring those Arsenical Fumes that have been retained so long in her bowels'.

Modern science remains baffled by the comings and goings of this deadly contagion. We know that bubonic plague is spread by infected fleas living on rats and humans. It is *not* spread from human to human by physical contact or even by human breath, except in the comparatively rare cases of pneumonic plague where the infection, having penetrated the lungs, is then breathed out by the sufferer in his or her brief remaining hours of painful life. The multiplication of rats and their fleas can be related to climatic factors – the rat flea *Xenopsylla cheopis* hibernates in frosty weather and flourishes at 20–25 degrees Celsius. But no one has convincingly connected particular conditions of heat or cold to the epidemic years – not least to September 1665, when plague hit England again with a vengeance. The bills of mortality mounted alarmingly – to seven thousand deaths a week by the end of the month – and the city streets sounded to the tolling of bells and the rumbling of plague carts as their drivers hooked up bodies left in doorways to convey them to the burial pits outside the city walls. Crosses were daubed on homes where infection had struck and their doors were boarded up, condemning those inside to almost certain death or – in just a few unexplained cases – to miraculous recovery.

Outside London, the plague spread wherever *X. cheopis* travelled, and it is thought to have reached the village of Eyam in Derbyshire that September in a box of tailor's samples and old clothing sent to Edward Cooper, a village trader. The clothes were damp on arrival, so Cooper's servant, George Vickers, placed them before the fire to dry. Within three days, a bluish-black plague-spot appeared on Vickers's chest, and he died the next day. Cooper followed him to the graveyard two weeks later, and by the end of October Eyam had suffered another twenty-six deaths. The mortality rate slowed during the hard Peak District winter to between four and nine a month, but with spring it rose again, and by midsummer 1666 over seventy of the village's 360 inhabitants had succumbed.

The old rector of Eyam, Thomas Stanley, had recently been ousted. A dissenter, he was one of the thousand or so Puritans who had refused to conform to the Church of England when, along with the monarchy, it had been restored six years earlier. So Stanley was deprived of his living, but he stayed on in Eyam, and seems to have collaborated with his young successor, the Revd William Mompesson, in face of the terrifying threat to their flock.

It was Mompesson, a married man with two children, who took the step that made Eyam famous – he urged his congregation to follow Jesus's words in the Gospel of St John: 'Greater love hath no man than this, that a man lay down his life for his friends.' Rather than fleeing the village and spreading the infection around the Peak District, argued the young rector, the community should stick together and help their fellow-men. This, clearly, was to risk their own lives in an act of extraordinary self-sacrifice. The congregation agreed, and for more than a year Eyam became effectively a huge plague house, shut off from the world. Their neighbours, meanwhile, who included the Earl of Devonshire at nearby Chatsworth, responded to their gesture by leaving food and other provisions at the outskirts of the village. Derbyshire was spared further plague, and Eyam paid the price, losing more than 260 inhabitants, some three-quarters of the population. Among the last to die was Mompesson's wife Catherine, who had gone from house to house during the outbreak, ministering to the sick.

The final burial took place on 11 October 1666, and Mompesson started assessing the damage. 'Our town has become a Golgotha, the place of a skull . . .' he wrote in November. 'I intend, God willing, to spend this week in seeing all woollen clothes fumed and purified . . .' Modern quarantine procedure suggests that this is the very first thing Eyam should have done. Had the fleas that were lurking in Edward Cooper's box of clothing been destroyed on day one, the villagers would have posed no threat to their neighbours. And even if the fleas had not been destroyed, those who left the village flealess could not have infected anyone they met.

In scientific terms, we can now say that the sacrifice of Eyam's villagers was probably unnecessary, and quite certainly counterproductive. By staying together they actually brought more humans, fleas and rats into close proximity, hugely increasing the mortality from a single source of infection. But if their lack of knowledge now seems a tragedy, does that invalidate the brave and selfless decision they took?

LONDON BURNING
1666

AT TWO O'CLOCK ON THE MORNING OF SUNDAY 2 September 1666, Thomas Farynor awoke to the smell of burning. Farynor bore the title of King's Baker – meaning that he baked ships' biscuits for the navy rather than bread for the King – and he lived above his bakery in Pudding Lane, not far from London Bridge. Dashing downstairs, he met with a blaze of such intensity that he snatched up his family and fled. Modern excavations have unearthed the carbonised remains of twenty tar barrels in the cellar below Pudding Lane, and it was probably their explosion that catapulted burning debris into the stables of the inn next door, setting fire to the hay piled up in the yard.

It had been a long hot summer. London's wood and wattle houses, roofed with straw, were tinderbox-dry, and a warm wind was blowing from the east. By three a.m. the city's fire-fighters were on hand, accompanied by the Lord Mayor Sir Thomas Bloodworth, tetchy at having had his sleep disturbed. He gave the conflagration a cursory glance, then returned to his bed. 'Pish!' he sniffed, 'a woman might piss it out!'

But while the Lord Mayor slept, the flames licked their way to the riverside, enveloping the wooden wharves and warehouses that were stacked to the rafters with merchandise waiting to burn. Tallow, oil, timber, coal – in no time an inferno was raging up the shoreline and had consumed a third of the houses on London Bridge. 'Rattle, rattle, rattle . . .' wrote one eyewitness, 'as if there had been a thousand iron chariots, beating together on the stones.' The fire was roaring along so fast that it caught any pigeons too slow to get out of its path, setting their feathers alight.

By Sunday lunchtime, Mayor Bloodworth's coarse complacency had turned to panic. Samuel Pepys found him sweating helplessly at the front line, a handkerchief tied round his neck. 'Lord, what can I do?' he cried. 'People will not obey me!'

Bloodworth's only recourse was the one reliable defence that the seventeenth century could offer against fire – to pull down blocks of houses to create firebreaks. But he found himself up against the fiercely protective instincts of some of the city's most powerful property owners, and it took royal intervention to get the firebreak policy under way. In fact, King Charles and his brother James were the fire-fighting heroes of that day, and of the three further days it took to bring the blaze under control. The King sent his Life Guards along to help, and the two brothers were soon out on the streets themselves, setting to with shovels and buckets of water. Working from five in the morning until nearly midnight, James came in for particular praise. 'If the Lord Mayor had done as much,' said one citizen, 'his example might have gone far towards saving the city.'

Thirteen thousand two hundred houses, 87 churches, and 44 merchant guild halls, along with the City's own Guildhall, Exchange, Custom House and the Bridewell Prison, were destroyed in the fire that started at Pudding Lane. For several nights the flames burned so brightly that they lit the horizon at Oxford, fifty miles away. One hundred thousand were made homeless – tent cities sprang up in the fields around the capital. And with no compensation available for rebuilding – at this date insurance existed only for ships – many were left destitute.

It was hardly surprising that a catastrophe of such magnitude should prompt a witch-hunt. When MPs gathered at the end of September they agreed to a man that papist saboteurs were to blame, and they set up a commission to prove it, solemnly gathering gossip about sinister French firework-makers and Catholic housewives from Ilford overheard predicting hot weather.

In fact, there is not the slightest evidence that the fire which started in Thomas Farynor's biscuit bakery in Pudding Lane in September 1666 was anything but an accident. And there was a certain half-heartedness in the Protestant attempts to pin the blame on the papists. Coupled with the 'blow' of the plague the previous year, people felt a depressing anxiety that the punishment might be the work of God himself – His judgement on a king and a monarchy that, in just a few years, had fallen sadly short of all that its restoration had promised.

TITUS OATES AND THE POPISH PLOT
1678/9

KING CHARLES II WAS PROUD TO HAVE FATHERED NO LESS than fourteen illegitimate children. His pursuit of pleasure summed up the spirit with which Restoration England threw off the drab constraints of the Puritan years. Strolling in the park with his knock-kneed, floppy-eared spaniels, the 'Merry Monarch' privately believed in his divine right to rule as totally as his father had, but unlike his father, Charles II masked his mission with the common touch. Orange-seller turned actress Nell Gwynne was the most popular of his many mistresses, famously turning jeers to cheers when anti-Catholic demonstrators jostled her carriage. Red-haired Nelly leaned out of the window. 'I am the *Protestant* whore!' she cried.

'King Charles II,' wrote John Evelyn, 'would doubtless have been an excellent prince had he been less addicted to women.' The King, explained Evelyn, was 'always in want to supply their immeasurable profusion'.

Women and wars drained the royal coffers. Under Charles, England's taxes rose to even higher levels than under the Commonwealth and Protectorate, but without the military triumphs that had made Cromwell's wars palatable. In June 1667 a marauding Dutch fleet entered the Thames estuary and sailed up the River Medway, where its fire ships destroyed half the English fleet. The Dutch cannon were clearly heard many miles away in fire-devastated London, while the newly renamed *Royal Charles* was captured and towed ignominiously back to Holland.

The humiliation in the Medway ended the Restoration honeymoon. Charles had been careful to avoid dissolving the 'Cavalier' Parliament that had been elected in the first joyously royalist flush of his return – at the end of every session he used the mechanism of prorogation (the temporary suspension of the Lords and Commons) to keep the Cavaliers returning. But these loyal merchants and country gentlemen distrusted the Roman Catholicism that permeated the royal court, and they disliked wasted taxes as much as the next man.

In 1670 Charles embarked on a disastrous course. Seeking extra funds that would diminish his reliance on Parliament, he made a secret pact with his cousin, the French King Louis XIV. In return for a French pension that, in the event, would be paid intermittently for the rest of his reign, he agreed not only to restore the rights of English Catholics but also, when the moment was right, personally to acknowledge the Catholic faith in which he had been brought up by his devout French mother, Henrietta Maria.

The secret clauses were negotiated at Dover as part of a deal creating an Anglo-French alliance against the Dutch, and to camouflage his betrayal Charles appointed two of his ministers to negotiate a 'cover' Treaty of Dover – without the sell-out over Catholicism. But it was not long before suspicions of under-the-table dealings emerged, and when Charles went before Parliament in 1674 to swear there had been no secret clauses, it was observed that his hand shook.

The King's problems were intensified by the fact that, despite his profusion of bastard children, he had produced no legitimate heirs. His marriage to the Portuguese Catherine of Braganza remained obstinately childless, and though faithless to his spouse in so many ways, Charles refused to discard her. This handed the succession squarely to his brother James, Duke of York, who, unlike Charles, was not prepared to disguise his faith. In 1673 James had resigned his post as Lord High Admiral rather than denounce the doctrine of transubstantiation (see p. 207) as required by the Test Act, Parliament's attempt to exclude non-Anglicans from public office. Thus the heir to England's ultimate public office openly declared himself a Roman Catholic.

With the present King living a lie and his successor conjuring up the prospect of a re-enactment of the fires of Smithfield, it was small wonder that Protestant England felt under threat – and on 17 October 1678 came the event that seemed to justify their wildest fears. The body of Sir Edmund Berry Godfrey, a prominent London magistrate, was found face down in a ditch on Primrose Hill, run through with a sword. Godfrey had been a rare London hero of the plague year. He had stayed in the capital overseeing mass burials and prosecuting grave robbers, and shortly before his death, it now turned out, he had embarked on a still more heroic mission: he was investigating allegations of a sinister 'Popish Plot' to murder the King and place James on the throne.

The allegations had been laid before the magistrate by one Titus Oates, an oily and pompous con man of the cloth, who had been expelled from his school, two Cambridge colleges, his Church of England ministry, the navy, and two Catholic colleges in Europe for offences that ranged from drunkenness to sodomy – with an ongoing strand of perjury. Oates's tabloid tales of dagger-wielding Jesuit assassins might normally have commanded little credence, but the murder of Sir Edmund Berry Godfrey – which was never solved – gave his

'Popish Plot' a horrid plausibility. The magistrate's body was put on public display, and enterprising tradesfolk hawked 'Edmund Berry Godfrey' daggers to citizens newly concerned with self-defence. In the panic that followed, further informers came crawling out of the woodwork, leading to the prosecution of more than twelve hundred Catholics in London alone and the execution of twenty-four innocent men and women on charges of treason.

Parliamentarians and Puritans now saw a pressing need to exclude the King's popish brother from the succession, and the bitter battle to impose this 'exclusion' on Charles produced rudimentary political parties. Campaigning for exclusion was a 'country' alliance of Puritans, populists and old parliamentary diehards – derided by their opponents as 'Whiggamores', a term of abuse for Scottish Presbyterian outlaws. In response, the 'Whigs' denounced the 'court' party of High Anglicans and loyal monarchists as 'Tories' (from the Gaelic word *toraighe* – an Irish label for Catholic bandits).

Outlaws versus bandits, Whigs versus Tories: thus, in mutual insult, was born the British two-party political system. By the early 1680s the rival groupings were proudly proclaiming their names, printing manifestos, financing newspapers and choosing candidates. They even issued coloured rosettes – red for Tories and true blue for Whigs – and in this, the first of their many great confrontations, the Whigs managed to build up the larger majorities in the House of Commons.

But though the Whigs had the votes, they found themselves helpless in face of the King's prerogative powers, which were still essentially those enjoyed by Charles I – it was as if Commonwealth, Protectorate and Restoration had never been. Whenever the Whigs got close to passing a bill that would exclude James, his brother dissolved Parliament, and after three bitterly debated sessions and three dissolutions, the exclusion crisis ran out of steam. The fabrications of Titus Oates were exposed, and for the last five years of his reign Charles II was able to rule without Parliament.

The King's guiding principle had always been that he 'did not wish to go again on his travels', and through charm, deceit and a general unwillingness on the part of his subjects to fight another Civil War, he succeeded. Charles II never had to climb another oak tree or blacken his face with soot again. On his deathbed, he called for a priest and formally converted to the faith of his childhood. But as the Merry Monarch headed for his Catholic heaven, his farewell words paid due homage to his licentious past – 'Let not poor Nelly starve'.

MONMOUTH'S REBELLION AND THE BLOODY ASSIZES
1685

JAMES, DUKE OF MONMOUTH, WAS CHARLES II'S ELDEST AND favourite son, the product of his first serious love affair – in 1649, with Lucy Walter, an attractive, dark-eyed Englishwoman living in Paris. This was the year of Charles I's execution, and it was later recounted that the nineteen-year-old prince, suddenly and tragically King-in-exile, fell so deeply in love with Lucy that he secretly married her.

Charles always denied that Lucy was his legitimate wife, but he showed great favour to his handsome firstborn, awarding him the dukedom – the highest rank of aristocracy – when the boy was only fourteen, and arranging his marriage to a rich heiress. Sixteen years later, in 1679, Charles entrusted him with the command of an English army sent to subdue Scottish rebels, and the thirty-year-old returned home a conquering hero.

As the exclusion crisis intensified, the Whigs embraced Monmouth as their candidate for the throne – here was a dashing 'Protestant Duke' to replace the popish James – and Monmouth threw himself into the part. He embarked on royal progresses, currying popular favour by taking part in village running races, and even touching scrofula sufferers for the King's Evil (see pp. 53-4). But Charles was livid at this attempt by his charming but bastard son to subvert the line of lawful succession. He twice issued proclamations reasserting Monmouth's illegitimacy.

The transition of rule from Charles to James II in February 1685 was marked by a widespread acceptance – even a warmth – that had seemed impossible in the hysterical days of the Popish Plot. Without forswearing his Catholic loyalties, James pledged that he would 'undertake nothing against the religion [the Church of England] which is established by law', and most people gave him the benefit of the doubt. At the relatively advanced age of fifty-two, the new King cut a competent figure, reassuringly more serious and hardworking than his elder brother.

But Monmouth, in exile with his Whig clique in the Netherlands, totally misjudged the national mood. On 11 June that year he landed at the port of Lyme Regis in Dorset with just eighty-two supporters and equipment for a thousand more. Though his promises of toleration for dissenters drew the support of several thousand West Country artisans and labourers, the local gentry raised the militia against him, and the duke was soon taking refuge in the swamps of Sedgemoor where King Alfred had hidden from the Vikings eight hundred years earlier. Lacking Alfred's command of the terrain, however, Monmouth got lost in the mists during an attempted night attack, and as dawn broke on 6 July his men were cut to pieces.

Nine days later the 'Protestant Duke' was dead, executed in London despite grovelling to his victorious uncle and offering to turn Catholic in exchange for his life. It was a sorry betrayal of the Somerset dissenters who had signed up for what would prove the last popular rebellion in English history – and there was worse to come. Not content with the slaughter of Sedgemoor and the summary executions of those caught fleeing from the field, James insisted that a judicial commission headed by the Lord Chief Justice, George Jeffreys, should go down to the West Country to root out the last traces of revolt.

Travelling with four other judges and a public executioner, Jeffreys started his cull in Winchester, where Alice Lisle, the seventy-year-old widow of the regicide Sir John Lisle, was found guilty of harbouring a rebel and condemned to be burned at the stake. When Jeffreys suggested that she might plead to the King for mercy, Widow Lisle took his advice – and was spared burning to be beheaded in the marketplace.

Moving on to Dorchester on 5 September, Jeffreys was annoyed to be confronted by a first batch of thirty suspects all pleading 'not guilty': he sentenced all but one of them to death. Then, in the interests of speed, he offered more lenient treatment to those pleading 'guilty'. Out of 233, only eighty were hanged.

By the time the work of the Bloody Assizes was finished, 480 men and women had been sentenced to death, 260 whipped or fined, and 850 transported to the colonies, where the profits from their sale were enjoyed by a syndicate that included James's wife, Mary of Modena. The tarred bodies and heads pickled in vinegar that Judge Jeffreys distributed around the gibbets of the West Country were less shocking to his contemporaries than they would be to subsequent generations. But his Bloody Assizes did raise questions about the new Catholic King, and how moderately he could be trusted to use his powers.

THE GLORIOUS INVASION
1688-9

THOSE WHO DISLIKED ENGLAND HAVING AN OPENLY Catholic monarch took comfort from the thought that James II could not live for ever. The King was comparatively old by seventeenth-century standards – in October 1687 he turned fifty-four, the age at which his brother had died – and his immediate heirs, his daughters Mary (twenty-five) and Anne (twenty-three), were both staunch Protestants. Mary, indeed, was married to the Dutch Protestant hero William of Orange, who had his own place in the English succession (see family tree p. xviii), and who was leading Holland's battle against the empire-building ambitions of Catholic France. (The 'Orange' in William's title referred to the French town near Avignon that had once belonged to his family.)

Mary and Anne were the surviving offspring of James's first marriage, to Anne Hyde, the daughter of Charles II's adviser in exile, Edward Hyde. Following her death in 1671 James had married an Italian Catholic, Mary, daughter of the Duke of Modena, and the couple had worked hard to produce a Catholic heir – Mary of Modena went through ten pregnancies in the decade 1674–84. But these had produced five stillbirths and five who died in infancy, so by the time James II came to the throne, Protestants could safely feel that his wife's reproductive capacity posed them no threat.

They had not reckoned on the visits that Queen Mary started making to the ancient city of Bath with its curative spa waters. Just before Christmas 1687 came alarming news – the Bath fertility treatment had worked. Mary of Modena was pregnant for an eleventh time, and early in June 1688, she gave birth to a healthy baby boy. Named James and styled Prince of Wales, this new arrival displaced his Protestant sisters from the succession and suddenly offered England the prospect of a Catholic Stuart monarchy in perpetuity.

English Protestants refused to believe James's luck – the birth had to be a fake. Pamphlets were rushed out asserting that the strapping baby was a miller's son, smuggled into the royal bed in a long-handled warming-pan. Vivid graphic images circulated, showing how the deception must have been carried out, and it was in vain that the King marshalled a chamberful of respected Protestant witnesses to swear to the genuineness of the birth. The story of the 'baby in the warming-pan' proved one of history's most persuasive conspiracy theories.

After three years on the throne, James was arousing widespread suspicion. He had promised not to undermine the established Church, but evidence was mounting that his true purpose was to steer England back towards Rome. By March 1688 a succession of moves favouring Catholics and dissenters had ousted more than twelve hundred members of the Church of England from public office, and though James claimed to be unbiased, even his own family dismissed as a popish ploy his recently cultivated tolerance towards nonconformists. 'Things are come to that pass now,' wrote his daughter Anne from London to her elder sister in Holland, 'that if they go on much longer, I believe no Protestant will be able to live.'

James was knocking the stilts from under his own conservative powerbase. The Anglican Tory squires who had welcomed his accession were incensed to see their own kind being replaced on the magistrates' benches by papists and Puritans – and seriously alarmed when Catholics were given positions of command in the King's rapidly growing standing army. On 30 June, less than three weeks after the birth of the Prince of Wales, seven senior peers, their signatures in code, sent a secret invitation to Mary's husband William of Orange to come over to England.

William needed no prompting. He spent that summer preparing an army and an invasion fleet – 463 vessels and forty thousand troops – along with sixty thousand pamphlets to explain his purpose. He did not intend to seize the crown, he said. His expedition was 'intended for no other design, but to have a free and lawful parliament assembled as soon as possible' – and to inquire, among other matters, 'into the birth of the pretended Prince of Wales'.

William's Dutch and German invasion force was larger than Philip of Spain had assembled for the Armada of 1588, but when the Dutch prince landed in Torbay in November a hundred years later, his success was by no means guaranteed. His foreign mercenaries might well have it in them to defeat the twenty-thousand-strong English army that was blocking their way to London. But shedding English blood would have ruined William's claim to be acting in English interests, and would also have exposed his basic reason for invading England – he wanted England's military might on Holland's side in its ongoing battle against Louis XIV.

William was fortunate that, at the moment of confrontation, James lost his nerve. Though debilitated by nosebleeds and insomnia, the King made haste to join his army on Salisbury Plain – only to return abruptly to London, where he discovered that his daughter Anne had deserted and joined the cause of her sister and brother-in-law. Lear-like, James raged against the perfidy of his daughters. Having sent the Queen and the Prince of Wales ahead of him, he fled Whitehall on 11 December by a secret passage, throwing the Great Seal of England petulantly into the Thames as he left.

At this point a band of overzealous Kent fishermen spoiled the plot. They arrested James at Faversham and dispatched him back to London – to William's embarrassed fury. The Dutch prince promptly returned his father-in-law to Kent, with an escort briefed to look the other way when they got the King to Rochester. At the second attempt, James made good his escape.

Six weeks later, on 13 February 1689, William and Mary accepted the English crown as joint sovereigns in return for their agreement to the passing by Parliament of a 'Bill of Rights' – a mutually convenient deal that has gone down in history as 'the Glorious Revolution'. This is generally taken to mean that 1688/9 marked the inauguration of England's constitutional monarchy – the moment when Parliament finally codified the control over the Crown that it had won in the Civil War, but had failed to secure in the reigns of Charles II and James II.

In fact, the Bill of Rights of 1689 said very little about the rights of individuals, and it would be more than a century before England's monarchy could truly be called 'constitutional'. In the horse-trading with Parliament that followed James II's effective abdication, the hard-headed William coolly defended his royal prerogatives, retaining his right to select his own ministers and to control the length of parliamentary sessions. Revolution? The year 1688/9 witnessed nothing so grass-roots or drastic in England – though from William's point of view his invasion had certainly enjoyed a glorious outcome.

ISAAC NEWTON AND THE PRINCIPLES OF THE UNIVERSE
1687

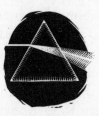

ISAAC NEWTON WAS BORN IN THE LINCOLNSHIRE VILLAGE OF Woolsthorpe in 1642, the year that England's Civil War began. A small and sickly baby, he had an unhappy childhood, discarded by his widowed mother at the age of three when she remarried a rich clergyman who had no time for Isaac. But a kindly uncle helped him to school in the nearby market town of Grantham, and in 1661 the nineteen-year-old won admission to Trinity College, Cambridge.

Newton was not an outstanding student. But in 1665 the plague came to Cambridge, the students were sent home, and it was back in Woolsthorpe that he experienced the revelation he loved to recount in later life. Sitting in the shade of an apple tree one day, he watched an apple drop to the ground. 'Why should this apple always invariably fall to the earth in a perpendicular line?' he remembered thinking. 'Why should it not fall upwards, sideways, or obliquely?'

Newton did not publish his ideas about the law of gravity for another twenty years, and some have suggested that his subsequent description of his famous Eureka moment was nothing more than an exercise in myth-making. But Isaac had come up with another big idea during his plague-enforced gap year at Woolsthorpe, and it is not surprising that falling apples should take a back seat while he explored this equally intriguing – and literally dazzling – phenomenon: the structure of light. 'In the beginning of the year 1666 . . .' he later wrote, 'I procured me a triangular glass prism, to try therewith the celebrated phenomena of colours . . . Having darkened my chamber, and made a small hole in my window shuts [shutters] to let in a convenient quantity of the sun's light, I placed my prism at his entrance that it might be thereby refracted to the opposite wall.'

The prevailing theory at this time was that a prism produced colours by staining, or dyeing, the light that passed through it. But in his study at Woolsthorpe, where we can see today exactly where the twenty-five-year-old boffin played with the colours of the rainbow, Newton set up a second prism. If each prism coloured the light, the hues should have deepened as they passed through the second refraction. In fact, they returned to being bright and clear – Newton had put white light's component colours back together again.

This was the discovery that made his name. In 1672 he was invited to publish his findings by the Royal Society of London for Improving Knowledge. This fellowship of inquiring minds had started life in Oxford and London during the Civil War when, lacking a fixed base, they called themselves the 'Invisible College'. Science was one of Charles II's more constructive interests, and in 1662 he had chartered the 'Invisible College' as the Royal Society, bestowing his patronage on the meeting and mingling of some extraordinary minds: Robert Boyle was working on the definition of chemical elements, together with the density, pressure and behaviour of gases; Robert Hooke was publicising the hidden world revealed by the microscope; Edmund Halley was investigating the movement of heavenly bodies like comets; and Christopher Wren, surveying the almost limitless architectural opportunities offered by fire-devastated London, was formulating a fresh vision of the structures required by city living.

Immediately elected a Fellow of the Royal Society for his work on 'opticks', Isaac Newton did not, in fact, get on very well with this illustrious fraternity. His troubled childhood had left him a solitary character, untrusting and morose. But it was a gathering of three more sociable Fellows that prompted the publication of his greatest work. Sitting in one of London's newly fashionable coffee houses one day in 1684, Halley, Wren and Hooke fell to discussing how to describe the movements of the planets, and shortly afterwards Halley visited Newton to put the question to him. Newton replied without hesitation: the planets moved in an ellipse. He had worked it out years earlier, he said, and when Halley asked to see his calculations, Newton promised to write them out for him.

The result was his *Principia Mathematica*, often described as the most important book in the history of science. In it Newton set out his three laws of motion, the second of these explaining the power of gravity and how it determined the motion of the planets and their moons, the movement of the tides and the apparently eccentric behaviour of comets. Halley used Newton's calculations to predict the course of the comet that would make him famous – Halley's Comet, which passed over England in 1682 and which he linked to reports of previous comet sightings in 1456, 1531 and 1607.

Having prompted Newton to write the *Principia*, it was Halley who extracted the manuscript from him, paid with his own money for its printing, and acted as its chief publicist, preparing reader-friendly summaries of Newton's often severely complicated ideas. Newton himself expressed his thoughts so dourly that students often avoided his lectures at Cambridge, and he spent his time 'lecturing to the walls'.

Today we see Isaac Newton as a pioneering scientist and the father of physics. In fact, the terms 'scientist' and 'physics' did not exist in his lifetime. Newton devoted long years of research to the ancient mysteries of alchemy and how base metals could be turned into gold. The modern scientists and historians involved in the 'Newton Project', a venture that will put all his ten million or so words on to the World Wide Web, report that more than a million of those words are devoted to alchemy, and another four million to lurid biblical prophecy – and particularly to the book of Revelation: the Whore of Babylon, the nature of the two-horned and ten-horned beasts and the Four Horsemen of the Apocalypse.

Yet between the lines of this ancient-sounding discourse lurks a radical and forward-thinking vision. Newton eagerly awaits the moment when 'the Word of God makes war with ye Beasts & Kings of ye earth' to create a 'new heaven, new earth & new Jerusalem'. This man, born with the Civil War and producing his master work in the years when the absolutist Stuart monarchy finally collapsed, is rightly identified with modernity. He prepared the brief by which Cambridge University would defend its independence against King James II, and in 1689 he was elected to the Parliament that put William and Mary on the throne.

More important, his explanation of how the universe operated by logical mechanical laws was to cause a profound alteration in human thought. The work of Newton, Halley, Hooke and their contemporaries upended the very basis of philosophy and human inquiry, making once divine areas the province of their own earthly research. All things were possible. Reason, logic and deduction would replace blind faith. Old ideas were questioned. New ideas were explored. No longer did God reside in the heavens; he existed in your mind if you could find him there – a transformation in thinking that truly was a glorious revolution.

JOHN LOCKE AND TOLERATION
1690

S NOW FELL HEAVILY IN HOLLAND IN THE WINTER OF 1683, and one of the victims of the cold was a lioness that died in the Amsterdam zoo. As Dutch academics gathered for the rare opportunity to dissect the corpse of an exotic beast, they were joined by an English doctor and philosopher, John Locke. Locke had recently arrived in Amsterdam and when he struck up a conversation with Philip van Limborch, a local professor of theology, the exchange between the two men soon extended far beyond the autopsy. They both had an interest, they discovered, in religious toleration – it was a burning issue of the moment – and van Limborch encouraged Locke to set his thoughts down on paper.

Locke, fifty-one, was a political exile in Holland. A small-time lawyer's son from the Somerset village of Wrington, he had been a teenager during the Civil War, then studied at Oxford University in the years following the death of Charles I. As religious sects quarrelled and the army made and unmade parliaments, the visionary chaos of Cromwell's England started pushing Locke to consider that there must be some more stable and rational way of government. The essence of civil society, he came to feel, should be a fair working contract between the governor and the governed, and this had inclined him to welcome Charles II's return at the invitation of Parliament in 1660.

But the restored King had proved, for all his charm, to be an absolutist like his father. Locke drifted into the Whig, or anti-royal camp, becoming a friend and medical adviser to Anthony Ashley Cooper, the Earl of Shaftesbury, who led the Whig attempt to exclude the future James II from the succession. When Charles defeated the third Exclusion Bill in 1681 and determined to rule without Parliament, Shaftesbury fled for his life to the Netherlands, dying there in 1683.

Later that year Locke decided that he too would be safer in the Netherlands, and so found himself, soon after his arrival, in the crowd that gathered around the lioness on the dissecting table.

Shadowed by Stuart agents and hiding under a variety of aliases, Locke was working on the philosophical text for which he would become most famous, *An Essay on Human Understanding*. 'The highest perfection of intellectual nature,' he wrote, 'lies in a careful and constant pursuit of true and solid happiness.'

Looking for happiness in this life might strike many today as the most obvious of goals to pursue, but it was heresy in an age when most people assumed they would only encounter and fully experience their God after they had died. Locke's suggestion that earthly life was something to be enjoyed here and now jarred on many of his contemporaries as 'atheistic'.

In fact, the philosopher was a devout Christian, and in the autumn of 1685 he was appalled by Louis XIV's sudden revocation of the freedom of worship that France's Protestants, the Huguenots, had enjoyed since 1598 under the Edict of Nantes. As Huguenot refugees fled persecution – England alone welcomed fifty thousand – Locke took up his Dutch friend van Limborch's suggestion and sat down to compose *Epistola de tolerantia, A Letter concerning Toleration*. Spiritual belief, Locke argued, was no business of the state, which should confine itself to the 'civil interests' that he defined as 'life, liberty, health and indolency [freedom from pain] of body, and the possession of outward things such as money, land, houses, furniture and the like'.

A century later Thomas Jefferson would combine these words with the key phrase from Locke's *Essay on Human Understanding* to produce his stirring battle cry for 'Life, Liberty and the Pursuit of Happiness'. The US Declaration of Independence would echo round the world.

In his own lifetime, however, Locke felt it safer to keep a low profile. Although he came back to England on 12 February 1689 on the same ship as Princess Mary – who, next day, would strike the deal with Parliament that made her husband and herself joint sovereigns – Locke found it prudent to keep some of his crucial essays anonymous. There was no author's name on *A Letter concerning Toleration*: the title page carried scrambled letters that were code for 'Locke' and 'Limborch', to whom the work was dedicated. Only Locke and the

Dutchman knew the code, and Locke acknowledged his authorship of the *Letter* and other works only in a codicil to his will signed the month before his death in October 1704.

By then, people were coming to see that Locke had put into words the essential values of the Glorious Revolution – and particularly in his *Two Treatises on Civil Government* that he published anonymously in 1690. Governments, he wrote, may not 'levy taxes on the people' without 'the consent . . . of their representatives'. No government, he argued, could be considered legitimate unless grounded in the consent of the people – and any ruler who attempted to exercise an arbitrary power 'is to be esteemed the Common enemy and Pest of mankind and is to be treated accordingly'.

Nowadays John Locke is thought of almost exclusively in terms of his political philosophy. He is studied at universities as the apostle of modern Western liberal democracy, as Marx was the apostle of Communism. But in his own lifetime he was a hands-on man of many talents – throwing himself into the vortex of thought and experiment that came to be known as the Enlightenment. Elected a member of the Royal Society, he served on a 'committee of experiments', and when his patron Lord Shaftesbury fell ill, he supervised the risky operation that drained an abscess on his liver. Above all, he spoke up for toleration, and was delighted when one of the first statutes of William and Mary's reign was an act that allowed Dissenters (though not Catholics) to worship in their own licensed meeting-houses.

'Toleration has now at last been established by law in our country,' he wrote triumphantly to his lioness autopsy friend, van Limborch. 'Not perhaps so wide in scope as might be wished for by you . . . Still, it is something to have progressed so far.'

'REMEMBER THE BOYNE!' – THE BIRTH OF THE ORANGEMEN

1690

AT THE BEGINNING OF JULY 1690, KING WILLIAM III AND his officers sat down for a picnic on the north bank of the River Boyne, thirty miles north of Dublin. On the other bank were massed the more numerous forces of James II, who, having fled from London the previous year, was now trying to recapture his kingdom with the help of his loyal Catholic subjects in Ireland and a contingent of crack French troops. The French King Louis XIV was backing James as part of his campaign for French and Catholic domination of Europe.

It was a momentous confrontation – the last between two rival kings of Britain. Either man could lose everything, and William nearly did when a stray shot from the southern bank came sailing across the river and smacked into his shoulder, sending him tumbling to the ground. The Jacobites (so named from the Latin for James – *Jacobus*) could not believe their luck. With one stray shot, it seemed, they had reversed the ousting of their Catholic champion the previous year.

But within hours William, calm as ever, was riding among his troops, with his arm in a sling – a token of God's providence and also of his cool Dutch courage. That night he showed his Dutch cunning as well. He dispatched a section of his troops west along the river to the ford of Rosnaree, making enough noise to persuade the Jacobite scouts and sentries that most of his army was on the move.

James responded by breaking camp and marching for Rosnaree with a major contingent to foil this flanking attack. But when the sun rose the next morning, the Jacobite troops that he had left by the Boyne peered through the river mists to see, with horror, that most of William's army was still in place. From having outnumbered their enemy, it was they who were now outnumbered – and one of the mysteries of that day is why the deposed King, when he reached Rosnaree and discovered he had fallen for a ruse, did not come marching back post-haste. James was strangely invisible at this moment that would decide his – and Britain's – destiny. The little figure of William with his bandaged arm, by contrast, was much in evidence as his men forded the river and fought their way uphill to eventual victory.

By the end of the following day William was riding into Dublin in triumph – while James, for the third and last time in his career, was escaping from the British Isles as a fugitive. 'I do now resolve,' he declared with resignation, 'to shift for myself.'

William was generous in victory. He allowed some eleven thousand Jacobite soldiers to go freely to France, where they became 'the Wild Geese' – a foreign legion of devil-may-care mercenaries who fought for the Catholic cause in the royal armies of Europe. William also promised Ireland's Catholics 'such privileges in the exercise of their religion . . . as they had enjoyed in the days of Charles II'.

But Ireland's victorious Protestants did not share their new King's spirit of tolerance. It was not easy to expunge the religiously entwined hatreds between settler and native that went back, via Oliver Cromwell's atrocities of the 1650s, to the original colonisation by the Normans. In the months before the Boyne, during the brief period when James II controlled the island, the Catholics had been merciless. Taking their revenge for centuries of subjection, they had dispossessed Protestants of their land, pushing them back to their northern strongholds in Ulster, and particularly to the town of Derry, where the local apprentice boys rationed the available oatmeal and horsemeat in a desperate siege that lasted 105 days before the army of 'King Billy' relieved them.

Now the Protestants in turn took their revenge. In 1691 Catholics were excluded from Ireland's Parliament and, the next year, from serving in the army; Protestants could carry firearms, but Catholics could not. In subsequent years Catholics were excluded from public office and prevented from building up large estates – all this making brutally clear that Ireland was, in effect, a colony and its Catholics second-class citizens. In 1720 the Declaratory Act laid down that while London had the right to veto acts passed by the Irish Parliament, Ireland must accept all legislation that Westminster might send the other way.

The hatreds have lingered poisonously into the present. At the Boyne, William of Orange's troops wore orange sashes, and to this day the Apprentice Boys and the bowler-hatted men of the Orange Order, now mainly concentrated in the counties of Northern Ireland, march proudly every July to commemorate the victory of King Billy. The annual 'marching season' seldom fails to bring Ireland's sectarian bigotry to the boil, with bitterness – and, not infrequently, bloodshed.

'Remember the Boyne!' The rest of the British Isles has come to see the factious anniversary of this battle as a peculiarly Irish obsession. In fact, the victory deserves wider celebration, since it guaranteed England and Scotland the benefits of the 'Glorious Revolution' – restraint, equality, and respect for the law. These were the forward-looking principles that the real King Billy made possible in his unexciting but effective way, and it seems unfair that the Orange King should have become the symbol for the perversely backward-looking values that still bedevil Northern Ireland.

'1690?' runs a message on the wall of one Catholic ghetto. 'Let's have a replay!'

BRITANNIA RULES THE WAVES – THE TRIANGULAR TRADE
1693

ON 18 NOVEMBER 1693 CAPTAIN THOMAS PHILLIPS WAS sailing his ship the *Hannibal* along the west coast of Africa, when he made a curious discovery. One of the young black soldiers on board, by the name of John Brown, was not a man but a woman. Her true sex had been discovered when she fell ill and the ship's surgeon had ordered a 'glister'. Administering this enema, or rectal poultice,

the surgeon's assistant 'was surpriz'd to find more sally-ports than he expected'.

Captain Phillips immediately arranged separate quarters for the young woman, and had the ship's tailor make up for her some female clothing. She had been living on the all-male ship for several months – she had fooled the recruiters of the Royal Africa Company and had enlisted in London to serve in one of their forts along the coast of 'Guinea', as West Africa was known. Was she one of the 'blackamoor' community that had existed in London for more than a century? The blackamoors were descendants, for the most part, of imported black African slaves – and this enterprising twenty-year-old probably disguised herself as a soldier to get back 'home' to Guinea. But what was her real name, and what had inspired her to hide under the identity of 'John Brown'?

History, sadly, gives us no answers to these questions, for having repaid Captain Phillips for his kindness by washing his linen, 'John Brown' disembarked with the other, truly male soldiers at Cape Coast Castle (in modern Ghana), vanishing from the pages of the captain's log and of any other surviving record. Yet her intriguing adventure does open the door on to the bizarre and scandalous commerce that would help make thousands of Englishmen very rich in the next century or so – the transatlantic slave trade, also known as the triangular trade.

The *Hannibal* had been sailing south on the first leg of this triangle when Captain Phillips discovered 'John Brown'. By this date English slave-traders had been travelling down to Guinea for more than thirty years with cargoes of cloth, guns, brass, knives, beads, mirrors, cooking pots, beer, cider, brandy and the occasional horse, which they would use to purchase slaves – men, women and children – captured by local traders and warrior chiefs. The soldiers on board the *Hannibal* were on their way to garrison the little beachside castles with which the Royal Africa Company, founded by Charles II, protected the slavers from attack.

The second leg of the triangle carried the slaves westwards across the Atlantic to be sold to the plantation owners in England's colonies in North America and the Caribbean – the *Hannibal* was heading for the sugar plantations on the island of Barbados. This so-called Middle Passage was marked by conditions of the most appalling barbarity, starting with the branding of each slave on the breast or shoulder with a hot iron – 'the place before being anointed with a little palm oil which caused but little pain', according to Captain Phillips, 'the mark [usually the first letter of the ship's name] being usually well in four or five days, appearing very plain and white'.

Shackled and stacked like so many books on a shelf, the captive Africans endured unspeakable squalor in the dark and fetid holds of the slave ships. One in eight died on the voyage. Twice a day they were taken up on deck, chained in pairs, for fresh air, a pint of water and two pints of soup. But infected by the urine and excrement in which they lay, many succumbed to 'the flux' – vomiting and diarrhoea. Other vessels would try to keep upwind of the slave ships, which were notorious for their noxious stink.

Unloaded for sale on the other side of the Atlantic, the human cargoes were poked and prodded, their jaws clamped open for teeth inspection, their private parts fondled, on occasions, and exposed to inspection of a still more demeaning sort. 'Do you not buy them and use them merely as you do horses to labour for your commodity?' protested Richard Baxter, the Puritan preacher. 'How cursed a crime it is to equal men to beasts.'

But few others saw it that way. African slaves provided cheap, sturdy labour – and profits. John Locke was an investor in the Royal Africa Company, along with most of the English court and the political elite. England was developing a profitable sweet tooth, along with a free-spending taste for other addictive substances – coffee, tobacco and rum (distilled from cane sugar). Only muscular young men who were acclimatised to working in a tropical climate could handle the back-breaking labour of the plantations that produced sugar, tobacco and also cotton.

These were the cargoes that now filled the slave ships – sluiced down and considerably cleaner than they had been on the Middle Passage – as they sailed home on the third and final leg of their triangular voyage that had lasted between a year and eighteen months. In the 1690s London provided both the start and the finish for most of these lucrative ventures, but Bristol would take over in the 1730s with roughly forty trips a year, and Liverpool took over after that. By the end of the eighteenth century this one-time fishing village at the mouth of the Mersey was a prosperous metropolis from whose grand stone quays and warehouses a hundred slave ships were sailing every year.

The profits of the triangular trade helped fuel the spectacular economic take-off that the whole of England – and later Scotland – would enjoy in the eighteenth century, along with the prosperous growth of Britain's overseas Empire and the control of the seas celebrated in 'Rule Britannia', the hit song of 1740: 'Britons never, never, never shall be slaves.'

But that would not prevent Britons from buying and selling them.

JETHRO TULL'S 'DRILL' AND THE MINER'S FRIEND

1701

LIKE MANY AN INNOVATOR, JETHRO TULL WAS SOMETHING of a crank. In 1701 he got annoyed when the labourers on his Oxfordshire farm refused to follow his instructions for planting sainfoin, a clover-like fodder plant that took its name from the French – literally, 'wholesome hay'. Educated at Oxford University and trained as a barrister, Jethro reckoned he had the wit, as he later put it, to 'contrive an engine to plant St Foin more faithfully than [paid] hands would do'. Machines, unlike 'hands', did not answer back. '[So] I examined and compared all the mechanical ideas that ever had entered my imagination.'

This gentleman farmer found his inspiration in the soundboard of a musical instrument – an organ, whose grooves and holes suggested to him a way that sainfoin seeds could be channelled into the earth at a controlled rate. To the rear of this device Jethro added the spikes of a harrow that would rake soil over the seed, and he named his new machine a 'drill' – 'because,' he explained, 'when farmers used to sow their beans and peas into channels or furrows by hand, they called that action drilling'.

Jethro Tull was ahead of his time. It would be a century and a half before factory-made mechanical seed drills were a common sight on English farms. Some of Jethro's theories actually held back farming progress – he opposed the use of manure, for example, on the grounds that it encouraged the spread of weeds. But *Horse-Hoeing Husbandry*, the book that he wrote to publicise his inventions, encouraged England's farmers to think in scientific and mechanical terms, and this made an important contribution to the movement that historians would later call the 'Agricultural Revolution'.

The efficient production of low-priced food meant that the typical eighteenth-century English family did not have to spend nearly everything it earned on bread, as was the case in France before 1789. They had spare money for shopping. Economists have identified this surplus purchasing power as one of the factors contributing to Britain's so-called *Industrial* Revolution, with people spending their spare cash on the consumer goods that started to emerge from the growing number of '[manu]factories'.

Many of these new factories would come to depend on the efficiencies made possible by harnessing the power of steam, and this breakthrough was first announced in the year after Jethro invented his drill.

The year 1702 saw the publication in London of *The Miner's Friend – or a Description of an Engine to raise Water by Fire* by Thomas Savery, a Devonian naval engineer who devised a means of powering ships by mechanical paddles. The navy turned down Savery's suggestion for a paddle-boat, but he had more luck with his 'Miner's Friend', a machine he devised to improve the efficiency and safety of Cornwall's tin mines. A coal-fired boiler heated water to produce steam. When cooled, the steam created a vacuum that drew up water from the mineshaft as a primitive pump.

This pumping action was improved a few years later by another Devonshire inventor, Thomas Newcomen, who collaborated with Savery and added a piston to his process. Newcomen's piston dramatically increased the volume of water that could be brought to the surface, and by the time of his death in 1729 more than a hundred such steam pumps were working in British tin and coal mines. Standing at the head of the pit shaft, Newcomen's heavy beam, rocking to and fro to the sighing of the steam and the creaking of the piston, was the technological marvel of the age.

But Newcomen did not die a wealthy man – the canny Savery had taken out a patent extending to 1733, which covered all engines that 'raised Water by Fire'. Like Jethro Tull, Newcomen furthered technological progress, but scarcely profited from it.

MARLBOROUGH CATCHES THE FRENCH SLEEPING AT THE VILLAGE OF THE BLIND

1704

AS DAWN ROSE ON 13 AUGUST 1704 OVER THE VILLAGE OF Blindheim in southern Germany, a French officer was horrified to wake and see the red and white uniforms of an English army advancing towards him in full battle array. Riding hell for leather back into the French camp, he found his troops in their tents fast asleep – they had all thought the English were miles away. The battle that followed at Blindheim (literally, 'the home of the blind') would rank as England's greatest military triumph since Agincourt, and would make the reputation of the general who accomplished it – John Churchill, Duke of Marlborough.

Churchill specialised in dawn surprises. Early on 24 November 1688 he had led four hundred officers and men out of the camp of King James II on Salisbury Plain to join the invading army of William of Orange – it was the key defection in the Dutchman's bloodless takeover. Rewarded with the earldom of Marlborough, Churchill would build a spectacular military career based on imagination, administrative ability and a willingness to lead from the front.

But Churchill's bravery was matched by his arrogance, vanity and deviousness – for many years he maintained a secret correspondence with the exiled James II and in 1694 even betrayed the battle plans for a British naval attack on the French port of Brest. Churchill also played domestic politics with the help of his equally ambitious wife Sarah, who used her position as best friend and confidante of Queen Mary's younger sister Anne to intrigue at court on her husband's behalf.

Following the death of Mary in 1694 and then William in 1702, Anne became Queen in her own right, and the Churchills, John and Sarah, made full use of the wealth and influence that went with being the power-couple behind the throne. In 1702 Sarah controlled the three main jobs in the new Queen's household – she was groom of the stool, mistress of the robes and keeper of the privy purse – while John, now Knight of the Garter, was 'Captain-General of her Majesty's land forces and Commander-in-Chief of forces to be employed in Holland in conjunction with troops of the allies'.

England was then at war with France, the so-called War of the Spanish Succession that followed the death of the mad and childless Carlos II of Spain. The conflict had been sparked in 1701 when Louis XIV backed his grandson Philip's claim to the entire Spanish Empire that included large areas of Italy. Not content with that, he had recognised James II's son, James Francis Edward Stuart (the child believed by Protestants to have been smuggled into the royal birthing bed in a warming pan), as 'King James III' of England. To resist the French King's bid for a 'universal monarchy', England, the Netherlands and Austria had banded together in a 'Grand Alliance' – and the Earl of Marlborough was given command of the English and Dutch forces.

Marlborough's problem was that Holland viewed its army primarily as a defence force. The Dutch did not want their soldiers deployed too far from home. So Marlborough did not tell his allies the full story as he headed south towards the River Mosel. Swinging eastwards, he made a series of forced marches, travelling from 3 to 9 a.m. in the morning in order to avoid the summer heat and the French spies. At every halt, masterly planning had fresh horses, food and clothing awaiting his troops – in Heidelberg there was a new pair of boots for every soldier. Meeting up with Prince Eugene, the Austrian commander, Marlborough went to view the enemy encampment at Blindheim from the top of a church tower on 12 August, and the two men agreed to make a surprise attack next day.

The allies were outnumbered by the Franco-Bavarian forces but they had surprise on their side, plus a disciplined aggression which Marlborough's training had instilled into the formerly despised English soldiery. 'The rapidity of their movements together with their loud yells, were truly alarming,' recalled one French officer.

By the end of the day, the Franco-Bavarian army had suffered some 20,000 killed and wounded, compared to 12,000 allies. As dusk fell, Marlborough scribbled a message to his wife on the back of a tavern bill: 'I have not time to say more but to beg you will give my duty to the Queen and let her know her army has had a glorious victory.'

When the message reached London eight days later the capital went wild. It was a memorable victory, overturning the country's reputation as an offshore also-ran. A service of thanksgiving was held in the newly built St Paul's Cathedral, printers turned out copies of the tavern-bill note, and Parliament voted Marlborough a dukedom and a huge sum of money. The Queen gave her friend's husband land from the old royal estate at Woodstock near Oxford, and on it the new Duke and Duchess of Marlborough would erect a magnificent palace named after the popular English rendering of Blindheim – Blenheim.

In the years that followed, Marlborough won victories at Ramillies (1706), Oudenarde (1708) and Malplaquet (1709). But the last of these cost thirty thousand allied lives – it was 'a very murdring battel', as Marlborough himself confessed, and English opinion began to turn against the war. The revelation that the great man had enriched himself from the sale of bread to his armies led to charges of embezzlement, and on New Year's Eve 1711 he was sacked by his wife's former best friend, Queen Anne.

Disabled by strokes, John Churchill died in 1722, pitifully broken in body and mind. But his palace at Blenheim remains a splendid memorial to a great general and an historic victory, and was to be the birthplace a century and a half later of another battling Churchill –

Winston. Britain's inspirational leader in the Second World War was a direct descendant. Until the birth in 1897 of his cousin John, in fact, Winston was in line to become the 10th Duke of Marlborough.

UNION JACK
1707

I N THE SPRING OF 1702 A SHORT-SIGHTED, BURROWING mammal became the hero of the Jacobite supporters of the old Catholic Stuart line. William III died from his injuries after his horse stumbled on a molehill in the park at Hampton Court, and the Jacobites thereupon raised their glasses to toast 'the little gentleman in black velvet'.

William had died childless, and Protestants worried at the similar lack of issue in his sister-in-law and successor, Queen Anne. In the seventeen years following her marriage in 1683 to her cousin Prince George of Denmark, Anne had endured no less than nineteen pregnancies that ended in five infant deaths, some thirteen miscarriages and just one healthy son who died at the age of eleven. This tragic succession of gynaecological failures left Anne an invalid for the rest of her life and presented Protestant England with a dilemma – after Anne, the next fifty-seven Stuarts in line to the throne were all Catholics.

Parliament's solution was the Act of Settlement of 1701. All fifty-seven Catholics were eliminated from the succession, which was handed to no. 58, the Protestant Sophia, Electress of Hanover, a descendant of James I's daughter Elizabeth (see family tree, p. xviii).

But Westminster failed to consult Scotland in arriving at this drastic solution, apparently assuming that the 'northern kingdom' would meekly go along with whatever monarch England chose for itself. The Scots were outraged. 'All our affairs since the union of the crowns have been managed by the advice of English ministers,' complained one member of the Scottish Parliament, referring to 1603 when James VI of Scotland became James I of England. 'We have from that time appeared . . . more like a conquered province than a free independent people.'

To reclaim Scotland's independence, its Parliament in Edinburgh passed an Act of Security asserting that, after Anne's death, Scotland would choose a Protestant Stuart of its own – who might not be a Hanoverian. Westminster's retort was the so-called Alien Act of March 1705. This threatened that unless Scotland adopted the Hanoverian succession by December, any Scot who found himself in England would be treated as an alien, and that Scottish imports of coal, cattle and linen would be banned.

'Never two Nations that had so much Affinity in Circumstances,' commented Daniel Defoe, 'have had such Inveteracy and Aversion to one another in their blood.'

Like a long-married couple wrangling, both sides made their points with feeling, but then decided to compromise. In April 1706 two teams of commissioners met in London to negotiate a union between the kingdoms, and they arrived at twenty-five articles of agreement with remarkable speed. Scotland and England would be separate no more: they would become a new single Kingdom of Great Britain with the same Hanoverian on the throne; a single Parliament in Westminster would be expanded to include forty-five Scottish MPs and sixteen Scottish peers; the whole of Great Britain would become a single free-trade zone using the English pound and English weights and measures; but Scotland would keep its own legal system, universities, local town charters and, above all, its own separate Presbyterian Church, the Kirk. All those distinct Scottish entities survive to this day – with the recent addition, in 1997, of a revived Scottish Parliament.

The very first article of the Act of Union, passed early in 1707, described the flag of this new United Kingdom – a combination of Scotland's diagonal white cross of St Andrew on a blue ground with the upright red cross of St George on white (Wales being considered part of England). In fact, Anglo-Scottish ships had been flying this design for more than a century as a small ensign on the bowsprit. Sailors knew it as the 'jack flag', but now it got a new nickname – the Union Jack.

MADE IN GERMANY
1714

IN SEPTEMBER 1714 KING GEORGE I ARRIVED IN LONDON IN A cavalcade of 260 horse-drawn coaches that took three hours to pass by. In the coaches were more than ninety of his German ministers and courtiers, his two German mistresses – one inordinately fat and the other contrastingly thin – and his much favoured Turkish grooms and body-servants, captured at the siege of Vienna in 1683. None of these companions spoke more than a few words of English, and nor did the King himself. Having passed most of his fifty-four years in the small north German state of Hanover, Georg Ludwig had to converse with his English ministers in a mixture of French and schoolroom Latin.

The family tree on p. xviii shows the complicated blood route by which Georg Ludwig of Hanover's descent from James I entitled him to become King George I of Great Britain, but his principal qualification was his Protestant faith. 'A Protestant country can never have stable times under a popish Prince,' declared Bishop Richard Willis in 1715, 'any more than a flock of sheep can have quiet when a wolf is their shepherd.'

Understanding this, England's Protestant elite – the gentry, merchants and nobility – flocked to greet the King in the Painted Hall at Greenwich. But the ordinary people felt resentment. On George's coronation day the following month, 'strange tumults and disorders' were reported in Bristol, Norwich, Birmingham and some thirty other towns in the south. In the subsequent months, disturbances became so commonplace in London, the Midlands and along the Welsh border that in July 1715 Parliament passed the Riot Act. This gave the authorities the power to 'read the riot act' to any gathering of twelve people or more: if they refused to disperse within an hour, they could be hanged.

That autumn, 'the Pretender', the tall and thin, white-faced James Francis Edward Stuart, son of James II, landed in Scotland in a bid to reclaim his throne. But though loyalists might secretly toast 'the King over the water', few were prepared to risk their lives. Only a few diehard Roman Catholics rallied to the small Jacobite army as it marched south. If German George was uninspiring, the fastidious, French-educated James III had even less charisma. His troops surrendered at Preston in November 1715, while James himself escaped to Scotland and thence to France.

So the English had to work up some enthusiasm for their short, pop-eyed German monarch, who demonstrated his enthusiasm for them by going off to Hanover every summer and staying there for as long as he could. When George was in London he spent as much time as possible with his fellow Germans, particularly his two mistresses, whom he visited on alternate nights, fat and thin, listening to music, playing cards and amusing himself with such pastimes as cutting out paper silhouettes. His problems with the language discouraged him from getting too involved in England's politics – and that suited England's politicians just fine.

SOUTH SEA BUBBLE
1720

THE WHEELER-DEALERS OF EIGHTEENTH-CENTURY LONDON loved to gather in the city's busy coffee houses. 'There was a rabble going hither and thither,' wrote one visitor, 'reminding me of a swarm of rats in a ruinous cheese store. Some came, others went; some were scribbling, others were talking . . . The whole place stank of tobacco.'

If the focus of the modern coffee bar is the hissing espresso machine, in Stuart and Georgian times it was the row of tall, black coffee pots warming in the open hearth. Many of London's coffee houses clustered around the Royal Exchange in the heart of the City between Cornhill and Threadneedle Street, and when the senior merchants of the Exchange called for quiet and expelled the jabbering stock-jobbers at the end of the seventeenth century, these forerunners of the modern stockbroker shifted their trading to the coffee hearths. For more than seventy years (until 1773), London's stock exchange gesticulated and shouted its business in the coffee houses of Exchange Alley, notably at Jonathan's and Garraway's.

Share-dealing in England went back over a century to the joint-stock companies set up to fund the Tudor voyages of discovery – with foreign exchange dealers, ship insurers and old-fashioned money-lenders all contributing to the profitable bustle of City life. This had taken on a new dimension in 1694 with the founding of the Bank of England, which borrowed from the general public at interest rates ranging from 8 or 9 to as much as 14 per cent in order to lend money to the government. Investors had rushed forward. In its first two weeks of business, the new Bank attracted some twelve hundred of them, including the King and Queen.

In 1711 the South Sea Company was founded as a rival investment opportunity to the Bank, with an exotic twist. The company was busy securing a monopoly of the Spanish slave trade and a share in other trading ventures in the tropics. Soaking up the money of investors great and small, the new institution, ever more ambitious, negotiated with the government to take over part of the National Debt. But this involved bribing ministers and courtiers, including the King's mistresses, with South Sea stock. And, to keep the price up, the company's promoters started making unrealistic promises, offering dividends they could not deliver. 'The town is quite mad about the South Sea,' wrote one observer in March 1720. 'One can hear nothing else talked of.'

By April, South Sea stock had risen from around 130 per cent to over 300, and speculation grew fiercer. 'Surprizing Scene in [Ex]Change Alley,' ran a report on 2 June. 'S. Sea in the morning above 900.'

Aristocrats, fashionable ladies and footmen all joined in the rush to stake their fortunes on South Sea stock. 'Everyone thirsts for more,' came one word of warning at the end of June as shares peaked at over 1000, 'and all this founded upon the machine of paper credit supported only by the imagination'.

Within the bubble grew smaller bubbles – a company to import walnut trees from Virginia, a project to improve the Greenland fisheries – and even 'a company for carrying on an undertaking of great advantage but nobody to know what it is'.

As canny investors realised the folly of the general hysteria and cashed in their shares, the value of South Sea stock began to fall. The bubble was pricked. By September 1720 it was down to 130, and hundreds of thousands of people who had sold land and property to buy near the peak were ruined. Bankruptcy listings in the *London Gazette* reached an all-time high. Suicides were reported, and panic was widespread. As the company directors fled the country, the King signed warrants for their arrest.

At the time, the monstrous bubble produced a shocking and unheard-of train of events. But today we are familiar with the sequence of boom and bust, insider trading, corruption and, finally, the show trials and the verdicts meted out to those with inky fingers. They are the all too familiar ingredients of the modern big-city scam.

BRITAIN'S FIRST PRIME MINISTER
1721–42

TOWARDS THE END OF AUGUST 1720 ROBERT WALPOLE MP fancied dipping his toes once again in the profitable waters of the South Sea Company. Four months earlier the hard-drinking and rotund Norfolk politician, who had recently been appointed

Paymaster General of the forces, had sold much of his stock at 300 per cent, and had pocketed a tidy profit. Now he sent off a hefty bid for more, greedily eyeing a price that was rising beyond the 1000 mark and seemed to promise him even more riches . . .

Luckily for Walpole, there was a delay in the mail and he never spent his money, thereby avoiding financial ruin and earning a reputation for prudence that he did nothing to dispel. The portly Paymaster General actually took on the job of sorting out the mess left by the South Sea Bubble, punishing the most obvious scapegoats but discreetly turning a blind eye to those – like the King and some of his favourite ministers – whose dealings had not been above reproach. In August 1721, Robert Walpole's act 'to restore the publick Credit' was passed by Parliament, and he gained a national pre-eminence that he would enjoy for two decades.

Aged forty-five in 1721, Walpole was the knowing and worldly master of Britain's evolving system of constitutional government. He was, as he said himself, 'no saint, no Spartan, no reformer'. In 1711 he had spent six months in the Tower and been briefly expelled from Parliament for embezzling government money. Politically he was a Whig, a successor of those who had opposed the absolutism of James II and had fought for parliamentary supremacy over the Crown, ushering in the Hanoverians. Not surprisingly George I favoured the Whigs over their Tory opponents, with their lingering allegiance to the Jacobite cause.

Walpole grasped the essence of the new consensus. The monarch might head the government, but the country was run by his ministers, whose authority depended upon Parliament and the House of Commons in particular. 'So great was Walpole's love of the Commons,' wrote the Earl of Chesterfield, 'that when going to face the House, he dressed as carefully as a lover going to see a mistress.'

When Walpole's stature reached the point at which most politicians claimed a peerage and moved up to the House of Lords, he chose to stay in the Commons – the chamber that mattered when it came to government revenue. There he remained for more than twenty years, exercising his power as the monarch's principal, or 'prime', minister – though Walpole himself eschewed the title, preferring to be known as First Lord of the Treasury. This is the official title borne by prime ministers to this day – you will not find the words 'Prime Minister' inscribed on any formal government list.

A genial and relaxed speaker, Walpole unashamedly used patronage to massage his majority in the Commons, handing out government jobs to create an army of dependable placemen – 'all men have their price' was another of his favourite sayings. He made a point of dining privately with every new Whig MP, and he was equally assiduous with his other font of power, the Crown. When George II succeeded his father in 1727, Walpole worked hard to secure the new King a massively generous Civil List, the parliamentary grant first established for William and Mary to cover not only the expenses of the sovereign, their family, household, parks and palaces, but also the salaries and pensions of ministers, judges and other public officials – the civil government, in fact.

Having secured £800,000 for the King, Walpole raised a further £100,000 for the Queen, Caroline of Ansbach. His rival, Sir Spencer Compton, had been cultivating the King's mistress Henrietta Howard, but Walpole had worked out that Henrietta exercised no political influence. Compton, he later commented, 'took the wrong sow by the ear'.

The farmyard phrase epitomised the country squire image on which Walpole built his career, playing the hard-riding, hard-drinking man of the soil for the sake of the landed gentry who voted with him year after year in the Commons. In reality, he was a sophisticated urbanite who built up a fabled art collection – his grandson sold the best of it to Catherine the Great of Russia – and he could skip around a balance sheet with the skill of any City merchant. He was a particular believer in the new science of statistics. Those who analysed Walpole closely called him the 'skreenmaster', because he hid the truth behind a plausible screen.

BORN AGAIN
1738

YOUNG JOHN WESLEY HAD NOT WANTED TO GO TO THE Bible-study meeting being held beside the old wall of the city of London one evening in May 1738. But as the 34-year-old clergyman listened to a reading from the works of Martin Luther, he realised that he was deeply stirred: 'about a quarter before nine . . . I felt my heart strangely warmed. I felt I did trust in Christ, Christ alone for salvation, and an assurance was given me that He had taken away my sins, even mine.'

John Wesley's 8.45 revelation would inspire him to take Christianity to the thousands of dispossessed and downtrodden in Georgian England – and to do so with passion. Strong feeling was not the religious style of the day. The Church of England was taking a rest after its centuries of upheaval. Anglican ministers, many of them relaxed and quite worldly gentlemen, dispensed the comforts of the faith to congregations for whom worship was often a matter of habit rather than burning conviction. Few vicars viewed the working classes as their priority, while the very shape and extent of their parishes, formed by the population patterns of pre-industrial England, would make it difficult for them to minister to the new mining and manufacturing communities that were soon to spring up all over the country.

It was to reach these people that John Wesley rode out into the fields in the early summer of 1739. In a series of over 150 outdoor meetings between April and June he set fire to the new 'Methodist' movement, so called after the attempts that John and his brother Charles, another clergyman, had made together at Oxford when they formed the 'Holy Club', its aim to practise what they saw as the 'methods' of the early Church – to pray and read together, to fast, to make regular confession, to visit prisoners in jail.

To these the energetic John added travelling. In the remaining fifty-two years of his life, the wiry five-foot-three-inch evangelist trekked some 4000 miles annually on horseback – a total of 208,000 miles (over 330,000 kilometres) – preaching at least two sermons a day, and frequently four or five, to congregations whose only shelter from the weather was often the foliage of a tree overhead: a 'Gospel Oak'.

Legend would trace Wesley's sense of mission back to a providential escape in his childhood when fire demolished his family's Lincolnshire home. As his parents realised with horror that John, the fifteenth of nineteen children, had been left inside, the six-year-old miraculously appeared at an upstairs casement window and was rescued seconds before the flaming roof collapsed. He was 'a brand plucked from the burning', and his followers took this as a metaphor for their own God-given salvation. Methodist lay preachers did not need to be ordained at Oxford or anywhere else: they were qualified simply by their ability to preach. And women played a prominent role in the movement.

The Church correctly viewed Wesley's preaching as subversive. It undermined their monopoly of the pulpit as he took his message to the poverty-stricken communities of London, Bristol, the Midlands and the north. In fact, his message was not subversive, nor was it revolutionary. Wesley himself tried to work within the Anglican communion – it was only after his death that the Methodists split from the Church of England – and he did not call directly for social change. But his 'Second Reformation' revived Martin Luther's exciting idea that a man could communicate directly with his God, finding new purpose in life through the vigour of spiritual rebirth – and this inspiring notion would, in due course, make its impact on social rebirth as well. The working-class movements of the nineteenth century owed much to the ethos of Methodism and the chapel. John Wesley would have shuddered, but he was one of the godfathers of socialism.

AFEW DAYS BEFORE HE WAS DUE TO BE EXECUTED, the highwayman Richard Turpin bought himself a new frock-coat and smart new footwear – he was planning to meet his death in style. The most wanted criminal in England had hired himself five mourners to escort him to the gallows, and as the cart carried him through the crowd that gathered on the outskirts of York, he bowed ceremoniously to left and right.

Turpin had spent his last days in prison entertaining visitors with jokes and drinks. Now, on Saturday 7 April, 1739, he climbed the ladder of the 'three-legged mare', the triangular gallows on York racecourse, stamping his left leg to subdue a tremor that betrayed his fear. The noose was placed around his neck and he spoke briefly to the executioner whose job it was to pull the ladder away. But the victim did the hangman's work for him. The frock-coated highwayman jumped boldly off the ladder – 'dying with as much intrepidity and unconcern,' according to one eyewitness, 'as if he had been taking [a] horse to go on a journey'.

Highwaymen were the bane of travellers in Georgian England, flourishing to the end of the eighteenth century. With the bank transfer system in its infancy, many people travelled with bags containing quite substantial sums of cash. Policing was primitive, and passengers on the stagecoaches that started operating in the early 1730s dreaded the thunder of hooves, the juddering pull to a halt and the cry, 'Your money or your life!'

Some of the earliest, mid-seventeenth-century highway robberies were carried out by renegade royalist army officers, and it may have been their cavalier style that inspired the legend of the highwayman as a latter-day Robin Hood. Balladeers and poets built on the idea of the gentleman footpad who treated his victims with gallantry, particularly when it came to the fairer sex.

But the record shows that the average highwayman was simply a mugger on horseback – and Dick Turpin was proof of that. A heavily pockmarked man with a vile temper and a penchant for brutality, he was a member of the notorious Essex Gang who specialised in raiding and terrorising remote farmhouses on the outskirts of London. In the course of their housebreaking, they tortured one old man of seventy and raped a servant girl at pistol point. Turpin himself held a defenceless elderly woman over an open fire until she revealed where the family savings were hidden – and it was only when his fellow gangsters were brought to justice in 1735 that he turned to highway robbery south of the Thames.

The thug was brought down by his temper. When London got too hot for him Turpin went north, where he settled in Yorkshire and survived undetected under the pseudonym of 'John Palmer' – until he got into a quarrel with his landlord, shooting his prize farmyard cockerel and threatening to kill the landlord too. The man complained and Palmer/Turpin was arrested.

The death of Richard Turpin was the subject of one contemporary pamphlet, but otherwise the criminal died unlamented – one among the thousands strung up on the gallows of Georgian England for offences ranging from petty theft to murder. But a century later the novelist William Harrison Ainsworth devised the story of a Yorkshire country gentleman, one Jack Palmer, who lived a secret life as a highwayman. Ainsworth had clearly read the account of Palmer/Turpin's last days in Yorkshire, and to this he added other tales, notably the account that Daniel Defoe wrote in the 1720s of a dramatic ride from London to York by an earlier highwayman, 'Swift Nicks'.

In 1834 Ainsworth brought these different sources together in his bestselling romance *Rookwood*, which treated his readers to a dashing account of Dick Turpin riding north on his beloved mare, to whom the novelist, probably drawing on a ballad of 1825, gave the name Black Bess: '[Turpin's] blood spins through his veins, winds round his heart, mounts to his brain. Away! Away! He is wild with joy . . . A hamlet is visible in the moonlight . . . A moment's clatter upon the stones and it is left behind.'

Ainsworth made the imaginary Black Bess the faithful heroine of his story, vividly describing how she gamely kept her master ahead of the chasing posse, and only sank to her knees when she had finally carried him to safety: 'Bess tottered, fell. There was a dreadful gasp – a parting moan – a snort; her eye gazed for an instant upon her master with a dying glare . . . a shiver ran through her frame. Her heart had burst.'

The first edition of *Rookwood* sold out rapidly and was reprinted in August that year. 'Dauntless' Dick Turpin and his mare soon became the subject of popular prints and illustrations, and it was not long before authenticating anecdotes sprang up along the Great North Road, where innkeepers related how Turpin had refreshed his brave mount with ale – they could even produce the ancient tankard from which Black Bess had drunk. Here was the gully she had cleared in one stride, there was the five-bar tollgate she had vaulted with ease – Dick Turpin and the gallant black mare he never rode had passed into history.

GOD SAVE THE KING!

1745

God save our noble King!
God save Great George our King!
God save the King!
Send him victorious,
Happy and glorious,
Long to reign o'er us,
God save the King.

WHEN THESE WORDS WERE SUNG IN PUBLIC FOR THE
first time in September 1745, the anxious crowd that filled the
London theatre rose to their feet, clapping wildly and calling for
encores. Various versions of the song had been around for some time,
in praise of a number of kings – the deposed James II among them.
But on this warm autumn evening, the song was addressed to the
Hanoverian monarch of the moment, George II, and the words were
sung with special fervour. It was effectively a prayer, since at that
moment 'Great George, our King' really did stand in need of saving –
along with the audience and all those whose interests were linked to
the survival of the German Protestant dynasty.

That July, the 24-year-old grandson of James II, Charles Edward
Stuart, the Young Pretender, whose aim was to make himself King
Charles III, had landed in Scotland. Through August the clans had ral-
lied to his cause, and in September the Highlanders marched on
Edinburgh. Even as anxious Londoners were singing 'God Save the
King!' the Scottish capital was going Stuart. Twenty-thousand excited
citizens cheered the claimant into the city, shouting out the romantic
nickname by which the Prince would be known to history – 'Bonnie
Prince Charlie'.

Fine-featured and willowy with rosebud lips and limpid brown eyes,
Charles Edward Stuart was bonny indeed. Born and brought up in
Rome by his father the Old Pretender, who had made his own bid for
the throne in 1715, Charles Edward Stuart spoke three languages
(English, French and Italian), and had a roster of accomplishments that
included riding, shooting, royal tennis, shuttlecock (modern bad-
minton), dancing, golf and playing the cello. He also had the knack of
bearing himself like a king: he looked particularly magnificent when
wearing a kilt and marching amongst the ranks, kicking up dust and
mud with his men.

The Young Pretender had a streak of daring that brought him early
success. He had set off on his adventure against his father's advice, and
once he had secured his position in Edinburgh he headed his army
south, marching down the west coast to outflank the English army and
capture the towns of Carlisle, Manchester, Preston and Wigan. By 4
December 1745 the five-thousand-strong Stuart army was in
Derby – just 127 miles from London, which was defended at that

moment by no more than two thousand regular troops plus local trained bands who had hurriedly gathered at Finchley.

With a quick dash south Bonnie Prince Charlie and his Highlanders could possibly have reached the capital ahead of George II's second son, the Duke of Cumberland, who was commanding the English army. Householders along the road from Derby to London started burying their gold, and in London itself there was a run on the banks on 'Black Friday', 4 December, as people withdrew their gold and silver. The King himself loaded a yacht with his treasures: God save the King indeed – and his riches too!

At this crucial moment, however, Charles Edward Stuart could not persuade his Scottish officers to march any further south. He had promised them armed support from France that had not been forth-coming, and – more serious – the local response had been depressing. As in 1715, English and Welsh Jacobites had chosen to stay at home rather than risk their lives and livelihood by rallying to the Stuart banner. Lacking funds, the Prince could only pay his men in food, and they were hankering for home. Reluctantly, Bonnie Prince Charlie turned his march back towards Scotland, with the Duke of Cumberland shadowing his retreat.

The showdown came on Culloden Moor in the Highlands the fol-lowing April, where Cumberland's superior artillery and cavalry pulverised the tired and hungry Stuart army. Bonnie Prince Charlie headed for the Western Isles with a price of £30,000 on his head, but no one betrayed him: for six months he eluded his red-coated pur-suers, thanks to loyalists like Flora MacDonald who ferried him to safety on the island of Skye – whence he could make good his escape to France.

'Speed bonnie boat like a bird on the wing, over the sea to Skye,' ran the song. 'Carry the lad that's born to be king over the sea to Skye.'

To this day, the poignant ballad enshrines Scotland's yearning for its bonnie Prince – while down south 'God Save the King' enjoyed a career of its own, becoming the melody that bands struck up to mark a royal appearance. When in 1788, forty-three years after the '45, the writer Fanny Burney accompanied George II's grandson, George III, on a trip to Cheltenham to take the waters, she reported how 'every five miles or so there were bands of the most horrid fiddlers scraping "God save the King" with all their might, out of tune, out of time and all in the rain'.

By the 1800s the song had become so established as the expression of patriotic sentiment that it became accepted as the 'national anthem' – the world's first, which other countries hastened to copy. Prussia, Denmark, Switzerland, Russia and even the United States adopted the melody of 'God Save the King' for a period, setting it to words of their own. Later they preferred to sing their own song. But to this day, when the England soccer team line up to play the tiny principality of Liechtenstein, the same tune gets repeated – so good they play it twice.*

DR JOHNSON'S DICTIONARY

B Y THE MIDDLE OF THE EIGHTEENTH CENTURY BRITAIN HAD a fair claim to being in the forefront of Europe's economic, scientific and political progress. Culturally, however, there was a void. While Italy had long boasted its own dictionary, the *Vocabulario degli Accademici*

*The playing of 'God Save the Queen' reflects the confusion as to whether the inhabitants of the British Isles are primarily British or, more fundamentally, English, Irish, Scottish or Welsh. Their sporting teams tend to prefer their own local anthems, 'Land of Our Fathers' (Wales), 'The Soldier's Song' (Ireland) and 'Flower of Scotland', with England's supporters favouring 'Jerusalem', 'Land of Hope and Glory' (at the Commonwealth Games) and, recently, at rugby matches, the African-American gospel hymn 'Swing Low, Sweet Chariot', originally sung in homage to the hat-trick of tries scored against Ireland in 1988 by Chris Oti, England's first black player for eighty years. When it comes to the Olympic Games, however, it is 'God Save the Queen' to which all British athletes stand to attention – and sometimes cry.

della Crusca, and France had *Le Dictionnaire de l'Académie française*, England had no almanac of its vibrant and expanding language. In 1746 a group of London publishers pooled resources to correct the omission, entrusting the making of a national dictionary to Samuel Johnson, an opinionated 36-year-old journalist of untidy appearance with a gift for creating extremely neat definitions. Angling, he once said, was 'a stick and a string, with a worm on one end and a fool on the other'.

The son of a struggling bookseller from Lichfield in Staffordshire, Johnson suffered in his childhood from scrofula, a tubercular disease of the lymph nodes contracted through infected milk. Popular belief held that the characteristic swellings, known as the 'King's Evil', responded to the royal touch, and in March 1712 the two-year-old Samuel was taken down to London by his mother to be 'touched' by Queen Anne in one of the last of these ceremonies ever held. For the rest of his life Johnson wore round his neck the gold 'touch piece' the Queen gave him, but he was not blessed with a cure. A subsequent operation to remove the swellings left his neck visibly scarred.

Also pockmarked with smallpox, Johnson was tall and stout with a curious stoop – 'almost bent double,' commented the writer Fanny Burney. 'His mouth is almost constantly opening and shutting as if he were chewing. He has a strange method of frequently twirling his fingers and twisting his hands. His body is in constant agitation, see-sawing up and down.'

Modern experts have diagnosed Johnson's grunts and head-rollings as St Vitus' Dance or Tourette's Syndrome. His friends knew the kindly spirit behind this intimidating exterior, and nicknamed him 'Ursa Major' – the Great Bear – revelling in his sharp wit. 'Let me see,' he once remarked, when reminded that the French Academy's forty members had taken forty years to compile their dictionary, while he was planning to write his, alone, in only three. 'Forty times forty is sixteen hundred. As three to sixteen hundred, so is the proportion of an Englishman to a Frenchman.'

In the event the task took him nine years. Working with five assistants who scribbled away in the attic of his home on the north side of Fleet Street, he produced definitions of more than forty-two thousand words, laced from time to time with his own wit and prejudice:

. . . Lexicographer. A writer of dictionaries, a harmless drudge.
Oats. A grain which in England is generally given to horses but in Scotland supports the people.

The dictionary was an instant success, republished in many editions, and Johnson was honoured with academic distinctions – Oxford University made him a Master of Arts and Dublin gave him a doctorate. As 'Dr Johnson', he became the great man of letters of his time, founding, with the painter Joshua Reynolds, 'The Club', whose members included the playwright and novelist Oliver Goldsmith, the orator Edmund Burke, the actor David Garrick and the biographer James Boswell, whose famous *Life of Johnson* has preserved many of the great man's sayings for posterity: 'patriotism is the last refuge of a scoundrel', 'when a man knows he is to be hanged in a fortnight it concentrates his mind wonderfully' – and his comment on the contracting of a second marriage after an unhappy first one, 'the triumph of hope over experience'.

Johnson's own marriage to Tetty, a widow twenty years his senior, was a love match, and after her death he filled his home with an eccentric ménage of oddballs: the blind and bad-tempered poet Anna Williams; an unlicensed surgeon, Robert Levet, along with a former prostitute named Poll, all tended by a black servant, Frank Barber, who had arrived as a boy from Jamaica. Johnson cared for them all, and developed a fierce aversion to the business of slavery. 'Here's to the next insurrection of the negroes in the West Indies,' was one of his toasts.

Johnson's robust views do not always square with the standards of today. 'A woman's preaching,' he declared, 'is like a dog walking on its hind legs. It is not done well but you are surprised to find it done at all.' But his honesty disarmed criticism. Confronted one day by an indignant complainant who demanded how, in his dictionary, he could have defined 'pastern' (a horse's ankle) as a horse's 'knee', he offered no excuse – 'Ignorance, madam, pure ignorance.'

GENERAL WOLFE AND THE CAPTURE
OF QUEBEC
1759

The curfew tolls the knell of parting day,
The lowing herd wind slowly o'er the lea,
The ploughman homeward plods his weary way,
And leaves the world to darkness, and to me.

GENERAL JAMES WOLFE WAS FAR FROM HOME ON THE night of 12–13 September 1759 as he quietly read the opening lines of Thomas Gray's *Elegy Written in a Country Churchyard*. The general was with his officers in a flat-bottomed boat, according to the young midshipman who later recounted the tale, drifting under cover of darkness down the ebb tide on Canada's St Lawrence River.

'I can only say, gentlemen,' declared Wolfe (who was not widely known as a poetry lover), 'that if the choice were mine, I would rather be the author of these verses than win the battle that we are to fight tomorrow morning.'

After months of inconclusive sparring, the British general had decided on a daring stroke to outwit the Marquis de Montcalm, commander of the troops defending Quebec, the capital of French Canada. By the light of a pale quarter-moon, the British general had embarked his 4600 red-coated soldiers on a flotilla of vessels that made their way silently downriver with muffled oarstrokes – to land at the foot of cliffs so steep that the French had not seriously fortified them.

As Scottish troops scrambled up the cliffs, a French sentry challenged them. Fortunately the leading Highlander was able to reply in convincing French, and his companions scrambled over the clifftop to surprise the hundred or so guards, most of whom were asleep. As dawn rose on the Heights of Abraham, the flat green plateau extending to the walls of Quebec, Montcalm was confronted by no less than seven battalions of British soldiers drawn up in order, ready to attack.

The battle for Quebec was part of the Seven Years War (1756–63), later described by Winston Churchill as the first ever 'world' war, since Britain, allied in Europe with Prussia, spread her battles with France, Russia, Spain and Austria beyond Europe and the Mediterranean to India, Africa, North America, the Pacific and the Caribbean. James Wolfe had learned his soldiering as an officer in the army of the Duke of Cumberland, seeing action in 1746 at Culloden, then playing his part in the merciless subduing of the Scottish Highlands that followed. Self-assured, flamboyant, and almost manic in his will to win, Wolfe was once accused of madness by George II's Prime Minister, the Duke of Newcastle.

'Mad, is he?' retorted the King. 'Then I hope he will bite some others of my generals.'

The high-flying 33-year-old got engaged to be married shortly before he embarked for Canada in 1759, and his fiancée Katherine Lowther presented him with a sixpenny copy of Thomas Gray's *Elegy* as a going-away present. Gray was the most popular poet of the age: his reverie among the gravestones of a country churchyard, 'far from the madding crowd', had caught the imagination of a society that, now on the cusp of industrialisation, was coming to value the countryside it had once taken for granted. 'Full many a flower is born to blush unseen,' ran one couplet, 'And waste its sweetness on the desert air.'

Wolfe himself was anything but a shrinking violet – so cocky and disdainful, in fact, that he was barely on speaking terms with many of his principal officers. His reference to 'the battle that we are to fight tomorrow morning' was the first that some of them had heard of his plan. He was also capable of indecision. When he got to the top of the cliff with an early wave of soldiers, he seems to have lost his nerve, according to one source, and impulsively sent down an order to unload no more soldiers in the cove.

But down on the beach his officers kept the boats coming – and up on the Heights of Abraham the French panicked. Instead of waiting for reinforcements who might have outflanked the exposed line of redcoats, Montcalm attacked in a rush. As his Canadian irregulars advanced, they were mown down by British musket-fire, and Montcalm himself sustained a fatal wound to his stomach.

By this stage of the battle, Wolfe also lay dying, shot down after he had stood on a rise in clear view and easy range of the enemy. The general had been ill for weeks, suffering severe bladder pains. High on opium, he was also weakened by bloodletting, the primitive duo of remedies that his physicians had prescribed for his fever and his tubercular cough, and it was hardly surprising if his behaviour was erratic. The evidence suggests that James Wolfe may have deliberately exposed himself to danger on the Heights of Abraham, knowing that he did not have long to live.

The general received the hero's death that he had yearned for – immortalised some years later by Benjamin West's epic painting *The Death of General Wolfe*. The capture of Quebec crowned a year of triumphs in a war that would lay the foundations of Britain's overseas empire, and the victor's embalmed body was honoured with a glorious state funeral and burial in Westminster Abbey. Wolfe's will gave instructions that five hundred guineas be spent on framing the portrait of his fiancée with jewels as his farewell present to her, and among his personal effects was the copy of Gray's *Elegy* that had been Katherine's parting gift. The little booklet reposes today in the archives of Toronto University, where you can see the underlinings the general made while he was planning the daring coup that brought him fame and victory. One underlining seems especially poignant: 'The paths of glory lead but to the grave.'

JAMES HARGREAVES AND THE SPINNING JENNY
1766

FOR CENTURIES THE SPINNING WHEEL STOOD IN THE corner of almost every hearth in England – the basis of the country's cottage industry. Whenever she had a spare half-hour or so, the woman (and quite often the man) of the house would sit down at the ungainly contraption to tease out raw wool into skeins that could then be sold for weaving. After the discovery of the Americas, it was often cotton wool that went on to the spindle, with merchants supplying bundles of the fluffy raw material to cottage spinners whom they paid under the 'putting-out' system to supply them with the finished thread. Many spinners were also weavers.

By the mid-eighteenth century the damp and industrious north-western county of Lancashire was a major centre of this domestic cotton production, and one day in the 1760s an overturned spinning wheel inspired James Hargreaves, a hand-loom weaver from the village of Oswaldtwistle, to devise a way of dramatically increasing production. Hargreaves was struck by the way that the overturned wheel kept on spinning – as did the usually horizontal spindle.

What would happen, the weaver wondered, if several spindles were to be placed upright, side by side? Might it not be possible to spin several threads at once? Working with a knife, Hargreaves shaped a primitive engine, or 'jinny', a single spinning wheel, with, eventually, as many as eight separate spindles.

The 'spinning jenny' (finally perfected, according to his daughter Mary, in 1766) turned ordinary cottage kitchens into mini-workshops – and the initial reaction from some was distrust. Angry neighbours raided Hargreaves' barn and burned the first twenty jennies he had built – on the grounds, according to Mary, that the machines would 'ruin the country'. If one jenny could do the work of eight spinners, reasoned the neighbours, that would put seven out of work.

In fact, the spectacular new spinning capacity of the Lancashire cottages and barns provided the basis for a cotton boom. The county became the English centre of cotton cloth production in the 1760s and 70s, turning out not just rough calicoes but delicate muslins, and as earnings rose, spinners and weavers took to parading the streets on paydays with £5 notes in their hatbands. Their wives drank tea out of the finest china.

The fine but tough yarns needed for these new fabrics were made possible by a host of mechanical innovations. Richard Arkwright, a barber and wigmaker from Preston, worked with a Warrington clockmaker, John Kay, to produce a 'frame' which used rollers to draw out and twist the yarn. Samuel Crompton, a Bolton weaver, devised a crossbreed of the jenny and frame that became known as the 'spinning mule'.

Edmund Cartwright, a poet-clergyman, thought he was enhancing this golden age of pastoral prosperity when he invented a power-loom operated by a caged bull that turned a huge treadmill. But bull power was soon supplanted by steam power, and by the end of the eighteenth century the old putting-out system was doomed. Steam- and water-powered workshops and factories could mass produce ever cheaper cotton thread and cloth. By 1801, the painter Joseph Farington was to note in his diary: 'In the evening I walked to Cromford [Derbyshire], and saw the children coming from their work out of one of Mr Arkwright's factories. These children had been at work from 6 or 7 o'clock this morning and it is now 7 in the evening.' The dark satanic mill had been created.

Lecturing on these events in the 1880s, the Oxford scholar and social reformer Arnold Toynbee coined the phrase 'Industrial Revolution' to describe the economic transformation of England that started in the 1760s. But modern scholars dispute this impression of dramatic upheaval, pointing out the gradual and incremental nature of the process that went from Hargreaves to Arkwright and Kay, from Samuel Crompton to Cartwright, and then on to James Watt, who modified Newcomen's engine (see p. 302) to bring steam power into the process – the Industrial Evolution, in fact.

CAPTAIN COOK – MASTER OF THE PILOTAGE

1770

THE SECRET OF GENERAL WOLFE'S DARING CAPTURE OF Quebec in 1759 was navigation – the mastery that the British navy achieved over the shoals of the treacherous St Lawrence River. 'The enemy has passed 60 ships of war where we hardly dared risk a vessel of 100 tons,' grumbled the French second-in-command, the Marquis de Vaudreuil, as he watched the British navigate their way upriver that June – and the star of those navigators was a thirty-year-old ship's master from Yorkshire, James Cook. Following the capture of Quebec, the young officer was awarded a special bonus of £50 (£5690 today) for 'indefatigable industry' in making himself the 'master of the pilotage'.

James Cook came from humble origins. The son of a Yorkshire farm labourer, he started work as a shop assistant before joining the crew of a dirty broad-bottomed colliery ship that transported coal from Tyneside down to London. For eleven years he learned his seamanship by battling the storms and shifting sandbanks of the North Sea, before he enlisted in 1755, aged twenty-six, as an ordinary sailor in the Royal Navy. In just two years, Able Seaman Cook took his Master's exams, qualifying himself 'to observe all coasts, shoals, and rocks, taking careful notes of the same'.

Cook had had only a few years of basic schooling at his home village of Whitby, so he spent his spare time at sea educating himself in Greek, mathematics and astronomy. After the conquest of Quebec he helped compile a chart of the Gulf of St Lawrence and spent much of the 1760s surveying the north and west coasts of Newfoundland. Every summer for five years he sailed and measured these chilly North Atlantic waters before returning to England to spend the winter drawing up his meticulous charts. Then, in 1768, came the invitation to participate in the 'greater Undertaking' – a scientific mission to measure the sun's distance from the earth, plus a secret mission from the King.

Venus was due to pass across the sun in June 1769, and the scientists of the Royal Society knew that the sun's location could be worked out by measuring the planet's passage from three different points on the globe. Lieutenant Cook, who was by now the navy's top navigational expert, was allocated the South Pacific leg of the experiment, setting sail on 25 August 1768 in the *Endeavour*, a sturdy, round-bottomed collier from his native Whitby. On board were eleven scientists, including the Eton-educated botanist Sir Joseph Banks, who was to become Cook's lifelong friend and supporter.

Only after the astronomical observation of June 1769 did Cook open his sealed orders – to steer onwards and locate, once and for all, the fabled Terra Australis, literally 'the land of the south' which Dutch navigators had first logged a century earlier. On 29 April 1770 the *Endeavour* put down anchor just south of modern Sydney in a cove that Cook named Botany Bay, after the large number of unusual plant species that Joseph Banks located there.

Banks himself was not complimentary. 'It resembled in my imagination the back of a lean cow,' he wrote of the weathered landscape, 'covered in general with long hair, but nevertheless where her scraggy hipbones have stuck out further than they ought, accidental rubbs and knocks have intirely bar'd them of their share of covering.'

Cook claimed this east coast of Terra Australis for George III, naming it New South Wales, before heading for England where he arrived in June 1771, almost three years after his departure. He had measured the passage of Venus accurately and charted some 4400 miles of New Zealand and Australian coastline. But equally remarkable was his feat in getting his crew home without succumbing to the sometimes fatal disease of scurvy, the occupational hazard of long voyages that caused sailors' limbs to swell and their gums to rot.

Twenty years earlier a Scottish doctor, James Lind, had established that scurvy – essentially vitamin C deficiency – could be prevented by the consumption of fresh lemon and lime juice, but it wasn't until 1795 that Lind's rations (which eventually gave British sailors the nickname 'Limeys') were officially adopted by the navy. Cook's preference was for a concentrated vegetable gel known as portable soup, along with carrot marmalade and sauerkraut – pickled, fermented cabbage.

'Few men have introduced into their ships more novelties in the way of victuals and drink than I have done,' wrote Cook, describing how he got his crew to gather cabbage palms and wild celery in New Zealand – to their disgust. They condemned this vegetable fare 'as stuff not fit for human beings to eat'.

One local curiosity in which they did show interest was the Polynesian tradition of tattooing, which they first encountered on the island of Tahiti. With time on their hands, several sailors and the young nature artist, Sydney Parkinson, 'underwent the operation' and proudly brought their tattoos home, starting a naval tradition that would later become a fashion statement.

In subsequent voyages Cook crossed the Antarctic Circle three times and discovered the South Sandwich Islands. In Alaska he proved definitively that there was no Northwest Passage, before turning back via Hawaii – where, in a tragic skirmish with islanders over a stolen boat in 1779, he was clubbed to death on the beach. Isolated in an angry crowd, he had ordered his men to 'Take to the boats' that were floating off the rocky shore, but why he did not take to the water himself remains a mystery. Perhaps Captain Cook was too brave or too proud to flee. But there is another explanation: like a surprising number of sailors in the old Royal Navy, the great navigator had never learned how to swim.

THE BOSTON TEA PARTY
1773

I N DECEMBER 1773 THREE BRITISH MERCHANT SHIPS LAY AT anchor in the harbour of Boston, Massachusetts, their holds filled with forty-five tons of tea. Packed in 342 wooden chests, there was enough of the dried leaf, it has been calculated, to brew twenty-four million cups of tea – and, offloaded from an overproduction in India, it was going at a bargain price.

Yet the tea seemed no bargain to the citizens of Boston who, for more than a decade, had been tussling with the British government over the troublesome question of tax. As London saw it, the two and a half million inhabitants of North America's thirteen colonies should pay for the protection provided by the British troops stationed there. But many Americans resented the meddling of a government that was three thousand miles away. In 1763, for instance, London had halted the colonists' land-grab of native 'Indian' territories by drawing the 'Proclamation Line' along the Appalachian Mountains, creating a boundary beyond which the colonists were forbidden to seize or purchase native land.

Over the years a succession of British governments had first imposed, then withdrawn, a variety of taxes and customs duties in the face of colonial non-compliance and opposition. But tea was the exception, retained by London less to raise revenue than to defend a point of principle. 'There must always be one tax to keep up the right,' declared King George III, who had succeeded his grandfather George II in 1760. 'And as such I approve of the tea duty.'

On the night of 16 December 1773, a group of fifty activists showed what they thought of the royal claim. Painting their faces with red ochre and lamp-black and dressing in blankets to disguise themselves as Indian warriors, these tomahawk-wielding 'Mohawks' boarded the three British merchantmen to smash open the tea chests and spill their cargoes into the waters of Boston harbour. Next morning, rowing-boats steered out into the brown slurry to push any still-floating cases under the water and make sure that the hated British tea was well and truly ruined.

'No taxation without representation!' declaimed Samuel Adams, the local brewer whose oratory had helped inspire the demonstration.

Britain's reaction to Boston's act of defiance was split. Lord Chatham, who, as William Pitt, had masterminded Britain's victories in the Seven Years War, counselled conciliation. He knew how difficult a long-distance quarrel with the colonies could prove, and he called for Britain to pull back from the dispute 'while we can, not when we must'. But George III and his Prime Minister, Lord North, felt that the colonists must be compelled to show more respect for the 'mother country'. So the port of Boston was closed and troops were sent to reinforce the garrison.

The colonists refused to be cowed. Money and supplies poured in to sustain the Boston population and local resistance forces were raised, the so-called minutemen who kept their weapons ready so they could fight the redcoats at a minute's notice. In April 1775 they clashed with British troops at the village of Lexington outside Boston. America's war with the mother country had begun.

On 4 July 1776 the representatives of all thirteen colonies gathered in Philadelphia as the 'United States', to pronounce their defiance in a Declaration of Independence. Most of its clauses recited their grievances and denounced George III – 'a prince whose character is marked by every act that may define a tyrant'. But the historic declaration is remembered today for the preamble which its framer, Thomas Jefferson, a radical young lawyer, drew from the thinking of John Locke: 'We hold these truths to be self-evident, that all men are created equal, that they are endowed by their Creator with certain inalienable rights, that among these are life, liberty and the pursuit of happiness.'

In the five years of war that followed, the colonists' forces were shrewdly led by George Washington, a Virginia landowner who had learned his fighting as a British officer during the Seven Years War. Far from home and fighting in impossible terrain, some of it dense forest, Britain's redcoats steadily lost ground – particularly after 1778 when

France weighed in on the American side. It was the arrival of the French fleet in Chesapeake Bay in October 1781 that led to the final surrender of the British forces, who marched out of Yorktown to the tune 'The World Turned Upside Down'.

'Oh God,' declared Lord North when he received the news, 'it is all over.'

So America had won its liberty, creating a new republic in which all men were created equal – except for those who happened to be slaves. Four of the first five US presidents were slave-owners, including Washington and Jefferson.

'How is it that the loudest yelps for liberty,' asked Samuel Johnson derisively, 'come from the drivers of negroes?'

And then there was the plight of the new republic's pre-existing underclass, the native Americans. Independence meant the end of the Proclamation Line with which Britain had protected the enticing expanses of native territories. The white 'Mohawks' of the Boston Tea Party had borrowed the warpaint of the 'Red Indians'. Now they were free to take over their land.

THOMAS CLARKSON – THE GIANT WITH ONE IDEA
1785

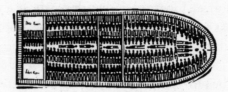

I own I am shocked at the purchase of slaves
And fear those who buy them and sell them are knaves.
What I hear of their hardships and tortures and groans
Is almost enough to draw pity from stones.
I pity them greatly, but I must be mum,
For how could we do without sugar and rum?

WILLIAM COWPER'S FLIPPANT POEM SUMMED UP MOST people's casual attitude to slavery in eighteenth-century England. Quakers were the exception – in 1774 all members of the Society of Friends agreed to have no dealings, personal or commercial, with slave-traders, and that same year John Wesley published an attack on slavery which helped swing Methodists against the commerce. By that date British slave-traders, sailing, for the most part, out of Bristol and Liverpool, had transported more than two million Africans across the Atlantic in conditions of unspeakable barbarity.

'I would do anything in my power,' Wesley later wrote, 'to the extirpation of that trade, which is a scandal not only to Christianity but to humanity.'

Then, in 1785, a young mathematics student at Cambridge University went in for a Latin essay competition. The topic was a philosophical question, 'Anne liceat invitos in servitutum?' – 'Is it lawful to make men slaves against their will?' – and Thomas Clarkson won the prize for a hard-hitting essay in which he tackled the question in terms of 'the Slavery and Commerce of the Human Species, particularly the African'. Clarkson was invited to read out his work (in Latin) to an admiring audience in the university Senate House, then set out immediately for London on horseback 'meditating [as he later recalled] on the horrors of slavery all the way'.

'I frequently tried to persuade myself,' he wrote, 'that the contents of my essay could not be true.'

But the more he reflected on all the evidence he had studied, the more the mathematics graduate felt the impact of its depressing truth, and he was feeling particularly grim as he came in sight of Wade's Mill in Hertfordshire, about thirty miles into his sixty-mile journey. Giving his horse a rest, he was sitting down on the turf at the roadside, holding the reins disconsolately, when 'a thought came into my mind that, if the contents of the essay were true, it was time some person should see these calamities to their end'.

Clarkson decided that he should be that person. He had been planning a career in the Church. Now he decided to dedicate his life to the eradication of slavery. In 1786 he had his prize-winning essay published in English and next year convened, in a Quaker bookshop, the first meeting of the Committee for Effecting the Abolition of the Slave

Trade. Headed by Clarkson, this twelve-man pressure group got Josiah Wedgwood, the great potter and social reformer, to devise for them a campaign badge that showed a manacled black slave on his knees, raising his chains to the motto: 'Am I not a man and a brother?'

The abolitionists' aim was an act of Parliament outlawing the trade, and in 1787 they recruited the Yorkshire MP William Wilberforce, who would become famous for his resolute championing of the cause in the initially hostile House of Commons. But the raw material of Wilberforce's speeches and the flood of local petitions that backed his Westminster campaign were largely the work of the indefatigable Clarkson, who mounted his trusty horse in the summer of 1787 and rode off for the slave port of Bristol. There he set to work gathering evidence, sitting in quayside taverns and persuading sailors to part with their 'souvenirs' – the manacles, whips and branding irons, along with the thumbscrews and forcible mouth-openers, that were the tools of the slavers' trade.

Then he headed north for Liverpool, where he picked up a particularly potent piece of propaganda – the plan of the local slave ship *Brookes*. Reprinted and widely circulated not just in Britain but in Europe and America, this graphic diagram showed how 609 slaves were crammed together, head to toe and side by side, on the notorious Middle Passage (see p.299). In the next seven years Clarkson would ride some thirty-five thousand miles setting up anti-slavery societies, making speeches – and risking his life as he recruited witnesses who could testify to the horrors of the profitable business. In Liverpool he narrowly escaped drowning at the hands of some enraged slavers.

When, after many battles and setbacks, the campaign to stop the slave trade finally triumphed in 1807, it was William Wilberforce who rightly received the credit for shepherding the Abolition Bill so tenaciously through Parliament. But it had been Thomas Clarkson who laid the groundwork, persuading 300,000 of the once apathetic British public to boycott sugar, and inspiring nearly 400,000 to sign petitions to Parliament. The prize-winning student who had got off his horse at Wade's Mill, then got back on and kept on riding, was, as the poet Samuel Taylor Coleridge put it, 'the moral steam engine' of the campaign to abolish slavery – 'the giant with one idea'.

THE MADNESS OF
KING GEORGE III
1788

IN AUGUST 1788 KING GEORGE III, FEELING ILL, DECIDED HE
should travel to the spa town of Cheltenham to take the waters. But
although the bitter-tasting purgative water opened his bowels most
effectively – he found 'a pint and a half the proper quantity to give him
two openings' – his health did not improve. Walking the elegant streets
with the Queen on his arm, he would raise his hat to total strangers
as if they were dear old friends. The fifty-year-old King was suffering
from agonising stomach pains and cramps in his legs. He found he
could not concentrate on the letters he received from his Prime
Minister, and he made numerous mistakes as his handwriting grew
large and shaky. 'I'm afraid,' he said, 'Mr Pitt will perceive I am not
quite in a situation to write at present.'

When he got back to London, the royal speech was slurred and his
dress so disordered when he appeared in public that the Lord
Chancellor, Lord Thurlow, felt he must advise His Majesty to go back
to his closet to readjust his clothing. One day in chapel, the King stood
bolt upright suddenly in the middle of the sermon and threw his arms
around the Queen and his daughters.

'You know what it is to be nervous,' he cried. 'But was you ever as
bad as this?'

As his agitation increased he could not stop talking, and though he
told his attendants to keep him quiet by reading aloud to him, he kept
on talking just the same. One day he fell on the shoulder of his 25-year-
old son, the Duke of York. 'I wish to God I may die,' he cried out. 'For
I am going to be mad!'

The future King George III had become heir to the throne at only
twelve years of age, when his father Frederick Prince of Wales fell

casualty to the newly fashionable game of cricket – struck on the head by a cricket ball and developing a fatal brain abscess. Nine years later, in 1760, the young king succeeded his grandfather George II, and set about making himself a hands-on monarch, proud to be the first of the Georges who was not brought up in Germany.

'Born and educated in this country,' he declared to the first Parliament of his reign, 'I glory in the name of Briton.'

Writing his own comments on the state papers and dating them to the day, hour and minute, George III was the last British king seriously to endeavour to rule the country himself. He believed that government should be directed by the Crown, not Parliament – but achieved exactly the opposite through his inflexible handling of the war against the American colonies. Determined to keep fighting after the British surrender at Yorktown in 1781, George was confronted by a clear majority in Parliament who wanted to sue for peace. His first reaction was to draft a letter of abdication. But on second thoughts, he decided to accept – and effectively obey – a Prime Minister, the Marquess of Rockingham, with whose policy he profoundly disagreed.

Modern experts have diagnosed the notorious 'madness' of George III as porphyria, 'the purple disease', so called because it turns its sufferers' urine deep red or purple. Mary Queen of Scots was said to have suffered from this rare disorder, which was hereditary and is presumed to have been passed down to George III through the Stuart line. Porphyrins are pigment cells, and an excess of these in the body leads to stomach cramps, constipation, rambling speech and hallucinations.

To counteract these symptoms, George's doctors resorted to a range of painful remedies that included blistering his shaven scalp and applying leeches to his forehead, to draw the poisonous matter from his brain. An alternative strategy sought to draw the bad humours down to the other end of his body by applying burning mustard plasters that opened wounds on his legs. Frequently confined in a straitjacket, with his arms tied round his back, the King was given strong purges then left in a room that was kept so cold that no one else could bear to stay in it for more than half an hour.

Not surprisingly enraged by these ordeals, the King nevertheless preserved something of his sense of humour, describing the seat to which he was frequently strapped immobile as his 'coronation chair'. Attempting a drawing as he was recovering in January 1789, he commented, 'Not bad – for a madman.'

Modern treatments for porphyria include sedation, maintaining the balance of electrolytes in the body, a high carbohydrate diet and the avoidance of sunlight. Nothing in the treatments that George III received corresponds to modern medical practice, but somehow he began to recover in the early months of 1789, and, as he got better, it became clear that the drama of his tragic disorder as reported in the newspapers had transformed England's view of the previously unpopular King. 'Compassion for his late sufferings,' reported Fanny Burney, 'seems to have endeared him now to all conditions of men.' In 1810 the fiftieth anniversary of George's accession prompted bonfires, fireworks, feasting and the lighting of beacons all over the country – Britain's first ever royal jubilee.

By this date, however, the 72-year-old King was drifting once more into mental confusion, possibly a return of his porphyria, compounded by senility. For the last ten years of his life, his authority was exercised by his son, the future George IV, as Prince Regent. But before the old King slipped finally into the darkness, he went to visit a lunatic asylum at Richmond where he enquired about how inmates were treated and the use of the straitjacket. Catching sight one day of his own canvas costume of torture that had been left out by accident, he calmed his embarrassed equerry.

'You needn't be afraid to look at it,' he said. 'Perhaps it is the best friend I ever had in my life.'

'BREADFRUIT BLIGH' AND THE
MUTINY ON THE BOUNTY
1789

WHEN CAPTAIN COOK WAS KILLED IN HAWAII IN 1779, one of the British officers charged with the grisly task of going from islander to islander, persuading them to hand back the dead hero's dismembered body parts, was Cook's 24-year-old sailing master, William Bligh. Having retrieved sufficient remains to carry out a burial at sea, Bligh then navigated his ship, the *Resolution*, north to the Bering Strait and back to England via Japan.

Before his death Cook had been examining the nutritional potential of a large, knobbly-skinned Polynesian fruit that had a sweet 'wheaten' taste – the breadfruit – and this provided the reason for the voyage that would make William Bligh famous. The breadfruit was a staple of the Pacific islanders' diet, and Cook noted how the climate and latitude of Owhyhee (as he called it) 'differs very little from that of the West India islands'. Why not transplant the breadfruit tree to the Caribbean, where it could provide cheap fodder for slaves, especially as the recent war with the colonies had cut off food supplies from America?

In 1786 the Society of Arts announced a prize and a gold medal for the first person to 'convey six breadfruit plants' from the South Seas to the West Indies, and Cook's friend the botanist Sir Joseph Banks put forward Bligh's name. HMAV* *Bounty* was elaborately modified into a floating greenhouse with two large skylights, three large air vents on each side, a rainwater irrigation system and a false floor cut full of holes to contain the plants for the nine-month voyage – His Majesty's Armed Potting Shed.

*His Majesty's Armed Vessel.

On 23 December 1787, the *Bounty* set sail for the Pacific via Cape Horn, with Fletcher Christian, an old friend of Bligh's, serving as master's mate. The two men had both risen from the ranks and had got to know each other on a previous ship, HMS *Cambridge*, where Bligh taught Christian how to navigate and had dined with him frequently. In his diary Christian claimed that Bligh treated him 'like a brother'.

Bligh ran a relaxed ship by the harsh standards of the time. He hired a fiddler to keep up the spirits of the crew and organised jig-dancing between five and eight every evening. 'Cheerfulness with exercise,' was his recipe for beating scurvy, along with Captain Cook's favoured diet of dried malt, sauerkraut and portable soup. But Bligh also had a temper,* and this was stretched when storms delayed the *Bounty*'s arrival in Tahiti. The breadfruit trees were now in their fruiting season and could not be transplanted for another five and a half months.

It must have seemed a good idea, after the rigours of the storm-tossed ten-month voyage, to let the crew of the *Bounty* relax in the luxuriant tropical surroundings of Tahiti. But here the seeds of the famous mutiny were sown – sun, sandy beaches, surf and, above all, affection and sex with the welcoming local women: after five and a half months of tropical tenderness, what man in his right mind would want to subject himself to the harshness of an eighteenth-century naval ship? By the time 1015 breadfruit plants had been potted up and placed in their slots in the floor of the Great Cabin on the *Bounty*, many of the crew had formed liaisons with local Tahitians whom they considered their 'wives'.

They lasted just three weeks at sea. On 27 April 1789, a fit of anger from Bligh over pilfered coconuts provoked Fletcher Christian and twenty-five of the crew to break open the ship's arms chest. Bligh was dragged from his bed and brought out on deck in his nightshirt with

---

*Modern research has established that Captain Bligh flogged his sailors less than any other British commander in the Pacific Ocean in the late eighteenth century. But he had a vicious tongue. After one incident he showered his officers and crew with an array of insults – 'damn'd Infernal scoundrels, blackguard, liar, vile man, Jesuit, thief, lubber, disgrace to the service, damned long pelt of a bitch' – and he told them he would make them 'eat grass like cows'.

his hands tied. With seventeen crew members that remained loyal to him, he was bundled into the *Bounty's* twenty-three-foot longboat and cast adrift with bread, water, salt pork, a little wine, four cutlasses, the carpenter's tool chest and a spare sextant.

From this point the story goes in several directions: the mutineers sailed back to be reunited with their 'wives' in Tahiti, where most elected to remain, sitting targets for the marines of HMS *Pandora* who were dispatched to arrest them in 1791. But Fletcher Christian and eight other mutineers sailed onwards in September 1789 with their Tahitian wives and six other islanders, to start a new life on the very outer limits of the known world, on the uninhabited island of Pitcairn. Here their descendants would eke out a bizarre and inbred existence, misfits to the present day.

Captain Bligh, meanwhile, carried out a feat of navigation and survival that remains unequalled in the annals of the sea. He piloted his open boat no less than 3600 miles (5800 kilometres) past the island of Fiji, across the Great Barrier Reef and along the uncharted north coast of Australia to Timor, the nearest European settlement. For forty-one days his eighteen men survived on such fish, turtles and seabirds as they could catch and eat raw, slaking their thirst on dribblings of rainwater.

Bligh returned home a hero, especially after he published his rapidly written *Narrative of the Mutiny on Board his Majesty's Ship Bounty*. After the formality of a court martial that cleared his name, the Admiralty sent him back to the South Seas on a voyage that did, finally, deliver several hundred breadfruit plants to the West Indies – as well as to the botanical gardens at Kew.

Bligh's subsequent career was curiously mutiny-prone. In 1797 he was captain of one of the several dozen warships that were taken over by their protesting crews in the massive mutiny at the Nore, the naval anchorage in the Thames near the Isle of Sheppey. In 1805 his attempts to clean up rum smuggling as governor of New South Wales pitched him against the corrupt local militia, who placed him under house arrest for more than a year. As before, an official inquiry exonerated him, and he became a respected vice-admiral, retiring to south London where his grave can be seen in the churchyard of St Mary-at-Lambeth.

According to his gravestone, William Bligh was famous as 'the celebrated navigator who first transplanted the bread-fruit tree from

Otaheite to the West Indies, bravely fought the battles of his country, and died beloved, respected, and lamented'. There is no mention of the M-word.

But the mutiny, of course, is the entire reason why William Bligh has been commemorated by Hollywood. His dramatic showdown with Fletcher Christian has inspired no less than four movies graced by the talents of Errol Flynn (1933), Charles Laughton and Clark Gable (1935), Marlon Brando and Trevor Howard (1962) and Anthony Hopkins and Mel Gibson (1984). The supporting casts have included David Niven, James Cagney, Laurence Olivier, Daniel Day-Lewis, and Liam Neeson. And all because he missed the breadfruit transplanting season.

THOMAS PAINE AND THE RIGHTS OF MAN
1791

R EPORTS OF THE SHOCKING EVENTS ON BOARD HMAV *Bounty* reached London as Britain was digesting the news of an even greater convulsion – the French Revolution. On 14 July 1789 enraged citizens had stormed the Bastille, the sinister royal fortress that loomed over eastern Paris. The stone-by-stone destruction of the hated prison foreshadowed the fate of the French monarchy itself in the months that followed, as Louis XVI and his wife Marie-Antoinette fell victim to the fury of the *sans-culottes* – literally, the trouserless ones – whose mob tactics took control of the Revolution. Most British sympathies were with the French royal family. But one Englishman, Thomas Paine, was so enthused by events in France that he crossed the Channel to give the Revolution his active support.

Thomas Paine was captain of the awkward squad – provocative, eloquent and happy to offend anyone in defence of the libertarian principles he espoused. No respecter of persons, Paine head-butted the status quo in the great English tradition of Wat Tyler, the Levellers, and radicals to the present day. Born in 1737, the son of a Quaker corset-maker in Norfolk, he displayed his egalitarian principles in a poem he was said to have written at the age of eight:

> *Here lies the body of John Crow,*
> *Who once was high but now is low.*
> *Ye brother crows take warning all,*
> *For as you rise, so must you fall.*

News of trouble in the colonies in 1774 attracted Paine to America, where he settled in Philadelphia and soon made his name as a loudly anti-British campaigning journalist. 'As it is my design to make those who can scarcely read understand,' he later explained, 'I shall therefore avoid every literary ornament and put it in a language as plain as the alphabet.'

In the autumn of 1775 he published *Common Sense*, a hard-hitting pamphlet that sold more than a hundred thousand copies and became the clarion call of revolution. 'Government by kings,' he wrote, 'runs contrary to the natural equality of man . . . in America THE LAW IS KING.'

When George Washington's army suffered setbacks in 1776, Paine rallied the colonists' spirit. 'These are the times that try men's souls,' he wrote in *The American Crisis*. 'Tyranny, like hell, is not easily conquered; yet we have this consolation with us, that the harder the conflict, the more glorious the triumph.'

Paine's private life was disorganised. He drank heavily and took pride in his spectacularly unkempt appearance. Suffering from scabies, the great polemicist stank from the noxious ointments that he used to cure this pimply rash. He was frequently in debt, and was happy to take employment with the newly independent American government to fund his erratic and extravagant lifestyle.

But Paine insisted that he served a higher cause. 'My principle is universal,' he wrote, 'my attachment is to all the world' – and in 1789 he found a new cause to champion. When Edmund Burke condemned the French Revolution, Paine responded furiously with *The Rights of Man*, arguing that it was not only France that suffered from its monarchy.

'It has cost England almost 17 millions sterling,' he wrote, 'to maintain a family imported from abroad, of very inferior capacity . . . Hereditary governments are verging to their decline and . . . revolutions on the broad basis of national sovereignty and government by representation, are making their way in Europe.'

The Rights of Man and *Common Sense* were the two best-selling pamphlets of the eighteenth century, with an international readership. In August 1792 Paine was one of seventeen foreigners accorded the honour of French citizenship, and the next month four of the revolutionary *départements* elected him to represent them in the new National Assembly. He chose to accept the invitation of Calais, crossing the Channel to a rapturous reception. Guns fired as the champion of liberty was presented with a revolutionary cockade, and the streets were lined with people shouting, '*Vive Thomas Paine!*' The mayor of Calais greeted him with a fervent embrace. 'I believe,' wrote one observer, 'he is rather fatigued with the kissing.'

When Paine reached Paris, however, and started work as a deputy, he found himself out of his depth. Speaking little French, he was lost in the rapid crossfire of revolutionary debate, and, deeply opposed to capital punishment, he found himself at odds with the fierce band of deputies who were intent on executing the King. 'France has been the first of European nations to abolish royalty,' he argued, through a translator, in his plea that Louis XVI be exiled to America. 'Let her also be the first to abolish the penalty of death.'

Paine's appeal was in vain. On 20 January 1793, the Convention narrowly voted that the ex-King should be dispatched to the guillotine, and as the death toll of 'the Terror' increased, the Englishman made no secret of his disenchantment. 'My friends were falling as fast as the guillotine could cut their heads off,' he later wrote to the Boston brewer, Samuel Adams, '. . . I expected, everyday, the same fate.'

At 4 a.m. on 28 December 1793 came the knock on his door. Assigned to the notorious prison of the Luxembourg, Paine succumbed to a fever that may have saved his life. Semi-conscious for several weeks, he was not fit enough to be herded into the carts of victims being transported to summary trial and execution – and then James Monroe, the American ambassador, intervened on his behalf. After nearly eleven months, Paine was finally released in November 1794 and taken to the safety of Monroe's Paris home.

It was impossible for the rebel to go home to England. In 1792 he had been tried in his absence and condemned as a traitor – a title that he proudly embraced. When, a few years later, he met the rising young general Napoleon Bonaparte (who claimed that he slept with a copy of *The Rights of Man* under his pillow), Paine was happy to discuss the prospects for an invasion of England, and even wrote two essays calling for a fleet of a thousand gunboats to carry French forces across the Channel. In 1802 he returned to America, his spiritual home, where he died seven years later.

Today his name still rouses passion. When the BBC recently screened a documentary in praise of Paine, the *Daily Telegraph* protested indignantly. 'He fought against his country in the American War of Independence and invited France to invade us during the French Revolution,' thundered an editorial, complaining that 'among decent Englishmen in his time his name was a synonym for treachery' – not to mention 'blasphemy' and 'debauchery'.

All this is true. But far bigger than his faults was Paine's inspiring big idea – that the rights of man, which include the (incompatible) rights of equality and liberty, are God-given at birth, and that governments are only good when they protect them.

MARY WOLLSTONECRAFT AND THE RIGHTS OF WOMAN

1792

It is time to effect a revolution in female manners – time to restore them to their lost dignity – and make them as a part of the human species.

Mary Wollstonecraft,
Vindication of the Rights of Woman

RECIPES FOR CHANGING THE WORLD FLOWED FROM THE presses during the 1790s. Inspired by the French Revolution, they made a torrent of passion-filled pamphlets, and until quite recently most historians felt that Tom Paine's *Rights of Man* held pride of place among them. But as we have sought to explain how society is changing in our own times, we have come to focus more closely on a friend of Paine's whose visionary work was derided at the time and overlooked for nearly two centuries – Mary Wollstonecraft and her *Vindication of the Rights of Woman*.

'I am not born to tread in the beaten track,' declared this brave, insurgent and ultimately tragic woman who is now seen as the first modern feminist. On her birth in April 1759 she was handed over by her mother to be breast-fed by a 'wet nurse' – the normal practice in middle and upper-class families. Mary would criticise wet-nursing bitterly in later life: a mother's love, she wrote, 'scarcely deserves the name, when it does not lead her to suckle her children'. But she felt still more anger at the behaviour of her father Edward, a drunken and violent tyrant who lorded it over his womenfolk, beating Mary, bullying his wife, and wasting the family fortune on a succession of snobbish attempts to become a country gentleman. As a child Mary would sleep on the landing outside her mother's door in a vain attempt to protect her from Edward Wollstonecraft's alcohol-fuelled anger.

Wives were considered to be the property of their husbands in the eighteenth century. The marriage laws were, in effect, property laws that gave a man ownership of his wife, her money and her children: divorce was virtually impossible.

'How short a time does it take,' reflected Fanny Burney after spending a few hours at a friend's wedding in the 1780s, 'to put an eternal end to a woman's liberty?'

It was taken for granted that a man could beat his womenfolk – a court case of 1782 confirmed that beating was legal, provided the stick was no thicker than the man's thumb. And the idea that a woman of quality might want to work to support herself was dismissed as downright crazy.

Mary was a working woman, compelled by her father's improvidence to earn her living as a nurse, seamstress, schoolmistress, governess and eventually as a campaigning writer. In 1787 at the age of twenty-eight she published *Thoughts on the Education of Daughters* in which she argued (as a girl who had hated playing with dolls) that women should pursue the same serious studies as men. Education, in her view, was the key to self-respect and hence to female empowerment, the theme of her great work *A Vindication of the Rights of Woman*, which she wrote in six furious weeks in 1792. 'I wish,' she explained, 'to persuade women to endeavour to acquire strength, both of mind and body.'

Mary's *Vindication* fiercely disputed the idea that women were the weaker sex. They were not naturally inferior, she argued, but they had tricked themselves into seeing their life's duty as the pleasing of men. 'Confined . . . in cages like the feathered race', she wrote disdainfully, women were raised as fine 'ladies' rather than as capable workers, with 'nothing to do but plume themselves, and stalk with mock majesty from perch to perch'. She was particularly alert to 'the selfish vanity of beauty' and poured scorn on society women, trapped in their carriages 'that drive helter-skelter about this metropolis . . . pale-faced creatures who are flying from themselves'.

Published in England, Ireland, France, Germany and the USA, Mary's trenchantly argued *Vindication* provoked strong feelings. Horace

Walpole, the gossipy youngest son of Sir Robert Walpole, denounced her as a 'hyena in petticoats'. But radical thinkers like Tom Paine applauded her and welcomed her to Paris in 1792, when she arrived to write her own account of the French Revolution – which, as the twentieth-century champion of women's writing, Virginia Woolf, later wrote, was not merely an event to Mary. 'The revolution . . . was an active agent in her own blood. She had been in revolt all her life – against tyranny, against law, against convention.'

In Paris she met Captain Gilbert Imlay, a handsome American land speculator with whom she defied convention by embarking on a tempestuous love affair, bearing a daughter out of wedlock in May 1794. But the romance cooled, and returning to London, Mary discovered that Imlay had a mistress. In despair she rented a rowing-boat that took her to Putney, where she threw herself from the bridge, having walked up and down in the pouring rain for half an hour to drench her clothes and make sure she would sink.

Mary was rescued. The recently established Royal Humane Society was offering rewards to boatmen who foiled would-be suicides, and one of these dragged Mary from the water. The mixture of depression and resolve that characterised her suicide attempt ran right through her life. Volatile and self-dramatising, with a deep-rooted sense of personal grievance, she was emotionally fragile, but she kept on fighting the male-dominated conventions of her day. In her uncompleted novel *Maria, or the Wrongs of Woman*, she advanced the shocking assertion that a woman could have sexual desires that were as strong as a man's.

In 1797 Mary fell pregnant again, by William Godwin, a critic and reformer in whom she finally found a soulmate. Godwin shared her contempt for marriage – Mary had condemned the institution as tyranny and legalised prostitution, deciding at the age of twelve that she would never marry and suffer her mother's fate. But she and Godwin married anyway, and enjoyed five months of happiness before Mary died that September, following the birth of another daughter.

This Mary, like her mother, would defy convention, running off with the poet Percy Bysshe Shelley and writing the myth-making novel *Frankenstein*, the story of a man who fashioned a creature that he thought he could control, but which escaped from his power and eventually destroyed him.

ENGLAND EXPECTS ...
1805

WHEN HE SPOTTED A POLAR BEAR PROWLING THE ICE near the island of Spitzbergen in the Arctic Ocean, the fifteen-year-old Horatio Nelson leapt over the rail of his ship and went in pursuit with a musket. But the beast outmanoeuvred the skinny-legged midshipman, rearing up angrily over him, and when the boy pulled the trigger, nothing happened. His powder was wet. Seizing his gun by the barrel, Nelson was about to club his adversary around the head when a cannon shot rang out from the ship behind him. Startled by the cannonball, the bear slunk away.

'Sir,' declared the apprentice officer defiantly and ungratefully to the captain who had saved him, 'I wished to kill a bear so that I might carry the skin to my father.'

This story from the youth of Admiral Lord Nelson sums up the man – fearless, single-minded, and just a little crazy. They were qualities Britain needed in the years between 1798 and 1805, when Nelson commanded the fleets that confronted Napoleon. By the time he fought the first of his great battles he had already lost his right arm and the sight of his right eye in action.

The evening of 1 August 1798 found Nelson at the mouth of the River Nile, where Napoleon had brought his armies for the conquest of Egypt. The French admiral Brueys did not believe that the British would actually attack – they had only just appeared over the horizon, and it was the end of the day. But Nelson's ships just kept on sailing hard at the enemy, starting to fire as dusk fell. The Battle of the Nile was fought in darkness, with the flashing broadsides of cannonfire eerily silhouetting the tussling ships.

'Nelson comes, the invincible Nelson!' the victorious admiral wrote proudly home to his wife Fanny. Already this 39-year-old was sometimes referring to himself in the third person. 'Almighty God has made me the happy instrument in destroying the enemy's fleet,' he wrote to Sir William Hamilton, the British ambassador at Naples.

The ambassador could hardly have imagined what would happen next. Landing in Naples on his way back from the Nile, Nelson fell hopelessly in love with Hamilton's wife Emma, an exuberant beauty who was famous for her 'Attitudes', posing in exotic and diaphanous costumes as if she were a figure on a classical Greek vase. The romance between Nelson and the glamorous Lady Hamilton became the talk of Europe, and though both remained married to their long-suffering spouses, in 1801 Emma bore Nelson a daughter whom they christened Horatia – a name not designed for secrecy.

Fiercely disapproving, King George III snubbed Nelson when he next met him, and Queen Charlotte made it clear that she would not receive Lady Hamilton at court. But Nelson's saucy love life only added to his celebrity status, which he cultivated to the hilt, glorying in his glittering array of medals and orders, and making sure that favourable accounts of his triumphs found their way into the newspapers.

The hero would surely have been delighted that the most famous anecdote about him – that he placed a telescope to his blind eye so as to ignore an order during the Battle of Copenhagen in 1801 – was a legend devised after his death. The detailed account by Colonel William Stewart who was standing beside him on the quarterdeck at the time makes clear that Nelson certainly did ignore a signal to leave off action. But his 'turning a blind eye' was not described until five years later (no contemporary picture shows him wearing an eye patch), and the detail of the telescope was added three years after that.

During his lifetime Nelson's charisma inspired intense loyalty in his sailors. 'Nelson is arrived,' wrote Captain Edward Codrington of HMS *Orion* in September 1805 when the admiral's black-and-yellow chequered flagship *Victory* joined the British fleet outside Cadiz. 'A sort of general joy has been the consequence.'

'Everything seemed, as if by enchantment, to prosper under his direction,' declared Cuthbert Collingwood, his second-in-command off the Spanish coast.

Inside Cadiz harbour lay the combined French and Spanish fleets, the key to Napoleon's hopes of invading England. So, as the enemy sailed out of Cadiz, their sails set for battle, the British admiral put his fleet on its mettle: 'Nelson confides [is confident],' ran the signal he drafted, 'that every man will do his duty.'

Someone suggested 'England' instead of 'Nelson', and Nelson happily passed that on to his flag lieutenant. But the signalling officer explained that 'confides' would need eight flags, while 'expects' could be broadcast with just three – and thus was transmitted, at 11.35 a.m. on 19 October 1805, the most famous battle signal in English history.

In the four-hour duel that followed, the British ships drove directly into the enemy line as they sailed past Cape Trafalgar. Grapeshot cut Nelson's secretary in half where he stood beside the admiral, and up in the rigging of one of the French ships a sniper lined his sights on the flamboyant, medal-emblazoned coat of the little British commander. The bullet broke Nelson's back, opened an artery, and entered his lung. 'They have done for me at last,' he gasped.

As he lay below decks in the medical cockpit, its walls painted red to camouflage the blood that splashed everywhere, he asked why the sailors were cheering. Thomas Hardy, the flag captain of *Victory*, told him that fourteen or fifteen enemy ships had surrendered. 'That is well,' responded Nelson, 'but I had bargained for twenty.'

He knew that he was dying. 'Take care of my dear Lady Hamilton,' he told his captain. 'Take care of poor Lady Hamilton. Kiss me, Hardy.'

In later years the Victorians could not bear the idea that Nelson had asked another man to kiss him, and came up with the suggestion that he really said 'Kismet', from the Persian word for 'fate' or 'destiny'. But the account by the surgeon Dr Beatty was quite definite. Captain Hardy kissed the dying man twice – on the cheek and on the forehead.

FANNY BURNEY'S BREAST

1811

ANNY BURNEY DID NOT HEAR THE NEWS OF NELSON'S
victory at Trafalgar until seven years after the battle. Having married a French nobleman, the sprightly novelist had moved to France, where Napoleon had decreed that all English people between the ages of eighteen and sixty should be regarded as prisoners of war: they were forbidden to write to, or receive letters from, their families in England.

We have already heard from Fanny Burney a couple of times in these tales. She was a wise and wry observer of life in George III's England, where her novels won high praise. 'Oh, you little character-monger you!' chuckled Dr Johnson, giving her a squeeze after reading her first romance, *Evelina*. Jane Austen, who was composing her own novels in these years, praised Fanny's books – 'in which the most thorough knowledge of human nature, the happiest delineation of its varieties, the liveliest of wit and humour, are conveyed to the world in the best chosen language'.

In 1793, at the age of forty-one, Fanny married the charming if penniless Alexandre d'Arblay, a royalist army officer who had fled the Revolution and was living in Surrey. So penniless was the ex-general that for weeks at a time the d'Arblays had to survive on nothing but the vegetables that he grew in the garden. The Peace of Amiens coaxed the family to Paris in 1802, hopeful of recovering the d'Arblay rank and property – Napoleon was looking for good officers, ex-royalists included. But the resumption of hostilities in May 1803 trapped Fanny in enemy territory, and for nearly a decade she lived in limbo.

Fanny Burney's novels are difficult to read today – their wordiness seems dated in a way that Jane Austen's style is not. But her personal journals and letters are often breath-taking in their sharp-eyed observation, and one agonising incident during her long French 'captivity' inspired some writing that has become a classic of medical history. In the summer of 1810 she started experiencing pains in her right breast and felt a lump that a gathering of eminent doctors diagnosed as cancerous.

'*Il faut s'attendre à souffrir* [you must be ready to suffer],' warned Antoine Dubois, one of the most famous surgeons in France and gynaecologist to the Empress Josephine, explaining that removal of the cancer was the only way of saving her life. '*Vous souffrirez beaucoup* [You will suffer greatly].'

Fanny insisted that her husband should not be a witness to the operation, and that she herself should be given only two hours' warning. Had she cried greatly in childbirth? she was asked. Good, came the reply – she should not restrain her screaming when the time came.

At this point the tale becomes gruesome, and the squeamish should read no further. But it stands as a reminder of how countless thousands of men, women and children went bravely under the surgeon's knife in the centuries before the development of anaesthetics in the 1840s. On 30 September 1811 Alexandre d'Arblay was inveigled out of the house on a pretext, and Fanny found herself confronted by seven men in black, the surgeons, plus their pupils and nurses. She saw two old mattresses covered by a sheet and was told to undress and lie down on them. She was given a glass of wine cordial, then blindfolded. She could see the glint of polished steel through the muslin and heard the surgeon ask, '*Qui me tiendra ce sein?* [Who will support the breast?]'

'*C'est moi, monsieur!*' cried out Fanny, holding her own breast – and the surgery began.

> *My dear Esther [she wrote to her sister], when the dreadful steel was plunged into the breast – cutting through veins, arteries, flesh, nerves – I needed no injunctions not to restrain my cries. I began a scream that lasted unremittingly during the whole time of the incision – and I almost marvel that it rings not in my ears still, so excruciating was the agony. When the wound was made and the instrument withdrawn, the pain seemed undiminished – but when again I felt the knife, describing a curve, cutting against the grain, if I may say so, then indeed I thought I must have expired.*

As the knife was withdrawn for the second time, Fanny concluded that the operation must be over.

Oh no! Presently the terrible cutting was renewed – and worse than ever, to sep-arate the bottom, the foundation of this dreadful gland, from the parts to which it adhered. I felt the knife wrackling against the backbone – scraping it! – I remained in utterly speechless torture.

Fanny had expected that only the tumour would be cut out. In fact, the seven strong men in black had held her down for a full twenty min-utes while her whole breast was removed. But the ghastly pain proved worth while. Fanny Burney was fifty-nine years old at the time of her operation and would survive to the age of eighty-eight: she lived twenty-nine years with no recurrence of the cancer.

WHO WAS NED LUDD?
1812

IN 1811 AND 1812 MYSTERIOUS LETTERS STARTED REACHING the mill owners of Nottinghamshire and Leicestershire, threatening them with the destruction of their machinery. The threats were sent in the name of Ned Ludd or sometimes General Ludd – and 'the General' proved as good as his word. Well disciplined bands of men began attacking mills and factories after dark in raids of military precision, smashing windows and breaking down doors to destroy the mechani-cal looms, or 'frames', that were cutting their wages and putting them out of work. It was an organised proliferation of the attacks that had been made in 1766 on James Hargreaves's first spinning jennies.

The attacks soon spread to Lancashire and the West Riding of

Yorkshire, where fearful householders listened behind closed shutters to the passing of the General's army – 'a measured, beating, approaching sound, a dull tramp of marching feet,' as Charlotte Brontë described it three decades later, basing her account on those of contemporary newspapers. 'It was not the tread of two, nor of a dozen, nor of a score of men; it was the tread of hundreds.'

'Hundreds' was an underestimate for the size of Ludd's army at its largest. According to the Nottingham correspondent of the *Leeds Mercury*, 'the Insurrectional state to which this county has been reduced . . . has no parallel in history since the troubled days of Charles the First'. At one stage in 1812 there were as many as twelve thousand government troops in the four northern counties trying to hold down the rebellion of the Luddites – a significant drain on the numbers that Britain could deploy in Europe in those years in its epic struggle with Napoleon.

The European war had much to do with the trouble in the factories. Thanks to Trafalgar and the enduring might of the British navy, Napoleon could not invade England. But he had used his control over mainland Europe – and, from 1812, his friendship with America – to wage history's first large-scale economic war, imposing a trade blockade on the British Isles. British merchants and manufacturers found they could not sell their goods. To cut their wage bills, they had to sack workers and make more use of machines. Then a series of bad harvests in the years 1808–12 forced up food prices just when ordinary folk had less money than ever to spend. 'I have five children and a wife,' testified one Manchester worker whose weekly wage was nine old pennies. 'I work sixteen hours a day to get that . . . It will take 2 [pence] per week coals, 1 [penny] per week candles. My family live on potatoes chiefly, and we have one pint of milk per day.'

A number of the disturbances classed as 'Luddite' were, in fact, food riots. In April 1812 police and the army had to intervene in Manchester when desperate women started taking the stock of dealers who were charging fifteen shillings (180 old pence, or twenty weeks' wages) for a load of potatoes.

'Nothing but absolute want could have driven a large and once honest and industrious body of people into the commission of excesses so hazardous to themselves, their family and their community,' protested Lord Byron, speaking in the House of Lords.

The poet was opposing the Frame-Breaking Bill of 1812 by which the government of the day, led by Spencer Perceval, made the destruction of machinery punishable by death. When Perceval himself was murdered a few months later in the lobby of the House of Commons – the only British Prime Minister ever to be assassinated – suspicion fell immediately upon the Luddites. In fact, the killer was a deranged businessman who had been ruined by the collapse of foreign trade.

The original Lud was a mythical king of Britain who was said to have built the first walls of London – Ludgate Hill is named after him. Lud may also have been the name of a Celtic river god, and this name links, in spirit at least, with the machine-breakers of 1811 and 1812, who rallied and drilled their forces in the woods. Some of the letters from 'General Ludd and his Army of Redressers' gave their address as Sherwood Forest, the home of Robin Hood, who was certainly not a real person but whose legend embodied deeply cherished values to those who felt oppressed.

The Luddites were fighting to protect a centuries-old, craft-based way of life that gave them livelihood and self-respect – and also enshrined a certain commitment to quality. Some of the most savage machine-smashings were directed at the new 'stocking frames', which mass-produced socks by crudely closing and stitching tubes of fabric. Nowadays questions of wages and job security can be approached through negotiation, but there was no collective bargaining in the early nineteenth century. Trades unions were illegal. 'Combinations' of workmen were prohibited by law* – so where else could reformers turn but to the General in the woods? As the authorities clamped down on the Luddites – several dozen were hanged or transported to penal servitude in Australia – the movement was forcibly suppressed.

*'An Act to Prevent Unlawful Combinations of Workmen' was passed in 1799, and was reaffirmed and supplemented by a second Combination Act the following year. Prompted by government fears of unrest and that revolution might spread from across the Channel, the combination laws drove trades union activity underground until their repeal in 1824–5. Even then fresh legislation undermined the workers' power to bargain collectively: they had to operate on the fringes of the law until 1860.

Today the word 'Luddite' is an insult directed at someone who is thought to be mindlessly blocking progress, particularly technological progress. But were the original Luddites being so mindless when they challenged the tyranny of progress for progress's sake? Quality of life, tradition, social justice – in our own age that bows so slavishly to the soulless commands of technology and the marketplace, we might reflect on the protest of General Ludd and keep our ears pricked for his tramp, tramp, tramp in the night.

WELLINGTON AND WATERLOO
1815

IN THE SPRING OF 1793 ARTHUR WESLEY, A 23-YEAR-OLD army officer who loved playing the violin, proposed to Kitty Pakenham, a dark-haired beauty three years his junior, who lived a day's ride from Dangan, the Wesley home in County Meath. The couple had known each other for several years and, as two young Anglo-Irish aristocrats, they seemed a well suited pair. But Tom, Kitty's elder brother, vetoed the match – the Wesleys were impoverished, and Arthur's army career was going nowhere.

The rejection devastated Arthur Wesley. He burned his violin and never played music again. Resolving to make himself a better officer, he started attending parade-ground drill sessions and applied for active military service abroad. A dozen years later he returned from India with the rank of major general, a knighthood and a fortune of £42,000 that was more than enough to keep Kitty Pakenham in style. The couple married in Dublin in April 1806.

It would be nice to report that the Wellesleys (Arthur changed the spelling of his surname in 1798) lived happily ever after. In fact, Arthur started repenting at the altar – 'She has grown ugly, by Jove!' he confided to his brother Gerald – and his marriage proved one of the least happy aspects of his glittering career. Kitty, for her part, soon gave up the impossible task of pleasing her demanding husband, who treated her like a child. 'She is like the housekeeper and dresses herself exactly like a shepherdess,' sneered one of Arthur's glossy lady friends, 'with an old hat made by herself stuck on the back of her head, and a dirty basket under her arm.' The couple had two sons together, but little happiness.

Arthur Wellesley was to win his famous title, Duke of Wellington, for the brave and dogged military campaigns he fought against the French forces occupying Spain and Portugal – the Peninsular War that marked the turning-point in the struggle against Napoleon. In August 1808 he landed north of Lisbon with the first detachment of just nine thousand British troops, sent to assist the popular revolt against the French Emperor's placing of his brother Joseph Bonaparte on the throne of Spain. In the next six years he retrained the Portuguese army, collaborated with the Spanish guerrillas, and welded his own, often outnumbered, forces into a grimly efficient fighting machine.

Wellington was as sternly disciplined with his soldiers as he was with himself – among his many innovations was a new system of military police. But his men were devoted to 'Atty' (for Arthur) or 'Nosey', as they called their hardworking general, who rose every morning at six and spent the day busying himself with every little detail of his army's welfare.

After fighting from the Atlantic to the Pyrenees, the British army invaded southwestern France in the spring of 1814, to hear that Napoleon, broken by his Russian campaign and finally defeated at the Battle of Leipzig, had abdicated. Wellington marched into Paris in triumph, but as someone disobligingly reminded him, all his peninsular victories had been won against Napoleon's marshals – he had never been compelled to face the French Emperor in battle.

'I am very glad I never was,' replied the Duke candidly. 'I would at any time rather have heard that a reinforcement of 40,000 men had joined the French army, than that he had arrived to take command.'

'Nosey' versus 'Boney' seemed a fanciful historical might-have-been as Wellington travelled to Vienna to join the victorious allies in the remaking of Europe, while Napoleon languished in exile on the island of Elba. But on 7 March 1815, as Wellington was pulling on his boots for his favourite relaxation, a ride to hounds, came the astonishing news that Bonaparte had escaped. The ex-Emperor had landed in the south of France with just a handful of men, and as he marched north towards Paris, the whole country turned to him.

Wellington faced a formidable task as he set about organising the allied armies with their different languages, training, experience and weaponry. He had to share responsibility for the defence of the Netherlands with the venerable Prussian general, Blücher, and he could get no reliable intelligence about his enemy's plans. 'I had never seen him have such an expression of care and anxiety upon his countenance,' recorded Lady Hamilton-Dalrymple as she sat beside Wellington at the Duchess of Richmond's ball, held in Brussels on 15 June that year.

'Napoleon has humbugged me, by God,' the Duke exclaimed as he received news, some time after midnight, that the French army was heading straight for Brussels. 'He has gained twenty-four hours' march on me.'

Calling for a map, he traced the position of the troops he had deployed to defend the city, and placed his thumb on a ridge to the southwest – 'I must fight him here.' His thumb was on a hamlet called Waterloo.

Wellington later described the battle as a 'pounding match'. Napoleon had never before encountered the obstinate skill with which the Duke had learned in the Peninsula to keep defending a fortified position, and the French wore themselves out attacking the disciplined blocks of British and allied troops. When Blücher arrived towards the end of the day, his Prussian soldiers tipped the balance. The French army broke and fled.

Waterloo confirmed Wellington's place as one of Britain's greatest ever military leaders, and he went on to a controversial career in politics, serving as Prime Minister from 1828 to 1830 – the windows of his home at Hyde Park Corner, Apsley House,* were smashed twice by

*Known as 'Number One, London' because it was the first house you met as you entered London through the tollgate.

angry mobs, enraged by his anti-libertarian views and policies. But the 'Iron Duke' would go quiet whenever Waterloo was mentioned, remembering the victims – some 17,000 British, 7000 Prussians and 26,000 French – whose lives were the price of victory. 'It is a bad thing to be always fighting,' he said. 'It is quite impossible to think of glory. Both mind and feelings are exhausted. I am wretched at the moment of victory . . . Next to a battle lost, the greatest misery is a battle gained.'

STONE TREASURES – MARY ANNING AND THE TERROR LIZARDS
1823

THE SOFT AND FOSSIL-RICH LIMESTONE CLIFFS OF LYME Regis on the border of Devon and Dorset are forever crumbling – it is as if the earth's crust has been turned inside out – and from an early age Mary Anning loved to walk with her dog among the debris, chipping out stone treasures with a little hammer and pickaxe that she carried, together with a basket. The Anning family eked out a living in the early years of the nineteenth century selling these 'snake stones' and 'verteberries' to visitors – they had a tiny tumbledown shop beside the beach. But Mary was much more than a beachcomber.

'The extraordinary thing about this young woman,' wrote one visitor in the 1820s, 'is that she has made herself so thoroughly acquainted with the science that the moment she finds any bones she knows to what tribe they belong. She fixes the bones on a frame with cement and then makes drawings and has them engraved.'

The twin disciplines of geology (the study of the earth), and palaeontology (the study of 'early things') were just developing, and as the experts heard of Mary's work they hurried down from their universities and learned societies to Lyme Regis. 'By reading and application,' wrote Lady Harriet Silvester, 'she has arrived to that degree of knowledge as to be in the habit of writing and talking with professors and other clever men on the subject and they all acknowledge that she understands more of the science than anyone else in this kingdom.'

If Mary Anning ever alighted on an especially large treasure, she would go for help, leaving her dog to guard the spot, and in December 1823 she needed a large digging party to unearth the fossilised bones of a nine-foot monster that seemed to be a cross between a turtle and a snake. Its spine alone comprised ninety 'verteberries', with fourteen ribs and three surviving fine-boned paddles instead of feet. Academics identified the discovery as the world's first ever complete example of a 'plesiosaur' – a 'near-lizard'.

Modern science sets the plesiosaurs in the Mesozoic era, living 245 to 65 million years ago in that distantly frightening period that most people today accept as 'prehistoric'. But in 1823 many preachers taught their congregations that God had made the world less than six thousand years previously, even fixing on a precise date – 4004 BC. According to the Book of Genesis, the whole of Creation was accomplished in just six days. How could a loving God have filled the earth with these sinister creeping things?* And how did the age of lizards fit in with the story of the Flood – or with Adam and Eve, for that matter? The Bible did not even mention the giant reptiles' existence.

Mary was a devout chapel-goer, but these questions did not trouble her. The little bonneted figure could frequently be seen scouring the Dorset cliffs, making her discoveries – among them some of the earliest and finest examples of ichthyosaurs (fish lizards), and the first British 'flying dragon', the pterodactyl (so named from the Greek *pteron*, wing, and *daktulos*, finger). By the time of her death in 1847 Mary had become the heroine of England's Jurassic coast, awarded annuities by Parliament, by the Geological Society and by the British Association for the Advancement of Science. But she would have

---

*The word 'dinosaur', coined in 1842, means 'terrible' or 'fearfully great' lizard.

traded them all for her name at the top of a learned article. As she remarked one day to a young woman with whom she went out fossilling, 'these men of learning have made a great deal by publishing works of which I furnished the contents'. They had 'sucked my brains,' said Mary – and then quietly resumed her chipping.

BLOOD ON THE TRACKS
1830

RAIN WAS FALLING GENTLY ON THE MORNING OF 15 September 1830, as crowds gathered in Lancashire to ogle an array of locomotive engines. Until quite recently all 'engines' had been stationary pieces of machinery – solidly fixed in one place. But the newly developed locomotive engines had the power to shift themselves (from the Latin words *loco*, to or from a place, and *motivus*, moving), and now, to mark the opening of this freshly built stretch of railway line running thirty-three miles between the growing connurbations of Liverpool and Manchester, the new locomotives were demonstrating how they could reliably transport both goods and people.

Pride of place went to the stubby and muscular-looking *Rocket*, a formidable assemblage of brass, iron and steel that had been bolted together by the father-and-son team of George and Robert Stephenson. With steam oozing from her twin pistons, angled on either side of her boiler like the haunches of some gigantic frog ready to leap forward along the track, the *Rocket* embodied all the power and menace that frightened people about the railways: birds would be killed by the smoke, warned the doom-mongers, and cows' milk would curdle as the noisy trains sped past; it was even suggested that passengers' lungs would collapse under the pressure of high speeds. On the other side of the Pennines, the Duke of Cleveland had held up the Stockton and Darlington line for three years for fear of what it would do to his foxes.

The *Mechanic's Magazine* for September 1830 sought to allay such fears. 'We think we shall not go too far in saying that [the new invention] will produce an entire change in the face of British society,' the journal told its readers, predicting the growth of what would become known as the suburb and the stockbroker belt. 'Living in the country will no longer be a term synonymous with every sort of inconvenience, and it will come to be a mere matter of choice whether a man of business works close by his country house or thirty miles from it.'

One particular advocate of the railways was the MP for Liverpool, William Huskisson, who had served as President of the Board of Trade in 1823. Huskisson had proved himself quite a reformer, cutting trade tariffs and angering many employers by arguing for the repeal of the Combination Acts so that workers could organise trades unions. Some of his wealthiest supporters owned shares in the local canals, whose transport business would be drastically undercut by the speed and economy of the new railway line between Liverpool and Manchester; but that did not stop Huskisson working hard to get the line approved by Parliament. It would benefit all classes of the local workforce, he told the Liverpool newspapers, and he prepared a speech to deliver on the evening of 15 September at the dinner that had been arranged to celebrate the grand opening of the line.

'The principle of a Railway is that of commerce itself,' he planned to say. 'It multiplies the enjoyment of Mankind by increasing the facilities and diminishing the labour by which the means of those enjoyments are produced and distributed throughout the world.'

William Huskisson never got to deliver his speech. The guest of honour at the railway opening was none other than the Duke of Wellington, who had been Prime Minister since January, and Huskisson travelled in one of the carriages that set off with the Duke and other VIPs eastwards from Liverpool at eleven o'clock that morning. Just before noon, after travelling nearly eighteen miles – halfway to Manchester – the convoy of carriages stopped at Parkside Station, and Huskisson got out to join the crowd milling around Wellington's carriage.

Suddenly a shout went up – 'An engine is approaching. Take care, gentlemen!' It was the *Rocket*, careering along the northern track in the opposite direction, from Manchester. 'You had better step in!' the Duke called down from his carriage to Huskisson, who was standing on the gravel between the two tracks. Most people had dashed for the embankment, but after havering to and fro, Huskisson chose to cling on to the carriage. There was a gap of just over four feet (1.25 metres) between the two lines, and the MP would have been safe if he had stayed in place. But losing his nerve, he made a grab for the door of the Duke's carriage, which swung open with his weight – right into the path of the advancing *Rocket*.

Flung down on to the track, Huskisson suffered ghastly injuries – the wheels of the locomotive passed over his left leg, crushing bone and muscle and spraying out blood, to the horror of the spectators. As the MP was rushed away for medical attention, the Duke reluctantly agreed to continue the ride to Manchester. But the celebratory dinner that night was a subdued affair, the tone set by a mournful toast to William Huskisson – 'May his sufferings be speedily assuaged, and his health restored.' By 11 p.m., in fact, when the toast was delivered, the local champion of the railway had already died, his agonies only partially relieved by heavy doses of laudanum (opium in alcohol).

Fifty thousand mourners attended the funeral of William Huskisson. Liverpool closed down for the day. But that did not deter people from using the railway. In its very first week the new line carried 6104 fare-paying passengers, and within twelve months that figure had risen to nearly half a million. Most of these were pulled by the *Rocket*, now beloved as a pioneer of locomotive transportation, fully justifying Huskisson's prophecies. But he would be remembered as a pioneer of another sort – the first passenger fatality in the age of high-speed mechanical travel.

THE LUNG POWER OF
ORATOR HUNT
1819–32

Henry 'orator' hunt owed his nickname to his prodigious lung capacity – he could project his voice like a trumpet. Such decibel power was precious to a public speaker in an age before microphones – and to make quite sure that the furthest member of his audience could also see him, the barrel-chested Hunt would complete the picture with a large white top-hat.

One sultry day in August 1819, Orator Hunt rose to bellow out his message to a crowd of some sixty thousand men, women and children who had gathered in St Peter's Fields, Manchester. They were working people mostly, rallying in the cause of parliamentary reform and the right of all men to vote by secret ballot. But Hunt had not got ten minutes into his speech when a party of blue-and-white-clad cavalrymen came clip-clopping round the corner, their drawn swords raised in front of them.

The meeting had been quiet until that point, and the crowd greeted the soldiers with a shout of goodwill. But the cavalry's response was to ride their horses fiercely into the rally. 'Their sabres were plied to hew a way through naked held-up hands and defenceless heads,' wrote one eyewitness. 'Women, white-vested maids and tender youths were indiscriminately sabred or trampled.'

Within ten minutes the soldiery had cleared St Peter's Fields of people, as they had been ordered to do by local magistrates, leaving at least eleven people dead and more than five hundred wounded in what became known – in a derisive reference to the recent British victory at Waterloo – as the 'Peterloo' Massacre. The Cheshire magistrates had hoped to silence Hunt by ordering his arrest, but instead they turned him into a national celebrity. More than three hundred thousand people cheered the orator through the streets on the way to one of his trials, and when he started writing from his prison cell his memoirs became a serial bestseller (in forty-six instalments) – dedicated 'To the Radical Reformers, Male and Female, of England, Ireland and Scotland'.

At first glance, Hunt seems an unlikely candidate for radical martyrdom. His ancestors were Norman, his great-great-grandfather was a loyalist who went into exile with Charles II, and he himself farmed three thousand acres (over 1200 hectares) on which he produced fine grains and employed the latest sheep-farming techniques. But when, following the failure of his marriage, he took up with the unhappy wife of a friend, he found himself shunned by 'polite' society. He reacted with prickliness – rows with the commanding officer of the local yeomanry and with his neighbours landed him in jail in 1800 and again in 1810 – and he developed a hatred of the landed upper classes who dominated nineteenth-century British life.

Their domination was most powerfully expressed through the rickety parliamentary system that dated back to medieval times. Ancient and decayed communities retained the right to send MPs to Westminster – the seven voters of Old Sarum in Wiltshire, for instance, returned two MPs to Parliament. Many of these 'rotten' or 'pocket' boroughs were in the south, while the new industrial communities of the Midlands and the north were under-represented: Manchester, Birmingham, Leeds and Sheffield had no MPs at all. Of the nearly fourteen million people living in England and Wales in 1831, only four hundred thousand or so had the vote: all these voters were men, and they had to step up on to the hustings to cast their vote in public.

Orator Hunt called for universal male suffrage by secret ballot – as people vote today. So long as men had to declare their allegiance publicly, he argued, they would feel compelled to toe the line of their bosses and landlords. At the end of the eighteenth century the Earl of Lonsdale controlled no fewer than nine constituencies on his various estates – his MPs were known as his 'ninepins': by one estimate, just 87 peers controlled 213 of the Commons' 658 seats.

By 1830 the stentorian trumpet of Orator Hunt was one of many voices calling for change. That autumn discontented labourers in Kent,

Sussex, Hampshire and Berkshire responded to the call of a mythical 'Captain Swing' – a southern version of General Ludd – to set fire to the harvest and to smash their masters' threshing machines. The hayricks were burning as Parliament assembled, creating a mood that swept aside the Duke of Wellington and his Tory government.

His replacement, the elegant and elderly Lord Grey, was no radical – he oversaw the rounding-up of two thousand 'Captain Swing' rioters, 19 of whom were executed, 481 transported, and 644 sent to prison. But Grey understood the need for concession. 'The principle of my reform is to prevent the necessity for revolution,' he told Parliament; '. . . reforming to preserve, not to overthrow.' Doggedly fighting and negotiating for more than a year, Grey finally saw his Reform Bill into law on 4 June 1832, abolishing the 'rotten' boroughs and doubling the size of the electorate by extending the vote to a variety of small property-holders.

Orator Hunt participated vigorously in the epic battle over Reform. He got himself elected as the MP for Preston in Lancashire and made no less than a thousand speeches *against* Grey's proposals, which he saw as a betrayal of 'the unrepresented seven millions of working men in England'. Reform was a trick, he complained, to get 'the middle classes, the little shopkeepers and those people, to join the higher classes'.

His argument had merit: 1832 marked the end of the old system – it was a genuine, hard-fought turning-point in which Hunt himself had played his part. But the expanded new electorate of 814,000 was still only one in five males – and without a secret ballot it was as vulnerable as ever to the arm-twisting of landlords and bosses, who would remain the masters of political Britain for decades to come.

Orator Hunt died in 1835, dispirited and poverty-stricken, but battling to the end. One of his projects, to rebuild the fortune that he lost in his political campaigning, was 'Hunt's Matchless Shoe-Blacking'. It promised your shoes a perfect shine, and on every bottle was embossed the legend: 'Equal Laws. Equal Rights. Annual Parliaments, Universal Suffrage and the Ballot.'

THE TOLPUDDLE MARTYRS
1834

PLOUGHMEN, LABOURERS, SHEPHERDS, COW-HERDS, PIGMEN, hedgers, thatchers, dairymen, blacksmiths, gamekeepers – for much of the nineteenth century the largest single group of British workers were the men who worked on the land, and often they were poorly paid. Ten shillings (50p) per week was considered the minimum on which a family could survive in the 1830s, but in the village of Tolpuddle in Dorset the day came when the farm labourers found themselves expected to make do on nine.

'After some months we were reduced to eight shillings,' related George Loveless, a labourer who also preached in the local Methodist chapels. 'This caused great dissatisfaction, and all the labouring men in the village, with the exception of two or three invalids, made application [for Poor Relief] to a neighbouring magistrate.'

There were just six able-bodied men living in Tolpuddle, whose picturesque name was of Anglo-Saxon origin, meaning marshy, low-lying land, probably belonging to a widow called Tola* – and they received short shrift from the bench. 'We were told that we must work for whatever our employers thought fit to give us, as there was no law to compel masters to give any fixed sum of money to their servants.' And there was worse to come – their wages were soon reduced to seven shillings, with the threat that six was not far behind.

In desperation, the Tolpuddle Six decided to form a Friendly Society of Agricultural Labourers to campaign for better wages – only to find themselves arrested on 24 February 1834 and marched in chains

---

*Tola owned the land in 1050. Nearby villages on the River Piddle (a variant of Puddle) included Affpuddle, almost certainly named after Alfridus who was the landowner in 987.

to the county town of Dorchester, where they were charged with taking part in an initiation ceremony at which illegal oaths had been administered.

The charge was an obscure one, deriving from a statute designed to punish naval mutiny. Moderate wage campaigning had been legal since the repeal of the Combination Acts in 1824. But the Dorset authorities, like the Manchester magistrates who ordered troops to arrest Orator Hunt in St Peter's Fields, were determined to crack down on what they viewed as revolutionary activity. At the Dorchester Assizes in March 1834, George Loveless and his five fellow labourers from Tolpuddle were found guilty, and dispatched to serve seven years in Australia as convict labourers.

The outcry was immediate. Twenty-five thousand workers marched through the streets of London in one of the largest peaceful demonstrations ever seen in the capital. 'Arise, men of Britain and take your stand!' exhorted the London–Dorchester Labourers' Committee. 'Rally round the standard of liberty! Or for ever lay prostrate under the hand of your land- and money-mongering taskmasters!' Within a year the Home Secretary Lord John Russell had granted the men conditional pardons. In 1836 the pardons became full, and in 1837 the six started coming home to a succession of celebratory processions and dinners, which most of them – modest souls – found deeply embarrassing.

The 'martyrs' had become symbols. The flagrant injustice of their deportation, coupled with the men's own meekness – and also, perhaps, the comical name of their little village – helped stimulate working-class consciousness. The year 1839 saw the beginnings of the Chartist movement, dedicated to securing a charter of reforms that included the right to vote of *all* adult males, not just property-holders, and a call for the introduction of the secret ballot. Chartist demonstrations and ongoing radical pressure would eventually result in the Second Reform Act of 1867, which considerably extended the franchise, along with the Ballot Act of 1872 which finally realised Orator Hunt's dream of the secret vote.

But by 1872 only one of the six martyrs was still living in Tolpuddle. The others had emigrated to Canada. Having been transported once against their will, they now transported themselves voluntarily, though they never gave the reason why, and they carefully hid their Tolpuddle identities from their new friends and neighbours. The famous five did not even tell their Canadian-born children about their past – they wanted to escape from all of that. There was more to life than being a symbol.

'I WILL BE GOOD' – VICTORIA BECOMES QUEEN

1837

PREPARING ONE DAY IN 1830 FOR A HISTORY LESSON IN HER solitary schoolroom at Kensington Palace, the eleven-year-old Princess Victoria opened her exercise book to be confronted by a family tree. Her governess had put it there for her to study. The table of descent explained the relationships inside the House of Hanover – Victoria's own family – and as the Princess started tracing her personal connection with her grandfather King George III, she worked out something that had been concealed from her until that point in her life.

'I see I am nearer the throne than I thought,' she said – in fact, she was almost certain to become Queen. As the impact of this awe-inspiring prospect sank in, the little girl burst into tears. Yet even in her most emotional moments there was always a part of Victoria that remained detached: 'I will be good,' she said.

The family table showed that, by 1819, George III's seven surviving adult sons had, astonishingly, failed to produce a single legitimate living heir between them. The men – most of them portly, all of them spoilt, and all degenerate or defective in different, ingenious ways – had fathered bastards aplenty. Their mistresses and messy love lives had prompted scandal and widespread contempt for the royal family. Only with the birth of Victoria in May 1819 had the direct succession become reasonably safe – though the sudden death of her father Edward, Duke of Kent (the old King's fourth son), eight months later, demonstrated the perils of becoming ill in an age of poor health care. He had caught a chill at the seaside.

Victoria's mother, the widowed Duchess, was determined to keep her daughter safe and close to her in every way. The girl was not allowed to go downstairs without holding someone's hand. She had to sleep in the same bedroom as her mother, and she was shielded from 'unsuitable' personal influences by a cocoon of rules and protocol known as the 'Kensington System'. The Princess scarcely ever met children of her own age – for amusement and simple affection her solitary playmate was her beloved dog Dash, a King Charles spaniel.

Critics suspected that the main purpose of the Kensington System was to secure the position of Sir John Conroy, a handsome but slippery Irish adventurer who had become the confidant of the Duchess – and sure enough, when Victoria fell seriously ill on a visit to Ramsgate in 1835, Conroy tried to force the weakened Princess to sign a document that would make him her private secretary when she became Queen. The Duchess joined in, with a crude mix of threats and emotional blackmail, but the ailing sixteen-year-old withstood their pressure.

Two years later, in the quiet dawn hours of 20 June 1837, the Lord Chamberlain and the Archbishop of Canterbury came hurrying through the trees to knock on the door of Kensington Palace. Roused from her sleep, the eighteen-year-old Victoria received them in her dressing-gown – to see the venerable old gentlemen fall on their knees in front of her. Her uncle William IV had died in the night, and she was now Queen.

That night, for the first time in her life, Victoria slept on her own. She ordered her things to be moved to her own quarters – and in the weeks that followed she firmly detached herself from her mother. When the Duchess sent requests to see her daughter she would often receive notes containing just one word, 'Busy'. Sir John Conroy was forbidden access to the new Queen's apartments at Buckingham Palace.

Victoria was displaying all the fortitude that would characterise her sixty-three years on the throne – the longest reign to date in the history of the British monarchy. The adjective 'Victorian', meaning stern and dutiful, derived directly from her character. But the little Queen (she was less than five feet tall) had a playful and deeply sentimental side. When she got back to Buckingham Palace on 28 June 1838 at the end of her solemn and arduous coronation ceremonies, Her Majesty rushed straight upstairs to give a bath to her best friend Dash.

'GOD'S WONDERFUL RAILWAY' – ISAMBARD KINGDOM BRUNEL

1843

ONE DAY IN 1843, ISAMBARD KINGDOM BRUNEL WAS entertaining some children with his favourite party trick. Brandishing a half-sovereign, the Victorian equivalent of a 50p piece, the ingenious engineer would make the coin appear to vanish down his throat, then pluck it dramatically from his ear. Unfortunately for Brunel, on this occasion he really did swallow the coin – it slipped down his throat to become lodged in his windpipe.

For weeks the famous maker of railways, bridges, tunnels, docks and ships coughed painfully. A distinguished surgeon cut a hole in the windpipe and fumbled his forceps inside – to no avail. So the engineer decided to adopt an engineering solution. He designed a rotating table to which he could be strapped, face down. The table was then upended, with Brunel's head pointing towards the floor. With gravity thus enlisted, and the help of some hearty back-slapping, the coin came tumbling out.

Newspapers had been following the saga with horrified fascination – *The Times* ran daily bulletins on Brunel's health – and the reappearance of the coin was a national event. 'It's out! It's out!' cried the great historian Thomas Macaulay as he went running down the street. Everybody knew what he meant.

Brunel had been making headlines since 1826 when, aged only twenty, he took over the ambitious project started by his father, the French engineer Marc Brunel, to build a tunnel under the Thames from Rotherhithe to Wapping in London's docklands – the world's first underwater walkway. Isambard ('Kingdom' was the surname of his English mother Sophia) nearly died when the river broke through the tunnel roof and swept him away; but the young man survived to repair the tunnel and stage a spectacular candle-lit dinner for the project's directors below the riverbed. Brunel understood how visionary engineering needed showmanship to sell it, and he made himself a celebrity in the process.

The merchants of Bristol decided to enlist his flair. They were planning a 'Great Western Railway' to link the port with London, and the 27-year-old took on the project, exploring on horseback the 110 miles of countryside between London and Bristol to plot out the route with the gentlest, and thus the speediest, gradients. This involved some tunnelling again – Brunel's two-mile-long tunnel at Box, west of Swindon, took almost six years to complete, and when the crews digging from each end met in the middle, in 1840, they were found to be only one and a quarter inches out of alignment. Over the Thames at Maidenhead, Brunel constructed an elegant, flat-arched bridge whose spans were so level they seemed to be held up by magic. To this day they remain the widest, flat, brick-built arches in the world.

With its engineering marvels and soaring cathedral-like stations (also designed by Brunel), the GWR became nicknamed 'God's Wonderful Railway'. In 1842 Queen Victoria chose the GWR for her first trip by train – and by that date the railway had an extra dimension. 'Why not make it longer and have a steamboat go from Bristol to New York?' Brunel had suggested when one GWR director expressed worries about the length of the track. So in 1837 he had launched the *Great Western*, a huge paddle-steamer that carried passengers across the Atlantic in fifteen days and managed the return voyage in one day less. In the spring of 1843 (at the same time that he was trying to extricate the half-sovereign from his throat) he launched an even larger vessel, the *Great Britain*, the first iron-hulled, screw-propeller-driven ship the world had ever seen.

But the *Great Britain* lost money for its investors. Fare-paying passengers seemed wary of the ship's gargantuan bulk, and their fears were realised when, after only three transatlantic return voyages, she ran aground on the coast of Ireland. Not for the first time, Brunel's visionary ambition outran the practicalities. Extending the GWR into Devon, he built an 'atmospheric railway' that did away with noisy, soot-showering locomotives. Connected by iron rods to a vacuum tube between the rails, the carriages were sucked along by the vacuum inside the tube that was created and maintained by pumping-stations along the track.

But Brunel's system depended on the air-tightness of a leather flap along the top of the tube. This opened and closed to allow the passage of the iron rod below each carriage, and its suppleness was maintained by men who patrolled the line, painting the leather with a mixture of lime soap and whale oil. Unfortunately the taste of the whale oil was immensely appealing to rats, and as the rodents tucked into the oily leather, the atmospheric railway kept losing its atmospheric pressure.

Brunel took responsibility for the failure of his bold experiment – and he died in the middle of another, the launching in 1859 of his monster of monsters the *Great Eastern*, a 692-foot (210-metre) paddle-steamer that displaced 28,000 tons, five times more than any ship then afloat. Designed to carry four thousand, the *Great Eastern* carried just thirty-six passengers on her maiden voyage and ended her days as a cable-laying ship.

Brunel was only fifty-three when he died, but he had crammed several lifetimes into one. Nowadays he would be called a workaholic. He laboured every day and most of the night in a cloud of tobacco smoke, chain-smoking cigars. He drove his workforce fiercely – a hundred men were killed hacking through the solid rock of Box Tunnel – and he was as hard on his family as he was on himself.

By the time of his death, the commercial world had come to view him as dangerously extravagant – and so he was, agreed Daniel Gooch, the friend and colleague who built his locomotives for the GWR. But, added Gooch, 'great things are not done by those who count the cost of every thought and act'.

RAIN, STEAM & SPEED – THE SHIMMERING VISION OF J. M. W. TURNER

1843

ONE JUNE EVENING IN 1843 A YOUNG WOMAN, JANE O'Meara, was travelling to London on the recently constructed Great Western Railway through a terrifying storm. Thunder roared and lightning flashed across the countryside, while torrents of sheeting rain attacked the windows – so Jane was surprised when one of the elderly gentlemen travelling in her First Class carriage asked if she would mind him putting down the rain-blurred window. He wanted to take a look outside.

Politely consenting, Jane was still more surprised when her travelling companion thrust his head and shoulders out into the storm and kept them resolutely there for nearly nine minutes. The old man was evidently engrossed by what he saw, and when he finally drew back in, drenched, the young woman could not resist the temptation to put her own head out of the window – to be astonished by a blurred cacophony of sound and brightness. The train was standing at that moment in Bristol Temple Meads Station, and the mingled impression of steam, sulphurous smoke and the flickering glow from the engine's firebox overwhelmed her – 'such a chaos of elemental and artificial lights and noises,' she later wrote, 'I never saw or heard, or expect to see or hear.'

Almost a year later, going to look at the new pictures being hung in that summer's Royal Academy exhibition, Jane O'Meara suddenly realised who the eccentric traveller must have been. For hanging on the gallery wall, depicted in swirling and unconventional swathes of paint, was the same scary yet compelling vortex of light and turbulence that she had seen from her GWR carriage window – *Rain, Steam & Speed* by J. M. W. Turner.

By 1844 Joseph Mallord William Turner was a renowned, controversial and highly successful artist. He was born sixty-nine years earlier to a poor barber-wigmaker near London's Covent Garden fruit and vegetable market, and a mentally fragile mother who ended her days in the Bethlehem hospital for lunatics – 'Bedlam'. Turner retained his gruff Cockney accent all his life, along with a shrewd commercial spirit that dated back to the days when he exhibited his first paintings in his father's shop window at one shilling (5p) each.

Turner's wild, tumultuous and almost abstract paintings were denounced as 'mad' by many Victorians. But the French painters Monet, Renoir, Pissarro and Degas would later pay tribute to the 'the illustrious Turner' as the artist whose interest in 'the fugitive effects of light' inspired their own great revolution in ways of seeing – Impressionism. Monet came to London as a young artist to study *Rain, Steam & Speed* which, from the moment of its first hanging in the Royal Academy, was acknowledged by both its admirers and its detractors to be an extraordinary creation. 'The world has never seen anything like this picture,' declared the novelist William Thackeray.

The central feature of the picture was the glowing 'chaos' of light and energy that had shocked Jane O'Meara in Temple Meads Station – transposed by Turner to Brunel's famous bridge at Maidenhead in the Thames Valley, one of the artist's favourite locales for sketching. Enveloped in smoke and mist, the dark and sinister funnel of the locomotive is dashing forwards out of the canvas, a black stovepipe cutting ferociously through the slanting rain, while in front of the careering train – only visible if you step up to the canvas and peer closely – runs a terrified little brown hare, the creature that used to symbolise speed in the age before machines.

Rain, Steam & Speed now hangs in the National Gallery in London's Trafalgar Square. Standing back from its foaming confusion of colours and textures, you cannot help but be struck by the majesty of the world's first great railway painting. You can also recapture the excitement of Jane O'Meara, putting her head out into the storm to see what had caught the visionary eye of Joseph Mallord William Turner.

PRINCE ALBERT'S
CRYSTAL PALACE
1851

ON 1 MAY 1851 QUEEN VICTORIA, DRESSED IN A PINK crinoline that sparkled with jewels and silver embroidery, rode in her carriage to Hyde Park to open the largest greenhouse the world had ever seen. Extending over nineteen acres and nicknamed the 'Crystal Palace', the soaring steel structure contained 294,000 panes of glass and was tall enough to accommodate the park's towering old elm trees – along with a hundred thousand extraordinary objects gathered from Britain, Europe, America, Australia, India and China: 'The Great Exhibition of the Works of Industry of All Nations'.

The Great Exhibition was the work of Victoria's husband, Prince Albert of Saxe-Coburg-Gotha. Victoria had not been impressed when the two first met as teenagers – the solemn young German had nodded off to sleep when the time came to start dancing. But he had learned to dance by the time they met again, on 10 October 1839. 'It is quite a pleasure to look at Albert when he galops and valses,' noted the young Queen appreciatively in her diary. 'My heart is quite going.'

Five days later *she* proposed to *him* (protocol forbade the other way round), and the couple embarked on a passionate marriage that produced nine children – Britain had her first sentimental 'royal family'. Paintings and the recently invented photographic camera showed the royal clan playing with dogs, enjoying country holidays and singing carols round the Christmas tree – a German tradition that Britain now adopted enthusiastically. When it came to politics, Albert understood the importance of royal neutrality, trying to moderate his wife's fierce likings and dislikings for her successive prime ministers; he also appreciated the role the monarchy could play in raising the national spirit.

This was why he encouraged the idea of the Great Exhibition when it was put to him – and the show's popularity went on to justify his faith. More than six million people, a quarter of the country's entire population, flocked to Hyde Park to inspect the wonders of the Crystal Palace in the six months it was open – Queen Victoria herself visited no less than thirty-four times. Among the exhibits were the massive Koh-i-noor diamond, the world's largest mirror which ran the full length of the Palace's Main Avenue, and an 'alarm bed' that tipped over to eject the sleeper out and on to the floor. The serried ranks of public conveniences erected by George Jennings, the sanitary engineer, were a much discussed novelty, operated by coin-in-the-slot locks that would give rise to the expression 'spend a penny'.

Queen Victoria was struck by a machine that manufactured envelopes – it folded the paper as if it had fingers – and there were more glimpses of the world's mechanical future on the American stands, which displayed the first typewriter and sewing machine along with the mechanical harvesters and threshers that were transforming the power and prosperity of the young United States.

'Dearest Albert's name is for ever immortalised,' wrote Victoria with satisfaction on the day the exhibition opened, and that proved even more the case after it had closed. The show made a handsome surplus, which funded a dream that the Prince had long been nursing – to build a permanent campus of national culture and learning in South Kensington. Albert would die in 1861, aged only forty-two, diagnosed with typhoid fever, the dirty-water disease that poisoned city life in the years before effective public health regulations. But the profits of his Great Exhibition made it possible for his dream to take shape on a swathe of land running down from Hyde Park – the huge, circular Albert Hall for concerts; Imperial College, Britain's premier institution for the teaching of science; the Science Museum; the Natural History Museum; and the domestic design and arts museum now named after Victoria and Albert.

The Crystal Palace itself was carefully dismantled, girder by girder, pane by pane, and started a new life on Sydenham Hill in south London, where it was rebuilt by its architect Sir Joseph Paxton as the centrepiece of a two-hundred-acre Victorian theme park – the world's first, featuring huge, lifesize models of dinosaurs set in a prehistoric swamp. Later came a rollercoaster, a cricket ground and a football club, Crystal Palace FC, a founder member of the Football Association.

From 1895 to 1914 the FA Cup Final was played beside the Crystal Palace, and the glorious glass edifice dominated the south London skyline until November 1936, when it was destroyed in a spectacular fire. The flames lit up the sky as far as Brighton. But the name lives on – and you can still go up Sydenham Hill to see the dinosaurs.

'WOMEN AND CHILDREN FIRST!' – THE *BIRKENHEAD* DRILL
1852

STEAMING OFF THE COAST OF SOUTH AFRICA LATE IN February 1852, HM Troopship *Birkenhead*, a paddle-steamer, was one of the first iron-hulled ships built for the Royal Navy. She was carrying British troops, many of them raw recruits, with a small consignment of wives and children, to fight in the Kaffir Wars – an empire-building enterprise to conquer the territory of the Xhosa people in the eastern Cape.*

The sea was calm, the sky bright with stars, and most of the six hundred or so passengers and crew were sound asleep. Looking over the port rail, the small group of sailors who were manning the watch could make out the distant outline of the shore to the left-hand side of the ship, when, just before 2 a.m., a loud crash brought the *Birkenhead* to a juddering halt. Travelling at 8 knots (nearly 15 kilometres per hour) the vessel had driven hard on to an uncharted rock.

Instantly the lower troop deck was flooded, and as water came pouring through a gash in the *Birkenhead*'s iron cladding dozens of sol-

---

*In modern times the liberated Xhosa have provided the first two presidents of democratic South Africa, Nelson Mandela and Thabo Mbeki.

diers were drowned in their hammocks. Up on deck the crew struggled to release the lifeboats, to find that most were rusted in their davits. Only three boats could be launched, and the ship's commander, Captain Robert Salmond, ordered that the twenty-plus women and children on board should be dispatched to safety, along with the sick.

Elsewhere on deck, Colonel Alexander Seton of the 74th Highlanders took command of the troops, ordering them to line up in their regimental groupings. Many were boys and young men who had been in uniform only a few weeks, but they quickly assembled in their ten detachments, rank after rank, in parade-ground formation.

Now came the moment that distinguished the sinking of the *Birkenhead* from the sad but not uncommon fate of many ships in the centuries before radar, sonar and satellite weather-forecasting. Seeing that the vessel would not stay afloat much longer – she sank, in fact, within twenty minutes of being holed – Captain Salmond gave the order to swim for the boats, only to be countermanded by his army opposite number, Colonel Seton.

'You will swamp the cutter containing the women and children!' cried the colonel. 'I implore you not to do this thing, and I ask you to stand fast!'

The four hundred or so young soldiers who had lined up on the deck of the *Birkenhead* obeyed him. A handful broke for safety, but that only served to emphasise the stolidity of the serried ranks who chose to stay, standing side by side as the ship sank towards the water. We do not know when and how the onrushing ocean finally overwhelmed the *Birkenhead*, but as the *Boy's Own Paper* told it, the young soldiers 'went down with her to their watery graves as if merely on parade'.

Every Victorian school child knew the story. Later immortalised in a poem by Rudyard Kipling, 'The Birkenhead Drill' was held to be the archetype for the 'stiff upper lip', that ideal of calm and stoic conduct in the face of hopeless circumstances which was the hallmark of the English gentleman. In fact, Colonel Seton who gave the order to 'stand fast' was Scottish, and the bulk of his men were Irish and Scots, many from the famous Highland regiment, the Black Watch.

When the liner *Titanic* sank in 1912, contempt would be poured on the men who saved their skins by getting into the lifeboats: they broke the rule established by the *Birkenhead* – 'Women and Children First'.

And two years later, with the outbreak of the First World War, it was unquestioning, *Birkenhead*-style obedience that sent young men on both sides over the tops of the trenches to their deaths. The Emperor William I, who in 1871 unified Germany, decreed that the story of the *Birkenhead* should be 'read on parade at the head of every regiment in the Prussian service' – high praise, indeed, since the Prussians were renowned as the best-disciplined army in the world.

There was just one disturbing footnote to the apparently simple tale of heroism. Among the two hundred or so survivors fortunate enough to have drifted to shore in the warm ocean – avoiding horrifying shark attacks, which claimed numerous lives – was a young officer, Ensign Lucas, who recalled his final conversation with Colonel Seton.

'Perhaps we'll meet ashore, sir,' said Lucas.

'I do not think we shall, Lucas,' replied the colonel, 'as I cannot swim a stroke.'

So the *Birkenhead* drill was inspired by a non-swimming landlubber who had little option but to stand fast nobly on the deck – and who then imposed that option on his four hundred noble men.

INTO THE VALLEY OF DEATH
1854

O N A SUNNY MORNING LATE IN OCTOBER 1854, WILLIAM Howard Russell, war correspondent of *The Times*, found himself sitting among the stones and thistles of a Russian hillside with a ring-side view of an ongoing battle. 'The silence is oppressive,' he wrote. 'Between the cannon bursts, one can hear the champing of bits and the clink of sabres in the valley below.'

To his right, Russell could see water sparkling in the harbour of

Balaclava, 'a patch of blue sea' in a green landscape, and through this deceptively beautiful scenery rode the Light Cavalry Brigade of the British army, their swords unsheathed.

Looking through his field glasses, the reporter counted the British sabres – 607, he reckoned. 'They swept proudly past, glittering in the morning sun in all the pride and splendour of war.' But Russell could also see the menacing guns of the enemy, the Russians, stretched out along both sides and, most formidably, across the end of the valley. 'We could scarcely believe the evidence of our senses!' he wrote. 'Surely that handful of men were not going to charge an army in position?'

There had been a dreadful misunderstanding. High on the hillside, not far from where Russell was sitting, the British commander Lord Raglan had seen the Russian cavalry making off with some captured British guns. Now they were proceeding over the hills to one side of the valley, and Raglan instructed his own cavalry 'to advance rapidly to the front, and try to prevent the enemy carrying away the guns'.

But down on the floor of the valley, Lord Lucan, commander of the British cavalry, had no sight of the guns to which Raglan was referring. The only guns he could see were the ones straight ahead, and it was towards those that he now directed the Light Brigade. 'They advanced in two lines, quickening their pace as they closed towards the enemy,' wrote the horrified reporter. 'A more fearful spectacle was never witnessed than by those who, without the power to aid, beheld their heroic countrymen rushing to the arms of death.'

Russell was not then aware of the ambiguity of Raglan's order, which might have been checked or better explained if the British chain of command had been communicating more clearly with each other. The upper crust of aristocratic officers – many of whom had purchased their promotions to the elevated ranks they held – had been feuding ever since their arrival in the Crimea,* and Lucan was a particularly stubborn and peppery character. The man from *The Times* described the consequences in dreadful detail.

---

*In 1853 British and French forces invaded the Crimean Peninsula in southern Russia, ostensibly to protect the interests of Ottoman Turkey, but primarily to check Russian ambitions in the Black Sea and the Mediterranean.

At the distance of 1200 yards the whole line of the enemy belched forth, from thirty iron mouths, a flood of smoke and flame, through which hissed the deadly balls. Their flight was marked by instant gaps in our ranks, by dead men and horses, by steeds flying wounded or riderless across the plain ... Through the clouds of smoke we could see their sabres flashing as they rode up to the guns and dashed between them, cutting down the gunners as they stood.

The Light Brigade's heroism was in vain: 'Wounded men and dismounted troopers flying towards us told the sad tale ... At twenty-five to twelve not a British soldier, except the dead and dying, was left in front of these bloody Muscovite guns.'

By Russell's count, less than two hundred of the six hundred brave cavalrymen who headed off down the mile-long valley made it back – and he filed his report on 'the melancholy loss' in a long handwritten dispatch that was carried back to England by ship and horse-borne courier, to be published in *The Times* of 14 November 1854. Never before had such graphic eyewitness details of war been conveyed so rapidly to the nation at home – and they caught the attention of the poet Alfred Tennyson, who, as he read the *Times* coverage, was particularly struck by the phrase 'hideous blunder'.

Tennyson had been working for months on a complicated love epic, *Maud: A Monodrama*, later famous for the refrain 'Come into the garden, Maud'. But on 2 December he took a few minutes' break to dash off what would become his most famous poem of all:

> *Half a league, half a league,**
> *Half a league onward,*
> *All in the valley of Death*
> *Rode the six hundred.*
> *'Forward, the Light Brigade!*
> *Charge for the guns!' he said:*
> *Into the valley of Death*
> *Rode the six hundred.*

*A league is three miles – about five kilometres

384

'Forward, the Light Brigade!'
Was there a man dismay'd?
Not tho' the soldier knew
Some one had blunder'd:
Their's not to make reply,
Their's not to reason why,
Their's but to do and die:
Into the valley of Death
Rode the six hundred.

Cannon to right of them,
Cannon to left of them,
Cannon in front of them
Volley'd and thunder'd . . .
Into the jaws of Death,
Into the mouth of Hell
Rode the six hundred.

'The Charge of the Light Brigade' was published in the London *Examiner* on 9 December, less than seven weeks after the event it commemorated. Two years earlier the Victorians, as they were now calling themselves, had unquestioningly celebrated the discipline of the four hundred young recruits who stood to attention as the foundering *Birkenhead* took them to their deaths. Now Tennyson's poem captured the more complicated mixture of emotions inspired by the Light Brigade's blind obedience to orders – and this new perspective derived from the first-hand account of William Howard Russell watching from his Russian hillside among the stones and thistles.

In fact, *The Times*'s casualty figures were incorrect. While only 195 men got back on horseback, many staggered back to camp later on foot. Modern research has suggested that just 110 of the six hundred died in action – Tennyson's poem, in other words, perpetuated a media mistake.

But Russell was the father of a new tradition. 'In his hands,' wrote his colleague Edwin Godkin of the *Daily News*, 'correspondence from the field really became a power before which generals began to quail . . .

I cannot help thinking that the appearance of the special correspondent in the Crimea . . . led to a real awakening of the official mind. It brought home to the War Office the fact that the public had something to say about the conduct of wars and that they are not the concern exclusively of sovereigns and statesmen.'

THE LADY OF THE LAMP AND THE LADY WITH THE TEACUP (PLUS THE ODD SIP OF BRANDY)
1854-5

FLORENCE NIGHTINGALE HEARD GOD'S VOICE FOR THE first time when she was sixteen years old. 'On 7 February, 1837,' she wrote, 'God spoke to me and called me to His service.' Like Joan of Arc, Florence heard the words quite clearly – but it took her seven years to work out what precise form God's service should take: that she should go into hospitals to tend the sick.

The wealthy and elegantly fashionable Nightingale family were horrified. To be a nurse was no occupation for a lady in the early years of the nineteenth century. Hospitals were degraded and dangerously infectious places – they gave off an odour of vomit and excrement that you could smell from the street. As for the women who were willing to work in such squalor, it was generally assumed that nurses were coarse and promiscuous, with a propensity to drink.

But God kept telling Florence what He wanted – she recorded the instructions in her painfully honest private notes and diaries – and at the age of thirty-three she took a job as superintendent of the Institute for the Care of Sick Gentlewomen in Distressed Circumstances in

London's Harley Street. Caring for ageing governesses was a respectable job to which her family could not reasonably object (although, in fact, they did).

Then in October 1854 the war correspondents started writing home from the Crimea. 'It is with feelings of surprise and anger,' wrote Thomas Chinery, the Constantinople correspondent of *The Times*, 'that the public will learn that no sufficient medical preparations have been made for the proper care of the wounded. Not only are there not sufficient surgeons . . . there are no dressers or nurses to carry out the surgeon's directions.'

The very day *The Times* dispatch appeared, Florence contacted Sidney Herbert, the Secretary at War, offering to take a group of English nurses to Turkey – while Herbert himself, the husband of one of her dearest friends, was writing Florence a letter that crossed in the post: 'There is but one person in England that I know,' he wrote, 'who would be capable of organising and superintending such a scheme.'

This happy confidence was not shared by the resentful male staff in the military hospitals of Scutari in Turkey, where Florence and her thirty-eight nurses landed in November 1854, just weeks after the Battle of Balaclava and the Charge of the Light Brigade. 'Abandon hope all ye who enter here' was the motto that Florence suggested for the rambling and dilapidated Barrack Hospital with its four grim miles of smelly wards. Her first order was for the supply of two hundred hard scrubbing brushes.

In the months that followed she rented a house near the hospital, installed large boilers and turned it into a laundry. Discovering that the food served to the wounded consisted mainly of gristly, over-boiled lumps of fatty meat, she arranged for Alexis Soyer, the celebrity chef of the day, to come out from London to reorganise the kitchens. Above all, she insisted on discipline, clean uniforms, and orderly working among her staff, laying the foundation for what would come to be known as the British nursing *profession*. In all of this, Florence set a personal example:

> She is a 'ministering angel' without any exaggeration . . . [declared John MacDonald, almoner of The Times *Crimea Fund*] and as her slender form glides quietly along each corridor, every poor fellow's face softens with gratitude at the sight of her. When all the medical officers have retired for the

night, and silence and darkness have settled down upon those miles of pros-
trate sick, she may be observed alone, with a little lamp in her hand, making
her solitary rounds.

A legend was born. Adored by the common soldiers and fêted by
the newspapers, the lady with the lamp became a national heroine –
and she hated it. 'The buz-fuz about my name,' she wrote, 'has done
infinite harm.'

All glory, in Florence's view, must go to God. She refused a
welcome-home reception because she felt deeply guilty that she had
not achieved *more* for her patients, and she spent the rest of her life
campaigning for army and hospital reform. She also fought to improve
the training of midwives and the conditions inside maternity ('lying-
in') hospitals, had a nursing school named after her, became an expert
on sanitation and related health issues in India, and conducted a survey
aiming to improve the lot of the 'Sick Poor' in workhouses.

Scarcely a day went by when Florence did not fire off a detailed
letter to promote or protect one of her causes, and, throughout it all,
she kept up her conversations with God, whom she eagerly looked forward to meeting face to face. When a friend dared suggest towards the
end that death must come as something of a rest after a busy life, Miss
Nightingale sat bolt upright on her pillows. 'Oh *no*,' she said with conviction, 'I am sure it is an *immense* activity.'

'I trust,' wrote William Howard Russell at the end of the Crimean
War, 'that England will not forget one who nursed her sick, who sought
out her wounded to aid and succour them, and who performed the last
offices for some of her illustrious dead.'

The renowned war correspondent wrote many words in praise of
Florence Nightingale, but on this occasion he was not referring to the
Lady with the Lamp. Equally brave and caring was a Jamaican-born
nurse of mixed race who had made her own way out to the Crimean
War – Mary Seacole.

Mary would speak proudly of her ethnic mix – she often called herself 'the yellow woman'. Her mother was a Jamaican 'doctress' who
administered local folk remedies, her father a Scottish soldier in the
local garrison: when she married, Mary went for an Englishman, the

sickly Edwin Horatio Hamilton Seacole, godson of the famous Horatio Nelson.

On Mr Seacole's death in 1844, Mary had to fend for herself. Using the Creole healing skills she had learned from her mother, she turned her house in Kingston, Jamaica, into a convalescent home for invalid officers, picking up hints about Western medicine from visiting surgeons. On a visit to Panama in 1850 she won her own laurels as a 'doctress' when a cholera epidemic broke out, and she took charge of the local village, deploying the bag of medical supplies that she carried with her everywhere.

As a young woman, Mary had travelled several times to England – she financed one trip by the sale of her West Indian preserves and pickles – and in 1854, just approaching her fiftieth birthday, she found herself in London again. Reading the horrifying reports of conditions in the Crimea, she was moved, like Florence Nightingale, to contact the Secretary at War Sidney Herbert – but she received a very different response. Presenting herself at the front door of the minister's home, she endured long hours of contemptuous glances from the white servants who came and went in the great hall, and was then told, without any interview, that her services were not required.

She encountered similar rejection from the managers of the Crimean Fund that had already backed Florence Nightingale's mission to Scutari – Mary stood outside in the winter darkness, the tears streaming down her cheeks. 'Did these ladies shrink from accepting my aid,' she later wrote, 'because my blood flowed beneath a somewhat duskier skin than theirs?'

Mary got to nurse the soldiers just the same, though. With the help of Mr Day, a shopkeeper friend of her late husband, she booked a passage to the Black Sea, where she set up a Crimean version of her Kingston care centre. So rose, in the spring of 1855, in the shantytown of camp followers that gathered round the siege of Sebastopol, a cluster of buildings which Mary christened the 'British Hotel'. There was a kitchen, a canteen, sleeping quarters, stables and pens for livestock. The compound extended over more than an acre, and above Mr Day's trading store fluttered a large Union Jack.

Standing on a little hill just a mile from British headquarters, the British Hotel became a home-away-from-home for officers and men, offering cups of tea and generous servings of alcohol, Welsh rarebit, Irish stew – and, on a few eagerly awaited days a week, Mrs Seacole's celebrated rice pudding. Mary made her sausages from the pigs she kept in the yard, and, as the fame of her cooking spread, officers from the allied French army started dropping in for meals.

But it was her medical skills that made 'Mother Seacole' famous. She sold medicine to those who could afford it – and gave it to those who couldn't. She visited the bedsides of the sick, and, going a step further than Florence Nightingale whose work was in the military hospitals behind the lines, she even went out on to the battlefield. As the dead were being picked over by corpse plunderers, the portly form of Mrs Seacole could be seen administering sips of brandy to the suffering. She tended enemy Russians as well as the British and the French: when Sebastopol finally fell in 1855, she was the first woman to enter, by special permission of the allied command, carrying her medicine bag.

Peace brought disaster for the firm of Seacole and Day. The partnership had recently expanded their compound and had bought in new stocks of food and livestock. But with their customers, the allied troops, returning home, they had to sell to the local Russians for a fraction of their outlay. When Mary got back to England in 1856, she found herself facing bankruptcy proceedings.

But the war reporters had made Mother Seacole famous – they dubbed her 'the Creole with the Teacup' – and her plight was taken up by *The Times*, which championed a fund to assist her. *Punch* magazine organised a four-day military gala in her honour that was attended by eighty thousand people, and when Mary published her memoirs, *The Wonderful Adventures of Mrs Seacole in Many Lands*, her chirpy, no-nonsense style helped make the book an instant success.

Florence Nightingale had mixed feelings. 'Anyone who employs Mrs Seacole will introduce much kindness,' she remarked ' – also much drunkenness and improper conduct.' Still fighting her battle to make nurses respectable, Florence did not approve of Mary's raucous parties at the British Hotel: 'I will not call it a "bad house" – but something not very unlike it . . . She was very kind to the men and, what is more, to the Officers, and did some good and made many drunk.'

If the severe and driven Florence was a role model for the Victorian age, the plump and easy-going Mary provides more of a heroine for ours. 'The yellow woman' died wealthy and well loved in London in 1881 at the age of seventy-six, having proved the value of what she once described as 'that one common language of the whole world – smiles'.

CHARLES DARWIN AND THE SURVIVAL OF THE FITTEST
1858

IMAGINE THAT YOU HAVE BEEN DEVOTING YOUR PRINCIPAL energies for nearly twenty years to a Very Big Idea – a concept so revolutionary that it will transform the way the human race looks at itself. And then one morning, you open a letter from someone you scarcely know (someone, to be honest, that you never took very seriously) to discover that he has come up with exactly the same idea – and that he has picked you as the person to help him announce it to the world.

This was the dilemma that confronted Charles Darwin in June 1858 as he opened a thin, well wrapped package from Ternate, an island in the Dutch East Indies. He could recognise the handwriting of Alfred Russel Wallace, a railway surveyor-turned-naturalist who made his living selling specimens to richer collectors – a year or so back Darwin had asked him to track down some Malayan poultry skins for him.

But on this occasion, Wallace was not peddling specimens. He was asking Darwin to read a short, handwritten essay about natural selection. During a bout of malaria that February, the naturalist had got to thinking about the life-and-death struggle between existence and extinction in beasts and plants; about the need to adapt; about the selective breeding of domestic and farmyard animals to improve or alter their characteristics, and about the way that species diverge into different forms – all the ingredients of what would come to be known as 'evolution'.

'I never saw a more striking coincidence!' exclaimed the mortified Darwin. 'If Wallace had my MS [manuscript] sketch written out in 1842 he could not have made a better short abstract [summary].'

In June 1842, Darwin, then thirty-three, had sketched out his own ideas about evolution. Dinosaur discoveries and other geological research had pushed him towards the concept of the earth undergoing long, slow changes over the millennia. A five-year journey in his twenties on the research vessel *Beagle* had shown him how different forms of life adapted to different environments, most notably in the Galapagos Islands. And then in 1838 he had first laid eyes on an ape, an orang-utan, at London Zoo, and had started to make notes on her human-like emotions.

But the young man could see the bitter controversy towards which his thinking was leading – the idea that mankind was not created by God in a single day as the Bible described, but was, rather, shaped gradually in a long chain of descent that linked human beings to other species, including apes. Darwin himself found the idea deeply shocking – 'It is like confessing to murder,' he told a friend – and he reflected on the persecution handed out to the early astronomers who had dared to suggest that the earth revolved around the sun.

Such fears had held Charles Darwin back for nearly twenty years. He kept delaying publication, looking for one more piece of evidence to protect himself and his theory from the widespread outrage he anticipated – and now Wallace's essay meant, as Darwin wrote to the great geologist Charles Lyell, that 'all my originality, whatever it may amount to, will be smashed'.

Wallace had asked Darwin to forward his essay to Lyell if he approved of it, and, despite his disappointment, Darwin did the honourable thing. He could have destroyed the letter and pretended it had never arrived. He could have delayed doing anything, while rushing ahead with his own publication. Instead he passed it on – 'I hope you will approve of Wallace's sketch,' he wrote, 'that I may tell him what you say.'

Honour was rewarded. Lyell conferred with the botanist Joseph Hooker who decided that the groundbreaking ideas of both Wallace *and* Darwin should be presented side by side as soon as possible – at the very next meeting of the Linnean Society.* Alphabetically and chronologically, Darwin took precedence in the memorable double presentation of 1 July 1858 – one of the great moments in the history of science – and some have claimed that this was a fix. Lyell and Hooker were both old friends of Darwin, and had been pushing the reluctant author to publish for years.

But when, weeks later in the Far East, Wallace found out that Lyell and Hooker had, without consulting him, assigned him the role of junior co-discoverer, he was all generosity, graciously thanking Hooker for the presentation that was 'so favourable to myself'. If he felt any resentment, he never once betrayed it. At the age of thirty-five the former railway surveyor, who had started his studies in the free libraries of Welsh mechanics' institutes, continued his researches to embark on a public career that would make him one of the best-known naturalists of his time – 'the Grand Old Man of Science', as he was often described. He also campaigned for socialism, spiritualism, the reform of the House of Lords and the Church of England, votes for women, the proper design of museums, the redistribution of land through the breaking up of the great noble estates, early 'green belts' (as we would call them) and the protection of historic monuments. Seldom short of a provocative and forward-looking idea, Wallace suggested that rather than going on strike, disgruntled employees should club together to buy out their bosses and prove they could do a better job themselves.

Darwin went on to become the grand old man of evolution, pushed by Wallace's challenge finally to write his masterpiece *The Origin of Species*,† which was published in November 1859 and has never been out of print since. Sharing so many ideas, the two men who might have been fierce enemies actually became warm friends, treating each other with genuine respect. As the principal protagonists of what came to be known as the 'survival of the fittest' theory, with all its competitive, dog-eat-dog connotations, Darwin and Wallace illustrated how generosity can be the cleverest survival technique of all.

*Britain's pre-eminent biology fellowship, named after the Swedish naturalist Carl Linnaeus, the father of modern plant and animal classification.
†Full title: *On the Origin of Species by Means of Natural Selection, or the Preservation of Favoured Races in the Struggle for Life.*

THE GREAT STINK – AND THE TRAGEDY OF THE *PRINCESS ALICE*
1878

> *Dead hogges, dogges, cats and well-flayed carrion horses,*
> *Their noisome corpses soyled the water's courses.*
> *Both swines and stable dung, beast-guts and garbage,*
> *Street-dust, with gardners' weeds and rotten herbage.*
> *And from these waters' filthy putrefaction,*
> *Our meat and drink were made, which breeds infection.*
>
> The River Thames described in 1632
> by John Taylor, 'the Water Poet'

DUMPING YOUR RUBBISH IN THE RIVER THAMES WAS A long-cherished London tradition. In 1357 King Edward III complained of the 'fumes and other abominable stenches' this caused – he banned butchers from fouling the water with entrails from the beasts they slaughtered. Henry VIII attempted a total ban on dumping of any sort. But the Thames grew more polluted with every generation, and with the coming of the Industrial Revolution it became positively poisonous. Cement works and factories poured their effluent into the river, and the development of improved water closets made things worse. By the middle of the nineteenth century some 250 tons of human excrement were being flushed, daily, into the tidal flow.

Matters came to a head in the hot dry summer of 1858 when Parliament draped its windows with sheets soaked in chloride of lime in a vain attempt to combat what newspapers described as the 'Great Stink'. Legislators had to abandon the building as unusable. Fleeing from the Chamber, his nose buried in a scented handkerchief, the fastidious Benjamin Disraeli resolved on action. As Chancellor of the

Exchequer he made funds available for an ambitious scheme to 'embank' the river.

The Thames's embankments, constructed in the 1860s, were the brainchild of Joseph Bazalgette, a friend of Brunel who, like Brunel, was the English-born son of a French immigrant family – in Bazalgette's case, of Huguenot descent. He reorganised London's thirteen hundred miles of sewers so they drained into a superhighway of gigantic pipes that ran alongside the water. On top of these were built the wide roads and tree-lined promenades of the Victoria, Albert and Chelsea Embankments – while, below the surface, the city's rechannelled sewage was carried eastwards to the mouth of the river, where the tide was supposed to sweep it away.

The trouble was that the massive new culverts did not extend that far downstream. Twice every twenty-four hours, at high tide, two massive apertures at Barking and Crossness spewed out 75 million gallons of untreated sewage on either side of the river – with tragic consequences in 1878, when the pleasure boat *Princess Alice* collided with the *Bywell Castle*, a merchant steamer, not far from Woolwich.

The collision in itself was tragic enough – over 650 drowned. It was the worst single disaster in Thames history. But one hour before the collision the outfalls at Barking and Crossness had released their 75 million gallons into the tide, and, as one correspondent to *The Times* described it, there was 'projected into the river two continuous columns of decomposed fermenting sewage, hissing like soda water with baneful gases'.

'The water was very dreadful and nasty,' reported one witness at the subsequent coroner's inquest. 'Both for taste and smell it was something [he] could hardly describe,' said another. One survivor reckoned he owed his life to immediately vomiting up everything he had swallowed, but others were not so fortunate. After the ghastly experience of struggling for life in the noxious brown soup, the papers reported mysterious instances of paralysis, illness and a rate of fatality which, as *The Times* put it, was 'exceedingly large' if judged 'as the mere effect of an immersion in water on a fine summer evening'.

Then watermen noticed that the bodies of the dead were rising to the surface after only six days. The expected period for a corpse to float was nine – and these bodies were more bloated than usual. They could not fit into conventional coffins. Covered in a strange slime, which reappeared when washed off, their stench was so revolting that the dockers hired to move them went on strike for better money. The virulently chemical nature of the river was suggested by the way that the dead women's dresses changed from blue to violet. One pharmaceutical chemist offered his own analysis: while diluted sewage, 'say one drop in 10,000', was known to produce fevers like typhoid, concentrated and actively decomposing sewage produced sulphuretted hydrogen that was 'relatively as fatal as prussic acid'.

This was the other side – the price, indeed – of all the mass-produced wonders in Prince Albert's Crystal Palace. The Victorian spirit of free enterprise and devil-take-the-hindmost was summed up in Samuel Smiles's *Self-Help* (published in 1859, the year after the Great Stink).* Typhoid fever was killing nearly fifteen hundred Londoners a year; in the course of one thirty-five-year cycle, outbreaks of cholera, another disease of polluted water, claimed thirty-six thousand more. But the idea that government should intervene was still seen by many as an unacceptable infringement of freedom. 'We prefer to take our chance of cholera and the rest,' declared *The Times*, '[rather] than be bullied into health.'

The sinking of the *Princess Alice* (named after Queen Victoria's third daughter) did produce some reform. The rules of navigation on the river were more rigidly enforced, and the Metropolitan Board of Works went back to Joseph (now Sir Joseph) Bazalgette for a new sewage strategy – to extract the solid waste and transport it far out to sea in a fleet of sludge boats. So the old Thames tradition of dumping survived more grandly than ever.

Self-Help was published on the same day, and by the same publisher (John Murray), as Charles Darwin's *Origin of Species*.

LORD ROSEBERY'S HISTORICAL HOWLER
1887

I N 1887 QUEEN VICTORIA HAD BEEN FIFTY YEARS ON THE throne, and Lord Rosebery wanted to give her a present to mark the occasion. The British public were celebrating with a jubilee (the word came from 'jobel', the Old Testament celebration that took its name from the blowing of the ram's horn trumpet), but Lord Rosebery wanted to offer a personal tribute. He had served as Victoria's Foreign Secretary the previous year and was widely tipped as a future Prime Minister.* What better gift than some memento of England's only other great and long-reigning queen, Elizabeth I? So Rosebery dispatched a dainty miniature portrait of 'Gloriana', with a letter expressing the hope that Her Majesty would accept this remembrance of her illustrious predecessor.

Queen Victoria was most touched. The 68-year-old monarch had a soft spot for the dashing young grandee – forty years old and noted for his eloquence. She wrote to Rosebery next day, thanking him for his 'kind and most valuable present, accompanied by such flattering words . . . I am delighted to possess this exquisite gem which I *intend* to *wear*' – underlining the two words to emphasise her pleasure.

But there was one problem. As a stickler for sometimes inconvenient truth, Queen Victoria felt she had to remind Lord Rosebery: 'I

---

*Archibald Philip Primrose, 5th Earl of Rosebery, became Prime Minister in 1894, but did not live up to his promise, resigning the following year. He is better remembered for his empire-based foreign policy in the tradition of 'splendid isolation' – he invented the phrase 'the British Commonwealth of Nations' – and as an owner of racehorses. He won the Derby three times. He was one of the last British prime ministers to sit in the House of Lords.

have no sympathy with my great Predecessor, descended as I am from her rival Queen, whom she so cruelly sacrificed.'

Lord Rosebery had made the common historical error of forgetting that the modern British monarchy does not descend from Queen Elizabeth I, who had no descendants, but from Mary Queen of Scots, who was executed by Elizabeth (see p. 237). It was Mary's son James who brought the Stuart dynasty south after Elizabeth died in 1603.

ANNIE BESANT AND 'PHOSSY JAW' – THE STRIKE OF THE MATCH GIRLS

1888

I will speak for the dumb. I will speak of the small to the great, and of the feeble to the strong. I will speak for all the despairing silent ones.
Motto of Annie Besant's halfpenny weekly, The Link

'PHOSSY JAW' WAS A DEADLY OCCUPATIONAL HAZARD THAT afflicted young women who worked in Victorian match factories, where the ends of the matchsticks were dipped into a combustible white phosphorus paste. The disease started with a toothache, followed by painful and unpleasant-smelling abscesses as the bone tissue rotted away. In its final stages, the remains of the phosphorus-infected jaw glowed in the dark a greenish-yellowy white. Surgical removal might save the sufferer's life; otherwise, convulsions, 'inflammation of the brain' and death through organ failure would inevitably result.

In June 1888 the journalist Annie Besant exposed the terrible life of the match girls in her campaigning weekly, *The Link*. At the Bryant &

May factory in east London, she reported, teenagers were paid only a few shillings a week, from which fines could be deducted by the management for such offences as talking too much, dropping matches, or going to the toilet without permission. The girls worked from 6.30 a.m. in summer (8 in winter) to 6 p.m., and were fined half a day's pay if they were late. Bryant & May, meanwhile, were paying huge dividends to their shareholders, so that a £5 share was valued at over £18.

A few days after her article appeared (under the title 'White Slavery in London'), Annie Besant heard female voices calling her name outside the office of *The Link* in Fleet Street. The match girls had come to see her. The Bryant & May management had asked them to sign letters saying they were happy and contented – the firm was planning to sue Annie for libel – and the women had refused.

'You had spoke up for us,' explained one, 'and we weren't going back on you.'

Soon afterwards one of their leaders was sacked, and all fourteen hundred match girls came out on strike. They had no union organisation, and they turned to Annie for help.

'A pretty hubbub we created,' Annie later recalled. 'We asked for money, and it came pouring in; we registered the girls for strike pay, wrote articles, roused the clubs, held public meetings . . .'

Annie Besant pioneered techniques of protest that are in use to this day. She took a delegation of the girls to lobby the House of Commons in their ragged, East End clothes, so the press could not help but note 'the contrast between these poor "white slaves" and their opulent sisters' of the West End. As the girls spoke to MPs 'in their own words', one pretty thirteen-year-old whipped off her bonnet to reveal a bald scalp from carrying heavy wooden palettes on her head.

Bryant & May were forced to climb down. They agreed to a package that included the abolition of all deductions and fines, and the provision of a breakfast room for their workers. The girls returned to work next day, victorious – and, following a further campaign in which Annie also took part, white phosphorus was eventually banned. It was replaced by red, which worked just as well in matches and had no deleterious side effects.

The strike of the match girls was a landmark in British labour history – it helped inspire the formation of trades unions all over the country, and it provided an early grass-roots triumph in the struggle for women's rights. But for Annie Besant, forty years old in 1888, it was just one in a lifetime of battles. In her twenties she had walked away from Frank Besant, a stiff-necked Lincolnshire vicar who made it a condition of their marriage that she attend holy communion every Sunday. In her thirties she was convicted, and narrowly escaped prison, for publishing a treatise on birth control that was deemed obscene. Following her victory with the match girls, she turned to the mystic cult of theosophy and became interested in the Eastern religions.

This took her out to India, where she campaigned for Indian Home Rule and adopted Indian dress, a white sari and white sandals – white being the Hindu colour of mourning. She was in mourning, she explained, for all the harm that British rule had done to the country, and the British returned the compliment by interning her for a while. Annie Besant died in Madras at the age of eighty-six, fighting so long as she had strength for all the despairing silent ones.

DIAMOND JUBILEE – THE EMPIRE MARCHES BY

1897

A S QUEEN VICTORIA DROVE OUT OF BUCKINGHAM PALACE on a sunny June morning in 1897, she leant from her carriage to press a specially mounted button, which, through the ingenuity of the electric telegraph, dispatched a greeting on her behalf to every corner of her worldwide Empire. Within sixteen minutes the first answer – from Ottawa in Canada – came clicking back.

The electric telegraph was just one of the many miracles that had transformed life in the sixty eventful years since the young Queen had received the Archbishop of Canterbury in her dressing-gown. 'Slavery has been abolished,' wrote her reforming Prime Minister, William Ewart Gladstone, proudly. 'A criminal code that disgraced the statute book has been effectually reformed.' Most men (but no women) could now vote by secret ballot. Free education was available to almost everyone. Gaslight illuminated homes and streets. One penny would buy a postage stamp which, when licked and applied to an envelope, would carry your letter to almost any corner of the country overnight. People were generally richer than their parents – and most would live longer, thanks to medical advances like anaesthesia and antiseptics. They could also travel quicker and further, thanks to railways and steamships – and a lucky few now considered it their right to take at least one holiday a year.

Queen Victoria had played no personal role in any of these transformations, over which she had presided as a sometimes grudging head of state. Overcome with grief at the premature death of her beloved Albert in 1861, she had withdrawn from the world for many years and was only reluctantly coaxed back to perform a few of her public duties – and then in a style that was dripping with disapproval. Of the many photographs of Britain's longest reigning monarch, only one shows her smiling.

But the grumpier the old Queen became, the more the world loved her. By 1897, aged seventy-eight, Victoria was by far the most famous woman on earth, her name bestowed on cities, rivers, lakes, bays and great waterfalls all over the planet. Ten years previously her half-century had been marked with a Golden Jubilee. Now the government proclaimed that her sixty years on the throne be celebrated as her Diamond Jubilee, and the Empire assembled in London to do her homage: the streets were fragrant with fresh-sawn green pine, as miles of wooden stands were thrown up to accommodate the spectators.

Headed by the tallest officer in the British army, six feet eight inches in his bare feet and riding a gigantic charger, the procession of sailors, military bands, clattering horses and colourfully garbed fighting men was forty-five minutes long. The Empire – almost literally – passed by. From Canada they came, from Australia, Africa, India, Borneo, Fiji, Hong Kong – Britain ruled nearly a quarter of the earth's landmass in 1897, eleven million square miles (28,000,000 square kilometres) coloured red in the atlases of the day. Bringing up the rear, hunched in her carriage, came the little widow in black to whom a quarter of the world's inhabitants paid homage.

The bells of St Paul's fell silent as the procession stopped in front of the cathedral for an open-air service – the Queen Empress was too lame to get down from her carriage. Lined up on the steps the assembled clerics and choirboys sang their way lustily through the hymns, in the last of which the Queen's carriage was supposed to start moving off. But, recalled the Bishop of London:

> the other carriages waited, and when the hymn was over there was a pause of intolerable silence. The Archbishop of Canterbury, with splendid audacity and disregard of decorum, interpreted what was in everyone's mind, and cried out 'Three cheers for the Queen!'
>
> Never were cheers given with such startling unanimity and precision. All the horses threw up their heads at the same moment, and gave a little quiver of surprise. When the cheers were over, the band and chorus, by an irresistible impulse, burst into 'God Save the Queen'.

Scarcely was the Queen round the corner when 'one of the choir boys, unable to restrain himself any longer, dashed from his place, leapt down the steps and filled his pockets with the gravel on which the wheels of the carriage had rested'.

As the boy sought to grasp the fleeting magic of the moment, operators of the recently invented movie camera were doing precisely the same. The 'cinematograph' had come to London only the previous year, but in June 1897 more than twenty rival newsreel companies set up their cameras along the ceremonial route. Pondering how to capture the splendours of the long, moving procession on film, they came up with a swivel device that would enable the previously immovable camera to swing from side to side and capture the full panorama. So the cinema's staple 'panning' shot owes its origin to Queen Victoria.

SLAUGHTER ON SPION KOP
1900

The tumult and the shouting dies;
The Captains and the Kings depart . . .
Far-called, our navies melt away;
On dune and headland sinks the fire:
Lo, all our pomp of yesterday
Is one with Nineveh and Tyre!
. . .

Lord God of Hosts, be with us yet,
Lest we forget – lest we forget!

THE POET RUDYARD KIPLING FELT UNEASY AT THE boastful pomp and circumstance of the Diamond Jubilee celebrations. Until 1897 the author of the *Jungle Books* (and later of the *Just So Stories*) had been known as a jingoistic* cheerleader of imperialism. But now he composed a doom-laden ode that he entitled 'Recessional',† comparing Britain's worldwide dominions to the once proud Old Testament empires of Assyria that crumbled into sand.

Kipling ended each verse with the warning 'Lest we forget!' and in less than three years the warning proved justified. In 1899 Britain was pouring troops into southern Africa in an attempt to discipline the Boers, the Dutch-speaking farmers who had settled the Cape before the arrival of the English, and they encountered bitter resistance. The

---

*The word comes from the Victorian music-hall song – 'We don't want to fight, but by jingo if we do, we've got the ships, we've got the men, and got the money too.'
†A hymn sung at the end of a church service, as the choir and clergy leave the church.

Boers correctly interpreted British interference as a land-grab – vast deposits of gold and diamonds had recently been discovered beneath the Boer territory of the Transvaal – and when the fighting started, their local knowledge gave them the upper hand.

One night in January 1900 some two thousand British troops, many of them conscripts from Liverpool serving in Lancashire regiments, were sent scampering up a *kopje* (little hill) known as the *spion* (look-out), about a dozen miles from the town of Ladysmith in Natal. The plan was to secure, under cover of darkness, a position from which they could fire down on the Boers. But next morning it became tragically clear that the opposite was the case. When the sun burned off the mist around 8 a.m., the British found themselves exposed to the enemy's pitiless fire streaking down from the surrounding hilltops that were higher than Spion Kop. 'The Boers was up above us, see,' one survivor told the author Thomas Pakenham many years later. 'They'd got us in a trap.'

In the interests of camouflage, the British army had recently switched its combat uniform from red to khaki, but the men on top of Spion Kop were sitting targets. With just twenty shovels between them, they had only been able to dig themselves a shallow trench across the top of the rocky hill, and the Boers were deadly shots.

'Shells rained in among us,' recalled another old survivor. 'The most hideous sights were exhibited – men blown to atoms, joints torn asunder. Headless bodies, trunks of bodies. Awful. Awful. You dared not lift your head above the rock or you were shot dead at once.'

Watching the slaughter was a young war correspondent for the *Morning Post* who bravely made his way to the foot of the hill. 'Men were staggering along alone, or supported by comrades, or crawling on hands and knees,' wrote the 26-year-old Winston Churchill. 'The splinters and fragments of shell had torn and mutilated in the most ghastly manner.'

Helping the wounded was another gigantic figure of twentieth-century history, Mohandas Gandhi, the inspiration of the Indian independence movement who was later known as the Mahatma ('Great Soul'). Then a 28-year-old barrister working in Durban's Indian community, Gandhi had volunteered his services as a stretcher-bearer, and would win a British campaign medal for his work in raising an ambulance corps of more than a thousand Indians.

By the time nightfall brought merciful relief from the bombardment, the young British commander Alec Thorneycroft had had enough. 'Poor boys, poor boys,' he kept muttering, giving the order to evacuate. 'Better six battalions safely off the hill than a mop-up in the morning.'

A shortage of signal-lamp oil meant Thorneycroft had not received a crucial message – the news that guns and reinforcements were on their way. Had the British held their ground they could have retained Spion Kop, since the Boers had suffered casualties themselves and were almost out of ammunition. They could not have sustained another day's attack and many of the farmers were preparing to ride away. Three hundred and twenty-two British soldiers had died, with 563 wounded, for nothing.

Six years later the fruitless sacrifice received its most famous memorial. Founded in 1892, Liverpool Football Club won its second League Championship in 1906 and decided to celebrate by building extra room for spectators at its Anfield ground – a tall embankment that could pack more than twenty thousand standing behind one of the goals. Ernest Edwards, the editor of the *Liverpool Post and Echo*, had a suggestion to make: that Anfield's new embankment should be named 'Spion Kop' as a memorial to 'all those local lads of ours' who gave their lives in Natal.

And so the 'Kop' became the inspirational heart of one of the most successful teams in English soccer history. Twenty minutes after kick-off on 1 September 1906, Joe Hewitt gave Liverpool the lead against Stoke City when he scored the first ever goal in front of the Kop, and Liverpool has gone on to win sixteen more League titles and five European Cups – 'Walk on, walk on, with hope in your heart, and you'll never walk alone . . .'

Well, not quite alone, for Edwards's idea had a London inspiration. In 1904 the Woolwich Arsenal football team, largely composed of military men and munitions workers at the Royal Arsenal workshops in Woolwich, southeast London, had decided to name their high new cinder embankment 'Spion Kop'. The name did not survive Arsenal's 1913 move across the river to their new stadium at Highbury, but by then the grieving munitions workers had inspired no less than sixteen other clubs, as well as Liverpool, to name their home hills after the men who scaled Spion Kop and did not come down again.*

EDWARD VII AND THE ENTENTE CORDIALE

1903

TWO HUNDRED THOUSAND BRITISH TROOPS VERSUS SIXTY thousand Boers – the war in South Africa should have been a walkover. But the elusive guerrilla tactics of the local Afrikaner farmers drove the British commander Lord Kitchener to repressive measures – the Boer farms were burned, their livestock was looted, and their dispossessed women and children were 'concentrated' into camps along the railway lines.

Surrounded by barbed wire, with inadequate food and germ-laden water, these 'concentration camps' became Britain's shame – some 24,000 Boer women and children and 14,000 interned Africans died in epidemics of dysentery, measles and enteric fever. Britain eventually 'won' the South African War (fought from 1899 to 1902), forcing the

---

*The kops of English football: Anfield (Liverpool); Bloomfield Road (Blackpool); Bramall Lane (Sheffield United); County Ground (Northampton Town); Elland Road (Leeds United); Highfield Road (Coventry City); Hillsborough (Sheffield Wednesday); Home Park (Plymouth Argyle); Leeds Road (Huddersfield Town); Meadow Lane (Notts County); Prenton Park (Tranmere Rovers); Racecourse Ground (Wrexham); Recreation Ground (Chesterfield); St Andrews (Birmingham City); Valley Parade (Bradford City); Filbert Street (Leicester City); York Street (Boston United).

Boers into what became the Union of South Africa. But it was a poor way to start the new century. 'When children are treated in this way and dying,' commented David Lloyd George, the campaigning Liberal MP, 'we are simply ranging the deepest passions of the human heart against British rule in Africa.'

The Boers were no saints. Among the 'freedoms' for which they were fighting was the right to treat the native, non-white inhabitants of southern Africa as slaves – their twentieth-century Afrikaner descendants would extend the existing system of racial segregation and give it their own name, 'apartheid'. But their fight against the might of the British Empire made them heroes in Europe. When Britain's new King, Edward VII, visited Paris in May 1903, hostile shouts of *Vive les Boers!* came ringing from the crowds.

'The French don't like us,' commented one of his courtiers.

'Why should they?' the King replied.

Fifty-nine years old when his mother Queen Victoria died in January 1901, Edward VII was determined to make the most of the short time left to him as King. He possessed an old-fashioned confidence that his job involved having an impact on national policy – and the test of that came on this same visit to the unwelcoming city of Paris, where cries of *'Vive Jeanne d'Arc!'* mingled with those in support of the Boers.

Edward liked France. As Prince of Wales, he had made many visits to the capital, where he had tried to disguise his identity by travelling as the 'Duke of Lancaster'. But his portly, bearded form was unmistakable, and the French detectives assigned to shadow him spent many a long afternoon waiting outside the apartments of countesses and courtesans – all of them beautiful.

Now King Edward applied his seductive royal glamour to the affairs of nations. 'Ah, Mademoiselle,' he said loudly to the actress Jeanne Granier, kissing her hand when he met her on his first evening in Paris, 'I remember how I applauded you in London where you represented all the grace, all the esprit of France.' Next day's papers reported the King's delight at being once more 'in this beautiful city', and when he got to the Town Hall he said it all – and more besides – in the language of his audience: Paris, he declared, was a city *'où je me trouve toujours comme si j'étais chez moi'.*

Edward VII had a warm and genial voice, husky with the brandy and cigars of which he was so fond. When speaking in public, he had always conveyed the impression that he found life a matter of the utmost enjoyment, and when this was allied in May 1903 to his fluent and self-confident French, the effect was electric. His claim to be feeling 'at home' received 'a tremendous ovation', recorded his adviser Frederick Ponsonby. 'He now seemed to have captured Paris by storm. From that moment everything changed wherever he went. Not only the King but all of the suite were received with loud and repeated cheering.' Crowds blocked the path of the royal carriage shouting, '*Vive Édouard!*' '*Notre bon Édouard!*' and even '*Vive notre roi!*' As Paris's new hero embarked for the Channel, the newspapers used words like *passionnant* to describe the popular farewell.

From the days of William III and Marlborough to the time of Napoleon (the 1690s until 1815), France and Britain had been locked in recurring conflict – a second Hundred Years War. But they had collaborated against Russia in the Crimea (1853–6) and they had recently found common cause in their fears about the rising power of Germany. Edward VII did not invent the rapprochement, but his spectacular success in Paris forced the pace. Serious negotiation started that summer, and on 8 April 1904 the Entente Cordiale was signed in London.

The 'warm understanding' resolved a set of relatively minor trade and territorial differences that had been aggravating relations between Britain and France – largely to do with who controlled what in various corners of their empires. It was not a military alliance. But it ended Britain's standoffish policy of 'splendid isolation' from her European neighbours, and now appears a prelude to the great events of the twentieth century. In two murderous world wars, British troops would find themselves fighting in Europe . . . in the defence of France.

CELLAR MURDERER CAUGHT BY WIRELESS – DR CRIPPEN

1910

Dr HAWLEY HARVEY CRIPPEN THOUGHT HE HAD GOT away with it. Early in 1910 he killed his wife Cora, having first sedated her – and maybe half-poisoned her – with hyoscine hydrobromide. Using his medical knowledge, Crippen then dismembered her body, disposing of her head, skeleton and internal organs so they were never found. He buried what was left in the cellar of their home at 39 Hilldrop Crescent in Holloway, north London, and started a new life there with his lover, Ethel le Neve, who was sighted about this time wearing Cora's jewellery.

When the police came round, prompted by suspicious neighbours, Crippen said Cora had gone to America. Then he and Ethel fled to Belgium, where they boarded a liner, the SS *Montrose*, sailing from Antwerp to Canada. Crippen shaved off his moustache and posed as John Philo Robinson, travelling with his sixteen-year-old son (Ethel in disguise). Unfortunately for the couple, the *Montrose* was equipped with one of the first of the Marconi Telegraph Company's new 'wireless' machines.

'Have strong suspicion that Crippen London cellar murderer and accomplice are amongst saloon passengers,' telegraphed the *Montrose*'s captain, Henry Kendall, on 22 July, as the liner sailed past the tip of Cornwall. 'Moustache shaved off, growing a beard. Accomplice dressed as a boy, voice, manner and build undoubtedly a girl.'

Captain Kendall had been reading the newspapers. A week earlier they had reported how Inspector Walter Drew of Scotland Yard had searched 39 Hilldrop Crescent following the flight of the couple, and had discovered a set of headless and bizarrely filleted human body parts – presumably the remains of Cora – buried beneath the coal-cellar floor. On receipt of Captain Kendall's cable, the detective headed for Liverpool to board SS *Laurentic*, a mail steamer due to reach Montreal three days ahead of the *Montrose*.

Captain Kendall's ship-to-shore broadcast was the first time that wireless telegraphy, developed by Guglielmo Marconi in the 1890s, had been used to catch a murderer. It also provoked the first tabloid melodrama of the twentieth century, since details of the captain's wireless message were leaked to the press. As reporters leapt on board the *Laurentic* with Inspector Drew, readers around the world were able to follow the race across the Atlantic day by day.

On the *Montrose*, meanwhile, Captain Kendall kept the story to himself. He made friends with the unsuspecting 'Robinsons', wiring details of their doings to the outside world. When he revealed that Dr Crippen was reading the thriller *The Four Just Men*, it sealed the fame of its author, Edgar Wallace.

The press was on hand when Inspector Drew, having arrived first in Montreal, disguised himself as a pilot and went on board the *Montrose*. 'Let me introduce you,' said the ever helpful Captain Kendall (who later published his memoirs, *Ship's Log*).

As 'Mr Robinson' extended his hand, Inspector Drew promptly grabbed it, whipping off his pilot's cap. 'Good morning, Dr Crippen,' said the detective (who would also publish his own memoir, *I Caught Crippen*). 'Do you remember me? I'm Inspector Drew from Scotland Yard.'

'Thank God it's over' was the fugitive's reported response. 'The suspense has been too great. I couldn't stand it any longer.'

In the trial that followed, the quiet-spoken doctor, with his wire-framed spectacles and droopy moustache, scarcely emerged as an ogre. He had sold homeopathic remedies, managed a deaf institute and tried his hand at dentistry in a succession of failed careers that his shrewish wife Cora used to deride. The hen-pecked Crippen consummated his relationship with Ethel only after he found Cora – a would-be opera singer – in bed with another man, and his main purpose at his trial was to avoid saying anything that might incriminate the woman he now loved.

In this he succeeded. Ethel le Neve was acquitted. Crippen was found guilty on 22 October, and spent the weeks until his execution exchanging ardent love letters with Ethel. Coupled with his humdrum appearance, his devotion somehow made his crime of passion, dismembering his wife's remains in a net-curtained suburban street, all the more shocking. He was hanged at Pentonville Prison on 23 November 1910.

Ethel le Neve changed her name after her acquittal and managed to avoid attention for the rest of her life. But her lover Dr Crippen, the Cellar Murderer, remains to this day one of the star waxwork attractions in Madame Tussaud's Chamber of Horrors.

'I MAY BE SOME TIME . . .' – THE SACRIFICE OF CAPTAIN OATES

1912

LAWRENCE OATES WAS A SCRUFFY-LOOKING CHARACTER, often to be seen in a battered old Aquascutum raincoat that he buttoned tightly round his neck. He was wearing it when he arrived at the London berth of the *Terra Nova*, Captain Robert Scott's expedition ship that was about to weigh anchor for the Antarctic in the spring of 1910. The crew 'never thought for one moment', according to the Irish explorer Tom Crean, 'that he was an officer'. 'But oh! he was a gentleman,' remembered Crean, 'quite a gentleman and always a gentleman.'

Educated at Eton and a Master of Foxhounds, Oates certainly had the resources of a gentleman – he contributed £1000 (the equivalent of £66,000 today) to the funds of the Antarctic expedition. He was indeed an officer, the only horse expert in a group of mainly naval adventurers – they nicknamed him 'The Soldier'.* Oates's job was to

---

*The captain's other nickname was 'Titus' after the notorious Oates (no relation) who stirred up national hysteria in the reign of Charles II over the so-called 'Popish Plot' (see pp. 280–4).

care for the ponies on which the British were relying to carry food and fuel to their supply dumps along the route to the South Pole.

But Scott had not thought to send Oates to Siberia to purchase the ponies, whose strength was crucial to the success of the expedition. When the animals arrived, Oates was horrified to find they were a 'wretched load of crocks'. He complained bitterly to Scott, cataloguing their faults in his diary – 'knock knees . . . aged . . . wind-sucker . . . lame' – along with equally bad news: a wire from the Norwegian explorer Roald Amundsen announcing that he was heading for the Pole: 'I only hope they don't get there first,' Oates recorded gloomily, 'it will make us look pretty foolish after all the fuss we have made.'

To pull their sleighs the Norwegians were relying on a large number of dogs (over two hundred), which they planned to slaughter systematically as they went along, feeding the meat to the survivors. Scott considered this inhumane. He was counting on just thirty-two dogs, Oates's ponies and three new-fangled motor sledges to get his men within striking distance, at which point they would drag their own sledges to the Pole and then back to 'One Ton' Depot, so called after the amount of stores it contained.

But this provoked another disagreement, since Oates felt they should site One Ton Depot closer to the Pole. He proposed killing the weakest of his ponies as meat to provide energy for the dogs – and the men – to move the contents of the depot a crucial ten miles or so closer to their destination.

'I have had more than enough of this cruelty to animals,' replied Scott, 'and I'm not going to defy my feelings for the sake of a few days' march.'

'I'm afraid you'll regret it, sir,' retorted Oates.

'Myself, I dislike Scott intensely,' the indignant Oates confided in a letter home to his mother, 'and would chuck the whole thing if it was not that we are a British Expedition and must beat those Norwegians . . . The fact of the matter is he is not straight; it is himself first, the rest nowhere, and when he has got all he can out of you, it is shift for yourself.'

Oates accurately pinpointed the ruthless streak in the self-obsessed Scott, and when the British reached the Pole on 18 January 1912 to discover that the Norwegians had, in fact, beaten them by more than a month, Oates made clear in his diary which expedition had been more rationally led: 'That man [Amundsen] must have had his head screwed on right . . . They seem to have had a comfortable trip with their dog teams – very different from our wretched man-hauling.'

Stumbling through ice and crevasses by day, shivering in damp sleeping-bags by night, the demoralised British team hauled their sledges back towards One Ton Depot, a 120-mile journey which they might have hoped to cover inside three weeks. But they were harassed by bitterly freezing weather – and by frostbite. Edgar Evans, the only member of the final five-man team who was not of the officer class, succumbed to delirium, finally collapsing and dying after four hard weeks in which his fatigue and confusion had held the whole party back. 'The absence of poor Evans,' noted Scott unsentimentally, 'is a help to the commissariat [food supply].'

Now it was Oates's turn to hold the party back. He was already walking with a limp, the legacy of a wound he had sustained in the Boer War, and the frostbite in his feet was turning gangrenous. It slowed his walking pace and, worse, his preparation time every day, as he struggled for two hours with the agonising pain of pulling his boots over his feet.

'Poor Titus is the greatest handicap,' Scott confided to his diary. 'He keeps us waiting in the morning until we have partly lost the warming effect of our good breakfast . . . It is too pathetic to watch him.' Unable to pull, Oates would collapse on a sledge whenever the party halted. 'If we were all fit, I should have hopes of getting through,' wrote Scott in his diary on 6 March, 'but the poor Soldier has become a terrible hindrance.'

It was now seventeen days since Evans had died, but Oates insisted on carrying on. On 11 March Scott handed out thirty opium tablets to each man, a suicide dose; but if this was a hint, Oates declined to take it. Malnutrition and the agony of his frostbitten hands and feet may have clouded his mind. He kept going through the motions, wrestling with his boots every morning, staggering out into the freezing white blindness.

He was a brave soul [wrote Scott on the 17th]. This was the end. He slept through the night before last, hoping not to wake, but he woke in the morning – yesterday. It was blowing a blizzard. He said, 'I am just going out-side and I may be some time.' He went out into the blizzard and we have not seen him since . . . We knew that poor Oates was walking to his death, but though we tried to dissuade him, we knew it was the act of a brave man and an English gentleman.

So Captain Oates passed into history. Scott and his other companions died some two weeks later, just eleven miles short of One Ton Depot – which raises several questions. Might they have survived if Scott had heeded Oates's advice to locate the depot further south? And might they possibly have been able to cover that further eleven miles if Captain Oates had made his sacrifice earlier – at the beginning of March, say – instead of lingering, 'a terrible hindrance' to his companions, until the 16th?

The truth has vanished long ago in the glaring white mist. The last words that Oates himself wrote were in his diary on 24 February 1912 – so everything we think we know about the last three weeks of his life, together with his now famous manner of dying, comes from the pen of Captain Scott, the man whom Oates described as 'not straight'.

THE KING'S HORSE AND EMILY DAVISON

1913

ON 14 JUNE 1913 LONDONERS FLOCKED BY THE THOUSAND to Epsom Downs in Surrey for an afternoon of beer and betting. It was Derby Day, and in the stands with his binoculars was the King himself, George V, the bearded son of the bearded Edward VII, whom he had succeeded in 1910. The King owned one of the less fancied

entries, a colt named Anmer,* and as the horses reached the halfway stage, the sharp bend at Tattenham Corner, Anmer had already fallen back in the chasing pack.

Suddenly there was a commotion in the crowd. 'I noticed a figure bob under the rails,' recounted one eyewitness in *The Times* next day. 'The horses were thundering down the course at a great pace bunched up against the rail.'

The figure was a forty-year-old university graduate and teacher, Emily Davison, a 'suffragette' – so called because of her campaigning for female suffrage, votes for women.

'The king's horse Anmer came up,' recounted another spectator, 'and Miss Davison went towards it. She put up her hand, but whether it was to catch hold of the reins or to protect herself I do not know. It was all over in a few seconds. The horse knocked the woman over with very great force, and then stumbled and fell, pitching the jockey violently onto the ground. Both he and Miss Davison were bleeding profusely.'

Anmer rolled over, got to his feet, and galloped off down the course to complete the race without his rider. The jockey, Herbert Jones, lay 'doggo' on the ground till the last horse had passed, then sat up gingerly – he had a bruised face and fractured rib, with mild concussion. But Emily Davison did not move. She lay crumpled and unconscious, thrown to the ground with such force that her spine had been fractured at the base of her skull. She never regained consciousness, and died four days later.

Emily Davison was a passionate member of the Women's Social and Political Union, led by Emmeline Pankhurst and her eldest daughter Christabel. The Pankhursts had campaigned for many years through the Independent Labour Party, the predecessor of the modern Labour Party, until the ILP, fearing that middle- and upper-class women would vote for their opponents, had grown lukewarm on female suffrage. Working men (who routinely banned women from their clubs) were as prejudiced as the males of other classes, realised the Pankhursts. So in 1903 they had founded the WSPU to fight on the

*The Derby takes its name from the sporting Earl of Derby who founded the race in 1780. Anmer was a wood where George V particularly enjoyed shooting, near the village of Anmer on the royal estate of Sandringham in Norfolk.

single issue of votes for women, demonstrating peacefully to start with, but resorting to law-breaking as they got arrested for 'obstruction'. 'Deeds not Words' was their motto, and their deeds became more extreme as feelings escalated.

Emily Davison's personal motto was 'Freedom against tyrants is obedience to God'. In 1909 she had written the words on slips of paper and tied them to rocks that she hurled at a carriage containing David Lloyd George, the Chancellor of the Exchequer – she had been sentenced to one month in prison.

This was one of seven prison terms that Emily served between 1909 and 1912 for offences that included obstruction and breaking windows in the House of Commons. Her longest sentence was six months for setting fire to public postboxes. 'Argument is no use,' she once said, defending the fierceness of suffragette demonstrations, 'writing, speaking, pleading – all no use.'

Going on hunger strike while in prison, Emily suffered the dreadful ordeal of forcible feeding: she was held down while a rubber tube was pushed down her throat or up her nostril, then, inevitably, vomited up the fatty brown soup that was poured down the tube. When she barricaded herself inside her cell to escape the feeding, the authorities flooded it with freezing-cold water. In furious protest, she threw herself down an iron staircase, knocking herself out and seriously damaging her spine. She was never free from pain again.

'I give my life,' she declared, 'as a pledge of my desire that women shall be free.'

So dramatic were some of Emily's protests that history has tended to assume she travelled to Epsom in June 1913 with her mind made up to die. But newsreel film of the incident suggests that she was only trying to slow Anmer down by grabbing his reins – and that was the impression of Jones, the royal jockey. In her pocket were found a return rail ticket, and two flags in the suffragette colours.

'She had concerted a Derby protest without tragedy,' explained Sylvia Pankhurst, Emmeline's second daughter ' – a mere waving of the purple-white-and-green at Tattenham Corner which, by its suddenness, it was hoped, would stop the race.'

Whatever the intentions of Emily Davison, her death did not impress people at the time, only confirming popular prejudice against the wildness of the suffragettes. 'She nearly killed a jockey as well as herself,' complained *The Times*, 'and she brought down a valuable horse . . . Reckless fanaticism is not regarded by [the public] as a qualification for the franchise.'

It took the terrible war of 1914–18 to transform attitudes, as women moved into offices, shops and factories to take over the jobs of men. Mrs Pankhurst suspended suffragette protests – it would be pointless, she argued, to fight for the vote without a country to vote in – and her conciliatory attitude prompted the politicians to climb down.

'Where is the man who would now deny to woman the civil rights she has earned by her hard work?' asked Edwin Montagu, the Minister of Munitions, in 1916. In June 1918, five months before the war ended, the vote was given to women over the age of 30 who were ratepayers (council-tax payers) or married to ratepayers. Ten years later suffrage was extended to all women, on the same terms as men.

In the short term, Emily Davison's gesture on Derby Day may have been counterproductive, but over the years it has come to be romantically symbolic of the fight for women's rights – and that was how her fellow campaigners saw it at the time:

Waiting there in the sun, in that gay scene, among the heedless crowd [wrote the journal Votes for Women *in June 1913], she had in her soul the thought, the vision of wronged women. That thought she held to her; that vision she kept before her. Thus inspired, she threw herself into the fierce current of the race. So greatly did she care for freedom that she died for it.*

WHEN CHRISTMAS STOPPED
A WAR
1914

I T STARTED WITH SMALL GLIMMERS OF LIGHT – COULD THEY possibly be candles? – flickering on the crusted mud of the enemy trenches a hundred yards or so away. The British sentries could not make them out. At first there were just one or two. Then more appeared, several dozen perhaps – miniature Christmas trees were being hoisted over the parapet, accompanied by strange but unmistakable sounds of jollity. The Germans were singing carols now: *Stille Nacht! Heilige Nacht!* – 'Silent Night, Holy Night'. It was Christmas Eve on the Western Front.

The Christmas trees were presents from the German homeland – tiny conifers shipped in by the thousand to raise morale and, presumably, to encourage their boys to fight more fiercely. But on 24 December 1914 their effect was quite the opposite, for the Germans started to clamber out of their fortified positions. And on the other side of the corpse-littered No Man's Land between the trenches, the British found themselves doing the same.

'I went out, and they shouted "No shooting!" and then somehow the scene became a peaceful one,' wrote Captain R.J. Armes of the 1st Battalion North Staffordshire Regiment in a letter home to his wife. 'All our men got out of their trenches and sat on the parapet. The Germans did the same and they talked to one another in English and broken English. I got on top of the trench and talked German and asked them to sing a German folk song, which they did; then our men sang quite well, and each side clapped and cheered the other.'

'It all happened spontaneously and very mysteriously,' remembered Major Leslie Walkinton, then a seventeen-year-old rifleman. 'A spirit stronger than war was at work that night.'

A bright full moon made for classic Christmas card weather. White frost had crispened and had even brought a certain beauty to the normally glutinous wastes of mud. Captain Armes saw the chance to clear the former turnip field of the dead of both sides, so he negotiated an agreement with his German counterpart. The two officers also agreed 'to have no shooting until midnight tomorrow'.

Similar agreements to celebrate Christmas Day peacefully were being negotiated up and down the war zone around Armentières near Lille in northern France. Elsewhere along the four hundred miles of the Western Front, which stretched from the English Channel to the Swiss border, hostilities continued. But in this little patch of Flanders, a bizarre and rather wonderful interlude was imposing itself upon the lethal squalor of the 'war to end all wars'.

Christmas morning started with burial services, the troops from both sides sometimes lining up together. 'Our padre gave a short sermon, one of the items of which was the 23rd Psalm,' wrote Lance Corporal Alex Imlah of the 6th Battalion Gordon Highlanders. 'Thereafter a German soldier, a divinity student I believe, interpreted the service to the German party. I could not understand what he was saying, but it was beautiful to listen to him because he had such an expressive voice.'

The service over, the two bands of men started fraternising. 'One can hardly believe them capable of the terrible acts that have been laid at their door,' Alex Imlah told his father. 'Some of them could speak English fluently, one of them had been a waiter at the Cecil Hotel, London, and I gathered from them they were pretty well tired of this horrible business.'

The British packages from home included Christmas cards and cigarettes from Buckingham Palace, plus plum puddings from the *Daily Mail*, which formed the basis of some lively barter. Beer, tins of jam, 'Maconochie's' (a canned vegetable stew) and cigars (the Kaiser's Christmas gift to his troops) all changed hands. 'I met a young German officer, and exchanged buttons as souvenirs,' remembered Captain Bruce Bairnsfather of the 1st Battalion Royal Warwickshire Regiment. 'With my wire-cutting pliers I removed a button from his tunic, and gave him one of mine in exchange. Later I was photographed by a German with several others, in a group composed of both sides.'

In several sectors of the Front the climax of Christmas Day was a series of knock-up football matches, using empty bully-beef cans where balls were not available – one match featured teams of fifty or so per side. Three–two in favour of the Germans was the only result recorded, but the losers did not seem to mind. 'There was not an atom of hate on either side that day,' remembered Bairnsfather.

Such a widespread flowering of peace and friendship had never been seen in the history of war, and it has prompted two myths – that it did not actually happen, or, alternatively, that the truth about 'the Christmas truce' was suppressed by the authorities. Sir John French, the morose commander of the British Expeditionary Force, certainly expressed his 'grave displeasure [at] the reports he has received on recent incidents of unauthorised intercourse with the enemy'. But there was no censorship of the numerous letters in which British officers and men sent home their tales of celebrating Christmas with the enemy, and these were picked up in the newspapers.

These letters also tell the stories of how eventually, and in different ways, the Christmas truce ended. One went like this: 'At 8.30 I fired three shots in the air and put up a flag with "Merry Christmas" on it,' wrote Captain J.C. Dunn of the Royal Welch Fusiliers, whose unit had celebrated with two barrels of beer sent over by the Saxons in the opposite trenches. 'The German captain appeared on the parapet. We both bowed and saluted and got down in our respective trenches, and he fired two shots in the air . . . The War was on again.'

PATRIOTISM IS NOT ENOUGH –
EDITH CAVELL
1915

T HE FIRST WORLD WAR STARTED ON 4 AUGUST 1914, WHEN
German armies marched into neutral Belgium, hoping to surprise
France and capture Paris. It was the outcome of a complicated series
of international manoeuvrings that had followed the assassination of
Archduke Franz Ferdinand, heir to the throne of Austria–Hungary, in
Sarajevo, Bosnia–Herzegovina, earlier that summer. Britain had been
trying to stay out of Europe's quarrels, but she felt impossibly menaced
by the prospect of a German army – and navy – off the English
Channel coast. By the end of August British troops were on their way
to help both the French and the Belgians.

After some early setbacks, the British Expeditionary Force that was
sent to France eventually played its part in helping to check the
Germans, digging the trenches of what became the Western Front. But
the regiments sent to Belgium fared less well. Defeated and outflanked,
many British, French and Belgian soldiers found themselves trapped
behind enemy lines. If they stayed in uniform they would be captured
by the Germans; if they disguised themselves as locals, they risked
being shot as spies. Just a few were fortunate enough to find shelter in
a nurses' training school on the outskirts of Brussels run by an English
matron, Nurse Edith Cavell.

She was a handsome woman, forty-seven years old, with high
cheekbones and a luxuriant mass of greying hair that she rolled on top
of her head in an elegant chignon. Sharp-eyed and upright, Miss Cavell
looked like a matron, exuding stern authority. She held a watch in front
of her at breakfast, and if any of her nurses arrived more than two minutes late they would be ordered to work an extra two hours. According
to one of her staff, she could be 'cold, distant and aloof'.

But matron did not hesitate when Lieutenant Colonel Dudley Boger and Company Sergeant Major Frank Meachin of the 1st Battalion Cheshire Regiment came to her door on a chilly, wet night in November 1914. Boger had a leg wound; he had grown a beard, and was dressed as a Belgian factory worker in a black hat and floppy tie. Meachin was also dressed as a labourer, with rolls of cloth packed between his shoulders to make him look like a hunchback. 'These men are fugitive soldiers,' Cavell told her assistant matron. 'Give them beds in the empty surgical house.'

Boger and Meachin were the first of two hundred such fugitives that Edith Cavell and her staff sheltered at her institute, feeding and tending them until they were strong enough to be on their way. As a young woman Edith had worked as a governess in Brussels for six years, then returned as a nurse in 1907 to pioneer the teaching of Florence Nightingale-style techniques in Belgium. She spoke fluent French and was a respected local figure, trusted by the Belgian underground network: with its assistance, many of her charges were able to find their way home.

'I am helping,' she wrote to her cousin in England, 'in ways I may not describe to you till we are free.'

The Germans announced repeatedly that anyone caught assisting enemy soldiers would be shot, but Edith kept on smuggling fugitives through the hospital. Often she would cook their food at night, serve it herself, then clean up the dishes to get rid of the evidence by dawn. She kept her diary sewn into a footstool.

Unfortunately not all of her fellow conspirators were so careful. One of her contacts in the escape network was arrested, having failed to destroy letters in which Edith's name was mentioned, and on 5 August 1915 the local head of the German secret police arrived at the hospital.

The Germans had no need to torture Edith to discover the truth. She was the daughter of an evangelical Norfolk vicar, and she declined to lie. The only incriminating evidence was a thank you postcard, thoughtfully and thoughtlessly sent by a grateful soldier who had made it home. Tried and found guilty in a single day, Edith's own honest words had effectively condemned her to death. On 12 October she was led out at dawn, blindfolded, and shot by two firing squads, each of eight men, at the national rifle range in Brussels. She was still wearing her nurse's uniform.

The outcry was immediate, both in Britain and around the world – the bitterness provoked by her killing was one of the reasons why there were no more Christmas truces in the trenches. Allied recruitment doubled for eight weeks following her death, and, effectively admitting a tragic error, the Kaiser gave orders that no more women were to be executed without his permission. After the war her body was brought back for a service of thanksgiving in Westminster Abbey, followed by burial at Norwich Cathedral.

Yet Edith Cavell was a war heroine with a difference. On the night before her execution, the English chaplain in Brussels came to offer her consolation, and found instead that the condemned woman had a powerful spiritual insight to offer him: 'Standing, as I do, in view of God and eternity,' she said, 'I realise that patriotism is not enough. I must have no hatred or bitterness towards anyone.'

YOUR COUNTRY NEEDS YOU! – THE SHEFFIELD PALS

1916

AS THE BRITISH ARMY GATHERED RECRUITS IN THE summer of 1914, it came up with an attractive offer – men who enlisted together could serve together. Whole neighbourhoods and communities were encouraged to sign up en masse with the promise that they would be able to train and fight together, side by side, as 'pals'.

France, Germany, Austria–Hungary and Russia were raising their armies on the basis of conscription, but Britain's Liberal government balked at making military service compulsory. Volunteers, it was felt, would fight with more spirit than conscripts, and the new War

Secretary, Lord Kitchener of Khartoum, was made the focus of a dramatic recruiting campaign.

Horatio Herbert Kitchener was a national war hero who in 1898 had conquered Khartoum – and, indeed, the entire Sudan – then had gone on to secure victory in the Boer War (loyal admirers did not mention his creation of the 'concentration camps'). 'K of K' had striking facial features – fierce, bright eyes and a handlebar moustache of quite extraordinary luxuriance. These figured in a brightly coloured poster in which the great man imperiously pointed directly at the viewer. 'Your Country Needs You!' ran the slogan, and men responded in their tens of thousands. In the 'rush to the colours' of August and September 1914, young friends marched together to the recruiting office, sometimes arm in arm and singing, to enlist in what became known as the pals' (or chums') battalions.*

At full strength a battalion consisted of 1107 officers and men, and in September the Sheffield Pals reached that number in just a few days' recruiting at the Corn Exchange. They were white-collar workers, for the most part – '£500-a-year businessmen,' recalled one recruit, 'stockbrokers, engineers, chemists, metallurgical experts, university and public school men, medical students, journalists, schoolmasters, shop assistants, secretaries, and all sorts of clerks'. 'To Berlin via Corn Exchange' read placards that captured the jingoistic atmosphere of the times.

Technically known as the 12th (Service) Battalion, York & Lancaster Regiment, the Sheffield Pals started their drill lessons at Bramall Lane, home of Sheffield United Cricket and Football Club. But the stamping of a thousand pairs of boots had a disastrous effect on the turf, and the pals moved on for twelve months of training in various camps, including a spell on Salisbury Plain alongside the 1st and 2nd Barnsley Pals and the Accrington Pals – all grouped together in the 94th Brigade (31st Division).

At the end of 1915, the 31st Division set sail for Egypt to defend the Suez Canal against the threat of a Turkish attack that did not

---

*More than fifty pals' battalions were formed in 1914/15 from communities all over the country. Among them were the 'bantam' battalions – men who were less than the regulation army height of 5 feet 3 inches (but taller than 5 feet).

materialise, thereby providing an unexpected holiday in the sun. The office pals from cold northern towns soaked up the late winter warmth of Alexandria – in eighteen months together they had neither lost a life nor fired a shot in anger. But in March 1916 the division was called back to Europe. Britain was preparing a massive assault on the German positions along the River Somme in northeastern France, and the Sheffield Pals had been assigned to capture the village of Serre.

It would be easy, they were told. For a week before their attack, the German positions would be subjected to a non-stop bombardment from the British guns. Nothing would survive – not even a rat – and at the end of June 1916, along the whole length of the Front, one and three-quarter million shells were duly rained down on the enemy. The battalions attacking Serre were instructed to walk steadily across No Man's Land – there was no need to run. Their job would be to occupy and rebuild the vacated German trenches, and they were loaded down with picks, shovels, rolls of wire and mallets accordingly.

At dawn on the morning of 1 July the pals consumed their iron rations, a special bar of chocolate, and a sandwich to give them energy as they went over the top, and at 7.30 a.m., when the British bombardment ceased, they rose to their feet and headed for the German lines – to be met by a devastating hail of bullets. While the pals had been training and travelling for a year, the Germans had been digging – shelving and fortifying their defences to create deep, shell-proof bunkers that they had shored up with concrete and corrugated iron. The British bombardment had claimed very few casualties, and had also made it obvious that an attack was on the way. The machine-gunners were ready.

As the Sheffield Pals moved forward, in four waves, they were mown down by a merciless fusillade. Half of the third and fourth waves did not even make it to No Man's Land. Those who reached the wire struggled vainly to cut it. To their right the Accrington Pals had greater success, actually reaching the German trenches, but they were driven back with horrendous losses – Kitchener's volunteers fell all along the Front. By sunset that day, some twenty thousand British soldiers lay dead along the Somme, with nearly forty thousand wounded – more than half the troops sent into action, and the greatest ever British loss in a single day of battle.*

The Sheffield Pals had lost more than five hundred, killed, wounded or missing, the pals of Accrington, Barnsley, Bradford, Durham and Leeds falling in similar numbers. They had signed up together, and they perished together – there was scarcely a street in the north of England that did not have a house with its blinds drawn that summer. Two days later the remnants of the Sheffield Pals were taken out of the line: their battalion had virtually ceased to exist.

In the months that followed, their numbers were rebuilt. Conscription was introduced in 1916, and the Sheffield City Battalion would go into battle again at Vimy Ridge in 1917, fighting bravely. But 'pals' they could never be again – not like the original £500-a-year businessmen and 'all sorts of clerks' who had marched to the Corn Exchange so blithely to swap their white collars for khaki.

A COUNTRY FIT FOR HEROES?
1926

EARLY IN NOVEMBER 1920, FOUR MILITARY SEARCH PARTIES set off from England to France on a gruesome mission. It was two years since the Great War had ended, and the soldiers were heading for the four principal battlefields, the Aisne, the Somme, Ypres and Arras, with orders to dig up one British body from each. They were

---

*The Somme offensive continued until 18 November 1916, with the British and the French eventually advancing some 7.5 miles (12 kilometres) – at a cost of some 420,000 British missing, dead or wounded, and a further 200,000 French casualties. German casualties were estimated at 500,000. The village of Serre remained untaken.

instructed to look for badges and scraps of uniform which identified the corpse as belonging to a British regiment, but to exclude bodies with any form of personal identification. The soldier they were looking for must be *unknown*.

Four such unidentifiable British bodies, each covered reverently with a Union Jack, were brought to a chapel in the Flanders town of St Pol, where an officer – blindfolded, according to some versions of what happened next – indicated which of the four should be placed in a waiting coffin made of oak from Hampton Court. The other three bodies were solemnly reburied, while the Unknown Warrior was taken to Boulogne, then across the English Channel, by warship, to Dover.

Silent crowds – many of them mothers, sisters and widows dressed in mourning – were waiting on the platform of every station through which the train would carry the Warrior from Dover to the capital. 'In the London suburbs,' wrote one reporter, 'there were scores of homes with back doors flung wide, light flooding out, and in the garden figures of men, women and children gazing at the great lighted train rushing past.'

On the morning of 11 November 1920, the anniversary of the Armistice* signed two years earlier, the Unknown Warrior was borne on a gun carriage drawn by six black horses to Westminster Abbey where an honour guard of one hundred VCs was waiting.†

'They buried him among the Kings,' read the text inscribed on his tomb, 'because he had done good toward God and toward his house.'** More than seven hundred thousand young Britons had died in the four years of the Great War, and a further 1.5 million had been wounded – one in ten males had vanished from an entire generation.

---

*From the Latin, *armistitium*, literally the arms-stopping, or truce, signed in France on the eleventh hour of the eleventh day of the eleventh month of 1918. This moment is marked today – as it was on 11 November 1920 – by the nationwide observance of two minutes' silence.

†Holders of the Victoria Cross, the supreme award for valour in battle, created after the Crimean War in the name of Queen Victoria (and manufactured from the metal of Russian guns captured at the siege of Sebastopol).

**Based on the Old Testament (2 Chronicles 24:16), these words were inscribed by Richard II on the tomb of his treasurer, John Waltham, Bishop of Salisbury, buried in Westminster Abbey.

Now it was the task of those who survived, said the Prime Minister David Lloyd George, 'to make Britain a fit country for heroes to live in'.

Things started off well, with a postwar boom. The old-age pension was doubled and unemployment insurance was extended to just about every worker in the country – here were the dividends of sacrifice. But Britain's once massive share of the world cake was starting to shrink. The USA's powerful intervention at the end of the war had made clear that the UK was no longer 'top nation' – and as manufacturers found their prices undercut by cheaper, better-quality goods from America and Japan, they resorted to the traditional remedies: cutting wages, demanding that their employees work longer hours for the same pay, or throwing them out of work.

In March 1926 a government commission investigating the coal industry recommended a reduction in wages. 'Not a penny off the pay, not a minute on the day,' was the militant response of the miners' union, which inspired the pit owners to their own act of solidarity – a lockout, which denied employment to all miners who were union members. The Trades Union Congress (TUC) promptly called on union members across the country to come to the support of the miners, and on 3 May that year Britain found itself in the throes of its first – and, so far, only – General Strike. The empires of Russia, Germany and Austria–Hungary had all been swept away by the social upheaval that marked the final stages of the Great War. Had revolution now come to Britain?

That was certainly the opinion of the gung-ho Chancellor of the Exchequer, Winston Churchill. He called in the army to deliver essential supplies, and also to guard the printing presses, on which he published the *British Gazette*, an aggressive government propaganda sheet. But calmer heads declined to inflame feelings. The recently founded British Broadcasting Company refused to put out official bulletins without presenting the strikers' point of view as well, while King George V used his influence behind the scenes to delay and effectively scuttle a government plan to impound union funds.

'Damned lot of revolutionaries!' exclaimed the pit owner Lord Derby when the King told him he felt sorry for the miners.

'Try living on their wages before you judge them,' was George V's response.

That proved to be the attitude of Britain as a whole. There was widespread sympathy for the miners. But people did not feel that the miner's plight, no matter how dire, justified the entire country being held to ransom. The strike may have been general, but its extent was far from universal. From the start, middle-class opinion lined up solidly behind the government, with university students driving buses and manning lorries to distribute vital supplies. After little more than a week the TUC felt compelled to call off their action, though the miners would defiantly remain out for months.

'Our old country can well be proud of itself,' wrote the King in his diary, 'as during the last nine days there has been a strike in which 4 million people have been affected, not a shot has been fired and no one killed. It shows what a wonderful people we are.'

His Majesty went too far. The General Strike did show that post-war Britain had the sense to hold back from the brink – but a land fit for heroes?

THE GREATEST HISTORY BOOK EVER

1930

TIMES WERE TOUGH IN THE EARLY 1930s. THE COLLAPSE OF the American stock market in October 1929 triggered a worldwide economic recession, the Great Depression, which hit Britain hard as a trading nation. By the end of 1930 the value of British exports had fallen by 50 per cent and unemployment had more than doubled to 2.5 million, a fifth of the country's insured workforce.

Walter Sellar and Robert Yeatman were better off than most. Having fought in the Great War (both were wounded – Yeatman was awarded the Military Cross), they met when they studied history together at Oxford. Graduating in 1922, Sellar went to work as a history teacher, while Yeatman entered the developing trade of advertising as a 'copywriter', devising snappy slogans and sales 'copy' for the Kodak camera company.

The two friends kept in touch, amusing each other with the problems they encountered in their very different careers, and Sellar's tales of the elementary mistakes that his pupils made in their history lessons prompted a brilliant idea: why not compile these schoolboy 'howlers' into a new sort of book that would not seek to impress or bewilder readers with its wealth of historical knowledge, but would, rather, amuse and even console them with its humour and its profusion of mistakes?

The result was *1066 and All That*, a slender volume of short paragraphs and humorous drawings that was first published in October 1930, went through eight more editions before the end of that year, and has remained in print ever since. If you have not read it – and even if you have – please turn to its pages as soon as you have finished this book and read the Sellar and Yeatman perspective on Woadicea, the Venomous Bead, Alfred the Cake (who 'ought never to be confused with King Arthur, equally memorable, but probably non-existent'), the Feutile System, Magna Charter and the Pheasants' Revolt, Richard Gare de Lyon, the Burglars of Calais, the Old Suspender and the Young Suspender, Katherine the Arrogant, Anne of Cloves, the Disillusion of the Monasteries, Broody Mary, the Spanish Armadillo, Shakespeare and his rhyming cutlets, the utterly memorable struggle between the Cavaliers (Wrong but Wromantic) and the Roundheads (Right but Repulsive), WilliamanMary, Rotten Burrows, the Industrial Revelation, Florence Nightingown, the Charge of the Fire Brigade, Queen Victoria's Jamboree, the Great War and the Peace to End Peace . . .

Arbitrarily classifying monarchs as 'Good Things' or 'Bad Things', Sellar and Yeatman gently lampooned the prevailing vision of history as an unstoppable progression of brave and clever actions on the way to Britain becoming 'top nation'. Their satire was so gentle at times as to pay affectionate homage to their target, but they sharpened their knives when it came to 'Justifiable Wars': *'War against Zulus. Cause: the Zulus. Zulus Exterminated. Peace with Zulus.'*

Their debunking was very much of its time, reflecting the disillusion of the 'lost generation', enticed towards destruction by promises that had proved to be empty. But their bigger point was timeless and brilliant: 'History is not what you thought,' they wrote in their Compulsory Preface (subtitled 'This means You'). '*It is what you can remember.*'

NOT CRICKET – 'BODYLINE' BOWLING WINS THE ASHES
1933

IT WAS A HOT AUGUST DAY, AND THE SHORT-PITCHED BALLS being hurled down the wicket by Yorkshire's W.E. ('Bill') Bowes were bouncing up sharply. They whistled round the ribs – and sometimes round the ears – of Douglas Jardine, Surrey's cool and lofty captain, whose head was protected by nothing more substantial than the patterned cloth of his exclusive Harlequin club cap. In 1932 it was not considered manly for cricketers to wear protective helmets.

'These things lead to reprisals,' complained Pelham 'Plum' Warner, the retired international cricketer-turned-coach, 'and when they begin, goodness knows where they will end.'

But Jardine did not complain. He liked to be challenged, and he had been thinking for some time about this aggressive style of bowling, then known as 'leg theory'. When attacking a right-handed batsman, a fast bowler would set as many as four or five fielders in a semicircle behind the batsman and to his left – the 'leg' side. He would then bowl fast 'bumpers' down the pitch, aimed more or less at the batsman's head and body, which confronted his victim with a difficult choice: he could either duck in an undignified manner, or else brandish his bat wildly in the hope the ball might end up at the boundary. Sometimes it would – but it would also bounce, quite regularly, into the hands of the waiting fielders.

Bowes and Jardine were both international players. They were due to sail that winter to Australia in an attempt to recapture the 'Ashes'* which Australia had won two years earlier, largely thanks to a phenomenal young batsman, Donald Bradman. This neat and businesslike little cricketer had notched up an average of 139 in the Ashes series of 1930 – in the Third Test at Leeds he had scored 334 in a single innings, a world Test batting record – and in 1932–3 it seemed likely he would perform even better on Australia's dusty wickets.

It was clear that England must find some way of neutralising Bradman, and Jardine reckoned that 'leg theory' was the answer. An austere and aloof character, he had been England's captain since 1931, and he knew that he had the bowlers to cause Bradman trouble. Even faster than Bowes were a strapping pair from the coalfields of Nottingham, Harold Larwood and Bill Voce, who could bowl at velocities approaching a hundred miles (160 kilometres) an hour. In the First Test, held at Sydney, Larwood's devastating speed claimed ten wickets, and prompted a local journalist to come up with a new word as he watched the Australian batsmen ducking and diving for their lives. Leg theory? Call it 'bodyline'.

The name stuck. Australia won the Second Test to level the series, but when they went in to bat in the Third Test at Adelaide ten days later, their captain W.M. Woodfull was felled by a ball from Larwood that struck him over the heart. Larwood had not been bowling 'leg theory', but for his next over – to the furious howls of the fifty-thousand-strong crowd – Jardine calmly set a threatening

---

*Following England's defeat by Australia in 1882, the *Sporting Times* published a mock obituary of English cricket which concluded: 'the body will be cremated and the ashes taken to Australia'. This prompted the burning of a cricket stump whose ashes were placed in an urn and presented to the English team next time it won. Since then the little black urn has been the trophy for which the two countries compete at cricket – though whichever side wins, the urn remains permanently at Lord's Cricket Ground in north London, headquarters of the MCC, the Marylebone Cricket Club, cricket's governing body since 1787. Until 1976 the English cricket team travelled under the name of the MCC who organised the tours.

semicircle of 'leg theory' fielders. A shaken Woodfull was dismissed for only 22. Bradman, bowled by Larwood, managed just 8.

That evening the English coach, Plum Warner, went to the Australian dressing-room to enquire after Woodfull's health. 'I don't want to speak to you, Mr Warner,' the angry captain replied. 'There are two teams out there; one is playing cricket, the other is not. It is too great a game to spoil. The matter is in your hands.'

When play resumed after the weekend, the popular little Australian wicket-keeper Bert Oldfield was knocked down by another fierce Larwood bouncer and retired hurt. Larwood had pitched to the offside, bowling to an off-side field, but as far as the Australians were concerned it was 'bodyline'. X-rays revealed a hair-line skull fracture.

'In our opinion it is unsportsmanlike,' ran an indignant cable from the Australian Board of Control to the MCC in London. 'Bodyline bowling has assumed such proportions as to menace the best interest of the game.' Whipped up by the press, feelings became so intense as to prompt talks between the governments of Britain and Australia – the harmony of the Empire seemed at stake.

To start with, the MCC backed their captain. They cabled Jardine their congratulations when the Third Test was won (England won the whole series 4–1, cutting Bradman's average down to a relatively fallible 56.57), and they forced the Australians to withdraw the word 'unsportsmanlike'.

But feelings changed, and so did the rules. 'Leg theory' was outlawed – captains could place no more than two fielders where Jardine placed four or five – and when Australia came to play in England in 1934, it was felt that sacrificial victims were required. The MCC requested that Harold Larwood apologise for his bowling in 1932–3, which he stoutly refused to do since he had simply bowled as instructed by his captain. So England's only bowler ever to top the bowling table five times would never play again for his country, while Jardine, aged thirty-three and at the height of his abilities, felt that the time had come to take a diplomatic retirement from Test cricket.

'Bodyline' bowling – hurling, or more usually bouncing the ball at the batsman – still remains a legal tactic in cricket. You may not do it with a 'leg theory' field set behind the batter, nor may you do it too often – law 42 on Fair and Unfair Play sets out the factors that the umpires must consider. But it remains the great divide between the boys' game of cricket and the girls' game of rounders (or baseball, as it is known in the USA): in rounders/baseball the pitcher is penalised if his ball hits the batter, with the statistics recording HBP (hit by pitch).

When, in the summer of 2005, England wanted to win back the Ashes, they turned to Andrew 'Freddie' Flintoff, a dashing batsman and fast bowler who peppered his deliveries with short-pitched balls that shot up fiercely at Australian bodies and heads. It was seventy years after the era of Jardine and Larwood, and the batsmen were now wearing helmets, but 'bodyline' could still get the job done – England won back the Ashes, and the award for player of the series went to Flintoff (24 wickets, 402 runs, 'hits' not recorded).

EDWARD THE ABDICATOR
1936

'THE MORE I THINK OF IT ALL,' WROTE EDWARD, PRINCE OF Wales, shortly after the First World War, 'the more certain I am that . . . the day for Kings & Princes is past, monarchies are out-of-date.' The Prince was touring the Empire to thank countries like Canada and Australia for their help to Britain during the war, but while publicly smiling, he was privately miserable. 'What an unnatural life for a poor little boy of 25,' he wrote after a busy day of shaking hands and posing for photographs. 'I do get so fed up with it & despondent about it sometimes, & begin to feel like "resigning"!!'

Handsome and charming, with a winning smile and a taste for cocktails and jazz, Edward Prince of Wales was the first young British royal to be a media celebrity. He was cheered and fêted wherever he travelled: his brightly coloured sweaters and his snazzy plus-fours* were copied as the latest fashion statements. But the more famous he grew, the more hollow and valueless he felt. 'How I loathe my job now,' he wrote, 'and this press-"puffed" empty "succès". I feel I'm through with it and long to die.'

The Prince resented the intrusion of the media. 'I can put up with a certain amount of contact with officials and newspapers on official trips,' he explained to one of his staff. 'It's when they get in on my private life that I want to pull out a gun and kill.' He was a young man in pain, the world's first and most spectacular case of celebrity burnout.

The Prince got little sympathy from his gruff father King George V, who had steered the British monarchy through the years of war and revolution that had brought down two European emperors and eight ruling sovereigns. In July 1917 the King renounced his family's German titles and dignities deriving from the House of Hanover and adopted a new, thoroughly British-sounding name, the House of Windsor. At the same time he had reinvented the style of the monarchy, with more emphasis on duty, going out to meet the public and 'setting a good example'. When the Prime Minister, Lloyd George, complained that heavy drinking among munitions workers was hampering the supply of ammunition to the Front, the King banned alcohol from royal occasions, offering his guests water, lemonade or ginger beer for three years until the war ended.†

The old King was particularly unhappy at his eldest son's mistresses – a series of glamorous married women with whom the Prince was seen around the nightclubs of London. British newspapers

---

*'Plus-fours' were loose knickerbockers often worn by golfers, deriving their name from the extra four inches (about 10 cm) of cloth required for the overhang at the knee.
†The King did not enjoy the sacrifice, which was greeted with ribaldry rather than respect, particularly since the announcement of the self-denying edict from Windsor was followed by the words: 'The Earl of Rosebery and the Rt. Hon. A.J. Balfour, M.P., have left the Castle.' Lloyd George himself did not stop serving alcohol in Downing Street.

discreetly looked the other way, but the disapproving father prophesied trouble. 'After I am dead,' he said gloomily, 'the boy will ruin himself in twelve months.'

George V died in January 1936, and at first Britain welcomed the modern style of the new King Edward VIII. Unlike his father, who had always refused to fly, Edward liked to travel by aeroplane, and, in another daring departure, would sometimes appear in public without a hat. But in December the Empire learned to its horror that his modern tastes extended to a tough and wise-cracking American girlfriend, Mrs Wallis Warfield Simpson, who had already divorced one husband and was in the process of divorcing Mr Simpson, her second.

Many people liked the fact she was American – the newspapers, who finally broke their silence five weeks after Mrs Simpson appeared in the divorce court, expressed their approval of her nationality. But 'two husbands living' presented an insuperable obstacle to a society that viewed divorce as a moral and social catastrophe. How could a double divorcee be bowed and curtsied to, or represent Britain to the world? For a start, royal etiquette prohibited divorced or even separated persons from being received at court.

After canvassing his cabinet colleagues and opinion around the Empire, the Prime Minister Stanley Baldwin told the King he would have to choose between his throne and Mrs Simpson – and Edward VIII did not hesitate. Whenever the King talked of Wallis, Baldwin later told his family, his face wore 'such a look of beauty as might have lighted the face of a young knight who had caught a glimpse of the Holy Grail'. On 11 December the King formally abdicated the throne, and gave his reason in a live broadcast to the nation. 'You must believe me when I tell you,' he said in a voice heavy with emotion, 'that I have found it impossible to carry the heavy burden of responsibility and to discharge my duties as King as I would wish to do without the help and support of the woman I love.'

While Edward's supporters seized joyously on the L-word, proclaiming his sacrifice the love story of the century, his critics found the romantic talk vulgar. They blamed Mrs Simpson, the wicked woman who had led the King astray. But if, sixteen years earlier, Edward had been genuine when he talked of 'resigning' from his 'unnatural' and 'out-of-date' job, then Mrs Simpson was not the reason for the abdication. She was the excuse he had finally found – his blessed release from the fearful and empty destiny of being royal.

PEACE FOR OUR TIME! –
MR CHAMBERLAIN TAKES A PLANE
1938

NEVILLE CHAMBERLAIN WAS A BIRDWATCHER – HE WOULD get up at five in the morning to study the songs of the various species. He knew more Shakespeare than any other British Prime Minister. A lover of music, he inspired the foundation of the Birmingham Symphony Orchestra, while also campaigning to move the city's 'working classes from their hideous and depressing surroundings to cleaner, brighter and more wholesome dwellings'. He was, in short, a thoroughly civilised, decent and well-meaning man. But it was his misfortune to believe that Adolf Hitler could be trusted.

When Chamberlain flew off to Germany to meet Hitler for the first time, on 15 September 1938, he quoted Hotspur in *Henry IV Part I* – he hoped, he said, to 'pluck from this nettle, danger, this flower, safety'. The danger went back to the Treaty of Versailles that redrew the map of Europe after the First World War, seeking to cut Germany and Austria down to size. Hitler's ambition, it seemed, was to reverse Versailles – the German people, he said, needed living space (*Lebensraum*) – and he had embarked on an unapologetic programme of rearmament and expansion: in 1936 German troops reoccupied the demilitarised Rhineland; in March 1938 they marched into Austria; now, just six months later, they were threatening to occupy Czechoslovakia in order to 'liberate' the three million German-speaking inhabitants of the Sudetenland, that part of the country bordering on Germany.

It was the first time that Chamberlain had ever flown any distance – perhaps it was an expression of his anxiety that he gripped his umbrella tightly as he got on and off the plane. It was also the first example of what would later be known as 'shuttle diplomacy', for he travelled to and from Germany three times between 15 and 30 September, negotiating with Germany, France, Italy and, nominally at least, with Czechoslovakia, in search of a peaceful solution. It was 'horrible, fantastic, incredible', he declared in one broadcast when he got home, that Britain might be drawn into war because 'of a quarrel in a far-away country between people of whom we know nothing'. The Royal Navy was mobilised, gas masks were distributed, and air-raid trenches were dug in Hyde Park.

Britain had no treaty obligation to defend Czechoslovakia. But France did, and if she was drawn into war with Germany, then Britain would almost certainly need to go to her defence. It was a rerun of 1914 – and less than a quarter of a century later the tragic slaughter of the Great War loomed very large in people's thinking. Britain was not militarily ready for war. More important, she was not psychologically ready to repeat the pain and sacrifice.

When Chamberlain returned from his third trip, this time to a hurriedly convened conference in Munich, he brought the news that people wanted to hear – 'peace with honour. I believe it is peace for our time.' Britain and France had forced Czechoslovakia to hand over the Sudetenland to Germany in return for a pledge of peace from Hitler, who had signed a separate declaration of friendship with Britain. This Anglo-German Declaration, said Chamberlain, was 'symbolic of the desire of our two peoples never to go to war with one another again', and he waved the piece of paper enthusiastically as he stepped down from his plane.

Britain went mad with relief. Frantic crowds massed along the road into London. Chamberlain, said the Scottish socialist James Maxton, had done 'something that the mass of the common people in the world wanted done'. He was received by the new King George VI on the balcony of Buckingham Palace and applauded by every newspaper except the left-wing *Reynolds News*. Downing Street was flooded with umbrellas sent by people expressing their gratitude to the Prime Minister who had brought them peace.

Munich was the fruit of 'appeasement', a foreign policy that successive British governments had been developing since 1931, based on the feeling that the Treaty of Versailles had saddled several countries – and Germany in particular – with legitimate grievances that threatened the stability of Europe. Anthony Eden, Foreign Secretary from 1935 to 1938, liked to point out the primary meaning of 'appease' in the dictionary – 'to bring peace, to settle strife'.

But peace depended on both sides sticking to what they had promised, and Adolf Hitler considered himself too clever and powerful for that. Intent on building his Third Reich,* he wanted the whole of Czechoslovakia – and more. In March 1939 German troops occupied Prague, then marched into Poland at the end of the summer.

'Everything I have worked for, everything that I have hoped for, everything that I have believed in my public life, has crashed into ruins,' said Chamberlain on 3 September, as he announced that Britain and Germany were now at war. When Hitler, following his conquest of Poland, suggested a European peace conference, Chamberlain rejected the idea with scorn. No reliance could be placed, he told his sister Ida, on anything the man said: 'the only chance of peace is the disappearance of Hitler and that is what we are working for'.

Chamberlain did not head the battle for long. In the spring of 1940 an Allied attempt to oust German troops from Norway failed ignominiously, and though it had been the project of the First Lord of the Admiralty, Winston Churchill, it was the architect of Munich who got the blame. Neville Chamberlain resigned as Prime Minister on 10 May 1940 and died later that year, an object of scorn. Appeasement became a dirty word, with connotations of treachery and cowardice, and the memory of Munich hangs over politics to this day: it was used to justify the British attack on Suez in 1956, and, more recently, the Anglo-American invasion of Iraq.

*Germany's first Reich, or empire, was the Holy Roman Empire, the confederation of German and central European states that dominated much of Europe in the Middle Ages. The second was the unified nation state of Germany that lasted from 1871 to 1918. Hitler's ambition was to create a *Drittes Reich*, a Third Empire, larger and longer-lived than either.

With hindsight we can see that Chamberlain was mistaken in trusting Hitler – he only postponed the inevitable by a year. But the cheers that greeted his piece of paper in September 1938 suggested he was far from alone in his wishful thinking. And was he really so wrong to try to stop a conflict which, as it turned out, would claim the lives of more than fifty million people?

DUNKIRK – BRITAIN'S ARMY SAVED BY THE LITTLE BOATS

1940

THE PORT OF DUNKIRK LIES ON THE WINDSWEPT northernmost coast of France, surrounded by gently rolling sand dunes. To the west, just over the horizon, lies England, and it was in hopes of somehow crossing the Channel and getting back home that a quarter of a million defeated British troops (along with some 120,000 French) came straggling through the grey-green grass at the end of May 1940.

They had only their rifles and whatever they could carry on their backs. They had forsaken their tanks and trucks and field guns. The equipment and supplies of two entire armies lay scattered behind them across the lowlands of Belgium – abandoned in haste as the British and French headed for the sea. On 10 May Hitler's troops had launched a massive, rolling onslaught through the Netherlands, Belgium and Luxembourg. The Germans called it *Blitzkrieg*, 'lightning war', and it had smashed open the route to Paris.

By coincidence, 10 May was the day on which, in London, Neville Chamberlain had resigned as Prime Minister, to be succeeded by Winston Churchill. 'I have nothing to offer,' he told the ministers who joined his Cabinet, 'but blood, toil, tears and sweat. We have before us an ordeal of the most grievous kind.' France was lost, and now Hitler had the prospect of taking nearly a quarter of a million British soldiers captive. On the 26th Churchill ordered the navy to head for Dunkirk, with the RAF overhead to give cover.

The problem was how to load the fleeing soldiers off the beaches, since the shallow coastal waters meant that the navy's destroyers and transport vessels had to anchor a quarter of a mile or more offshore. So the call went out to the yacht clubs and seaside resorts of southeast England for the help of a second navy: paddle-steamers and motor-boats, fishing smacks, tugs, yachts, lifeboats and 'All aboard the *Skylark!*' pleasure-boats – just about anything that would float. This oddly assorted flotilla, the 'Armada of the Little Ships', embarked from England on a mercifully calm sea and headed for the beaches of Dunkirk.

Watching from the dunes, a British artillery officer described the scene:

From the margin of the sea, at fairly wide intervals, three long thin black lines protruded into the water, conveying the effect of low wooden breakwaters. These were lines of men, standing in pairs behind one another far out into the water, waiting in queues till boats arrived to transport them, a score or so at a time, to the steamers and warships that were filling up with the last survivors.

Behind them Dunkirk was in flames: 'the whole front was one long continuous line of blazing buildings, a high wall of fire, roaring and darting in tongues of flame, with the smoke pouring upwards'. Above, in the smoke-filled sky, British planes fought it out with the Stuka dive-bombers of the Luftwaffe (the German air force, literally 'air weapon'). 'One bomber that had been particularly offensive,' wrote C. H. Lightoller, a retired naval officer who had sailed his yacht *Sundowner* across the Channel, 'itself came under the notice of one of our fighters, and suddenly plunged vertically into the sea just about fifty yards astern of us. It was the only time any man ever raised his voice above a conversational tone, but as that big black bomber hit the water, they raised an echoing cheer.'

For nine days and nights the evacuation continued round the clock.

Churchill had predicted that 30,000 men might be lifted off; Admiral Ramsay, the officer in charge of the rescue, hoped for 45,000. In the event, virtually everyone who made it to the Dunkirk beaches, some 330,000 men – 220,000 British, 110,000 French and Belgian – was miraculously saved.

Churchill was rightly cautious in his relief: 'Wars are not won by evacuations,' he warned the House of Commons. But saving the vast bulk of the professional army provided Britain with the practical means to keep on fighting – and, more vitally, gave the country a new sense of purpose. In certain respects, the story of the little boats was exaggerated: many had sailed for money, a good number were commanded by active naval officers, and it was the 'big ships' of the Royal Navy that transported the vast majority of the soldiers home.

But if it was a myth, it was a necessary and inspiring myth, symbolising how ordinary people could make a difference. In the weeks that followed, over a million men enrolled in the Local Defence Volunteers; roadblocks and concrete pillboxes sprang up all over the countryside; signposts were removed or craftily rearranged to fool invaders; and the coast was wreathed with barbed wire. 'We shall fight on the beaches,' proclaimed Churchill, 'we shall fight on the landing grounds, we shall fight in the fields and in the streets, we shall fight in the hills; we shall never surrender.'

Britain had drifted rather vaguely through the opening months of what had been known as the 'phoney war'. Now she started to believe in herself – and helped others to believe in her too. Previously detached, America removed the restrictions on getting involved in the European conflict: half a million rifles were dispatched to Britain in the first weeks of June 1940, for, as the *New York Times* explained to its readers, the issues at stake had been made clear at Dunkirk:

In that harbour, such a hell on earth as never blazed before, at the end of a lost battle, the rags and blemishes that had hidden the soul of democracy fell away. There, beaten but unconquered, she faced the enemy, this shining thing in the souls of free men, which Hitler cannot command. It is in the great tradition of democracy. It is a future. It is victory.

BATTLE OF BRITAIN –
THE FEW AND THE MANY
1940

WHEN HITLER HEARD IN THE MIDDLE OF JUNE 1940 THAT the French government was ready to sue for peace, he instructed them to send their negotiators to the town of Compiègne in northern France. This was where Germany's generals had signed the Armistice in November 1918 at the end of the First World War, in a railway carriage that had been triumphantly preserved in the local museum. Hitler had the carriage taken out of the museum and met the French inside it on the 22nd of that month. After they had signed their humiliating surrender, handing over two-thirds of France to German occupation, the Führer (leader) had the railway carriage taken back to Berlin as his own trophy of war, then ordered that the Armistice site be obliterated.

After Dunkirk, no one could doubt that Hitler was planning some equally gleeful humiliation for London. He ordered his generals to start planning an invasion, codenamed *Seelöwe* (sea lion), to be preceded by a massive aerial attack that would wipe out the RAF. The staff of Hermann Goering, commander of the Luftwaffe, reckoned they could deal with RAF Fighter Command in four days or so of pitched battle, then spend four weeks bombing Britain's major cities and munitions factories into oblivion.

On 10 July the Germans put the first stage of their strategy into practice – dive-bombing merchant ships in the English Channel: apart from sinking vital cargoes, their plan was to lure British fighter planes out to give battle. Since the Luftwaffe probably had three times more planes than the RAF, it would be only a matter of time before Britain was defenceless.

Winston Churchill conjured up another of his ringing declamations in tribute to the airmen who took part in the great battle that followed. 'Never in the field of human conflict was so much owed by so many to so few,' he declared on 20 August, and the young heroes of the RAF who were 'scrambling' as many as five times a day into the skies above southern England that summer were certainly 'few' in number – no more than two thousand or so. But every fighter pilot depended on a massive and complex pyramid of support staff – radar technicians, the observer corps, searchlight and barrage-balloon operators, chart plotters, telephone operators, telephone engineers, dispatch riders, signallers and runway repair crews, not to mention the mechanics who produced, maintained and repaired the fighter planes that enabled the Few to win their dogfights. The inside story of the Battle of Britain was the triumph of the Many.

This formidably efficient back-up organisation, unparalleled in aerial warfare to that point, was the work of Air Marshal Sir Hugh Dowding, a cagey character generally disliked by his fellow airmen, who nicknamed him 'Stuffy'. In fact, 'Stuffy' had some most original and unstuffy personal interests that included theosophy* and a belief in fairies, angels, flying saucers and the possibility of intelligent communication between the living and the dead. As one of the first pilots in the Royal Flying Corps (which became the RAF) and a squadron commander in the First World War, he had experimented with Marconi's discovery that messages could be transmitted without connecting cables. He claimed to be 'the first person, certainly in England if not the world, to listen to a wireless telephone message from the air', and he had no doubt that technical superiority was the first principle of aerial warfare.

Dowding's second principle was not to risk expensive machines and the lives of trained airmen unnecessarily. So when the Germans started their *Kanalkampf* in July, dive-bombing in the Channel, he refused to be tempted. He sent up a few fighters, but kept his main squadrons in reserve. Earlier that summer he had successfully persuaded Churchill not to send too many precious Spitfires to the hopeless cause of saving France from the Germans. The secret of success in the coming battle for Britain would be to keep planes in the sky.

*Theosophy was a movement seeking a universal truth common to all religions. Among its adherents was Annie Besant (see pp.398–400).

In this key objective Dowding was aided by another abrasive but effective character, Lord Beaverbrook, the Canadian proprietor of the *Daily Express* whom Churchill brought into his Cabinet in May 1940 as Minister of Aircraft Production. Manufacture was already running smoothly – 163 new Spitfires came out of the factories that August, along with 251 Hurricanes. But in three short months Beaverbrook dramatically stepped up the maintenance and repair of existing aircraft: 35 per cent of all planes issued to pilots in the Battle of Britain were repaired rather than new; 61 per cent of all damaged planes were returned to active service, and the remaining 39 per cent were 'cannibalised' for spare parts.

The Germans could not match this turn-around rate – as they could not match the planes themselves. The Supermarine Spitfire and the Hawker Hurricane were highly manoeuvrable 'eight-gun' fighters (they had four machine-guns mounted in each wing) and they rapidly disposed of the once-feared Stuka dive-bomber. They also proved more than equal to Germany's best fighter, the Messerschmitt 109, that was handicapped by low fuel capacity: if a Messerschmitt got to London it could fight for only ten minutes before having to turn tail and head back to base.

No one realised it at the time, but from mid-August to mid-September, each day of the Battle of Britain saw the RAF lose significantly fewer planes than the Luftwaffe – 832 in total to Germany's 1268. On 17 September Hitler postponed the invasion of Britain, deciding that Russia offered a more attractive target, and at the end of October he effectively admitted defeat when he switched from daytime fighter attacks to night-time bombing.

A few days later, on 9 November 1940, Neville Chamberlain died, a victim of bowel cancer that spared him long enough to see the results of a far-sighted policy. As Chancellor of the Exchequer through the rocky years of the early 1930s, Chamberlain had insisted that the bulk of defence spending be allocated to aerial rearmament, and had raised income tax to five shillings (25p) in the £ to pay for it. So behind the famous Few and the anonymous Many, as organised in the complex back-up system devised by 'Stuffy' Dowding, was the unlikely and unwarlike figure of Neville Chamberlain.

CODE-MAKING, CODE-BREAKING – 'THE LIFE THAT I HAVE'

1943

L EO MARKS WAS SOMETHING OF A LONER AT SCHOOL – HE loved to retreat into his own private world of word puzzles and codes. So as Britain fought its intelligence war with Germany, the young code enthusiast was an obvious candidate for Bletchley Park, the mansion 'somewhere in the country' that was the centre of the nation's code-breakers. Bletchley's great coup was its deciphering, early in the war, of the German 'Enigma' encoding machine that gave Britain advance knowledge of enemy war plans.

To his initial disappointment, the 22-year-old was the one member of his induction course who did not move on to Bletchley. He was sent instead to the London offices of SOE, the Special Operations Executive, which organised the resistance movements behind German lines, following Churchill's order to 'set Europe ablaze'. Leo's job was not to break codes, but to create them for the agents that SOE was parachuting behind the enemy lines, and he rapidly rose to become SOE's head of communications. In his few hours off work, he met and fell in love with Ruth, a nurse who was training for air ambulance work – only to lose her in 1943 when she was killed in an air crash.

Distraught with grief, the code-maker went up on to the nearest roof, and as he gazed up at the stars he imagined Ruth among them, mentally transmitting to her a poem:

> *The life that I have*
> *Is all that I have*
> *And the life that I have*
> *Is yours.*

The love that I have
Of the life that I have
Is yours and yours and yours.

A sleep I shall have
A rest I shall have
Yet death will be but a pause.

For the peace of my years
In the long green grass
Will be yours and yours and yours.

A few months later, in the spring of 1944, Leo was organising the codes for Violette Szabo, a young French resistance worker who had been working under cover in German-occupied France, helping to blow up bridges and railway lines to interrupt the Nazis' supply lines. Violette was due to be parachuted back into enemy territory to help prepare the ground for D-Day, the Allied invasion of northern France, but she was having trouble remembering her code. Every secret agent had to memorise a verse whose letters created a code that was unique to them, and Violette kept forgetting hers – until, in desperation, Leo produced the lines that he had written for Ruth.

'I could learn this in a few minutes,' she said, and when Leo tested her next day, her codes were word-perfect. As a token of gratitude, she presented him with the perfect present for a code-master – a miniature chess set.

Later that summer SOE received news that Violette had been ambushed in France and transported to the German labour camp of Ravensbrück. A few weeks later came worse news. After brutal torture by the Gestapo, she had been executed – shot through the back of the head as she knelt, holding hands with two other captured female agents.

After the war, Violette Szabo's life story was made into a film, *Carve Her Name with Pride*, and many thousands of cinema-goers were moved by her code poem 'The Life That I Have'.

'Dear Code-Master,' wrote one eight-year-old boy in his own personally devised code, which Leo had to work hard to decipher. 'She was very brave. Please, how does the poem work? I'm going to be a spy when I grow up.'

A covering letter from the boy's father explained that his son was desperately ill, so Leo sent the invalid a present – Violette's own chess set, with an invitation, when he got better, to come and meet some of her fellow agents. The SOE's master cryptographer composed his reply in the eight-year-old's personal code, and was delighted to hear that his letter had helped the child rally for a month. The miniature chess set and the memorable code poem were at his bedside when he died.

VOICE OF THE PEOPLE
1945

WINSTON CHURCHILL WROTE ALL HIS OWN SPEECHES. He would spend as many as six or eight hours polishing and rehearsing his words to get the impact just right – and it was worth the effort. 'Let us therefore brace ourselves to our duties,' he declaimed in Parliament on 18 June 1940, 'and so bear ourselves that, if the British Empire and its Commonwealth last for a thousand years men will still say, "This was their finest hour."'

He cracked jokes: 'When I warned them [the French government] that Britain would fight on alone whatever they did,' he related at the end of December 1941, 'their generals told their Prime Minister and his divided Cabinet, "In three weeks England will have her neck wrung like a chicken." Some chicken! [Pause] Some neck!'

By the beginning of 1942 Britain had been at war for more than two years and the tide of fortune was starting to change. Three weeks earlier, on 7 December 1941, Japan had bombed the US fleet at anchor in Pearl Harbor on the island of Oahu in Hawaii, bringing America actively on to Britain's side. At the same time the USSR, as a result of Hitler's decision to attack her earlier that year, became an unlikely but extremely powerful ally. 'So we had won after all,' Churchill later wrote in his memoirs. 'We should not be wiped out. Our history would not come to an end.'

Germany and Japan would continue to fight – peace was still nearly four years away. But in 1942 people were already dreaming about the life they wanted when war was over, and their dreams were expressed by the social reformer William Beveridge, who took advantage of a government invitation to inquire into the social services to prepare a report that was effectively a blueprint for a cradle-to-grave 'welfare state'. After the war, proposed Beveridge, a free health service, family allowances, and universal social insurance should produce 'freedom from want by securing to each a minimum income sufficient for subsistence'.

Published in December that year, the Beveridge Report received a cool response from Churchill, but it struck a chord with the war-weary public. Six hundred and thirty-five thousand copies were sold – the best-selling government White Paper in history.*

Churchill would have done well to heed the sales figures. On 8 May 1945 he stood on the balcony of Buckingham Palace alongside King George VI to celebrate VE (Victory in Europe) Day, a solid-gold national hero. Britain had stood up to the tyranny of Hitler's Germany, and the credit for surviving and meeting that challenge was very personally Churchill's: his was the vision and resolution, his were the sweet and inspiring words.

But in the election that followed, the vision and the sweetness abandoned the great orator. 'My friends, I must tell you,' he said in his opening broadcast of the campaign, attacking the plans of the Labour Party, 'that a Socialist policy is abhorrent to the British ideas of freedom.' From statesman to politician again, in one short step. 'Some form of Gestapo', he claimed, would be needed to enforce the apparatus of state control that went with the Labour Party's plans to take over national resources.

---

*'White Papers' set out the proposals of government departments for future policy following a process of consultation and research. Originally they were bound with white covers.

This language horrified those who shared the vision of William Beveridge, but it would take some time to discover the nation's verdict. The votes of British servicemen all over the world had to be gathered and counted, so there was a three-week interlude between polling day on 5 July and the announcement of the result. On the 15th Churchill flew to Potsdam, outside Berlin, for a victory conference with the new US President Harry Truman and Joseph Stalin, the leader of Soviet Russia, then flew back to London for the verdict – to discover on the 26th that he had been defeated, and catastrophically. Labour had won power in a landslide victory of 393 seats to 213. The British people wanted change, and after the hardships and sacrifices of war, they liked the sound of the welfare state. Churchill had outlived his usefulness.

The Potsdam Conference was still going on, and was not due to finish until 2 August. So it was the quiet and modest Clement Attlee, leader of the Labour Party and now Prime Minister, who flew out to Berlin to represent Britain in the final discussions. Truman, who was accustomed to American elections at regular, preplanned intervals, and Stalin, who was accustomed to no elections at all, must have been rather confused by Churchill's rapid disappearance and replacement. But that was how democracy had come to work in Britain.

DECODING THE SECRET OF LIFE
1953

YOUNG FRANCIS CRICK WAS ALWAYS ASKING QUESTIONS. To keep him quiet, his mother gave him a children's encyclopae-dia, and it was through reading what the encyclopaedia had to say about galaxies and the hundred trillion cells in the human body, amongst other things, that he decided to become a scientist. It worried him, however, that science had already made so many discoveries. Would there be any left for him?

'Don't you worry,' said his mother. 'When you grow up there will be plenty left for you to discover.'

Crick was twenty-three years old when Britain went to war in 1939. Since he was doing research work in physics, he was co-opted by the Admiralty to help develop magnetic and acoustic mines. Then, with the return to peace, he went to Cambridge, keen to apply the precise techniques of physics and chemistry to the big questions of biology – what is life, for example, and how is it passed on?

'It was generally accepted,' he later recalled, 'that almost every cell has a complete set of instructions located in its genes which determines how the cell grows, metabolizes and functions in relation to other cells. It was also thought that these genes reside on the cell's chromosomes, which were known to consist of both protein and deoxyribonucleic acid [DNA].'

DNA was a mystery to most scientists, but in 1951 Crick met a young American geneticist, James D. Watson, who shared his hunch that DNA was the key to unlocking the identity of living organisms. With his shirt hanging out and his shoelaces often untied, Watson was the archetypal boffin. He arrived in Cambridge with a crew cut, but soon let his hair grow long and straggly so as not to be mistaken for a US airman, of which there were many in East Anglia – after the war they had stayed on at their bases to confront the new threat of Soviet Russia.

Crick and Watson got their break when Maurice Wilkins, a bio-chemist from King's College, London, showed them the X-ray diffraction image of DNA that he had made with his colleague Rosalind Franklin. This showed a coil, or helix – a key feature of the molecule. Wilkins and Franklin were on the brink of identifying DNA themselves, but they did not work as a team. Franklin felt that Wilkins patronised her, and she retaliated by refusing to show him her work.

Crick and Watson, meanwhile, struck creative sparks off each other in a wild and exploratory working partnership. When one suggested an idea, the other would try to shoot it down, but without malice. They were building huge improvised models of how they imagined the molecule to be, working with brass rods, metal cutouts, drinking straws and plasticine, like children in a preschool playgroup. They would fiddle with the model, argue a bit, have a cup of tea, move the rods some more – until suddenly, on the morning of Saturday 28 February, 1953, hey presto!

'We've discovered the secret of life!' announced Crick as he and Watson walked into the Eagle, an old coaching inn in the middle of Cambridge, where they liked to take lunch. Their breakthrough had been to visualise DNA as a double helix – a winding spiral staircase, each side of which reflected the other. The balustrades were the complementary components of DNA, held together by the rungs, which were hydrogen bonds. If the rungs were broken in two, the ladder could peel apart, with each side becoming the template for a new ladder. So DNA could go on unzipping itself and copying itself indefinitely.

The Englishman and the American announced their discovery in the journal *Nature* that April with more modesty than they had displayed in the public bar of the Eagle. 'It has not escaped our notice,' they wrote in what has been described as the greatest scientific understatement of all time, 'that the specific pairing we have postulated immediately suggests a possible copying mechanism for the genetic material.' In fact, the article had little popular impact. Britain was preoccupied with the forthcoming coronation of the young Queen Elizabeth II, and it was another nine years before Crick and Watson were awarded the Nobel Prize for their discovery, along with Maurice Wilkins (Franklin would have been honoured as well, had she not died of cancer in 1958).

Nowadays everyone is aware of DNA – murderers and rapists are trapped by its evidence, sheep are cloned with its technology, and we worry about the effects of genetic modification on our crops. It is possible for each of us to predict our own personal chances of long life or of obesity, demystifying what used to be matters of providence, fate, or even morality. Religion, philosophy and the law have yet to adapt to this: if we happen to be genetically programmed to eat, procreate or lose our temper to an excessive degree, how can our greed, lust or anger be condemned as sins or crimes? 'It wasn't me, Guv: it was my DNA.'

History itself will have to be rewritten as DNA research changes our perspective on how the motors of human personality and achievement operate. To paraphrase *1066 and All That*, Crick and Watson's extraordinary discovery confronts us with 'the cause of nowadays', and that seems a good point at which to end this particular history book. Indeed, it brings us full circle. In 1997 Oxford University's Institute of Molecular Medicine extracted mitochondrial DNA material from the tooth cavity of Cheddar Man, Britain's oldest complete skeleton, who lived in the caves of the Cheddar Gorge, Somerset, some 7000 years BC and came to a violent end (see p. 3). Mitochondrial DNA is inherited unchanged in the maternal line, and having taken swabs from the cheeks of twenty local people, the Oxford scientists announced that they had found a direct match, a blood relation across nine thousand years and some four hundred generations – Adrian Targett, aged forty-two, a local history teacher who lived less than a mile from the caves. Sometimes the past is closer than we think.

EXPLORING THE ORIGINAL SOURCES

I hope this book leaves you with a curiosity, perhaps even a passion, for the original sources on which our history is based: Julius Caesar's thoughts as he first caught sight of the white cliffs; Bede and his sparrow; Orderic Vitalis describing the survivors of the *White Ship* clinging to the wreckage in the night sea; Piers the Ploughman; Fanny Burney undergoing her operation without anaesthetic; William Howard Russell listening to the champing of bits of the Light Brigade. These centuries-old writings need not be intimidating. In the 'Further Reading' pages that follow, you can find many books that contain the full version of these texts, in translation where necessary, and often in paperback.

But in recent years we have gained a still more accessible resource. Most of the great historical texts are now available, free and online. On www.georgetown.edu/faculty/ballc/oe/oe-texts.html, for example, you can find an index of sites that host electronic editions of Old English texts, translations and images of Anglo-Saxon manuscripts. By clicking on the listed links you can access complete versions of works like Bede's *Ecclesiastical History*, *Piers the Ploughman* and various versions of *Beowulf* – your own desktop digital scriptorium. The Online Medieval and Classical Library at the University of California at Berkeley, www.omacl.org, includes the complete run-through of the Anglo-Saxon Chronicle. At Fordham University, the Internet History Sourcebooks project, www.fordham.edu/halsall, covers ancient, medieval and modern history, arranging all the texts by topic. Look under, say, 'slavery', or 'Roman sports and games', and you can find a selection of texts on each subject.

Tap in www.oxforddnb.com, and you will gain access to a truly great British enterprise – the *Oxford Dictionary of National Biography*, a compilation of 55,557 British lives, male and female, famous and infamous, brave, tragic, comic – and sometimes downright disgraceful. In bound, paper form, the ODNB comprises sixty volumes. Electronically, it supports a website which offers unrivalled search facilities – you can look up everyone who has the same name as you, for example, the same birthday, or who ever lived in the same locality. It offers you a 'biography of the day' and full-colour illustrations.

You will be lucky if you get the ODNB for Christmas. It costs over £7000. But most public libraries now stock it or have electronic access to it, so if your local library does not, you should ask that they do so without delay. Thanks to electronic access, I have been able to rummage in this extraordinary treasure trove, using the reader number on my ticket to my own local library in Westminster. Sitting at home at my computer, at any hour of the day or night, I have been able to access the documented stories of our greatest heroes and villains, including the mythical ones – King Arthur, Robin Hood, Ned Ludd, Captain Swing and the Unknown Warrior.

The Institute of Historical Research at London University offers a comprehensive index to every serious history website you can imagine: www.history.ac.uk/ihr/resources/index.html. For a beginner – especially someone interested in their family history – the best place to go is the appealing and diverse site offered by the National Archives, www.nationalarchives.gov.uk. The BBC offers additional material to its excellent history programming on www.bbc.co.uk, and it is always worth checking out Spartacus on www.spartacus.schoolnet.co.uk and the History Learning Site: www.historylearningsite.co.uk. Go to the History Place, www.historyplace.com/speeches, and you will discover a collection of memorable orations, from Elizabeth I's Armada speech, to Winston Churchill's 'Blood, Toil, Tears and Sweat'.

Lege Feliciter, as the Venerable Bede would say – May you read happily! And if you are in search of some old-fashioned words on paper, try these excellent general histories:

GENERAL HISTORIES OF ENGLAND

Ackroyd, Peter, *Albion: The Origins of the British Imagination* (London, Chatto & Windus), 2002.

Brewer's Dictionary of Phrase and Fable, Millennium Edition (London, Cassell), 2001.

Carey, John (ed.), *The Faber Book of Reportage* (London, Faber and Faber), 1987.

Churchill, Winston S., *A History of the English-speaking Peoples*, 4 volumes (London, Cassell), 2002.

Davies, Norman, *The Isles: A History* (London, Papermac), 2000.

Diamond, Jared, *Guns, Germs and Steel* (London, Vintage), 1998.

Dickens, Charles, *A Child's History of England*, (Oxford, Oxford University Press), 1998.

Ekwall, Eilert, *The Concise Oxford Dictionary of English Place Names* (Oxford, Clarendon Press), 1960.

Fernández-Armesto, Felipe, *Truth – A History and a Guide for the Perplexed* (London, Black Swan), 1998.

The Oxford Companion to British History, rev. and ed. John Cannon (Oxford, Oxford University Press), 2002.

Rogers, Everett M., *Diffusion of Innovations* (New York, The Free Press), 1995.

Schama, Simon, *A History of Britain*, 3 volumes (London, BBC Worldwide), 2001–2.

Scruton, Roger, *England – an Elegy* (London, Pimlico), 2001.

Strong, Roy, *The Story of Britain: A People's History* (London, Pimlico), 1998; *The Spirit of Britain: A Narrative History of the Arts* (London, Pimlico), 2000.

Weir, Alison, *Britain's Royal Families: The Complete Genealogy* (London, Pimlico), 2002.

Wood, Michael, *In Search of England: Journeys into the English Past* (London, Penguin Books), 2000.

FURTHER READING AND PLACES TO VISIT

c.7150 BC: *Cheddar Man*

The bones of Cheddar Man can be seen at the Natural History Museum in London. There is a replica of his skeleton at Gough's Cave in Cheddar, Somerset, part of the exhibition 'Cheddar Man and the Cannibals': www.cheddarcaves.co.uk. See www.ucl.ac.uk/boxgrove for details of the excavation of Britain's very earliest human remains, the half-million-year-old legbone found at Boxgrove in Sussex. Catherine Hills offers an accessible and scholarly account of our country's earliest waves of uninvited immigrants.

Hills, Catherine, *Blood of the British: From Ice Age to Norman Conquest* (London, George Philip with Channel 4), 1986.

c.325 BC: *Pytheas and the Painted People*

In *The Extraordinary Voyage of Pytheas the Greek*, Barry Cunliffe pulls together the fragments of our knowledge about this remarkable man, taking us by the hand on a delightful stroll through Celtic Gaul and Britain. If you would like to visit Stonehenge on the summer solstice in the company of modern Druids, ring the English Heritage hotline on 0870 333 1186. Paul Newman writes well about the prancing white horses on the hills.

Cunliffe, Barry, *The Extraordinary Voyage of Pytheas the Greek* (London, Penguin Books), 2002.

Newman, Paul, *Lost Gods of Albion: The Chalk Hill Figures of Britain* (Trowbridge, Sutton Publishing), 1999.

55 BC: *The Standard-bearer of the 10th*

You can't do better than read Julius Caesar's own story of hitting Britain's beaches, contained in his account of his campaigns in Gaul.

Caesar, Julius, *The Gallic War*, trans. Carolyn Hammond (Oxford, Oxford University Press), 1996.

AD 1–33: *And Did Those Feet? Jesus Christ and the Legends of Glastonbury*

Michael Wood's poetic work of reportage *In Search of England* (see General Histories, above) tackles the fantasies of Glastonbury gently but firmly. For the sacred, visit www.glastonburyabbey.com. For the profane, you can find out about the annual pop music festival on www.glastonburyfestivals.co.uk.

AD 43: *The Emperor Claudius Triumphant*

Barbara Levick's recent biography paints a sympathetic portrait of the crippled emperor. You can find out how to visit the Roman remains at Colchester at www.colchestermuseums.org.uk.

Levick, Barbara, *Claudius* (London, Routledge), 2002.

AD 61: *Boadicea, Warrior Queen*

Shrewdly separating fact from fiction, Antonia Fraser refers to the warrior queen as Boudicca when dealing with verifiable events, and as Boadicea when legend takes over. Tacitus's *Annals* provides an almost contemporary version of the revolt. The Museum of London has a standing exhibit on what happened when Boadicea came to town: www.museum-london.org.uk.

Fraser, Antonia, *The Warrior Queens: Boadicea's Chariot* (London, Phoenix), 2002.

Tacitus, *Annals of Imperial Rome*, trans. and intro. Michael Grant, rev. edn (London, Penguin Books), 1996.

AD 122: *Hadrian's Wall*

After many years of restoration, Rome's great English pleasure palace is now open again at Bath: www.romanbaths.co.uk. To visit Hadrian's Wall, consult www.hadrians-wall.org.

Drinkwater, J. F., and Drummond, A., *The World of the Romans* (London, Cassell), 1993.

AD 410–c.600: *Arthur, Once and Future King*

Enter 'King Arthur' in your search engine and more than a million pages will vie to take you back to Camelot. So read the man who started it all – the twelfth-century chronicler Geoffrey of Monmouth, in accessible paperback. Of the real-life Arthurian sites, Tintagel Castle in Cornwall comes closest to what Hollywood would lead you to expect. For a genuine and spectacular taste of the Dark Ages, you have the choice of the British Museum or the Sutton Hoo burial site in Suffolk to see *Beowulf* brought to life: www.thebritishmuseum.ac.uk; www.suttonhoo.org

Carver, Martin, *Sutton Hoo, Burial Ground of Kings?* (London, British Museum Press), 1998.

Monmouth, Geoffrey of, *The History of the Kings of Britain*, trans. Lewis Thorpe (London, Penguin Books), 1966.

c.AD 575: *Pope Gregory's Angels*

Here is our first chance to sample the writing of Bede, who tells his story of the Angles in the slave market, complete with Gregory's excruciating puns.

Bede, *Ecclesiastical History of the English People* (trans. Leo Sherley-Price, intro. D. H. Farmer), (London, Penguin Books), 1990.

AD 597: *St Augustine's Magic*

After describing Augustine's arrival in Canterbury, Bede went on to relate how the pagan altars around England became Christian. Maps showing the spread of Christianity in Anglo-Saxon England are among the many original features of David Hill's indispensable atlas. The original St Augustine's throne has long vanished, but if you visit Canterbury you can see the marble chair made in the early 1200s that stands near Thomas Becket's shrine.

Hill, David, *An Atlas of Anglo-Saxon England* (Toronto, University of Toronto Press), 1981.

AD 664: *King Oswy and the Crown of Thorns*

The gothic ruins of the Abbey of Whitby will be familiar to devotees of *Dracula* – Bram Stoker wrote his famous novel looking up at it. Today you can look down from the abbey on to the bracing sea view enjoyed by the guests of St Hilda at the synod in 664. Legend has it that the migrating geese who rest on the headland on their way down from the Arctic every year are pilgrims paying tribute to her memory: www.whitby.co.uk.

c.AD 680: *Caedmon, The First English Poet*

You can read Caedmon's 'Hymn' in the gem-like anthology of Anglo-Saxon verse compiled by the poet Kevin Crossley-Holland, together with the complete text of *Beowulf*, *The Dream of the Rood* and a bawdy collection of Anglo-Saxon riddles.

Crossley-Holland, Kevin (ed. and trans.), *The Anglo-Saxon World: An Anthology* (Oxford, Oxford University Press), 1984.

AD 672/3–735: *The Venerable Bede*

www.bedesworld.co.uk offers a flavour of the old monastery at Jarrow, with visitor information. Brown and de Hamel provide well-illustrated accounts of how the writing studios at such monasteries produced their masterpieces. Bede's spirit is now said by some locals to flit between Durham Cathedral, where his bones rest, and Anthony Gormley's magnificent statue, the *Angel of the North*, in Gateshead.

Brown, Michelle P., *Anglo-Saxon Manuscripts* (London, The British Library), 1991.

de Hamel, Christopher, *Medieval Craftsmen: Scribes and Illuminators* (London, British Museum Press), 1997.

AD 878: *Alfred and the Cakes*

Start with the original, Bishop Asser's *Life of King Alfred*. Then turn to the much criticised Alfred Smyth, who maintains that Asser was a forgery. There is not much marshland left in the Somerset Levels these days, but you can get a feeling of how the waters once swirled around the sedge when you look out from the train between Taunton and Bruton on a wet winter's day. On summer afternoons, you can climb up the great tower built at Athelney in the eighteenth century to commemorate Alfred's adventures in the swamps.

Keynes, Simon, and Lapidge, Michael (trans.), *Alfred the Great: Asser's Life of King Alfred and Other Contemporary Sources* (London, Penguin Books), 1983.

Smyth, Alfred P., *King Alfred the Great* (Oxford, Oxford University Press), 1995.

AD 911–18: *The Lady of the Mercians*

From this point onwards, and for the next two centuries, we can enjoy the acerbic comments of the compilers of the *Anglo-Saxon Chronicle*. Kathleen Herbert and Henrietta Leyser offer different takes on the role of women in medieval society.

Herbert, Kathleen, *Peace-Weavers and Shield-Maidens: Women in Early English Society* (Hockwold-cum-Wilton, Anglo-Saxon Books), 1997.

Leyser, Henrietta, *Medieval Women* (London, Phoenix), 1997.

Swanton, Michael (trans. and ed.), *The Anglo-Saxon Chronicle* (London, J. M. Dent), 1997.

AD 978–1016: *Ethelred the Unready*

Corfe Castle in Dorset, the site of the killing of Ethelred's half-brother Edward, is all that a castle should be, with a history of warfare that extends as late as the Civil War of the 1640s – see www.corfe-castle.co.uk. Michael Swanton's anthology contains Archbishop Wulfstan's famous denunciation of the evils of the reign of Ethelred – the Sermon of the Wolf to the English. To get a glimpse of the life created by the Danes whom Ethelred tried to slaughter, head for Jorvik (York to us), the place that a surprising number of Vikings called home: www.jorvik-viking-centre.co.uk.

Swanton, Michael (trans. and ed.), *Anglo-Saxon Prose* (London, J. M. Dent), 1993.

c.AD 1010: *Elmer the Flying Monk*

Elmer went by many names in the documents –Aethelmaer, Eilmer, Aylmer and even Oliver – all derived from readings and misreadings of the original account of his flight by his fellow-monk William of Malmesbury. At Malmesbury Abbey the Friends of the Abbey bookshop sells a full account of the flight, including the researches of Dr Lynn White Jr, President of the US Society for the History of Technology. If you want the Friends to send you a copy of the book you will have to send them a book of stamps, since they do not have credit card facilities.

Malmesbury, William of, *Gesta Regum Anglorum, The History of the English Kings*, volume 2, general intro. and commentary by R. M. Thomson with M. Winterbottom (Oxford, Clarendon Press), 1999.
Woosnam, Maxwell, *Eilmer, Eleventh-century Monk of Malmesbury: The Flight and the Comet* (Malmesbury, Friends of Malmesbury Abbey), 1986.

AD 1016–35: *King Canute and the Waves*

Few of King Canute's attempts to make himself an English gentleman have survived. The story of how he tried to turn back the waves provides a great opportunity to dip into Henry of Huntingdon, the sharpest of the post-Norman chroniclers.

Huntingdon, Henry of, *The History of the English People 1000–1154*, trans. Diana Greenway (Oxford, Oxford University Press), 2002.

AD 1042–66: *Edward the Confessor*

The Westminster Abbey that we see today was started in the reign of Henry III, but it is the obvious place to experience the dream of the Confessor – particularly in the cloisters, where you get the flavour of the monastic buildings attached to the great church. The abbey's website displays an interpretation of what the Confessor's original abbey probably looked like: www.westminster-abbey.org. Debby Banham offers a wonderful insight into the everyday life of mid-eleventh-century monks through an analysis of the sign language they used when they were not allowed to speak – 'Pass my underpants, please.'

Banham, Debby (ed. and trans.), *Monasteriales Indicia: The Anglo-Saxon Monastic Sign Language* (Hockwold-cum-Wilton, Anglo-Saxon Books), 1996.

c.AD 1043: *The Legend of Lady Godiva*

Call up 'Godiva' on your search engine and you will have difficulty finding the strictly historical sites. The Harvard professor Daniel Donoghue has written a stimulating analysis of the Godiva legend, which includes a translated text of Roger of Wendover.

Donoghue, Daniel, *Lady Godiva: A Literary History of the Legend* (Oxford, Blackwell Publishing), 2003.

1066: *The Year of Three Kings*

Tracking the most graphic evidence for the events leading up to the Battle of Hastings requires a trip across the Channel to Bayeux in Normandy: www.bayeux-tourism.com. But almost better than a visit, Martin Foys's new CD-Rom enables you to scroll the whole tapestry and magnify images so that individual stitches can be seen.

Foys, Martin K., *The Bayeux Tapestry Digital Edition* (Woodbridge, Boydell & Brewer), 2003.

1066: *The Death of Brave King Harold*
Battle Abbey in East Sussex – said to be built on the very spot where Harold's body was found – is open the year round and English Heritage guides will show you round the famous battlefield. The pioneering work of David Hill and John McSween has yet to be published but is summarised, with some illustrations, in Lawson's exhaustive study.

Hill, David, and McSween, John, *The Bayeux Tapestry: The Establishment of a Text*, forthcoming.
Lawson, M. K., *The Battle of Hastings*, 1066 (Stroud, Tempus), 2002.

1070: *Hereward the Wake and the Norman Yoke*
Once again, Michael Wood (see General Histories, above) is the most readable. His account of the Norman Yoke starts memorably with his encounter as a teenager with the great general, Montgomery of Alamein – with Clement Attlee playing a supporting role. Castle websites abound. Start with www.castles.org and www.castles-abbeys.co.uk. And if you missed Marc Morris's television series, don't miss his book.

Morris, Marc, *Castle* (London, Channel 4), 2003.

1086: *The Domesday Book*
The Public Record Office has been rebranded as the National Archives. It remains an airy temple of documentary delights. There is a small exhibition room on the ground floor where you can view Domesday in its glass case, in the company of a changing selection of themed exhibits: www.nationalarchives.gov.uk.

Roffe, David, *Decoding Domesday* (Woodbridge, Suffolk, Boydell & Brewer), 2007.

1100: *The Mysterious Death of William Rufus*
You can visit William Rufus's magnificent banqueting hall in the Palace of Westminster – www.parliament.uk/parliament/guide/palace.htm. To get the flavour of a Norman royal hunting preserve, visit the New Forest in Hampshire – ideally with a copy of Duncan Grinnell-Milne's book, which treats William Rufus's killing in the style of a murder mystery.

Grinnell-Milne, Duncan, *The Killing of William Rufus: An Investigation in the New Forest* (Newton Abbot, David & Charles), 1968.

1120: *Henry I and the* White Ship

Once again a trip to Normandy is in order. From the lighthouse on the cliffs beside Barfleur you can see the rock on which the *White Ship* foundered. The account by Orderic Vitalis is one of the most gripping passages in any of the medieval chronicles.

Chibnall, Marjorie (trans. and ed.), *The Ecclesiastical History of Orderic Vitalis*, volume 6, Books XI, XII and XIII (Oxford, Clarendon Press), 1978.

1135–54: *Stephen and Matilda*

This is where we say goodbye to the *Anglo-Saxon Chronicle*, whose description of the civil war horrors around Peterborough provides a rousing, if tragic, conclusion.

Davis, R. H. C., *King Stephen 1135–1154* (London, Longman), 1990.

1170: *Murder in the Cathedral* and AD 1174: *A King Repents*

The stunning stained-glass windows in Canterbury Cathedral's Trinity Chapel, which were created within half a century of Thomas Becket's death, tell the story of his murder and the miracles that followed. Henry VIII tried his best to eradicate the cult of St Thomas in the sixteenth century, but the aura of the martyr survives. Frank Barlow's study of Becket is a particularly fine biography.

Barlow, Frank, *Thomas Becket* (London, The Folio Society), 2002.

1172: *The River-bank Take-away*

You can read the full text of William FitzStephen's description of London in Frank Stenton's Historical Association leaflet. The Museum of London is the place to go for imaginative exhibits on the medieval city: www.museum-london.org.uk.

Stenton, Frank, *Norman London, An Essay* (London, Historical Association), 1934.

1189–99: *Richard the Lionheart*

Coeur de Lion has been well served by his biographers, with John Gillingham the most notable. Should you be lucky enough to go sailing down the River Danube, look out for the site of Richard's imprisonment, Castle Durnstein, the archetypal baronial fortress. Lying buried side by side in Fontevrault Abbey by the River Loire, Richard and his parents, Henry II and Eleanor of Aquitaine, make a poignant family scene.

Gillingham, John, *Richard the Lionheart* (London, Yale), 1999.
Nelson, Janet L. (ed.), *Richard Coeur de Lion in History and Myth*, Medieval History series (London, King's College), 1992.

1215: *John Lackland and Magna Carta*

You can see John's tomb in Worcester Cathedral. When it was opened in the eighteenth century, the King's skeleton was measured. Lackland was found to be just 5ft 5ins tall. Two of the surviving copies of Magna Carta from June 1215 can be seen at the British Library, with the other two at Lincoln and Salisbury Cathedrals.

Breay, Claire, *Magna Carta: Manuscripts and Myths* (London, The British Library), 2002.

1225: *Hobbehod, Prince of Thieves*

Errol Flynn and Kevin Costner convey the fanciful modern vision. Holt, Keen and Spraggs explain how that vision developed over the centuries, with some fruitful comparisons to the legends of Hereward the Wake and highwaymen like Dick Turpin.

Holt, J. C., *Robin Hood* (London, Thames & Hudson), 1989.
Keen, Maurice, *Outlaws of Medieval Legend* (London, Routledge), 1987.
Spraggs, Gillian, *Outlaws and Highwaymen: The Cult of the Robber in England* (London, Pimlico), 2001.

1265: *Simon de Montfort and his Talking-place*

A monument near Evesham Abbey beside the River Avon in Worcestershire recalls the death of Simon de Montfort on 4 August 1265, surrounded by the royalist forces and fighting against impossible odds. As a song of the time put it, it was 'the murder of Evesham, for *bataile non it was*'.

Maddicott, J. R., *Simon de Montfort* (Cambridge, Cambridge University Press), 1994.

Treharne, R. F., *Simon de Montfort and Baronial Reform: Thirteenth-Century Essays*, ed. E. B. Fryde (London, Hambledon Press), 1986.

1284: *A Prince Who Speaks No Word of English*

Jan Morris has composed the definitive Welsh diatribe demolishing the legend of the Prince of Wales. Caernarfon Castle itself, like Harlech, Conway and Edward's other great castles, survives triumphantly – as the eighteenth-century Welsh antiquarian Thomas Pennant put it, 'the magnificent badge of our servitude'. For full details consult the Welsh Historic Monuments website – www.cadw.wales.gov.uk.

Morris, Jan, *The Princeship of Wales* (Llandysul, Gomer Press), 1995.

Prestwich, Michael, *The Three Edwards: War and State in England 1272-1377* (London, Weidenfeld & Nicolson), 1980.

1308: *Piers Gaveston and Edward II*

Pierre Chaplais has recently advanced the argument that the relationship between Edward II and Piers Gaveston was non-sexual. Nice try. Kenilworth Castle, home of 'the black hound of Arden', is well worth the visit. Originally fortified by King John, it later passed to John of Gaunt. At Berkeley Castle, halfway between Bristol and Gloucester, Edward II's dungeon is open to the public in the summer months.

Chaplais, Pierre, *Piers Gaveston: Edward II's Adoptive Brother* (Oxford, Clarendon Press), 1994.

1346: *A Prince Wins His Spurs*

At Nottingham Castle you can see the secret passage by which the young Edward III claimed his right to rule England. It is known as Mortimer's Hole, and is the only surviving part of the original twelfth-century motte-and-bailey fortress. For visiting times see www.nottinghamcity.gov.uk. Donald Featherstone's book is a fascinating study of the men and the weapon that got England off to such a deceptively good start in the Hundred Years War.

Featherstone, Donald, *The Bowmen of England: The Story of the English Longbow* (Barnsley, Pen & Sword Books), 2003.

1347: *The Burghers of Calais*

Auguste Rodin's melodramatic bronze makes up the curious quintet of historical monuments around the Houses of Parliament in Westminster. To the north, Boadicea, galloping beside the Thames in her scythe-wheeled chariot. To the west, Oliver Cromwell, looking stern. In the car park, Richard the Lionheart, with his sword raised towards Palestine. And to the south, in the public gardens, not far from the suffragette Emmeline Pankhurst, the six haggard burghers, dressed in rags and with ropes around their necks – six self-important Frenchmen decisively put in their place. The French clearly have a different view: the town of Calais commissioned Rodin to create the group of life-sized burghers in 1885, and the original casting stands outside the town hall – an enduring reminder of French fortitude in the face of English beastliness.

Sumption, Jonathan, *The Hundred Years War: Trial by Battle* (London, Faber), 1990.

1347–9: *The Fair Maid of Kent and the Order of the Garter*

Every June the Queen processes through Windsor Castle with her modern fraternity of knights – who are not so Arthurian these days, counting politicians among their numbers and even a supermarket magnate, Lord Sainsbury of Preston Candover. At any time of year you can view the splendours of St George's Chapel and the rest of the castle, which is now a far cry from its original wooden motte-and-bailey structure: www.royal.gov.uk.

Collins, Hugh, *The Order of the Garter: Chivalry and Politics in Late Medieval England* (Oxford, Oxford University Press), 2000.

1348–9: *The Great Mortality*

Philip Ziegler has written the definitive study of the Black Death with his usual erudition and grace. Norman Cantor's more recent study concentrates on the consequences. Rosemary Horrox offers a fine array of contemporary sources – not least the complaints that the plague reflected God's anger at indecent clothes and the disobedience of the young.

Cantor, Norman F., *In the Wake of the Plague: The Black Death and the World It Made* (London, Pocket Books), 2002.

Horrox, Rosemary (ed.), *The Black Death* (Manchester, Manchester University Press), 1994.

Ziegler, Philip, *The Black Death* (London, The Folio Society), 1997.

1376: *The Bedside Manner of a Plague Doctor*

You can see examples of John Arderne's medical drawings for the removal of *fistulae in ano* and the gruesome surgical instruments he employed in Peter Murray Jones's well illustrated book.

Murray Jones, Peter, *Medieval Medicine in Illuminated Manuscripts* (London, The British Library), 1998.

1377: *The Dream of Piers the Ploughman*

Set aside a day to read this rambling epic right through from beginning to end – preferably on a summer's afternoon, on a bank beside a stream in the Malvern Hills.

Langland, William, *Piers the Ploughman*, trans. and intro. J. F. Goodridge (London, Penguin Books), 1966.

1381: *The 'Mad Multitude'*

Walk around the echoing arcades of modern Smithfield, and you can imagine under your feet the open meadow where Wat Tyler rode out on his pony to meet Richard II. If you get there early enough in the morning you can observe the porters and butchers of the modern meat-market, which will also, presumably, become part of history one day. Dobson's classic volume presents readable extracts from all the main contemporary sources.

Dobson, R. B., *The Peasants' Revolt of 1381* (London, Macmillan), 1983.

1387: *Geoffrey Chaucer and the Mother Tongue*

You can visit Chaucer's grave in Westminster Abbey, the memorial that inspired Poets' Corner. To read the very earliest editions of *The Canterbury Tales* as printed by William Caxton in the 1470s and 1480s, visit the British Library website, www.bl.uk/treasures/caxton/homepage.html – and for a wonderfully bawdy modern English version, read the classic translation by Nevill Coghill.

Coghill, Nevill, *The Canterbury Tales* (Harmondsworth, Penguin Books), 1951.

1399: *The Deposing of King Richard II*

Nigel Saul has written the definitive biography. Christopher Given Wilson has pulled together the contemporary sources.

Given Wilson, Christopher (ed.), *Chronicles of the Revolution, 1397–1400: The Reign of Richard II* (Manchester, Manchester University Press), 1993.
Saul, Nigel, *Richard II* (London, Yale University Press), 1997.

1399: *'Turn Again, Dick Whittington!'*

For an evocative flavour of Whittington's London, visit the medieval gallery at the Museum of London, or its website: www.museumoflondon.org.uk.

1399: *Henry IV and His Extra-virgin Oil*

A recent academic conference has assembled the latest research and thinking on this enigmatic king.

Dodd, Gwilym, and Biggs, Douglas, *Henry IV: The Establishment of the Regime, 1399–1406* (York, Medieval Press), 2003.

1415: *We Happy Few – the Battle of Azincourt*

The two English films of *Henry V* by the Shakespearian giants of their respective generations are regularly rerun on television. Laurence Olivier's sun-filled idyll was shot in neutral Ireland during World War II, with the Irish army playing the bowmen of England. Kenneth Branagh's 1989 version presents, surely in deliberate contrast, a dark, brooding and rain-drenched interpretation.

1429: *Joan of Arc, the Maid of Orleans*

Marina Warner has written the definitive interpretation; George Bernard Shaw, the classic play. For transcriptions of Joan's trial, visit: <u>archive.joan-of-arc.org.</u>

Warner, Marina, *Joan of Arc, the Image of Female Heroism* (London, Weidenfeld & Nicolson), 1981.

1440: A *'Prompter for Little Ones'*

Nicholas Orme's playful and original book is the inspiration for this chapter. The metal toys uncovered by Tony Pilson and the Mud Larks are exhibited in the medieval galleries at the Museum of London: <u>www. museumoflondon.org.uk</u>.

Orme, Nicholas, *Medieval Children* (London, Yale University Press), 2001.

1422–61, 1470–1: *House of Lancaster: the Two Reigns of Henry VI*

David Starkey's rereading of the 'Royal Book' of court etiquette has cast a new light on the supposed shabbiness of Henry VI. The Paston Letters, England's earliest set of family correspondence, provides a human picture of how the wars disturbed – and did not disturb – ordinary life. The original manuscripts of the Paston Letters are in the British Library, while <u>www.lib.virginia.edu</u> has all 421 letters or 1380 kilobytes' worth!

Starkey, David, 'Henry VI's Old Blue Gown', *The Court Historian*, vol. 4.1 (April 1999).

1432–85: *The House of Theodore*

Knowing that Pembrokeshire is Tudor country gives an extra dimension to visiting this south-west corner of Wales. Henry VII was born inside the thirteenth-century curtain walls of Pembroke Castle, <u>www.pembrokecastle.co.uk</u>, ten miles from Milford Haven where he landed in 1485 to claim the throne.

1461–70, 1471–83: *House of York: Edward IV, Merchant King*

Warwick Castle, the home of Warwick the Kingmaker, who made and was then unmade by Edward IV, was recently voted Britain's most popular castle, ahead of the Tower of London. With its gardens landscaped by 'Capability' Brown in a later century, it is today impressively maintained by Madame Tussaud's: www.warwick-castle.co.uk.

Seward, Desmond, *The Wars of the Roses* (London, Robinson), 1995.

1474: William Caxton

Caxton is buried within yards of the site of his printing press, in St Margaret's, the little church that is so often overlooked in the shadow of Westminster Abbey. Along with his edition of *The Canterbury Tales*, the British Library has digitised a number of his works on www.bl.uk treasures/caxton/homepages.html. To read his charming, often eccentric publisher's prefaces, visit www.bartleby.com.

Painter, George, *William Caxton: A Quincentenary Biography of England's First Printer* (London, Chatto & Windus), 1976.

1483: Whodunnit? The Princes in the Tower

The little princes were lodged by their uncle in the relatively luxurious royal apartments of the Tower. Visit the dungeons and watch the water come creeping under Traitors' Gate to enjoy the sinister chill of this fortress, prison, and high-class beheading place: www.hrp.org.uk. Dockray presents the contemporary evidence on the mystery, so you can make up your own mind.

Dockray, Keith, *Richard III: A Source Book* (Stroud, Sutton), 1997.

1484: The Cat and the Rat

'Now is the winter of our discontent . . .' Laurence Olivier's 1955 film portrayal of Richard III is the ultimate version of Shakespeare's crookback baddie. It might seem strange that the fullest and fairest exposition of this film is to be found on www.r3.org, the website of the Richard III Society, founded to clear and glorify the King's name. But that is the nature of this deservedly thriving association of historical enthusiasts.

1485: The Battle of Bosworth Field

This account of the battle is based on the recent book by Michael K. Jones. Virginia Henderson examines the legend of the Tudor Rose in her article on Henry VII's chapel in Westminster Abbey, while Illuminata's compendium of heraldic badges contains all you need to know about symbolic roses, Tudor and otherwise.

Henderson, Virginia, 'Retrieving the "Crown in the Hawthorn Bush": the origins of the badges of Henry VII', in *Traditions and Transformations in Late Medieval England*, ed. D. Biggs, S. D. Michalove and A. Compton Reeves (Leiden, Brill), 2002.
Jones, Michael K., *Bosworth 1485* (Stroud, Tempus), 2002.
Siddons, Michael Powell, *Heraldic Badges of England and Wales* (London, Illuminata for the Society of Antiquaries), 2005.

1486–99: *Double Trouble*

Again, www.r3.org, the website dedicated to his bitterest enemy, contains the most comprehensive and the latest material on Henry VII, and it is difficult not to recommend another visit to Westminster Abbey to view Henry's eerily lifelike death mask in the museum in the corner of the Cloisters.

1497: *Fish 'n' Ships*

www.matthew.co.uk relates the 1997 recreation of Cabot's historic voyage of exploration and the building of the modern replica *Matthew*, which can be visited in Bristol and, from time to time, cruised upon in the still waters of Bristol Harbour. Cocktails are served at sunset on the quarter deck.

Pope, Peter E., *The Many Landfalls of John Cabot* (Toronto, University of Toronto Press), 1976.

1500: *Fork in, Fork Out*

Stanley Chrimes has written the classic biography. Thompson's collection of essays re-evaluates the idea that Henry was a 'new' and non-medieval monarch.

Chrimes, Stanley B., *Henry VII* (Yale, Yale University Press), 1999.
Thompson, B. (ed.), *The Reign of Henry VII* (Stanford, Stanford University Press), 1995.

1509–33: *King Henry VIII's 'Great Matter'*

Built by Thomas Wolsey, Hampton Court breathes the grandiose spirit of its founder and, even more, that of the man who confiscated it from the cardinal, Henry VIII. The King enjoyed three honeymoons here, could entertain five hundred diners at one sitting, and worked up a sweat in the 'real' tennis court. In the garden is the famous maze: www.hrp.org.uk.

Thurley, Simon, *Hampton Court: A Social and Architectural History* (London, Yale University Press), 2003.

1525: *'Let There Be Light' – William Tyndale and the English Bible*

This account is largely based upon Brian Moynahan's revealing and passionate book.

Moynahan, Brian, *William Tyndale: If God Spare My Life* (London, Little, Brown), 2002.

1535: *Thomas More and His Wonderful 'No-Place'*

To read the complete text of *Utopia*, visit the electronic library of Fordham University that contains so many wonderful original sources: www.fordham.edu/halsall/mod/thomasmore-utopia.html. Thomas More himself is buried in two places: his body in the Tower of London, and his head, retrieved by his devoted daughter Margaret Roper, in the Roper Vault at St Dunstan's Church, Canterbury.

1533–7: *Divorced, Beheaded, Died . . .*

Scarisbrick and Starkey share the honours in the large and distinguished field of those who have written about Henry VIII, his wives and his world.

Scarisbrick, J. J., *Henry VIII* (London, Eyre & Spottiswoode), 1968.
Starkey, David, *Six Wives: The Queens of Henry VIII* (London, Chatto & Windus), 2003.

1536: *The Pilgrimage of Grace*

In recent years the work of Eamon Duffy, Christopher Haigh and

Diarmaid MacCulloch has done honour to the strength of traditional Catholic faith and practice in sixteenth-century England. They have shown how the Reformation did not so much reform as re-form – and in a variety of complex ways.

Duffy, Eamon, *The Stripping of the Altars: Traditional Religion in England c.1400–c.1580* (London, Yale University Press), 1992.

Haigh, Christopher (ed.), *The English Reformation Revised* (Cambridge, Cambridge University Press), 1987.

MacCulloch, Diarmaid, *Reformation: Europe's House Divided 1490–1700* (London, Penguin Books), 2004.

1539–47: . . . *Divorced, Beheaded, Survived*

Henry VIII is buried in the centre of the nave in St George's Chapel, Windsor, in the company of the wife for whom he overturned his country and who bore him the healthy male heir he desired so much: www.royal.gov.uk.

1547–53: *Boy King – Edward VI, 'The Godly Imp'*

Some grammar schools apart, there are few Tudor remnants dating from the boy king's short reign – and, sadly, an almost endless catalogue of Christian art destroyed by the whitewash brush and the plundering fingers of those who 'purified' the Church in Edward's name. Chris Skidmore makes a brilliant debut in his lucid biography.

Skidmore, Christopher, *Edward VI: The Lost King of England* (London, Orion), 2006.

1553: *Lady Jane Grey – the Nine-day Queen*

Jane Grey spent her youth in Sudeley Castle at Winchcombe near Cheltenham in Gloucestershire, where Henry VIII's last wife, Catherine Parr, lies buried. In the Civil War it was for a time the headquarters of the dashing Prince Rupert: www.sudeleycastle. co.uk. Now you can hire it for your wedding.

1553–8: *Bloody Mary and the Fires of Smithfield*

If one man created the legend of Bloody Mary, it was John Foxe, who painstakingly compiled the stories of her victims and brought them together in his *Book of Martyrs* – probably the bestselling book of the sixteenth-century and, arguably, the most influential. For the complete text visit www.ccel.org/f/foxe. Jasper Ridley's lucid modern account is largely based on Foxe.

Ridley, Jasper, *Bloody Mary's Martyrs* (London, Constable), 2001.

1557: *Robert Recorde and His Intelligence Sharpener*

The School of Mathematics and Statistics at Scotland's University of St Andrews has produced an excellent account of Robert Recorde's life and mathematical research work on: www-history.mcs.st-andrews.ac.uk/history/Biographies/Recorde.html Adam Hart-Davis provides the details of his horseshoe brain-teaser:

Hart-Davis, Adam, *What the Tudors and Stuarts Did for Us* (London, Boxtree), 2002.

1559: *Elizabeth – Queen of Hearts*

David Starkey concentrates on the early years of Elizabeth. Christopher Haigh's 'profile in power' is the best condensed analysis of her life.

Haigh, Christopher, *Elizabeth I* (London, Longman), 1988.
Starkey, David, *Elizabeth* (London, Chatto & Windus), 2000.

1571: *That's Entertainment*

The contemporary descriptions in this chapter come from Liza Picard's brilliant evocation. If you can't visit the Globe in Southwark, you can enjoy Tom Stoppard's whimsical but scenically accurate *Shakespeare in Love*, now on DVD.

Picard, Liza, *Elizabeth's London: Everyday Life in Elizabethan London* (Weidenfeld & Nicolson), 2003.

1585: *Sir Walter Ralegh and the Lost Colony*

Ralegh once owned Sherborne Castle in Dorset, though there is not much left of it today after Oliver Cromwell's Civil War siege:

www.sherbornecastle.com. And, in the spirit of Sir Walter himself, let me not fail to mention my own biography of the great man, sadly just out of print!

Lacey, Robert, *Sir Walter Ralegh* (London, Phoenix Press), 2000.

1560–87: Mary Queen of Scots

Inns and castles where Mary Queen of Scots is said to have stayed are almost as numerous as those that boast 'Queen Elizabeth Slept Here'. Tutbury overlooks the valley of the river Dove in Staffordshire: www.tutburycastle.com. Nothing much remains of Fotheringhay near Oundle where she was executed, but nearby is the beautiful fifteenth-century church of St Mary and All Saints. Antonia Fraser's biography is definitive.

Fraser, Antonia, *Mary Queen of Scots* (London, Weidenfeld & Nicolson), 1969.

1588: Sir Francis Drake and the Spanish Armada

Drake lived at Buckland Abbey, eleven miles north of Plymouth. This beautiful thirteenth-century Cistercian monastery had been spared destruction in the Dissolution when Henry VIII granted it to Sir Richard Grenville, whose grandson Richard, himself a naval hero, sold it to Sir Francis: www.nationaltrust.org.uk.

Cummings, John, *Francis Drake: The Lives of a Hero* (London, Weidenfeld & Nicolson), 1995.

Hanson, Neil, *The Confident Hope of a Miracle: The True Story of the Spanish Armada* (London, Corgi), 2004.

1592: Sir John's Jakes

Named in honour of the modern populariser of the water closet, www.thomas-crapper.com graphically sets out the tale of sewage through the ages in more detail than most would consider strictly necessary. Again, Adam Hart-Davis provides a lively summary.

Hart-Davis, Adam, *What the Tudors and Stuarts Did for Us* (London, Boxtree), 2002.

1603: *By Time Surprised*

Outliving three husbands, that other Elizabeth, Bess of Hardwick, Countess of Shrewsbury, built up a fortune that she devoted to building the redoubtable Hardwick Hall, near Chesterfield in Derbyshire. Tel.: 01246 850430. Mercifully spared the 'improvements' of later generations, it is a remarkable example of a great Elizabethan country house.

1605: 5/11: *England's First Terrorist*

The cellar where Guy Fawkes stacked his gunpowder was destroyed in the fire of 1834 that devastated the medieval Houses of Parliament, but thanks to the Tradescants you can still see his lantern in the Ashmolean Museum, Oxford.

Fraser, Antonia, *The Gunpowder Plot: Terror and Faith in 1605* (London, Weidenfeld & Nicolson), 1996.

1611: *King James's 'Authentical' Bible*

James VI and I's own prolific writings have been skilfully edited by Rhodes, Richards and Marshall. McGrath tells the story of the Bible he inspired.

McGrath, Alister, *In the Beginning: The Story of the King James Bible* (London, Hodder & Stoughton), 2001.

Rhodes, Neil, Richards, Jennifer, and Marshall, Joseph, *King James VI and I: Selected Writings* (Aldershot, Ashgate), 2003.

1616: *'Spoilt Child' and the Pilgrim Fathers*

The sentimental Disney cartoon film *Pocahontas* enraged her descendants, who set out their objections on their website: www. powhatan.org. The best source on the Pilgrim Fathers remains William Bradford's first-hand account which is extracted, along with many other original documents, on the excellent www.mayflowerhistory.com.

Bradford, William (ed. S. E. Morison), *Of Plymouth Plantation 1620–47* (New York, Alfred A. Knopf), 1954.

1622: *The Ark of the John Tradescants*

The Tradescants, father and son, are buried in the beautiful St Mary-at-Lambeth, just across the Thames from the House of Commons. The church was saved from destruction in 1977 by the Tradescant Trust ,who turned it into the world's first Museum of Garden History, complete with its own replica seventeenth-century knot garden of box trees: www.museumgardenhistory. org.

Leith-Ross, P., *The John Tradescants* (London, Peter Owen), 1984.

1629: *God's Lieutenant in Earth*

Charles I's cradle can be seen at Hatfield House in Hertfordshire, where Elizabeth I, a virtual prisoner, was brought the news that her sister Mary had died and she had become Queen. We see Hatfield today as it was rebuilt in the reign of James I by Robert Cecil: www.hatfield-house.co.uk

1642: *'All My Birds Have Flown'*

It is difficult to better C. V. Wedgwood's classic account of this episode. Tristram Hunt movingly brings together the voices of the time.

Hunt, Tristram, *The English Civil War at First Hand* (London, Phoenix), 2003.
Wedgwood, C. V., *The King's War* (London, HarperCollins), 1955.

1642–8: *Roundheads v. Cavaliers*

No study of the Civil War can omit the inspired and seminal work of Christopher Hill. Blair Worden shows how the Civil Wars have been fought through the subsequent centuries.

Hill, Christopher, *Puritanism and Revolution: Studies in Interpretation of the English Revolution* (London, Secker & Warburg), 1958.
Royle, Trevor, *The Wars of the Three Kingdoms 1638–1660* (London, Little, Brown), 2004.
Worden, Blair, *Roundhead Reputations. The English Civil Wars and the Passions of Posterity* (London, Penguin Books) 2001.

1649: *Behold the Head of a Traitor!*

The magnificent Banqueting House from which Charles I walked to his execution still stands opposite Horse Guards Parade in Whitehall. Designed by Inigo Jones as a setting for the plays and pageants of Ben Jonson, it is decorated with ceiling panels that illustrate Charles's disastrous theories on the nature of kingship: one tableau shows James I rising to heaven after his death like a latter-day Christ, to take his place among the immortals. www.hrp.org.uk.

1653: *'Take Away This Bauble!'*

The remains of Oliver Cromwell, like those of the other regicides, were dug up and dismembered after the Restoration. His rotting head was set on a pole outside Westminster Hall for a quarter of a century. But you can see his death mask, warts and all, in the Museum of London, www.museumoflondon.org.uk, and you can visit the house where he lived from 1636 to 1647 in St Mary's Street, Ely. Tel.: 01353 662062.

Hill, Christopher, *God's Englishman: Oliver Cromwell and the English Revolution* (London, Weidenfeld & Nicolson), 1970.

Morrill, John (ed.), *Oliver Cromwell and the English Revolution* (London, Longman), 1990.

1655: *Rabbi Manasseh and the Return of the Jews*

The dark oak benches from the Creechurch Lane synagogue, which opened in 1656, were moved in 1701 to the Spanish and Portuguese Synagogue in Bevis Marks Street, now Britain's oldest synagogue. Built by a Quaker, the exterior resembles a nonconformist chapel, while the interior reflects the influence of Sir Christopher Wren. Tel.: 020 7626 1274.

1660: *Charles II and the Royal Oak*

Richard Ollard colourfully recreates Charles II's adventures after the Battle of Worcester – and we are now entering the age of the great diarists, whom Liza Picard quotes along with a host of other contemporary sources in her intimate-feeling social history of the period.

Bowle, John (ed.), *The Diary of John Evelyn* (Oxford, Oxford University Press), 1983.

Latham, R. (ed.), *The Shorter Pepys* (London, Bell & Hyman), 1985.

Ollard, Richard, *The Escape of Charles II* (London, Constable), 1986.

Picard, Liza, *Restoration London* (London, Weidenfeld & Nicolson), 2001.

1665: *The Village That Chose to Die*

Every year on Plague Sunday (the last Sunday in August) the modern inhabitants of Eyam hold an outdoor service to commemorate the heroic sacrifice of their predecessors. In 2000, Eyam's enterprising little museum was awarded the Museum of the Year Shoestring Award. www.eyammuseum.demon.co.uk.

Bell, Walter George, *The Great Plague in London* (London, Folio Society), 2001.

1666: *London Burning*

The tragedy of the Great Fire produced the finest building of the seventeenth century, and arguably England's finest building ever. *'Lector, Si Monumentum Requeris, Circumspice'* ('Reader, if you seek a monument, then look around you') runs Sir Christopher Wren's inscription beneath the dome of St Paul's. Since Saxon times all five churches on this spot had been destroyed by fire. Wren designed the sixth as a sparkling symbol of London's rebirth, and he was there to witness its completion thirty-five years later. In the cathedral library you can see the huge and fabulously expensive oak model that the architect constructed to persuade Charles II to back his revolutionary concept. www.stpauls.co.uk.

Bell, Walter George, *The Great Fire of London in 1666* (London, Folio Society), 2003.

1678/9: *Titus Oates and the Popish Plot*

John Dryden's poem *Absalom and Achitophel* feverishly evokes the hysteria of the Popish Plot and the exclusion crisis. J. P. Kenyon recounts the story masterfully.

Kenyon, J. P., *The Popish Plot* (New York, Sterling), 2001.

1685: *Monmouth's Rebellion and the Bloody Assizes*

Christopher Lee starred as Judge Jeffreys in *The Bloody Judge* (1970), a film that has now acquired cult status. It is available on the DVD *The Christopher Lee Collection* by Blue Underground.

1688–9: *The Glorious Invasion*

Lord Macaulay virtually invented modern history, and his great five-volume work remains the classic study of the 1688/9 turning-point. Eveline Cruickshanks coldly dissects his Whig interpretation, but without destroying it.

Cruickshanks, Eveline, *The Glorious Revolution* (London, Macmillan), 2000.

Macaulay, T. B., *The History of England from the Accession of James II.* The five volumes of Macaulay's classic are currently in print at three publishers (R.A. Kessinger Publishing, the University Press of the Pacific, and Indypublish.com). The book is also accessible online at a variety of websites, including www.strecorsoc. org/macaulay/title.html#contents and www.gutenburg.org/ etext/1468.

1687: *Isaac Newton and the Principles of the Universe*

There are modern apple trees in the orchard of Woolsthorpe Manor near Grantham in Lincolnshire, Isaac Newton's birthplace. Tel.: 01476 860338. The best account of the ferment of science and superstition surrounding the birth of the Royal Society is Lisa Jardine's sparkling study of Newton's great rival, Robert Hooke. The project to put all ten million of Newton's words on the web can be accessed on www.newtonproject.ic.ac.uk.

Jardine, Lisa, *The Curious Life of Robert Hooke* (London, HarperCollins), 2004.

1690: *John Locke and Toleration*

www.oregonstate.edu/instruct/phl302/philosophers/locke.html provides a good timeline of Locke's career and also has links to an online version of his *Essay on Human Understanding*.

Goldie, Mark (ed.), *John Locke, Political Essays* (Cambridge, Cambridge University Press), 1997.

Tully, James H. (ed.), *John Locke: A Letter concerning Toleration* (Indianapolis, Hackett), 1983.

1690: 'Remember the Boyne!' – the Birth of the Orangemen

See www.geocities.com/Athens/2430/map.html for a map of the battle, and www.bcpl.net/~cbladey/battle.html for an eyewitness account. For the Orangemen, see www.orangenet.org.

Lenihan, Padraig, *1690: Battle of the Boyne* (Stroud, Tempus), 2003.

1693: *Britannia Rules the Waves – the Triangular Trade*

Facsimile pages of Thomas Phillips's voyage in the *Hannibal* provide the illustrations for Dr Steve Murdoch's article about the female John Brown on the website: www.historycooperative.org/journals/whc/1.2/murdoch.html. James Walvin relates the early history of African immigrants in Britain.

Thomas, Hugh, *The Slave Trade: History of the Atlantic Slave Trade 1440–1870* (New York, Simon & Schuster), 1987.

Walvin, James, *Black Ivory: Slavery in the British Empire* (Oxford, Blackwell), 2001.

1701: *Jethro Tull's 'Drill' and the Miner's Friend*

At the start of their career, the pop group Jethro Tull chose a different name every week. They played well enough on the evening for which they happened to have picked out the name of the seed-drill inventor to be invited back – so the name stuck, with its connotations of eccentric inventiveness. www.historyguide.org features a lecture on the origins of the Industrial Revolution – along with stimulating answers to the question 'What is history?'

1704: *Marlborough Catches the French Sleeping at the 'Village of the Blind'*

Two recent books tell the story of John Churchill's brilliant victory – then there is the biography of the great man by his famous twentieth-century descendant. To inspect the glories of Blenheim, visit www.blenheimpalace.com.

Chandler, David, *Blenheim Preparation: The English Army on the March to the Danube* (London, Spellmount), 2004.

Churchill, Winston S., *Marlborough, His Life and Times* (London, 4 vols, Harrap), 1933–8.

Spencer, Charles, *Blenheim: Battle for Europe* (London, Weidenfeld & Nicolson), 2004.

1707: *Union Jack*

For details of the Union Jack, and everything you ever wanted to know about vexillology (the scientific study of flags and related emblems), see www.flaginstitute.org.

1714: *Made in Germany*

Plumb's remains the classic account of Britain's early Hanoverian years.

Hatton, Ragnhild, *George I* (Yale, Yale University Press), 2001.

Plumb, J.H., *The First Four Georges* (London, Collins), 1956.

1720: *The South Sea Bubble*

Charles Mackay's *Extraordinary Popular Delusions and the Madness of Crowds* is still useful as the first historical account of the bubble www.econlib.org/library/Mackay/macEx.html.

Balen, Malcolm, *A Very English Deceit* (London, Fourth Estate), 2002.

1721–42: *Britain's First Prime Minister*

Jeremy Black provides a modern updating of Plumb's classic.

Black, Jeremy, *Walpole in Power* (Stroud, Tempus), 2001.

Plumb, J. H., *Sir Robert Walpole: The Making of a Statesman* and *The King's Minister* (London, Cresset Press), 1956 and 1961.

1738: *Born Again*

For the modern version of John Wesley's preaching to the multitudes, wherever they might be, visit www.methodist.org.uk. Wesley's letters and sermons can be found on a website run by the Wesley Center for Applied Theology at the Northwest Nazarene Christian University in Idaho: http://wesley.nnu.edu.

Hattersley, Roy, *John Wesley: A Brand from the Burning* (London, Little, Brown), 2002.

1739: *Dick Turpin – 'Stand and Deliver!'*

This account of the myth of Dick Turpin is largely based on the pioneering work of James Sharp. For additional historical detail consult the irresistibly named www.stand-and-deliver.org.uk.

Sharp, James, *Dick Turpin: The Myth of the English Highwayman* (London, Profile Books), 2004.

1745: *God Save the King!*

Frank McLynn began the modern reassessment of Bonnie Prince Charlie. For a Scottish view of the Battle of Culloden – and of other things – consult the website www.highlanderweb.co.uk.

McLynn, Frank, *Charles Edward Stuart: A Tragedy in Many Acts* (Oxford, Oxford Paperbacks), 1991.

1755: *Dr Johnson's Dictionary*

There are numerous popular editions of James Boswell's classic *Life of Johnson*, rich in colour and anecdote. If you want to see where the Doctor worked on his dictionary, you can visit his house, just off Fleet Street in London. See www.drjohnsonshouse.org. To track down a spicy quotation or insult, go to the Samuel Johnson Sound Bite Page on www.samueljohnson.com.

Lynch, Jack, *Samuel Johnson's Dictionary: Selections from the 1755 Work That Defined the English Language* (London, Atlantic Books), 2004.

1759: *General Wolfe and the Capture of Quebec*

Canadian websites do James Wolfe proud. www.uppercanadahistory.ca contains a graphic account of the battle on the Heights of Abraham, and you can view the copy of Gray's *Elegy* given to Wolfe by his fiancée Katherine Lowther on http://rpo.library.utoronto.ca/poem/882.html.

McLynn, Frank, *1759: The Year Britain Became Master of the World* (London, Jonathan Cape), 2004.

1766: *James Hargreaves and the Spinning Jenny*

Ironbridge Museum in Shropshire is a shrine to the wonders of the Industrial Revolution: www.ironbridge.org.uk. Two excellent websites dedicated to the cotton industry are www.cottontimes.co.uk and www.spinningtheweb.org.uk. These provide links with many places to visit in Derbyshire and Lancashire, including the Lewis Museum of Textile Machinery and Sir Richard Arkwright's Masson Mills Working Textile Museum, www.masson mills.co.uk.

1770: *Captain Cook – Master of the Pilotage*

The Captain Cook Memorial Museum is yet another reason for visiting the Yorkshire port of Whitby: www.cookmuseumwhitby.co.uk. Click on www.winthrop.dk/jcook.html and you will be greeted by a stirring rendition of 'Rule Britannia', along with links to books and portraits of Captain Cook, and provocative thoughts on Cook's promise to go 'farther than any other man has been before me . . . as far as I think it possible for a man to go'.

1773: *The Boston Tea Party*

Stanley Weintraub provides a fresh look at the American War of Independence, questioning the assumption that all justice resided with the rebels. John Steele Gordon takes the story forward to explain how the USA, which occupies 6 per cent of the world's landmass and has 6 per cent of its people, has come to account for nearly one third of the world's gross domestic product.

Gordon, John Steele, *An Empire of Wealth* (New York, HarperCollins), 2004.

Weintraub, Stanley, *Iron Tears: America's Battle for Freedom, Britain's Quagmire, 1775–1783* (New York, Simon & Schuster), 2005.

1785: *Thomas Clarkson – the Giant with One Idea*

Adam Hochschild describes how Thomas Clarkson ignited the anti-slavery movement and helped choose William Wilberforce as its figurehead. Wilberforce's abolition speech in the House of Commons on 12 May 1789 drew heavily on Clarkson's research and can be read at www.brycchancarey.com/abolition/wilberforce2.htm. His house can be visited in Hull: www.hullcc.gov.uk.

Hochschild, Adam, *Bury the Chains: The First International Human Rights Movement* (London, Macmillan), 2005.

1788: *The Madness of King George III*

Of the many biographies, Christopher Hibbert has written the most amiable. Alan Bennett's play and film *The Madness of King George* is the work of a serious history student, based closely on such contemporary sources as Fanny Burney. You can see the superb library that the King created between 1760 and 1820, stacked shelf on shelf in a crystal tower in the lobby of the modern British Library in London – the last place that the King, mad or sane, would have wanted it to be.

Hibbert, Christopher, *George III: A Personal History* (London, Penguin), 1999.
Lacey, Robert, 'The library of George III: collecting for Crown or nation?', *The Court Historian*, vol. 10, 2 (Dec. 2005), pp. 137–47.

1789: *'Breadfruit Bligh' and the Mutiny on the* Bounty

Visiting William Bligh's grave in Lambeth, just across the river from the Houses of Parliament, provides a double bonus, since the Church of St Mary-at-Lambeth also houses the Museum of Garden History. The Pitcairn Islands Study Center contains one of the world's largest collections of historical material relating to the mutiny on the Bounty – www.lareau.org/bounty.html, complementing the links to be found on http://library.puc.edu/pitcairn.html.

1791: *Thomas Paine and the Rights of Man*

Every year on the nearest Saturday to 8 June, the day of his death, members of the Thomas Paine Society gather at the statue of Paine in Thetford, Norfolk, his birthplace: www.thomaspainesociety.org. The Society also organises lectures by modern radical thinkers, from Germaine Greer to Tony Benn, in the Paine tradition. www.thomaspaine.org is the exhaustive website of the Thomas Paine National Historical Association in America.

1792: *Mary Wollstonecraft and the Rights of Woman*

You can read the text of *A Vindication of the Rights of Woman* on www.bartleby.com/144 and also on www.orst.edu/instruct/phl302/ philosophers/wollstonecraft.html.

Todd, Janet, *Mary Wollstonecraft: A Revolutionary Life* (London, Weidenfeld & Nicolson), 2000.

Tomalin, Claire, *The Life and Death of Mary Wollstonecraft* (London, Penguin), 1992.

1805: *England Expects . . .*

The recent bicentennial of the Battle of Trafalgar stimulated a flood of books about Nelson. Janet MacDonald shows how a navy sails on its stomach.

Coleman, Terry, *Nelson: The Man and the Legend* (London, Bloomsbury), 2002.

MacDonald, Janet, *Feeding Nelson's Navy: The True Story of Food at Sea in the Georgian Era* (London, Chatham Publishing), 2004.

1811: *Fanny Burney's Breast*

You can read the text of Fanny Burney's novel *Evelina*, an eighteenth-century *Bridget Jones's Diary* written in letter form, on http://digital.library.upenn.edu/women/burney/evelina/evelina. html. The harrowing tale of her breast removal can be read in Nigel Nicolson's brilliant little book.

Nicolson, Nigel, *Fanny Burney, Mother of English Fiction* (London, Short Books), 2002.

1812: *Who Was Ned Ludd?*

Ned Ludd may not have existed, but he has earned an entry in the *Oxford Dictionary of National Biography*, along with Robin Hood, King Arthur and his near-contemporary, Captain Swing. The National Archives Learning Curve presents five striking contemporary documents, including a handbill inciting weavers to revolt and one offering a £200 reward to catch men who wrecked machines: www.learningcurve.gov.uk/politics/g3.

Thompson, E.P., *The Making of the English Working Class* (London, Gollancz), 1963.

1815: *Wellington and Waterloo*

English Heritage now takes care of 'Number One, London', Wellington's home at Apsley House at Hyde Park Corner: www.english-heritage.org.uk/server/show/ConProperty.410. Fletcher, Howarth and Keegan analyse the battle from different viewpoints. Hibbert's intimate biography is a classic.

Fletcher, Ian, *A Desperate Business: Wellington, the British Army and the Waterloo Campaign* (London, Spellmount), 2001.

Hibbert, Christopher, *Wellington: A Personal History* (London, HarperCollins), 1998.

Howarth, David, *Waterloo: A Near-Run Thing* (Gloucestershire, Windrush Press), 1997.

Keegan, John, *The Face of Battle: A Study of Agincourt, Waterloo and the Somme* (London, Pimlico), 2004.

1823: *Stone Treasures – Mary Anning and the Terror Lizards*

Every year the Philpott Museum at Lyme Regis is the focus of a festival celebrating Mary Anning and her pioneering of England's Jurassic coast: www.lymeregismuseum.co.uk/fossils.htm. Dr Hugh Torrens, the geological expert on Mary's life and work, is currently searching for two ichthyosaur fossils whose current whereabouts are unknown. He suspects they are probably sitting in a museum or someone's personal collection gathering dust, so if you think you know their location, please contact Dr Torrens at gga10@keele.ac.uk.

Cadbury, Deborah, *The Dinosaur Hunters* (London, Fourth Estate), 2000.

Freeman, Michael, *Victorians and the Prehistoric: Tracks to a Lost World* (New Haven, Yale University Press), 2004.

McGowan, Christopher, *The Dragon Seekers* (New York, Perseus), 2001.

1830: *Blood on the Tracks*

This account of William Huskisson's death is largely based on Simon Garfield's recent book, which sheds revealing light on the politician's early career. Rail lovers will already know that the Mecca and Medina of locomotive collections are close to each other in Yorkshire at the Darlington Railway Centre and Museum (www.drcm.org.uk), which offers a virtual tour, and at the National Railway Museum at York (www.nrm.org.uk).

Garfield, Simon, *The Last Journey of William Huskisson* (London, Faber), 2003.

1819–32: *The Lung Power of Orator Hunt*
Edward Pearce, the modern parliamentary reporter, paints an insightful sketch of Orator Hunt in his historical account of Reform. The Act itself can be viewed at the National Archives website: www.nationalarchives. gov.uk/pathways/citizenship/struggle_democracy/getting_vote.htm.

Pearce, Edward, *Reform! The Fight for the 1832 Reform Act* (London, Jonathan Cape), 2003.

1834: *The Tolpuddle Martyrs*
The modern cult of the martyrs owes much to the centenary organised by the Trades Union Congress in 1934. Annual rallies have been held ever since in Tolpuddle, where there is a museum and a row of six cottages for retired agricultural workers, each one bearing the name of one of the martyrs: www.tolpuddlemartyrs.org.uk.

Trades Union Congress, *The Book of the Martyrs of Tolpuddle, 1834–1934* (London, TUC), 1934.

1837: '*I Will Be Good*' – *Victoria Becomes Queen*
The world's libraries are overloaded with chunky biographies of Queen Victoria, but the best two studies are the perceptive little volumes by Walter Arnstein and Lady Longford, each of them the distillation of a lifetime's study and thought. Lynne Vallone had a lucky break when she stumbled on boxes in the Royal Archives containing the earnest young Victoria's exercise books, notes on her behaviour during lessons, and some stray bits of blotting paper with little sketches on them – plus a watercolour map that she reprinted in *Becoming Victoria*.

Arnstein, Walter, *Queen Victoria* (Basingstoke, Palgrave Macmillan), 2004.

Longford, Lady Elizabeth, *Queen Victoria* (Pocket Biography Series) (London, Sutton Publishing), 2000.

Vallone, Lynne, *Becoming Victoria* (New Haven, Yale University Press), 2001.

1843: 'God's Wonderful Railway' – Isambard Kingdom Brunel

Depending on where you live, you can experience the soaring vision of Brunel by visiting Paddington or Bristol Temple Meads railway stations, the Clifton Suspension Bridge, or the Royal Albert Bridge crossing the Tamar at Saltash, near Plymouth. You can also tread the deck of the *Great Britain*, now at rest near the replica of John Cabot's *Matthew* in the floating docks at Bristol (another of IKB's achievements).

Brindle, Steve, *Brunel: The Man Who Built the World* (London, Weidenfeld & Nicolson), 2005.

Fox, Stephen, *The Ocean Railway* (London, HarperCollins), 2003.

Griffiths, Denis, with Andrew Lambert and Fred Walker, *Brunel's Ships* (London, Chatham Publishing), 1999.

1843: Rain, Steam & Speed – the Shimmering Vision of J.M.W. Turner

When he died in 1851, Turner bequeathed to the nation all his paintings, which he described as 'his children', along with his brushes, paint-smeared palettes and a myriad of his busy, often rain- and spray-spattered notebooks. You can see these on display in a sequence of wonderful rooms at the Tate Britain gallery in Pimlico, London: www.tate.org.uk. But you will have to go to the National Gallery in Trafalgar Square to see *Rain, Steam & Speed*. John Ruskin reproduced the details of Jane O'Meara's memorable train journey with Turner in volume 35 (p. 600) of his collected works.

Ruskin, John, *Works* (London, George Allen), 1908.

1851: Prince Albert's Crystal Palace

Michael Leapman's is the latest book to capture the magic of Prince

Albert's Great Exhibition, whose splendours are commemorated on a number of websites, notably www.victoriastation.com.

Leapman, Michael, *The World for a Shilling* (London, Headline), 2001.

1852: 'Women and Children First!' – the Birkenhead Drill
The *Boy's Own Paper* for 1 November 1884 contains the classic account of the *Birkenhead*'s sinking. The estimable Wikipedia project is not always reliable, but this link does contain the list of all those who perished – together with details of the unproved rumour that the *Birkenhead* went down with three tons of gold coins that had been secretly stored below decks in the ammunition chambers: http://en.wikipedia.org/wiki/HMS_Birkenhead

1854: Into the Valley of Death
Cecil Woodham-Smith wrote the classic account of this misadventure. Terry Brighton presents a modern reassessment. Philip Knightley's ground-breaking book recounts the career of William Howard Russell, along with the history of 'the war correspondent as hero, propagandist and myth maker from the Crimea to Vietnam'. The first casualty of war is, of course, the truth.

Brighton, Terry, *Hell Riders: The True Story of the Charge of the Light Brigade* (London, Henry Holt), 2004.
Knightley, Philip, *The First Casualty* (London, André Deutsch), 1975.
Woodham-Smith, Cecil, *The Reason Why* (London, McGraw-Hill), 1953.

1854–5: The Lady of the Lamp and the Lady with the Teacup (plus the Odd Sip of Brandy)
Just across the Thames from the Houses of Parliament, the Florence Nightingale Museum in St Thomas's Hospital contains, among other memorabilia, Florence Nightingale's pet owl, Athena, stuffed and preserved in a glass case: www.florence-nightingale.co.uk. Thames Valley University hosts a handsome website www.maryseacole.com, and the Department of Health offers monetary awards to black and minority ethnic nurses, midwives and health visitors working in the

NHS in honour of Mary Seacole: http://www.rcn.org.uk/aboutus/ scholarshipawards/rcnmembers.php.

Salih, Sara (ed.), *Wonderful Adventures of Mrs Seacole in Many Lands* (London, Penguin), 2005.

Woodham-Smith, Cecil, *Florence Nightingale, 1820–1910* (London, Fontana), 1969.

1858: Charles Darwin and the Survival of the Fittest

You could spend your whole life reading books about Darwin – and another lifetime studying the work of Alfred Russel Wallace (the spelling of whose middle name was perpetuated from a mistake made when his birth was recorded).

Browne, Janet, *Charles Darwin* (New York, Knopf), 2002.

Slotten, Ross A., *The Heretic in Darwin's Court: The Life of Alfred Russel Wallace* (New York, Columbia University Press), 2004.

1878: The Great Stink – and the Tragedy of the Princess Alice

This account is largely based on Jonathan Schneer's evocative history of the Thames, as entrancing and meandering as the river itself. For more on the remarkable architect of London's sewers, go to www.bbc.co.uk/history, and search for Joseph Bazalgette.

Schneer, Jonathan, *The Thames: England's River* (London, Little, Brown), 2005.

1887: Lord Rosebery's Historical Howler

The file copy of Queen Victoria's letter to Lord Rosebery is in the Royal Archives at Windsor, RA/VIC/F47/49, reproduced by gracious permission of H. M. the Queen. The original is in the Rosebery Archive at the National Library of Scotland, MS10064, ff 114-17.

Rhodes James, Robert, *Rosebery* (London, Weidenfeld & Nicolson), 1963.

1888: Annie Besant and 'Phossy Jaw' – the Strike of the Match Girls

Annie's philosophical journey from minister's wife to atheist to theosophist is graphically described in http://womenshistory. about.com/od/freethought/aannie_besant.htm. For the horrors of phossy jaw, visit http://en.wikipedia.org/wiki/Phossy-jaw.

1897: Diamond Jubilee – the Empire Marches By
Kuhn's seminal work describes the transformation of the British monarchy in the latter part of Queen Victoria's reign. Hudson illuminates the work behind the two great royal festivals.

Hudson, Roger, *The Jubilee Years 1887–1897* (London, Folio Society), 1996.
Kuhn, William, *Democratic Royalism: The Transformation of the British Monarchy 1861–1914* (London, Macmillan), 1996.

1900: Slaughter on Spion Kop
From the 1902 account by Arthur Conan Doyle (creator of Sherlock Holmes), the Boer War has been well served by lively authors, of which Thomas Pakenham is the finest. www.anglo-boer.co.za/index.html offers a 'virtual museum' of Boer War history to stroll through.

Pakenham, Thomas, *The Boer War* (London, Folio Society), 1999.

1903: Edward VII and the Entente Cordiale
Oxford's Bodleian Library gathered some unusual news clippings to mark the centenary of the Entente Cordiale, which can be reached via www.bodley.ox.ac.uk, then searching for Entente Cordiale. If you would like to win an endowed post-graduate scholarship to study in Paris, go to www.entente-cordiale.org.

Dunlop, Ian, *Edward VII and the Entente Cordiale* (London, Constable), 2004.
Heffer, Simon, *Power and Place: The Political Consequences of King Edward VII* (London, Weidenfeld & Nicolson), 1998.

1910: Cellar Murderer Caught by Wireless – Dr Crippen
The Metropolitan Police website gives major coverage to one of its most famous cases, and while you are visiting www.met.police.uk/history, why not sample more stories from the Crime Museum – Jack the Ripper, the Brides in the Bath murders, and the dreadful doings of the Kray twins?

Smith, David James, *Supper with the Crippens: A New Investigation into One of the Most Notorious Cases of the Twentieth Century* (London, Orion), 2005.

1912: 'I May Be Some Time . . .' – the Sacrifice of Captain Oates

The Scott Polar Research Institute – www.spri.cam.ac.uk – in Cambridge, has Captain Oates's reindeer-skin sleeping bag on display. The archives are rich with the letters and diaries of Polar explorers (north and south) – though Scott's diary of his last expedition is at the British Museum in London.

Limb, Sue, and Cordingley, Patrick, *Captain Oates, Soldier and Explorer* (London, Batsford), 1982.

Scott, R. F., *Scott's Last Expedition: The Journals of Captain R. F. Scott* (London, Pan), 2003.

1913: The King's Horse and Emily Davison

The admirable Spartacus website shows a photograph of Emily Davison at her graduation, along with extracts from contemporary newspapers and female memoirs: www.spartacus.schoolnet.co.uk/Wdavison.htm. For more on the suffragette movement, visit www.historylearningsite.co.uk/women%201900–1945.htm, as well as the history website of the BBC, www.bbc.co.uk/history, which has a rich archive on women's movements in Britain and abroad.

1914: When Christmas Stopped a War

www.firstworldwar.com is an encyclopaedic survey of the Great War, month by month, reproducing posters, memoirs, diaries and primary documents of all sorts, together with photographs and battlefield maps. Bruce Bairnsfather became the cartoonist of trench warfare, creating the character 'Old Bill'.

Marsay, Mark (ed.), *The Bairnsfather Omnibus* (Scarborough, Great Northern Publishing), 2000.

Weintraub, Stanley, *Silent Night: The Remarkable Christmas Truce of 1914* (London, Simon & Schuster), 2001.

1915: *Patriotism Is Not Enough – Edith Cavell*

'Humanity, Fortitude, Devotion, Sacrifice' is the inscription on the tall stone memorial to Edith Cavell which offers an inspiring sight outside the National Portrait Gallery, just off Trafalgar Square in London. The Edith Cavell website is a lovingly tended garden of tributes and memorabilia including photographs of the Norfolk rectory where she grew up, and the interior of the cell in which she spent her final hours: www.edithcavell.org.uk.

1916: *Your Country Needs You! – the Sheffield Pals*

www.firstworldwar.com contains detailed entries on the Pals' regiments and also on the ghastly battles of the Somme offensive. Extracts from Richard Sparling's detailed history of the Sheffield Pals can be found on their website, www.pals.org.uk/sheffield.

Sparling, Richard, *History of the 12th (Service) Battalion, York and Lancaster Regiment* (Sheffield, J. W. Northend), 1920.

1926: *A Country Fit for Heroes?*

www.aftermathww1.com dates itself from Armistice Day, 32,282 days ago by the end of March 2007. The purpose of the site is to recall what happened 'when the boys came home'. Kenneth Rose's prize-winning biography recounts the drama of the General Strike as seen from Buckingham Palace.

Rose, Kenneth, *George V* (London, Phoenix), 2000.

1930: *The Greatest History Book Ever*

'Histories have previously been written with the object of exalting their authors. The object of this History is to console the reader. *No other history does this.*'

Sellar, W. C., and Yeatman, R. J., *1066 and All That* (London, Methuen), 1930.

1933: *Not Cricket – 'Bodyline' Bowling Wins the Ashes*

www.cricinfo.com will connect you with the *Wisden Cricketers' Almanack*, the bible of the game. www.lords.org is the detailed and helpful website of the MCC, which will tell you how to visit the museum at Lord's, where you can see the little urn containing the Ashes. For detailed score sheets of every Test Match in the bodyline series, see www.334notout.com.

Frith, David, *Bodyline Autopsy: The Full Story of the Most Sensational Test Cricket Series* (London, Aurum Press), 2003.

1936: *Edward the Abdicator*
Edward VIII's abdication speech can be read in full on www.historyplace.com/speeches/edward.htm. Philip Ziegler wrote the official and definitive biography (not always the same thing). Rupert Godfrey edited the letters in which the young Prince of Wales expressed his despair at his royal lot.

Godfrey, Rupert (ed.), *Letters from a Prince: Edward Prince of Wales to Mrs Freda Dudley Ward, March 1918–January 1921* (London, Time Warner Books), 1999.
Ziegler, Philip, *Edward VIII* (London, HarperCollins), 1990.

1938: *Peace for Our Time! – Mr Chamberlain Takes a Plane*
Keith Robbins brilliantly captures the touch-and-go atmosphere of 1938 in his comprehensive study. Parker shows how 'appeasement' should mean much more to us than another word for 'caving in'.

Parker, R.A.C., *Chamberlain and Appeasement* (London, Macmillan), 1993.
Robbins, Keith, *Munich* (London, Cassell), 1968.

1940: *Dunkirk – Britain's Army Saved by the Little Boats*
The Association of Dunkirk Little Ships commemorates the heroes who crossed the Channel and gives details of surviving boats when they come up for sale: www.adls.org.uk.

Wilson, Patrick, *Dunkirk* (Barnsley, Pen & Sword Books), 1999.

1940: *Battle of Britain – the Few and the Many*
www.battleofbritain.net and www.the-battle-of-britain.co.uk provide detailed lists of the combatants on both sides. Among them was Joseph

Frantisek of the Polish Air Force, with 17 confirmed kills. He flew with 303 Squadron (named after the Polish hero, General Tadeusz Kosciuszko), which claimed to have downed 126 enemy planes, the highest number achieved by any fighter squadron engaged in the Battle of Britain.

Craig, Phil, and Clayton, Tim, *Finest Hour* (London, Hodder & Stoughton), 1999.
Olsen, Lynne, and Cloud, Stanley, *A Question of Honor: The Kosciuszko Squadron* (New York, Knopf), 2003.

1943: *Code-making, Code-breaking – 'The Life That I Have'*
Like Leo Marks, Alan Turing was an unconventional character whose creativity made an immense contribution to the secret war effort – working at Bletchley Park, he cracked the secret of the Enigma code. His intriguing and ultimately tragic story can be read on www.turing.org.uk. The official story is recounted on www.bletchleypark.org.uk, which tells you how you can visit Bletchley Park near Milton Keynes in Buckinghamshire.

Marks, Leo, *Between Silk and Cyanide: A Code-Maker's Story, 1941–1945* (London, HarperCollins), 1998.
Montefiore, Hugh Sebag, *Enigma: The Battle for the Code* (London, Weidenfeld & Nicolson), 2000.

1945: *Voice of the People*
You can hear Winston Churchill speak when you click on the website of the Churchill Society. www.churchill-society-london.org.uk also includes the text of his famous 'Iron Curtain' speech delivered at Fulton, Missouri, in 1946.

Harris, Jose, *William Beveridge: A Biography* (Oxford, Clarendon Press), 1997.
Reynolds, David, *In Command of History: Churchill Fighting and Writing the Second World War* (London, Longman), 1992.

1953: *Decoding the Secret of Life*
The finest account of DNA's decoding is James D. Watson's own engaging memoir on the search for the double helix. Before his death,

Francis Crick recounted his side of the story in a long interview which can be read on www.accessexcellence.org, along with other articles about the pair. Brenda Maddox's award-winning book documents the tale of the 'Dark Lady' of DNA.

Maddox, Brenda, *Rosalind Franklin* (London, HarperCollins), 2003.
Watson, James D., *The Double Helix: A Personal Account of the Discovery of the Structure of DNA* (London, Penguin), 1999.

ACKNOWLEDGEMENTS

History, according to the polymath Felipe Fernández-Armesto, is like 'a nymph glimpsed between the leaves: the more you shift perspective, the more is revealed. If you want to see her whole, you have to dodge and slip between many different viewpoints.'

Peering through those leaves has been a consuming passion of my life, and my first thanks must be to the generations of scholars whose research has parted so many branches. The preceding source notes set out the particular authors on whom I have relied, and I owe a further debt to the historians I have consulted personally while researching and writing this book: John Allen, Walter Arnstein, Andrew Barclay, Jonathan Conlin, Jacqueline Eales, Richard Eales, Christopher Haigh, Mary Hollingsworth, David Hill, J. Patrick Hornbeck II, Anna Keay, John McSween, Philip Revill, Keith Robbins, Kenneth Rose, Christopher Skidmore, Alfred Smyth, David Starkey, Simon Thurley, Lynne Vallone, Yvonne Ward and Patrick Wormald.

My thanks to Nigel Rees for helping me to track down several fugitive quotations, and also to Moyra Ashford, who helped me through the first three-quarters of the enterprise. I am grateful for the research assistance of Orlando Athill, Charles Donovan, Nabil Al-Khowaiter, Margaret Smyth, Christine Todd, and Jacqueline Williams, and for the painstaking help of the following archivists and academic experts: Elizabeth Anionwu of the Mary Seacole Centre for Nursing Practice, Thames Valley University; Pam Clark and Julie Snelling in the Royal Archives at Windsor; Elizabeth Finn and Margaret Sparks at Canterbury Cathedral; Sheila Mackenzie, National Archives of Scotland; Tony Trowles in the Muniments Room at Westminster Abbey; and Glenys Williams, Archivist of the MCC at Lord's – with a special mention to Matthew Engel of *Wisden* for his masterly exposition of 'leg theory'. My thanks to the partners of the John Sandoe bookshop, and to the librarians and archivists at the British Library, the London Library, the National Archives, and at my own, local public library in the west minster.

This omnibus edition was originally published as three separate volumes, and the earlier volumes prompted a host of friendly letters from readers, some of whom suggested tales that are included here. My thanks to Phil Turton for proposing the 'bodyline' tour as a modern morality tale, and to Clive Fairweather who passed on the vivid tableau of J. M. W. Turner sticking his head out of the railway carriage window, plus that even more dark and stormy Victorian episode, the sinking of the *Birkenhead*.

There is a sense in which Peter Furtado, the editor of *History Today*, initiated this project by inviting me to contribute to his column on historical beginnings, 'Point of Departure'. It made me realise there was nothing I would more enjoy than re-examining the stories on which I was brought up – and it has reminded me of the debt I owe to the history teachers who encouraged me at Bristol Grammar School: Charles Peter Hill, Maurice Isaac, John Millward and Roy Avery. Before them was my mother, who bought me my first history book, H. E. Marshall's *Our Island Story*, as well as my father, who dis-approved so much of the companion volume, *Our Empire Story* – 'Don't you know we haven't got an empire any more?'

At my publishers Little, Brown, in London and New York, my thanks go to Peter Cotton, Ursula Mackenzie, Elizabeth Nagle, Sue Phillpott and David Young – with particular gratitude to Roger Cazalet and Viv Redman, inspirers of the woad plant, the miniature chess set and the other illustration ideas so brilliantly realised by Fred van Deelen.

This is my last book launched by my agent of so many years, Michael Shaw, but how kind of him to groom such an able successor in Jonathan Pegg. My thanks to his assistants, Camilla Goslett and Shaheeda Sabir.

I have written this book for adults – or, perhaps, for children of my own age – and I have dedicated it to my own three children, Sasha, Scarlett and Bruno, whom I deeply love and admire and from whom I have learned to learn so much. My brilliant and original wife Sandi deserves much of the credit for their brilliance and originality, as well as for her help with the starting and the visualisation of this book.

The enterprise took longer than I expected, as my own life changed in ways for which I had not planned. My thanks to my friends Prentis Hancock, Myrto Cutler, Harry Moore and Gregorio Kohon for keeping my own tale a happy one – and to Jane Rayne, for surprising me in many happy ways, not least by producing this curious and useful aide-memoire from her diary:

> Willie, Willie, Harry, Stee,
> Harry, Dick, John, Harry Three;
> One, two, three Neds, Richard Two,
> Harrys Four, Five, Six – then who?
> Edwards Four, Five, Dick the Bad,
> Then Harrys (twain), and Ned the Lad.
> Mary, Bessie, James the Vain,
> Charlie, Charlie, James again.
> Will and Mary, Anna Gloria,
> Georges four, then Will, Victoria.
> Edward Seven, George and Ted,
> George the Sixth, now Liz instead.

Forty-one monarchs – half a dozen memorable rhyming cutlets . . .

Robert Lacey, March 2007
www.robertlacey.com

INDEX

abacus, 77
Abolition of the Slave Trade
Bill (1807), 336
Accrington Pals, 424–6
Acre, 95, 96
Act in Restraint of Appeals
(1533), 197
Act of Settlement (1701), 306
Act of Succession (1534), 203
Act of Union (1707), 307
actors, 229–30
Adams, Samuel, 333, 345
Adelaide, 432
adultery, 270
aeroplanes, 436, 444–5
Aethelflaed, 'Lady of the
Mercians', 40–2
aethelings, 43, 77
Africa, 325, 401, 402, 407 *see
also* South Africa; West
Africa
Agincourt, Battle of, 158–61,
162, 164, 303
Agricola, Gnaeus Julius, 17
agriculture, 5, 18, 215, 301–2,
367 'Captain Swing'
disturbances, 368
AIDS, 133
Ainsworth, William
Harrison, 317–18
Alaska, 331
Alban, St, 25, 98
Albert, Prince, 378–9, 396,
401
Albert Hall, 379
Albion, 4–5, 129
Aldgate, 148, 272
Alexandria, 425
Alien Act (1705), 307
Alfonso (son of Edward I),
113
Alfred, King, 36–9, 40, 42, 50,
285
and *Anglo-Saxon Chronicle*,
38
and burning of cakes, 37–8,
39, 48

described as 'Father of the
Royal Navy', 38
will of, 40–1
Algonquins, 249
America(s), 188–9, 191, 202,
232, 249–50
constitution, 251
discovery of, 327
religious freedom, 268
see also Canada; United
States of America
Amiens, Peace of, 353
Amsterdam, 270, 272, 293
Amundsen, Roald, 412–13
amusements, 229–30
Angel-cynn, family of the
English, 40
Angevin Empire, 82, 83
Angles, 24
invasion and settlement of
Britain, 19–20, 20–1
Anglesey, 15, 113
Anglo-Saxon Chronicle, 38, 40,
41, 42, 45, 48, 68, 69–70,
81–2
Anglo-Saxons, 25
aetheling system, 43
Canute's attempt to
reconcile Danes and
Anglo-Saxons, 49–50
conversion to Christianity
by missionaries from
Rome, 24, 25–7
and famine, 35
invasion of Britain and
settlement of, 20–2
landscape, 35–6
legal discrimination against
by Normans, 70–1
and Norman Conquest,
61–2, 65
pagan gods, 25–6
preaching of Christianity
by Irish monks, 27–8
resistance against Vikings,
37, 40 41, 44–5
women, 40, 42

Anmer (racehorse), 415, 416
Anne, Queen, 54, 286–7, 288,
304, 305, 306, 322
Anne of Cleves, 210–12
Anning, Mary, 361–3
Anno Domini system of
dating, 33
anticlericalism, 147–8, 197
Antonine Wall, 18
Antwerp, 200, 409
Anjou, 80, 82, 97, 108, 122
appeasement, 438–9, 440
Apprentice Boys, 298
Aquitaine, 82, 97, 108
Antoninus, Emperor, 18
Arabs, 95
archaeologists, 3, 140
archery, 123
architecture, 166–7, 173
Arctic Ocean, 350
Arderne, John, 134–6
Arkwright, Richard, 328
Armenia, King of, 150
Armentières, 419
Armes, Captain R.J., 418–19
Arminianism, 256
army
Catholics excluded, 297
and General Strike, 428
and Luddite disturbances,
356
and 'Peterloo', 366
Prussian, 381–2
reform, 388
tallest officer, 401
army regiments
Black Watch, 381
Cheshire Regiment, 422
Gordon Highlanders, 419
North Staffordshire
Regiment, 418
Royal Warwickshire
Regiment, 419
Royal Welch Fusiliers, 420
York & Lancaster
Regiment, 424
Arsenal Football Club, 191–2

505

Arthur of Brittany, nephew
of John, 101
Arthur, King, 2, 22, 129
Arthur, Prince, 192, 194, 195
arts, patronage of, 254, 257
Ashmole, Elias, 253
Aske, Robert, 208–9
'assizes', 84
astronomy, 224–5, 291, 330,
392
Athelney, 38
Athelstan, King, 42
Atlantic Ocean, 188, 253,
299–300, 329, 335
atmospheric railway, 375
Attlee, Clement, 450
Augustine, St, 25–7, 28
Austen, Jane, 353
Australia, 330, 342, 378, 401,
434
cricket in, 431–4
transportation to, 357, 370
Austria, 304, 325, 437
Austria–Hungary, 421, 428
Avon Gorge, 1
Avon River, 188
Azincourt, Battle of
see Agincourt, Battle of

Bacon, Francis, 192, 226
Bairnsfather, Captain Bruce,
419
Balaclava, Battle of, 382–3, 387
Baldwin, Stanley, 436
Balfour, A. J., 435n
Ball, John, 139–40, 144–5
Ballot Act (1872), 370
Bampton, John, 141
Bank of England, 310
Bankes, Sir John, 261
Bankes, Lady Mary, 261
Banks, Sir Joseph, 330, 340
Baptists, 271
Barbados, 299
Barbary Coast, 154, 252
Barber, Frank, 323
Barbon, Praise-God
('Barebone'), 269
Barfleur, 77
Barking, 395
Barnet, Battle of (1471), 167
Barnsley Pals, 424, 426
Bath, 287
Battle, Sussex, 61 see also
Hastings; Senlac
Battle of Britain, 160, 443–5
Baxter, Richard, 263, 300
Bayeux Tapestry, 59–60, 61,
62–4, 65

Bazalgette, Joseph, 395, 396
Beagle, 392
Beatty, Dr, 352
Beaufort, Lady Margaret,
170–1, 183, 185, 186, 193
Beaulieu, Hampshire, 187
Beaverbrook, Lord, 445
Becket, Thomas, 83–91, 98,
146, 156, 202, 208
becomes a martyr after hair
shirt discovery, 89
confrontation with Henry
II over Church, 83,
84–7
declaration of as a saint and
pilgrimage to tombs,
89–90
murder of, 87–8
Bede, Venerable, 28, 32–5, 48
Belgium, 409, 421–2, 440
Ben Israel, Rabbi Manasseh,
270–1, 272
benefit of clergy, 84, 91
Benoît, Antoine, 63
Berbers, 154
Bering Strait, 340
Berkeley Castle, 120
Berkshire, 368
Berlin, 424, 443, 450
Bertha (wife of King
Ethelbert of Kent), 25
Besant, Annie, 398–400, 444n
Besant, Frank, 400
Bethlehem hospital
('Bedlam'), 377
Beveridge, William, 449–50
Bible, 31, 195, 196, 198–9, 203,
215, 225, 270, 362, 392, 397,
427n
Book of Daniel, 271
Book of Revelation, 271
and divine right, 254
in English, 199–200, 236, 271
King James, 248–9
New Testament, 199, 200
Tyndale's translation,
199–200, 249
Bill of Rights, 289
bin Laden, Osama, 95
biological warfare, 132
Birkenhead, 380–2, 385
Birmingham, 308, 367
Birmingham Symphony
Orchestra, 437
birth control, 400
bishops, 258, 262, 271
Bishops' Wars, 258
Black Death, 131–3, 137, 148,
155, 276

Black Prince, Edward the
(son of Edward III), 124,
128, 137, 140
Black Sea, 383n, 389
Blenheim, Battle of, 303–5
Blenheim Palace, 305–6
Blair, Tony, 97
Blake, William, 11–12
Bletchley Park, 446–7
Bligh, Captain William,
340–3
Blitzkrieg, 440
Blois, 80 see also Stephen
Blondel, legend, 97
Bloodworth, Sir Thomas, 279
Bloody Assizes, 285–6
Blücher, General Gebhard
von, 360
Bluebeard, 162
Boadicea, 14–16, 17, 184
Aethelflaed compared to,
41
Boer War, 403–7, 413, 424
Boger, Lieutenant Colonel
Dudley, 422
Boleyn, Anne, 195–6, 200,
204–6, 225
coronation, 204
execution, 205
Boleyn, George, 196, 200
Bolingbroke, Henry see
Henry IV, King
Bolton, 236, 328
Bonaparte, Joseph, 359
Book of Common Prayer see
Prayer Book
Borneo, 401
Boscobel House, 273
Boston Tea Party, 332–4
Boswell, James, 323
Bosworth, Battle of (1485),
183–5, 186, 193
Botany Bay, 330
Bothwell, James, Earl of, 235
Boulogne, 427
Bounty, 340–3
Bouvines, Battle of (1214), 101
Bowes, W. E. ('Bill'), 431–2
Box Tunnel, 375
Boyle, Robert, 291
Boyne, Battle of the, 296–8
Boy's Own Paper, 381
Bradford, William 251, 252
Bradford Pals, 426
Bradman, Donald, 432–3
Bradshaw, John, 266
breast cancer, 354–5
Breda, Declaration of, 275
Brentwood, 141

INDEX

Brest, 304
Brewster, William, 251, 252
Brighton, 380
Brinton, Thomas, 132–3
Bristol, 188, 189, 190, 308, 315
  railway links, 374, 376–7
  and slave trade, 300, 335–6
British Association for the
  Advancement of Science,
  362
British Broadcasting
  Company (BBC), 428
British Commonwealth,
  397n, 448
British Empire, 301, 326,
  400–2, 407, 436, 448
British Expeditionary Force,
  420, 421
British Gazette, 428
British Isles
  changing landscape of, 3, 4,
  5
  early exploration of by
    Pytheas, 4–5
  inhabitants, 321n
Brittany, 183
Brontë, Charlotte, 356
Brookes, 336
'Brown, John', 28–9
Brueys, Admiral François,
  350
Bruges, 174, 175
Brunel, Isambard Kingdom,
  373–5, 377, 395
Brunel, Marc, 374
Brussels, 200, 360, 422
Bryant & May, 398–9
bubonic plague, 132, 133, 276
Buckingham, George Villiers,
  Duke of, 253, 255, 256
Buckingham Palace, 373, 400,
  419, 438, 449
Buckinghamshire, 257
Burgundy, Duchy of, 161
burhs, 38, 41
Burke, Edmund, 323, 345
Burney, Esther, 354
Burney, Fanny, 320, 322, 339,
  348, 353–5
  Evelina, 353
Bury St Edmunds, 37
Buxton, 237
Byron, Lord, 357
Bywell Castle, 395

Cabot, John, (Zuan Caboto)
  1, 189–90, 232
Cadiz, 351–2
Caedmon, 30–1, 209

Caernarfon Castle, 113
Caernarfon, Edward of *see*
  Edward II
Caesar, Gaius Julius
  Claudius copies, 13
  and invasion of Britain,
  7–9
  and reform of Western
  calendar, 9
Caesarean birth, 9
Calais, 158, 164, 223, 345
  siege of and surrender to
  English, 125–7, 128
Caledonians, 18
calendar, 26, 28
  Anno Domini system, 33
  Julian, 9
California, 238
Calne, Wiltshire, 259
Cambridge, 335, 451–2
Cambridge University, 224,
  282, 291
  King's College, 167
  Trinity College, 290
Camelot, 22
Canada, 324–5, 370–1, 401,
  409, 434
canals, 364
cannibalism and post-ice age,
  4
Canterbury, 25, 27, 29, 90,
  141–2, 146
Canterbury, Archbishop of,
  27, 85
  and Edward II, 119–20
  John and disputed election,
  100
  rights of, 86
  Simon Sudbury, 141–2
'Canterbury Water', 90
Canute, King, 46, 48–50, 52,
  270
  attempt to reconcile Danes
  and Anglo-Saxons,
  49–50
  and Christianity, 49
  law code, 50
  and the waves, 48–9
Cape Coast Castle, 299
Cape Cod, 251
Cape Horn, 341
Caracalla, Emperor, 19
Caribbean, 299, 325, 340 *see*
  also West Indies
Carisbrooke Castle, 265
Carlisle, 236, 319
Carlos II, King of Spain, 304
Caroline, Queen, 313
Cartwright, Edmund, 328

castles
  building of by William the
  Conqueror, 66–7
  building of Welsh by
  Edward I, 113, 114
Catesby, Sir William, 181–2
Catherine of Braganza,
  Queen, 282
Catherine of France, Queen,
  162, 170, 171, 183
Catherine the Great, 313
Catholic
  Church/Catholicism 24,
  28–9, 84, 198, 207, 215–16,
  220–1, 223, 226, 296–8,
  306, 309
  and astronomy, 224
  blamed for Great Fire of
  London, 280
  and Gunpowder Plot, 245
  laws against, 245–6, 247
  under James II, 287
  under Restoration and
  Popish Plot, 281–2
  ritual and symbolism,
  206–7, 214–15, 220
  see also Church
cats, 155
cattle, 307
Cavaliers, 262, 264, 281
Cavell, Edith, 421–3
Caxton, William, 174–6, 207
CCR5-delta 32 mutation, 133
Cecil, Robert, Lord Salisbury,
  243, 244, 246, 252
Cecil, William, Lord
  Burghley, 226, 227, 236,
  243
Celtic cross, 27
Celtic fringe, 21
Celts, 5–6, 8, 21
  and Anglo-Saxons, 21
  in battle, 6
  language, 5
  religious rituals, 6
  and Roman invasion, 9
  settlements and way of life,
  5–6
  trade with Rome, 6
Chalus, 97
Chamberlain, Ida, 439
Chamberlain, Neville,
  437–41, 445
Channel *see* English Channel
Charing Cross, 114, 115
Charles I, King, 254–60,
  262–7, 283, 356
  accession, 254
  adopts 'cavalier', 262

507

Charles I, King – *continued*
childhood, 254
confrontations with
Parliament, 255–60,
262, 264, 266
correspondence captured,
263
and divine right, 254, 255, 263
enters Commons, 260–1
execution, 266–7, 284
flees to Isle of Wight, 265
High Church policies, 256,
268
martyrdom, 274
masques, 258
patronage of the arts, 254,
257
raises army, 260
signs Strafford's attainder,
258
taken prisoner, 264
tried for treason, 266–7,
269
Charles II, King, 178, 268,
273–4, 287, 289, 293, 299,
367, 441n
belief in divine right, 281
Catholicism, 282, 284
death, 283–4
and Duke of Monmouth,
284–5
education, 271
and Great Fire of London,
279
illegitimate children, 284–5
interest in science, 290–1
mistresses, 280–1
and Parliament, 281, 283
and Popish Plot, 282–3
restoration, 275
in Royal Oak, 273
succession, 282, 283, 284
Treaty of Dover, 281–2
Charles V, Emperor, 195
Charles VI, King of France,
161–2, 168
Charles VII, King of France
see
Dauphin, the
Charles, Prince, 43, 114
Charlotte, Queen, 337, 351
Chartist movement, 370
Chartley, 237
Chatsworth House, 237, 277
Chaucer, Geoffrey, 146–9, 175
Cheddar Man, 3–4, 5, 7, 457,
453
Cheke, John, 214
Chelsea, 201, 203

Cheltenham, 320, 337
Chesapeake Bay, 250, 334
Cheshire, 171, 366
Chesterfield, Earl of, 312
childhood, in Middle Ages,
165–6
China, 232, 378
Chinery, Thomas, 387
chivalry, 160, 167
cholera, 389, 396
Christian, Fletcher, 341–3
Christianity, 25, 94, 151
conversion of Anglo-
Saxons, 25–7
and crusades, 94, 95–6, 8,
109–10
differences between
Canterbury and Celtic
monks, 27–9, 32
preaching of to northern
inhabitants by Irish
monks, 27–8
Christmas trees, 378, 418
Church, 176, 202–3, 213
ceremonial, 255, 256
and common law, 84–5,
91
conflict between Becket
and Henry II over, 83,
84–7
conflict with King John,
100–1
corruption, 147–8, 197, 207
English, 196, 198, 226
giving generously to, 55
as landowner, 226
'lock-out' by clergy in King
John's reign, 100
power of clerics, 84
Roman, 199, 200
Church of England
(Anglican Church), 213,
245, 256, 257, 274, 314–15
abolished, 271
bishops, 258, 271
under James II, 285, 287
restoration, 277
Churchill, John *see*
Marlborough, Duke of
Churchill, Winston, 160, 306,
315
and Boer War, 404
election defeat, 450
and General Strike, 428
and Second World War,
439, 440–2, 443–5,
446, 448–9
speeches, 448
and welfare state, 449

cinematograph, 402
Civil List, 313
Civil War, 260, 261–3, 283,
289, 291
aftermath, 269, 270–1,
274–5
Second, 265–6
statistics, 261–2
Clarkson, Thomas, 335–6
class system, 368
Claudius, Emperor, 13–14
Cleveland, Duke of, 364
Cleves, 210, 212
coal, 307, 329, 428
Codrington, Captain
Edward, 351
'Coeur de Lion' *see* Richard I
coffee houses, 291, 309–10
coinage, 40, 199, 215, 226, 248
Colchester
attack on by Boadicea, 15
Roman advance on, 13
Coldstream, 274
Coleridge, Samuel Taylor, 336
Collingbourne, Sir William,
182
Collingwood, Admiral
Cuthbert, 351
colonies, 233, 238, 249–52
transportation to, 286
Columba, St, 28
Columbus, Christopher, 188,
189, 191
Combination Acts (1799,
1800), 357n, 364, 370
common law, 84
and Church, 84–5, 91
Commonwealth, 268, 271–2,
274, 275, 281, 283
Communism, 295
Commynes, Philippe de, 174,
182–3
Compiègne, 443
Compton, Sir Spencer, 313
concentration camps, 406,
424
confessor saints, 51
Conroy, Sir John, 372
Constantine, Emperor, 25
Constantinople, 387
constitutional history
and Provisions of Oxford,
108–9, 110–11, 117
see also Good Parliament
(1376);
Magna Carta;
Ordinances;
Parliament
constitutions, 251, 289

Cook, Captain James, 329–31, 340
Cooper, Edward, 277, 278
Cooper, Samuel, 267
Copenhagen, Battle of (1801), 351
Copernicus, Nicolaus, 224
Corfe Castle, 261
Cornwall, 5, 6, 21, 215, 302, 409
    Earldom of, Gaveston awarded, 116
cotton, 300, 327–8
Council of Fifteen, 109
Council of State, 268
court etiquette, 167
    lifestyle, 173
    masques, 257
Court of High Commission, 259
Court of Star Chamber, 258, 259
Covent Garden, 377
Coventry, 55–6, 56–7, 58, 236
Cowper, William, 344–5
Cox, Richard, 214
Cranmer, Thomas, 214, 215, 218, 226
    recantations and execution, 222–3
Crataegus monogyna praecox, the 'Holy Thorn', 11
Crean, Tom, 411
Crécy, Battle of (1346), 123–5, 128, 164
Creechurch Lane synagogue, 272
Crew, Sir Randolph, 255
Crick, Francis, 450–3
cricket, 338, 431–4
    'Ashes', 432, 434
crime and punishment
    criminal code, 401
    death penalty, 346, 357
    policing, 316
    transportation, 357, 368, 370–1
    see also executions
Crimean War, 382–6, 387–90, 408, 427n
Crippen, Cora, 409–10
Crippen, Dr Hawley Harvey, 409–11
Cripplegate, 167
Croatoans, 233–4
Cromford, Derbyshire, 328
Crompton, Samuel 328

Cromwell, Oliver, 263, 265–6, 267–72, 293, 297
    death, 270, 274
    health, 268
    proclaimed Lord Protector, 269
    Puritan faith, 268
    and return of Jews, 272
    welcoming of religious diversity, 271–2
Cromwell, Richard, 274
Cromwell, Thomas, 203, 205, 207–8, 210–12
crossbows, 97, 124
Crossness, 395
crusades, 94, 95–6, 98, 109–10, 151, 161
Crystal Palace, 378–80, 396
Culloden, Battle of (1746), 320, 325
Culpeper, Thomas, 212
Cumberland, 209
Cumberland, Duke of, 320, 325
'Curthose' see Robert, son of William I
Cymbeline (Cunobelimus), 129
Czechoslovakia, 437–9

Daily Express, 445
Daily Mail, 419
Daily News, 385–6
Daily Telegraph, 346
dancing, 269
Daedalus, 46
Danegeld payments, 37, 44
Dangan, County Meath, 358
Danube, River, 96
d'Arblay, Alexandre, 353–4
Darnley, Henry Stuart, Lord, 235
Darwin, Charles, 391–3, 396n
Dash (dog), 372, 373
dating system, 33
Dauphin, the (King Charles VII of France), 162–4
Davison, Emily, 415–17
Davison, William, 237
Day, John, 188, 190
days of the week origin of, 26
D-Day, 447
de Montfort, Simon (Earl of Leicester), 109–12
de Monstrelet, Enguerrand, 164
dead reckoning, 150
Declaration of the Army (1647), 265

Declaratory Act (1720), 297
Dee, Dr John, 225, 232, 242
Defoe, Daniel, 307, 317
defrutum, 18
Degas, Edgar, 377
Deira, 24
democracy, 150, 295, 450
    extension of suffrage, 367–8, 370
    patronage, 313
    rotten boroughs, 367–8
    secret ballot, 367, 368, 370, 401
    women's suffrage, 393, 401, 415–17
Denmark, 321
deposition, 151–2, 156, 168, 180, 270
Deptford, 238
Denys, St, 98
Derby, 41–2, 319–20
Derby, Lord, 428
Derby, the, 397n, 414–17
Derbyshire, 277
Dereham, Thomas, 212
Derry, 297
destrier, Norman warhorse, 61, 67
Despenser, Hugh the elder (Earl of Winchester), 119
Despenser, Hugh the younger, 119
Devon, 274, 361, 375
Devonshire, Earl of, 277
dictionaries, 321–3
Diggers, 271, 272
dinosaurs, 362–3, 380, 392
Dio Cassius, 14
discovery, voyages of, 188–91, 202, 232
Disraeli, Benjamin, 394–5
Dissenters, 295
Dissolution of Monasteries, 185, 208–9, 221
divorce, 436
dogs, 372, 373, 412
DNA, 451–3
Domesday Book, 57, 58, 69–72
Domrémy, 161, 162
Dorchester, 261, 286, 370
Dorset, 261, 361, 362, 369
Dover, 427
Dover, Treaty of, 281–2
Dowding, Air Marshal Sir Hugh, 444–5
Downing Street, 438
Drake, Francis, 232, 238–41, 244

drama, 229–30, 257
Drew, Inspector Walter, 409–10
Druids, 6, 15, 27
Dublin, 296, 323, 358
Dubois, Antoine, 354
Duchy of Lancaster, 151
Dudley, Edmund, 194, 217, 255
Dudley, Guildford, 218, 219
Dunkirk evacuation, 440–2, 443
Dunn, Captain J. C., 420
Durban, 404
Durham Pals, 426
Durnstein Castle 96, 466
Dussindale, Battle of (1549), 217
Dutch East Indies, 391
dysentery, 406

Ealdgyth, 60
Eanfled, Queen, 28
East Anglia, 20, 35, 36, 41, 215, 219, 263
Easter, 26, 27, 28, 29
Eden, Anthony, 439
Edinburgh, 235, 248, 307, 319
Edgehill, Battle of (1642), 262, 266
Edington, battle of (878), 38
Edith Swan-Neck, 60, 64
Edith (wife to Edward the Confessor), 52, 53
Edith-Matilda (wife to Henry I), 77
Edmund, Duke of York, 168
Edmund, Earl of Warwick, 186, 187
Edmund, King, 36–7, 49
Edmund, St, 298
education, 32, 108, 174, 348, 401
Edward the Confessor, 51–4, 107, 206
succession to, 58–60
Edward I, King, 'Longshanks', 112–15, 272
and birth of son in Wales, 113
and Gaveston, 116
'Hammer of the Scots', 114
held hostage by Simon de Montfort and escape, 110, 111, 112
Welsh campaigns, 113
Edward II, King, 113, 115–20, 180
death, 120

deposition of and imprisonment, 119–20
and Despensers, 119
and Gaveston, 115–18
and Parliament, 117, 118
Scottish campaign, 118–19
unkingly characteristics, 117
Edward III, King, 119, 121–3, 128–30, 137, 168, 394
and Battle of Crécy, 124
and Countess of Salisbury, 128
death, 140
death of daughter Joan to the plague, 133
military campaigns, 122–3
and Order of the Garter, 129–30
and siege of Calais, 125–7
Edward IV, King, 168–9, 172–3, 180
architectural achievements, 173
business acumen, 172–3
death, 173, 177
Edward V, King, 173, 177, 181
Edward VI, King, 206, 213, 214–16, 221, 224
death, 218
education, 214, 218
illness, 217
Edward VII, King, 114, 407–8, 414
Edward VIII, King, 434–7
Edward the Elder, King of Wessex, 41, 42
Edwards, Ernest, 405
Egypt, 161, 350, 424
El Dorado, 250–1
Elba, 360
Eleanor of Aquitaine (wife to Henry II), 82, 97, 122
Eleanor of Provence (wife to Henry III), 108
Eleanor of Castile (wife to Edward I), 113, 114
Eleven Years Tyranny, 258
Eliot, Sir John, 255–6, 259
Eliot, T. S., 85
Elizabeth, Princess (daughter of James I), 186, 193
Elizabeth of York, Queen, 186, 193
Elizabeth I, Queen, 205, 213, 216, 225–8, 230, 232, 255, 398
accession and coronation, 225, 227, 232
advisers, 226, 236

birth, 204–5
burial in Westminster Abbey, 245
death, 242–3, 244
declared illegitimate, 218
excommunicated, 236
finances, 226
Gloriana the Virgin Queen, 227, 228, 231
'Golden Speech', 228
marriage policy, 227, 235, 244
and Mary, Queen of Scots, 234, 235–7
progresses, 227
religious compromise, 226
and Spanish Armada, 239–40
succession, 243–4
water closet, 241–2
Elizabeth II, Queen, 43, 178, 452
Elizabeth, Queen Mother, 74
Elmer the flying monk, 46–7, 60
Emma (wife to Ethelred II and to Canute), 44, 51–2, 55
Empson, Richard, 194, 255
enclosures, 215
Endeavour, 330
English Channel, 4, 346, 421, 427, 440, 441
bombing in, 443–4
crossing by snecca, 77
Engla-lond, 40, 43
English language, 31, 38–9, 71, 145, 174, 215, 271, 308, 309
Caxton's, 176
Chaucerian, 146, 148–9
Elizabethan, 233
and King James Bible, 248–9
Tyndale's, 199–200, 226, 249
English Revolution, 270
Englishness, 2
Alfred and, 40
Bede's pride in, 34
'Enigma' code, 446
Enlightenment, 295
Entente Cordiale, 408
enteric fever, 406
Epsom Downs, 414, 416
Erasmus, 201–2
Essex, 20, 259, 243
Essex Gang, 317
Ethelbert, King of Kent, 25–7
Ethelred (ruler of Mercia), 41
Ethelred II, the Unready, 41, 43–6, 49, 51, 145

contract with nobles and
    clerics, 45, 101, 145
Eton College, 166–7, 173, 411
Eugene, prince, 305
Evans, Edgar, 413
Evelyn, John, 270, 281
Evesham, Battle of (1265), 111
'Excalibur', 96
exchequer, 76–7, 141
Exclusion Bill (1681), 293
exclusion crisis, 283, 284
executions, 158, 160, 167, 181,
    209, 228–9, 266, 283
  Anne Boleyn, 205
  Charles I, 266–7
  Duke of Monmouth, 285
  Duke of Northumberland,
    219
  Earl of Essex, 243
  Edmund Dudley, 194, 217
  Gunpowder Plotters, 247
  Joan of Arc, 164
  Katherine Howard, 212
  Lady Jane Grey, 219, 221
  Mary, Queen of Scots, 237
  Perkin Warbeck, 187
  Protestant martyrs, 221–3
  Sir Thomas More, 204
  Sir Walter Raleigh, 251
  Sir William Collingbourne,
    182
  Thomas Cromwell, 212
  Thomas Strafford, 259
  William Tyndale, 200–1
    249
Exeter, 215
Eyam, Derbyshire, 277–8

factories, 302, 328
  match, 398–400
  women working in, 417
Fairfax, Sir Thomas, 263
famines, 34, 108–9
Farington, Joseph, 328
farming see agriculture
Farynor, Thomas, 278, 280
Faversham, Kent, 288
Fawkes, Guy, 244–7, 253
Felton, John, 255
Fens, 48, 67
Ferdinand, King of Spain,
    192
feudalism, 70
feudal system, phrase coined
    by Adam Smith, 70
Fifth Monarchists, 271
Fiji, 342, 401
film stars, 342
Finch, Sir John, 256

Finchley, 320
First World War (Great
    War), 12, 262, 382, 417,
    418–28, 429, 434, 444
  alcohol during, 435
  Armistice, 427, 443
  casualties, 427
  Christmas truce, 418–20,
    423
  conscription, 426
  Europe after, 438
  pals' battalions, 424–6
  recruitment, 423–4
fishing, 188–9
FitzStephen, Captain
    Thomas, 77, 78
FitzStephen, William, 91–3
FitzUrse, Reginald, 87
Fitzwarren, Alice, 153
Fitzwarren, Sir Hugh, 153, 154
Flanders, 419, 427
fleas, 132, 276
Fleet Street, 322, 399
Flint Castle, 151
Flintoff, Andrew 'Freddie',
    434
Florida, 232
Foliot, Gilbert, Bishop of
    London, 85, 86
Fontevrault Abbey, 97
food and drink
  breadfruit, 340–1, 343
  and Celts, 6
  and Cheddar Man, 3
  coconuts, 341
  coffee, 300
  in hospital, 387
  packages, 419
  pepper and bland food, 33
  on polar expeditions, 412
  and Roman Britain, 18
  rum, 300, 334
  at sea, 330–1, 341–2
  sugar, 300, 334, 336
  tea, 332
  wine from Gascony, 122
food prices, 302
food riots, 356
football, 123, 420
  clubs, 379–80, 405–6
Football Association, 379–80
Forkbeard see Sweyn
Fotheringhay Castle, 237
Frame-Breaking Bill (1812),
    357
Framlingham Castle, 218–19
France, 82, 108, 162, 163, 183,
    214, 348, 359
  and American War of

Independence, 334
and Battle of Crécy, 123–5
Catholic, 286
Charles II escapes to, 273
English prisoners of war in,
    353
in First World War, 419,
    421, 423, 425
food prices, 302
Henry Bolingbroke in exile,
    151
Henry V's campaigns,
    158–60, 162
and Hundred Years War,
    122–3
Jacobites and, 297, 309, 320
and Mary, Queen of Scots,
    234, 236
military tactics, 123
and Order of the Star,
    130
peace with, 150, 257
relations with Britain,
    407–8
religious intolerance, 294
and Second World War,
    438, 440–1, 443, 445,
    447
and siege of Calais, 125–7
troops in Britain, 106
at war with Britain, 243,
    304–5, 325
Francois II, King of France,
    234
Franklin, Rosalind, 451, 452
Franz Ferdinand, Archduke,
    421
Frederick, Prince of Wales,
    337–8
French, Sir John 420
French Academy, 322
French language, 176
French Revolution, 343–6,
    349, 353
Furness, Lancashire, 186

Gaddafi, Muammar, 95
Galapagos Islands, 392
games, 165, 194
Gandhi, Mohandas
    ('Mahatma'), 404–5
Garrick, David, 323
garum, 18
Gascony, 82, 108, 122
gaslight, 401
Gaul/Gauls, 5, 8
Gaunt, John of see John of
    Gaunt
Gaveston, Piers 115–18

General Strike, 428–9
Genoa, 189
Geoffrey of Anjou, 80, 82
Geoffrey of Brittany, son of
    Henry II, 99, 101
Geoffrey of Lynn, 165, 166
Geoffrey of Monmouth, 129,
    459
Geological Society, 362
geology, 361–2
George I, King, 308–9, 311, 312
    mistresses, 308, 309, 310
George II, King, 313, 319–20,
    325, 332, 338
George III, King, 320, 353, 371
    and American colonies,
        332–3, 338
    'madness' of, 337–9
    and Nelson, 351
    and voyages of discovery, 330
George IV, King, 339
George V, King, 178, 414–15
    and General Strike, 428–9
    reinvention of monarchy,
        435–6
George VI, King, 438, 449
George, Prince of Denmark,
    306
George, St, 98, 130, 190
Germany, 160, 161, 195, 199,
    210, 222, 338, 348, 408
    and First World War, 423,
        428
    and Second World War,
        437–9, 446, 449
    unified, 382, 439n
Gesta Herwardi Incliti Exulis et
    Militis, 68–9
Gestapo, 447, 449
Gethin, Euan, 131
Gilbert, Humphrey, 232
Gilbert and Robert of Clare,
    75
Gladstone, William Ewart,
    401
Glastonbury Abbey
    (Somerset), 11
Globe theatre, 230
Glorious Revolution, 286–9,
    298, 295
Gloucester, 221–2
Gloucestershire, 153, 199
Glyndwr, Owain, 156, 157
'God Save the King/Queen'
    see national anthem
Godfrey, Sir Edmund Berry,
    282
Godiva, Lady (Godgifu of
    Mercia), 55–8, 60, 71

Godkin, Edwin, 385–6
gods, Anglo-Saxon, 25, 26
Godwin, Earl of Wessex, 52,
    53
Godwin, William, 349
Goering, Hermann, 443
Golden Hind, 238
Goldsmith, Oliver, 323
Gooch, Daniel, 375
Good Parliament (of 1376),
    137–8, 140
Gordon, Lady Katherine, 187
Gospel Oak, 315
Gospels, 10
gout, remedy for, 134
government
    and Council of Fifteen, 109
    and exchequer, 76–7, 141
    and Provisions of Oxford,
        108–9, 110–11, 117
Grand Banks, 189
Grand Remonstrance, 259
Granier, Jeanne, 407
Grantham, 290
Gravesend, 250
gravity, 290
Gray, Thomas, 325–6
Great Britain, 375
Great Chronicle of London,
    177, 180
Great Depression, 429
Great Eastern, 375
Great Exhibition, 378–9
Great North Road, 318
Great Seal of England, 288
'Great Stink', 394–5
Great Western, 374
Great Western Railway, 374,
    375, 376
Greek, 199, 214, 218
Greenland, 311
Greenwich, 194, 217
    Painted Hall, 308
Gregorian chant, 24
Gregory I, Pope
    sending of missionaries to
        Britain to convert
        Anglo-Saxons, 25, 26–7
    and wordplay in slave
        market in Rome, 23–4
Grenville, Richard, 232
Grey, Lady Jane, 217–19
    executed, 219, 221
    marriage, 218
    proclaimed Queen, 218–19
Grey, Lord, 368
Grim, Edward, 86, 87–8
Grosseteste, Robert (Bishop
    of Lincoln), 110

'Guinea', 299
Gunnhilda (sister of Sweyn
    Forkbeard), 45
gunpowder, 126
Gunpowder Plot (1605),
    244–7
Gutenberg, Johann, 175
Guthrum, Danish King, 37,
    38
Guy of Amiens, Bishop, 64
Gwynne, Nell, 281, 284

Hadrian, Emperor, 17
Hadrian's Wall, 17–18, 19
Halidon Hill, Battle of (1333),
    123
hairstyles
    differences between Anglo-
        Saxons and Normans,
        61
    tonsure, 28, 29
Hales, Sir Robert, 142
Halley, Sir Edmund, 60, 291,
    292
Halley's Comet, 60
Hamburg, 200
Hamilton, Lady Emma,
    351–2
Hamilton, Sir William, 351
Hamilton-Dalrymple, Lady,
    360
'Hammer of the Scots' see
    Edward I
Hampden, John, 258, 259
Hampshire, 368
Hampton Court, 196, 205–6,
    260, 265, 306, 427
    conference (1604), 245, 248
Hanover, 308, 309
Hardraada, Harald (King of
    Norway), 60
Hardy, Captain Thomas, 352
Hargreaves, James, 327–8, 355
Harington, Sir John, 241–2,
    243
Harley Street, 386
Harold, King
    and Battle of Hastings,
        61–2
    claim to throne of England
        and fighting for, 54,
        58–61
    death, 62–5
    as Earl of Wessex, 52, 53
Harrison, William, 229
Hart-Davis, Adam, 224
Hartha Canute, 52, 60
Hastings, Battle of (1066),
    61–2, 64

Hatfield House, 252
Hawaii, 331, 340, 448
Hawkins, Sir John, 232
Hazelrig, Arthur, 259
Hebrew, 199, 218
Heidelberg, 305
Hengist ('the stallion'), 21
Henrietta Maria, Queen, 257, 281
  dancing in masques, 258
  flees to Holland, 260
Henry of Huntingdon, 48, 463
Henry I, King, 72–3, 75, 76–9, 83, 101
  death, 80
  and government accounting, 76–7
  succession problems, 80
  and the White Ship 77, 78–9
Henry II, King, 82, 98–9, 122
  and Church, 84–5, 91
  conflict with Becket over Church, 83, 84–7
  law and order under, 84
  repentance of, 90
  and son John, 99
Henry III, King, 106, 107–8, 112
  and de Montfort, 109
  and parliament, 111
  and Provisions of Oxford, 108–9, 110
  and rebuilding of Westminster Abbey, 107
  unpopularity, 110
Henry IV, King (Henry Bolingbroke), 151–2, 154, 156–8, 168
  advisers, 153, 157
  coronation, 156
  disability, 157, 158
  exile, 151
  pilgrimage to Jerusalem, 151, 157
  sense of humour, 156, 157–8
  usurpation, 151–2, 153, 156, 157–8
Henry V, King (Henry of Monmouth), 154, 158–61, 166, 168
  campaigns in France, 158–60, 161
  death, 160–1
  as 'Prince Hal', 157
  regent of France, 162
  religious conviction, 158, 160
  speeches, 159

Henry VI, King, 166–9, 170, 172, 214
  architectural achievements, 166–7, 173
  death, 169
  deposition, 168, 180
  mental breakdown, 168
  succession, 166
Henry VII, King (Henry Tudor), 182–5, 191–3, 217, 243
  death, 192–3
  distrustfulness and cunning, 214, 226
  finances, 191–2, 193, 226
  as Henry Tudor, 171, 182–3
  marriage, 186
  and pretenders, 186–7
  takes crown, 185
  victory at Bosworth, 183–5
  and voyages of discovery, 189–90
Henry VIII, King, 193–7, 201, 205–6, 210–13, 237, 249, 394
  accession and coronation, 193–4
  advisers, 196, 208
  break with Rome, 198, 200, 213, 220, 221, 255
  Catholicism, 203, 209, 214
  'close stool', 241
  death, 213, 214, 217
  dissolution of monasteries, 208, 209
  divorce, 195–6, 197, 200, 203
  executions, 194, 200, 204, 205, 212, 217
  interest in artillery, 239
  marriages, 192, 194, 197, 205, 211, 212, 213
  named Fidei Defensor, 199
  obstinacy, 216
  physique and accomplishments, 193–4, 212
  son's education, 214
  Thames pageant, 210
Henry, Prince (Henry VIII's son), 194–5
Henry, Prince (James I's son), 254
Henry the Younger, eldest son of Henry II, 85, 99
herbal remedies, 134–5
Herbert, Sidney, 387, 389
heresy, 200–1, 203, 221
Hereward the Wake, 2, 67–9, 71, 105

Herlève, (Arlette of Falaise), mother of William I, 53
heroic failure, 22
heroism, 1, 91
Hewitt, Joe, 405
highwaymen, 316–19
Hilda, Abbess of Whitby, 30–1, 40
Hilda, St, 209
Hill, David, 63
Himmler, Heinrich, 65
history 1–2
  truth of, 9, 37–8, 48
Hitler, Adolf, 437–9, 440, 442, 443, 445, 449
Hobart, Sir Miles, 256
Hobbehod see Hood, Robin
Hobbes, Thomas, 271
Holbein, Hans, 210
Holland see Netherlands
Holland, Sir Thomas, 128
Holles, Denzil, 256, 259
Holmby House, Northamptonshire, 264
Holy Roman Empire, 439n
Holy Thorn, 11
homosexuality, 116
  and monarchy, 117
Hong Kong, 401
Honorius, Emperor, 19–20
honours system, 173
Hood, Robin, 104–6, 316, 357
Hooke, Robert, 291, 292
Hooker, Joseph, 392–3
Hooper, Bishop John, 221
Hopton, Sir Ralph, 262
Horsa ('the horse'), 21
Hotspur, see Percy, Henry
Howard, Henrietta, 313
Howard, Katherine, 212
Howard of Effingham, Lord, 239, 240
Howland, John, 252
Hoxton, 246
Hudson, Michael, 265–6
Huguenots, 231, 294
Hull, 200
human sacrifice, 6
Hundred Years War, 122–3, 137, 150, 164, 408
Hunt, Henry 'Orator', 366–8, 370
hunting, 172
  Magna Carta and laws protecting royal hunting forests, 102
  and Norman kings, 74
Huntingdon, 268
Huskisson, William 364–5

Hussein, Saddam, 95
Hyde, Anne, 287
Hyde, Edward, 274, 287
Hyde Park, 378–9, 438
'Hymn of Creation',
    Caedmon's, 30, 31

Icarus, 46
ice ages, 3, 4
Iceland, 90
Iceni, 14–15
Ilford, 280
Imlah, Lance Corporal Alex,
    419
Imlay, Captain Gilbert, 349
Imperial College, 379
Impressionism, 377
Independent Labour Party, 415
India, 325, 332, 358, 378, 388,
    401
    Home Rule campaign, 400
    independence movement,
        404
Industrial Revolution, 302,
    328, 394
industrialisation, 302, 327–8,
    367 see also factories;
    Luddites; railways
Ine, King, 21
ink, 33
Interdiction by Pope of King
    John' England, 100
Inuit (Eskimos), 191
Iona, island of, 27, 28
Iraq, 439
Ireland, 24, 27, 34, 117, 186,
    188, 240, 243, 257, 296–8,
    348
    anthem, 321n
    Cromwell and, 268, 270
    Parliament, 297–8
    Richard II in, 151
    Sir Walter Ralegh in, 231
    see also Northern Ireland
Ireton, Henry, 265
Irish monks
    preaching Christianity to
        northern inhabitants of
        England, 27–8, 29
Ironside, Edmund (son of
    Ethelred II), 45
Isabella, Queen (wife to
    Edward II), 115, 116, 119,
    121, 122
Isabella, Queen of Spain, 192
Isle of Wight, 265
Isle of Sheppey, 342
Israel, 5
Italy, 172, 195, 304, 321–2, 438

Jacobites, 296–7, 306, 312
    rebellions, 309, 319–20
Jaffa, 96
Jakes, 242
Jamaica, 323
James, Duke of Monmouth,
    284–5
James I (and VI of Scotland),
    King, 235, 243–4, 248,
    250, 254, 307, 309, 398
    and Bible, 248–9
    and divine right, 254, 255
    favourites, 253, 255
    religious policy, 245
    and Sir Walter Ralegh,
        250–1
James II, King, 284–9, 293,
    303, 304, 319
    absolutism, 312
    accession, 285, 287
    and Battle of Boyne, 296–7
    and Bloody Assizes, 285–6
    Catholicism, 282, 285, 286,
        287
    descendants of, 304, 309,
        319
    escape and abdication,
        288–9
    exclusion, 283
    and Great Fire of London,
        279
    and Monmouth's
        Rebellion, 285–6
    and Popish Plot, 282–3
    rule in Ireland, 297
    son born, 287
James IV, King of Scotland,
    187, 192, 234
James V, King of Scotland,
    234
James, Edward Stuart (Prince
    of Wales), 287, 288
Japan, 340, 428, 448
Jardine, Douglas, 431–4
Jarrow, 32–3
Jefferson, Thomas, 294, 333,
    334
Jeffreys, Judge George, 285–6
Jennings, George, 379
Jerome, St, 199
'Jerusalem', 10, 11–12
Jerusalem, 11, 95, 151, 157, 158
Jesus Christ, 10–12, 28
    dating of history from birth
        of, 33
    and Glastonbury legend of
        the Holy Thorn, 11
    setting foot in England
        myth, 10, 12

Jews, 270
    expulsion from England by
        Edward I (1290),
        114–15, 272
    persecution of, 94–5
jihad, holy war, 95
jingoism, 403n, 424
Joan (daughter of Edward
    III), 133
Joan of Arc, 161–4, 407
    condemned as witch, 164
    virginity, 163
    voices, 162, 163, 386
Joan of Kent (Countess of
    Salisbury), 128–9, 142
John of Gaunt, Duke of
    Lancaster, 138, 140–1, 142,
    149, 151, 168, 170
John II, King of France, 137
John, King, 'Lackland',
    99–103, 105, 108
    conflict with the Church,
        100–1
    death, 103, 106
    lost jewels of, 103
    and Magna Carta, 101–2
John, King of Bohemia, 124
John, St, 131
Johnson, Dr Samuel, 54,
    322–3, 334, 353
Jones, Herbert, 415, 416
Joseph of Arimathea, 10–11, 12
Josephine, Empress, 354
Joyce, Cornet George, 264
judiciary, 84
Julian calendar, 9, 28

Kaffir Wars, 380
Katherine of Aragon, Queen,
    194–5, 204, 208, 220
    divorce, 195–6, 197, 200,
        203, 222
    marriage to Henry VIII,
        192, 194–5
    marriage to Prince Arthur,
        192, 194, 195
    pregnancies, 194–5, 205
Kay, John, 328
Kelston, Somerset, 241
Kempen, Thomas (Thomas à
    Kempis), 171
Kendall, Captain Henry,
    409–10
Kensington Palace, 271–2
Kent, 259, 265, 288, 367–8
    language, 176
    uprising, 219, 221
Kent, Duchess of, 372
Kent, Edward, Duke of, 372

Kew Gardens, 342
Khartoum, 424
kidney stones, remedy for, 134–5
kings *see* monarchy
King's Cross Station, 16
'King's Evil', 54, 284, 322
King's Lynn, 165
Kingston, Jamaica, 389
Kipling, Rudyard, 381
  'Recessional', 403–4
Kitchener, Horatio Herbert, Lord, 406, 424, 425
knights, 159, 173
Knox, John, 234

La Rochelle, 162
Labour Party, 415, 449–50
Labrador, 189
'Lackland' *see* John
Lady of the Mercians *see* Aethelflaed
Ladysmith, 404
Lambeth, 253
lampreys, 80
Lancashire, 171, 327–8, 355, 363
  regiments, 404
Lancaster, House of, 168, 186
land ownership/land owners
  and Church, 196, 197, 207
  and Dissolution of Monasteries, 209
  early Saxon and Britons, 20–1
  enclosures, 215
  losing of Anglo-Saxon to Normans, 70–1
  and women, 40
landscape, 3, 4, 5, 35–6
Langland, William, 136–7, 138–9, 140
Larwood, Harold, 432–4
Latimer, Bishop Hugh, 215, 222
Latin, 31, 57, 165, 174, 199, 215, 218
Laud, William, 256, 257–9
Laurentic, 410
law
  and 1225 version of Magna Carta, 107
  common, 84–5, 91
  under Henry II, 84
  see also Church
law code
  of Canute, 50
  of Ethelbert, 26
  of Ine, 21

lawyers, 197, 202
Lear, legendary king, 129
Le Bel, Jean, 124, 125
lebensraum, 437
le Neve, Ethel, 409–10
Leeds, 367
Leeds Mercury, 356
Leeds Pals, 426
legends, 2, 21–2, 129
  see also individual legends
Leicester, 42, 184, 263
Leicestershire, 185, 355
Leipzig, Battle of, 359
Lenthall, William, 260
Leofric of Mercia, 52–3, 55–7, 60
Leonardo da Vinci, 201
Leopold, Duke of Austria, 96
Levellers, 265, 271, 272, 344
Levet, Robert, 323
Lewes, Battle of (1264), 110, 111, 112
Lexington, 333
Lichfield, 322
Liechtenstein, 321
Life Guards, 279
Light Brigade, Charge of the, 382–6, 387
Lightoller, C.H., 441
Lille, 419
Lincoln, Abraham, 251
Lincolnshire, 315, 400
Lind, James, 330
Lindisfarne, Abbey of, 36
linen, 307
Lindsey, 20
Link, The, 398–9
Linnaean Society, 393
Lionel, Duke of Clarence, 135
'Lionheart' *see* Richard I
Lisbon, 359
Lisle, Alice, 285
Lisle, Sir John, 285
Lithuania, 151
Liverpool, 404, 410
  Football Club, 405
  railway, 363–4
  and slave trade, 300–1, 335–6
Liverpool Post and Echo, 405
Lloyd George, David, 114, 407, 416, 428, 435, 435n
Local Defence Volunteers, 442
Locke, John, 293–5, 333
  An Essay on Human Understanding, 294
  A Letter concerning Toleration, 294–5

Two Treatises on Civil Government, 295
Loire River, 86
Lollards, 142, 158, 199, 221
London ('Londinium'), 69, 91–3, 153, 230, 260
  attack on by Boadicea, 15
  Cecil Hotel, 419
  coffee houses, 309–10
  demonstrations in, 308, 370
  Diamond Jubilee in, 401–2
  Entente Cordiale signed, 408
  Great Fire of, 278–80
  and Jacobite rebellion, 319–20
  poverty in, 315
  railway links, 374, 376
  and Second World War, 443, 445
  sewage disposal, 394–6
  stock exchange, 310
  Unknown soldier buried, 427
  see also individual places
London Bridge, 146, 241, 275, 278, 279
London Examiner, 385
London Gazette, 311
London Zoo, 392
Londsdale, Earl of, 367
longbow, 123
'Longshanks' *see* Edward I
Lord's cricket ground, 432n
Louis XIV, King of France, 281, 288, 294, 296, 304
Louis XVI, King of France, 343, 345
Loveless, George, 369, 370
Lovell, Francis, Lord, 182
Low Countries, 161, 239
Lowther, Katherine, 325, 326
Lucan, Lord, 383
Lucas, Ensign, 382
Lud, King, 357
'Ludd, General', 355–8, 368
Luddites, 368
Ludgate Hill, 357
Ludlow, 177
Luftwaffe, 441, 443
lunar calendar, 28
Luther, Martin, 198–9, 200, 203, 207, 208, 314, 315
Luxembourg, 440
Lyell, Charles, 392–3
Lyme Regis, 285, 361–2

Macaulay, Thomas, 374
MacDonald, Flora, 320

MacDonald, John, 387
McSween, John, 63
Madame Tussaud's, 411
Madoc (legendary Prince of Wales), 232
Madras, 400
Magna Carta (1215), 101–2, 106, 107, 108, 109
Magno, Allesandro, 229
Maidenhead railway bridge, 374, 377
Major, John, 145
major generals, 269, 272
malaria, 392
Malmesbury Abbey, 46, 47
Malory, Sir Thomas, 178, 207
Malplaquet, Battle of, 305
Mancetter, Warwickshire, 15, 16, 184
Manchester, 319, 356, 367
  railway, 363, 364–5
  St Peter's Fields, 366–7, 370
Mancini, Dominic, 180
Mandela, Nelson, 380n
Mandeville, Viscount, 259
Manox, Henry, 212
Mantes, 72
manuscripts, writing of, 33
Marconi, Guglielmo, 409, 444
Margaret, Princess, 192
Margaret of Anjou, Queen, 167
Marie-Antoinette, Queen, 343
Marion, Maid, 105–6
Marks, Leo, 446–8
Marlborough, John Churchill, Duke of, 303–6, 408
Marlborough, Sarah, Duchess of, 304, 305
marriage, 348, 349 see also divorce
Marshall, H. E.
  Our Island Story, 1
marshes see wetlands
Marston Moor, Battle of (1644), 262
martyrs, 98
Marx, Karl, 295
Mary I, Queen, 203, 205, 208, 213, 220–1, 224
  accession, 219, 220
  advisers, 221
  birth, 195
  Catholicism, 215–16, 217, 220–1, 223
  death, 223

declared illegitimate, 218, 222
  marriage, 219, 221
  persecution of Protestants under, 220–3
Mary II, Queen, 286–7, 288, 289, 294–5, 304, 313
Mary, Queen of Scots, 234–7, 243, 244, 338, 398
  abdication, 235
  Catholicism, 234, 236, 245
  execution, 237
  marriage with Bothwell, 235
  marriage with Darnley, 235
  reburied in Westminster Abbey, 245
Mary of Modena, Queen, 286, 287, 288
Marylebone Cricket Club (MCC), 432n, 433
masques, 258
match girls' strike, 399–400
mathematics, 224–5
Matilda (daughter of Henry I), 80, 81, 82–3
Matilda du Perche, 78
Matthew, 189
Maundy Thursday, 206, 220
Maxton, James, 438
Mayerne, Turquet de, 268
Mayflower, 251, 252
Mbeki, Thabo, 380n
Meachin, Company Sergeant-Major Frank, 422
measles, 392
Mechanics' Magazine, 364
medicine, 134–5, 205
  anaesthetics, 354, 401
  antiseptics, 401
  hospitals, 386–8
  nursing, 386–8
  surgery, 354–5, 398
Mediterranean Sea, 325, 383n
Medway River, 281
Melville, Sir James, 235–6
mercers, 154, 174
merchants, 154, 196, 197, 209, 255, 272, 281
Mercia, 20, 41–2, 52
Merlin the Magician, 129
'Merrie Men', 105
Methodists, 314–15, 335
Michelangelo, 201
Middle Ages, 146
Middle Passage, 299–300, 336
Milford Haven, 183
mining, 302–3, 428
Minos, King of Crete, 46

minutemen, 333
missionaries
  conversion of Anglo-Saxons to Christianity by Irish, 27–8
  sent by Pope Gregory to convert Anglo-Saxons, 24, 25–7
Mompesson, Revd William, 277, 278
monarchs and monarchy
  abolition, 265, 268
  absolute, 254
  constitutional, 289
  deposition, 270
  distinguished from subjects, 267
  divine right, 150, 254, 263, 281
  form of address, 150
  and homosexuality, 117
  and Magna Carta, 101–2, 106, 107, 108
  mistakes of, 143
  and Ordinances (1311), 117–18
  power, 167, 197
  and Provisions of Oxford (1258), 108–9, 110–11, 117
  Restoration, 274–5, 277, 280
  social contract between King and subjects, 45, 50, 101, 107, 145
  style of crown, 156
monasteries, dissolution of, 185, 208–9, 221
Monck, George, 274–5
Monet, Claude, 377
Mongols, 131–2
monks
  Anglo-Saxon, 32
  Irish, 27–8, 29
Monmouth, Henry of see Henry V, King
monopolies, 243
Monroe, James, 346
Mont, Christopher, 210
Montagu, Edwin, 417
Montcalm, Louis-Joseph, Marquis de, 324, 325–6
Monteagle, Lord, 246
Montreal, 410
Montrose, 409–10
More, Sir Thomas, 196, 199, 201–4, 205
  execution, 204
  on Richard III and Princes in the Tower, 178–9, 179–80
  Utopia, 202

Morning Post, 404
Mortimer, Roger, Earl of
    March, 119, 120, 121–2
Mortimer's Cross, Battle of
    (1461), 170
Morton, Cardinal John,
    191–2, 196
Mosel River, 304
Mousehold Heath, 215
Muggletonians, 271
Munich agreement, 438–9
music, 194, 287
Muslims, 94
    fighting against by
        crusaders, 95
mutinies
    Bounty, 341–3
    mutiny on the *Bounty* films,
        343

Nore, 342
Nantes, Edict of, 294
Naples, 351
Napoleon Bonaparte, 240,
    351, 353, 356, 408
    invasion plans, 346, 352
    and Waterloo, 359–60
Naseby, Battle of (1645), 263,
    264, 266
Natal, 404, 405
national anthem, 318–19,
    320–1, 402
National Gallery, 377
native Americans, 332–3, 334
Natural History Museum,
    379
natural selection, 391–3
Nature, 452
navigation, 329–30
navy *see* Royal Navy
Nazis
    and Bayeux Tapestry, 65
Nelson, Admiral Horatio,
    350–2, 389
Nelson, Fanny, 350
Nelson, Horatio, 351
Nennius, 22
Nero, 14
Netherlands, 187, 195, 243,
    247, 251, 252, 260, 275,
    281, 285, 287, 288, 293,
    304, 440
Neville, Richard, Earl of
    Warwick ('the
    Kingmaker'), 168–9, 172,
    182
New England, 189, 251
New Forest, 74
New Model Army, 263–5

breach with Parliament,
    264–5
New Palace Yard, 251
New South Wales, 330, 342
New World, 188, 189, 191, 232,
    233, 238, 249, 253
New York, 374
New York Times, 442
New Zealand, 330–1
Newbolt, Sir Henry, 240–1
Newcastle, Duke of, 325
Newcomen, Thomas, 302–3,
    328
Newfoundland, 188, 189, 232,
    329
newspapers, 258, 283
    see also individual titles
Newton, Isaac, 289–92
Nightingale, Florence, 386–91
Nile, Battle of the (1798), 350
Nobel Prize, 452
Nore mutiny, 342
Norfolk, 217, 394, 422
Norfolk, Duke of, 203–4,
    208–9, 212
Norman Conquest, 61–2, 65,
    70, 145, 148
'Norman Yoke', 67
Normandy, 53, 76, 97, 101, 108,
    167
Normandy, Duke of *see*
    Richard of Normandy,
    William the Conqueror
Normans, 44, 53, 297
    and Battle of Hastings,
        61–2
    and Jews, 94
    legal discrimination of
        against Anglo-Saxons,
        71
    uprisings against William
        the Conqueror and
        putting down of
        resistance, 67
North America, 299, 325, 332
    see also Canada; United
        States of America
North, Frederick Lord, 333,
    334
North Sea, 329
North West Passage, 232
Northern Ireland, 223, 298 *see
    also* Ireland
Northumberland, Earl of, 151
Northumberland, John
    Dudley, Duke of, 217–19
Northumbria, 20, 52
Northampton Castle, 85
Norway, 439

Norwich, 423
Nottingham, 105, 356, 432
Nottingham, Sheriff of, 105
Nottinghamshire, 355
Nova Scotia, 189
Novgorod, 36

Oahu, 448
Oates, Captain Lawrence,
    411–14
Oates, Titus, 282, 283
Odo, Bishop, 59, 62, 63
Offa, King of Mercia, 41
old-age pension, 428
Old Sarum, Wiltshire, 367
Oldfield, Bert, 433
Olivier, Laurence, 160
Olympic Games, 321n
O'Meara, Jane, 376–7
optics, 290
Orange, 287
Orange Order, 298
Order of the Garter, 129–30,
    142
Order of the Golden Fleece,
    130
Order of the Star, 130
Ordinances (1311), 117–18
Orion, 351
Orleans, 163
Oswaldtwistle, 327
Oswy, King of Northumbria,
    27–9
Ottawa, 400
Oudenarde, Battle of, 305
outlaws, 104
Oxford, 222, 261, 262, 280, 290
    Ashmolean Museum, 253
    University, 224, 301, 314,
        323, 430, 453
Oxford, Provisions of *see*
    Provisions of Oxford

Pacific Ocean, 325, 330, 341,
    341n
paganism, 25–6, 50
Paine, Thomas, 343–6, 347,
    349
    The American Crisis, 344
    Common Sense, 345
    The Rights of Man, 345, 346,
        347
Pakenham, Kitty, 358–9
Pakenham, Thomas, 404
Palace of Westminster, 53, 73
palaeontology, 361–2
Palestine, 94, 95, 161
'Palmer, John' *see* Turpin,
    Dick

Panama, 389
Pandora, 342
Pankhurst, Christabel, 415
Pankhurst, Emmeline, 415, 416
Pankhurst, Sylvia, 416
pantomimes, 153, 155
papacy, 24
parchment, preparation of, 33
Paris, 271, 284, 353, 359, 421
    Edward VII visits, 407–8
    during French Revolution, 343, 346, 349
    in Second World War, 439
Paris, Matthew, 107–8, 109
Parkinson, Sydney, 331
Parliament
    anticlericalism, 197
    Barebones (Nominated), 269
    breach with army, 264–5
    Cavalier, 281
    and Charles I and Civil War, 255–63, 264–5, 266
    and Charles II, 281, 282–3
    and Edward II, 117, 118, 119–20
    and Edward III, 137–8
    and Edward VI, 218
    and Elizabeth I, 226, 227, 243
    and George III, 338
    and Glorious Revolution, 287–8, 289, 295
    Good (of 1376), 137–8, 140
    and 'Great Stink', 394–5
    Gunpowder Plot, 244–7, 253
    Henry VI attends as a child, 166
    and Henry VIII, 203
    House of Commons, 213, 227, 255–6, 257–60, 262, 268–9, 281, 283
    House of Lords, 259, 262, 268, 281, 393
    Irish, 297–8
    and James I, 248
    language, 148
    and Mary I, 221
    and Ordinances (1311), 117–18
    party system, 283
    passes legislation, 308, 312, 336
    Pride's purge, 266, 269, 274–5
    prorogation, 281

and Provisions of Oxford (1258), 111
and railways, 364
and Restoration, 293
rewards Marlborough, 305
rewards Mary Anning, 362
and Richard II, 150
rules Commonwealth, 268–9
Rump, 269, 274–6
Scottish, 307
and union of kingdoms, 307
welcomes Henry IV, 156
Westminster meeting place, 175
Parma, Duke of, 239, 240
Parr, Catherine, 213, 218
Parry, Hubert, 12
Patrick, St, 23, 27, 34
Pauntley, Gloucestershire, 154
Paxton, Sir Joseph, 379
Peak District, 41
Pearl Harbour, 448–9
Peasants' Revolt (1381), 139–45, 148, 149, 151
Peeping Tom, 58
Pembroke, 171
Peninsular War, 359, 360
penny post, 401
Pepys, Samuel, 155, 275, 279
Perceval, Spencer, 357
Percy, Henry 'Hotspur', 151
Percy family, 156, 157
Perrers, Alice, 137, 138
Peter, St, 29
Peterborough, 67, 82
'Peterloo' Massacre, 366–7
Petition of Right, 255, 257, 259
Philadelphia, 344
Philip II, King of France, 99, 102
Philip II, King of Spain, 219, 221, 233, 238, 288
Philip IV, King of France, 122, 126–7, 132
Philippa of Hainault, Queen (wife to Edward III), 127, 128, 139
Phillips, Captain Thomas, 298–300
phossy jaw, 398
physics, 292
Picquigny, Treaty of (1475), 173
Picts, 18, 19
Piddle River, 369n
Piers the Ploughman, 196–9

Pilgrim Fathers, 251–2
Pilgrimage of Grace, 208–9
pilgrimages, 146, 147, 151, 157
Pilson, Tony, 165–6
piracy, 232, 239, 252
Pissarro, Camille, 377
Pitcairn, 342
Pitt, William (the elder), Lord Chatham, 333, 337
Pius V, Pope, 236
plague, 131–3, 135, 137, 139, 148, 276–8, 280, 282, 290
Plantagenets, 82, 150
plants, 252–3
Platter, Thomas, 230
plunder, 262
plus-fours, 435n
Plymouth, 238, 239, 250, 251
Plymouth Colony, 251
pneumonic plague, 132, 276
Pocahontas, 249–50
poetry
    and Caedmon, 30–1
Poland, 439
political parties, 283
poll tax, 141, 145
ponies, 412
Ponsonby, Frederick, 408
Pontefract, 152
Pontius Pilate, 11
poor, 138
Pope, 24, 26, 44, 84, 100
    see also individual names
Popish Plot, 282–3, 284, 411n
porphyria, 339
Portsmouth, 255
Portugal, 232, 359
potatoes, 232
Potsdam Conference, 450
Powhatan, 249, 250
Prasutagus, 14
Prayer Book (Book of Common Prayer), 215, 217, 222, 226, 236, 258, 271
Presbyterian Church (Kirk), 307
Presbyterianism, 265
Preston, 309, 319, 328, 368
pretani, 6
pretenders, 186–7
Pride, Colonel Thomas, 266, 269
prime ministers, official title of, 312–13
primogeniture, 43
Primrose Hill, 282
Princes in the Tower, 173, 177–81, 185, 186, 187
Princess Alice, 395–6

printing, 175–6, 200
progresses, 227, 285
Protectorate, 272, 274, 281, 283
Protestants/Protestantism,
    198–9, 214, 218, 219, 226,
    238, 245, 247, 282, 297,
    306, 308
    Dutch, 247, 262
    French, 231
    and James II, 286–7
    Marian persecutions of,
        220–3
    Scottish, 234–5, 236
Provisions of Oxford (1258),
    108–9, 110–11, 117
Prussia, 321, 325
Prynne, William, 258–9
public conveniences, 379
Pudding Lane, 278, 279
Punch, 390
Puritans, 256, 262, 263
    and James II, 287–8
    in Parliament, 257, 259, 269,
        271
    and Restoration, 274, 277,
        283
    sects, 265
Putney, 349
Putney Debates, 265
Pym, John, 259, 260
Pytheas, 4–5, 6

Quakers, 271, 335, 344
Quebec, 324–5, 326, 329

radiocarbon dating, 7
Raglan, Lord, 383
railways, 363–5, 373–5, 401
    Turner's painting of, 376–7
Rainsborough, Colonel
    Thomas, 265
Rais, Gilles de, 162
Ralegh, Sir Walter, 231–4, 243
    conspiracy, 250
    El Dorado expedition,
        250–1
    executed, 251
Ralf the Timid, 53
Ramillies, Battle of, 305
Ramsay, Admiral Sir
    Bertram, 442
Ramsgate, 372
Ranters, 271
Ratcliffe, Sir Richard, 182
rats, 132, 276
Ravensbrück labour camp,
    447
Recorde, Robert, 224–5
Reform Bill (1832), 368

Reformation, 198, 207, 209,
    221, 222
    Oak, 215
    Scottish, 234
regicide, 152, 169, 180–1, 266,
    275
relics, 208
religion, 141–2
    and Celtic rituals, 6
    and paganism, 25–6
    toleration of, 270–2, 287,
        293, 294–5, 297
    see also Catholicism;
        Christianity;
        Protestantism/Protesta
        nts; Church
Renaissance, 201
Renoir, Auguste, 377
Resolution, 340
Restoration, 280–1, 283
Reynolds, Joshua, 323
Reynolds News, 438
Rhineland, 437
Richard, Duke of York, 177,
    187
Richard I, the Lionheart,
    93–8, 99, 117, 160
    and brother John, 99–100
    capture and imprisonment
        by Leopold, 96, 97, 99
    and crusades, 94, 95–6
    death, 99
    and Jews, 95
    legends surrounding, 93–4,
        96–7
    loves music, 96–7
    at Nottingham, 105
Richard II, King, 128, 140,
    142–3, 144, 145, 147,
    149–52, 154, 157, 427n
    campaign in Ireland, 151
    death, 152
    deposition, 151–2, 156, 168,
        180
    nicknamed 'the Redeless',
        153
    rules without Parliament,
        150
    self-image, 150
Richard III, King, 181–2, 186,
    187
    Battle of Bosworth, 183–5
    courage, 184–5
    death, 185
    physique, 179
    and the Princes in the
        Tower, 173, 177–81, 186
    religious observance, 179
    seizure of power, 181, 183

Richard of Normandy, Duke,
    44
Richmond, 196, 242, 339
Richmond, Charlotte,
    Duchess of, 360
Ridley, Bishop Nicholas, 222
Rievaulx Abbey, 209
Riot Act (1715), 308
ritual and symbolism, 209,
    254, 256
    Catholic, 206–7, 214–15,
        220
    Cromwell rejects, 269
    Elizabethan, 226, 227
Rizzio, David, 235
Roanoke, 233, 250
Robert the Bruce, 114, 118
Robert 'Curthose' (son of
    William the Conqueror),
    72, 73, 76
Robert of Merton (Beckett's
    confessor), 89
Rochefort, Guillaume de, 181
Rochester, 289
Rochford, Lady, 212
Rocket, 363, 365
Rockingham, Charles,
    Marquess of, 338
Rolf, John, 250
Roger of Wendover, 55–6, 57
Roman Catholicism see
    Catholic Church
Roman Empire/Romans, 242
    attacks on by Picts, 19
    and Boadicea's revolt,
        14–16, 17
    building of Hadrian's Wall,
        17–18
    dating system, 33
    departure from Britain
        after barbarian attacks,
        19, 20
    fortifications built against
        threat from Angles and
        Saxons, 19
    invasion of Britain by
        Claudius, 13–14
    invasions of Britain by
        Caesar, 7–9
    legionaries, 19
    occupation of Britain and
        settlements, 17, 18–19
Rome, 6–7, 37, 90, 195, 198
Roper, Margaret, 203
Roper, William, 201
Rose theatre, 229–30
Rosebery, Archibald, Earl of,
    296–8, 306, 309, 397–8,
    435n

Rotherhithe, 374
rotten boroughs, 367–8
Rouen, 164
Roundheads, 262, 273
Royal Academy, 376–7
Royal Africa Company, 299–300
Royal Air Force (RAF), 441, 443–4
Royal Charles, 275, 281
Royal Flying Corps, 444
Royal Humane Society, 349
royal jubilees, 339, 397, 400–2, 403
Royal Navy, 302, 329, 331, 380, 438 and Dunkirk, 441, 442
Royal Society, 290, 295, 330
Royal Society of Arts and Commerce, 340
Rufus, William *see* William II, King
'Rule Britannia', 301
Runnymede, 101–2
Rupert of the Rhine, Prince, 262
Russell, Lord John, 370
Russell, William Howard, 382–4, 385, 388
Russia, 252, 321, 325, 359, 408, 423, 428
  foundation of, 36
  Hitler attacks, 449
  see also Crimean War; Soviet Union

St Albans, 15
  Abbey of, 56
  Battle of, 168
St Lawrence River, 324, 329
St Mary-at-Lambeth churchyard, 342
St Paul's Cathedral, London, 51, 182, 192, 272, 305, 402
  on Whit Sunday, 207, 214
St Pol, 427
saints, 51
  confessor saints, 51
  patron saints, 94, 130
  see also individual names
Saladin, 95
Salisbury Plain, 303, 424
Salmond, Captain Robert, 381
Saltwood Castle, 86–7
Sandlake *see* Senlac
Sandringham, 415n
sans-culottes, 343
Sarajevo, 421

Savery, Thomas, 302, 303
Sawley Abbey, 209
Saxon Shore, 19, 20
Saxons, 19, 22
  invasion of Britain and settlement of, 19–20, 20–1
  see also Anglo-Saxons
scabies, 344
Scheveningen, 275
schools, 174
Science Museum, 379
Scotland, 21, 149, 214, 234, 240, 298, 301
  anthem, 321n
  campaign against by Edward I, 114
  campaign against by Edward II, 118–19
  campaign against by Edward III, 123
  diet, 323
  in Civil War, 268, 273, 274
  integrated into United Kingdom, 306–7
  Jacobite rebellions, 309, 319–20
  Parliament, 307
  and Prayer Book, 258
  Presbyterians, 258, 283
  religion, 234–5, 236
  subduing of Highlands, 325
  union of crowns, 248
Scotland Yard, 409–10
Scott, Captain Robert, 411–14
Scott, Sir Walter, 167
scrofula, 53–4, 322
Scrooby, Northamptonshire, 251, 252
scurvy, 330
Scutari, Turkey, 387, 389
Seacole, Edwin Horatio Hamilton, 389
Seacole, Mary, 388–91
Sebastopol, siege of, 389–90, 427n
Second Reform Act (1872), 370
Second World War, 15, 65, 437–48, 450
  see also Battle of Britain; Dunkirk evacuation
sects, 265, 270–2
Sedgemoor, Battle of (1685), 285
Sellar, Walter, 429–31
Senlac, 61, 62
Separatism, 251, 268

serfdom, 102, 139
Serre, 425, 426n
Seton, Colonel, Alexander, 381–2
Seven Years War (1756–63), 325, 333
Seville, 238
Seymour, Jane, 205–6, 210, 217
Shaftesbury, Anthony Ashley Cooper, Earl of, 293, 295
Shakespeare, William 129, 157, 173, 244, 437
  Henry V, 160
  Henry VI, Part 1, 167, 437
  The Merry Wives of Windsor, 230, 232
  Richard II, 152
  Richard III, 179, 184–5
Sheffield, 237, 367
  Corn Exchange, 424, 426
Sheffield Pals, 424–6
Shelley, Mary, 349
Shelley, Percy Bysshe, 349
Sherwood Forest, 104, 105, 357
ship money, 257–8, 259
ships, 239 *see also* individual names
Shoreham, Sussex, 273
Shrewsbury, 183
Siberia, 412
Sicily, 108
Siculus, Diodorus, 6
'Silent Night', 418
Silvester, Lady Harriet, 362
Simnel, Lambert, 186, 190
Simpson, Mrs Wallis Warfield, 436
Siward of Northumbria, Earl, 52–3
Skye, 320
slave trade, 298–301, 310
  abolition of, 335–6
slaves/slavery, 21, 23–4, 323, 334–5, 401, 407
smallpox, 322
Smiles, Samuel, 396
Smith, Adam, 70
Smith, Sir Thomas, 247
Smithfield, 149, 223, 247, 282
snakeships, 77
snecca, 77
social contract
  between Ethelred the Unready and nobles, 45, 101, 145
socialism, 315, 393
Somerset, 285

Somerset, Edward Seymour,
    Duke of (Protector), 217
Somerset Levels, 35–6
Somme, Battle of the, 425
'Song of the Battle of
    Hastings', 64
Sophia, Electress of Hanover,
    306
South Africa, 380, 406–7
    apartheid, 407
    see also Boer War
South Pole, 412
South Sandwich Islands, 331
South Sea Bubble, 310–12
Southwark, 229
Soviet Union, 450, 451
Soyer, Alexis, 387
Spain, 195, 236, 240, 325, 359
    colonies, 191, 232
    peace with, 257
    war against England, 238,
        240, 243
Spanish Armada, 233,
    238–40, 243, 288
Speaker, 137–8
Special Operations Executive
    (SOE), 446–8
spinning and weaving, 327–8
Spion Kop, 404–5
spiritualism, 393
Spitzbergen, 350
Sporting Times, 432n
sports, 123, 194, 269
Staffordshire, 35
Stalin, Josef, 450
Stamford Bridge, Battle of, 61
Stamford, Lincs, 94, 101
standard-bearer of the 10th
    legion, 8
Stanley, Thomas, 277
Stanley, Thomas, Lord, 171,
    183, 184
Stanley, Sir William, 184–5
Stanley family, 183–4
steam power, 202–3, 328
steamships, 374–5, 401
Stephen of Blois, King, 80–1,
    83, 84
Stephen, sea captain to
    William I, 77
Stephenson, George, 363
Stephenson, Robert, 363
Stewart, Colonel William, 351
Stockton and Darlington
    railway, 364
Stony Stratford, 188, 181
Stothard, Charles, 63
Stow, John, 238
Strafford, Thomas

Wentworth, Earl of,
    257–9
Straits of Dover, 239
Straw, Jack, 140, 144–5
Strode, William, 259
Stuart, Charles Edward
    (Bonnie Prince Charlie,
    the Young Pretender),
    319–21
Stuart, James Francis Edward
    (the Old Pretender), 304,
    309, 319
Stuart, House of, 192, 287
Stubbs, John, 227
Sudbury, Simon (Archbishop
    of Canterbury), 142
Sudan, 424
Sudetenland, 48
Suez Canal, 424–5, 439
Suffolk, Henry Grey, Duke
    of, 218, 219
suffragettes, 415–17
suicides, 353, 431
Surrey, 353, 431
Sussex, 20, 259, 368
Sweyn Forkbeard, King of
    Denmark, 45, 49
Swindon, 374
'Swing, Captain', 368
Switzerland, 161, 222, 321
Sydenham Hill, 379–80
Sydney, 330, 432
Symonds, Richard, 186, 187
Syria, 161
Szabo, Violette, 447–8

Tacitus, 7, 14, 16, 17
Tahiti (Otaheite), 331, 341–2
Tamworth, 41
Targett, Adrian, 453
tattooing, 331
taxation, 56–7, 97, 100, 108,
    141, 150, 295, 332
    and Charles I, 255, 256,
        257–8
    and Charles II, 281
    and Elizabeth I, 227, 243
    'Morton's Fork', 192
    under protectorate, 274
    ship money, 257–8, 259
Taylor, John, 'the Water Poet',
    394
telegraph, 400
1066 and All That, 429–31, 453
Tennyson, Alfred Lord, 85,
    384–5
Ternate, 391
Terra Nova, 411
Test Act, 282

Teutonic Knights, 151
Thackeray, William
    Makepeace, 377
Thames River, 13, 15, 91–2,
    146, 166, 170, 196, 201,
    204, 241, 253, 377
    disasters, 395–6
    embankments, 395
    estuary, 176, 281
    fishing, 154
    frozen, 266
    Great Seal thrown in, 288
    Henry VIII's pageant, 210
    Maidenhead bridge, 374,
        377
    mudflats, 165
    navigation rules, 396
    sewage and pollution,
        394–6
    south bank, 230
    tunnel under, 374
Thames Valley, 35
Thanksgiving, 251
Thatcher, Margaret, 145
theatres, 229–30, 250
theosophy, 400, 444
Thorneycroft, Alec, 405
Thurlow, Edward, Lord, 337
tides, Bede studies, 33
    Canute and, 48–9
Tilbury, 239
Times, The, 373, 382, 383–5,
    387, 390, 395–6, 415, 417
Timor, 342
Tinchebrai, Battle of (1106),
    76
Tintern Abbey, 209
Titanic, 381
tobacco, 232–3, 300
Tolkein, J.R.R., 21
Tolpuddle Martyrs, 369–71
tonsure see hairstyles
Torbay, 288
Tories, 283, 288, 312, 368
Toronto University, 326
Tostig, son of Godwin, 60, 61
Tournai, 187
Tower Green, 205
Tower Hill, 187
Tower of London, 66, 91, 151,
    169, 219, 237, 256, 312
    Henry VI imprisoned, 169
    Princes in, 173, 177–81, 185,
        186, 187
    Richard II imprisoned, 203
    Sir Walter Ralegh
        imprisoned, 251
towns, 102 see also burhs;
    London

Toynbee, Arnold, 328
toys, 165–6
trade, 153–4, 172, 174, 188, 253, 356
Celtic trade with Rome, 6
Trades Union Congress (TUC), 428
trades unions, 357, 364, 399–400
Tradescant, Hester, 253
Tradescant, John (father), 252–3
Tradescant, John (son), 252–3
Trafalgar, Battle of, 352, 353, 356
transubstantiation, 207, 209, 222, 282
Transvaal, 404
Triennial Act (1641), 259
Trevisa, John, 120
Troyes, Treaty of (1420), 162
trial by jury, 84
Truman, Harry, 450
Trussell, Sir William, 120
Tudor, Edmund, Earl of Richmond, 170
Tudor, Henry see Henry VII, King
Tudor, House of, 170–1
double rose symbol, 193
Tudor, Jasper, Earl of Pembroke, 170, 171, 183, 184
Tudor, Margaret, 234
Tudor, Owen (Owain ap Maredudd ap Tydwr), 170
Tull, Jethro, 301–3
Turkey, 383n, 387
Turner, Joseph Mallord William, 376–7
Turpin, Dick, 316–18
Tutbury, Staffordshire, 236
Tyburn, 228–9
Tyler, Wat, 140, 141–4, 145, 149, 344
Tyndale, William, 196, 199–200, 203, 207, 208
and English language, 199–200, 226, 248–9
execution, 200–1, 249
translation of Bible, 199–200, 249
Tyneside, 329
typhoid, 379, 396
Tyrel, Walter, 74–5
tywysogion, 'Princes' of Wales, 113

Ulster, 297
unemployment, 429
insurance, 428
Union Jack, 307, 389, 427
United States of America, 250, 321, 346, 348, 378, 409
Declaration of Independence, 294, 333
economic power, 379, 428
and First World War, 428
Napoleon and, 356
and Second World War, 442, 448–9
War of Independence, 333–4, 338, 344, 346
see also Boston Tea Party
Unknown Soldier, 427
USSR see Russia; Soviet Union

van Limborch, Philip, 293, 294–5
Vaudreuil, Pierre, Marquis de, 329
VE Day, 449
Vega, Lope de, 238
Venice, 180
Vergil, Polydore, 190
Versailles, Treaty of, 437–8
Vespucci, Amerigo, 202
Vickers, George, 277
Victoria, Queen, 270, 374, 378–9, 396, 427n
childhood and accession, 371–3
death, 407
visits Great Exhibition, 379
jubilees, 397–8, 400–2
marriage, 378
Victoria and Albert Museum, 63, 379
Victoria Cross, 427n
Victory, 351–2
Vienna, Congress of, 359–60
Vienna, siege of, 308
Vienne, Sir John de, 126, 127
Vikings, 40, 188, 285
attacks on England and settlement of, 36–7, 44, 45, 47
massacre of Danes living in England by Ethelred and consequences, 44–5
resistance to by Anglo-Saxons, 40, 41
resistance to by King Alfred, 37, 38

Rus in Novgorod, 36
settle in Normandy, 44
villein, 102
Vimy Ridge, Battle of, 426
vin claret, 122
Virgil, 176
Virgin Mary, 11, 148, 156
Virginia, 233, 249, 311
Virginia Company, 250
Vitalis, Orderic, 78–9
Voce, Bill, 432

Wade's Mill, Hertfordshire, 335, 336
wages, 148, 190
Wales, 21, 156, 171, 183, 265, 307, 321n, 367
birth of Edward I's son in, 113
campaigns against by Edward I, 113
Wales, Princes of, 113–14, 125
Walkinton, Major Leslie, 418
Wallace, Alfred Russel, 391–3
Wallace, Edgar, 410
Wallace, William 'Braveheart', 114
Waller, Sir William, 262
Walpole, Horace, 348–9
Walpole, Sir Robert, 311–13, 349
Walsingham, Sir Francis, 236, 237
Walter, Lucy, 284
Waltham (Essex), 172
Waltham Abbey (Essex), 64, 209
Wapping, 374
war correspondents, 385–6
War of the Spanish Succession, 304
Warbeck, Perkin (Pierquin Wesbecque), 187
warfare, 174
archers, 159, 161
knights, 159
pikemen, 183, 184
see also weapons
Warkworth, John, 169
Warner, Pelham ('Plum'), 431, 433
Warrington, 328
Wars of the Roses, 152, 167, 169, 174, 262
Warwick, Earl of, 118
Warwick the Kingmaker see Neville, Richard, Earl of Warwick
Wash, the, 103, 106

Washington, George, 333–4, 344
Waterloo, Battle of (1815), 360–1, 366
Watson, James D., 451–2
Watt, James, 328
Wavrin, Jehan de, 159
weapons, 123
  crossbows, 97, 124
  gunpowder, 126
  longbow, 123
Wedgwood, Josiah, 336
welfare state, 428, 449–50
weights and measures, 102
Wellington, Arthur Wellesley, Duke of, 358–61, 364–5, 368
Wentworth, Thomas see Stafford, Earl of
Welsley, Arthur, see Wellington
Wesley, Charles, 314
Wesley, John, 314–15, 335
Wessex, 20, 37–8, 39, 40, 52
West, Benjamin, 326
West Africa, 299
West Indies, 323, 340, 342
  see also Barbados; Jamaica
Western Isles, 320
Westminster, 156, 192, 253, 256, 260
  Great Hall, 73–4, 193, 266
  Palace, 191
Westminster Abbey, 51, 54, 66, 107, 142, 150, 157, 225, 246, 326, 423, 427
  Chapter House, 175
  Mary, Queen of Scots reburied, 245
  Princes in the Tower reburied, 178, 180, 185
Weston, Father William, 245
wetlands, 35–6, 48, 67
wet-nursing, 347
whale oil, 375
Whigs (Whiggamores), 283, 284, 293, 312–13
Whitby, 329
Whitby Abbey, 209
White, John, 233
White Ship, 77–9, 80, 81
white papers, 449n
Whitehall, 242, 246, 260, 288
  Banqueting House, 266
Whitelocke, Bulstrode, 262
Whittington, Sir Richard, 152–5, 174
  cat, 153–4, 155
  'Longhouse', 154, 241

Mayor of London, 154
  public works, 154
Wigan, 319
Wilberforce, William, 336
'Wild Geese', 297
Wilhelm, Kaiser, 419, 423
Wilkins, Maurice, 451, 452
William the Aetheling (Henry I's son), 77–8, 79, 80
William the Bastard, Duke of Normandy
  see William the Conqueror
William I, Emperor, 382
William the Conqueror (William I of England), 66–7, 69–70, 76, 108
  becomes king, 62, 66
  castles built, 66–7
  death and succession to, 72–3
  and the Domesday Book, 70
  and Harold's death, 64
  resistance to by Hereward the Wake, 67–8
  and succession contest to Edward the Confessor, 54, 59–60, 61
  uprisings against and putting down of resistance by, 67
William II, King (Rufus), 72–5, 81, 101 117
William III, King, 286, 288–9, 292, 303–4, 313, 408
  death, 306
  in Ireland, 296–8
William IV, King, 372
William of Malmesbury, 47, 64, 74, 75
William of Wales, Prince, 43
Williams, Anna, 323
Willis, Bishop Richard, 308
wills, 40–1
Winchester, 285
Windsor, 167, 180
  St George's Chapel, 173, 206
wine, 122
wireless, 409–10, 444
witan, 45, 111
Wittenberg, 198, 203
woad plant, 6
Wolfe, General James, 324–6, 329
Wollstonecraft, Edward, 347–8

Wollstonecraft, Mary, 347–9
  Maria, or the Wrongs of Woman, 349
  Thoughts on the Education of Daughters, 348
  A Vindication of the Rights of Woman, 347–9
Wolsey, Cardinal Thomas, 196, 199, 200, 203
  death, 196
women, 347–9
  Anglo-Saxon, 40, 41
  executed, 422
  preaching, 323
  suffrage, 393, 401, 415–19
  war work, 417
  wife-beating, 348
  see also birth control; marriage
Women's Social and Political Union, 415–16
Woodcroft Hall, 266
Woodfull, W.M., 432
Woodstock, 305
Woolf, Virginia, 349
Woolsthorpe, Lincolnshire, 290
Woolwich, 395, 405
Worcester, 57
  Battle of, 273, 275
workhouses, 388
World War I see First World War
World War II see Second World War
Worms, 200
Wren, Christopher, 291
Wright, Professor W., 178
Wrington, Somerset, 294
writings, 7
Wycliffe, John, 142, 199, 249

Xhosa people, 380

Yeatman, Robert, 429–31
Yersin, Alexandre, 131
York, 36, 247, 260, 262, 316, 317
York, Duke of, 337
York, House of, 168, 186
Yorkshire, 151, 265, 317, 329, 431
  West Riding, 355–6
Yorktown, 334, 38

Zela (Turkey), 9